THE SALVATION ARMY YEAR BOOK

THE
SALVATION ARMY
YEAR BOOK

2007

INTERNATIONAL
MISSION STATEMENT

The Salvation Army, an international movement, is an
evangelical part of the universal Christian Church.
Its message is based on the Bible. Its ministry is motivated by love
for God. Its mission is to preach the gospel of Jesus Christ and
meet human needs in his name without discrimination.

THE SALVATION ARMY
INTERNATIONAL HEADQUARTERS
101 QUEEN VICTORIA STREET, LONDON EC4P 4EP, UNITED KINGDOM

First published 2006

COPYRIGHT © 2006 THE GENERAL OF THE SALVATION ARMY

ISBN 0 85412 750 X

Editor: Major Trevor Howes

Editor-in-Chief: Major Charles King

Cover design by Berni Georges
Full-colour inserts by Nathan Sigauke
Maps by Katie Baddams

Printed in the United Kingdom
by
Polestar Wheatons Ltd
Exeter, Devon, England

Annual reports in this edition mostly cover the period 1 May 2005 to 30 April 2006. The staff lists and details of centres of work are generally accurate to 31 August 2006.

Statistics are those for the year ending December 2005.

Officers and lay staff serving in countries other than their own are counted in the statistics of the territory/command in which they are serving.

The 'Officers on Active Service' section is as accurate as possible at the time of going to press.

Contents

Articles of special interest

Foreword by the General 1
'Another Door Will Open' – possibilities for global expansion
                                        by Commissioner Paul du Plessis 3
'For Want of a Better Name' – the centenary of the Home League
                                        by Lieut-Colonel Jenty Fairbank 5
'A Shield of Faith and a Shield from Harm' – opposing sex-trade trafficking
                                        by Commissioner Helen Clifton 7
'The Sally Ann Story' – the emerging Fair Trade venture
                                        by Commissioner Berit Ødegaard 9

Facts and figures

What is The Salvation Army? 11
The Doctrines of The Salvation Army 12
Founders of The Salvation Army 13
Glossary of Salvation Army terms 14
Salvation Army History (chronological table)....................................16
Significant Events 2005-2006 21
The High Council 22
Generals Elected by a High Council 23
Countries where The Salvation Army is at work................................27
International Statistics 29
Salvation Army Periodicals 31
Books Published 2005-2006...33
Ministries and Fellowships..34
Salvation Army Honours 36
International Emergency Services 38
International Projects and Development Services 40
Community Development Grants..41

Reports, staff lists and addresses

International Headquarters 42
    International Trustee Company..45
    Reliance Bank Limited 45
    International College for Officers..46
    Salvation Army Leaders' Training College of Africa 47
    Overseas Service Funds 48
    International Administrative Structure 50

(Continued on the next page)

Contents (continued)

Australia 52
    Eastern.....................................53
    Southern 60
Bangladesh..................................70
Belgium 72
Brazil 74
Canada and Bermuda..................78
Caribbean....................................88
Congo (Brazzaville)....................93
Congo (Kinshasa) and Angola ..96
Denmark 100
Eastern Europe..........................103
Finland and Estonia 106
France 109
Germany and Lithuania 113
Ghana 116
Hong Kong and Macau 119
India
    National 125
    Central 127
    Eastern.....................................131
    Northern 134
    South Eastern 137
    South Western 140
    Western....................................143
Indonesia...................................147
Italy...151
Japan 153
Kenya...156
Korea 159
Latin America North 163
Liberia.......................................168
Malawi 170
Mexico 172

Netherlands, The, and Czech
    Republic 176
New Zealand, Fiji and Tonga...181
Nigeria 188
Norway, Iceland and
    The Færoes 191
Pakistan.....................................195
Papua New Guinea 198
Philippines, The 201
Portugal.....................................206
Rwanda 208
Singapore, Malaysia and
    Myanmar.................................210
South America
    East...214
    West...217
Southern Africa 223
Spain 227
Sri Lanka 229
Sweden and Latvia 232
Switzerland, Austria and
    Hungary 237
Taiwan 241
Tanzania.....................................243
Uganda.......................................245
United Kingdom 247
USA
    National 255
    Central 257
    Eastern.....................................263
    Southern 271
    Western....................................277
Zambia 286
Zimbabwe 289

Officers on Active Service 292
Retirements from Active Service 321
Retired Generals and Commissioners 328
Promotions to Glory 336
Abbreviations...342
International direct dialling 343
Index 344

FOREWORD

by General Shaw Clifton

International leader of The Salvation Army

GOD has graciously and lovingly led The Salvation Army through another year. The struggle against suffering, sin and Hell goes on apace. It grows more and more intense as exploitation, secularism and materialism tighten their already iron grip on so many of the peoples of the world. Poverty is unremitting. Even in the richest, most developed nations The Salvation Army is needed to provide food, clothing and shelter for the neglected. The yawning gap between rich and poor grows ever wider.

Neither bodily nor spiritual need knows set seasons. If anything will grind down a person to the point of desperation it is spiritual or material poverty. The Salvation Army's part is to offer help, restoring dignity in the sacred name of Jesus Christ.

General Shaw Clifton and Commissioner Helen Clifton

Seeing a person in all the complex fullness of their being, the needs of the heart and of the spirit become our concern too. We offer Christ as the Saviour, as the Door of Heaven, to any who will listen.

In the sudden disaster we are called forth. I feel immensely proud of the compassionate and professional emergency response of Salvationists in the face of large-scale suffering, whether it be caused by natural phenomena or evil human deeds.

We still say that the absence of basic material provision for all – income, food, clean water, shelter, education – is a very great evil. Human suffering does not diminish. Dignity is an inherent right that should not need to be argued for. Salvationists are called to be proactive in matters of social justice, analysing intelligently the root causes of

1

the wrongs and using our considerable influence where it will count. All this while bringing to victims what measure of relief we can.

Christ is our energy, our resource. He is our Head. We are his Army. The articles in the pages that follow in this 2007 edition of *The Salvation Army Year Book* brim over with information. We publish the book *soli Deo gloria* – to the glory of God alone.

May every reader find herein cause to bless the God and Father of our Lord Jesus Christ who, by his Holy Spirit, makes it all possible.

International Headquarters, London
September 2006

On their first day in office as The Salvation Army's international leaders, General Shaw Clifton and Commissioner Helen Clifton (World President of Women's Ministries) arrive at International Headquarters with the newly appointed Chief of the Staff, Commissioner Robin Dunster *(right)*

ANOTHER DOOR WILL OPEN

Commissioner Paul du Plessis outlines possibilities for The Salvation Army's global expansion

IN 1970 the door closed and Salvationists were absorbed into The Protestant Church of Algeria; the excitement of work in Vietnam turned to disappointment as financial constraints prompted withdrawal in 2000; and when exit concluded emergency relief to Nicaragua in the 1980s some wondered whether the door would ever open again. And will the flag fly over a Salvation Army in China once more?

As the International Self-Denial Fund staggered under the weight of expansion into Eastern Europe, a decade of caution was inevitable. New models for financing were emerging but International Headquarters recognised it should be open to changing opportunities and challenges.

Fresh vision emerged during a 2003 retreat with Patrick Johnstone, co-author of *Operation World*. 'Plan for growth,' was his challenge; 'not to do so is to plan for decline'. The Holy Spirit was at work in the heart of IHQ.

Tribal

The Spirit was at work elsewhere. From the 1980s an American-Polish Salvationist felt convinced about Poland. That selfsame Spirit was at work in two Greek Salvationists in Australia. In 1992 they wrote asking to start the work in their homeland. Two Greek officer-couples are now serving in the UK Territory.

And the same Spirit was at work in Mali. André Togo is not yet 30 years old. Converted in Sierra Leone, he joined a local church; back in Mali he planted two. In a dream his mother told him to join a uniformed church marching with tambourines, drums and brass. Searching the internet, he discovered it. It was The Salvation Army's Vancouver War College, and things grew from there.

Tribal relatives across the northern border of Ghana have pleaded for Salvationists to ignore a man-made border with Burkina Faso. 'Come over and help us' is repeated, and other doors open.

Medical

There are more-formal approaches. In 1999 the North Korean ambassador to Switzerland started requesting aid. It began by subsidising two medical students; now there are yoghurt factories with scope for more. A government official in Solomon Islands has repeatedly invited the Army, his support and membership promised.

The National Council of Churches in Sudan asked the Army to join an ecumenical strategy to offset the Islamisation of Southern Sudan; at the same time Tear Fund asked The Salvation Army's Africa Regional Team to assist with its programmes there. Considered decisions have to be taken prayerfully.

The renewing Spirit inspires and empowers for mission. The Army grows not by its own energy but fuelled by the Spirit.

Mizo Salvationists have a burden to carry the gospel into Nepal and Bhutan. They start with ministry to Nepalis within Mizoram, and special training for Nepali evangelists. When the Indian Ocean tsunami hits the Andaman Islands a Salvation Army presence is reborn in relief programmes.

Meanwhile Salvationists working in the Gulf meet regularly in Dubai, Muscat and Kuwait. What about their request for an officer-pastor? Is this the door to West Asia and the Middle East?

Cultural

Reconnaissance becomes inevitable as doors appear to open. A Kenyan officer serving in Rwanda visits Burundi and finds a ready-made Army wanting to join the international family; a Melanesian territorial commander accompanied by an American public relations officer visits Solomon Islands; a Dutch-Danish couple explore Warsaw.

Support teams are set up; task forces multiply; multinational membership sensitive to cultural dynamics is the norm. What kind of work will be established?

Colonel Vibeke Krommenhoek, team leader of Project Warsaw, writes: 'The focus is to develop the corps from a cell-church structure, because here is evangelism, spiritual growth and service to the community by local disciples. Social work will develop with the growth of the corps, but not at its expense.'

The colonel radiates enthusiasm. She observes: 'New openings need to be linked to persons, not necessarily neighbouring territories.'

As doors open elsewhere the emphasis may be on social and community development where actions can speak louder than words. That's the case in China where the door is open for cooperation with other agencies, theological colleges and churches. This may one day permit wider expression of The Salvation Army's integrated mission, but not now.

We could force entry, pushing our way in uninvited. But a century of experience has taught this Army to go gently and wisely. We just keep seeking, keep asking and keep knocking – and another door will be opened.

The Army returns to Nicaragua in 2007. Hallelujah!

Commissioner du Plessis retired in 2006 from the appointment of Commissioner for World Evangelisation, IHQ

OPERATION DESERT ROSE

'The desert shall ... blossom as the rose' (Isaiah 35:1)

Operation Desert Rose (ODR) is a Salvation Army prayer initiative on behalf of people in the Middle East and North Africa. Here is the home of Judaism and Islam. Here conflict erupts easily and the Israeli-Palestinian question remains unresolved. Here is the least-evangelised part of the world.

If you are willing to be a minute-a-day ODR prayer partner, email: IHQ-CFWE@salvationarmy.org – adding the subject heading: Operation Desert Rose. You will receive a short information sheet and regular prayer guides.

FOR WANT OF A BETTER NAME

Lieut-Colonel Jenty Fairbank highlights the Home League centenary

ALTHOUGH 'mothers meetings' were held at some Christian Mission stations they formed no part of the early Salvation Army programme. Not until the winter of 1902/3 was a 'Women's Corps Auxiliary' launched – by Major and Mrs Harvey Banks at Fenelon Falls, Canada.

A similar gathering, organised by Mrs Commissioner Fanny Jolliffe in January 1904 at East Finchley, UK, was possibly the prototype of that 'Important New Departure' headlined in *The War Cry* of 9 February 1907.

Florence Booth, daughter-in-law of the Army's Founders, was reported as having 'undertaken a new, interesting, and … difficult … yet needful crusade … nothing less than an attempt to help mothers by advice, sympathy, and friendship, in the management of their homes.' The Home League was born!

No doubt already confronted by the patronising attitudes that would stalk it through the years, Mrs Colonel Catherine Higgins, first General Secretary of this new departure, pointed out that it was in no sense a 'mothers meeting' but a 'help one another society'.

Emblem

Whereas *The War Cry* welcomed the inauguration of the Home League, *The Deliverer* and *All the World* reported Florence Booth herself as being less than enthusiastic about its name, not foreseeing that a century later the same name would be upholding the same aims in every country of the Army world, its emblem a house on the Bible, its fourfold programme Worship, Education, Fellowship, Service.

By its 50th anniversary the Home League internationally numbered more than 277,000 members. We search the 2007 *Year Book* in vain for a comparative statistic in this centenary year, however.

In the closing decades of the 20th century changing socio-economic factors triggered significant developments in the Army's women's programme, so instead

Home league members in Malawi enjoy a craft class led by Mission Team members from USA Central

of a simple Home League membership figure the current *Year Book* gives a Women's Ministries entry of 505,856 members (all groups).

To unpack that parenthetical 'all groups' would be to discover Kingdom-building at its most creative. Editorial constraints requiring that the focus of this article be the centenary of the Home League itself, the numerous evidences of late-20th century 'thinking outside the box' developing from it must wait a future occasion for their unpacking.

Edge

Meanwhile, although this centenarian 'help one another society' in some long-established territories sometimes looks to be limping behind its progeny, the developing world's home leagues continue to be at the cutting edge of community ministry.

Never could Florence Booth have imagined a volcanic eruption in 2005 would lead to the establishing of a new home league in Papua New Guinea – that fledgling territory where one divisional headquarters still has no telephone. People from Manam Island, evacuated to the mainland by The Salvation Army, built a hall at Pottsdam on the north coast, began meetings and a home league, before requesting an officer be appointed.

Across the Indian Ocean the aftermath of the 2004 Boxing Day tsunami throbs with reports of not only home league ministry to victims in the affected territories but also sacrificial giving by home league members throughout the world in support of this and associated disaster relief work.

In drought-ravaged Kenya, where one home league managed to raise enough funding to dig a borehole, five new Sudanese home league members at Kakuma not only attend Sunday meetings but also form part of the strategy for reaching into Sudan itself in future days.

Neighbouring Uganda's advanced level of deforestation resulted in a divisional director for women's ministries attempting to increase awareness of the environment by challenging home leaguers to plant trees around their corps halls. With junior home league members as young as nine, a fine show of trees should result – despite HIV/Aids leaving some of these youngsters too ill to take part.

Let Cabayaoasan Corps in The Philippines be the final example of home league growth. An unmarried male corps officer ensures women's ministries are alive and active. He was tasked to handle spiritual aspects of a newly formed women's community project, the majority of whose recipients were non-believers.

The fruit of his using Women and Family modules was the enrolment of four new home league members, two of whom are now senior soldiers. With home league attendance increased by 150 per cent, it isn't surprising that the territorial home league banner was awarded to his corps. As that CO (quoting the Founder) said: 'Truly my best men are women' – or in his case shouldn't it be, 'Truly my best woman is a man'?

Lieut-Colonel Fairbank retired in 2000. Her appointments included Editor-in-Chief/Publishing Secretary, UK, and Archivist/Director of the International Heritage Centre.

A SHIELD OF FAITH AND A SHIELD FROM HARM

Commissioner Helen Clifton writes of The Salvation Army's opposition to the evil of sex-trade trafficking

'Take up the shield of faith, with which you can extinguish all the flaming arrows of the evil one' (Ephesians 6:16); 'He is a shield to those who take refuge in him' (Proverbs 30:5 – both texts *New International Version*)

THE 'shield' emblem of The Salvation Army's mission takes on a powerful and biblical significance when associated with opposing the twin evils of commercial sex exploitation and human trafficking. The sex industry makes a cheap commodity of the most sacred and intimate of human relationships. Opposing this abuse is a core issue for The Salvation Army.

In recent years trade in vulnerable women has reached a scale that shocks the world. Still modern culture accepts the existence of brothels, massage parlours, lap-dancing clubs, sex tourism and pornography available at the click of a button, all in the name of freedom and personal choice.

In fact, freedom is the last word which should be associated with these matters. Many women, girls, men and boys are trapped in an underworld of crime and fear, disguised by a veneer of glamour and easy money.

The slave trade flourishes everywhere, bringing cheap labour across borders, enticing and coercing vulnerable people into working for minimal wages and keeping very young women in conditions of fear and exploitation.

Prevention, protection, prosecution – and prayer – are key elements in the battle. The Salvation Army, with its international networks and influence, joins others in the fight against an evil which touches nearly every country on earth.

Prevention includes education, awareness-raising and empowerment. Those who are most poor are most vulnerable to being trafficked or having their children trafficked. Therefore, every programme which encourages independence, self-worth and freedom of choice is a plank in our strategy.

No easy exit

Prevention also means fighting the demand – and here we face the sad truth that many 'customers' who pay for sex acts are neither poor nor uneducated. However, their education falls short of teaching them that the women apparently available for their pleasure are hurting and trapped in an evil trade from which there is no easy exit.

Pornography is often a factor, being addictive, presenting women as objects, destroying healthy relationships and creating the demand for more and more novelty and younger and younger girls. This culture leaves the door wide open for exploitation and crime.

Protection includes seeing trafficked individuals as victims or survivors, to be cared for and rehabilitated rather than left to fend for themselves and face probable retrafficking. Safe accommodation, with due attention to risk factors, is crucial and The Salvation Army has a professional record in this field.

Support required to house victims of trafficking includes access to legal advice, language facilities, health services, trauma counselling and activities which help recovery. Repatriation may be necessary and here The Salvation Army's international or state-wide services come into play.

Have a chance

Prosecution of perpetrators means advocating for laws and policies which enable and resource police to intervene and punish offenders, across national boundaries. Education also needs to be in place in prisons where men (and some women) involved in criminal networks have a chance to break the cycle of evil in which they are embroiled.

The Salvation Army is engaging with these issues in more and more places, is fundraising for programmes and is ready to work day and night for the care of victims. It has a history of opposing sex slavery, particularly in the UK (1885) and Japan (1900).

Today, programmes are in place in the USA, where the Army has been particularly active in advocacy at the heart of government, and where internet tools have been developed for training and reporting; in the UK,

where awareness-raising and fundraising have accompanied victim support; in Africa, where training and safe houses are being established; and in The Philippines, India, Bangladesh and Sri Lanka, to name just a few examples.

In a year in which 100 years of women's ministries will be marked and celebrated worldwide, it is appropriate that combatting trafficking for commercial sex exploitation should be one of the priorities for an Army whose shield remains a symbol of strong faith, spiritual warfare and protection of the weak.

Commissioner Clifton is World President of Women's Ministries

A trafficking rescue centre in India Western

THE SALLY ANN STORY

Commissioner Berit Ødegaard reports on The Salvation Army's emerging Fair Trade venture

SLOWLY yet steadily 'Sally Ann' is becoming more than some people's nickname for The Salvation Army. It has become the trademark under which The Salvation Army's Fair Trade scheme is developing.

It started in Bangladesh, where underprivileged people were given the possibility to support themselves by learning a handicraft in order to produce goods which they later sold. In time, the products were branded 'Sally Ann' and a shop was opened in Dhaka, where participants in the programme were able to develop and control their own sales.

Contacts between The Salvation Army in Bangladesh and Norway gave birth to the idea of developing the project internationally. In July 2003 the first Sally Ann shop opened in Oslo. Mainly products from Bangladesh were sold to start with, then goods from Kenya, Tanzania and Peru were added soon after.

Income-generating projects have been part of The Salvation Army's programme from the beginning. William Booth looked at 'darkest England' and asked, 'What is the use of preaching the gospel to people whose whole attention is concentrated upon a mad, desperate struggle to keep themselves alive?'

And so was established a variety of programmes to alleviate poverty.

The emerging Sally Ann concept is one such programme. Good, healthy business practices will be applied and the whole Salvation Army world will be able to take part on an equal basis. For 'fair trade' represents the most efficient way of partnering with the poor, and within this area the Army has particular capabilities for success due to its international structure, networks and objectives.

People who are marginalised because of poverty are given a way out of their deprived situation, not by charity but by using their working abilities and skills as they are guided in the setting up of sustainable businesses in a sound working environment, always keeping in mind that the Fair Trade regulations – giving fair pay, ensuring a good working environment and offering long-term business relationships – are adhered to.

Good products

In addition to Norway's shop in Oslo there is one in Dhaka (Bangladesh), and Stockholm (Sweden) opened one in June 2006. Products such as beadwork, baskets, shirts, knitted scarves and hats, cushions, table runners, place mats, greetings cards and boxes are being sold.

The concept is not built on the fact that people will purchase because they necessarily want to support The Salvation Army's work, but rather because these are good products which they will want to buy and use, and for this reason want to come back and buy more. Only in this way will the concept be sustainable.

Now that the Sally Ann concept has been shown to work, providing income for workers, vital funds for the Bangladesh Command and a means by which The Salvation Army has become more widely known in Norway, the concept is being taken to a whole new level, with International Headquarters setting up a desk that will enable Sally Ann to be the Fair Trade wing of the international Salvation Army.

An International Sally Ann Council (ISAC), chaired by the Secretary for Mission Product Development and Marketing and with members from the territories involved, was inaugurated in October 2006. The council is the overall guardian of the Fair Trade concept and will meet twice yearly. Sally Ann schemes will be overseen by the Programme Resources Department at IHQ. In order for Sally Ann to reach its full potential, expert advice is needed both on the business side and on the International Fair Trade arena.

Four territories are at present involved in production and three in retail, with Bangladesh doing both. However, the potential for Sally Ann is limitless and in the next few years it is expected that several more territories will become involved in both the production and retail side.

The vision of the people who started the project, and those who have followed, is to develop Sally Ann into a viable international Fair Trade organisation

with as many territories as possible around the world participating. Along with the countries involved so far, we are looking at the best possible international structure of Sally Ann, as it develops from a rather small project into a sustainable operation.

Always bearing in mind that it is a concept based upon the key principle of Fair Trade, we are making sure that the people for which the concept was intended are the ones who benefit and that the Army's key principles and values are upheld. The Sally Ann story so far has been exciting and innovative – but with the plans that are now under way, what has gone before is just the beginning of something really big.

Commissioner Ødegaard is Secretary for Mission Product Development and Marketing in the Programme Resources Department, IHQ

FAIR TRADE BY THE SALVATION ARMY

SALLY ANN

Enhanced by photographs from Norwegian international photographer Knut Bry, *Sally Ann – Poverty to Hope* by Colonel Bo Brekke tells the story of The Salvation Army's Fair Trade venture. *Sally Ann – Poverty to Hope* is available from SP&S Ltd (tel [44] (0)20 7367 6580) at £9.99 plus £2.95 p&p.

WHAT IS THE SALVATION ARMY?

THE Salvation Army is a worldwide evangelical Christian church with its own distinctive governance and practice. The Army's doctrine follows the mainstream of Christian belief and its articles of faith emphasise God's saving purposes.

Its religious and charitable objects are 'the advancement of the Christian religion ... and, pursuant thereto, the advancement of education, the relief of poverty, and other charitable objects beneficial to society or the community of mankind as a whole'.*

The Movement, founded in London, England, in 1865 by William and Catherine Booth, has spread to many parts of the world.

The rapid deployment of the first Salvationists was aided by the adoption of a quasi-military command structure in 1878 when the title 'The Salvation Army' was brought into use. A similarly practical organisation today enables resources to be equally flexible.

Responding to a recurrent theme in Christianity which sees the Church engaged in spiritual warfare, The Salvation Army has used to advantage certain soldierly features such as uniforms, flags and ranks to identify, inspire and regulate its endeavours.

Evangelistic and social enterprises are maintained, under the authority of the General, by full-time officers and employees, as well as soldiers who give service in their free time. The Army also benefits from the support of many adherents and friends, including those who serve on advisory boards.

Leadership in The Salvation Army is provided by commissioned and ordained officers who are recognised as fully accredited ministers of religion.

Salvationists accept a disciplined and compassionate life of high moral standards which includes abstinence from alcohol and tobacco.

From its earliest days The Salvation Army has accorded women equal opportunities, every rank and service being open to them, and from childhood the young are encouraged to love and serve God.

Raised to evangelise, the Army spontaneously embarked on schemes for the social betterment of the poor. Such concerns developed, wherever the Army operates, in practical, skilled and cost-effective ways. Evolving social services meet endemic needs and specific crises worldwide. Highly trained staff are employed in up-to-date facilities.

The need for modernisation and longer-term development is under continual review. Increasingly the Army's policy and its indigenous membership allow it to cooperate with international relief agencies and governments alike.

The Army's partnership with both private and public philanthropy will continue to bring comfort to the needy, while the proclamation of God's redemptive love revealed in Jesus Christ offers individuals and communities the opportunity to know spiritual fulfilment here on earth and a place in Christ's eternal Kingdom.

*Salvation Army Act 1980

THE DOCTRINES OF
THE SALVATION ARMY

We believe that the Scriptures of the Old and New Testaments were given by inspiration of God, and that they only constitute the Divine rule of Christian faith and practice.

We believe that there is only one God, who is infinitely perfect, the Creator, Preserver and Governor of all things, and who is the only proper object of religious worship.

We believe that there are three persons in the Godhead – the Father, the Son and the Holy Ghost, undivided in essence and co-equal in power and glory.

We believe that in the person of Jesus Christ the Divine and human natures are united, so that he is truly and properly God and truly and properly man.

We believe that our first parents were created in a state of innocency, but by their disobedience they lost their purity and happiness, and that in consequence of their fall all men have become sinners, totally depraved, and as such are justly exposed to the wrath of God.

We believe that the Lord Jesus Christ has by his suffering and death made an atonement for the whole world so that whosoever will may be saved.

We believe that repentance towards God, faith in our Lord Jesus Christ, and regeneration by the Holy Spirit, are necessary to salvation.

We believe that we are justified by grace through faith in our Lord Jesus Christ and that he that believeth hath the witness in himself.

We believe that continuance in a state of salvation depends upon continued obedient faith in Christ.

We believe that it is the privilege of all believers to be wholly sanctified, and that their whole spirit and soul and body may be preserved blameless unto the coming of our Lord Jesus Christ.

We believe in the immortality of the soul; in the resurrection of the body; in the general judgment at the end of the world; in the eternal happiness of the righteous; and in the endless punishment of the wicked.

FOUNDERS OF THE SALVATION ARMY

William Booth

The Founder and first General was born in Nottingham on 10 April 1829 and promoted to Glory from Hadley Wood on 20 August 1912. He lived to establish Army work in 58 countries and colonies and travelled extensively, holding salvation meetings. In his later years he was received in audience by emperors, kings and presidents. Among his many books, *In Darkest England and the Way Out* was the most notable; it became the blueprint of all the Army's social schemes. It was reprinted in 1970.

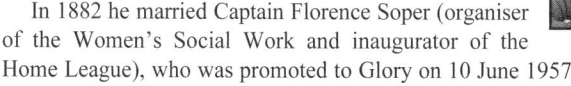

Catherine Booth

The Army Mother was born in Ashbourne on 17 January 1829 and promoted to Glory from Clacton-on-Sea on 4 October 1890. As Catherine Mumford, she married William in 1855. A great teacher and preacher, she addressed large public meetings in Britain with far-reaching results, despite ill health. Her writings include *Female Ministry* and *Aggressive Christianity*.

William Bramwell Booth

The eldest son of the Founder, and his Chief of the Staff from 1880 to 1912, Bramwell (as he was known) was born on 8 March 1856. He was largely responsible for the development of the Army. His teaching of the doctrine of holiness and his councils with officers and young people were of incalculable value.

In 1882 he married Captain Florence Soper (organiser of the Women's Social Work and inaugurator of the Home League), who was promoted to Glory on 10 June 1957.

During his time as General (1912-1929), impetus was given to missionary work. Published books include *Echoes and Memories* and *These Fifty Years*. He was appointed a Companion of Honour shortly before his promotion to Glory from Hadley Wood on 16 June 1929.

GLOSSARY OF SALVATION ARMY TERMS

Adherent: A member of The Salvation Army who has not made a commitment to soldiership.

Advisory Board: A group of influential citizens who, believing in the Army's programme of spiritual, moral and physical rehabilitation and amelioration, assist in promoting and supporting Army projects.

'Blood and Fire': The Army's motto; refers to the blood of Jesus Christ and the fire of the Holy Spirit.

Cadet: A Salvationist who is in training for officership.

Candidate: A soldier who has been accepted for officer training.

Chief of the Staff: The officer second in command of the Army throughout the world.

Chief Secretary: The officer second in command of the Army in a territory.

Citadel: A hall used for worship.

Colours: The tricolour flag of the Army. Its colours symbolise the blood of Jesus Christ (red), the fire of the Holy Spirit (yellow) and the purity of God (blue).

Command: A smaller type of territory, directed by an officer commanding.

Command leaders: An officer commanding and spouse in their joint role of sharing spiritual leadership and ministry, providing pastoral care and exemplifying the working partnership of officer couples.

Commission: A document conferring authority upon an officer, or upon an unpaid local officer, eg, secretary, treasurer, bandmaster, etc.

Congress: Central gatherings often held annually and attended by most officers and many soldiers of a territory, command, region or division.

Corps: A Salvation Army unit established for the preaching of the gospel and to provide Christian-motivated service in the community.

Corps Cadet: A young Salvationist who undertakes a course of study and practical training in a corps, with a view to becoming efficient in Salvation Army service.

Corps Sergeant-Major: The chief local officer for public work who assists the corps officer with meetings and usually takes command in his/her absence.

Dedication Service: The public presentation of infants to the Lord. This differs from christening or infant baptism in that the main emphasis is upon specific vows made by the parents concerning the child's upbringing.

Division: A number of corps grouped together under the direction of a divisional commander (may also include social service centres and programmes), operating within a territory or command.

Divisional Commander: The officer in charge of the Army in a division.

Envoy: A local officer whose duty it is to visit corps, societies and outposts, for the purpose of conducting meetings. An envoy may be appointed in charge of any such unit.

General: The officer elected to the supreme command of the Army throughout the world. All appointments are made, and all regulations issued, under the General's authority (see under High Council – p 22).

General Secretary: The officer second in charge of the Army in a command (or, in some territories, a large division).

Halfway House: A centre for the rehabilitation of alcoholics or parolees (USA).

Harbour Light Centre: A reclamation centre, usually located in inner city areas.

High Council: (See p 22)

Home League: (See p 34)

International Headquarters (IHQ): The offices in which the business connected with the command of the worldwide Army is transacted.

International Secretary: A position at IHQ with responsibility for the oversight and coordination of the work in a specific geographical zone or functional category, and for advising the General on zonal and worldwide issues and policies.

Junior Soldier: A boy or girl who, having professed conversion and having signed the junior soldier's promise, becomes a Salvationist.

League of Mercy: Salvationists who visit prisons, hospitals and needy homes, in their own time, bringing the gospel and rendering practical aid (see p 35).

Lieutenant: A Salvationist giving service to the Army for an agreed period of time without becoming a commissioned officer.

Local Officer: A soldier appointed to a position of responsibility and authority in the corps; carries out the duties of the appointment without being separated from regular employment or receiving remuneration from the Army.

Medical Fellowship: (See p 35)

Mercy Seat or Penitent Form: A bench provided as a place where people can kneel to pray, seeking salvation or sanctification, or making a special consecration to God's will and service. The mercy seat is usually situated between the platform and main area of Army halls as a focal point to remind all of God's reconciling and redeeming presence.

Officer: A Salvationist who has left secular concerns at God's call and has been trained, commissioned and ordained to service and leadership. An officer is a recognised minister of religion.

Officer Commanding: The officer in charge of the Army in a command.

Order of Distinguished Auxiliary Service: (See p 37)

Order of the Founder: (See p 36)

Outpost: A locality in which Army work is carried out and where it is hoped a society or corps will develop.

Pastoral Care Council: Established in each corps for the care of soldiers, etc, and maintenance of the membership rolls. Previously called the census board.

Promotion to Glory: The Army's description of the death of Salvationists.

Ranks of Officers: Captain, major, lieut-colonel, colonel, commissioner, General.

Red Shield: A symbol identifying a wide range of Army social and emergency services.

Red Shield Appeal: A financial appeal to the general public; also known as the Annual Appeal in some countries.

Red Shield Centre: A club for military personnel.

Salvation: The work of grace which God accomplishes in a repentant person whose trust is in Christ as Saviour, forgiving sin, giving meaning and new direction to life, and strength to live as God desires. The deeper experience of this grace, known as holiness or sanctification, is the outcome of wholehearted commitment to God and enables the living of a Christlike life.

Self-Denial Appeal: An annual effort by Salvationists and friends to raise funds for the Army's worldwide operations.

Sergeant: A local officer appointed for specific duty, usually in a corps.

Society: A company of soldiers who work together regularly in a district, without an officer, but with the approval of the divisional commander.

Soldier: A converted person at least 14 years of age who has, with the approval of the pastoral care council, been enrolled as a member of The Salvation Army after signing the Soldier's Covenant.

Soldier's Covenant: The statement of beliefs and promises which every intending soldier is required to sign before enrolment. Previously called 'Articles of War'.

Territorial Commander: The officer in command of the Army in a territory.

Territorial leaders: A territorial commander and spouse in their joint role of sharing spiritual leadership and ministry, providing pastoral care and exemplifying the working partnership of officer couples. The chief secretary is the second-in-command of the territory.

Territory: A country, part of a country or several countries combined, in which Salvation Army work is organised under a territorial commander.

Young People's Sergeant-Major: A local officer responsible for young people's work in a corps, under the commanding officer.

Chronological Table of Important Events in Salvation Army History

1829　Catherine Mumford (later Mrs Booth, 'the Army Mother') born at Ashbourne, Derbyshire (17 Jan); William Booth born at Nottingham (10 Apr).

1844　William Booth converted.

1846　Catherine Mumford converted.

1855　Marriage of William Booth and Catherine Mumford at Stockwell New Chapel, London (16 Jun).

1856　William Bramwell Booth (the Founder's eldest son and second General of the Army) born in Halifax (8 Mar).

1858　William Booth ordained as Methodist minister (27 May). (Accepted on probation 1854.)

1859　*Female Teaching*, Mrs Booth's first pamphlet, published (Dec).

1860　Mrs Booth's first public address (27 May, Whit Sunday).

1865　**Rev William Booth began work in East London** (2 Jul); The Christian Mission, founded; Eveline (Evangeline) Cory Booth (fourth General) born in London (25 Dec).

1867　First Headquarters (Eastern Star) opened in Whitechapel Road, London.

1868　*The East London Evangelist* – later (1870) *The Christian Mission Magazine* and (1879) *The Salvationist* – published (Oct).

1874　Christian Mission work commenced in **Wales** (15 Nov).

1875　*Rules and Doctrines of The Christian Mission* published.

1876　*Revival Music* published (Jan).

1878　First use of the term 'Salvation Army' – in small appeal folder (May); 'The Christian Mission' became **'The Salvation Army'**, and the Rev William Booth became known as the General; deed poll executed, thus establishing the doctrines and principles of The Salvation Army (Aug); first corps flag presented by Mrs Booth at Coventry (28-30 Sep); *Orders and Regulations for The Salvation Army* issued (Oct); brass instruments first used.

1879　First corps in **Scotland** opened (24 Mar) and **Channel Islands** (14 Aug); cadets first trained; introduction of uniform; first corps band formed in Consett; issue No 1 of *The War Cry* published (27 Dec).

1880　First training home opened, at Hackney, London; first contingent of SA officers landed in the **United States of America** (10 Mar); SA work commenced in **Ireland** (7 May); children's meetings commenced at Blyth (30 Jul); SA work extended to **Australia** (5 Sep).

1881　Work begun in **France** (13 Mar); *The Little Soldier* (subsequently *The Young Soldier*) issued (27 Aug); *The Doctrines and Disciplines of The Salvation Army* prepared for use at training homes for Salvation Army officers; Headquarters removed to Queen Victoria Street, London (8 Sep).

1882　The Founder's first visit to France (Mar); former London Orphan Asylum opened as Clapton Congress Hall and National Training Barracks (13 May); work begun in **Canada** (21 May), **India** (19 Sep), **Switzerland** (22 Dec) and **Sweden** (28 Dec).

1883　Work begun in **Sri Lanka** (26 Jan), **South Africa** (4 Mar), **New Zealand** (1 Apr), **Isle of Man** (17 Jun) and **Pakistan** (then a part of India); first prison-gate home opened in Melbourne, Australia (8 Dec); *The Doctrines and Disciplines of The Salvation Army* published in a public edition.

1884　Women's Social Work inaugurated; *The Soldier's Guide* published (Apr); work begun in **St Helena** (5 May); *The Salvation Army Band Journal* issued (Aug); *All the World* issued (Nov).

1885　*Orders and Regulations for Divisional Officers* published (10 Jun); *The Doctrines of The Salvation Army* published; Purity Agitation launched; Criminal Law Amendment Act became law on 14 Aug; trial (began 23 Oct) and acquittal of Bramwell Booth – charged, with W. T. Stead, in connection with the 'Maiden Tribute' campaign.

1886　Work begun in **Newfoundland** (1 Feb); first International Congress in London (28

Salvation Army History

May-4 Jun); *The Musical Salvationist* issued (Jul); first Self-Denial Week (4-11 Sep); first slum corps opened at Walworth, London, by 'Mother' Webb (20 Sep); work begun in **Germany** (14 Nov); *Orders and Regulations for Field Officers* published; the Founder first visited the United States and Canada.

1887 Work began in **Italy** (20 Feb), **Denmark** (8 May), **Netherlands** (8 May) and **Jamaica** (16 Dec); the Founder's first visit to Denmark, Sweden and Norway.

1888 Young people's work organised throughout Great Britain; first food depot opened, in Limehouse, London (Jan); work begun in **Norway** (22 Jan); first junior soldiers' brass band (Clapton); the Army Mother's last public address at City Temple, London (21 Jun).

1889 Work begun in **Belgium** (5 May) and **Finland** (8 Nov); *The Deliverer* published (Jul).

1890 Work begun in **Argentina** (1 Jan); *Orders and Regulations for Soldiers of The Salvation Army* issued (Aug); the Army Mother promoted to Glory (4 Oct); *In Darkest England and the Way Out*, by the Founder, published (Oct); work begun in **Uruguay** (16 Nov); banking department opened (registered as The Salvation Army Bank, 1891; Reliance Bank Ltd, 28 Dec 1900).

1891 The Founder publicly signed 'Darkest England' (now The Salvation Army Social Work) Trust Deed (30 Jan); £108,000 subscribed for 'Darkest England' scheme (Feb); Land and Industrial Colony, Hadleigh, Essex, established (2 May); International Staff Band inaugurated (Oct); work begun in **Zimbabwe** (21 Nov) and **Zululand** (22 Nov); the Founder's first visit to South Africa, Australia, New Zealand and India; the charter of The Methodist and General Assurance Society acquired.

1892 Eastbourne (UK) verdict against Salvationists quashed in the High Court of Justice (27 Jan); Band of Love inaugurated; League of Mercy begun in Canada (Dec).

1893 Grace-Before-Meat scheme instituted; *The Officer* issued (Jan).

1894 Second International Congress (Jul); work begun in **Hawaiian Islands** (13 Sep) and **Java** (now part of **Indonesia**) (24 Nov); naval and military league (later

red shield services) established (Nov); Swiss Supreme Court granted religious rights to SA (Dec).

1895 Work begun in **British Guiana** (now **Guyana**) (24 Apr), **Iceland** (12 May), **Japan** (4 Sep) and **Gibraltar** (until 1968).

1896 Young people's legion (Jan) and corps cadet brigades (Feb) inaugurated; work begun in **Bermuda** (12 Jan) and **Malta** (25 Jul until 1972); first SA exhibition, Agricultural Hall, **London, England** (1-10 Aug).

1897 First united young people's meetings (later termed 'councils') (14 Mar); first International Social Council in **London, England** (28, 29 Sep); first SA hospital founded at Nagercoil, India (Dec).

1898 *Orders and Regulations for Social Officers* published; work begun in **Barbados** (30 Apr) and **Alaska**; first united corps cadet camp at Hadleigh (Whitsun).

1899 First bandsmen's councils, Clapton (10 Dec).

1901 Work begun in **Trinidad** (7 Aug).

1902 Work begun in **St Lucia** (Sep) and **Grenada**.

1903 Migration Department inaugurated (became Reliance World Travel Ltd, 1981; closed 31 May 2001); work begun in **Antigua**.

1904 Third International Congress (24 Jun-8 Jul); Founder received by King Edward VII at Buckingham Palace (24 Jun); Founder's first motor campaign (Aug); work begun in **Panama** (Dec).

1905 The Founder campaigned in the Holy Land, Australia and New Zealand (Mar-Jun); first emigrant ship chartered by SA sailed for Canada (26 Apr); opening of International Staff Lodge (later College, now International College for Officers) (11 May); work begun in **St Vincent** (Aug). Freedom of London conferred on the Founder (26 Oct); Freedom of Nottingham conferred on the Founder (6 Nov).

1906 *The YP* (later *The Warrior*, then *Vanguard*) and *The Salvation Army Year Book* issued; Freedom of Kirkcaldy conferred on the Founder (16 Apr).

1907 Anti-Suicide Bureau established (Jan); Home League inaugurated (28 Jan); *The Bandsman and Songster* (later *The Musician*) issued (6 Apr); honorary degree of DCL, Oxford, conferred on the Founder (26 Jun); work begun in **Costa Rica** (5 Jul).

1908 Work begun in **Korea** (Oct).

1909 Leprosy work commenced in **Java** (now part of **Indonesia**) (15 Jan); SA work begun in **Chile** (Oct).

1910 Work begun in **Peru**, **Paraguay** and **Sumatra** (now part of **Indonesia**).

1912 Founder's last public appearance, in Royal Albert Hall, London (9 May); **General William Booth promoted to Glory** (20 Aug); **William Bramwell Booth appointed General** (21 Aug).

1913 Inauguration of life-saving scouts (21 Jul); work begun in **Celebes** (now part of **Indonesia**) (15 Sep) and **Russia** (until 1923).

1914 Fourth International Congress (Jun).

1915 Work begun in **British Honduras** (now **Belize**) (Jun) and **Burma** (now **Myanmar**); life-saving guards inaugurated (17 Nov).

1916 Work begun in **China** (Jan until 1951), in **St Kitts** and in **Portuguese East Africa** (now **Mozambique**) (officially recognised 1923).

1917 Work begun in **Virgin Islands** (USA) (Apr); chums inaugurated (23 Jun); Order of the Founder instituted (20 Aug).

1918 Work commenced in **Cuba** (Jul).

1919 Work begun in **Czechoslovakia** (19 Sep until 1950).

1920 Work begun in **Nigeria** (15 Nov) and **Bolivia** (Dec).

1921 Work begun in **Kenya** (Apr); sunbeams inaugurated (3 Nov).

1922 Work begun in **Zambia** (1 Feb), **Brazil** (1 Aug) and **Ghana** (Aug); publication of a second *Handbook of Salvation Army Doctrine*.

1923 Work begun in **Latvia** (until 1939).

1924 Work begun in **Hungary** (24 Apr until 1949), in **Surinam** (10 Oct) and **The Færoes** (23 Oct).

1927 Work begun in **Austria** (27 May), **Estonia** (31 Dec until 1940) and **Curacao** (until 1980); first International Young People's Staff Council (May-Jun).

1928 General Bramwell Booth's last public appearance – the stonelaying of the International (William Booth Memorial) Training College (now William Booth College), Denmark Hill, London (10 May).

1929 First High Council (8 Jan-13 Feb); **Comr**

Edward J. Higgins elected General; General Bramwell Booth promoted to Glory (16 Jun); Army work begun in **Colombia** (until 1965).

1930 Inception of goodwill league; Order of the Silver Star (now Fellowship of the Silver Star) inaugurated (in USA, extended to other lands in 1936); work begun in **Hong Kong**; Commissioners' Conference held in London (Nov).

1931 Work begun in **Uganda** and the **Bahamas** (May); The Salvation Army Act 1931 received royal assent (Jul).

1932 Work begun in **Namibia**.

1933 Work begun in **Yugoslavia** (15 Feb until 1948), Devil's Island, **French Guiana** (1 Aug until closing of the penal settlement in 1952) and **Tanzania** (29 Oct).

1934 Work begun in **Algeria** (10 Jun until 1970); second High Council elected Commander Evangeline Booth General (3 Sep); work begun in **Congo (Kinshasa)** (14 Oct); **General Evangeline Booth took command of The Salvation Army** (11 Nov).

1935 Work begun in **Singapore** (28 May).

1936 Work begun in **Egypt** (until 1949).

1937 Work begun in **Congo (Brazzaville)** (Mar), **The Philippines** (6 Jun) and **Mexico** (Oct).

1938 Torchbearer group movement inaugurated (Jan); *All the World* re-issued (Jan); work spread from Singapore to **Malaysia**.

1939 Third High Council elected Comr George Lyndon Carpenter General (24 Aug); **General George Lyndon Carpenter took command of The Salvation Army** (1 Nov).

1941 Order of Distinguished Auxiliary Service instituted (24 Feb); International Headquarters destroyed in London Blitz (10 May).

1943 Inauguration of The Salvation Army Medical Fellowship (16 Feb) (SA Nurses' Fellowship until 1987).

1944 Service of thanksgiving to mark the centenary of the conversion of William Booth (in 1844) held in St Paul's Cathedral, London (2 Jun).

1946 Fourth High Council elected Comr Albert Orsborn General (9 May); **General Albert Orsborn took command of The Salvation Army** (21 Jun).

1948 First Army worldwide broadcast (28 Apr).

1950 Work begun in **Haiti** (5 Feb); first TV broadcast by a General of The Salvation Army; official constitution of students' fellowship; first International Youth Congress held in London (10-23 Aug); reopening of Staff College (later International College for Officers) (10 Oct).

1954 Fifth High Council elected Comr Wilfred Kitching General (11 May); **General Wilfred Kitching took command of The Salvation Army** (1 Jul).

1956 Work begun in Port Moresby, **Papua New Guinea** (31 Aug); first International Corps Cadet Congress (19-31 Jul).

1959 Over-60 clubs inaugurated (Oct).

1962 Work begun in **Puerto Rico** (Feb).

1963 Sixth High Council elected Comr Frederick Coutts General (1 Oct); Queen Elizabeth the Queen Mother declared International Headquarters open (13 Nov); **General Frederick Coutts took command of The Salvation Army** (23 Nov).

1965 Queen Elizabeth II attended the International Centenary commencement (24 Jun); Founders' Day Service held in Westminster Abbey, London (2 Jul); work re-established in **Taiwan** (pioneered 1928) (Oct).

1967 Work begun in **Malawi** (13 Nov).

1969 Seventh High Council elected Comr Erik Wickberg General (23 Jul); *The Salvation Army Handbook of Doctrine* new edition published (Aug); **General Erik Wickberg took command of The Salvation Army** (21 Sep).

1970 Work begun in **Bangladesh** with cyclone relief measures (25 Nov).

1971 Work begun in **Spain** (23 Jul) and **Portugal** (25 Jul).

1972 Work begun in **Venezuela** (30 Jun).

1973 Work begun in **Fiji** (14 Nov).

1974 Eighth High Council elected Comr Clarence Wiseman General (13 May); **General Clarence Wiseman took command of The Salvation Army** (6 Jul).

1975 Work begun in **Costa Rica**.

1976 Work begun in **Guatemala** (Jun); **Mexico and Central America Territory** (now **Latin America North Territory** and **Mexico Territory**) formed (1 Oct).

1977 Ninth High Council elected Comr Arnold Brown General (5 May); **General**

Arnold Brown took command of The Salvation Army (5 Jul).

1978 Fifth International Congress (30 Jun-9 Jul), with opening ceremony attended by HRH the Prince of Wales.

1979 The Salvation Army Boys' Adventure Corps (SABAC) launched (21 Jan).

1980 Inauguration of International Staff Songsters (8 Mar); The Salvation Army Act 1980 received royal assent (1 Aug); work begun in **French Guiana** (1 Oct).

1981 Tenth High Council elected Comr Jarl Wahlström General (23 Oct); **General Jarl Wahlström took command of The Salvation Army** (14 Dec).

1984 International Conference of Leaders held in **Berlin, East Germany** (1-10 May).

1985 Work begun in **Colombia** (21 Apr) and **Marshall Islands** (1 Jun); second International Youth Congress (17-23 Jul) held in **Macomb, Illinois, USA**; work begun in **Angola** (4 Oct) and **Ecuador** (30 Oct).

1986 Work begun in **Tonga** (9 Jan); *Salvationist* first issued (15 Mar); 11th High Council elected Comr Eva Burrows General (2 May); **General Eva Burrows took command of The Salvation Army** (9 Jul); International Development Conference held at Sunbury Court, **England** (1-4 Sep).

1988 Work begun in **Liberia** (1 May); International Conference of Leaders held in **Lake Arrowhead, California, USA** (6-16 Sep).

1989 Work begun in **El Salvador** (1 Apr).

1990 Work begun in **East Germany** (Mar), **Czechoslovakia** (May), **Hungary** (Jun) and re-established in **Latvia** (Nov); sixth International Congress held in London (29 Jun-8 Jul); **United Kingdom Territory** established (1 Nov).

1991 Restructuring of **International Headquarters** as an entity separate from UK Territory (1 Feb); work reopened in **Russia** (6 Jul); International Conference of Leaders held in **London, UK** (30 Jul-9 Aug).

1992 Opening of new **USA National Headquarters** building in Alexandria, VA (3 May).

1993 The 12th High Council elected Comr Bramwell H. Tillsley General (28 Apr); **General Bramwell H. Tillsley took command of The Salvation Army** (9 Jul); work begun in **Micronesia**.

1994 General Bramwell H. Tillsley retired due to ill health (18 May); 13th High Council elected Comr Paul A. Rader General (23 Jul); **General Paul A. Rader took command of The Salvation Army immediately**; work begun in **Guam** and **Micronesia**.

1995 International Conference of Leaders held in **Hong Kong** (19-28 Apr); all married women officers granted rank in their own right (1 May); work begun in **Dominican Republic** (1 Jul); work reopened in **Estonia** (14 Aug); following relief and development programmes, work begun in **Rwanda** (5 Nov).

1996 Work begun in **Sabah (East Malaysia)** (Mar).

1997 International Youth Forum held in Cape Town, **South Africa** (Jan); first-ever congress held in **Russia/CIS**; Salvation Army leaders in **Southern Africa** signed commitment to reconciliation for past stand on apartheid; work begun in **Botswana** (20 Nov).

1998 International Conference of Leaders held in **Melbourne, Australia** (12-20 Mar); publication of a fourth Handbook of Doctrine entitled *Salvation Story* (Mar); International Commission on Officership opened in **London, England** (Oct).

1999 International Education Symposium held in **London, England** (Mar); work begun in **Romania** (May); 14th High Council elected Comr John Gowans General (15 May); **General John Gowans took command of The Salvation Army** (23 Jul).

2000 International Commission on Officership closed and subsequent Officership Survey carried out (Mar-May); work begun in **Macau** (25 Mar); The Salvation Army registered as a denomination in **Sweden** (10 Mar); International Conference of Leaders held in **Atlanta, Georgia, USA** (22-25 Jun); seventh International Congress held in **Atlanta, Georgia, USA** (28 Jun-2 Jul) (first held outside UK); work begun in **Honduras** (23 Nov).

2001 International Conference for Training Principals held in **London, England** (Mar); International Theology and Ethics Symposium held in **Winnipeg, Canada** (Jun); International Music Ministries Forum held in **London, England** (Jul); International Poverty Summit held on the Internet and Lotus Notes Intranet (Nov 2001-Feb 2002).

2002 The 15th High Council elected Comr John Larsson General (6 Sep); **General John Larsson took command of The Salvation Army** (13 Nov).

2004 International Conference of Leaders held in **New Jersey, USA** (29 Apr-7 May); International Music and Other Creative Ministries Forum (MOSAIC) held in **Toronto, Canada** (Jun); New International Headquarters building at 101 Queen Victoria Street, **London, England,** opened by Her Royal Highness, The Princess Royal (9 Nov); IHQ Emergency Services coordinates disaster relief work after Indian Ocean tsunami struck (26 Dec).

2005 Indian Ocean Tsunami Summit held in **London, England** (Jan); Eastern Europe Command redesignated Eastern Europe Territory; Singapore, Malaysia and Myanmar Command redesignated Singapore, Malaysia and Myanmar Territory (both 1 Mar); International Literary and Publications Conference held at **Alexandria, Virginia, USA** (22-29 Apr); European Youth Congress held in **Prague, Czech Republic** (4-8 Aug); All-Africa Congress held in **Harare, Zimbabwe** (24-28 Aug); work in **Lithuania** officially recognised by IHQ, and Germany Territory redesignated Germany and Lithuania Territory (Sep); 'Project Warsaw' launched to begin Army's work in **Poland** (23-25 Sep); East Africa Territory redesignated Kenya Territory, with Uganda Region given command status (1 Nov)

2006 The 16th High Council elected Comr Shaw Clifton General (28 Jan); **General Shaw Clifton took command of The Salvation Army** (2 Apr); Salvation Army Scouts and Guides World Jamboree held in **Almere, The Netherlands** (Aug); 2nd International Theology and Ethics Symposium held in **Johannesburg, South Africa** (Sep)

SIGNIFICANT EVENTS 2005-2006

2005

June

United Kingdom Territory with the Republic of Ireland: Salvationist Brian Oxley was appointed MBE (Member of the Order of the British Empire) in the Queen's Birthday honours, published on 11 June. The citation not only recognised his important contribution to The Salvation Army's international emergency work but also acknowledged the value of the Army's role in international relief work.

Hong Kong & Macau Command: The command celebrated the 50th anniversary of its training college.

July

South America West Territory: Lieut-Colonel Jorge Nery, OF, was promoted to Glory on 15 July. He had been Divisional Commander, Bolivia, for 25 years and much of The Salvation Army's work there can be attributed to his tireless efforts. In retirement the colonel mentored many young people who went on to become officers.

August

USA: The business publication *NonProfit Times* named Commissioner W. Todd Bassett (the then National Commander) in its Power and Influence Top 50 in the not-for-profit sector, and listed The Salvation Army as the most recognisable name in religious social service.

October

Finland & Estonia Territory: The Salvation Army celebrated the 10th anniversary of its work in Estonia.

2006

January

High Council: Commissioner Shaw Clifton was elected The Salvation Army's 18th General on 28 January.

USA: The Salvation Army's national leaders attended the signing into law of The Trafficking Victims Protection Reauthorisation Act (TVPRA) of 2005 by President George W. Bush.

Italy: The Salvation Army was represented at the Third Ecumenical Assembly, held in Rome.

April

USA National Headquarters: A record $370 million in public donations was received for the ongoing hurricane disaster recovery efforts.

USA Western Territory: On 18 April, The Salvation Army participated in the 100th annual commemoration of the 1906 San Francisco earthquake. Salvationists played an important part in the survival of San Francisco after that massive natural disaster.

July

Poland: The Salvation Army was officially registered as a church in Poland. It was added to the country's register of churches on 21 June and official confirmation of this step was given by the authorities on 12 July.

We needed to register as a church and not as anything else. The reason for this is that we are fundamentally a church with a social profile, and not a humanitarian organisation with church activities. We believed the registration was a priority in order to be effective in our mission and an equal partner with other churches in Poland.

– Colonel Vibeke Krommenhoek (Project Warsaw Team Leader) on The Salvation Army being granted official registration as a church in Poland

THE HIGH COUNCIL

THE High Council was originally established by William Booth in 1904 as a safeguard to allow the removal from office of an incumbent General who had become, for whatever reason, unfit to continue to exercise oversight, direction and control of The Salvation Army. Should such an allegation be made and receive significant support from officers of the rank of commissioner, a High Council would be called to decide upon the matter and to appoint a successor should the General be found unfit.

The Founder intended, however, that the normal method of appointment would be for the General in office to select his or her successor, but only one General – Bramwell Booth in 1912 – was ever selected in this way.

By November 1928, Bramwell Booth had been absent from International Headquarters for seven months on account of illness, and a High Council was called. The 63 members, being all the commissioners on active service and certain territorial commanders, gathered at Sunbury Court near London on 8 January 1929 and eventually voted that the General, then aged 73, was 'unfit on the ground of ill-health' to continue in office. On 13 February 1929 the High Council elected Commissioner Edward Higgins as the Army's third General.

Subsequently, a commissioners' conference agreed to three major constitutional reforms later passed into law by the British Parliament as the Salvation Army Act 1931, namely:

i. the abolition of the General's right to nominate his or her successor, and the substitution of the election of every General by a High Council;

ii. the fixing of an age limit for the retirement of the General;

iii. the creation of a trustee company to hold the properties and other capital assets of the Army, in place of the sole trusteeship of the General.

The High Council is currently constituted under provisions of the Salvation Army Act 1980 as amended by deeds of variation executed in 1995 and 2005.

Since 1929, High Councils have been held in 1934 (electing General Evangeline Booth), 1939 (General Carpenter), 1946 (General Orsborn), 1954 (General Kitching), 1963 (General Coutts), 1969 (General Wickberg), 1974 (General Wiseman), 1977 (General Brown), 1981 (General Wahlström), 1986 (General Burrows), 1993 (General Tillsley), 1994 (General Rader), 1999 (General Gowans), 2002 (General Larsson) and 2006 (General Clifton). The next is currently scheduled to convene in January 2011.

High Councils are normally called by the Chief of the Staff and have usually met at Sunbury Court but can meet anywhere in the United Kingdom. Since 1995 the High Council has been composed of all active commissioners except the spouse of the General, and all territorial commanders.

GENERALS ELECTED BY A HIGH COUNCIL

The place and date at the beginning of an entry denote the corps from which the General entered Salvation Army service and the year

Edward J. Higgins

Reading, UK, 1882. General (1929-34). b 26 Nov 1864; pG 14 Dec 1947. Served in corps and divisional work, BT; at the International Training Garrison, as CS, USA; as Asst Foreign Sec, IHQ; Brit Comr (1911-19); Chief of the Staff (1919-29). CBE. Author of *Stewards of God*, *Personal Holiness*, etc. m Capt Catherine Price, 1888; pG 1952.

Evangeline C. Booth

General (1934-39). b 25 Dec 1865; pG 17 Jul 1950. Fourth daughter of the Founder, at 21 years of age she commanded Marylebone Corps, its Great Western Hall being the centre of spectacular evangelistic work despite riotous opposition. As Field Commissioner this experience was used to advantage throughout Great Britain (1888-91). Her father appointed her to train cadets in London (1891-96), then as TC, Canada (1896-1904), and then Commander of the Army in the United States of America (1904-34). Author of *Toward a Better World*; *Songs of the Evangel*, etc.

George L. Carpenter

Raymond Terrace, Aus, 1892. General (1939-46). b 20 Jun 1872; pG 9 Apr 1948. Appointments included 18 years in Australia in property, training and literary work; from 1911 to 1927 at IHQ for most part with General Bramwell Booth as Literary Secretary; from 1927 to 1933 further service in Australia, including CS, Aus E; TC, S America E (1933-37); TC, Canada (1937-39). Author of *Keep the Trumpets Sounding*; *Banners and Adventures*, etc. m Ens Minnie Rowell, 1899; pG 1960. Author of *Notable Officers of The Salvation Army*; *Women of the Flag*, etc.

Albert W. T. Orsborn

Clapton, UK, 1905. General (1946-54). b 4 Sep 1886; pG 4 Feb 1967. Served as corps officer and in divisional work in BT; Chief Side Officer at the ITC (1925-33); CS, New Zealand (1933-36); TC, Scotland and Ireland (1936-40); Brit Comr (1940-46). CBE, 1943. Writer of many well-known Army songs. Author of *The House of My Pilgrimage*, etc. m Capt Evalina Barker, 1909; pG 1942. m Major Evelyn Berry, 1944; pG 1945. m Comr Mrs Phillis Taylor (née Higgins), 1947; pG 1986.

Wilfred Kitching

New Barnet, UK, 1914. General (1954-63). b 22 Aug 1893; pG 15 Dec 1977. Served in BT corps, divisional and NHQ appointments, then as CS, Aus S (1946-48); TC, Sweden (1948-51); Brit Comr (1951-54). Composer of many distinctively Salvationist musical works. Hon LLD (Yonsei, Korea), 1961; CBE, 1964. Author of *Soldier of Salvation* (1963) and *A Goodly Heritage* (autobiography, 1967). m Adjt Kathleen Bristow (Penge, 1916), 1929; pG 1982.

Frederick Coutts

Batley, UK, 1920. General (1963-69). b 21 Sep 1899; pG 6 Feb 1986. Served in British Territory in divisional work (1921-25) and as corps officer (1925-35); for 18 years in Literary Department, IHQ; writer of *International Company Orders* (1935-46); Editor of *The Officers' Review* (1947-53); Asst to Literary Secretary (1947-52); Literary Secretary (1952-53); Training Principal, ITC (1953-57); TC, Aus E (1957-63). Author of *The Call to Holiness* (1957); *Essentials of Christian Experience* (1969); *The Better Fight* (1973); *No Discharge in this War* (1975), *Bread for my Neighbour* (1978); *The Splendour of Holiness* (1983), etc. Order of Cultural Merit (Korea), 1966; Hon Litt D (Chung Ang, Korea), 1966; CBE, 1967; Hon DD (Aberdeen), 1981. m Lt Bessie Lee, BSc, 1925; pG 1967. m Comr Olive Gatrall (Thornton Heath, 1925), 1970, pG 1997.

Erik Wickberg

Bern 2, Switz, 1925. General (1969-74). b 6 Jul 1904; pG 26 Apr 1996. Served as corps officer in Hamilton, Scotland; in Germany as Training (Education) Officer, and Private Secretary to CS and TC (1926-34); at IHQ as Private Secretary to IS and Asst to Under Secretary for Europe (1934-39); in Sweden as IHQ Liaison Officer (1939-46), and DC, Uppsala (1946-48); CS, Switz, (1948-53); CS, Sweden (1953-57); TC, Germany (1957-61); Chief of the Staff (1961-69). Commander, Order of Vasa, 1970; Order of Moo Koong Wha (Korea), 1970; Hon LLD (Korea), 1970; Grand Cross of Merit, Federal Republic of Germany, 1971; King's Gold Medal (Grand Cross) (Sweden), 1980. Author of *Inkallad* (*God's Conscript*) (autobiography, Sweden, 1978) and *Uppdraget* (*The Charge – My Way to Preaching*) (1990). m Ens Frieda de Groot (Berne 1, Switz, 1922), 1929;

pG 1930. m Capt Margarete Dietrich (Hamburg 3, Ger, 1928), 1932; pG 1976. m Major Eivor Lindberg (Norrköping 1, Swdn, 1946), 1977.

Clarence Wiseman

Guelph, Ont, Canada, 1927. General (1974-77). b 19 Jun 1907; pG 4 May 1985. Served as corps officer and in editorial work in Canada; Chaplain with Canadian forces overseas (1940-43); Senior Representative, Canadian Red Shield Services Overseas (1943-45); in Canada, as divisional commander (1945-54), Field Secretary (1954-57) and Chief Secretary (1957-60); TC, East Africa (1960-62); Training Principal, ITC (1962-67); TC, Canada and Bermuda (1967-74). Order of Canada, 1976, Hon LLD, Hon DD (Yonsei). Author of *A Burning in My Bones* (1980) and *The Desert Road to Glory* (1980). m Capt Jane Kelly (Danforth, Ont, Canada, 1927), 1932; pG 1993. Author of *Earth's Common Clay*; *Bridging the Year*; *Watching Daily*.

Arnold Brown

Belleville, Can, 1935. General (1977-81). b 13 Dec 1913; pG 26 Jun 2002. Served in corps, editorial, public relations and youth work in Canada (1935-64); Secretary for Public Relations at IHQ (1964-69). Chief of the Staff (1969-74); TC, Canada and Bermuda (1974-77). MIPR, Hon LDH (Asbury, USA); Freeman, City of London; Hon DD (Olivet, USA), 1981; Officer, Order of Canada, 1981. Author of *What Hath God Wrought?*; *The Gate and the Light* (1984); *Yin – The Mountain the Wind Blew Here* (1988); *With Christ at the Table* (1991); *Occupied Manger – Unoccupied Tomb* (1994). m Lt Jean Barclay (Montreal Cit, Can, 1938), 1939. Author of *Excursions in Thought* (1981).

Jarl Wahlström

Helsinki 1, Fin, 1938. General (1981-86). b 9 Jul 1918. pG 3 Dec 1999. Served in corps, youth and divisional work in Finland; as Second World War Chaplain to Finnish armed forces; in Finland as a divisional commander (1960-63), Training Principal, Secretary of Music Dept (1963-68), Chief Secretary (1968-72); as CS, Canada & Bermuda (1972-76); TC, Finland (1976-81); TC, Sweden (1981); Knight, Order of the Lion of Finland, 1964; Order of Civil Merit, Mugunghwa Medal (Korea), 1983; Hon DHL (W Illinois), 1985; Paul Harris Fellow of Rotary International, 1987; Commander, Order of the White Rose of Finland, 1989. Author of *A Traveller's Song* and *A Pilgrim's Song* (autobiography, Finnish/ Swedish, 1989). m Lt Maire Nyberg (Helsinki 1, 1944).

Eva Evelyn Burrows

Fortitude Valley, Qld, Aus E, 1951. General (1986-93). b 15 Sep 1929. Appointed to corps in British Territory, before post-graduate studies; served at Howard Institute, Zimbabwe (1952-67), Head of Teacher Training (1965), Vice-Principal (1965-67); as Principal, Usher Institute (1967-70); Asst Principal, ICO (1970-74), Principal (1974-75); Leader WSS (GBI) (1975-77); TC, Sri Lanka (1977-79); TC, Scotland (1979-82); TC, Australia Southern (1982-86). BA (Qld); M Ed (Sydney); Hon Dr of Liberal Arts (Ehwa Univ, Seoul), 1988; Hon LLD (Asbury, USA), 1988; Paul Harris Fellow of Rotary International, 1990; Hon DST (Houghton), 1992; Hon DD (Olivet Nazarene Univ), 1993; Hon Dr Philosophy (Qld), 1993; Hon Dr of University (Griffith Univ), 1994; Companion of Order of Australia, 1994; Living Legacy Award from Women's International Center, USA, 1996.

Bramwell Harold Tillsley

Kitchener, Ont, Can, with wife née Maude Pitcher, 1956. General (1993-94). b 18 Aug 1931. Served in corps, youth, training college and divisional appointments in Canada, including Training Principal (1974-77), Provincial Commander in Newfoundland (1977-79) and DC, Metro Toronto (1979-81). Principal, ITC (1981-85); CS, USA Southern (1985-89); TC, Australia Southern (1989-91). In 1991 appointed Chief of the Staff. Retired in 1994 due to ill health. BA University of Western Ontario. Has written extensively for SA periodicals. Author of *Life in the Spirit*; *This Mind in You*; *Life More Abundant*; *Manpower for the Master*.

Paul Alexander Rader

Cincinnati Cit, USA E, w wife née Frances Kay Fuller, BA (Asbury), Hon DD (Asbury Theol Seminary) 1995, Hon LHD (Greenville) 1997, 1961. General (1994-99). b 14 Mar 1934. Served in corps prior to transfer to Korea in 1962. Served in Korea in training work (1962-73), as Training Principal (1973), Education Secretary (1974-76), Asst Chief Secretary (1976-77) and Chief Secretary (1977-84); in USA Eastern as Training Principal (1984-87), divisional commander (1987-89) and CS (1989); as TC, USA Western (1989-94). BA, BD (Asbury); MTh (Southern Baptist Seminary); D Miss (Fuller Theological Seminary); Hon LLD (Asbury); 1984 elected to board of trustees of Asbury College; 1989 elected Paul Harris Fellow of Rotary International; Hon DD (Asbury Theol Seminary), 1995; Hon LHD (Greenville), 1997; Hon DD (Roberts Wesleyan), 1998.

John Gowans

Grangetown, UK, 1955. General (1999-2002). b 13 Nov 1934. Served in British Territory as corps and, divisional youth secretary, National Stewardship Secretary and divisional commander; Chief Secretary, France (1977-81); in USA Western as Programme Secretary (1981-85) and DC, Southern California (1985-86); TC, France (1986-93); TC, Australia Eastern & PNG (1993-97); TC, UK (1997-99). Paul Harris Fellow of Rotary International; Hon DLitt (Yonsei, Korea); Freedom of the City of London (2000). Songwriter. Author of *O Lord!* series of poetry books and *There's a Boy Here* (autobiography, 2002). Co-author with John Larsson of 10 musicals. m Lt Gisèle Bonhotal (Paris Central, France, 1955) 1957.

John Larsson

Upper Norwood, UK, 1957. General (2002-06). b 2 Apr 38. Served in corps; at ITC; TYS (Scotland Territory); NYS (British Territory); CS, S Am W (1980-84); Principal, ITC (1984-88); Assistant to Chief of the Staff for UK Administrative Planning, IHQ (1988-1990); TC, UK (1990-93); TC, NZ (1993-96); TC, Swdn (1996-99); Chief of the Staff (1999-2002). BD (London). Author of *Doctrine without Tears* (1964); *Spiritual Breakthrough* (1983); *The Man Perfectly Filled with the Spirit* (1986); *How Your Corps Can Grow* (1989), etc. Composer of music and co-author with John Gowans of 10 musicals. m Capt Freda Turner (Kingston-upon-Thames, UK, 1964) 1969.

Shaw Clifton

Edmonton, UK, with wife née Helen Ashman, 1973. General (2006-present). b 21 Sep 45. Served as corps officer in British Territory; in Literary Department, IHQ (1974); in Zimbabwe as Vice Principal, Mazoe Secondary School (1975-77) and CO, Bulawayo Citadel (1977-79); in further BT corps appointments (1979-82, 1989-92); at IHQ as Legal & Parliamentary Secretary (1982-89); in UK as DC, Durham & Tees (1992-95); in USA Eastern as DC, Massachusetts (1995-97); as TC, Pakistan (1997-2002); TC, New Zealand, Fiji & Tonga (2002-04); TC, UK (2004-06). LLB (Hons), AKC (Theol), BD (Theol) (Hons), PhD. Author of *What Does the Salvationist Say?* (1977); *Growing Together* (1984); *Strong Doctrine, Strong Mercy* (1985); *Never the Same Again* (1997); *Who are these Salvationists?* (1999); *New Love – Thinking Aloud About Practical Holiness* (2004), etc.

The Army has been raised up by God. We are sustained in being an Army by God. The Army belongs to God. The General is under God. Your new General is under God. There is no other place to be. Under God – only under God – am I willing to accept this sacred responsibility. Only under God can it be done. Only under God can the heavy burden be carried.

– General Shaw Clifton, speaking at his welcome and dedication meeting in Kensington Town Hall, London, on 8 April 2006

COUNTRIES WHERE THE SALVATION ARMY IS AT WORK

THE Salvation Army is at work in 111 countries. A country in which the Army serves is defined in two ways:

(i) Politically

(ii) Where the General has given approval to the work, thus officially recognising it, ensuring it has legal identity and a Deed Poll is published to acknowledge this.

As far as political status is concerned, for the Army's purposes, three categories are recognised:

(a) Independent countries, eg USA and New Zealand;

(b) Internally independent political entities which are under the protection of another country in matters of defence and foreign affairs, eg The Færoes, Isle of Man, Puerto Rico;

(c) Colonies and other dependent political units, eg Bermuda, French Guiana, Guam, Guernsey, Jersey, Virgin Islands.

Administrative subdivisions of a country such as Wales and Scotland in the UK are not recognised as separate countries for this purpose. The countries fulfilling the quoted criteria, with the date in brackets on which the work was officially recognised, are as follows:

Angola ....(1985)	China ....(1916)	Estonia ....(1927)
Antigua ....(1903)	Colombia ....(1985)	...........................(1995)
Argentina ....(1890)	Congo (Brazzaville)	
Australia.............(1881)	...........................(1937)	Færoes, The ....(1924)
Austria ....(1927)	Congo (Kinshasa)	Fiji ....(1973)
	...........................(1934)	Finland...............(1889)
Bahamas.............(1931)	Costa Rica ....(1907)	France ....(1881)
Bangladesh..........(1970)	...........................(1975)	French Guiana ....(1980)
Barbados ....(1898)	Cuba....................(1918)	
Belgium ....(1889)	Czech Republic ..(1919)	Georgia ....(1993)
Belize ....(1915)	...........................(1990)	Germany ....(1886)
Bermuda.............(1896)		Ghana.................(1922)
Bolivia ....(1920)	Denmark ....(1887)	Grenada ....(1902)
Botswana ....(1997)	Dominican Republic	Guam ....(1994)
Brazil ....(1922)	...........................(1995)	Guatemala ....(1976)
		Guernsey ....(1879)
Canada ....(1882)	Ecuador ....(1985)	Guyana...............(1895)
Chile...................(1909)	El Salvador ....(1989)	

27

Countries where The Salvation Army is at work

Haiti ....(1950)
Honduras ....(2000)
Hong Kong ....(1930)
Hungary ....(1924)
..............................(1990)

Iceland ....(1895)
India ....(1882)
Indonesia ....(1894)
Ireland, Republic of
 (Eire) ....(1880)
Isle of Man..........(1883)
Italy ....(1887)

Jamaica ....(1887)
Japan ....(1895)
Jersey ....(1879)

Kenya..................(1921)
Korea ....(1908)

Latvia ....(1923)
..............................(1990)
Lesotho ....(1969)
Liberia ....(1988)
Lithuania ....(2005)

Macau ....(2000)
Malawi ....(1967)
Malaysia..............(1938)
Marshall Islands..(1985)
Mexico ....(1937)
Micronesia ....(1993)
Moldova..............(1994)
Mozambique ......(1916)
Myanmar ....(1915)

Netherlands, The
..............................(1887)
New Zealand ......(1883)
Nigeria ....(1920)

Norway ....(1888)
Pakistan ....(1883)
Panama................(1904)
Papua New Guinea
..............................(1956)
Paraguay ....(1910)
Peru ....(1910)
Philippines, The
..............................(1937)
Poland ....(2005)
Portugal ....(1971)
Puerto Rico ....(1962)

Romania..............(1999)
Russia..................(1913)
..............................(1991)
Rwanda ....(1995)

St Christopher Nevis
 (St Kitts) ....(1916)
St Helena ....(1884)
St Lucia ....(1902)
St Maarten ....(1999)
St Vincent ....(1905)
Singapore ....(1935)

South Africa........(1883)
Spain ....(1971)
Sri Lanka ....(1883)
Suriname ....(1924)
Swaziland............(1960)
Sweden................(1882)
Switzerland ....(1882)

Taiwan ....(1965)
Tanzania..............(1933)
Tonga ....(1986)
Trinidad and Tobago
..............................(1901)

Uganda................(1931)
Ukraine ....(1993)
United Kingdom (1865)
United States of
 America ....(1880)
Uruguay ....(1890)

Venezuela ....(1972)
Virgin Islands ....(1917)

Zambia ....(1922)
Zimbabwe ....(1891)

A micro-credit group in India Northern Territory

INTERNATIONAL STATISTICS
(as at 1 January 2006)

Countries and other territories where
SA serves (see pp 27-28) 111
Languages used in SA work, including
some tribal languages....................175
Corps, outposts, societies, new
plants and recovery churches....14,966
Goodwill centres................................758
Officers 25,966
Active..17,131
Retired..8,835
Auxiliary-captains...............................134
Lieutenants 582
Envoys/sergeants, full-time............1,174
Cadets..912
Employees...................................106,695
Senior soldiers 1,062,453
Adherents....................................190,214
Junior soldiers 368,149
Corps cadets..................................43,488
Senior band musicians..................23,273
Senior songsters...........................97,677
Other senior musical group
members.....................................66,257
Senior and young people's
local officers 119,160
Women's Ministries (all groups) –
members 505,856
League of Mercy – members......106,647
SAMF – members..........................7,015
Over-60 clubs – members..........109,295
Men's fellowships – members......58,507
Young people's bands –
members 17,164
Young people's singing
companies – members..............90,562
Other young people's music
groups – members....................61,249
Sunday schools – members........616,946
Junior youth groups
(scouts, guides, etc, and clubs) –
members..................................218,023
Senior youth groups – members......60,684

Corps-based community development
programmes..............................22,103
Beneficiaries/clients............1,109,716
Thrift stores/charity shops
(corps/territorial)........................1,583
Recycling centres 23

Social Programme
Residential
Hostels for homeless and transient....606
Capacity 34,681
Emergency lodges...............................185
Capacity 12,013
Children's homes 218
Capacity 9,320
Homes for the elderly........................149
Capacity 8,655
Homes for the disabled 46
Capacity 1,667
Homes for the blind 8
Capacity 374
Remand and probation homes..............61
Capacity 1,221
Homes for street children....................37
Capacity 837
Mother and baby homes......................48
Capacity 1,325
Training centres for families 19
Capacity 447
Care homes for vulnerable people 59
Capacity 1,071
Women's and men's refuge
centres 87
Capacity 2,690
Other residential care
homes/hostels 88
Capacity 4,748

Day Care
Community centres............................539
Early childhood education centres....114
Capacity 6,028

Day centres for the elderly 154
    Capacity 9,100
Play groups..158
    Capacity 4,664
Day centres for the hearing
    impaired 15
    Capacity 122
Day centres for street children 11
    Capacity 645
Day nurseries 196
    Capacity 11,569
Drop-in centres for youth..................276
Other day care centres 603
    Capacity 14,886

Addiction Dependency

Non-residential programmes 375
    Capacity 29,452
Residential programmes....................167
    Capacity 9,235
Harbour Light programmes 35
    Capacity 65,031
Other services for those with
    addictions 116
    Capacity 6,785

Service to the Armed Forces

Clubs and canteens...............................24
Mobile units for service personnel......38
Chaplains 19

Emergency Disaster Response

Disaster rehabilitation schemes 429
    Participants 173,255
Refugee programmes –
    host country 16
    Participants 7,523
Refugee rehabilitation programmes....12
    Participants 6,470
Other response programmes..............185
    Participants 54,262

Services to the Community

Prisoners visited 297,456
Prisoners helped on discharge....127,429
Police courts – people helped 329,727
Missing persons – applications 10,264
    Number traced..............................6,745
Night patrol/anti-suicide –

    number helped........................351,064
Community youth programmes 764
    Beneficiaries 49,075
Employment bureaux –
    applications 304,634
    initial referrals......................91,262
Counselling – people helped......311,672
General relief – people
    helped 13,686,003
Emergency relief (fire, flood,
    etc) – people helped............2,796,246
Emergency mobile units 2,372
Feeding centres 612
Restaurants and cafes........................226
Thrift stores/charity shops
    (social)...................................1,430
Apartments for elderly 629
    Capacity 8,268
Hostels for students, workers, etc.......57
    Capacity 2,977
Land settlements (SA villages,
    farms etc) 13
    Capacity 402
Social Services summer camps 193
    Participants 30,470
Other services to the community
    (unspecified)....................................76
    Beneficiaries.......................6,411,694

Health Programme

General hospitals 20
    Capacity 2,203
Maternity hospitals.............................13
    Capacity 247
Other specialist hospitals 16
Capacity 1,906
Specialist clinics.................................77
    Capacity 387
General clinics/health centres 151
    Capacity 578
Mobile clinics/community health
    posts 37
Inpatients...................................260,509
Outpatients 1,030,748
Doctors/medics...................................920
Invalid/convalescent homes 27
    Capacity 11,487

Health education programmes
(HIV/Aids, etc) 419
Beneficiaries.............................450,894
Day care programmes.........................18

Education Programme
Kindergarten/sub primary..................700
Primary schools 946
Upper primary and middle
schools 201
Secondary and high schools..............191
Colleges and universities......................3
Vocational training schools/centres ...133

Pupils...482,870
Teachers..15,834
Schools for the blind (included in
above totals)....................................25
Schools for the disabled (included in
above totals)....................................10
Boarding schools (included in
above totals)....................................16
Evening schools 5
Colleges, universities, staff training
and development study and distance
learning centres...............................16

SALVATION ARMY PERIODICALS
BY TERRITORY/COMMAND

Australia National: *Kidzone, Warcry*

Australia Eastern Territory: *Creative Ministry, Pipeline, Venue, Women in Touch*

Australia Southern Territory: *Kidzone, On Fire, Warcry*

Belgium Command: *Espoir* (French), *Strijdkreet* (Flemish)

Brazil Territory: *Notas e Notícias, O Oficial, Rumo Magazine*

Canada and Bermuda Territory: *Edge for Kids, En Avant, Faith & Friends, Foi & Vie, Salvationist*

Caribbean Territory: *The War Cry*

Congo (Brazzaville) Territory: *Le Salutiste*

Congo (Kinshasa) and Angola Territory: *Echo d'Espoir*

Denmark Territory: *Mennesker & Tro, Kids Alive, Vision-Mission, Young Connection*

Eastern Europe Territory: *Vestnik Spaseniya* (*The War Cry*), *The Officer* (both Russian)

Finland and Estonia Territory: *Krigsropet* (Swedish), *Nappis, Sotahuuto* (both Finnish)

France Territory: *Avec Vous, Le Bulletin de la Ligue du Foyer, Le Fil, Le Magazine, L'Officier, Quand Même*

Germany and Lithuania Territory: *Danke, Der Kriegsruf, Heilsarmee-Forum*

Ghana Territory: *Salvationist Newsletter*

Hong Kong and Macau Command: *Army Scene, The War Cry*

India Central Territory: *Home League Magazine, Udyogasthudu, Yovana Veerudu, Yudha Dwani*

India Eastern Territory: *Sipai Tlangau* (Mizo *War Cry*), *The Officer, Young Salvationist, Chunnunpar* (all Mizo)

India Northern Territory: *Home League Quarterly* (Hindi), *Mukti Samachar* (Hindi and Punjabi), *The Officer* (Hindi)

India South Eastern Territory: *Chiruveeran* (Tamil), *Home League Quarterly, Poresathan* (Tamil), *The Officer* (Tamil)

India South Western Territory: *Home League Quarterly* (Malayalam/English), *The Officer, Youdha Shabdan, Yuva Veeran* (all Malayalam)

India Western Territory: *Home League Quarterly, The Officer, The War Cry,*

The Young Soldier (all Gujarati and Marathi)

International Headquarters: *All the World, Global Exchange, The Officer, Words of Life*

Italy Command: *Il Bollettino dell' Unione Femminile, Il Grido di Guerra*

Japan Territory: *Home League Quarterly, The Officer, The Sunday School Guide, Toki-no-Koe*

Kenya Territory: *Sauti ya Vita* (English and Kiswahili)

Korea Territory: *Home League Programme Helps, Loving Hands Sponsorship Magazine, The Officer, The War Cry*

Latin America North Territory: *Voz de Salvación (Salvation Voice), Arco Iris de Ideas (Rainbow of Ideas)*

The Netherlands and Czech Republic Territory: *Dag in Dag Uit, Heils-en Strijdzangen, InterCom, Strijdkreet, Voor Werk* (all Dutch), *Prapor Spásy* (Czech)

New Zealand, Fiji and Tonga Territory: *War Cry*

Nigeria Territory: *Salvationist, The Shepherd, The War Cry*

Norway, Iceland and The Færoes Territory: *Herópid* (Icelandic), *FAbU nytt, Krigsropet, Frelsesoffiseren* (all Norwegian)

Pakistan Territory: *Home League Quarterly, The War Cry* (Urdu)

Papua New Guinea Territory: *Tokaut*

The Philippines Territory: *Home League Programme Aids, The War Cry*

Singapore, Malaysia and Myanmar Territory: *The War Cry*

South America East Territory: *El Cruzado, El Oficial, El Salvacionista, El Mensajero*

South America West Territory: *El Grito de Guerra, El Trebol*

Southern Africa Territory: *Echoes of Mercy, Home League Highlights, Home League Resource Manual, Outer Circle Newsletter, SAMF Newsletter, The Reporter, The War Cry*

Sri Lanka Territory: *Yudha Handa*

Sweden and Latvia Territory: *FA-musikant, Stridsropet, William*

Switzerland, Austria and Hungary Territory: *Espoir* (French), *Dialog* (German), *Dialogue* (French), *IN* (French and German), *Just 4 U* (French), *Trialog* (German), *Klecks* (German)

Taiwan Region: *Taiwan Regional News*

United Kingdom Territory with the Republic of Ireland: *Kids Alive!, Salvationist, The War Cry*

USA National: *The War Cry, Word & Deed – A Journal of Theology and Ministry, Women's Ministries Resources, Young Salvationist*

USA Central Territory: *Central Connection*

USA Eastern Territory: *¡Buenas Noticias!, Cristianos en Marcha* (both Spanish), *Good News, Priority!, Ven a Cristo Hoy* (Spanish)

USA Southern Territory: *Southern Spirit*

USA Western Territory: *Caring, New Frontier, Nuevos Fronteras* (Spanish)

Zimbabwe Territory: *Zimbabwe Salvationist, ZEST*

A LITERARY LEGACY

'Our issues of *The War Cry* and tabloids present one of the most consistent and compelling records of the history of the Christian Church, reporting on the details and drama of God at work in the Army he has called to serve in the trenches of life. God's work in our Movement has inspired a literary legacy of which every Salvationist can be proud, and which offers a treasure trove of insight and inspiration.' – *Colonel Henry Gariepy*

Books Published during 2005-06

Finland and Estonia Territory
The Salvation Army in Estonia 1927-1940 and 1995-2005
Pelastusarmeija Virossa 1927-1940 ja 1995-2005 (Finnish)
Päästearmee Eestis 1927-1940 ja 1995-2005 (Estonian)

India Eastern Territory
*Manipuri (Meitei) Song Book**
Discovery (Discipling Programme for Young People) (Mizo)*
Senior Sunday School Bible Lessons (Mizo)*
Young People's Bible Lessons – Senior, Intermediate, Junior, Primary and Beginners (Mizo)*

India South Western Territory
Discovery (Discipling Programme for Young People) (Malayalam)*
*Malayalam Song Book**

International Headquarters
Adventurers Junior Soldiers Training Course (International Literature Programme)
Discovery Corps Cadet Studies (International Literature Programme)
The Salvation Army Year Book 2005

Japan Territory
Servant Leadership – How to Make it Happen by Robert Street (Japanese)
We Need Saints! by Chick Yuill (Japanese)

Korea Territory
Corps Cadet Lessons (Courses F and G)
Corps Cell Group Study Manual 2006
Daily Home Bible Studies for Salvationist Families 2006
Summer Bible School 2006 (handbook and workbooks)
Young People's Company Lessons 2006 (manual and workbooks)

South America West Territory
La Primera Familia Disfuncional (*The First Dysfunctional Family*) by A. Kenneth Wilson (Spanish)*
40 Días con el Salvador (*40 Days with the Saviour*) by Henry Gariepy (Spanish)*
Liderazgo de Siervos (*Servant Leadership*) course

material from Personnel Development Dept, IHQ (Spanish)*
Salvation Army Ceremonies Book (Spanish)*
Guidelines for the League of Mercy (Spanish)*
Orders and Regulations: Corps Secretaries and Treasurers, Bands and Brigades, Divisional Commanders, Work Among Young People, Local Officers (Spanish)*

Southern Africa Territory
Chi-Cheddi – a three-year Sunday school curriculum written and produced by the children's section of the Youth Dept

United Kingdom Territory
Eagle's Wings by Alan Crossland
Getting to Know William Booth of The Salvation Army (teachers' and pupils' books) by Elisabeth Smith, illustrated by Berni Georges
Lasting Joys by Muriel Yendell (autobiography)

Books on the web, available on www.salvationarmy.org.uk
Closer Communion by Clifford Kew
Community in Mission by Philip Needham
In Darkest England and The Way Out by William Booth
Marching On! (The Salvation Army, Its Origin and Development) by Malcolm Bale
Salvation Story – Salvationist Handbook of Doctrine
Strong Doctrine, Strong Mercy by Shaw Clifton
The Art of Prayer by John Murfitt
Outlines of Cadets' Bible Lessons

USA National
Beside Still Waters by Marlene Chase
Soldiers of the Cross by Norman H. Murdoch
The Life and Ministry of William Booth by Roger J. Green

USA Eastern Territory
Heartwork of Hope – a directed journal by JoAnn Streeter Shade

USA Western Territory
Lyssa Lamb by Debora Bell, illustrated by Ronda Gilger

* Published with the assistance of a grant from the International Literature Programme, IHQ

MINISTRIES AND FELLOWSHIPS

WOMEN'S MINISTRIES

THE ideal basic unit of society is the home and family, where women play a vital and definitive role. Furthermore, as natural providers of hope, women play an important part in shaping society. Therefore, any fellowship of women in which Christian influence is exerted and practical help given benefits not only the individual and the family, but also the nation.

Women's Ministries provide a programme of meetings and other activities based on the fourfold aim of the Army's international women's organisation, the Home League, which was inaugurated in 1907. Those aims are Worship, Education, Fellowship, Service. The motto of the Home League is: 'I will live a pure life in my house' (Psalm 101:2 *Good News Bible*).

The mission of Women's Ministries is to bring women into a knowledge of Jesus Christ; encourage their full potential in influencing family, friends and community; equip them for growth in personal understanding and life skills; address issues which affect women and their families in the world.

A Women's Ministries
Centenary Challenge

from the World President of Women's Ministries

WILLIAM BOOTH, Founder of The Salvation Army, had a large heart of compassion and – like the Lord Jesus – was known to shed tears over suffering humanity. The women in Booth's life shared his concern. His wife Catherine, along with their daughters and daughters-in-law, wanted women to be empowered and offered inclusion. The Salvation Army is a place where women can shed their tears of spiritual longing, disappointment, repentance, sorrow and joy. Here they can find acceptance, faith for the future and opportunities for Christian service.

It is in this spirit that 100 years of Women's Ministries are being celebrated during 2007. A logo for the centenary year *(above)* shows a teardrop, representing a softened heart. The slogan 'While Women Weep' has been translated into many languages. The English initials of www represent a challenge to extend the network of The Salvation Army wherever women want to belong.

Women's Ministries has been an area of vibrant activity and witness for the gospel since the launch of the Home League in January 1907. The Founder's fighting spirit – to lift up the fallen and free the captives – continues to be a hallmark of Women's Ministries. In this centenary year, may the name of Jesus bring hope and joy to every home in every land!

THE LEAGUE OF MERCY AND COMMUNITY CARE MINISTRIES

THE League of Mercy began in 1892 in Canada and is made up of people of all ages whose mission is to engage in a caring ministry. The main objective of the League of Mercy is to respond to the spiritual and social needs of the community. The ministry is adapted according to the local situation, the size of its membership and the skill of its members, and endeavours to follow Christ's injunction, 'Inasmuch as ye have done it unto one of the least of these my brethren, ye have done it unto me' (Matthew 25:40 *Authorised Version*).

THE FELLOWSHIP OF THE SILVER STAR

THE Fellowship of the Silver Star, inaugurated in the USA in 1930 and extended worldwide in 1936, expresses gratitude to parents or other significant life mentors of Salvation Army officers.

THE SALVATION ARMY MEDICAL FELLOWSHIP

THE Salvation Army Medical Fellowship, instituted in 1943 by Mrs General Minnie Carpenter, is an international fellowship of dedicated medical personnel. Physical suffering in our world today challenges both the medical and the physical and emotional resources of medical personnel. The fellowship encourages a Christian witness and application of Christian principles in professional life while at the same time being involved with practical  application in hospitals, clinics and various other places of medical care. The motto of the Fellowship is: 'If we walk in the light, as he is in the light, we have fellowship one with another' (1 John 1:7 *Authorised Version*).

THE SALVATION ARMY STUDENTS' FELLOWSHIP

THIS fellowship started in Norway in 1942 and later spread to other countries, receiving an official constitution in 1950. It comes under the world presidency of the General. The aim of the fellowship is to unite Salvationist students and graduates of universities, colleges and other centres of higher education in Christian fellowship and such Salvation Army service as may be appropriate.

THE SALVATION ARMY BLUE SHIELD FELLOWSHIP

IN 1974 the Blue Shield Fellowship was formed by two British Salvationist policemen to provide friendship and support to Christian policemen as they face present-day challenges. Membership is open to both active and retired police officers, and there are members in many countries.

SALVATION ARMY HONOURS

ORDER OF THE FOUNDER

Instituted on 20 August 1917 by General Bramwell Booth, the Order of the Founder is the highest Salvation Army honour for distinguished service

HISTORY OF THE ORDER

IN 1917, five years after the death of William Booth, his son, General Bramwell Booth, inaugurated the Order of the Founder 'to mark outstanding service rendered by officers and soldiers such as would in spirit or achievement have been specially commended by the Founder'.

The first awards were made in 1920 to 15 officers and one soldier. Three years later, seven officers and one local officer were honoured, but since then the awards have been made much more sparingly and, to date, 151 officers and 90 lay Salvationists have been recognised with the Army's highest honour – a mere 241 in total over 90 years.

The first presentation was to a soldier, Private Herbert Bourne, for outstanding Christian witness and service during military service in the First World War. A few senior leaders such as Commissioner Henry Howard, General Evangeline Booth and Commissioner Catherine Bramwell-Booth have been recipients but, much more commonly, faithful and devoted service by less well-known personalities has been acknowledged.

The honour is rarely given because every nomination is carefully scrutinised by a panel of senior leaders at International Headquarters. Salvationists have every reason to be proud of those who have been awarded this outstanding recognition for meritorious Christian example, witness and service.

Recipients of the Order of the Founder 2005-06

Brigadier Gertrude McClennan Purdue (USA Southern Territory). The exemplary Christian witness of Brigadier Gertrude McClennan Purdue was demonstrated in her tireless work on behalf of others, her personal efforts to promote racial reconciliation, her pastoral ministry with people of all ages and circumstances, and her persistent encouragement and mentoring of hundreds. Admitted to the Order of the Founder on 21 August 2005.

Geoffrey John Dalziel (Australia Southern Territory). Displaying exemplary Salvationism and spiritual leadership as a local officer of outstanding influence, and being of impeccable moral character, John

Dalziel was the face and voice of The Salvation Army in the Australian media. In clearly delineating the ethical standards and compassionate ministry of the Movement he enhanced the reputation of The Salvation Army with the Australian community at large. Admitted to the Order of the Founder on 3 November 2005.

Commissioner (Dr) Harry Williams (United Kingdom Territory with the Republic of Ireland). As a plastic surgeon and strategic health administrator Commissioner Harry Williams applied his gifts to all sectors of society, but especially the disadvantaged. His gifts as a Salvation Army leader created new directions in territories, in international development

and ecumenically. His gifts as a writer and artist enabled many to know more of his observations of God's world, God's ways and God's people. Admitted to the Order of the Founder on 17 November 2005.

Commissioner (Dr) Harry Williams is admitted to the Order of the Founder by General John Larsson in a meeting at IHQ

ORDER OF DISTINGUISHED AUXILIARY SERVICE

On 24 February 1941 General George Carpenter instituted this order to mark the Army's appreciation of distinguished service rendered by non-Salvationists who have helped to further its work in a variety of ways

Recipient of the Order of Distinguished Auxiliary Service 2005-06

Mr Merrill R. Fie (USA Western Territory) received the order in recognition of his vision, leadership, generosity and compassion in advancing the mission and ideals of The Salvation Army. Admitted to the Order of Distinguished Auxiliary Service on 12 December 2005.

Responding to the Call

by Major Cedric Hills (International Emergency Services Coordinator, IHQ)

OSCAR WILDE is credited with this wonderful observation: 'To expect the unexpected shows a thoroughly modern intellect.' Recent years have witnessed dramatic changes for the emergency responder as powers of intellect have combined with developments in modern technology to help us predict future emergencies and reduce the occurrence of unexpected disasters.

Weather forecasts and computer graphics predicting the path and strength of incoming weather hazards are fascinating. As Hurricanes Katrina and Rita moved towards the southern states of the USA in 2005 such forecasts enabled managers of Salvation Army emergency disaster services to preposition huge numbers of response vehicles, supplies and personnel.

But despite modern aids, the expected became the unexpected as levees were breached – hazard became disaster and then tragedy. The disaster in New Orleans prompted the largest emergency response ever mounted by The Salvation Army.

The 'luxury' of preparation time was not afforded to families living in the Kashmir regions of India and Pakistan. A massive earthquake of magnitude 7.6 hit the region on 8 October 2005. With its epicentre in Pakistan's North-West Frontier Province, the town of Balakot was destroyed in an instant.

The earthquake came unexpectedly and the residents of this community received no evacuation warnings. More than a year after this disaster The Salvation Army's relief team is still working among impacted families in the region.

These were two very different disasters; both prompted swift action from The Salvation Army with teams of emergency relief workers responding to the call and on site within hours.

Recent experience has shown that training personnel is one of the most effective ways in which we can be ready for the unexpected. During the past 12 months trainers from the International Emergency Services (IES) have conducted disaster preparedness courses in Sri Lanka, India, Iraq, UK and USA. Personnel are being equipped to respond to local disasters and to reinforce work in other countries when local resources become overwhelmed.

June 2006 saw the launch of the first intensive international training programme, with three delegates commencing a 12-month internship programme. Placements to emergency programmes around the world will provide a diverse training experience. Stimulating the intellect and enhancing the 'heart for service' with practical skills will make for a better response to future unexpected events.

Generous response to international appeals for assistance has enabled us to provide grants to disaster work around the globe. Recent support has been given to Congo (Kinshasa), Zimbabwe, Uganda, Rwanda, Nigeria, Romania, Chile, Brazil, Bolivia, Peru, India, Indonesia, The Philippines, Malawi, Tanzania and Kenya.

Intellect should suggest that extended periods of drought would cause suffering. However, governmental and media complacency allowed the 'unexpected' to develop over four years in eastern Africa. Four successive seasons of drought left thousands starving and prompted the launch of the international 'Sub Sahara Famine Appeal' early in 2006.

Once the problem had been highlighted, support came quickly and generously. With the assistance of international emergency personnel, interventions were launched in Kenya, Tanzania and Malawi. An extensive programme of water storage and transportation schemes made water available to hundreds of rural communities. A 'food for fees' programme provided much-needed food supplies to secondary (boarding) schools and a food ration distribution was mounted in Malawi.

While the main role of the IES section at IHQ focuses on supporting territorial emergency responses, we are also charged with coordinating responses in areas where there is no existing Salvation Army presence. One major programme came to an end in Spring 2006. A ceremony of thanksgiving, held in Kuwait, brought to a close a three-year community recovery programme in Iraq.

During this time thousands of families benefited from Salvation Army assistance, with help including the building of new homes and schools, the provision of water supplies, distribution of livestock, job creation schemes and much more.

Practical assistance was enhanced by stimulation of intellect and training, with almost 1,000 Iraqi personnel from humanitarian organisations, community groups and government departments attending Capacity Building training programmes supported by The Salvation Army across southern Iraq.

Although The Salvation Army's own programme there is officially over, we continue to mentor the Iraq Salvation Humanitarian Organisation (a newly created local independent NGO) as it continues the vital work of recovery for the people in Iraq.

Expecting the unexpected may be an oxymoron but the IES continues to prepare and equip Salvation Army emergency relief teams for that moment when they respond to the call.

A Salvation Army bowser located in Kenya by the IES

Aligning Hearts with Christ's Presence

by Captain Ted Horwood (International Projects and
Development Services Secretary, IHQ)

THE Salvation Army believes that the poverty experienced by much of the world is unacceptable. The International Projects and Development Services (IPDS) attempts to facilitate the Army's mission by operating as a catalyst for sustainable change through its network of community development programmes.

From a Christian perspective, change involves more than delivering effective projects. For those who are implementing projects throughout the Army world, the term 'community development' means transformation. Projects provide an entry into communities, families and individuals where traditional forms of evangelism may not be appropriate or feasible.

For the thousands of Salvation Army officers, personnel and volunteers working around the world, 'community development' is an expression of Christ's presence working in and through their lives.

For those participating at the community level, 'community development' represents hope. Hope for peace, while living in societies in conflict. Hope for love in reconciling families and seeking relationships with Jesus. Hope for a better life where water, education, food and recognition of human rights are in short supply.

And lastly, for those providing funds and offering services, 'community development' represents participation. We align ourselves with what God is already doing in a community.

For example, Nepal is the world's only Hindu kingdom. Less than two per cent of the population is Christian. Yet, near the border of Nepal The Salvation Army in India operates a school for deaf children. Ministry to the pupils and their families has caused the establishment of four corps of primarily Nepalese worshippers converted from the Hindu religion.

The past year has also seen a stronger establishment of ministry alongside people at a public refuse disposal site. On the island of Tonga, a socially neglected community of desperately poor people was scraping

The Salvation Army operates a community health project in this deprived community of Patangata, Tonga

40

a living by unearthing scrap metal. Their healthcare needs were appalling, but also an entry point for the grace and mercy offered by project personnel. As a result of relationships built through a project, soldiers were enrolled and home groups established. But to a greater extent hope was offered in the name of Jesus.

IPDS facilitates this vital ministry of mercy by linking concerns and capacity with resources and participation in an attempt to align our hearts with Christ's presence.

FUNDING THE MINISTRY

The Salvation Army wishes to thank those listed below who, during 2005, assisted in its ministry to some of the world's most vulnerable people through community development projects. These involved:

♦ **Combating the HIV/Aids pandemic** ♦ **Developing savings and loans groups**
♦ **Promoting healthy communities** ♦ **Supporting formal and non-formal educational services** ♦ **Improving access to safe water and sanitation** ♦ **Supporting social service programmes to the aged, the marginalised and the young** ♦ **Responding to disaster-hit areas**

Country	Donor	US $
Australia	Eastern & Southern Territories	1,618,034
	AusAID (through SAADO)	977,130
Canada	Canada and Bermuda Territory	250,000
Germany	Christoffel Blindenmission	153,671
	Dr Walter Herter	112,353
	Kindernothilfe	471,695
Netherlands	The Netherlands and Czech Republic Territory	1,218,969
	Kerk in Actie	635,496
Norway	NORAD	1,636,749
	Operation One Day Work	205,686
	Royal Norwegian Ministry of Foreign Affairs	489,667
Sweden	Dispurse Foundation	22,373
	Radio Help	10,613
	Swedish Ecumenical Council for Women	6,292
Switzerland	Bread for All	148,417
	Solidarity Third World	49,594
	Stanley Thomas Johnson Foundation	23,000
	Swiss Government	947,173
	Swiss Solidarity	752,599
United Kingdom	UK Territory with the Republic of Ireland	2,743,351
	Hope HIV	275,187
	Oxfam (tsunami support)	9,333
	Tear Fund (tsunami support)	954,062
USA	SAWSO	30,072,505
	USAID	1,952,139
TOTAL		**US$ 45,736,088**

INTERNATIONAL HEADQUARTERS

Postal address: The Salvation Army,
101 Queen Victoria Street, London EC4P 4EP, United Kingdom

Tel: (020) 7332 0101 (national); [44] (20) 7332 0101 (international)
Fax: (020) 7332 8019; email: websa@salvationarmy.org
web site: www.salvationarmy.org

General
SHAW CLIFTON
(2 April 2006)

Chief of the Staff
COMMISSIONER ROBIN DUNSTER
(2 April 2006)

The General directs Salvation Army operations throughout the world through the administrative departments of International Headquarters, which are headed by international secretaries. The Chief of the Staff, a commissioner appointed by the General to be second-in-command, is the Army's chief executive whose function is to implement the General's policy decisions and effect liaison between departments. As well as the handling of day-to-day business and the allocation of resources, International Headquarters is concerned with strategic, long-range planning, and functions as a resource centre for the worldwide Army and a facilitator of ideas and policies.

The Christian Mission Headquarters, Whitechapel Road, became the Army's first International Headquarters in 1880. However, the Founder soon decided that a move into the City of London would be beneficial and in 1881 IHQ was moved to 101 Queen Victoria Street. Sixty years after this move the IHQ building was destroyed by fire during the Second World War. The rebuilt International Headquarters was opened by Queen Elizabeth, the Queen Mother, in November 1963.

When it was decided to redevelop the Queen Victoria Street site, IHQ took up residence at William Booth College, Denmark Hill, in 2001. Three years later, in October 2004, IHQ returned to 101 Queen Victoria Street and the new building was opened by Her Royal Highness The Princess Royal on 9 November.

INTERNATIONAL MANAGEMENT COUNCIL

The International Management Council (IMC), established in February 1991, sees to the efficiency and effectiveness of the Army's international administration in general. It considers in detail the formation of international policy and mission. It is composed of all IHQ commissioners, and meets monthly with the General taking the chair.

Sec: Lt-Col Miriam Frederiksen
Asst Sec: Maj Richard Gaudion

GENERAL'S CONSULTATIVE COUNCIL

The General's Consultative Council (GCC), established in July 2001, advises the General on broad matters relating to the Army's mission strategy and policy. The GCC is composed of all officers who qualify to attend a High Council, and operates through a Lotus Notes database. Selected members also meet four times a year at IHQ with the General taking the chair.

Sec: Lt-Col Miriam Frederiksen
Asst Sec: Maj Richard Gaudion

ADMINISTRATION DEPARTMENT

The Administration Department is responsible for all matters with which the Chief of the Staff deals; for the effective administration of IHQ; for IHQ personnel; for international external relations; for providing legal advice; and for ensuring that the strategic planning and monitoring process is implemented and used effectively.

International Secretary to the Chief of the Staff

COMR ROBERT STREET (1 Jul 2006)

Sec for Administration: Lt-Col Michael Williams

Executive Sec to the General/Research and Planning Sec: Lt-Col Miriam Frederiksen

P/S to the General: Maj Richard Gaudion

P/S to the Chief of the Staff: Maj Rob Garrad

Sec for Spiritual Life Development and International External Relations: Comr Linda Bond

United Nations Rep (New York): Lt-Col Jerry Gaines

General's Representative for Global Evangelisation: Col Dick Krommenhoek

International Youth Ministries Coordinator/ Leader, Project Warsaw (Poland): Col Vibeke Krommenhoek

International Doctrine Council: Chair: Comr William Francis

Sec for IHQ Staff Development: Comr Nancy Roberts, BS, MA

Legal and Parliamentary Sec: Maj Peter J. M. Smith (Solicitor of the Supreme Court)

INTERNATIONAL PERSONNEL DEPARTMENT

The International Personnel Department works in the interests of international personnel in support of the Chief of the Staff and the zonal international secretaries. Responsibilities include facilitating the personal and vocational development of all personnel, their pastoral care and physical well-being. The department exists to encourage and facilitate the sharing and appropriate deployment of personnel resources on a global basis; to assist in the identification of officers with potential for future leadership; to monitor training and development; to register and coordinate all offers for international service.

International Secretary for Personnel

COMR LYN PEARCE, BA (1 Dec 2004)

Under Sec: Maj Albertine Wolterink

Sec for International Training and Leader Development: Lt-Col Ian Southwell, BSc, BEd

Medical Consultant: Dr John Thomlinson, MB, ChB, FRCOG

BUSINESS ADMINISTRATION DEPARTMENT

The Business Administration Department is responsible for international accounting, auditing, banking, property and related matters. The International Secretary for Business Administration has the oversight of the finance functions in territories and commands.

International Secretary for Business Administration

COMR WILLIAM ROBERTS, BS, MA (1 Feb 2005)

Finance Sec: Lt-Col Ann Woodall, MA, MSc, PhD, FCCA

Chief Accountant: Maj Jeffrey Wills, BCom, FCA

Acting Chief International Auditor: Col Gordon Becker, FFA, FAAI, AMIA, MFBA

Auditors: Lt-Col Gustave Allemand; Lt-Col John Rowlanes, ASCA; Maj Randall Sjogren, CFM; Maj John Warner MSc, FAIA, FCIS

Facilities Manager: Mr Graham Twist

Information Technology Manager: Mr Mark Calleran

Property Manager: Mr Graham Reynolds

Travel Manager: Mr Mark Edwards

PROGRAMME RESOURCES DEPARTMENT

The mission of the Programme Resources Department is to participate with others in envisioning, coordinating, facilitating and raising awareness of programmes that advance the global mission of The Salvation Army.

International Secretary for Programme Resources

COMR B. DONALD ØDEGAARD, Cand Mag (11 Jul 2005)

Under Sec: Maj Stephen Yoder

Sec for Mission Product Development and Marketing: Comr Berit Ødegaard

Communications Sec/Editor-in-Chief/Literary Sec: Maj Charles King

   Editor *All the World*: Mr Kevin Sims

   Editor *Global Exchange*: Maj Morag Yoder

   Editor *The Officer*: Maj Charles King

Editor *The Year Book*: Maj Trevor Howes
Writer *Words of Life*: Retired General John Gowans
International Literature Programme Sec: Maj Helen Bryden

Editorial fax: (020) 7332 8079

International Projects and Development Services Sec: Capt Ted Horwood, BA

International Health Programme Consultant: Dr Ian Campbell, MBBS, MRCP (UK), DRCOG (UK)

Community Development Consultant (HIV/Aids and Health): Mrs Alison Rader Campbell, BA, MSc

Regional Coordinator, Programme Facilitation Team (HIV/Aids, health development, mission) SPEA/South Asia: Mr Jerry Mua, CHW, RN, BAppHSc

International Emergency Services:
Coordinator: Maj Cedric Hills
Field Operations and Training Officer: Capt Elizabeth Haywood
Field Operations Officer: Capt Mike McKee

WOMEN'S MINISTRIES

World President of Women's Ministries
COMR HELEN CLIFTON, BA

World Secretary for Women's Ministries and World President, SA Scouts, Guides and Guards
COMR JANET STREET

Women's Ministries Administrative Asst: Capt Teresa Everett

ZONAL DEPARTMENTS

The zonal departments are the main administrative link with territories and commands. The international secretaries give oversight to and coordinate the Army's work in their respective geographical areas.

AFRICA
International Secretary

COMR AMOS MAKINA (1 Jul 2004)

Under Secs:
Africa East: Major Stephen Moriasi
Africa West: Lt-Col Joan Dunwoodie
fax: (020) 7332 8231
Sec WM: Comr Rosemary Makina
Regional Consultant HIV/Aids: Mr Ben Bofu

AMERICAS AND CARIBBEAN
International Secretary

COMR WILLIAM FRANCIS, BA, M Div, Hon DD (1 Apr 2003)

Under Sec: Maj Joan Canning
fax: (020) 7332 8199

Sec WM: Comr Marilyn Francis, BA, MA

EUROPE
International Secretary

COMR HASSE KJELLGREN, BSc (1 Nov 2006)

Under Sec: Maj Theodoor Wolterink
fax: (020) 7332 8209

Sec WM: Comr Christina Kjellgren
Officer for European Affairs: Maj Göran Larsson

SOUTH ASIA
International Secretary

COMR LALKIAMLOVA (1 Jan 2004)

Under Sec: Lt-Col John Dyall
fax: (020) 7332 8219

Sec WM: Comr Lalhlimpuii

SOUTH PACIFIC AND EAST ASIA
International Secretary

COMR ROY FRANS (1 Jun 2006)

Under Sec: Maj Alison Cowling
fax: (020) 7332 8229

Sec WM: Comr Arda Frans

STATISTICS

Officers 62 **Employees** 71

We want International Headquarters to be a place where people walk through the doors and feel the love of Christ
– General Shaw Clifton, speaking at his welcome to IHQ on 3 April 2006

The Salvation Army International Trustee Company

Registered Office: 101 Queen Victoria Street, London EC4P 4EP

Registration No 2538134. Tel: (020) 7332 0101

Company Secretary: Lieut-Colonel Ann Woodall

DIRECTORS: Comr Robin Dunster (Chair), Comr William Roberts (Managing Director and Vice Chair), Mr Andrew Axcell, Comr William Francis, Comr Roy Frans, Comr Hasse Kjellgren, Comr Lalkiamlova, Comr Amos Makina, Comr Donald Ødegaard, Comr Lyn Pearce, Maj Peter Smith, Mr Trevor Smith, Comr Robert Street, Lt-Col Ann Woodall.

The company is registered under the Companies Acts 1985 and 1989 as a company limited by guarantee, not having a share capital. It has no assets or liabilities, but as a trustee of The Salvation Army International Trusts it is the registered holder of Salvation Army property both real and personal including shares in some of the Army's commercial undertakings. The company is a trust corporation.

Reliance Bank Limited

Faith House, 23-24 Lovat Lane, London EC3R 8EB

Tel: (020) 7398 5400; fax: (020) 7398 5401; email: info@reliancebankltd.com
web site: www.reliancebankltd.com

Chairman: Commissioner William Roberts
Managing Director: Trevor J. Smith, ACIB

Banking Manager and Company Secretary: Michael R. Meads, ACIB
Finance Manager: Kevin Dare, BA (Hons), CIMA; Operations Manager: Paul Underwood, ACIB;
Business Development Manager: Hazel Edwards

DIRECTORS: Comr William Roberts (Chairman), Comr Robert Street, Lt-Col Ann Woodall, Lt-Col William Cochrane, Maj Jeffrey Wills, Maj John Wainwright, Maj David Hinton, Mr Trevor Smith, Mr Michael Meads, Mr Philip Deer, Mr Edward Ashton, Mr Gerald Birkett, ACIB.

Reliance Bank Limited is an authorised institution under the Banking Act 1987, is regulated by the Financial Services Authority and registered under the Companies and Consumer Credit Acts.

OWNED by The Salvation Army through its controlling shareholders – The Salvation Army International Trustee Company and The Salvation Army Trustee Company – Reliance Bank accepts sterling and foreign currency deposits, carries on general banking business, and provides finance for Salvation Army corporate customers and private and business customers.

The bank can grant mortgages, personal loans and overdrafts, and also provides travel currency, cheques and safe custody facilities. It offers current accounts, together with a Reliance Bank Visa Debit Card, fixed deposits and savings accounts, and is involved in money transmission transactions both within the UK and abroad. Internet banking and telephone banking services are also offered.

The bank pays at least 75 per cent of its taxable profits by means of Gift Aid donation to its controlling shareholders.

Brochures are available on request, or visit the bank's web site:
www.reliancebankltd.com

STATISTICS
Employees 21

International College for Officers

The Cedars, 34 Sydenham Hill, London SE26 6LS, UK

Tel: [44] (020) 8693 3290/4976; fax: [44] (020) 8693 5909

Principal: Commissioner Margaret Sutherland, MA, ARCO (1 Jul 2004)

During the International Congress held at the Crystal Palace, Sydenham, London, in 1904, Commissioner Henry T. Howard voiced what he saw as the young Salvation Army's need for leaders inspired with the aggressive spirit of Salvationism. William Booth took up the idea and the International Staff Training Lodge was opened at Clapton on 11 May 1905.

The present building was brought into service in 1950, when General Albert Orsborn declared it to be 'an investment in the great intangibles without which our cogs and wheels would soon be rusty and dead'. In 1954, a broadening of scope promoted a change of name to the International College for Officers.

MISSION STATEMENT OF THE ICO

The Salvation Army's International College for Officers exists to further develop officers by:

- ☐ **nurturing personal holiness and spiritual leadership**
- ☐ **providing opportunity to experience the internationalism of the Army**
- ☐ **encouraging a renewed sense of mission and purpose as an officer.**

THE aims of the ICO have in essence remained unchanged since the college began, although they have been stated in different ways over the years. A revised mission statement has been crafted and is reproduced above.

While the aims remain the same, the curriculum evolves to respond to the challenges of the 21st century. In the past year, a lecture on global evangelisation has been introduced in response to the way the Holy Spirit has led The Salvation Army's top leadership to consider possible future openings in countries where the Army is not yet at work.

A recent session focused on social justice issues under the heading 'Hope for the World'. This was so successful that a similar session is planned in 2007.

While there has been for some time a series of lectures on world religions, the emphasis now is particularly, though not exclusively, on Islam and the challenge that this poses to Christian believers.

From 2007 every alternate session will be a translation session. This will bring its own challenges, particularly from an administrative perspective, but is part of the ICO's commitment to meet the needs of the Salvation Army world in all its diversity.

STATISTICS
Officers 4 **Employees** 5

STAFF
Programme Sec and Asst Principal:
  Maj Linda Markiewicz
Business Sec: Maj Steven Howard
Personnel Sec: Maj Janice Howard

The Salvation Army Leaders' Training College of Africa

16 Private Rd, off General Booth Rd, Braeside, Harare, Zimbabwe

Postal Address: PO Box GT 650, Graniteside, Harare, Zimbabwe

Tel: [263] (4) 743 039; fax: [263] (4) 743 010; email: leadcoll_africa@sal.salvationarmy.org

Principal: Major David Sterling, BA (12 Feb 2002)

Prompted by the request of territorial leaders of Africa, The Salvation Army Leaders' Training College of Africa (SALT College) was established in 1986. Its purpose is to coordinate officer and local officer in-service training across the continent through SALT College distance-learning courses and seminars, implemented by an extension training officer in each territory.

THE Salvation Army Leaders' Training College of Africa (SALT College) is passionately committed to student development in Africa. Facilitating distance learning in 14 countries across the continent, it reports to territorial leaders through the International Secretary for Africa and aims to develop informed, theologically-aware Christian leaders for effective Army service.

The diverse college roll includes officers, local officers and soldiers. Guided and encouraged by extension training officers (ETOs), students work in either English, French, Portuguese or Kiswahili.

During 2005 there were 351 new student registrations and 334 subject passes at certificate level, with 19 students achieving their final Certificate in Salvation Army Ministry award. Captain Luke Msikita (Malawi Command) commented in his *Management 1* evaluation: 'This was a practical subject I took right after being commissioned. It was a tool to solve problems, plan strategies and manage the church. It reinforced the theory I learned in college with good outcomes in my corps.'

Captains Aggressive Nakalonga and Britius Munkombwe (Zambia Territory) and Major Lewis Mukawo (Zimbabwe Territory) all completed the Australian College of Theology Associate in Theology (ThA) award with merit. A wider range of ThA optional subjects now includes Ethics and the Christian Faith, Church History, Christian Leadership and Management, and World Religions. Students comment that these studies extend their understanding, deepen spiritual life and enrich their corps ministry.

Since the upgrading of the computerised student database, every active student receives a transcript listing their achievements. Another exciting development is the inauguration of the SALT College Board of Studies. This evaluates study materials and examinations, monitors students' progress, and reviews course content and delivery. The aim is one of continuous improvement to enable students to achieve their study goals.

STATISTICS

Officers 4 Employees 5

STAFF

Senior Tutor: Maj Brenda Sterling, MA
Asst to the Principal: Capt Filankembo Mayala
Tutor: Capt Dorcas Mayala

OVERSEAS SERVICE FUNDS 2005-2006 INCOME

	International Self-Denial Contributions £	International Self-Denial Special £	Special Projects £	Donations via IHQ £	Total £
Australia Eastern	535,365		358,163	302,458	1,195,986
Australia Southern	408,970		41,781	571,503	1,022,254
Bangladesh	697				697
Belgium	1,784			3,653	5,437
Brazil	8,655				8,655
Canada	855,360		1,353,775	301,888	2,511,023
Caribbean	15,844			26,382	42,226
Congo (Brazzaville)	19,275				19,275
Congo (Kinshasa) & Angola	20,642				20,642
Czech Republic	1,122				1,122
Denmark	47,500			4,824	52,324
Kenya (East Africa)	17,937				17,937
Eastern Europe	6,064			2,717	8,781
Finland	41,448		28,517	9,321	79,286
France	12,819			32,662	45,481
Germany	46,000			104,646	150,646
Ghana	4,270				4,270
Hong Kong	50,626		703,750	185,490	939,866
India Central	27,972				27,972
India Eastern	16,120				16,120
India Northern	13,374				13,374
India South Eastern	21,053				21,053
India South Western	16,910				16,910
India Western	13,650				13,650
Indonesia	18,924				18,924
Italy	7,809			38,338	46,147
Japan	69,829		49,717	14,535	134,081
Korea	49,292			72,460	121,752
Latin America North	7,036			1,138	8,174
Malawi	861				861
Mexico	9,949			58	10,007
Myanmar	675				675
Netherlands	125,071		538,038	313,330	976,439
New Zealand	215,669		449,874	89,186	754,729
Nigeria	6,302				6,302
Norway	272,655		971,702	338,738	1,583,095
Pakistan	1,728			550	2,278
Papua New Guinea	2,513				2,513
Philippines	3,923			1,143	5,066
Portugal	1,286			438	1,724
Rwanda	399				399
Singapore & Malaysia	53,430		14,258	191,648	259,336
South America East	4,172				4,172
South America West	13,335				13,335
Southern Africa	11,965				11,965
Spain	3,971			16,267	20,238
Sri Lanka	812			573	1,385
Sweden	83,087		305,042	113,642	501,771
Switzerland	373,310		1,012,542	440,858	1,826,710
Taiwan	4,001			6,256	10,257
Tanzania	2,550				2,550
United Kingdom	1,416,960		1,463,369	669,057	3,549,386
USA Central	2,151,623	129,095	984,772	201,033	3,466,523
USA Eastern	2,075,128	136,924	818,649	673,112	3,703,813
USA Southern	2,326,334	188,411	1,800,002	558,154	4,872,901
USA Western	1,465,249	26,895	1,306,154	41,035	2,839,333
USA SAWSO			710,418	822,567	1,532,985
Zambia	5,282				5,282
Zimbabwe	40,000			1,297	41,297
TOTAL	£ 13,028,587	£ 481,325	£ 12,910,523	£ 6,150,957	£ 32,571,392

OVERSEAS SERVICE FUNDS 2005-2006 EXPENDITURE

	Support of Overseas Work	Special Projects	Donations via IHQ	Total
	£	£	£	£
Africa, General	9,130			9,130
Americas, General	18,279			18,279
Austria	27,897			27,897
Bangladesh	125,868	105,479	806	232,153
Brazil	667,788	369,560	19,845	1,057,193
Caribbean	599,832	1,005,180	23,519	1,628,531
Congo (Brazzaville)	378,563	115,265	89,994	583,822
Congo (Kinshasa) & Angola	413,603	162,393	14,033	590,029
Czech Republic	312,249	105,795	1,408	419,452
Kenya (East Africa)	552,308	583,491	23,248	1,159,047
Eastern Europe	1,573,725	416,764	86,884	2,077,373
Estonia	8,681	72,011	8,832	89,524
Europe, General			37,216	37,216
Fiji & Tonga		395,122		395,122
France		111,216		111,216
Germany (East)	102,166	39,178	23,709	165,053
Ghana	140,314	207,854	4,471	352,639
Hong Kong	9,308	79,053	6,590	94,951
Hungary	56,946	60,809		117,755
India National Secretariat	65,413	38,949		104,362
India Central	165,208	199,222	13,529	377,959
India Eastern	70,894	173,262	22,469	266,625
India Northern	214,037	475,031	14,859	703,927
India South Eastern	173,193	583,598	3,791	760,582
India South Western	253,278	586,723	7,067	847,068
India Western	169,286	461,624	16,622	647,532
Indonesia	35,154	709,038	7,472	751,664
Italy	123,518	87,217		210,735
Korea	19,965	46,487	2,021	68,473
Latin America North	471,210	327,042	29,417	827,669
Latvia (Sweden)	84,561	176,396	17,239	278,196
Liberia	108,110	90,660	1,663	200,433
Lithuania (Germany)		3,906		3,906
Malawi	71,921	104,064	1,667	177,652
Mexico	281,456	324,974	16,398	622,828
Mozambique	113,698	94,653	2,150	210,501
Myanmar	62,355	117,772	12,133	192,259
Nigeria	141,022	61,124	109,969	312,115
Norway		51,045		51,045
Pakistan	326,544	555,350	4,207	886,101
Papua New Guinea	342,422	231,632	193,007	767,061
Philippines	299,721	626,301	13,553	939,575
Poland			29,575	29,575
Portugal	196,316	116,994	10,000	323,310
Rwanda	76,976	37,360	23,335	137,671
Singapore & Malaysia	38,072	156,441		194,513
South America East	363,139	161,151	56,314	580,604
South America West	372,511	578,585	79,117	1,030,213
South Asia, General	14,689			14,689
Southern Africa	145,107	288,687	9,467	443,261
SPEA, General	5,889	1,467	285	7,641
Spain	260,650	148,791	15,862	425,303
Sri Lanka	55,795	577,180	10,973	643,948
Taiwan	52,259	115,917	11,271	179,447
Tanzania	128,824	192,431	7,998	329,253
Uganda	34,801	29,315	29,786	93,902
USA Southern			66,567	66,567
Zambia	246,279	198,141	18,364	462,784
Zimbabwe	307,095	352,823	33,888	693,806
SALT College	47,666		144	47,810
TOTAL	£ 10,935,691	£ 12,910,523	£ 1,232,734	£ 25,078,948

International Administrative Structure

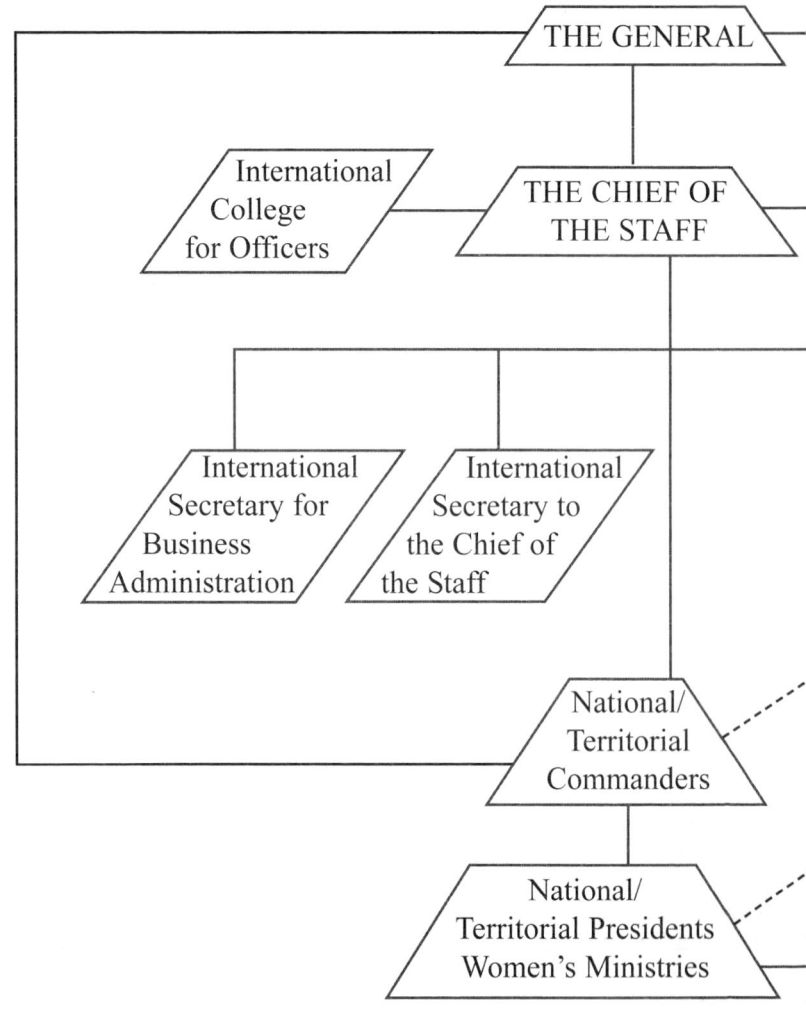

World President and World Secretary for Women's Ministries

International Secretaries (Zonal)

International Secretary for Personnel

International Secretary for Programme Resources

Secretaries for Women's Ministries

Officers Commanding/ IHQ Regional Commanders

Command Presidents Women's Ministries

AUSTRALIA

National Secretariat: 2 Brisbane Ave, Barton, Canberra, ACT 2600

Postal address: PO Box 4256, Manuka, ACT 2603, Australia

tel: [61] (02) 6273 3055; fax: [61] (02) 6273 1383; email: John.Staite@aue.salvationarmy.org

Two Christian Mission converts, John Gore and Edward Saunders, pioneered Salvation Army operations on 5 September 1880 in Adelaide. These were officially established on 11 February 1881 by the appointment of Captain and Mrs Thomas Sutherland. In 1921 the work in Australia was organised into Eastern and Southern Territories with headquarters in Sydney and Melbourne.

A National Secretariat serving the whole of Australia and funded jointly by both territories was established in 1987.

Periodicals: *Kidzone*, *Warcry*

THE National Secretariat represents the views of both Australian territories to the Australian Government as required or requested by both territorial commanders. It addresses issues of spiritual, moral, ethical and social welfare by means of written submissions, personal dialogue with members of parliament and attendance at open forums.

It also negotiates of funding from the Australian Government. The office monitors overseas aid community development projects funded jointly with the Australian Agency for International Development (AusAID).

Investment in China continues through an integrated development programme with activities in eight counties in collaboration with Switzerland. These activities include biogas, HIV and health education, teacher training, micro-credit lending, agricultural training and road building.

A partnership with four Salvation Army territories in India resulted in an extension to the Self-help Savings and Loan Group (SHG) process. A pro-gramme to prevent trafficking of small children for sexual purposes operates in the India Western Territory.

A second electricity-generating windmill in India has been funded and will become a long-term source of income through the sale of electricity to the Government of India. It will promote self-sufficiency for the India Central Territory.

In North Korea (DPRK) a third yoghurt-packaging machine is being funded jointly with the Switzerland, Austria and Hungary Territory and contributing to the health and income of local people. Two water projects are being undertaken in Myanmar and Kenya. Three southern India tsunami projects, funded by The Salvation Army in Australia and other SA donors, are helping to restore the lives of the people affected.

National Sec: Lt-Col John Staite

Overseas Development Consultant: Mr Gordon Knowles, BA, Grad Dip Admin, M Dev Admin

Editorial Department: 1-9 Drill St, Hawthorn, Vic 3122; tel: (03) 9818 1438; fax: (03) 9819 4864 .

Editor-in-Chief: Maj Laurie Robertson

Red Shield Defence Services: PO Box 3246, Manuka, ACT 2603; tel: (02) 6273 2280; fax: (02) 6273 1383

Chief Commissioner: Capt Robert Stephens

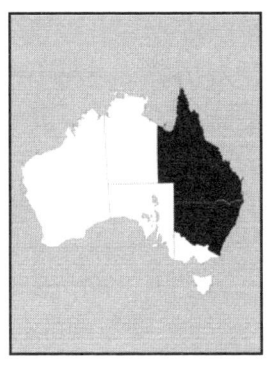

AUSTRALIA EASTERN TERRITORY

Territorial leaders:
Commissioners Leslie and Coral Strong

Territorial Commander:
Commissioner Leslie Strong (1 Mar 2003)

Chief Secretary:
Lieut-Colonel Geanette Seymour
(1 Aug 2006)

Territorial Headquarters: 140 Elizabeth Street, Sydney, NSW 2000

Postal address: PO Box A435, Sydney South, NSW 1235, Australia

tel: [61] (02) 9264 1711 (10 lines); fax: [61] (02) 9266 9638; web site: www.salvos.org.au

Zone: South Pacific and East Asia
States included in the territory: New South Wales, Queensland, The Australian Capital Territory (ACT)
Languages in which the gospel is preached: Cantonese, English, Korean, Mandarin
Periodicals: *Creative Ministry, Pipeline, Venue, Women in Touch*

A CENTRE for problem gamblers is a new venture in the territory. A partnership between the Fairfield Returned Soldiers League Club and The Salvation Army, the centre was opened in October 2005 after the club had recognised its responsibility to provide assistance to people affected by problem gambling.

At the conclusion of the senior school year (November 2005) school-leavers participated in Schoolies Week, gathering at tourist spots to celebrate the completion of their secondary education. As usual, young Salvationists joined members of other churches to provide chaplaincy to the students; this year they were instrumental in leading more than 100 young people to Christ.

'Built on Rock' seminars, teaching

Salvationists the Army's biblical foundations and its Wesleyan holiness heritage, were an initiative in the territory. Speakers included Majors Malcolm and Barbara Robinson (Canada and Bermuda) and Commissioner Linda Bond (IHQ). The Communication Department produced videos and DVDs of these speakers as part of a study course for distribution throughout the territory and overseas.

'Godscape' – a conference for people interested in all types of media presentation and production – attracted delegates from across the territory and already new contributors are providing material for Army publications because of this resource.

Major Barbara Sampson (New Zealand, Fiji and Tonga), the writer of *Words of Life*, was guest speaker at the Women's Bible Convention held over two weekends in February 2006, in two different states. More than 600 women participated in the teaching and fellowship.

The Visionaries Session of cadets was commissioned in December 2005, then in March 2006 the Heralds of the Good News Session was welcomed to the school for officer training with an open day for family and friends.

The cadets had a territorial welcome with a difference by travelling to several New South Wales and Queensland corps to conduct the Sunday meetings. All corps received a special DVD introducing each cadet to the territory.

Recognition of employees who had given faithful service was an innovation during the year under review. The territory, which has more than 4,000 employees, presented Service Recognition Awards to staff who had completed 5-9 (bronze), 10-19 (silver) and 20+ (gold) years' service.

New buildings were opened at Capricorn Region Corps, Redlands Corps and the Salvo Care Line (24-hour phone counselling service) at Five Dock, Sydney. The Salvo Care Line was a project of the Rotary Club of Sydney which, over two years, contributed much of the cost of the facility's building. There were also new openings of extensions at Panania Corps and at Campbelltown Women's Shelter.

STATISTICS

Officers 964 (active 546 retired 418) **Cadets** (1st Yr) 9 (2nd Yr) 12 **Employees** 4,052
Corps 174 **Outposts/Corps plants** 56 **Institutions** 62 **Community Care Services** 128 **Thrift stores/Charity shops** 238
Senior Soldiers 9,867 **Adherents** 2,901 **Junior Soldiers** 695
Personnel serving outside territory Officers 34 Layworkers 15

STAFF

Personnel: Maj Peter Farthing
Programme: Lt-Col Lynette Green
Business: Lt-Col John Hodge
Asst Chief Sec: Maj Brian Holley
Asst Sec for Business: Maj Peter Holley
Audit: Mr Tim Green
Candidates: Capt Alwyn Robinson
College of Further Education & Training: Maj Philip Cairns
Counselling Service: Major (Dr) Christine Unicomb
Editor-in-Chief and Sec for Communications: Maj Ken Sanz
Emergency Services: Maj Kevin Hentzschel
Finance: Mr Ian Minnett
Information Technology: Mr Wayne Bajema
Legal: Maj Peter Holley
Mobilise for Mission:
　Corps Programme Dept: Major Colin Daines
　Music and Creative Arts: Mr Graeme Press
　Youth: Major Ian Channell
Moral and Social Issues Council: Maj Margaret Sanz
Property: Capt Edwin Cox
Public Relations: Maj Mark Campbell
Red Shield Defence Services: Capt Robert Stephens
Rep to Nat Council of Churches: Maj Graham Harris
Salvationist Supplies: Mr Graham Lang
Salvos Stores: Mr Neville Barrett
Social Programme Dept: Maj Cec Woodward
Sydney Staff Songsters: S/L Graeme Press
Women's Ministries: Comr Coral Strong (TPWM) Maj Glenys Holley (TSWM)

DIVISIONS

Australian Capital Territory and South NSW: 2-4 Brisbane Ave, Barton 2600, PO Box 4224, Kingston 2604; tel: (02) 6273 2211; fax: (02) 6273 2973; Maj Rodney Ainsworth
Central and North Queensland: 54 Charles St,

North Rockhampton, QLD 4701, PO Box 5343, CQMC, Rockhampton, QLD 4702; tel: (07) 4999 1999; fax: (07) 4999 1915; Maj Gary Baker

Newcastle and Central NSW: 94 Parry St, PO Box 5319, Newcastle West 2302; tel: (02) 4926 3466; fax: (02) 4926 2228; Maj Peter Laws

North NSW: 4 Salmon Ave, PO Box 1180, Armidale 2350; tel: (02) 6771 1632; fax: (02) 6772 3444; Maj John Rees

South Queensland: 342 Upper Roma St, Brisbane 4000, GPO Box 2210, Brisbane, Qld 4001; tel: (07) 3222 6699; fax: (07) 3229 3884; Maj Wayne Maxwell

Sydney East and Illawarra: 61-65 Kingsway, Kingsgrove 2208, Locked Bag 888, Kingsgrove 1480; tel: (02) 9336 3320; fax: (02) 9336 3359; Lt-Col Ian Hamilton

The Greater West: 93 Phillip St, Parramatta, 2150, PO Box 66, Parramatta, NSW 2124; tel: (02) 9635 7400; fax: (02) 9689 1692; Maj Kelvin Alley

COLLEGE OF FURTHER EDUCATION

Bexley North, NSW 2207: 32a Barnsbury Grove, PO Box 226; tel: (02) 9502 0460; fax: (02) 9502 4177; email: COFE@aue.salvationarmy.org

SCHOOL FOR OFFICER TRAINING

Bexley North, NSW 2207: 120 Kingsland Rd, PO Box 63; tel: (02) 9502 1777; fax: (02) 9554 3298

SCHOOL OF THEOLOGY

Bexley North, NSW 2207: 32a Barnsbury Grove, PO Box 237; tel: (02) 9502 0432; fax: (02) 9502 0476

SCHOOL FOR LEADERSHIP TRAINING

Stanmore, NSW 2048: 97 Cambridge St; tel: (02) 9557 1105; fax: (02) 9550 2005

SCHOOL FOR YOUTH LEADERSHIP

Lake Munmorah, NSW 2259: 42 Greenacre Ave; tel: (02) 4358 8886; fax: (02) 4358 8882

HERITAGE CENTRE

Bexley North, NSW 2207: 120 Kingsland Rd, PO Box 226; tel: (02) 9502 0424; fax: (02) 9554 9204; email: AUEHeritage@aue.salvationarmy.org; Envoy George Hazell, OF

RECOVERY SERVICES COMMAND

Sydney: 85 Campbell St, Surry Hills 2010; tel: (02) 9212 4000; fax: (02) 9212 4032; Maj Jennifer Cotterill

BRIDGE ADDICTION RECOVERY PROGRAMME
(Drugs, alcohol and other substances)

Brisbane: 'Moonyah', 58 Glenrosa Rd, PO Box 81, Red Hill 4059; tel: (07) 33690922; fax: (07) 3369 9294 (acc men 76 Detox Unit 13 Halfway House 3)

Canberra: Canberra Recovery Services Centre, 5-13 Mildura St, Fyshwick 2609, PO Box 4181, Kingston 2604; tel: (02) 6295 1256/1644; fax: (02) 6295 3766 (acc men 37 Halfway House 3)

Fountaindale: 'Selah', 60 Berkeley Rd, Berkeley Vale, PO Box 5019, Chittaway 2261; tel: (02) 4388 4588; fax: (02) 4389 1490 (acc women 36)

Gold Coast: 'Fairhaven', 497 Parklands Drive, Southport 4215; PO Box 482, Ashmore City 4214; tel: (07) 5594 7288; fax: (07) 5594 7218 (acc men 54 Detox Unit 11 Halfway House men 3 Halfway House women 9)

Hunter Region Recovery Services –
  Morisset: 'Endeavour Community', 8 Russell Rd, PO Box 346, Morisset 2264; tel: (02) 4973 4146/4156; fax: (02) 4973 4173 (acc men 26)

  Morisset: 'Miracle Haven', Russell Rd, PO Box 93, Morisset 2264; tel: (02) 4973 1495/1644; fax: (02) 4970 5807 (acc men 84)

  Newcastle: 100-102 Hannell St, PO Box 125, Wickham 2293; tel: (02) 4961 1257; fax: (02) 4965 3295 (acc men 19)

Leura: 'Blue Mountains Recovery Services Centre', 6 Eastview Ave, Leura; PO Box 284, Wentworth Falls 2782; tel: (02) 4782 7392; fax: (02) 4782 7392 (acc men 22)

Shoalhaven: Bridge Program, 4 Smith Lane, Nowra 2541; tel: (02) 4422 4604; fax: (02) 4422 4672

Sydney: 'Catherine Booth House', 348 Elizabeth St, PO Box 750, Surry Hills 2010; tel: (02) 9211 7300/1543; fax: (02) 9211 3598 (acc women 25)

Sydney: 'William Booth House Recovery Services Centre', 56-60 Albion St, Surry Hills 2010, PO Box A127, Sydney South 1232; tel: (02) 9212 2322; fax: (02) 9281 9771 (acc men 8 Assessment Phase 31 ReStart Phase 17 ReEntry Phase 24 Aftercare 20)

Townsville: 'Rehabilitation Services Centre',

312-340 Walker St; PO Box 803, Townsville 4810; tel: (07) 4772 3607; fax: (07) 4772 3174 (acc men 26 Detox Unit 6 Halfway House 4)

Salvos Stores

General Manager: Mr Neville Barrett

ACT and Monaro Area: 5-15 Mildura St, Fyshwick 2609, PO Box 4181, Kingston; tel: (02) 6295 1644; fax: (02) 6295 3766 (retail stores 8)

Brisbane: 80 Glenrosa Rd, PO Box 81, Red Hill, 4059; tel: (07) 3369 0922; fax: (07) 3368 6344 (retail stores 18)

Central Coast Area Administration Office: 342 Mann St, Gosford 2250; tel: (02) 4325 3101; fax: (02) 4325 4879 (retail stores 4)

Gold Coast: 497 Parklands Drive, Southport 4215; tel: (07) 5571 5777; fax: (07) 5574 4893 (retail stores 12)

Illawarra Area: 29 Ellen St, Wollongong 2500; tel: (02) 4228 5644; fax: (02) 4228 1040 (retail stores 7)

Newcastle: 900 Hunter St, Newcastle 2300; tel: (02) 4961 3889; fax: (02) 4961 2623 (retail stores 9)

Sydney: 5 Bellevue St, St Peters 2044; tel: (02) 9519 1477; fax: (02) 9516 2924 (retail stores 12)

Sydney West: 4 Archbold Rd, Minchinbury 2770; tel: (02) 9625 8883; fax: (02) 9625 2253 (retail stores 10)

Townsville: 314-340 Walker St, PO Box 803, Townsville 4810; tel: (07) 4772 3844; fax: (07) 4772 3084 (retail stores 5)

AERIAL SERVICE

Flying Service Base: 107 Transmission St, Mt Isa

CONFERENCE AND HOLIDAY HOMES

Budgewoi, NSW 2262: Holiday Cottage, 129 Sunrise Ave; tel: (02) 4399 3921 (acc 6)

Cairns, Qld 4870: 281-289 Sheridan St; bookings through DHQ Rockhampton; tel: (07) 4999 1902 (5 motel units)

Caloundra, QLD 4551: 4 Michael Street, Golden Beach

Collaroy Beach, NSW 2097: Peck Cottage, 11/1041 Pittwater Rd; tel: (02) 9972 0243

Collaroy, NSW 2097: The Collaroy Centre, Homestead Ave, Collaroy Beach, PO Box 11; tel: (02) 9982 9800 (office); (02) 9982 6570 AH; fax: (02) 9971 1895

Margate, QLD 4019: 2 Duffield Rd; tel: 0414 614 215

Tugun, QLD 4224: Holiday Unit, 3/15 Elizabeth St; tel: (07) 3222 6666

RED SHIELD DEFENCE SERVICES

RSDS Administration, Canberra ACT; tel: (02) 6273 2280; fax: (02) 6273 1383

Gallipoli Barracks, Brisbane, QLD: RSDS representative; tel: (07) 3332 7943

Holsworthy Military Camp, Sydney, NSW: RSDS representative; mobile: 0428 680 556

Kokoda Barracks, QLD: RSDS representative; tel: (07) 5541 6569

Lavarack Barracks, Townsville, QLD: RSDS representative; tel: (07) 4771 8571

Royal Military College, Duntroon, ACT: RSDS representative; mobile: 0417 236 183

Singleton Infantry Centre, NSW: RSDS representative; tel: (02) 6570 3279

SOCIAL SERVICES

Aged Care

Arncliffe, NSW 2205: Macquarie Lodge, 171 Wollongong Rd; tel: (02) 9556 6900; fax: (02) 9567 5043 (acc nursing home 65 hostel 49 units 99)

Balmain, NSW 2041: Montrose, 13 Thames St, PO Box 2; tel: (02) 9818 2355; fax: (02) 9818 5062 (acc hostel men 44)

Bass Hill, NSW 2197: Weeroona Village, 14 Trebartha St; tel: (02) 9645 3220; fax: (02) 9645 1390 (acc hostel 44 units 44 respite care 1)

Burwood, NSW 2134: Shaftesbury Court, 75a Shaftesbury Rd; tel: (02) 9560 4457 (acc units 35)

Canowindra, NSW 2804: Moyne, Eugowra Rd, PO Box 156; tel: (02) 6344 1475; fax: (02) 6344 1902 (acc nursing home 29 hostel 44)

Chelmer, QLD 4068: Warrina Village, 35 Victoria Ave, PO Box 239, Indooroopilly 4068; tel: (07) 3379 9800; fax: (07) 3278 1127 (acc nursing home 40 hostel 42 units 13)

Collaroy, NSW 2097: Elizabeth Jenkins Place, 21 Eastbank Ave, PO Box 14 Collaroy Beach; tel: (02) 9982 9244; fax: (02) 9971 4716 (acc nursing home 41 hostel 112)

Dee Why, NSW 2099: Pacific Lodge, 15 Fisher Rd, PO Box 109; tel: (02) 9982 8090; fax: (02) 9982 9174 (acc hostel 59)

Dulwich Hill, NSW 2203: Maybanke, 80 Wardell Rd, PO Box 286; tel: (02) 9560 4457;

fax: (02) 9569 1301 (acc nursing home 39 hostel 38)

Goulburn, NSW 2580: Gill Waminda, 2 Combemere St, PO Box 233; tel: (02) 4821 6533; fax: (02) 4821 7405 (acc hostel 67)

Marrickville, NSW 2204: Bethesda, 80 Victoria Rd, PO Box 286 Dulwich Hill 2203; tel: (02) 9519 7079; fax: (02) 9565 1327 (acc nursing home 46)

Merewether, NSW 2291: Carpenter Court, 46 John Pde, PO Box 246; tel: (02) 4963 4300; fax: (02) 4963 6489 (acc 42)

Narrabundah, ACT 2604: Mountain View, Goyder St, PO Box 61; tel: (02) 6295 1044 (acc 65)

Narrabundah, ACT 2604: Karingal Court, 11 Boolimba Cresc; tel: (02) 6295 1044; fax: (02) 6295 1473 (acc 36)

Parkes, NSW 2870: Rosedurnate, 46 Orange St, PO Box 100; tel: (02) 6862 2300; fax: (02) 6862 3756 (acc nursing home 29 hostel 45 units 17)

Port Macquarie, NSW 2444: Bethany, 2-6 Gray St, PO Box 2016; tel: (02) 6584 1127; fax: (02) 6584 1045 (acc nursing home 50 hostel 40)

Riverview, QLD 4303: Moggill Ferry Road, PO Box 6042; tel: (07) 3282 1000; fax: (07) 3282 6929 (acc nursing home 50 hostel 143 units 44)

Rockhampton, QLD 4700: Bethesda Hostel, 58 Talford St, PO Box 375; tel: (07) 4922 3229; fax: (07) 4922 3455 (acc hostel 50 respite care 1)

Resident Funded Accommodation

Collaroy, NSW 2097: Warringah Place, 1039 Pittwater Rd, PO Box 395; tel: (02) 9971 1933; fax: (02) 9971 4155 (acc self care units 64 serviced apartments 44)

Erina, NSW 2250: Woodport Village, 120-140 The Entrance Rd; tel: (02) 4365 2660; fax: (02) 4365 1812 (acc hostel 79 nursing home 96 units 67)

Northmead, NSW 2152: The Willows, 226 Windsor Rd, PO Box 551, Baulkham Hills, 1755; tel: (02) 9686 2288; fax: (02) 9686 2961 (acc hostel 48 units 142)

Crisis Accommodation and Day Care (Aged)

'Burrangiri', 1-7 Rivett Place, PO Box 65, Rivett, ACT 2611; tel: (02) 6288 1488; fax: (02) 6288 0321 (acc 15 day care 20)

Children's Services (Child care centres and family day care and after-school programmes)

Carina, QLD 4152: 202 Gallipoli Rd; tel: (07) 3395 0744

Gladstone, QLD 4680: 198 Goondoon St; tel: (07) 4972 2985: fax: (07) 4972 7835

Macquarie Fields, NSW 2564: Eucalyptus Drive, PO Box 1; tel: (02) 9605 4717; fax: (02) 9618 1492

Counselling Service

Head Office: Rhodes, NSW 2138, PO Box 3096; tel: (02) 9743 4535

Brisbane, QLD 4122: 5/46 Mt Gravatt-Capalaba Rd, Upper Mount Gravatt, PO Box 6266, Upper Mt Gravatt; tel: (07) 3349 5046

Campbelltown: Refer to Penrith Office

North Lyneham, ACT 2602: Ste 3, Southwell Park Offices, Montford Cresc; tel: (02) 6248 5504

Penrith, NSW: Ste 15, Lethbridge Ct, 20-24 Castlereagh St, PO Box 588; tel: (02) 4731 1554

Pine Rivers, QLD 4501: 27-29 Lawnton Pocket Rd, Lawnton, QLD; tel: (07) 3285 2401

Tuggeranong, ACT 2900: Ste 3, Southwell Park Offices, Montford Cresc, PO Box 2324, North Lyneham 2902; tel: (02) 6248 5504

Moneycare Financial Counselling Service

Brisbane, 4001: 342 Upper Roma St, PO Box 2210; tel: (07) 3222 6621; fax: (07) 3229 3884

Campbelltown, NSW 2560: 27-31 Rudd Rd, PO Box 204 Leumeah; tel: (02) 4620 7482

Campsie, 2194: 30 Anglo Rd, PO Box 399; tel: 9787 5375; fax: 9718 6775

Central Qld 4701: 54 Charles St, North Rockhampton, PO Box 5343 CQMC 4702; tel: (07) 4999 1999; fax: (07) 4999 1915

Dickson, ACT 2602: 4 Hawdon Pl, PO Box 1038; tel: 6247 1340 (Direct Line), 6247 3635; fax: 6257 2791

Eastlakes, Belmont, NSW 2280: 360 Pacific Highway; tel: (02) 4945 1912; fax: (02) 4945 1930

Foster House, Surry Hills 2010: 5-19 Mary St; tel: (02) 8218 1242; fax: (02) 9211 6837

Kingsgrove, 1480: 61-65 Kingsway, Locked Bag 888; tel: 9336 3320; fax: 9336 3359

Lethbridge Park, 2150: 2-6 Bougainville Rd; tel/fax: (02) 9835 2756

Newcastle West, NSW 2302: DHQ, Union and Parry Sts; tel: (02) 4926 0231; fax: (02) 4926 2228

Parramatta, 2150: Ste 1, 2nd Fl, 95 Phillip St,

PO Box 3681; tel: 9633 5011; fax: 9633 5214

Taree, NSW 2430: 140a Victoria St;
tel: (02) 6592 4404; fax: (02) 6892 4405

Tuncurry, NSW 2428: 7 South St;
tel: (02) 6554 6101; fax: (02) 6555 3347

Crisis and Supported Accommodation (Homeless persons programmes)

Adults

Broken Hill, NSW 2880: Catherine Haven,
198 Wolfram St, PO Box 477;
tel: (08) 8087 1999

Cairns North, QLD 4870: Centennial Lodge,
369 Sheridan St, PO Box 140N;
tel/fax: (07) 4031 4432 (acc men 23 women 5)

Carrington, NSW 2294: The Anchor, PO Box
134, Cnr Young and Cowper Sts;
tel: (02) 4961 6129; fax: (02) 4961 4038
(acc men 18)

Chermside, QLD 4032: Glen Haven, 1000
Gympie Rd, PO Box 82, Aspley, QLD 4034;
tel: (07) 3350 3455; fax: (07) 3256 3601
(acc women/children units 10)

Griffith, NSW 2680: Anzac St;
tel: (02) 6964 3388 (acc men)

Kemblawarra, NSW 2505: 'Carinya Cottage',
1/3 Kemblawarra Rd, PO Box 269,
Warrawong 2502; tel: (02) 4276 2968;
fax: 4276 1412 (acc women and children 38)

Leeton, NSW 2705: 9 Mulga St;
tel: (02) 6953 4941 (client units)

Mackay, QLD 4740: Samaritan House,
Shakespeare St, PO Box 6642;
tel: (07) 4957 7644 Silent (acc mothers and
children, families 4)

Merewether, NSW 2291: Clulow Court,
49 Frederick St, PO Box 414, The Junction
2291; tel: (02) 4963 6616 (acc women 8)

Mount Isa, QLD 4825: 'Serenity House',
4 Helen St, PO Box 2900; tel: (07) 4743 3198
(acc women)

Southport, QLD 4215: Still Waters, 173 Wardoo
St, PO Box 888, Ashmore City 4214;
tel: (07) 5591 1776 (acc men 20 women 16
family units 6)

Spring Hill, QLD 4004: Pindari, 28 Quarry St,
PO Box 159; tel: (07) 3832 1491 (acc hostel
148 flats 11 medical centre 3)

Surry Hills, NSW 2010: Foster House,
5-19 Mary St; tel: (02) 9212 1065;
fax: (02) 9218 1248 (acc men 201)

Surry Hills, NSW 2010: Samaritan House,
348 Elizabeth St, PO Box 583, Surry Hills;
tel: (02) 9211 5794; fax: (02) 9212 5430
(acc women 38)

Tewantin, QLD 4565: 26 Donella St, PO Box
671; tel: (07) 5447 1184; fax: (07) 5447 1854
(acc families)

The Junction (Newcastle), NSW 2291: Faith
Cottage, 28 Farquhar St, PO Box 366;
tel: (02) 4969 4275 (acc mothers and
children 16)

Toowoomba, QLD 4350: 5 Russell St, PO Box
2527; tel: (07) 4632 5239; fax: (07) 4639 1821
(acc men)

Toowoomba, QLD 4350: 5 Russell St, PO Box
2527; tel: (07) 4639 1998 (acc Family Crisis)

Youth

Bundaberg QLD 4670: The Salvation Army Youth
Refuge, 71 Woongarra St, Bundaberg 4670;
tel: (07) 41513400; fax: (07) 41526044

Canberra, ACT 2601: Oasis Support Network,
PO Box 435; tel: (02) 6248 7191;
fax: (02) 6249 8116

Fortitude Valley, QLD 4006: 20 Baxter St, PO
Box 701; tel: (07) 3854 1245;
fax: (07) 3854 1552

Newcastle, NSW 2293: The Ark, 116-120 Hannell
St, PO Box 94 Wickham; tel: (020) 4969 8066;
fax: (02) 4969 8073 (acc 24)

Surry Hills, NSW 2010: Oasis Youth Support
Network, 365 Crown St, PO Box 600
Darlingshurst 1300; tel: (02) 9331 2266

Wyong, NSW 2259: Oasis Youth Support,
5 Hely St, PO Box 57, Wyong;
tel: (02) 4353 9799; fax: (02) 4353 9550

Handicapped Persons: Accommodation

Toowoomba, QLD 4350: Horton Village, 2 Curtis
St, PO Box 289; tel: (07) 4639 4026 (acc 30)

Family Tracing Service

Brisbane, QLD 4000: 342 Upper Roma St, GPO
Box 2210, Brisbane 4001; tel: (07) 3236 5544;
fax: (07) 3221 6228

Sydney, NSW 2000: PO Box A435, Sydney South,
1232; tel: (02) 9211 0277; fax: (02) 9211 2044

Special Search Service

Sydney, NSW 2000: 85 Campbell St, Surry Hills
2010, PO Box A435, Sydney South, 1232;
tel: (02) 9211 6491, 1300 667 366 Australia
Wide; fax: (02) 9211 2044

Court and Prison Ministry

Brisbane, QLD 4000: 342 Upper Roma St, GPO
Box 2210, Brisbane 4001; tel: (07) 3222 6670

Sydney South, NSW 1232: PO Box
Corrective Services Ministry NSW/ACT

Parramatta, NSW 2105: 30-32 Smith St;
tel: (02) 9687 9005; fax: (02) 9687 9544

Community Service

Brisbane, QLD 4003: 97 Turbot St, PO Box
13688, George St 4003; tel: (07) 3211 9230;
fax: (07) 3211 9234

Broken Hill, NSW 2880: Algate House
Community Ctr, 463 Lane St, PO Box 477;
tel: (08) 8088 2044

Campsie, NSW 2194: 30 Anglo Rd, PO Box 399;
tel: (02) 9787 2333; fax: (02) 9718 6775

Canberra, ACT 2602: 4 Hawdon Pl, Dickson,
PO Box 1038 Dickson; tel: (02) 6247 3635

Dulwich Hill: 54 Dulwich St;
tel: (02) 9569 4511; fax: (02) 9569 4677

Eastern Beaches, NSW 2022: 41 Brisbane St,
PO Box 1505, Bondi Junction;
tel/fax: (02) 9389 6186

Greenslopes, QLD 4120: 627 Logan Rd; PO
Box 221 Stones Corner; tel: (07) 3394 4184

Illawarra, NSW 2500: Northcliffe Dr,
Kemblawarra 2505, PO Box 6102 Wollongong;
tel: (02) 4275 1188; fax: (02) 4275 2944

Inala, QLD 4077: 83 Inala Ave, PO Box 1050;
tel: (07) 3372 1889

Inner City (Sydney), NSW 2000: 339 Crown St,
Surry Hills 2010; tel: (02) 9360 1000

Ipswich, QLD 4305: 14 Ellenborough St;
PO Box 227; tel: (07) 3812 2462

Logan City, QLD 4114: Shop 5, 41 Station Rd,
Woodridge, PO Box 816; tel: (07) 3808 2564

Macquarie Fields, NSW 2564: Eucalyptus Drive,
PO Box 1; tel: (02) 9605 4771

Maroubra, NSW 2035: 100 Boyce Rd, PO Box
321; tel: (02) 9314 2166; fax: (02) 9344 3160

Nerang, QLD 4211: Shop 5, Dalmar Centre,
43-45 Price St, PO Box 599; tel: (07) 5596 0764

Newcastle West, NSW 2302: 12-16 Union St;
tel: (02) 4929 2300

Northern Beaches, NSW 2099: 1 Fisher Rd,
PO Box 210, Dee Why; tel: (02) 9981 4472

St George, NSW 2208: 302 Kingsgrove Rd,
PO Box 472 Kingsgrove 1480;
tel: (02) 9150 7700; fax: (02) 9150 7711

Southport, QLD 4215: 48 Nind St, PO Box 1680;
tel: (07) 5591 2729

Townsville, QLD 4810: 165 Ross River Rd,
Mundingburra, PO Box 1152 Aitkenville MC
QLD 4814; tel: (07) 4755 0722

Wynnum/Capalaba, QLD 4178: 107 Akonna St,
PO Box 701; tel: (07) 3393 4713

Zillmere, QLD 4034: 8/35 Handford Rd,
PO Box 182, Zillmere; tel: (07) 3865 1416;
fax: (07) 3865 1705

Hostels for Students

Marrickville, NSW 2204: Stead House,
12 Leicester St, PO Box 3015;
tel: (02) 9557 1276 (acc women 25)

Toowong, QLD 4066: 15 Jephson St, PO Box
1124; tel: (07) 3371 1966 (acc 66)

Telephone Counselling Service

Salvo Care Line, NSW 2046: 1 Barnstaple Rd,
Five Dock 2046; tel: (02) 8736 3297 (office)
(02) 9331 6000 (24-hr counselling);
(02) 9331 2000 (suicide prevention);
(02) 9360 3000 (youth line)

Salvo Care Line, QLD 4000: 342 Upper
Roma St, GPO Box 2210, Brisbane 4001;
tel: (07) 3222 6678 (24-hr counselling)

Work Skill Training

Bundaberg QLD 4670: The Salvation Army
Tom Quinn Community Centre, 8 Killer St,
Bundaberg 4670; tel (07) 41533557;
fax: (07) 41511746

Job Link, Blacktown, NSW 2148: 15-21 Boiler
Close, PO Box 20; tel: (02) 9831 4247

Newcastle Youth Crisis and Training Service:
The Ark, 116-120 Hannell St, PO Box 94
Wickham NSW 2293; tel: (02) 4969 8066;
fax: (02) 4969 8073

This Way Up Furniture Co: 46 Maitland Rd,
Islington 2296; tel: (02) 4969 5695;
fax: (02) 4969 5665

JPET

Caboolture, QLD 4510: Unit 1, 75 King St;
tel: (07) 5428 2811

Fortitude Valley, QLD 4006: 20 Baxter St;
tel: (07) 3854 1245

Lawnton, QLD 4501: 27-29 Lawnton Pocket Rd;
tel: (07) 3285 8522

Redcliffe, QLD 4020: Shop 4, 3 Violet St;
tel: (07) 3283 5977

Employment Plus

National Office: Level 3, 10 Wesley Court, East
Burwood, VIC 3151; tel: 136 123 Australia
Wide

NSW State Office: 1st Floor, 125 Main St, PO
Box 747, Blacktown, NSW 2148;
tel: (02) 8825 1500; fax: (02) 8825 1525

QLD State Office: 895 Ann St, Fortitude Valley,
QLD 4006; tel: (07) 3250 8900;
fax: (07) 3250 8925

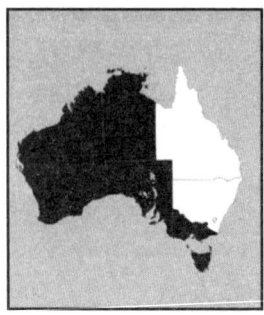

AUSTRALIA SOUTHERN TERRITORY

Territorial leaders:
Commissioners James and Carolyn Knaggs

Territorial Commander:
Commissioner James Knaggs (1 Aug 2006)

Chief Secretary:
Lieut-Colonel John Jeffrey (1 Mar 2003)

Territorial Headquarters: 3-7 Hamilton St, Mont Albert 3127, Vic

Postal address: Locked Bag 1, Mont Albert 3127, Victoria, Australia

Tel: [61] (03) 9896 6000; fax: [61] (03) 9899 2337; email: Salvosaus@aus.salvationarmy.org;
web site: www.salvationarmy.org.au

Zone: South Pacific and East Asia

States included in the territory: Northern Territory, South Australia, Tasmania, Victoria,
Western Australia

Languages in which the gospel is preached: Cantonese, English, Mandarin, local aboriginal languages

Publications: *Kidzone, On Fire, Warcry*

HUNDREDS of Salvationists signing a Declaration of War during the final meeting of the South Australian Divisional One Mission Conference in November 2005 was one of many highlights of the event that celebrated the 125th anniversary of The Salvation Army commencing in Australia. The declaration affirmed the Army's commitment to continue the war against sin by proclaiming the gospel, alleviating suffering and promoting social justice.

Another significant celebration was the 40th anniversary of the Red Shield Appeal in Australia. The appeal results increased significantly in 2005 despite Australians having given hundreds of millions of dollars already that year to tsunami relief appeals. The territory's result on doorknock day was up 17 per cent on the previous year.

The Salvation Army was at the forefront of evangelistic outreach and in the provision of practical assistance during the Commonwealth Games in Melbourne (March 2006). A total of 20,000 copies of the Army's children's magazine *Kidzone* and 4,000 copies of *Warcry* were distributed at games-associated events.

There were mixed emotions for Salvationists during June and July 2005 as 15 Salvation Army-owned aged care facilities changed hands. The territory had made the decision previously (for financial reasons) that it needed to decrease the number of aged care centres it maintained. Arrangements had been made with the new owners for Salvation Army chaplains to still be attached to the centres that were sold. The territory now has four centres serving the marginalised aged.

In the Queen's Birthday honours (June 2005) Brigadier Stella Bywaters OF received the nation's highest award when she became a Companion of the Order of Australia. The citation listed her 'decades of service to the international community during an unsafe and dangerous period in Uganda'.

Later in the year Territorial Communications Director John Dalziel was admitted to the Order of the Founder during a celebration rally at Waverley Temple conducted by Chief of the Staff Commissioner Israel L. Gaither. The citation noted his influence in promoting the Army's message throughout Australia and also commended him for his spiritual leadership as a local officer at Camberwell Corps.

The territory's developing world child sponsorship programme celebrated 25 years of operation in 2006. During the 2004/05 financial year A$432,916 (US$325,163) was sent to 2,184 children in 23 countries from 1,767 sponsors.

The launch of a revamped junior soldier programme in the early part of 2006 involved revised content and packaging, including spreading the word via CD-ROMS.

The territory has combined with Australia Eastern, New Zealand, Fiji and Tonga and Papua New Guinea Territories in a history project called *Keeping It Alive*. The three-year project will culminate in the release of a series of DVDs, CD-ROMs, a coffee table book and youth-oriented literature that tells the story of The Salvation Army in the region.

Mission undergirded with prayer continues to be the main focus of the territory.

STATISTICS

Officers 890 (active 490 retired 400)
Lieutenants 59 **Cadets** (1st Yr) 12 (2nd Yr) 35 **Employees** 5,510
Corps 164 **Outposts** 9 **Social Centres/ Programmes** 218 **Family Stores** 202 **Family Support Centres** 72 **Outback Flying Service** 1
Senior Soldiers 9,318 **Adherents** 2,970 **Junior Soldiers** 1,255
Personnel serving outside territory Officers 31 Layworkers 2

STAFF

Asst Chief Sec: Lt-Col Elaine Hood
Asst to Chief Sec/Events/Projects: Lt-Col Lyndon Spiller
National Editor-in-Chief: Maj Laurie Robertson
Business Administration: Lt-Col Brian Hood
  Asst Business Sec: Capt Malcolm Roberts
  Audit: Mr Cameron Duck
  Family Stores: Mr Allen Dewhirst
  Finance: Mr Gregory Stowe
  Information Technology: Mr Larry Reed
  Legal: Capt Malcolm Roberts
  Property: Mr David Perry
  Public Relations: Maj Wayne Pittaway
  SA Supplies: Mrs Jean Roper
Leader Development: Lt-Col Elaine Hood
  Training Principal: Maj Frank Daniels
  Asst Sec Leader Development: Maj Colin Corkery
Personnel: Maj Ray Finger
  Asst Personnel Sec: Maj Bryce Mouchemore
  Asst Personnel Sec – Officer Resource Unit: Maj Leanne Ruthven
  Candidates: Maj Diane Corkery
  Human Resources: Mr John Cullinan
  Overseas Personnel: Lt-Col Julie Spiller
  Pastoral Care: Maj Graeme Faragher
  Spiritual Development: Maj Robert A. Paterson

Programme: Maj John Vale
  Corps Programme: Maj Kelvin Merrett
  Family Tracing: Maj Barbara Munro
  Melbourne Staff Band: B/M Ken Waterworth
  Melbourne Staff Songsters: S/L Brian Hogg
  Social Programme: Maj Graeme Rigley
  Youth: Capt Simon Damen
Women's Ministries: Comr Carolyn Knaggs
  (TPWM) Lt-Col Judith Jeffrey (TSWM)
  Director: Maj Adele Vale
  Child Sponsorship: Mrs Wendy Smith
  Fellowship of the Silver Star: Maj Aylene
  Finger

DIVISIONS

Eastern Victoria: 347-349 Mitcham Rd,
  Mitcham, Vic 3132; tel: (03) 8872 6400;
  Maj Ronald Clinch
Melbourne: 69 Bourke St, Melbourne, Vic 3000;
  tel: (03) 9653 3213; Maj Rodney Barnard
Northern Victoria: Bramble St, Bendigo, Vic
  3550; tel: (03) 5443 4288; Lt-Col Jocelyn
  Knapp
South Australia: 39 Florence St, Fullarton, SA
  5063; tel: (08) 8379 9388; Maj Dennis Rowe
Tasmania: 'Maylands', 27 Pirie St, Newtown, Tas
  7008; tel: (03) 6278 7184; Maj Allan Daddow
Western Australia: 333 William St,
  Northbridge, WA 6003; tel: (08) 9227 7010;
  Maj Iain Trainor
Western Victoria: 209a Dana St, Ballarat, Vic
  3350; tel: (03) 5331 3088; Maj Peter Walker

REGION

Northern Territory: 49 Mitchell St, Darwin, NT
  0800; tel: (08) 8981 8188; Maj Ritchie Watson

OFFICER TRAINING COLLEGE

Parkville, Vic 3052: 303 Royal Parade;
  tel: (03) 9347 0299

ARCHIVES AND HERITAGE CENTRES

Melbourne, Vic 3000: Territorial Archives and
  Museum, 69 Bourke St, PO Box 18137,
  Collins St E, Melbourne, Vic 8003;
  tel: (03) 9653 3201
Nailsworth, SA 5083: Heritage Centre, 2a
  Burwood Ave; tel: (08) 8342 2545
Northbridge, WA 6003: Historical Society
  Display Centre, 3rd Floor, 333 William St;
  tel: (08) 9227 7010

CONFERENCE AND HOLIDAY CENTRES

Bicheno, Tas 7215: Holiday Home, 11 Banksia St
Busselton, WA 6280: Unit 2, 12 Gale St;
  tel: (08) 9227 7010

Daylesford, Vic 3460: Holiday Flat, Unit 5/28
  Camp St
East Geelong, Vic 3219: Geelong Conference
  Centre, Adams Court, Eastern Park;
  tel: (03) 5226 2121
Mount Dandenong, Vic 3767: Holiday Home, 6
  Oakley St
Ocean Grove, Vic 3226: Holiday Home,
  4 Northcote Rd
Victor Harbor, SA 5211: Red Shield Memorial
  Camp, 22 Bartel Blvd; tel: (08) 8552 2707
  (acc 148)
Weymouth, Tas 7252: Weymouth Holiday Camp,
  Walden St; tel: (03) 6382 6359 (acc 32)

EMPLOYMENT PLUS

National Office: Burwood, Vic 3151, Level 3,
  10 Wesley Crt; tel: (03) 9847 8700; Maj John
  Simmonds
State Offices: 5
Service Delivery Centres: New South Wales 23;
  Queensland 16; South Australia 12;
  Tasmania 4; Victoria 31; Western Australia 7
Enquiries: tel: 136 123

FLYING PADRE AND OUTBACK SERVICES

PO Box 43289, Casuarina, NT 0811;
  tel: (08) 8945 0176; Capt David Shrimpton

RED SHIELD DEFENCE SERVICES

Puckapunyal, Vic 3662: Representative
  tel: (03) 5793 1294
Robertson Barracks, NT 0800: Representative
  tel: (08) 8935 2526, 8981 7663

SOCIAL SERVICES

Pathways Accommodation and Support
(including Personal Support Programme,
Community Connections Programme,
and Homeless Services)
43b Wyndham St, Shepparton, Vic 3630;
  tel: (03) 5821 2131

Pathways Shepparton
43a & 43b Wyndham St, Shepparton Vic 3630;
  Postal Address: PO Box 7352, Shepparton,
  Vic 3632;
  email: pathways@aus.salvationarmy.org

Homelessness Support Service
Outreach Connections: tel: (03) 5821 2131;
  fax: (03) 5822 4424
Family Support Services
Tel: (03) 5822 4420; fax: (03) 5821 7627

Adult Services

Abbotsford, Vic 3067: The Anchorage,
81 Victoria St; tel: (03) 9417 5820

Geelong, Vic 3216: Community Access,
Community Support, Adult Outreach,
1 Riverview Tce; tel: (03) 5243 3364

Kensington, Vic 3031: Community Outreach,
133 Rankins Rd; tel: (03) 9372 2488

New Town, Tas 7008: Accommodation and
Housing for the Aged, 115 New Town Rd;
tel: (03) 6278 3256

North Melbourne, Vic 3051: Community Aged
Care, Food Services, Cleaning Maintenance,
9 Roden St; tel: (03) 9329 5777

Aboriginal Ministry

Alice Springs, NT 0870: Aboriginal Programme,
88 Hartley St; tel: (08) 8951 0207

Swan Hill, Vic 3585: 190 Beveridge St;
tel: (03) 5033 1718

Chaplaincy
Police, Fire and Emergency Services

Darwin NT 0800 (PFES): tel: 0407 797 197

Kununurra WA (FES)

Child Care and Family Services

Balga, WA, 6061: Family Day Care and Long
Day Care, 10-18 Lavant Way;
tel: (08) 9349 7488

Ballarat, Vic 3550: 6 Crompton St;
tel: (03) 5329 1100

Bendigo, Vic 3552: Fairground Family Access
Programme, 65-71 Mundy St;
tel: (03) 5441 5405

Melton, Vic 3337: Melton Foster Care,
38 Station Rd; tel: (03) 9747 8310

North Coburg, Vic 3031: 2/828 Sydney Rd;
tel: (03) 9353 1011

Sunshine, Vic 3020: Child and Adolescent
Services, 34 Devonshire Rd;
tel: (03) 9312 3544

Sunshine, Vic 3020: Intensive Case
Management Services, 34 Devonshire Rd;
tel: (03) 9312 3544

Sunshine, Vic 3020: Home-Based One-to-One
Care, 34 Devonshire Rd; tel: (03) 9312 3544

Intensive Living and Learning
Environments – ILLE Programmes

St Albans; Taylor's Lakes; Sunshine; North
Altona; Kealba; Melton

Contact through Westcare, 34 Devonshire Rd,
Sunshine; tel: (03) 9312 3544

Children's Homes and Cottages

Sunshine, Vic 3020: Westcare, 34 Devonshire
Rd, Sunshine; tel: (03) 9312 3544

Community Programmes

Bendigo Vic. 3552: Community Programmes
including Youth Ministries, Personal Support
Programme, Creative Arts and Technology,
Gravel Hill Community Gardens, HillSkills
Workshop, Hilltop Café, Fairground
Children's Contact Service, 65 -71 Mundy
Street; tel: (03) 5442 7699

Berri, SA 5343: Riverland Community Services,
20 Wilson St; tel: (08) 8582 3182

Brunswick, Vic 3056: 256 Albert St;
tel: (03) 9387 6746

Hawthorn, Vic 3122: Hawthorn Project,
16 Church St; tel: (03) 9851 7800

Hawthorn, Vic 3122: Homeless Outreach
Project, 16 Church St; tel: (03) 9851 7800

Hawthorn, Vic 3122: Community Connection
Project, 16 Church St; tel: (03) 9851 7800

Hawthorn, Vic 3122: Equity and Access Project,
16 Church St; tel: (03) 9851 7800

Hawthorn, Vic 3122: Multiple and Complex
Needs Initiative, 16 Church St;
tel: (03) 9851 7800

Kununurra, WA 6743: Community Outreach
Centre, 106 Coolibah Drive; tel: 0429 802 885

Mornington, Vic 3931: PYFS, Reconnect
Programme, Shop 9, 234 Main St;
tel: (03) 5976 2231

Port Augusta, SA 5700: Community Services, 35
Flinders Tce; tel: (08) 8641 1021

Rosebud, Vic 3939: Peninsula Community
Support Programme, 17-19 Ninth Ave;
tel: (03) 5986 7268

Crisis Services

Balga, WA 6061: Family Accommodation
Programme, 10-18 Lavant Way;
tel: (08) 9349 7488

Croydon, Vic 3136: Gateways Crisis Services,
PO Box 1072; tel: (03) 9725 8455

Frankston, Vic 3199: Peninsula Counselling
Service, 37 Rossmith Ave East;
tel: (03) 9784 5050

Frankston, Vic 3199: Peninsula Crisis Centre,
37 Rossmith Ave East; tel: (03) 9784 5050

Geraldton, WA 6530: Family Crisis
Accommodation, 42 Ainsworth St;
tel: (08) 9964 3627

Leongatha, Vic 3953: GippsCare Domestic
Violence Outreach Service, 51 McCartin St;
tel: (03) 5662 4502

St Kilda, Vic 3128: Inner South Domestic
Violence Service, 27 Grey St;
tel: (03) 9536 7730, toll free: 1800 627 727

St Kilda, Vic 3182: Verve Programme, 31 Grey
St; tel: (03) 9536 7780

Australia Southern Territory

St Kilda, Vic 3182: 27 Grey St;
 tel: (03) 9536 7777
St Kilda, Vic 3182: St Kilda Crisis
 Accommodation, 31 Grey St;
 tel: (03) 9536 7730, toll free 1800 627 727
St Kilda, Vic 3182: Health and Information,
 29 Grey St; tel: (03) 9536 7703,
 toll free 1800 627 727
St Kilda, Vic 3182: Access Health Service,
 31 Grey St; tel: (03) 9536 7780
St Kilda, Vic 3182: Inner South Domestic
 Violence Services, 29 Grey St;
 tel: (03) 9536 7720

Emergency Accommodation

Albany, WA 6330: 152-160 North Rd;
 tel: (08) 9841 1068 (acc family units 2)
Alice Springs, NT 0870: 11 Goyder St;
 tel: (08) 8952 1434 (acc service, single men,
 dual diagnosis)
Ballarat, Vic 3350: Karinya, 6 Crompton St;
 tel: (03) 5329 1100 (acc mothers 8)
Berri, SA 5343: Riverland Community Services,
 20 Wilson St; tel: (08) 8582 3182 (acc 30)
Bunbury, WA 6230: Cnr Bussell H'way and
 Timperly Rd; tel: (08) 9721 4519
 (acc family units 2)
Burnie, Tas 7320: 24 View Rd;
 tel: (03) 6431 5791 (acc 61)
Darwin, NT 0800: 49 Mitchell St;
 tel: (08) 8981 5994 (acc 64, family units 5)
Geraldton, WA 6530: Ainsworth St;
 tel: (08) 9964 3667 (acc family units 3)
Hobart West, Tas 7000: 15 Lansdowne Cresc;
 tel: (03) 6234 5777 (acc 16 exit houses 2)
Horsham, Vic 3400: 12 Kalkee Rd;
 tel: (03) 5382 1770 (acc family units 3 single 3)
Jacana, Vic 3047: 23 Sunset Blvd;
 tel: (03) 9309 6289 (acc family units 4
 community houses 6)
Kalgoorlie Boulder, WA 6430: Oberthur St;
 tel: (08) 9021 2255 (acc family units 2)
Sale, Vic 3850: Cnr Cunningham and Marley
 Sts; tel: (03) 5144 4564 (acc 6)
Shepparton, Vic 3630: 23 Middleton St;
 tel: (03) 5821 2131 (acc extended care house 1
 family units 3 single women unit 1 single men
 units 2)
Stawell, Vic 3380: 26-30 Ligar St;
 tel: (03) 5358 4072 (youth and singles)
Sunbury, Vic 3429: 27-37 Anderson St;
 tel: (03) 9740 8844
Sunshine, Vic 3020: 1 St Andrew St;
 tel: (03) 9364 9744

Emergency Family Accommodation

Burnie, Tas 7320: Oakleigh House, 24 View Rd;

tel: (03) 6431 5791 (acc 61)
Darwin, NT 0800: 49 Mitchell St;
 tel: (08) 8981 5994 (family units 5)
Horsham, Vic 3400: 12 Kalkee Rd;
 tel: (03) 5382 1770 (acc family units 3
 single 3)
Port Augusta, SA 5700: 35 Flinders Tce; tel:
 (08) 8641 1021 (acc 65)
St Kilda, Vic 3182: 27 Grey St;
 tel: (03) 9536 7730 (acc 20)

Family Outreach (Community Programme)

Brunswick, Vic 3056: 256 Albert St;
 tel: (03) 9387 6746
Geelong, Belmont, Vic 3216: Kardinia,
 1 Riverview Tce; tel: (03) 5243 3364
Jacana, Vic 3047: 23 Sunset Blvd;
 tel: (03) 9309 6289
Moonah, Tas 7008: 73 Hopkins St;
 tel: (03) 6228 0910
Port Augusta, SA 5700: 35 Flinders Tce;
 tel: (08) 8641 1024
Seymour, Vic 3660: Pathways, 6 Tallarook St;
 tel: (03) 5799 1581

Family Stores

Administration: Noble Park, Vic 3174;
 400 Princes H'way; tel: (03) 9707 9999
Stores: Northern Territory 6; South Australia 39;
 Tasmania 10; Victoria 92; Western
 Australia 45

Family Support Services

Aberfoyle Park, SA 5159: The Hub Worship and
 Community Complex; tel: (08) 8370 5003
Adelaide, SA 5000: 277 Pirie St;
 tel: (08) 8227 0199
Albany, WA 6330: 152-160 North Rd;
 tel: (08) 9841 1068
Alice Springs, NT 0870: 88 Hartley St;
 tel: (08) 8951 0206
Armadale, WA 6112: 57 Braemore St;
 tel: (08) 9497 1803
Arndale, Kilkenny, SA 5009: 1-7 Gray;
 tel: (08) 8445 2044
Bairnsdale, Vic 3875: 63 McLeod St;
 tel: (03) 5152 4201
Balga, WA 6061: 10-18 Lavant Way;
 tel: (08) 9349 7488
Ballarat, Vic 3350: 102 Eureka St;
 tel: (03) 5337 0600
Beechworth, Vic 3747: 35 Ford St;
 tel: (03) 5728 3245
Benalla, Vic 3672: 72 Fawkner Dr;
 tel: (03) 5762 6396
Bendigo, Vic 3550: 65-71 Mundy St;
 tel: (03) 5442 7699

Bentleigh, Vic 3204: 87 Robert St;
tel: (03) 9557 2644

Bentley, WA 6102: Dumond St;
tel: (08) 9458 1855

Berwick, Vic 3806: Cnr Parkhill Dr and Ernst
Wanke Rd; tel: (03) 9704 1940

Box Hill, Vic 3128: 17-23 Nelson Rd;
tel: (03) 9890 2993

Broadford, Vic 3658: 25-27 Powlett St;
tel: (03) 7584 1635

Brunswick, Vic 3056: 256 Albert St;
tel: (03) 9387 6746

Burnie, Tas 7320: 99 Wilson St;
tel: (03) 6431 8722

Busselton, WA 6280: Kent St; tel: (08) 9754 2733

Camberwell, Vic 3124: 7 Bowen St;
tel: (03) 9889 2468

Campbelltown, SA 5074: Cnr Roma Grv and
Florentine Ave; tel: (08) 8365 2301

Carrum Downs, Vic 3201: 1265 Frankston-
Dandenong Rd; tel: (03) 9782 0383

Castlemaine, Vic 3450: 47 Kennedy St;
tel: (03) 5470 5389

Chelsea, Vic 3196: 4 Swan Walk;
tel: (03) 9773 1027

Colac, Vic 3250: 35 Corangamite St;
tel: (03) 5231 1178

Cranbourne, Vic 3977: 1 New Holland Dr;
tel: (03) 5991 1777

Darwin, Anula, NT 0812: Cnr Lee Point Rd and
Yanyula Dr; tel: (08) 8927 9566

Doncaster, Vic 3109: 37 Taunton Street;
tel: (03) 9842 4744

Doveton, Vic 3177: 1A Frawley Rd;
tel: (03) 9793 3933

Echuca, Vic 3564: 50-52 Sturt St;
tel: (03) 5482 6722

Ellenbrook, WA 6069: Cnr Highpoint and
Woodlake Blvds; tel: (08) 9296 7172

Ferntree Gully, Vic 3156: 37 Wattletree Rd;
tel: (03) 9752 3604

Frankston, Vic 3200: 15 Forest Dr;
tel: (03) 9776 9155

Geelong, Vic 3220: 26-28 Bellerine St;
tel: (03) 5223 2434

Geraldton, WA 6530: 42 Ainsworth St;
tel: (08) 9965 2467

Glenroy, Vic 3046: 2 Finchley Ave;
tel: (03) 9300 4099

Greensborough, Vic 3088: 2 Flodden Way;
tel: (03) 9434 6990

Healesville, Vic 3777: 114 Maroondah Hwy;
tel: (03) 5962 2486

Heathridge, WA 6027: 36 Christmas Ave;
tel: (08) 9401 3408

Hobart, Tas 7000: 250 Liverpool St;
tel: (03) 6231 1345

Horsham, Vic 3400: Cnr Kalkee Rd and
Lynott St; tel: (03) 5382 1770

Ingle Farm, SA 5098: Cnr Bridge and Maxwell
Rds; tel: (08) 8264 4166

Kalgoorlie/Boulder, WA 6430: Oberthur St;
tel: (08) 9021 2255

Karratha, WA 6714: 2 Bond Pl;
tel: (08) 9185 2148

Keilor, Vic 3037: 2a Roseleigh Boulevard;
tel: (03) 9390 6111

Kwinana, WA 6167: Cnr Medina Ave and Hoyle
Rd; tel: (08) 9439 1585

Kyabram, Vic 3620: 24 Unitt St;
tel: (03) 5853 2684

Launceston, Tas 7250: 7 Cameron St;
tel: (03) 6334 2950

Leongatha, Vic 3953: 52 Anderson St;
tel: (03) 5662 4670

Marion, SA 5047: Cnr Sturt and Morpett Rd,
Seacombe Gdns; tel: (08) 8377 0001

Mandurah, WA 6210: Lot 5 Lakes Rd;
tel: (08) 9535 4951

Maryborough, Vic 3465: 58 High St;
tel: (03) 5461 2789

Melbourne, Vic 3000: 69 Bourke St;
tel: (03) 9653 3259

Merriwa, WA 6030: 26 Jenolan Way;
tel: (08) 9305 2131

Mildura, Vic 3500: 1401-1415 Etiwanda Ave;
tel: (03) 5021 2229

Moonee Ponds, Vic 3040: Cnr Mount Alexander
Rd & Buckley St; tel: (03) 9375 3249

Mooroolbark, Vic 3138: 55 Manchester Rd;
tel: (03) 9727 4777

Morley, WA 6062: 565 Walter Rd;
tel: (08) 9279 4500

Mountain View, Vic 3154: 1 The Basin - Olinda
Rd; tel: (03) 9762 3490

Mt Gambier, SA 5290: Cnr Gray and Wyatt Sts;
tel: (08) 8725 9900

Narrogin, WA 6312: Doney St;
tel: (08) 9881 4004

Noarlunga, Morphett Vale, SA 5162: 186
Elizabeth St; tel: (08) 5382 1600

Northam, WA 6401: Wellington St;
tel: (08) 9622 1228

Northbridge, WA 6003: Perth - 333 William St;
tel: (08) 9328 1690

Norwood, SA 5067: 55 George St;
tel: (08) 8332 0283

Oakleigh, Vic 3166: 50 Atherton Rd;
tel: (03) 9563 0786

Pakenham, Vic 3810: 51 Bald Hill Rd;
tel: (030) 5941 4906

Palmerston, NT 0830: Cnr Temple Tce and
Woodroffe Ave; tel: (08) 8932 2103
Playford, Elizabeth East, SA 5112: Cnr Kinkaid
Rd and Aylwin St; tel: (08) 8255 8811
Plenty Valley, Vic 3075: Cnr Morang Dr and
Fred Hollows Way, Mill Park;
tel: (03) 9436 9200
Port Lincoln, SA 5606: 41 Marine Ave;
tel: (08) 8682 4296
Preston, Vic 3072: 263 Gower St;
tel: (03) 9471 9111
Ringwood, Vic 3134: 47 Wantirna Rd;
tel: (03) 9879 2894
Rivervale, WA 6103: Cnr Norwood Rd and
Francisco St; tel: (08) 9355 2799
Rochester, Vic 3561: Cnr Elizabeth and Ramsay
Sts; tel: (03) 5484 1364
Rockingham, Cooloongup, WA 6168: Cnr Read
St and Willmot Dr; tel: (08) 9527 3460
Rosebud, Vic 3940: 2 Melaleuca Ave;
tel: (03) 5986 4206
Rowville, Vic 3178: Police Rd;
tel: (03) 9701 0491
Seymour, Vic 3660: Victoria St;
tel: (03) 5799 2583
Shepparton, Vic 3630: 43a Wyndham Street:
tel (03) 5831 1551
St Arnaud, Vic 3478: 14 Queens Ave:
tel: (03) 5495 1385
Sunshine, Vic 3020: 34 Devonshire Rd;
tel: (03) 9312 4624
Swan Hill, Vic 3585: 190 Beveridge St;
tel: (03) 5033 1718
Swan View, WA 6056: 371-379 Morrison Rd;
tel: (08) 9294 2811
Tea Tree Gully, Modbury, SA 5092: 138
Reservoir Rd; tel: (08) 8264 8729
Traralgon, Vic 3844:
Latrobe Valley Community Services Network,
Admin Office, 51-57 Post Office Pl;
tel: (03) 5174 1955
Moe, Vic 3825: 18-22 George St;
tel: (03) 5126 1683
Morwell, Vic 3840: 160 Commercial Rd;
tel: (03) 5133 9366
Traralgon, Vic 3844: 51-57 Post Office Pl;
tel: (03) 5174 7153
Wangaratta, Vic 3677: 13-17 Garnet Ave;
tel: (03) 5722 1129
Warragul, Vic 3820: 120 Burke St;
tel: (03) 5623 1090
Warrnambool, Vic 3280: Cnr Lava and
Henna Sts; tel: (03) 5561 6844
Waverley, Glen Waverley, Vic 3150: 958 High
Street Rd; tel: (03) 9803 2587

Werribee, Vic 3030: 1-3 Thames Blvd;
tel: (03) 9731 1344
Whyalla, Whyalla Norrie, SA 5608: 5-7
Viscount Slim Ave; tel: (08) 8645 7101
Wodonga, Vic 3690: 210 Lawrence St;
tel: (03) 6024 2886
Wonthaggi, Vic 3995: McKenzie St;
tel: (03) 5672 1228

Family Tracing Service

Adelaide, Fullarton, SA 5063: 39 Florence St;
tel: (08) 8379 9388
Darwin, Anula, NT 0812: Cnr Lee Point Rd and
Yanyula Dr; tel: (08) 8927 6499
Hobart, New Town, Tas 7008: 27 Pirie St;
tel: (03) 6278 7184
Perth, Northbridge, WA 6003: 333 William St;
tel: (08) 9227 7010
Victoria and Inter-Territorial enquiries only:
Mont Albert, Vic 3127: 3-7 Hamilton St;
tel: (03) 9896 6000

Home and School Support Service

Broadford, Vic 3658: 25-27 Powlett St;
tel: (03) 5784 1635

Hostels for Homeless Men

Abbotsford, Vic 3067: Anchorage Hostel,
81 Victoria Crescent; tel: (03) 9417 8520
Adelaide, SA 5000: Towards Independence, 277
Pirie St; tel: (08) 8223 4911 (acc 75)
Alice Springs, NT 0870: 11 Goyder St;
tel: (08) 8952 1434 (acc 27)
Darwin, NT 0820: Sunrise Centre, Lot 5344
Salonika St; tel: (08) 8981 4199 (acc 26)
Melbourne North, Vic 3051: The Open Door,
166 Boundary Rd; tel: (03) 9329 6988 (acc 45)
Melbourne West, Vic 3003: Flagstaff Crisis
Accommodation, 9 Roden St;
tel: (03) 9329 4800 (acc 64)
Perth, Mount Lawley, WA 6050: Tanderra
Hostel, 68 Guildford Rd;
tel: (08) 9271 1209 (acc 27)
Perth, WA 6000: Lentara, Cnr Short and Nash
Sts; tel: (08) 9328 3102 (acc 55)
St Kilda, Vic 3182: St Kilda Crisis
Accommodation Centre, 31 Grey St;
tel: (03) 9525 4473 (acc 20)

Hostels for Homeless Youth

Fitzroy, Vic 3065: 12 Tranmere St;
tel: (03) 9489 1122
Frankston, Vic 3199: 37 Rossmith Ave East;
tel: (03) 9784 5050 (4 houses)
Kalgoorlie/Boulder, WA 6430: 10 Park St;
tel: (08) 9091 1016 (acc 12)

Lansdale, WA 6065: Lansdale House, 460
Kingsway; tel: (08) 9302 1433 (acc 8)

Leongatha, Vic 3953: GippsCare Cross-target
Transitional Support, 51 McCartin St;
tel: (03) 5662 4502

Mirrabooka, WA 6061: Oasis House, 68-70
Honeywell Blvd; tel: (08) 9342 6785
(acc adolescents 8)

Pooraka, SA 5095: Muggy's, 88 Henderson Ave;
tel: (08) 8260 6617 (acc 10)

Salisbury, SA 5108: Burlendi, 22 Spains Rd;
tel: (08) 8281 6641 (acc 8)

Shepparton, Vic 3630: Brayton, 360 River Rd;
tel: (03) 5823 2277

St Kilda, Vic 3182: 27 Grey St;
tel: (03) 9536 7730

Hostels for Intellectually Disabled Persons

Manningham, SA 5086: Red Shield Housing
Network Services, 109 Hampstead Rd;
tel: (08) 8368 6800 (properties 310)

Social Housing – SASHS

Adelaide, Manningham, SA 5086: Red Shield
Housing Network Services, 109 Hampstead
Rd; tel: (08) 8368 6800

Box Hill, Vic 3128: 31-33 Ellingworth Pde;
tel: (03) 9890 7144

Geelong, Grovedale, Vic 3216: Barwon South
West Region, 142 Torquay Rd;
tel: (03) 5244 2500

Hawthorn, Vic 3122: EastCare Housing
Services, 16 Church St; tel: (03) 9851 7800

Hobart, Tas 7000: Red Shield Housing,
223 Macquarie St; tel: (03) 6223 8050

Kew, Vic 3101: EastCare Housing Services,
85 High St; tel: (03) 9851 7800

Leongatha, Vic 3953: Gippsland Region, 51a
McCartin St; tel: (03) 5662 4538

Melbourne, Vic 3000: SACHS, 69 Bourke St;
tel: (03) 9653 3288

Newtown, Tas 7008: 117 Main Rd;
tel: (03) 6278 2817

Sunshine, Vic 3020: Western Metropolitan
Region, 27 Sun Cres; tel: (03) 9312 5424

Warragul, Vic 3820: 64 Queen St;
tel: (03) 5622 0351

Warrnambool, Vic 3280: 70 Henna St;
tel: (03) 5561 6844

Mobile Ministry

Karratha, WA 6714: 1 Nelson Court;
tel: (08) 9144 2895

Darwin, Jingili, NT 0810: 5 Murphy St (Flying
Padre); tel: (08) 8945 0176

Independent Units for Intellectually Handicapped Persons

Ottoway, SA 5013: Centennial Ct, 30-32 Edward
St; tel: (08) 8341 0413 (acc 18)

Men's Support Service

Medina, WA 6167: Cnr Hoyle Rd and Median
Ave; tel: (08) 9439 1585

Migrant and Refugee Services

Brunswick, Vic 3056: 12-14 Tinning St; tel: (03)
9384 8334

Non-Residential Domestic Violence Programme

Adelaide, SA 5000: Central Violence Intervention
Project, 440 Morphett St; tel: (03) 8231 0655

Prison Chaplaincy, Police Court, Probation Work

Adelaide, Manningham, SA 5086: 109
Hampstead Rd; tel: (08) 8368 6800

Alice Springs, NT 0870: 88 Hartley St;
tel: (08) 8951 0200

Ballarat, Vic 3350: tel: (03) 0409 963 673

Bendigo, Vic 3552: Bramble St;
tel: (03) 5443 4288

Darwin, Anula, NT 0812: Cnr Lee Point Rd &
Yanula Dr; tel: (08) 8927 5189

Darwin, Stuart Park, NT 0820: Lot 5043
Salonika St; tel: (08) 8981 4199

Geelong, Vic 3220: Gordon St;
tel: (03) 5225 3353

Hobart, Tas 7000: Prison Support Service, 250
Liverpool St; tel: (03) 6234 1870

Horsham, Vic 3400: 12 Kalkee Rd;
tel: (03) 5382 1770

Manningham, SA 5086: 109 Hampstead Rd;
tel: (08) 8368 6800

Perth, Northbridge, WA 6003: 333 William St;
tel: (08) 9227 7010

Sale, Vic 3869: PO Box 45, Yinnar, Vic;
tel: (03) 5169 1503

Swan Hill, Vic 3583: 190 Beveridge St;
tel: (03) 5033 1718

Wangaratta, Vic 3677: 13-17 Garnet Ave;
tel: (03) 5722 1129

West Melbourne, Vic 3033: Senior Courts and
Prisons Chaplain, 9 Roden St;
tel: (03) 9329 6022

Wodonga, Vic 3690: PO Box 130, Beechworth,
Vic 3747; tel: (03) 5728 3245

Red Shield Hostels

Alice Springs, NT 0870: 11 Goyder St;
tel: (08) 8952 1434 (acc 27)

Darwin, NT 0800: 49 Mitchell St;
tel: (08) 8981 5994 (acc 64, 5 family units)

Rehabilitation Services

Abbotsford, Vic 3067: Detox Unit, 81 Victoria Cres; tel: (03) 9495 6811

Adelaide, SA 5000: Central Violence Intervention Programme, 118 Wright St; tel: (08) 8231 0655

Adelaide, SA 5000: Sobering Up Unit, 62A Whitmore Sq; tel: (08) 8212 2855 (acc 25)

Adelaide, SA 5000: Warrondi Stabilisation Unit, 146 Gilbert St; tel: (08) 8212 1215 (acc 22)

Bendigo, Vic 3550: Bendigo Bridge Community Outreach, 65-71 Mundy St; tel: (03) 5442 8558

Bendigo, Vic 3550: Northern Victoria Drug and Alcohol Coordinator and Administration, 65-67 Mundy St; tel (03) 5442 7931

Box Hill, Vic 3128: Aurora Women's Accommodation Service, 310 Elgar Rd; tel: (03) 9890 4549

Brunswick, Vic: Outreach Service, 256 Albert St; tel: (03) 9387 6746

Corio, Vic 3214: Geelong Adult Withdrawal Unit; tel: (03) 5243 3364

Darwin, Stuart Park, NT 0820: Drug and Alcohol Services – Top End, Lot 5344, Salonika St; tel: (08) 8981 4199 (acc 26)

Geelong, Vic 3220: Geelong Bridge, Goldsworthy St; tel: (03) 5275 3500

Gosnells, WA 6110: Harry Hunter Adult Rehabilitation, 2498 Albany H'way; tel: (08) 9398 2077

Hawthorn, Vic 3122: Aurora Women's Accommodation Service, 16 Church St; tel: (03) 9851 7800

Hawthorn, Vic 3122: Drug and Alcohol Counselling Programme, 16 Church St; tel: (03) 9851 7800

Highgate, WA 6003: Bridge House, 15 Wright St; tel: (08) 9227 8086 (acc 27)

Hobart, Tas 7008: The Bridge Programme, Creek Rd; tel: (03) 6278 8140

Kew, Vic 3101: Drug and Alcohol Counselling Programme, 85 High St; tel: (03) 9851 7800

Kilmore, Vic 3664: Overdale Rural Residential Programme, 455 O'Grady's Rd; tel: (03) 5782 2744 (acc 10)

Preston, Vic 3072: Bridgehaven, 1a Jackman St; tel: (03) 9480 6488 (acc 15)

St Kilda, Vic 3182: The Bridge Centre, 12 Chapel St; tel: (03) 9521 2770

Swan Hill, Vic 3585: 190 Beveridge St; tel: (03) 5033 1718

The Basin, Vic 3154: New Hope Rehabilitation Centre, Basin-Olinda Rd; tel: (03) 9762 1166

Warrnambool, Vic 3280: 52-54 Fairy St; tel: (03) 5561 4453

Rural Outreach Worker

Eaglehawk, Vic 3556: 51 Church St; tel: (03) 5446 8135, mobile: 0429 337 408

Senior Citizens' Residences

Adelaide, SA 5000: Linsell Lodge, 430 Morphett St; tel: (08) 8231 4687 (acc hostel 53)

Clarence Park, SA 5034: Jean McBean Ct, 35 Mills St; tel: (08) 8231 4687 (acc units single 10 double 4)

Footscray, Vic 3011: James Barker House, 78 Ryan St; tel: (03) 9689 7211 (acc 45)

Fremantle North, WA 6159: Hillcrest, 23 Harvest Rd; tel: (08) 9335 9955 (acc hostel 49 nursing home 30 day care 30)

Geelong, Belmont, Vic 3216: Kardinia, 1 Riverview Tce; tel: (03) 5243 3364 (acc hostel 27 day care 12 with extended care)

Gosnells, WA 6110: Seaforth Gardens, 2542 Albany H'way; tel: (08) 9398 5228 (acc hostel 53 units 50)

Lenah Valley, Tas 7008: Macfarlane Ct, 16-22 Ratho St (acc units single 22 double 8)

New Town, Tas 7008: Barrington Lodge, 21 Tower Rd; tel: (03) 6228 2164 (acc res beds 10)

Soup Runs

Adelaide, SA 5000: 277 Pirie St (care of Adelaide Congress Hall; tel: (08) 8223 7776

Melbourne, Vic 3001: 69 Bourke St; tel: (03) 9653 3222

Perth, Northbridge, WA 6003: 333 William St; tel: (08) 9328 1690

Telephone Counselling Service

Perth, WA 6000: Salvo Care Line, Cnr Short and Nash Sts; tel: (08) 9227 8655

Women's Refuge Centres

Ballarat, Vic 3350: Karinya; tel: (03) 5329 1100 (mothers 8)

Darwin, NT 0801: Catherine Booth House, PO Box 189; tel: (08) 8981 5928 (acc 8)

Fullarton, SA 5063: Bramwell House, PO Box 305; tel: (08) 8379 7223 (acc 5 adults with children)

Geelong, Belmont, Vic 3216: Kardinia Women's Services; tel: (03) 5241 9149

Highgate, WA 6003: Byanda/Nunyara; tel: (08) 9328 8529 (acc 43)

Hobart, Tas 7000: McCombe House; tel: (03) 6243 5777 (acc 16)

Karratha, WA 6714: tel: (08) 9185 2807 (acc 16)
Richmond, Vic 3121: Mary Anderson Lodge,
Refer Crossroads; tel: (03) 9353 1011

Youth and Family Services
Alice Springs, NT 0870: Towards Independence,
88 Hartley St; tel: (08) 8951 0203
Box Hill, Vic 3128: Intensive Case Management
Service, 31-33 Ellingworth Pde;
tel: (03) 9890 7144
Box Hill, Vic 3128: Specialist Consulting and
Assessment Service, 31-33 Ellingworth Pde;
tel: (03) 9890 7144
Box Hill, Vic 3128: Children in Residential Care
Education Support, 31-33 Ellingworth Pde;
tel: (03) 9890 7144
Box Hill, Vic 3128: Work and Recreation
Program with Education, 31-33 Ellingworth
Pde; tel: (03) 9890 7144
Box Hill, Vic 3128: Residential Youth Services,
31-33 Ellingworth Pde; tel: (03) 9890 7144
Box Hill, Vic 3128: Leaving Care,
31-33 Ellingworth Pde; tel (03) 9890 7144
Box Hill, Vic 3128: JJHIP (Juvenile Justice
Housing Initiative Pathways);
tel: (03) 9890 7144
Brunswick, Vic 3056: Creative Opportunities,
10-18 Tinning St; tel: (03) 9386 7611
Darwin, Anula, NT 0812: Towards Independence,
Cnr Lee Point Rd & Yanula Dr;
tel: (08) 8927 5189
Kew, Vic 3101: The Hawthorn Project, 85 High
St; tel: (03) 9851 7800
Leongatha, Vic 3953: GippsCare Adolescent
Community Placement, 51 McCartin St;
tel: (03) 5662 4502
Melbourne, Vic 3000: Melbourne Counselling,
69 Bourke St; tel: (03) 9653 3250
Moonee Ponds, Vic 3039: Crosslink
Employment Services, 33a Taylor St;
tel: (03) 9372 0675
Mornington, Vic 3931: Peninsula Home and
Community-Based Care Services, Shop 9, 234
Main St; tel: (03) 5976 2231
Mornington, Vic 3931: Peninsula Adolescent
Community Placement, Shop 9, 234 Main St;
tel: (03) 5976 2747

Mornington, Vic 3931: Peninsula High Risk
Adolescent Programme, Shop 9, 234 Main St;
tel: (03) 5976 2747
Mornington, Vic 3931: Peninsula Special
Support Unit, Shop 9, 234 Main St;
tel: (03) 5976 2747
Mornington, Vic 3931: Peninsula Supported
Independence, Shop 9, 234 Main St;
tel: (03) 5976 2747
Mornington, Vic 3931: Reconnect Program,
Shop 9, 234 Main St; tel: (03) 5976 2747
Northbridge, WA 6003: Crossroads West –
Perth, 333 William St; tel: (08) 9328 1600
North Coburg, Vic 3058: Transitional Support,
Independent Living Programmes, (including
Youth Services, Transitional Support
Accommodation for Youth (TSAY), Anger
Management, Reconnect), 2/828 Sydney Rd;
tel: (03) 9353 1011
Salisbury, SA 5108: CHIPS Internet Cafe, 20B
John St, Salisbury; tel: (08) 8285 9406
Shepparton, Vic 3630: Brayton Young Activities
Service, 360 River Rd; tel: (03) 5823 2277
Shepparton, Vic 3630: Brayton Young Offenders
Pilot Programme, 360 River Rd;
tel: (03) 5823 2277
Shepparton, Vic 3630: Strengthening Families
and Sexual Abuse Prevention, 360 River Rd;
tel: (03) 5823 2277
Shepparton, Vic 3630: JPET, 360 River Rd;
tel: (03) 5821 8144
Swan Hill, Vic 3585: Y-Space, 5 Campbell St;
tel: (03) 5033 1411

**Youth Centres for Homeless
Unemployed**
Mornington, Vic 3931: Peninsula JPET, Shop 8,
234 Main St; tel: (03) 5976 5500
Mornington, Vic 3931: Burnt Toast Cyber Cafe,
Shop 7, 234 Main St; tel: (03) 5976 5500
North Coburg, Vic 3058: 2/828 Sydney Rd; tel:
(03) 9353 1011
St Kilda, Vic 3182: Crisis Centre, 29 Grey St;
tel: (03) 9536 7777
Wonthaggi, Vic 3995: GippsCare Cyber Café
Net, 59 McBride Ave; tel: (03) 5672 5506

*The declaration affirmed the Army's commitment
to continue the war against sin by
proclaiming the gospel, alleviating suffering and
promoting social justice*

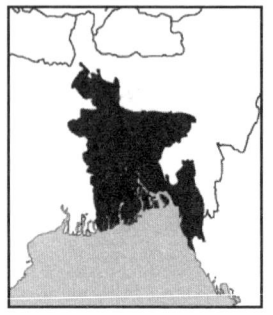

BANGLADESH COMMAND

Officer Commanding:
Lieut-Colonel Ethne Flintoff (1 Jul 2002)

General Secretary:
Major Joginder Masih (1 Sep 2005)

Command Headquarters: House 96, Road 23, Banani, Dhaka

Postal address: GPO Box 985, Dhaka 1000, Bangladesh

tel: [880] (2) 9882836/7; fax: [880] (2) 8823568; email: ban_leadership@ban.salvationarmy.org;

Work in Bangladesh commenced as a relief operation following a severe cyclone in 1970. On 21 April 1980 the Army was incorporated under the Companies Act of 1913. Bangladesh was upgraded to command status on 1 January 1997.

Zone: South Asia
Country included in the command: Bangladesh
'The Salvation Army' in Bengali: Tran Sena
Languages in which the gospel is preached: Bengali, English

DURING 2005 – 'A Year for Children and Youth' – representatives from all corps in the command were brought together for a youth leadership seminar. They discussed their vision and plans for youth involvement and creativity in corps and mission outreach.

Several corps held Bible seminars for children and youth throughout the year. Newly formed youth groups became involved in corps worship and prayer ministries. Musical instruments were supplied to a number of corps for youth worship ministry.

A 'mailbox club' using Bible teaching notes for children aged 10 to 14 years was launched in all corps and became very popular.

Development projects covered such matters as HIV/Aids, education,

discouraging child marriage and sexuality. Adolescent training in issues relevant to youth began in several corps.

A 'Together in Mission' conference enabled officers and senior employees to learn and discuss methods of self-support through fundraising and income-generation projects for local self-sustainable mission. All development projects received fresh outside donor funding. New goals were set to assist corps and communities in becoming self-reliant.

Officers' councils with the theme 'Servant Leadership' were held in both districts, the first sessions being led by Commissioners John and Elizabeth Nelson. The councils were of great blessing to all officers.

STATISTICS
Officers active 65 **Cadets** (1st Yr) 10
Employees 295
Corps 27 **Outposts** 17 **Institution** 1 **Schools** 14
Clinics 9 **HIV/Aids Counselling Centres** 2
Senior Soldiers 1,494 **Adherents** 547 **Junior Soldiers** 177

STAFF
Director of Finance: Mrs Sarah Biswas
Information Technology Development:
Mr Palash (Paul) Baidya
Projects: Capt Elizabeth Nelson
Training : Maj Ingrid Larsen
Women's Ministries: Lt-Col Ethne Flintoff
(CPWM) Maj Shanti Masih (CSWM)
Youth and Translation: Mrs Smriti Baroi

DISTRICTS
South Western: PO Box 3, By-Pass Rd,
Karbala, Jessore 7400; tel: (0421) 68758;
Capts Ganendro and Shefali Baroi
Dhaka: Hse 96, Rd 23, Banani, Dhaka 1213;
tel: (0171) 546012; Capts Alfred and Dipti Mir

TRAINING COLLEGE
Genda, Savar, Dhaka; tel: (02) 7712614

COMMUNITY WORK
HIV/Aids Counselling Centres: Jessore, Old
Dhaka
Micro-Credit Projects: Dhaka Mirpur, Jessore,
Khulna
Income-generating Cooperatives: Jessore,
Khulna

EDUCATIONAL WORK
Adult Education: Jessore, Khulna
Schools for the Hearing Impaired: Dhaka
(acc 30); Jessore (acc 30)
Primary Schools: (pupils 2,963)
Jessore: Arenda, Bagdanga, Fatepur, Ghurulia,
Kholadanga, Konejpur, Ramnagar,
Sitarampur, Suro
Khulna: Andulia, Komrail, Krisnanagar
Gopalgonj: Rajapur
**Integrated education for sighted and visually
impaired:** Savar (pupils 180)
Vocational Training: Dhaka, Jessore, Khulna

MEDICAL AND DEVELOPMENT WORK
**Urban Health and Development Project
(UHDP):**
Mirpur Clinic, Dhaka, with Leprosy and TB
Control Programmes

**Community Health and Development Projects
(CHDP):**
Jessore: New Town and Kholadanga Clinics,
with Leprosy and TB Control Programmes
Village Clinics: Fatepur, Ghurulia, Konejpur,
Ramnagar, Sitarampur and mobile clinic to
five villages
Khulna: Andulia Clinic

SOCIAL WORK
Integrated Children's Centre (Sishu Niloy),
Savar (acc 50)

ECONOMIC DEVELOPMENT
Sally Ann Bangladesh (Fair Trade)
(employees 24)
Production units: 13
Shop: Dhaka
Knitting Factories: Genda, Savar, Dhaka
(staff 9 trainees 20)

**Some of the children who attended
a young people's Bible seminar in
Bangladesh *(see inside front cover)***

BELGIUM COMMAND

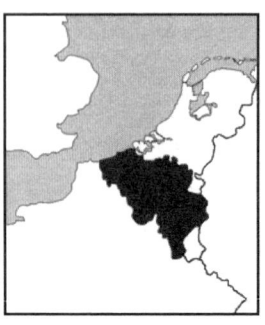

Command leaders:
Majors Christian and Joëlle Exbrayat

Officer Commanding:
Major Christian Exbrayat (1 Aug 2003)

General Secretary:
Major Noélie Lecocq (1 Aug 1999)

Command Headquarters: Place du Nouveau Marché aux Grains, 34, 1000 Brussels, Belgium

Tel address: Salvation Brussels; tel: [32] (02) 513 39 04; fax: [32] (02) 513 81 49
web sites: www.armeedusalut.be; www.legerdesheils.be

Salvation Army operations, which were pioneered on 5 May 1889 by Adjutant and Mrs Charles Rankin and Captains Velleema and Hass, are now carried out among both French and Flemish-speaking people. Legal recognition was granted by Act 1007 on 8 December 1930.

Zone: Europe
Country included in the command: Belgium
'The Salvation Army' in French: Armée du Salut; in Flemish: Leger des Heils
Languages in which the gospel is preached: Flemish, French
Periodicals: *Espoir* (French), *Strijdkreet* (Flemish)

THE Christmas period in Belgium is a significant time when The Salvation Army has its Christmas kettles on the streets during the whole of December. It is an opportunity for Salvationists to give strong visible testimony to the Belgian people.

Supporting them in this for several years now, members of Hull Icehouse Band have travelled from the UK at their own expense for a long weekend to play carols and assist with the street collections. They also take part in Sunday worship, visiting a different corps each year. In a 'twinning' exchange, the band from Jumet Corps went to Hull and experienced an enriching weekend.

During the 2005 Christmas period Captain Jean Olekhnovitch (Public Relations) was invited to present The Salvation Army's work in Belgium during a television programme. Excerpts from the broadcast appear on the command web site.

A three-day evangelistic campaign was held in Verviers Corps during Easter weekend. The participation of Brussels 2 Corps's African community made a dynamic impact at open-air witness in the town centre.

In the year under review more than 300 youngsters enjoyed summer camps and long weekends at the Army's youth centre in Spa. The

Members of the African community in Brussels 2 Corps make a dynamic impact during open-air witness at Belgium's national congress

camps are always fully booked. Some 30 home league members also gathered at Spa for their annual camp. Earlier in the year the command's home league rally took place in the industrial town of Seraing.

A few years ago the command was troubled by a financial crisis. Today, the difficulties are more related to a lack of human resources, particularly national officers. This is an area requiring attention and prayer.

STATISTICS

Officers 34 (active 21 retired 13) **Auxiliary-Captains** 2 **Lieutenants** 3 **Employees** 93 **Corps** 10 **Institutions** 7 **Stores** 3 **Youth Centre** 1 **Senior Soldiers** 253 **Adherents** 128 **Junior Soldiers** 55

STAFF

Candidates/Youth: Capt Ariane Olekhnovitch
Editor: Murielle Stievenart-Volet
Family Tracing: Murielle Stievenart-Volet
Finance: Capt Jean Olekhnovitch, Capt Marc Dawans
Personnel: Maj Noélie Lecocq
Property: Maj Noélie Lecocq
Public Relations: Capt Jean Olekhnovitch
Social: Maj Noélie Lecocq
Women's Ministries: Maj Joëlle Exbrayat (CPWM)

SOCIAL SERVICES

Hostels for Men
Home Georges Motte, Bd d'Ypres 24, 1000 Brussels; tel: (02) 217 61 36 (acc 75)
'Le Foyer', Centre d'accueil, rue Bodeghem 27-29, 1000 Brussels; tel: (02) 512 17 92 (acc 70)

Family Aid (food, counselling)
Bd d'Ypres 26, 1000 Brussels; tel: (02) 223 10 44

Guidance Centre (Housing help and Recovery Dept)
102 rue de l'église ste Anne, 1180 Brussels; tel: (02) 414 19 16

Refugee Centre
1000 Brussels, 'Foyer Selah', Bld d'Ypres 28; tel: (02) 219 01 77 (acc 90)

Mother and Child Home
Chaussée de Drogenbos 225, 1180 Brussels; tel: (02) 376 17 01 (acc mothers 14 children 25)

Children's Home
'Clair Matin', rue des Trois Rois 88, 1180 Uccle-Brussels; tel: (02) 376 17 40 (acc 41)

SHOPS

Antwerp: Ballaerstraat 94, 2018 Antwerpen
Brussels: bld d'Ypres 24, 1000 Brussels
Courcelles: rue Général de Gaulle 145, 6180 Courcelles
Liège: 6 Quai Bonaparte, 4000 Liège

YOUTH/CONFERENCE CENTRE

Villa Meyerbeer, route de Barisart 256, 4900 Spa; tel: (087) 77 49 00

BRAZIL TERRITORY

Territorial leaders:
Commissioners Peder and Janet Refstie

Territorial Commander:
Commissioner Peder Refstie (1 Dec 2006)

Chief Secretary:
Lieut-Colonel Torben Eliasen (1 Jul 2001)

**Territorial Headquarters: Rua Juá 264 - Bosque da Saúde,
04138-020 São Paulo, SP**

**Postal address: Exército de Salvação; Caixa Postal 46036, Agência Saúde
04046-970 São Paulo, SP, Brazil**

Tel address: Salvation Army; tel: [55] (011) 5591 7070; fax: [55] (011) 5591 7074

email: exercitodesalvacao@salvos.org.br; web site: www.exercitodesalvacao.org.br

Pioneer officers Lieut-Colonel and Mrs David Miche unfurled the Army flag in Rio de Janeiro on 1 August 1922.

The Salvation Army operates as a national religious entity, Exército de Salvação, having been so registered by Presidential Decree 90.568 of 27 November 1984. All its social activities have been incorporated in APROSES (Assistência e Promoção Social Exército de Salvação) since 1974 and have had Federal Public Utility since 18 February 1991.

Zone: Americas and Caribbean
Country included in the territory: Brazil
'The Salvation Army' in Portuguese: Exército de Salvação
Language in which the gospel is preached: Portuguese
Periodicals: *Notas e Notícias, O Oficial, Rumo Magazine*

'GROWING in the Word' was the theme for 2006, chosen in line with the Territorial Strategic Plan. The investment of Mission Support project funding allowed in-service training seminars to be held for all active officers, aiming to equip and train dedicated people in all aspects of mission.

The seminars emphasised the need to sustain the mission, with Christian Stewardship being the foundation and sustenance of human and financial resources. The first participants were territorial leaders, THQ departmental heads and divisional commanders. The themes and material were then used at five divisional seminars held in the first half of the year.

With some 50 per cent of the country's 180 million-plus population being under 25 years of age, Salvationists in Brazil accepted with great enthusiasm the General's global challenge to focus on children and youth during 2005. The territory's programmes were creatively refocused so as not to exclude those who were readily included by Jesus when he said: 'Let the children come to me ... for the Kingdom of God belongs to such as these' (Mark 10:14 *New International Version*).

The Brazilian government has approved a new civil code which requires that all organisations wishing to remain or become legal must fulfill this new set of laws. As The Salvation Army in Brazil operates under two different legal entities – church and social – two new constitutions were written under which the Movement now functions.

Salvationists praise God that the new law is not creating any restriction to the existing religious freedom in this immense country. They continue to trust him for what is to come and remain confident in God's word of assurance: 'The earth is the Lord's, and everything in it' (Psalm 24:1 *NIV*).

STATISTICS

Officers 164 (active 137 retired 27) **Cadets** (1st Yr) 7 (2nd Yr) 5 **Employees** 225
Corps 47 **Outposts** 5 **Social Institutions** 32
Senior Soldiers 1,912 **Adherents** 135 **Junior Soldiers** 641
Personnel serving outside territory Officers 2

STAFF

Personnel: Maj Márcio Mendes
Candidates: Maj Nara Strasse
Editor-in-Chief/Communications: Maj Paulo Soares
Education: Maj Jurema Mendes
Finance: Maj Joan Burton
Legal/Property: Maj Giani Azevedo
Music: Maj Paulo Soares
National Band: B/M Antônio Oliveira
National Songsters: S/L Vera Sales
Social: Mrs Marilene Oliveira
Training: Lt-Col Deise Eliasen
Women's Ministries: Comr Janet Refstie (TPWM) Maj Jurema Mendes (TSWM) Maj Iolanda Camargo (ORRO/FT/ORWM)
Youth: Maj Márcio Mendes (responsible)

DIVISIONS

North East: Rua Conde de Irajá, 135, 50710-310 Recife, PE; tel/fax: (81) 3227-1764; email: regional.ne@salvos.org.br; Maj Maruilson Souza
Paraná and Santa Catarina: Rua Mamoré 1191, 80810-080 Curitiba, PR; tel/fax: (041) 336-8624; email: regional.pr@salvos.org.br; Maj Verônica Jung
Rio de Janeiro and Minas Gerais and Centre West: Rua Visconde de Santa Isabel no 20, salas 712/713, 20561-210, Rio de Janeiro, RJ; tel/fax: (21) 3879-5594; email: regional.rj@salvos.org.br; Maj Edgar Chagas
Rio Grande do Sul: Rua Machado de Assis 255, 97050-570, Santa Maria, RS; tel/fax: (55) 3222-1935; email: regional.rs@salvos.org.br; Lt-Col Tomas de Sá
São Paulo: Rua Taguá 209, Liberdade 01508-010, São Paulo, SP; tel/fax: (11) 3275-0777; email: regional.sp@salvos.org.br; Maj Oscar Sanchez

TRAINING COLLEGE

Rua Juá 264, Bosque da Saúde, 04138-020, São Paulo-SP; tel: (11) 5071-5041

SOCIAL WORK

Children's Homes and Day Centres

Arco Verde: 'Maria Felisbina de Souza' Home, Av Antonio Pires 1790, 35715-000, Prudente de Moraes-MG; tel: (31) 3711-1370 (acc 50)
Joinville: 'João de Paula', Rua 15 de Novembro 3165, 89216-201, Joinville-SC; tel: (47) 453-0588 (acc 50)
Paranaguá: 'Honorina Valente', Rua Manoel Jordão Cavalheiro s/no, 83200-000, Paranaguá-PR; tel: (41) 423-6115 (acc 36)
Pelotas: Av Fernando Osório, 6745, 96065-000, Pelotas-RS; tel: (53) 273-6909 (acc 30)
Rio de Janeiro: Méier, Rua Garcia Redondo 103, 20775-170, Rio de Janeiro-RJ; tel: (21) 2595-5694 (acc 50)
Suzano: 'Lar das Flores', Rua Gal. Francisco Glicério 3048, 08665-000, Suzano-SP; tel: (11) 4747-1098 (acc 30)
Uruguaiana: Rua Gal. Câmara 1403, 97500-281, Uruguaiana-RS; tel: (55) 3412-4930 (acc 50)

Clinics (medical and dental)

Porto Alegre: 'Dr Leopoldo Rössler', Av São Pedro 1116, 90230-123, Porto Alegre-RS; tel: (51) 3342-4170

An art class for girls is part of the Women's Ministries programme in Uruguaiana Childrens' Home, Brazil

Suzano: 'Lar das Flores', Rua Gal. Francisco
Glicério 3048, 08665-000, Suzano-SP;
tel: (11) 4747-1098

Community Centres
*Cubatão: 'Vila dos Pescadores', Rua Amaral
Neto 211, 11531-070, Cubatão-SP;
tel: (13) 3363-2111
*Curitiba: Rua Manoel de Abreu 247, 80215-060,
Curitiba-PR; tel: (41) 363-1537
Guarulhos: Rua NS Aparecida 10, 07111-190,
Guarulhos-SP; tel: (11) 6409-1500
*Itaquaquecetuba: Rua Antônio Fugas 190,
08572-730, Itaquaquecetuba-SP;
tel: (11) 4640-4304
*Recife: 'Centro Comunitário Integração',
Rua Conde de Irajá, 108/135, 50710-310,
Recife-PE; tel: (81) 3228-4740
*Rio de Janeiro: 'Nova Divinéia', Rua Bambuí 36,
20561-210, Rio de Janeiro-RJ;
tel: (21) 2298-2574
(These centres have programmes for children
at risk)*

Crèches and Kindergartens
Carmo do Rio Claro: 'Recanto da Alegria',
Rua Luiz Amélio Freire 260, 37150-000,
Carmo do Rio Claro-MG; tel: (35) 3561-2175
(acc 100)

Cubatão: 'Recanto dos Sirizinhos', Rua Amaral
Neto 211, 11531-070, Cubatão-SP;
tel: (13) 3363-2111 (acc 300)
Guarulhos: Rua NS Aparecida 10, 07111-190,
Guarulhos-SP; tel: (11) 6409-1500 (acc 50)
Recife: 'Centro Comunitário Integração', Rua
Conde de Irajá 108, 50710-310, Recife-PE;
tel: (81) 3228-4740 (acc 420)
São Gonçalo: 'Arca de Noé', Rua Rodrigues da
Fonseca 315, 24.610-000, São Gonçalo-RJ;
tel: (21) 2604-9821 (acc 150)
São Paulo: 'Ranchinho do Senhor', Rua Bertioga
470/480, 04141-100, São Paulo-SP;
tel: (11) 5589-4609 (acc 60)
Suzano: 'NUDI - Lar das Flores', Rua Gal.
Francisco Glicério, 3048, 08665-000,
Suzano-SP; tel: (11) 4747-1098 (acc 160)

Centres for Street Children
Curitiba: Rua Bartolomeu Lourenço de Gusmão
5167, 81730-040, Curitiba-PR;
tel: (41) 286-3662 (acc 11)
São Paulo: Rua Taguá 209, Liberdade, 01508-010,
São Paulo-SP; tel: (11) 3275-0644 (acc 50)
São Paulo: Rua Diogo Vaz 248, Cambuci,
01527-020, São Paulo-SP; tel: (11) 3271-8511
(acc 10)

Mother and Baby Home
São Paulo: Rancho do Senhor, Rua Caramurú 931, 04138-020, São Paulo-SP; tel: (11) 275-4487 (acc mothers 25 babies 18)

Old People's Home
Campos do Jordão: Lar do Outono, Rua João Rodrigues Pinheiro 335, 12460-000, Campos do Jordão-SP; tel: (12) 262-2154 (acc 24)

Prison Work
Piraí do Sul and Carmo do Rio Claro

Social Services Centres
Santa Maria: Rua Jerônimo Gomes 74, 97001-970, Santa Maria-RS; tel: (55) 3221-8922
São Paulo: Rua Taguá 209, 01508-010, São Paulo-SP; tel: (11) 3209-5830

Students' Residences
Brasília: Av L2 Sul, 610B Mod 69, 70259-970, Brasília-DF; tel: (61) 443-3332 (acc 20)
Santa Maria: Rua Jerônimo Gomes, 74, 97050-350, Santa Maria-RS; tel: (55) 3222-1935 (acc 26)

Territorial Camp
Suzano: Rua Manuel Casanova 1061, 08664-000, Suzano-SP; tel: (11) 4476-3843

Thrift Stores
São Paulo:
Salvashopping I, Av Santa Catarina 1781, 04146-020, São Paulo-SP; tel: (11) 5563-1442
Salvashopping II: Av Cupecê 3254, 04366-000, São Paulo-SP; tel: (11) 5563-9937

MEDIA MAN PLAYS SANTA ON TWO WHEELS

Santa's sleigh is replaced by a motorcycle as Territorial Communications Director John Dalziel (Australia Southern Territory) sets off on a Christmas toy run. For many years John Dalziel was the face and voice of The Salvation Army in the Australian media. He was admitted to the Order of the Founder in 2005 *(see page 36)*.

CANADA AND BERMUDA TERRITORY

Territorial Commander:
Commissioner M. Christine MacMillan
(22 Jun 2003)

Chief Secretary:
Colonel Glen Shepherd (22 Jun 2003)

**Territorial Headquarters: 2 Overlea Blvd, Toronto,
Ontario M4H 1P4, Canada**

tel: [1] (416) 425-2111; fax: [1] (416) 422-6201;
web sites: www.salvationarmy.ca and www.armeedusalut.ca

There are newspaper reports of organised Salvation Army activity in Toronto, Ontario, in January 1882, and five months later the Army was reported holding meetings in London, Ontario. On 15 July the same year, Major Thomas Moore, sent from USA headquarters, established official operations. In 1884 Canada became a separate command. The League of Mercy originated in Canada in 1892. An Act to incorporate the Governing Council of The Salvation Army in Canada received Royal Assent on 19 May 1909.

The work in Newfoundland was begun on 1 February 1886 by Divisional Officer Arthur Young. On 12 January 1896 Adjutant (later Colonel) Lutie Desbrisay and two assistant officers unfurled the flag in Bermuda.

Zone: Americas and Caribbean
Countries included in the territory: Bermuda, Canada
Languages in which the gospel is preached: Creole, English, French, Indian languages (Gitxsan, Nisga'a, Tsimshian), Korean, Lao, Portuguese, Spanish, Thai
Periodicals: *Edge for Kids*, *En Avant*, *Faith & Friends*, *Foi & Vie*, *Salvationist*

THE Toronto Grace Health Centre marked its 100th anniversary in 2005 with an outdoor birthday party in May and another day of celebration in September. People born at the hospital over the years were invited to attend the day-long festivities. A fixture on the Toronto scene for more than a century, the former maternity hospital now specialises in palliative care. Its impact and influence can still be felt by those who were helped in any way by its professional and caring services.

In June 2005 Salvationists from Newfoundland and Labrador gathered for their 119th annual congress, during which 21 new captains were commissioned. Stemming from the international Year for Children and Youth, the congress theme – 'Open Door to Tomorrow' – was enriched by the showcasing of gifts and talents from the younger generation.

Later in June the Canadian Staff Band embarked on a 10-day tour of Western Canada, playing to packed halls and receptive crowds in Victoria, Vancouver, Calgary, Edmonton and Saskatoon. A highlight was an outdoor performance at the

SaskTel Saskatchewan Jazz Festival, where the band's Christian message made an impact on many listeners.

Company 150, a new performing arts mission team, ministered throughout southern Ontario during July and August. The 10 young people, aged 16 to 25, challenged many people through their creative outreach.

Throughout the late spring and summer, Army volunteers ably assisted workers and victims at various natural disasters, including record-setting floods in Calgary that saw many residents of southern Alberta driven from their homes. In Montreal, an agreement was signed between The Salvation Army and other relief agencies to ensure better co-ordination of emergency disaster services.

In September the first cadets were enthusiastically welcomed at the new college for officer training in Winnipeg – 23 members of the Heralds of the Good News Session.

During October a group of 12 women conducted a short-term mission in Manta, Ecuador, where they visited a new women's shelter built by money raised through a territorial women's ministries project. The team led meetings, conducted Bible studies, taught crafts and were involved in various other practical ministries.

In November 150 delegates from across the territory met at Jackson's Point Confrence Centre for a long-anticipated territorial symposium. Designed to open lines of communication and provide grassroots feedback that could be incorporated into the territory's future direction, the event sparked ongoing discussion on a wide range of issues crucial to the Army's mission.

A unique witness opportunity came by way of participation in the Toronto Santa Claus Parade to launch the Christmas season. The composite band and timbrelists were greeted happily by more than 500,000 viewers along the parade route who cheered the message of the traditional carols.

Early in the new year the Editorial Department restructured its magazine ministry to communicate better with Salvationists across the territory. In May 2006 *The War Cry* and *Horizons* were combined into an expanded monthly magazine, *Salvationist*. In addition to receiving Army news and information, readers would now be engaged at a deeper level with spiritual formation topics and exciting new mission opportunities.

At the same time the department took over the territorial website, Salvationist.ca, to enhance its communication abilities and allow more-timely publication of ministry reports. A new youth website, SendtheFire.ca, was also launched as a means of connecting young Salvationists across the territory and equipping them to live for Christ.

STATISTICS

Officers 1,888 (active 994 retired 894) **Cadets** (1st Yr) 23 (2nd Yr) 13 **Employees** 9,936
Corps 328 **Outposts** 12 **Institutions** 110
Bible College 1
Senior Soldiers 21,182 **Adherents** 53,139
 Junior Soldiers 3,825
Personnel serving outside territory Officers 33
 Layworkers 4

STAFF

Personnel: Maj Jean Moulton
Programme: Lt-Col David Hiscock
Business: Maj Neil Watt
Asst Chief Sec: Maj James Champ
Corps Ministries: Maj Floyd Tidd
Editor-in-Chief and Literary Sec:
Lt-Col Raymond Moulton
Finance: Mr Paul Goodyear
Information Technology: Mr Robert Plummer
National Recycling Operations: Mr John
Kershaw
Property: Maj Pearce Samson
Public Relations and Development:
Mr Graham Moore
Social: Mrs Mary Ellen Eberlin
Training: Maj Sandra Rice (Winnipeg)
WCBC Bible College: Dr Donald Burke
Women's Ministries: Comr M. Christine
MacMillan (TPWM) Col Eleanor Shepherd
(TSWM)

DIVISIONS

Alberta and Northern Territories: 9618 101A
Ave NW, Edmonton, AB T5H OC7;
tel: (780) 423-2111; fax: (780) 425-9081;
Maj Robert Ratcliff
Bermuda: PO Box HM 2259, 10 North St,
Hamilton, HM JX BERMUDA;
tel: (441) 292-0601; fax: (441) 295-3765;
Maj Douglas Lewis
British Columbia: 103-3833 Henning Dr,
Burnaby, BC V5C 6N5; tel: (604) 299-3908;
fax: (604) 299-7463; Maj William Blackman
Manitoba and Northwest Ontario: 55 Donald
St, Ste 500, Winnipeg, MB R3C 1L8;
tel: (204) 946-9101; fax: (204) 975-1010;
Maj Wilbert Abbott
Maritime: Metropolitan Pl, 99 Wyse Rd, Suite
1420, PO Box 54, Dartmouth, NS B3A 4S5;
tel: (902) 455-1201; fax: (902) 453-2192;
Maj Brian Peddle
Newfoundland and Labrador West: 157
Airport Blvd, Gander, NF A1V 1K6;
tel: (709) 256-6088/7135;
fax: (709) 256-7955
Newfoundland and Labrador East: 21 Adams
Ave, St John's, NF A1C 4Z1;
tel: (709) 579-2022/3; fax: (709) 576-7034;
Maj Raymond Rowe
Ontario Central: 1645 Warden Ave,
Scarborough, ON M1R 5B3;
tel: (416) 321-2654; fax: (416) 321-8136;
Lt-Col Donald Copple
Ontario East: 4 Cataraqui St, Ste 201,
Kingston, ON K7K 1Z7;

tel: (613) 547-6111/6112/8051;
fax: (613) 547-9940; Maj Kenneth Bonnar
Ontario North: 76 Coldwater St E, Orillia, ON
L3V 1W5; tel: (705) 325-4416;
fax: (705) 325-4667; Maj Eric Bond
Ontario Great Lakes: 371 King St, London, ON
N6B 1S4; tel: (519) 433-6106;
fax: (519) 433-0250; Maj Alfred Richardson
Quebec: 2050 Stanley St, Ste 500, Montreal, QC
H3A 3G3; tel: (514) 288-2848;
fax: (514) 288-4657; Lt-Col Gilbert St-Onge
Saskatchewan: 2240 13th Ave, Regina, SK
S4P 3M7; tel: (306) 757-1631/2;
fax: (306) 757-5357; Maj Larry Martin

COLLEGE FOR OFFICER TRAINING

Winnipeg Campus: 100-290 Vaughan St,
Winnipeg, MB R3B 2N8; tel: (204) 924-5606

EDUCATION

The William and Catherine Booth College,
447 Webb Pl, Winnipeg, MB R3B 2P2;
tel: (204) 947-6701/6950;
fax: (204) 942-3856; Interim President: Dr
Donald Burke (acc 104)

ETHICS CENTRE

447 Webb Pl, Winnipeg, MB R3B 2P2;
tel: (204) 957-2412; fax: (204) 957-2418;
email: ethics.centre@can.salvationarmy.org;
Dr James Read

SALVATION ARMY ARCHIVES

Archives: 26 Howden Rd, Scarborough, ON
M4H 1P4
Museum: 2 Overlea Blvd, Toronto, ON M4H 1P4;
tel: (416) 285-4344; fax: (416) 285-7763; Col
John Carew

NATIONAL RECYCLING OPERATIONS

2 Overlea Blvd, Toronto, ON M4H 1P4;
tel: (416) 425-2111; fax: (416) 422-6167
Atlantic Region: 1127 Champlain St,
Dieppe, NB E1A 1P9; tel: (506) 857-8477;
fax: (506) 858-0453
Montreal Region: 1620 Notre Dame W,
Montreal QC H3J 1M1; Tel: (516) 935-7128;
fax:514-935-6093
Ontario Central Region: 2360 South Service
Rd W, Oakville, ON L6L 5M9;
tel: (905) 825-9208; fax: (905) 825-9182
Ottawa & Thunder Bay Region: 6-1280 Leeds
Ave, Ottawa, ON K1B 3W3;
tel: (613) 247-1435; fax: 613-247-2243
Prairies Region: 1-111 Inksbrook Dr,

Winnipeg, MB R2R 2V7; tel: (204)-954-1504;
fax: (204)-953-1505

Western Canada Region: 2520 Davies Ave,
Port Coquitlam, BC V3C 4T7;
tel: (604) 944-8747; fax: (604) 944-3158

SOCIAL SERVICES (UNDER THQ)
Family Tracing Services
2 Overlea Blvd, Toronto, ON M4H 1P4;
tel: (416) 422-6291; fax: (416) 422-6221

Hospitals (public)
Rehabilitation
Montreal, QC H4B 2J5, Catherine Booth
Hospital, 4375 Montclair Ave

General (B Class)
Scarborough, ON M1W 3W3, Scarborough
Hospital – Grace Division, 3030 Birchmount
Rd; tel: (416) 495-2400

Windsor, ON N9A 1E1, Hotel-Dieu Grace
Hospital, 1030 Ouellette Ave;
tel: (519) 973-4444

Winnipeg, MB R3J 3M7, Grace General
Hospital, 300 Booth Dr; tel: (204) 837-8311

Complex Continuing Care
Toronto, ON M4Y 2G5, Toronto Grace Health
Centre, 650 Church St; tel: (416) 925-2251

SOCIAL SERVICES (UNDER DIVISIONS)
Hospitals (public)
General (B Class)
Calgary, AB T2N 4J8, Grace Women's Health
Centre, 1441 29 St NW; tel: (403) 670-2200

Hospice
Calgary, AB T2N 1B8, Agape Hospice, 1302
8 Ave NW; tel: (403) 282-6588 (acc 20)

Regina, SK S4R 8P6, Wascana Grace Hospice,
50 Angus Rd; tel: (306) 543-0655 (acc 10)

Richmond, BC V6X 2P3, Rotary Hospice,
3111 Shell Rd; tel: (604) 244-8022 (acc 10)

Winnipeg, MB R3J 3M7, Grace Hospice, 300
Booth Dr; tel: (203) 837-8311 (acc 257)

Adult Services to Developmentally Handicapped
Fort McMurray, AB T9H 1S7, 9919 MacDonald
Ave; tel: (780) 743-4135

Hamilton, ON L8S 1G1, Lawson Ministries,
1600 Main St W; tel: (905) 527-6212 (acc 21)

Toronto, ON M4K 2S5, Broadview Village,
1132 Broadview Ave (Residential Living for
Developmentally Handicapped Adults);

tel: (416) 425-1052; fax: (416) 425-6579
(acc 160)

Winnipeg, MB R3A 0L5, 324 Logan Ave;
tel: (204) 946-9418

Adult Services Mental Health
Toronto, ON M6K 1Z3, Dufferin Residence, 248
Dufferin St; tel: (416) 531-3523 (acc 23)

Westmount, QC H3Z 1V1, 4102 Dorchester
Blvd W; tel: (514) 932-5306 (acc 12)

Sheltered Workshops
Etobicoke, ON M8Z 4P8, Booth Industries, 994
Islington Ave; tel: (905) 255-7070 (acc 160)

Toronto, ON M3A 1A3, 150 Railside Rd;
tel: (416) 693-2116 (acc 44)

Addictions and Rehabilitation Centres (Alcohol/Drug Treatment)
Men
Calgary, AB T2G 0R9, 420 9th Ave SE;
tel: (403) 410-1150 (acc 34)

Edmonton, AB T5H 0E5, 9611 102 Ave NW;
tel: (780) 429-4274 (acc 158)

Glencairn, ON L0M 1K0, PO Box 100;
tel: (705) 466-3435/6 (acc 35)

Hamilton, Bermuda HM JX, PO Box HM 2238;
tel: (441) 292-2586 (acc 10)

Kingston, ON K7L 1C7, 562 Princess St;
tel: (613) 546-2333 (acc 24)

Mission, BC V2V 4J5, PO Box 3400;
tel: (604) 826-6681 (acc 171)

Sudbury, ON P3E 1C2, 146 Larch St;
tel: (705) 673-1175/6 (acc 32)

Toronto, ON M4K 3P7, 450 Pape Ave;
tel: (416) 363-5496 (acc 80)

Vancouver, BC V6A 1K8, 119 East Cordova St;
tel: (604) 646-6800 (acc 70)

Victoria, BC V8W 1M2, 525 Johnson St;
tel: (250) 384-3396 (acc 109)

Winnipeg, MB R3B 0A1, 72 Martha St;
tel: (204) 946-9401 (acc 32)

Women
Toronto, ON M5R 2L6, The Homestead, 78
Admiral Rd; tel: (416) 921-0953 (acc 18)

Vancouver, BC V6P 1S4, The Homestead, 975
57th Ave W; tel: (604) 266-9696 (acc 32)

Residential Services (Hostels, Emergency Shelters)
Men
Barrie, ON L4M 3A5, Bayside Mission Centre,
16 Bayfield St; tel: (705) 728-3737 (acc 32)

Brampton, ON L6T 4M6, Wilkinson Road
Shelter, 15 Wilkinson Rd; tel: (905) 452-6335
(acc 60)

Canada and Bermuda Territory

Brantford, ON N3T 2J6, Booth Centre, 187 Dalhousie St; tel: (519) 753-4193/4 (acc 32)

Calgary, AB T2G 0J8, Booth Centre, 631 7 Ave SE; tel: (403) 262-6188 (acc 276)

Calgary, AB T2G 0R9, Centre of Hope, 420 9th Ave; tel: (403)410-1111

Halifax, NS B3K 3A9, 2044 Gottingen St; tel: (902) 422-2363 (acc 49)

Hamilton, ON L8R 1R6, Booth Centre, 94 York Blvd; tel: (905) 527-1444 (acc 75)

London, ON N6C 4L8, Centre of Hope, 281 Wellington St; tel: (519) 661-0343 (acc 253)

Mississauga, ON L5C 1T9, Mavis Shelter, 3190 Mavis Rd; tel: (905) 848-8922 (acc 24)

Montreal, QC H3J 1T4, Booth Centre, 880 Guy St; tel: (514) 932-2214 (acc 195)

New Westminster, BC V3L 2K1, 32 Elliot St; tel: (604) 526-4783 (acc 10)

Oakville, ON L6L 6X7, Lighthouse Shelter, 750 Redwood Sq; tel: (905) 339-2918 (acc 25)

Ottawa, ON K1N 5W5, Booth Centre, 171 George St; tel: (613) 241-1573 (acc 142)

Pembroke, Bermuda HM JX, 5 Marsh Lane; tel: (441) 295-5310 (acc 83)

Quebec City, QC G1R 4H8, Hotellerie, 14 Côte du Palais; tel: (418) 692-3956 (acc 60)

Regina, SK S4P 1W1, 1845 Osler St; tel: (306) 569-6088 (acc 75)

Regina, SK S4P 1W1, Waterston Centre, 1865 Osler St; tel: (306) 566-6088 (acc 40)

Richmond, BC V6X 2P3, Richmond House Emergency Shelter, 3111 Shell Rd; tel: (604) 276-2490 (acc 10)

Saint John, NB E2L 1V3, 36 St James St; tel: (506) 634-7021 (acc 75)

St Catharine's, ON L2R 3E7, Booth Centre, 184 Church St; tel: (905) 684-7813 (acc 21)

St John's, NL A1E 1C1, Wiseman Centre, 714 Water St; tel: (709) 739-8355/8 (acc 30)

Saskatoon, SK S7M 1N5, 339 Avenue C S; tel: (306) 244-6280 (acc 50)

Thunder Bay, ON P7A 4S2, CARS, 545 Cumberland St N; tel: (807) 345-7319 (acc 46)

Toronto, ON M5T 1P7, 167 College St; tel: (416) 979-7058 (acc 108)

Toronto, ON M4M 2G9, 312 Broadview Ave; tel: (416) 465-6970 (acc 60)

Toronto, ON M5C 2H4, 107 Jarvis St; tel: (416) 368-0324 (acc 100)

Toronto, ON M5A 2R5, 135 Sherbourne St; tel: (416) 366-2733 (acc 427)

Vancouver, BC V6B 1K8, Belkin House, 555 Homer St; tel: (604) 681-3405 (acc 198)

Vancouver, BC V6A 1K7, James McCready Residence, 129 East Cordova St; tel: (604) 646-6800 (acc 44)

Vancouver, BC V6A 1K7, The Haven, 128 East Cordova St; tel: (604) 646-6800 (acc 40)

Windsor, ON N9A 7G9, 355 Church St; tel: (519) 253-7473 (acc 133)

Winnipeg, MB R3B 0J8, 180 Henry Ave; tel: (204) 946-9460 (acc 208)

Women

Brampton, ON L6X 3C9, The Honeychurch Family Life Resource Center, 535 Main St N; tel: (905) 451-4115 (acc 24)

Brampton, ON L6T 4M6, Wilkinson Road Shelter, 15 Wilkinson Rd; tel: (905) 452-6335 (acc 24)

Mississauga, ON L5C 1T9, Mavis Shelter, 3190 Mavis Rd; tel: (905) 848-8922 (acc 24)

Montreal, QC H3J 1M8, L'Abri d'Espoir, 2000 Notre Dame W; tel: (514) 934-5615 (acc 36)

Quebec City, QC G1R 4H8, Maison Charlotte, 14 Cote du Palais; tel: (418) 692-3956 (acc 25)

Toronto, ON M6P 1Y5, Evangeline Residence, 2808 Dundas St W; tel: (416) 762-9636 (acc 71)

Toronto, ON M6J 1E6, Florence Booth House, 723 Queen St W; tel: (416) 603-9800 (acc 60)

Vancouver, BC V5Z 4L9, Kate Booth House, PO Box 38048 King Edward Mall; tel: (604) 872-0772 (acc 12)

Vancouver, BC V6B 1G8, The Crosswalk, 138-140 W Hastings St; tel: (604) 669-4349

Family

Mississauga, ON L5A 2X3, SA Peel Family Shelter, 2500 Cawthra Rd; tel: (905) 272-7061 (acc 148)

Montreal, QC H3J 1M8, L'abri e'espoir, 2000 rue Notre-Dame oust; tel: (514) 934-5616 (acc 25)

Youth

Sutton, ON L0E 1R0, 20898 Dalton Rd, PO Box 1087; tel: (905) 722-9076

Community and Family Services

Abbotsford, BC V2S 5V2, 33933 Cyril St; tel: (604) 852-9305

Ajax, ON L1S 2L8, 35 King Cresc; tel: (905) 683-0454

Bathurst, NB E2A 1A4, 112 Main St; tel: (506) 548-5270

Belleville, ON K8N 3B3, 295 Pinnacle St; tel: (613) 968-6834

Bowmanville, ON L1C 2N8, 75 Liberty St S; tel: (905) 623-2185

Brampton, ON L6T 2J6, 115 West Dr; tel: (905) 451-8840

Brandon, MB R7A 1R8, 9 Princess St E;
tel: (204) 727-4334

Brantford, ON N3T 2J9, 2 Darling St;
tel: (519) 752-7814

Bridgewater, NS B4V 2K7, 199 Dominion St;
tel: (902) 543-5471

Brockville, ON K6V 3B6, 175 First Ave;
tel: (613) 342-5211

Burlington, ON L7P 1A8, 2054 Mountainside
Dr; tel: (905) 637-3894

Calgary, AB T2B 0X6, 1826 36 St SE;
tel: (403) 220-0445

Cambridge, ON N1R 4J5, 12 Shade St;
tel: (519) 623-1221

Campbell River, BC V9W 2M4, 291 McLean St;
tel: (250) 287-3720

Campbelltown, NB E3N 2G8, 110B Roseberry
St; tel: (506) 753-6592

Charlottetown, PEI C1A 1S4, 190 Fitzroy St;
tel: (902) 892-8870

Chatham, ON N7L 5H1, 46 Orangewood Blvd;
tel: (519) 354-1430

Chilliwack, BC V2P 2N4, 45746 Yale Rd;
tel: (604) 792-0001

Cobourg, ON K9A 1K5, 66 Swayne St;
tel: (905) 373-9440

Collingwood, ON L9Y 3K2, 162 St Marie St;
tel: (705) 445-9222

Corner Brook, NL A2H 4C7, 61 Broadway;
tel: (709) 639-1719

Cornwall, ON K6J 3Z8, 500 York St;
tel: (613) 932-8311

Courtenay, BC V9N 8P1, 10-2966 Kilpatrick
Ave; tel: (250) 383-5133

Cranbrook, AB V1C 4Y5, 533 Slater Rd NW;
tel: (250) 426-3612

Dauphin, MB R7N 0Z4, 38 2nd Ave NE;
tel: (204) 638-3764

Dawson Creek, BC V1G 2G6, 1019 103rd Ave;
tel: (250) 782-8669

Deer Lake, NL A8A 1W7, 13 A Main St;
tel: (709) 635-3377

Drumheller, AB T0J 0Y4, 242 First St W;
tel: (403) 823-2722

Duncan, BC V9L 3P9, 280 Trans Canada Hwy;
tel: (250) 746-8669

Edmonton, AB T5H 0C7, 9620 101A Ave NW;
tel: (780) 424-9222

Elliott Lake, ON P5A 1H3, 96 Dieppe Ave;
tel: (705) 848-2417

Essex, ON N8M 1A7, 26 Talbot St S;
tel: (519) 776-4750

Etobicoke, ON M8W 3B7, 5 Thirtieth St;
tel: (416) 252-1289

Etobicoke, ON M9W 4K9, 2152 Kipling Ave N;
tel: (416) 743-1282

Fenelon Falls, ON K0M 1N0, 42 Bond St W;
tel: (705) 887-1408

Fernie, BC V0B 1M0, 741 2nd St;
tel: (250) 423-4661

Flin Flon, MB R8A 1S6, 3 Hemlock Dr;
tel: (204) 687-7812

Fort Frances, ON P9A 2C2, 316 Victoria Ave;
tel: (807) 274-3871

Fort McMurray, AB T9H 1S7, 9919 MacDonald
Ave; tel: (780) 791-9903

Fort St John, BC V1J 1Y6, 10116 100 Ave;
tel: (250) 785-0500

Fredericton, NB E3A 1C8, 146 Main St;
tel: (506) 453-1706

Gananoque, ON K7G 1H9, 120 Garden St;
tel: (613) 382-3105

Gander, NL A1V 1A9, 111 Memorial Dr;
tel: (709) 256-4480

Georgetown, ON L7G 5K8, 271 Mountainview
Rd; tel: (905) 877-9470

Gibsons, BC V0N 1V0, PO Box 1625;
tel: (604) 886-3665

Glace Bay, NS B1A 5V1, 40 Union St;
tel: (902) 849-7886

Goderich, ON N7A 3H8, 303 Suncoast Dr;
tel: (519) 524-4188

Grand Bay East, NL A0N 1K0, PO Box 620;
tel: (709) 695-7153

Grand Falls Windsor, NL A2B 1C7, 27 Park St;
tel: (709) 489-7751

Grande Prairie, AB T8V 3Y1, 9525 83 Ave;
tel: (780) 532-3720

Gravenhurst, ON P1P 1E7, 620 Muskoka Rd N;
tel: (705) 687-7271

Guelph, ON N1E 1E9, 210 Victoria Rd S;
tel: (519) 836-9360

Halifax, NS B3K 3A9, 2038 Gottingen St;
tel: (902) 422-1598

Hamilton, Bermuda, 92 Reid St;
tel: (441) 292-5159

Hamilton, ON L8R 3N3, 80 Bay St N;
tel: (905) 540-1888

Happy Valley/Goose, NL A0P, PO Box 52, St
A; tel: (709) 896-2756

High River, AB T1V 1G3, 22 4th Ave SE;
tel: (403) 653-7530

Huntsville, ON P1H 1W4, 4 Mary St E;
tel: (705) 789-3398

Ingersoll, ON N5C 2T5, 192 Thames St S;
tel: (519) 485-4961

Jacksons Point, ON L0E 1L0, 1816 Metro Rd;
tel: (905) 722-4613

Kamloops, BC V2B 3L7, 175 Leigh Rd;
tel: (250) 376-1754

Kelowna, BC V1Y 2A4, 1449 Ellis St;
tel: (250) 860-3442

Kemptville, ON K0G 1J0, 2 Oxford St W St;
tel: (613) 258-3583

Kenora, ON P9N 1T8, 104 Matheson St S;
tel: (807) 468-8918

Kentville, NS B4N 1K7, 401 Main St;
tel: (902) 678-4534

Kingston, ON K7L 3S5, 326 Alfred St;
tel: (613) 548-4411

Kirkland Lake, ON P2N 2C7, 6 Sylvanite Ave;
tel: (705) 567-6151

Kitchener, ON N3M 2C8, 300 Gage Ave Unit 1;
tel: (519) 745-4215

Labrador City/Wabush, NL A2V 1G3, PO Box
369; tel: (709) 944-3200

Leamington, ON N8H 1T6, 88 Setterinton St;
tel: (519) 326-0319

Lethbridge, AB T1J 0E3, 1212 2 Ave S;
tel: (403) 328-2860

Lindsay, ON K9V 3L8, 30 Peel St;
tel: (705) 878-5331

Listowel, ON N4W 2C8, 625 Main St E;
tel: (519) 291-2331

Lloydminster, AB T9V 2P9, 2302 53rd Ave;
tel: (306) 825-4840

London, ON N6C 4L8, 281 Wellington St;
tel: (519) 434-1651

Maple Ridge, BC V2X 3K4, 22777 Dewdney
Trunk Rd; tel: (604) 463-8296

Medicine Hat, AB T1B 3R3, 164 Stratton Way
SE; tel: (403) 526-9699

Midland, ON L4R 1R1, 555 Dominion Ave;
tel: (705) 526-2751

Milton, ON L9T 5B2, 100 Nipissing Rd;
tel: (905) 875-1022

Miramichi, NB E1V 1L8, 1447 (Unit 4) King
George Hwy; tel: (506) 622-7826

Mississauga, ON L5A 2X4, 3173 Cawthra Rd;
tel: (905) 279-3941

Mississauga, ON L5N 4W8, 3020 Vanderbilt
Rd; tel: (905) 824-0452

Mississauga, ON L5L 1V3, 2460 The
Collegeway; tel: (905) 607-2151

Moncton, NB E1E 2B5, 528 St George Blvd;
tel: (506) 389-9901

Montreal, QC H4E 1C8, 1545 Cabot St;
tel: (514) 766-2155Moose Jaw, SK S6H 0Y9,
175 1st Ave NE; tel: (306) 692-5899

Naniamo, BC V9R 4S6, 19 Nicol St;
tel: (250) 754-2621

Napanee, ON K7R 1H2, 12 Mill St;
tel: (613) 354-2550

Neepawa, MB R0J 1H0, 309 Davidson St;
tel: (204) 476-5869

Nelson, BC V1L 4E9, 601 Vernon St;
tel: (250) 352-3488

New Glasgow, NS B0K 2A0, 134 James St;
tel: (902) 752-3299

New Liskeard, ON P0J 1P0, 260 Whitewood
Ave; tel: (705) 647-1588

New Westminster, BC V3L 3A9, 325 6th St;
tel: (604) 521-2421

Newmarket, ON L3Y 8G8, 415 Pickering Cres;
tel: (905) 895-0577

Niagara Falls, ON L2G 3V6, 4609 Crysler Ave;
tel: (905) 354-2834

North Bay, ON P1B 1C4, 134 McIntyre St E;
tel: (705) 474-7859

North Vancouver, BC V7M 1N2, 105 12th St W;
tel: (604) 988-7225

North York, ON M3A 1A3, 150 Railside Rd;
tel: (416) 285-0080

North York, ON M2M 2L4, 25 Centre Ave;
tel: (416) 225-6683

Oakville, ON L6L 1Z1, 1225 Rebecca St;
tel: (905) 827-6523

Orillia, ON L3V 3L7, 157 Coldwater Rd W;
tel: (705) 326-3472

Oshawa, ON L1H 1B2, 45 King St E;
tel: (905) 723-7422

Ottawa, ON K1N 5W5, 165 George St;
tel: (613) 241-5188

Owen Sound, ON N4K 5P7, 365 14th St W;
tel: (519) 371-0957

Parksville, BC9P 2H6, 866 Webley Rd;
tel: (250) 248-8793

Pasadena, NL A0L 1K0, 12 Third Ave;
tel: (709) 686-5209

Peace River, AB T8S 1E1, 9710 74th Ave;
tel: (780) 624-5980

Pembroke, ON K8A 5N9, 484 Pembroke St W;
tel: (613) 735-5601

Penticton, BC V2A 5G6, Unit 121 – 1550 Main
St; tel: (250) 492-5624

Perth, ON K7H 1R9, 40 North St;
tel: (613) 267-4652

Peterborough, ON K9H 2H6, 219 Simcoe St;
tel: (705) 742-4391

Port Alberni, BC V9Y 1V9, 4815 Argyle St;
tel: (250) 723-6913

Portage La Prairie, MB R1N 0S6, 220 Duke
Ave; tel: (204) 857-4672

Powel River, BC V8A 3A6, 4500 Joyce Ave;
tel: (604) 485-6067

Prince Albert, SK S6V 4V3, 900 Central Ave;
tel: (306) 763-6078

Prince George, BC V2L 3C7, 835 3rd Ave;
tel: (250) 564-4000

Prince Rupert, BC V8J 1R3, 25 Grenville Crt;
tel: (250) 624-6180

Quebec City, QC G1J 2C3, 1125 De La
Canardiere; tel: (418) 641-0050

Canada and Bermuda Territory

A group of 12 women in the Canada and Bermuda Territory formed a 'Workers Together' mission team to visit and assist fellow-Salvationists in Ecuador. Two of the team *(left)* prepare gifts ready to distribute at an old people's residence *(below)*.

Quesnel, BC V2J 2N9, 374 McLean St;
  tel: (250) 635-1829
Red Deer, AB T4N 5E9, 4837 54 St;
  tel: (403) 346-6145
Regina, SK S4P 3M7, 2240 13th Ave;
  tel: (306) 757-4600
Renfrew, ON K7V 4A3, 8 Argyle St S;
  tel: (613) 432-7721
Richmond, BC V7C 3W7, 8280 Gilbert Rd;
  tel: (640) 277-2424
Ridgetown, ON N0P 2C0, 7 Eric St N;
  tel: (519) 674-2472
Robert's Arm, NL A0J 1R0, PO Box 130;
  tel: (709) 652-3571
Saint John, NB E2L 3S1, 27A Prince Edward St;
  tel: (506) 634-1633
Salmon Arm, BC V1E 1H6, 191 2nd Ave NE;
  tel: (250) 832-9194
Sarnia, ON N7T 1B3, 228 Davis Rd;
  tel: (519) 334-1142
Sault Ste Marie, ON P6C 3K9, 670 John St;
  tel: (705) 759-4143
Scarborough, ON M1H 2W6, 2085 Ellesmere
  Rd; tel: (416) 438-2573
Seal Cove, NL A0K 5E0, PO Box 100;
  tel: (709) 531-2305
Sherbrooke, QC J1H 5C7, 112 Rue Wellington
  Sud Suite 101; tel: (819) 566-6298
Simcoe, ON N3Y 3V3, 184 Colborne St N;
  tel: (519) 426-3640

Smiths Falls, ON K7A 3Z5, 243 Brockville St;
  tel: (613) 3563
Springdale, NL A0J 1T0, PO Box 127;
  tel: (709) 673-3576
St-Hubert, QC J4T 2S5, 3228 Grande Allée;
  tel: (450) 676-8060
St Albans, AB T8N 6A7, 165 Liberton Dr;
  tel: (780) 458-1937
St Anthony, NL A0K 4S0, PO Box 699;
  tel: (709) 454-3172
St Catharines, ON L2M 7N5, 400 Niagara St;
  tel: (905) 935-4311
St John's, NL A1C 4Z1, 21 Adams Ave;
  tel: (709) 726-0393
St Mary's, ON N4X 1A9, 220 Queens St E;
  tel: (519) 284-4822
St Thomas, ON N5P 1Y8, 105 Edward St;
  tel: (519) 633-4509
Stephenville, NL A2N 3A3, PO Box 464;
  tel: (709) 643-3482
Stratford, ON N4Z 1C8, 230 Lightbourne Ave;
  tel: (519) 271-2762
Strathroy, ON N7G 1X4, 26 Front St W;
  tel: (519) 245-5398
Sudbury, ON P3E 4S1, 107 Lome St;
  tel: (705) 566-8151
Summerside, PEI C1N 1B2, 163 Water St;
  tel: (902) 888-3870
Surrey, BC V3W 8V3, 4-13570 78th Ave;
  tel: (604) 507-4860

Sussex, NB E4E 1S8, 95 Main St;
tel: (506) 433-5461

Sydney, NS B1P 2V6, 152 Victoria Rd;
tel: (902) 562-5442

Sydney Mines, NS B1V 2B8, 9 Fraser Ave;
tel: (902) 736-2548

Terrace, BC V8G 2N5, 3236 Kalum St;
tel: (250) 635-1829

The Pas, MB R9A 1E3, 345 Lathlin Ave;
tel: (204) 623-2811

Thompson, MB R8N 1W2, 305 Thompson Dr;
tel: (204) 677-3658

Thunder Bay, ON P7A 4S2, 545 Cumberland St
N; tel: (807) 344-7300

Tillsonburg, ON N4G 1R7, 110 Concession St
W; tel: (519) 842-9491

Toronto, ON M3N 1J3, 20 Yorkwoods Gate;
tel: (416) 398-1566

Toronto, ON M6H 2X4, 789 Dovercourt Rd;
tel: (416) 532-4511

Toronto, ON M5A 3P1, 77 River St;
tel: (416) 304-1982

Trail, BC V1R 1N3, 2030 Second Ave;
tel: (250) 386-3814

Trenton, ON K8V 1L9, 244 Dundas St E;
tel: (613) 392-9905

Trois-Rivieres, QC G9A 6H7, 1610 rue
Ste-Marie; tel: (819) 371-3224

Truro, NS B2N 7B8, 14 Outram St;
tel: (902) 893-1862

Vancouver, BC V5V 4B8, 3213 Fraser St;
tel: (604) 872-7676

Vernon, BC V1T 2M7, 3303 32nd Ave

Victoria, BC V8T 4E3, 2695 Quadra St;
tel: (250) 386-8521

Wallaceburg, ON N8A 1M8, 17 Gillard St;
tel: (519) 627-1163

Welland, ON L3B 3W3, 30 East Main St;
tel: (905) 735-5700

Westville, NS B2H 5E3, 134 James St;
tel: (905) 752-3299

Whitby, ON L1N 6S5, 607 Palace St;
tel: (905) 430-3454

White Rock, BC V4B 2G4, 15417 Roper Ave

Whitehorse, YT Y1A 1J5, 4169 4th Ave;
tel: (867) 668-2327

Williams Lake, BC V2G 1R3, 272 Borland St;
tel: (250) 392-2429

Windsor, ON N9A 7G9, 355 Church St;
tel: (519) 253-7473

Winnipeg, MB R3B 0J8, 180 Henry Ave;
tel: (204) 945-9485

Winnipeg, MB R3A 0L5, 324 Logan Ave;
tel: (204) 946-9136

Woodstock, ON N4V 1E9, 769 Juliana Dr;
tel: (519) 539-6166

Yarmouth, NS B5A 4K3, 259 Main St;
tel: (902) 742-7749

Correctional and Justice Services
Community Programme Centres

Barrie, ON L4M 5A1, 400 Bayfield St, Ste 255;
tel: (705) 737-4140

Burnaby, BC V5C 6N5, 3833 Henning Dr;
tel: (604) 299-3908

Calgary, AB T2G 0R9, 420 9th Ave SE;
tel: (403) 410-4119

Charlottetown, PE C1A 1S5, 203 Fitzroy St

Chilliwack, BC V2P 2N4, 45742B Yale Rd;
tel: (604) 792-8581

Guelph, ON N1L 1H3, 1320 Gordon St;
tel: (519) 836-9360

Halifax, NS B3J 1Y9, 1329 Barrington St,
Halifax; tel: (902) 429-6120

Kingston, ON K7K 4B1, 472 Division St;
tel: (613) 549-2676

Kitchener, ON N2H 2M2, 151 Frederick St,
Ste 502; tel: (519) 742-8521

London, ON N6B 2L4, 281 Wellington St;
tel: (519) 432-9553

Medicine Hat, AB T1A 0E7, 874 2 St E;
tel: (403) 529-2111

Moncton, NB E1C 1M2, 68 Gordon St;
tel: (506) 853-8887

Ottawa, ON K1Y K1N, 171 George St;
tel: (613) 725-1733

Peterborough, ON K9H 2H6, 219 Simcoe St;
tel: (705) 742-4391

Prince Albert, SK S6V 4V3, 900 Central Ave;
tel: (306) 763-6078

Regina, SK S4P 3M7, 2240 13th Ave;
tel: (306) 757-4711/2

Saint John, NB E2L 1V3, 36 St James St;
tel: (506) 634-7021

St Catharines, ON L2R 3E7, 184 Church St;
tel: (905) 684-7813

St John's, NL A1C 4Z1, 21 Adams Ave;
tel: (709) 726-0393

Saskatoon, SK S7M 1N5, 339 Avenue C S;
tel: (306) 244-6280

Stoney Creek, ON L8J 3Y1, 300 Winterberry Dr;
tel: (905) 573-0635

Thunder Bay, ON P7A 4S2, 545 Cumberland
St N; tel: (807) 345-5785

Toronto, ON M5A 3P1, 77 River St;
tel: (416) 304-1974

Winnipeg, MB R3A 0L5, 324 Logan Ave,
2nd Floor; tel: (204) 949-2100

Adult/Youth Residential Centres

Brampton, ON L6X 1C1, 44 Nelson St W;
tel: (905) 453-0988

Dartmouth, NS B3A 1H5, 318 Windmill Rd;
tel: (902) 465-2690

Dundas, ON L9H 2E8, 34 Hatt St;
tel: (905) 627-1632

Ilderton, ON N0M 2A0, PO Box 220;
tel: (519) 666-0600

Kitchener, ON N2G 2M4, 657 King St E;
tel: (519) 744-4666

Moncton, NB E1C 8P6, 64 Gordon St,
PO Box 1121; tel: (506) 858-9486

Sydney, NS B1P 1B4, 571 Esplanade;
tel: (902) 564-0032

Toronto, ON M4X 1K2, 422 Sherbourne St;
tel: (416) 964-6316/967-6618

Whitehorse, YT Y1A 6E3, 91678 Alaska
Highway; tel: (867) 667-2741

Yellowknife, NWT X1A 1P4, 4927 45th St;
tel: (867) 920-4673

Health Services
Long-Term Care/Seniors' Residences

Brandon, MB R7A 3N9, Dinsdale Personal Care
Home, 510 6th St; tel: (204) 727-3636
(acc 60)

Calgary, AB T3C 3W7, Jackson/Willan Seniors'
Residence, 3015 15 Ave SW;
tel: (403) 249-9116 (acc 18)

Edmonton, AB T5X 6C4, Grace Manor, 12510
140 Ave; tel: (780) 454-5484 (acc 100)

Kitchener, ON N2H 2P1, A. R. Goudie Eventide
Home, 369 Frederick St; tel: (519) 744-5182
(acc 80)

Montreal, QC H4B 2J4, Montclair Residence,
4413 Montclair Ave; tel: (514) 481-5638
(acc 50)

New Westminster, BC V3L 4A4, Buchanan
Lodge, 409 Blair Ave; tel: (604) 522-7033
(acc 112)

Niagara Falls, ON L2E 1K5, The Honourable
Ray and Helen Lawson Eventide Home,
5050 Jepson St; tel: (905) 356-1221
(acc 100)

Ottawa, ON K1Y 2Z3, Ottawa Grace Manor,
1156 Wellington St; tel: (613) 722-8025
(acc 128)

Regina, SK S4R 8P6, William Booth

Special Care Home, 50 Angus Rd;
tel: (306) 543-0655 (acc 81)

Riverview, NB E1B 4K6, Lakeview Manor, 50
Suffolk St; tel: (506) 387-2012/3/4 (acc 50)

St John's, NL A1A 2G9, Glenbrook Lodge, 105
Torbay Rd; tel: (709) 726-1575 (acc 114)

St John's, NL A1A 2G9, Glenbrook Villa, 107
Torbay Rd; tel: (709) 726-1575 (acc 20)

Toronto, ON M4S 1G1, Meighen Retirement
Residence, 84 Davisville Ave;
tel: (416) 481-5557 (acc 84)

Toronto, ON M4S 1J6, Meighen Manor, 155
Millwood Rd; tel: (416) 481-9449 (acc 168)

Vancouver, BC V5S 3T1, Southview Terrace,
3131 58th Ave E; tel: (604) 438-3367/8 (acc 57)

Victoria, BC V9A 7J6, Matson Sequoia
Residence, 554 Garrett Pl Ste 211;
tel: (250) 383-5821 (acc 30)

Victoria, BC V9A 4G7, Sunset Lodge, 952 Arm
St; tel: (250) 385-3422 (acc 108)

Winnipeg, MB R2Y 0S8, Golden West
Centennial Lodge, 811 School Rd;
tel: (204) 888-3311 (acc 116)

Immigrant and Refugee Services

Toronto, ON M5A 1Z1, 7 Labatt Ave Suite B116;
tel: (416) 360-6036

Women's Multi-Service Programmes (and unmarried mothers)

Hamilton, ON L8P 2H1, Grace Haven,
138 Herkimer St; tel: (905) 522-7336
(acc 12)

London, ON N6J 1A2, Bethesda Centre, 54
Riverview Ave; tel: (519) 438-8371 (acc 14)

Ottawa, ON K1Y 2Z3, Bethany Hope Centre,
1140 Wellington St; tel: (613) 725-1733

Regina, SK S4S 7A7, Grace Haven, 2929 26th
Ave; tel: (306) 352-1421 (acc 7)

Saskatoon, SK S7K 0N1, Bethany Home,
802 Queen St; tel: (306) 244-6758 (acc 15)

Thunder Bay, ON P7B 1E3, 219 Pearl St;
tel: (807) 345-3772

Children's Treatment Facilities

Calgary, AB T3C 1M6, Children's Village, 1731
29 St SW; tel: (403) 246-1124 (acc 40)

Regina, SK S4S 0X5, Gemma House, 3820 Hill
Ave; tel: (306) 586-5388 (acc 8)

Company 150, a new performing arts mission team of 10 young people, aged 16 to 25, challenged many people through their creative outreach

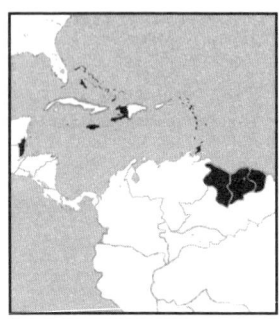

CARIBBEAN TERRITORY

Territorial leaders:
**Commissioners Raymond and
Judith Houghton**

Territorial Commander:
Commissioner Raymond Houghton
(1 Jul 2006)

Chief Secretary:
Lieut-Colonel Raphael Mason (1 Jun 2005)

Territorial Headquarters: 3 Waterloo Rd, Kingston 10, Jamaica

Postal address: PO Box 378, Kingston 10, Jamaica, WI

Tel address: Salvation Kingston Jamaica; tel: [1876] 929 6190/91/92; fax: [1876] 929 7560;
web site: www.salvationarmycarib.org

In 1887 The Salvation Army 'opened fire' in Kingston, and thence spread throughout the island of Jamaica and to Guyana (1895), Barbados (1898), Trinidad (1901), Grenada (1902), St Lucia (1902), Antigua (1903), St Vincent (1905), Belize (1915), St Kitts (1916), Suriname (1924), the Bahamas (1931), Haiti (1950), French Guiana (1980) and St Maarten (1999). The General of The Salvation Army is a Corporation Sole in Jamaica (1914), Trinidad and Tobago (1915), Barbados (1917), Belize (1928), Guyana (1930), the Bahamas (1936) and Antigua (1981).

Zone: Americas and Caribbean
Countries included in the territory: Antigua, Bahamas, Barbados, Belize, French Guiana, Grenada, Guyana, Haiti, Jamaica, St Kitts, St Lucia, St Maarten, St Vincent, Suriname, Trinidad and Tobago
'The Salvation Army' in Dutch: Leger des Heils; in French: Armée du Salut
Languages in which the gospel is preached: Creole, Dutch, English, French, Surinamese
Periodicals: *The War Cry*

THE territory continues to move forward in mission under its vision statement theme, 'Together – Building Tomorrow, Today'. At the end of December 2005 key roll figures showed continued increases, with women's ministries being a particularly encouraging area. Since year end December 2000, the senior soldiers roll has recorded an increase of 22 per cent. This increase continues to be led mainly by the Haiti Division.

The international Year for Children and Youth was positively featured throughout the territory. The territorial junior soldiers roll again increased and much-needed renewed emphasis was given to the future officers fellowship in some divisions, notably Eastern Jamaica Division. A youth congress in the Barbados Division, led by Captains Kendall and Katrina Matthews (USA Central) proved successful.

During February 2006, in Grenada, the prime minister and government ministers participated in the ceremony when the then territorial leaders (Commissioners John and Betty Matear) officially concluded a repair project on 150 homes. The territorial commander preached at the National Independence Day ecumenical service and the corps's new community facilities were officially opened. It was a joy to witness the impact being made in the corps and community by recently commissioned officers Captains Derrick and Abena Miller.

Much-needed property development and improvement have taken place in Trinidad and Tobago, funded by the division. In Jamaica significant repair and new building work was carried out in the aftermath of Hurricane Ivan. The TC dedicated the newly refurbished Bramwell Booth Memorial Hall, home of Kingston Central Corps, and also opened the reconstructed Windsor Lodge Children's Home.

Relationships with the territory's 'Partners in Mission' continue to develop on all fronts and this is particularly true with neighbouring partner, USA Southern Territory. A number of work/mission teams, along with music sections, have visited the Caribbean and in March 2006 second-year cadets and training college staff conducted a mission campaign in Trinidad.

A number of Caribbean officers and soldiers had the opportunity to participate in training and mission-focused events sponsored by the USA Southern Territory.

In June 2005 leaders from the 10 divisions and regions met at the Territorial Executive Conference in Kingston, Jamaica. The then Chief of the Staff Commissioner Israel L. Gaither and Commissioner Eva D. Gaither were special guests and also led the commissioning of six captains of the Preparers of the Way Session.

Following the General's decision to transfer the Dominican Republic Region to the Latin America North Territory and return the Belize Region to the Caribbean Territory, transfer meetings were held during July 2005 in the respective territories, led by International Secretary Commissioner William Francis.

STATISTICS
Officers 293 (active 216 retired 77) **Cadets** (1st Yr) 8 (2nd Yr) 8 **Employees** 1,035
Corps 126 **Outposts** 59 **Institutions** 59 **Schools** 167
Senior Soldiers 9,228 **Adherents** 1,145 **Junior Soldiers** 3612
Personnel serving outside territory Officers 9

STAFF
Business: Maj Ward Matthews
Coordinator for Disasters/Services: Capt Michele Matthews
Editor: Capt Prescilla Kellman
Field/Property: Lt-Col Sydney McKenzie
Projects/Sponsorship: Capt Michele Matthews
Training: Maj Rosemarie Brown
Women's Ministries: Comr Judith Houghton (TPWM) Lt-Col Winsome Mason (TSWM & TWMS, inc HL) Lt-Col Trypheme McKenzie (TLOMS & TWAS)
Youth and Candidates: Capt Jonathan Kellman

DIVISIONS
Antigua: PO Box 2, 36 Long St, St John's; tel: [1 268] 562-5473; fax: [1 268] 462-9134; Maj Stanley Griffin
Bahamas: PO Box N 205, Nassau, NP; tel: [1242] 393-2340; fax: [1242] 393-2189; Maj Lester Ferguson
Barbados: PO Box 57, Reed St, Bridgetown; tel: [1246] 426-2467; fax: [1246] 426-9369; Maj Dewhurst Jonas

Guyana: PO Box 10411, 237 Alexander St, Lacytown, Georgetown; tel: [592] 22 72619/ 54910; fax: [592] (22) 50893; Maj Sinous Theodore

Haiti: PO Box 301, Port-au-Prince; tel: [509] 222-4502; fax: [509] 510-3671; Maj Ron Busroe

Jamaica Eastern: Box 153, Kingston; 153B Orange St, Kingston; tel: [1876] 922-6764/ 0287; fax: [1876] 967-1553; Maj Devon Haughton

Jamaica Western: PO Box 44, Lot #949 Westgreen, Montego Bay, St James; tel: [1876] 952-9312; fax: [876] 952-3778; Maj Keith Graham

Trinidad and Tobago: (temporary DHQ) 131-133 Henry St, Port-of-Spain, Trinidad, PO Box 248, 27 Edward St, Port-of-Spain; tel: [1868] 625-4120; fax: [1868] 625-4206; Maj Dewhurst Jonas

REGIONS

Belize: PO Box 64, 41 Regent St, Belize City; tel: (501)2273 365; fax: (501) 2278 240; email: salvationarmyrhqbelize@yahoo.com; Maj Errol Robateau

Suriname: PO Box 317, Henck Arron Straat 172, Paramaribo; tel: [597] 47-3310; fax: [597] 41-0555; email:salvationarmy@inbox.com; Maj Kervin Harry

COUNTRIES NOT IN DIVISIONAL OR REGIONAL LISTS

French Guiana: Route de la Madeleine, Cite Mortin, Boite Postale 329, 97327 Cayenne Cedex, Guyane Francaise; tel: [594] 594-315832

Grenada: Grenville St, St George's, Grenada; tel: [1473] 440-3299

St Kitts: PO Box 56, Cayon Rd, Basseterre, St Kitts; tel: [1869] 465-2106; fax: [1869] 465-4429

St Lucia: PO Box 6, High St, Castries, St Lucia; tel: [1758] 452-3108; fax: [1758] 451-8569

St Maarten: 59 Union Rd, Cole Bay, PO Box 5184, St Maarten, Netherlands Antilles; tel: [599] 580-8588

St Vincent: Melville St, PO Box 498, Kingstown, St Vincent; tel: (809) 456-1574; fax: [1784] 456-1082

TRAINING COLLEGE

Jamaica: GPO Box 437, 174 Orange St, Kingston; tel: [1876] 922-2027; fax: [1876] 967-7541

CITY WELFARE OFFICES

Bahamas: 31 Mackey St, Nassau NP

Jamaica: 57 Peter's Lane, Kingston

COMMUNITY CENTRES

Bahamas: Freeport, Grantstown

Barbados: Checker Hall, St Lucy, Wellington St, Bridgetown, Wotton, Christchurch

Jamaica:
Rae Town Goodwill Centre, 24 Tower St, Kingston; tel: [1876] 928-5770/930-0028
Allman Town, 18-20 Prince of Wales St, Kingston 4; tel: [1876] 92-27279

FEEDING CENTRES

Antigua: Meals on wheels (60)

Bahamas: Mackey St and Grantstown, Nassau

Barbados: Reed St, Bridgetown

Belize: 9 Glynn St, Belize City (acc 50)

Guyana: 6-7 Water St, Kingston, Georgetown (Soup Kitchen); Third Avenue, Bartica

Haiti: Port-au-Prince (Nutrition Centre)

Jamaica: Peter's Lane, Kingston; Jones Town, Kingston; Spanish Town, St Catherine; May Pen, Clarendon; St Ann's Bay, St Ann; Port Antonio, Portland; Montego Bay, St James

Suriname: Gravenstraat 126, Paramaribo

For Children

Bahamas: Nassau, Mackey St

Grenada: St Georges

Guyana: Georgetown, Bartica, Linden

St Vincent: Kingstown

MEDICAL WORK

Haiti: Bethel Maternity Home and Dispensary, Fond-des-Negres
Bethesda TB Centre, Fond-des-Negres
Primary Health Care Centre and Nutrition Centre, Port-au-Prince

Jamaica: Rae Town Clinic, 24 Tower St, Kingston; tel: (876) 928-1489/930-0028

PRISON, PROBATION AND AFTERCARE WORK

Antigua, Grenada, Guyana (Georgetown, Bartica, New Amsterdam), Jamaica, St Kitts, Suriname, Tobago, Trinidad

Prison Visitation Services

Belize: directed by Regional Commander

RETIRED OFFICERS' RESIDENCES

Jamaica: Francis Ham Residence, 57 Mannings Hill Rd, Kingston 8; tel: (876) 924-1308 (acc 7)

Barbados: Long Bay, St Phillip

Guyana: East La Penitence

Women Salvationists in Bangladesh witness on a march prior to a home league rally

Above: Home league members in Congo (Brazzaville) prepare for worship at the start of a women's rally

Right: Passionate prayers during the Junior Home League Convention in Congo (Kinshasa) and Angola Territory

Above: The Ladies' Brass Band of Waterweg Corps, in the Netherlands

Right: New home league members are welcomed in an enrolment ceremony at Rochester Corps (Australia Southern Territory)

Above: A self-help group in India Northern Territory

Left: Distributing saris to poor women in India South Eastern Territory

Above: Home league members in Ghana take part in a market-place meeting

Left: Celebrating the 72nd anniversary of the Home League in Indonesia

Below: A craft class at a women's camp in Latvia

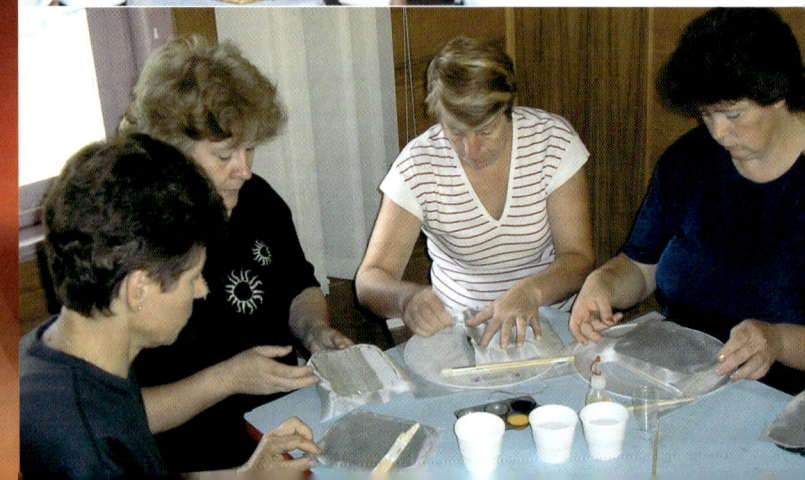

SOCIAL SERVICES
Blind and Handicapped
Adults

Bahamas: Visually Handicapped Workshop, Ivanhoe Lane, PO Box N 1980, Nassau NP; tel: (242) 394-1107 (acc 19)

Jamaica: Francis Ham Residence (home for blind women), 57 Mannings Hill Rd, Kingston 8; tel: (876) 924-1308 (acc 30)

Children (schools)

Bahamas: School for the Blind, 33 Mackay St, PO Box N 205, Nassau NP; tel: (242) 394-3197 (acc 15)

Jamaica: School for the Blind and Visually Impaired, 57 Mannings Hill Rd, PO Box 562, Kingston 8; tel: (876) 925-1362 (residential acc 120)

Deaf/Blind Unit, 57 Mannings Hill Rd, Kingston 8 (residential acc 20)

Vocational Training (Women)

Jamaica: Evangeline Residence, Kingston; Port Antonio, Portland

St Vincent: Melville St, Kingstown

SOCIAL SERVICES
Children
Day Care Centres (nurseries)

Barbados: Wellington St, Bridgetown (acc 50) Wotton, Christchurch (acc 50)

Grenada: St Georges (acc 25)

Jamaica: Allman Town, Kingston (acc 40) Havendale, Kingston (acc 16) Lucea, Hanover (acc 30) Montego Bay, St James (acc 40) Rae Town, Kingston (acc 50)

St Lucia: Castries (acc 50)

St Vincent: Kingstown (acc 20)

Trinidad: San Juan (acc 20)

Homes

Antigua: St John's Sunshine Home (acc 12)

Haiti: Bethany, Fond-des-Negres (acc 22) La Maison du Bonheur, Port-au-Prince (acc 52)

Jamaica:
Hanbury Home, PO Box 2, Shooter's Hill PO, Manchester; tel: [1876] 603-3507 (acc 90)
The Nest, 57 Mannings Hill Rd, Kingston 8; tel: [1876] 925-7711 (acc 45)
Windsor Lodge, PO Box 74, Williamsfield PO, Manchester; tel: [1876] 963-4031 (acc 80)

Suriname: Ramoth, Henck Arron Straat 172, PO Box 317, Paramaribo; tel: [597] 47-3310 (acc 62)

Playgrounds

Jamaica: Rae Town, Kingston; Lucea, Hanover; Montego Bay, St. James

Suriname: Henck Arron Straat 126, Paramaribo

Schools
Basic (kindergartens)

Antigua: St John (acc 150)

Barbados: Checker Hall (acc 50) Wellington St (acc 10) Wotton (acc 20)

Guyana: Bartica (acc 90)

Haiti: Aquin (acc 72) Carrefour (acc 23) Duverger (acc 50) Fond-des-Negres (acc 114) La Colline (acc 35) Laferonnay (acc 40) LeBlanc (acc 40) Vieux Bourg (acc 70)

Jamaica: Bath (acc 25) Bluefields (acc 49) Cave Mountain (acc 30) Cave Valley (acc 75) Falmouth (acc 86) Great Bay (acc 40) Kingston Allman Town (acc 150) Kingston Havendale (acc 90) Kingston Rae Town (acc 100) Lime Hall (acc 83) Linstead (acc 65) Lucea (acc 200) May Pen (acc 60) Montego Bay (acc 240) Port Antonio (acc 50) St Ann's Bay (acc 36) Savanna-la-mar (acc 110) Top Hill (acc 93)

St Kitts: Basseterre (acc 80)

St Lucia: Castries (acc 100)

Trinidad and Tobago: San Fernando (acc 80) Scarborough, Tobago (acc 70) Tragarette Rd, Port-of-Spain (acc 20)

Home Science

Barbados: Project Lighthouse (acc 12)

Haiti: Aquin, Carrefour, Desruisseaux, Duverger, Fond-des-Negres, Gros Morne, Vieux Bourg

Primary Schools

Belize: 12 Cemetery Road, Belize City; tel: (501) 227-2156 (acc 250)

Haiti: Abraham (acc 171) Arcahaie (acc 210) Aquin – William Booth (acc 400) Bainet (acc 156) Balan (acc 156) Baptiste (acc 60) Bas Fort National (acc 198) Bellamie (acc 130) Bellegarde (acc 245) Belle Riviere (acc 140) Boco Lomond (acc 250) Bodoun (acc 80) Brodequin (acc 140) Campeche (acc 100) Carrefour/Desruisseaux (acc 235) Cayot (acc 175) Couyot (acc 140) Dessources (acc 125) Duverger (acc 190) Fond-des-Negres (acc 630) Gardon (acc 250) Gros Morne (acc 200) Guirand (acc 130) Jacmel (acc 40) Kamass (acc 100) L'Azile (acc 190) Laferonnay (acc 100) L'Homond (acc 250) La Jovange (acc 171) La Zandier (acc 170) La Colline (acc 275) Le Blanc (acc 105)

La Fosse (acc 500) Lilette (acc 110) Limbe (acc 35) Luly (acc 210) Mapou (acc 80) Montrouis (acc 250) Moulin (acc 150) Peirigny (acc 165) Petit Goave (acc 200) Plaisance (acc 216) Port-au-Prince – College Verena (acc 1,410) Port-de-Paix (acc 100) Puits Laurent (acc 200) Rossignol (acc 230) St Louis du Sud (acc 75) St Marc (acc 235) Vieux Bourg (acc 440) Violette (acc 120)

Evening Schools
Guyana: Happy Heart Youth Centre, New Amsterdam (acc 20)
Haiti: Port-au-Prince (acc 83)

Secondary Schools
Haiti: Port-au-Prince (acc 450); Gros-Morne (acc 85)

SOCIAL SERVICES
Men and Women
Centre for Homeless
Belize: Raymond A. Parkes Home, 18 Cemetery Rd, Belize City; tel: (501) 207-4309 (acc 24)

Eventide Homes
Trinidad: Senior Citizens' Centre, 34 Duncan St, Port-of-Spain; tel: [868] 624-5883 (acc 57)

SOCIAL SERVICES
Men
MacKenzie Guest House: Rainbow City, PO Box 67, Linden Co-op MacKenzie, Guyana; tel: [592] 444-6406 (acc 30)

Hostels and Shelters
Guyana:
Men's Hostel, 6-7 Water St, Kingston, Georgetown; tel: [592] 226-1235 (acc 40)
Drug Rehabilitation Centre, 6-7 Water St,

Kingston, Georgetown; tel: [592] 226-1235 (acc 20)
Jamaica:
Men's Hostel, 57 Peter's Lane, Kingston; tel: [1876] 922-4030 (acc 25)
William Chamberlain Rehabilitation Centre, 57 Peter's Lane, Kingston (acc 25)
Suriname: Night Shelter, Ladesmastraat 2-6, PO Box 317, Paramaribo; tel: [597] 4-75108 (acc 31)
Trinidad: Working Lads' Hostel, 154a Henry St, Port-of-Spain; tel: 36514 (acc 28)

SOCIAL SERVICES
Women
Eventide Homes
Belize: Ganns Rest Home, 60 East Canal St, Belize City; tel: (501) 227 2973 (acc 12)
Guyana: 69 Bent and Haley Sts, Wortmanville, Georgetown; tel: [592] 226-8846 (acc 22)
Suriname:
Elim Guest House, Gravenstraat 126, PO Box 317, Paramaribo; tel: [597] 47-2735 (acc 15)
Emma House, Dr Nassylaan 76, PO Box 2402, Paramaribo; tel: [597] 4-73890 (acc 22)

Hostels and Shelters
Bahamas: Women and Children's Emergency Residence, Grantstown, PO Box GT 2216, Nassau NP; tel: [242] 323-5608 (acc 14)
Jamaica: Evangeline Residence, 153 Orange St, Kingston; tel: 922-6398 (acc 48)
Trinidad: Geddes Grant House, 22-24 Duncan St, Port-of-Spain; tel: 623-5700 (acc 36)
Josephine Shaw House, 131-133 Henry St, Port-of-Spain; tel: 623-2547 (acc 106)
Night Shelter, 34 Duncan St, Port-of-Spain; tel: 624-5883 (acc 10)

Key roll figures showed continued increases, with women's ministries being a particularly encouraging area. The senior soldiers roll has recorded an increase of 22 per cent . . . the junior soldiers roll again increased and much-needed renewed emphasis was given to the future officers fellowship.

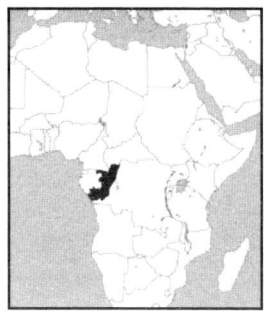

CONGO (BRAZZAVILLE) TERRITORY

Territorial leaders:
Commissioners Mfon J. and Ime Akpan

Territorial Commander:
Commissioner Mfon J. Akpan (1 Apr 2004)

Chief Secretary:
Lieut-Colonel Ambroise Zola (1 Apr 2004)

**Territorial Headquarters: Rue de Reims, Brazzaville,
République du Congo**

Postal address: c/o Africa Department, International Headquarters, 101 Queen Victoria St,
London EC4P 4EP, United Kingdom

tel: [242] 881144; email: ads_congo_brazzaville@yahoo.com

In 1937 The Salvation Army spread from Léopoldville to Brazzaville, and in 1953 French Equatorial
Africa (now Congo) became a separate command. Commissioner and Mrs Henri Becquet were the
pioneers. The command was upgraded to a territory in December 1960.

Zone: Africa
Country included in the territory: The Republic of Congo
'The Salvation Army' in French: Armée du Salut; in Kikongo: Nkangu a Luvulusu; in Lingala: Basolda
    na Kobikisama; in Vili: Livita li Mavutsula
Languages in which the gospel is preached: French, Kikongo, Kituba, Lingala, Vili
Periodical: *Le Salutiste*

NEARLY 900 soldiers – senior and junior – were enrolled during the visit of General John Larsson and Commissioner Freda Larsson to the territory in August 2005. In one of the meetings, to mark the international Year for Children and Youth, the General enrolled 401 junior soldiers and many young people sought Christ at the mercy seat. General Larsson also opened Nkuoikou Clinic, where every day more than 50 patients receive medical attention.

Some of the territory's Salvationists were to hear the General again later that month when the territory sent

44 delegates to the All-Africa Congress in Harare (Zimbabwe). Many of them sponsored themselves to attend. A women's timbrel group among the delegates presented an excellent display.

Specialist doctors from Kinshasa spent two weeks in one of the clinics in Brazzaville to carry out eye surgery. Nearly 150 people had operations and many others received medication.

A maternity department has been added to Loua and Dolisie clinics, while at the clinic in Mongali an ophthalmology department was established. Yangui Clinic still waits for repairs after it was damaged during the civil war.

Twenty villages have benefited from the supply of building material such as roofing sheets, to help in the reconstruction of homes destroyed during the civil war.

The year 2006 started with a day of prayer for all staff in the chapel at territorial headquarters, with similar meetings being organised for officers and soldiers of the two divisions in the Brazzaville area. Some 750 people attended and experienced moments of spiritual blessing.

Later in January the Kouilou Division was divided into two, with the launching of Pointe Noire Division and Tchitondi District. The ceremony was conducted by the territorial commander in the presence of a crowd of Salvationists and representatives from administrative authorities.

Another 30 cadets have been commissioned as officers and are happily serving the Lord. Seminars were held for the benefit of officers and staff responsible for finance and involved in women's ministries.

From 1 April 2006 the territory took on the cabinet system of leadership, appointing secretaries for personnel, business administration and programme.

The territory's Salvationists are grateful to God for the peace in the country that has made it possible for them to achieve their objectives for the year under review.

STATISTICS

Officers 274 (active 233 retired 41) **Cadets** (2nd Yr) 30 **Employees** 126
Corps 95 **Outposts** 54 **Maternity Unit** 1 **Clinics** 6 **Centres** 2 **Schools** 12
Senior Soldiers 21,176 **Adherents** 1,514 **Junior Soldiers** 5,276 **Recruits** 4,687
Personnel serving outside territory Officers 4

STAFF

Sec for Personnel: Maj Prosper Bakemba
Sec for Programme: Maj Alexis Sakamesso
Sec for Busness Administration: Maj Jean Pierre Sonda
Extension Training: Maj Anatole Massengo
Financial Administrator: Sgt Jean Mayandu
Health Services Coordinator: Capt Grégoire Mamete
Projects: Sgt Edy Seraphin Kanda
Property: Capt Aristide Samba
Public Relations: Capt Pascal Matsiona
Social: Maj Cécile Loukoula
Territorial Bandmaster: Sgt Sensa Malanda
Territorial Songster Leader: Wilfrid Milandou
Training: Maj Frédéric Diandaga
Women's Ministries: Comr Ime Akpan (TPWM) Lt-Col Alphonsine Zola (TSWM) Maj Monique Bakemba (THLS)
Youth and Candidates: Capt Pierre Mounsambote

DIVISIONS

Brazzaville 1: BP 20, Brazzaville; tel: 21 13 15; Maj Eugène Bamanabio (mobile: 5 58 63 92)

Twenty villages have benefited from the supply of building material such as roofing sheets, to help in the reconstruction of homes destroyed during the civil war. . . . Salvationists are grateful to God for the peace in the country.

Brazzaville 2: tel: 68 95 14; Maj Antoine Massielé (mobile: 5 35 53 21)

Pointe Noire: BP 686, Pointe Noire; tel: 94 00 16; Maj François Mavouna (mobile: 5 58 68 08)

Lekoumou: BP 20, Brazzaville; tel: 58 63 92; Maj Alexandre Mabanza

Louingui: BP 20, Brazzaville; Maj Jérôme Nzita (mobile: 5 47 09 75)

Mbanza-Ndounga: BP 20, Brazzaville; Maj Daniel Taty (mobile: 5 38 76 31)

Niari: BP 85, Dolisie; Captain Urbain Loubacky Tel 5364319

Yangui: BP 10, Kinkala; Maj Patrick Tadi (mobile: 5 56 38 72)

DISTRICTS

Bouenza: BP 20, Brazzaville; Maj Jean-Pierre Douniama (mobile: 5 39 50 87)

North: BP 20, Brazzaville; Maj Gabin Mbizi (mobile: 5 31 35 09)

Tchitondi: c/o THQ; Maj Alphonse Mayamba-Debi

TRAINING COLLEGE

Nzoko, BP 20, Brazzaville; tel: 56 95 72

SOCIAL AND EDUCATIONAL CENTRES

Day Care Centre: Ouenze Corps, Brazzaville
Guest House: Pointe-Noire
Yenge Home for the Needy: Nzoko

Institute for the Blind: BP 20 Brazzaville
John Swinfen Primary School: Loua
Commissioner V. Makoumbou Nursery School: Nzoko

HEALTH SERVICES

Clinic and Eye Treatment Centre:
Moukoundji-Ngouaka: BP 20, Brazzaville
Clinics with Maternity Units:
Dolisie: BP 235, Dolisie
Loua: BP 20, Brazzaville
Moungali: BP 20, Brazzaville
Nkayi: BP 229, Nkayi

A Salvation Army drum serves as the mercy seat as people are led to Christ during an open-air meeting in the Brazzaville area

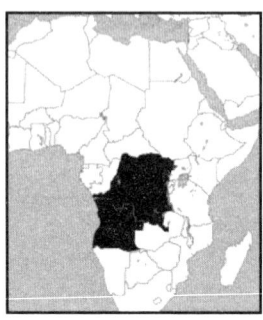

CONGO (KINSHASA) AND ANGOLA TERRITORY

Territorial leaders:
**Commissioners Jean B. and
Véronique Ludiazo**

Territorial Commander:
Commissioner Jean B. Ludiazo (1 Feb 2002)

Chief Secretary:
Lieut-Colonel Onal Castor (1 Nov 2003)

**Territorial Headquarters: Ave Ebea 23, Kinshasa-Gombe,
Democratic Republic of Congo**

Postal address: Armée du Salut 8636, Kinshasa 1, Democratic Republic of Congo

tel: [243] 997-526050

The first Salvation Army corps was established in Kinshasa in 1934 by Adjutant (later Commissioner) and Mrs Henri Becquet. By decree of Léopold III, Armée du Salut was given legal status, with powers set out in a Deed of Constitution, on 21 February 1936. Work spread to Congo (Brazzaville) in 1937 and 16 years later it became a separate command. Work in Angola was officially established in 1985.

Zone: Africa
Countries included in the territory: Democratic Republic of Congo, Angola
'The Salvation Army' in French: Armée du Salut; in Kikongo: Nkangu a Luvulusu; in Lingala: Basolda na Kobikisa; in Portuguese: Exército de Salvação; in Swahili: Jeshi la Wokovu; in Tshiluba: Tshiluila Tsha Luhandu
Languages in which the gospel is preached: Chokwe, French, Kikongo, Lingala, Portuguese, Swahili, Tshiluba, Umbundu
Periodical: *Echo d'Espoir*

GOD crowned each meeting with hundreds of seekers when Chief of the Staff Commissioner Israel L. Gaither and Commissioner Eva D. Gaither visited the territory during October 2005. Another highlight of their visit was the enrolment of 356 senior soldiers, 325 junior soldiers and 750 junior home league members.

That same month saw the 70th anniversary of Salvation Army schools. The celebration events concluded during the annual soldiers'

congress. Many people received certificates of recognition for their outstanding contribution and service to the Army's schools programme through the years.

At the end of April 2005 a territorial youth congress had marked the international Year for Children and Youth and among those attending this special event was Captain Blaise Kombo, then Territorial Youth and Candidates Secretary, Congo (Brazzaville). The first ever Junior

Home League Convention attracted 1,300 young girls from across the territory.

In July 2005 the territorial commander commissioned 10 new captains of the Preparers of the Way Session; three months later 12 cadets of the Heralds of the Good News Session were welcomed.

In August two new sections were opened as a result of the beginning of Army work in South Kivu Province and in the north of Bandundu Province. Two officer-couples were appointed to lead these new sections.

Work/mission teams from the USA Western Territory carried out two notable projects in August and September. The first team funded, built and completely furnished Mbenseke Primary School. This modern facility has eight classrooms, two offices, and toilets for boys, girls and staff. A second team repaired the site at Mbanza-Nzundu Camp.

For its 'Fight Against Sex Trafficking' project during 2005 the territory received funding from the Norway, Iceland and The Færoes Territory. The project's objectives are: (1) Preventing child prostitution; (2) Providing psychological care, leading to reconciliation and rehabilitation; (3) Pleading for sexual victims who cannot defend themselves. Already more than 510 sex workers have been identified and helped through this project.

In March 2006 the girls' choir of Kinshasa Central Corps released its first album. The year also marked the 20th anniversary of the National Band and National Songsters.

The Territorial Task Force has completed its strategic planning and proposed the way forward for the next five years.

STATISTICS

Officers 441 (active 357 retired 84) **Cadets** 12 **Employees** 4,257 **Pupils** 76,490
Corps 175 **Outposts** 238 **Health Centres** 27 **Maternity Hospitals/Clinics** 5 **Other specialist hospitals** 1 **Other specialist clinics** 4 **Institutions** 5
Schools: Secondary 110 **Primary** 165 **Boarding** 2 **Maternal** 7 **University** 1
Senior Soldiers 19,539 **Recruits** 3,054 **Adherents** 4,810 **Junior Soldiers** 7,055
Personnel serving outside territory Officers 6

STAFF

Sec for Personnel: Maj Eugene Dikalembolovanga
Sec for Programme: Maj Emmanuel Nsumbu
Candidates & Youth: Capt Norbert Makala
Development & Emergency Services: Maj Graçia Matondo
Editorial/Literature: Capt Denis Mafuta
Extension Training: Maj Jabhron Kibenga
Finance:
Information Technology: Sgt Mbumu Muba Jean-Marc
Medical: Dr David Nku Imbie
Music: Maj L. M. Ntoya Kapel
  Sgt Jean-Marc Mbumu (Bandmaster)
  Sgt Joseph Nsilulu (Songster Leader)
Property: Mr Claude Huguenin
Public Relations: Maj Esaie Ntembi
Schools Coordinator: Mr Raymond Luamba Ntolani
Social: Maj Odile Dikalembolovanga (Sec)
  Miss Pauline Mavitu (HIV/Aids Section)
Training: Maj Norbert Nkanu
Women's Ministries: Comr Véronique Ludiazo (TPWM) Lt-Col Edmane Castor (TSWM) Maj Lydia Isabel Matondo (Women's Development Programmes) Maj Clémentine Nsumbu (LOMS) Maj Angélique Lukau (Vocational Training/Literacy) Maj Marie-José Ntembi (JHLS)

DIVISIONS

Bas-Fleuve/Océan: BP 123, Matadi; Maj Simon Nzeza Biyenga (mobile: 0819065803)
Inkisi: Armée du Salut, Kavwaya, BP 45, Inkisi;

Maj Célestin Pepe Pululu (mobile: 0999938248)

Kasaï-Occidental: BP 1404, Kananga;
Maj Sébastien Lubaki Mbala
(mobile: 0998449971)

Kasangulu: BP 14, Kasangulu; Maj Jean-Baptiste
Mayisilwa Mata (mobile: 0998519443)

Kinshasa 1: BP 8636, Kinshasa; Maj Nsoki
Joseph Bueya (mobile: 0815184323)

Kinshasa 2: BP 8636, Kinshasa;
Lt-Col Ferdinand Nzolameso Nlabu
(mobile: 0816891161)

Kisangani: BP 412, Kisangani; Capt Dieudonné
Nzuzi Tsilulu (mobile: 0997015174)

Luozi: Armée du Salut, Luozi; Maj Isidore
Mayunga Matondo (mobile: 0990023962)

Mbanza-Ngungu: BP 160; Maj Henri Masamba
Nangi (mobile: 0815201681)

Sud-Katanga: BP 2525, Lubumbashi;
Maj Sébastien Makani Diantezulua
(mobile: 0816057064)

REGION

Angola: Exército de Salvação, Caixa Postal
1656-C, Luanda; Maj Emmanuel Manu
Mpanzu (mobile: [244] 92315211)

DISTRICTS

Bandundu: Armée du Salut, Bandundu;
Maj Abraham Dongya Naniwambote
(mobile: 0998235058)

Isiro: BP 135

SECTION

Tanganyika: BP 556; under supervision of
Sud-Katanga

TRAINING COLLEGE

BP 8636, Kinshasa

UNIVERSITY

William Booth University: BP 8636, Kinshasa;
Rector: Dr Mpiutu ne Mbodi Gaston

**Home league members at a women's camp in the Congo (Kinshasa) and
Angola Territory are joyous in their praise of God**

ATTACHED TO THQ
Conference Centre: Mbanza-Nzundu

MEDICAL WORK
Health Centres

Kinshasa: Amba (Kisenso), Bakidi (Selembao), Bomoi, Bopeto (Ndjili), Boyambi (Barumbu), Elonga, Esengo (Masina), Kimia (Kintambo), Molende (Kingasani)

Bas-Congo: Kasangulu, Boko-Mbuba, Kifuma, Kingantoko, Kingudi, Kinzambi, Kintete, Nkalama, Shefu, Kavwaya, Kimayala, Mbanza-Nsundi, Mbanza-Nzundu

Kananga: Moyo

Kisangani: Libota, Mokela, Dengue

Clinic: Maj Leka (Maluku/Kinshasa)

Dental Clinics: Boyambi (Barumbu), Elonga (Masuna), Kasangulu (Bas-Congo)

Diabetic Clinic: Kananga

Foot Clinic: Boyambi

Maternity Units: Bomoi Kinshasa (acc 60); Kasangulu, Bas-Congo (acc 13); Kavwaya, Bas-Congo maternity + centre (acc 14) Maluku Kinshasa (acc 12)

SECONDARY SCHOOLS
Kinshasa

Institut Scientifique Bandal; Collège Gabriel Becquet (Selembao); Collège Bimwala; ITC Bimwala; Institut Dianzenza; Institut Dizolele (Ndjili); Institut Ilona; ITC Kwamouth; Institut Lukubama; Collège John Mabwidi; Institut Mabwidi; Institut Pédagogique Masina; Lycée Matonge; Lycée Technique de Matonge; ITS Mbala; ITA Menkao; ITC Ndjili-Kilambu; Institut Ngizulu; ITC Nsakala; ITC Ntolani; ITI Ntolani; Institut Rwakadingi; Institut Tasi; Institut Tshangu 1; Institut Tshangu 2; ITC Selembao; Institut Wabaluku; Institut Yanda Mayemba; 44 primary schools

Bas-Congo

Institut Boyokani (Matadi); Institut Diakanwa; Institut Kavwaya, BP 45 Inkisi; Institut Beti 1; Institut Beti 2; Institut Kimbumba-Nord; Institut Bongo-Bongo; Institut Kingudi; Institut Pédagogique Kasi; Institut Dikal

(Lufuku); Institut Dizolele 1; Institut Dizolele 2; ITP Kintete; Institut Kimayasi; Institut Kinzadi; CS Kimbongo; Institut Kinzambi 1 (Kasangulu); Institut Kinzambi 2 (Luozi); Institut Ludiazo; Institut Mikalukidi; Institut Kitundulu; Institut Kivunda; Institut Kumba Ndilu; ITS Kumbi; ITC Lovo; Institut Maduma; Institut Mananga; Institut Maneka; Institut Manionzi; Institut Matanda; Institut Mateso; Institut Nkundi (Mbanza-Ngungu); CS Nsanga-Mamba; ITC Mbanza-Nsanda; ITA Mbanza-Nsundi; Institut Mbanza-Nzundu; Institut Mwala-Kinsende; ITA Nsangi-Kialelua; Institut Ndandanga; ITC Ngongolo; Institut Shefu; Institut Sombala; Institut Sundi-Mamba; Collège William Booth (Kasangulu); Institut Viaza; 68 primary schools

Province Orientale (Kisangani)

Institut Batiampanga, Institut Bonsomi; Institut Elikya; Institut Ketele; Institut Wagenia; 16 primary schools

Kasaï-Occidental (Kananga)

Institut Bena-Leka; Institut Bena-Mbiye; Institut Bobumwe; Institut Muzemba, Institut Mwanza-Ngoma; Institut Tshitakanioka; 10 primary schools

Sud-Katanga (Lubumbashi)

ITC Wokovu (Katuba); 4 primary schools

Bandundu

Institut Elonga; Institut Kwango; Institut Mabwidi; Institut Ngampo Maku; Institut Ngobila; Institut Makaya; Institut Wembe; Institut Luvua Kabeya; 8 primary schools

Equateur

ITM Bukaka; ITCA Lihau; Institut Mambune; Institut Masobe; Institut Mokuta; Institut Yambo; ITCA Yamwe; Institut Yangola; 5 primary schools

SOCIAL SERVICES
Old People's Home: Kinshasa-Kintambo (acc 28)

Children's Home and Community Child Care: Kinshasa (acc 8)

Development and Emergencies: Kavwaya, Mbanza-Nzundu, Impini, Mato, Kasungulu

Vocational Training Centres: Barumbu, Kinshasa (acc 47); Lubumbashi, Sud-Katanga (acc 64); Ndjili (acc 90)

Another highlight was the enrolment of 356 senior soldiers, 325 junior soldiers and 750 junior home league members

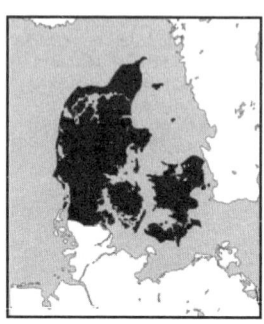

DENMARK TERRITORY

Territorial leaders:
Colonels Michael and Ina Marvell

Territorial Commander:
Colonel Michael Marvell (1 Nov 2004)

Chief Secretary:
Major Graham Owen (1 Nov 2005)

**Territorial Headquarters: Frederiksberg Allé 9,
1621 Copenhagen V, Denmark**

tel: [45] 33 31 41 92; fax: [45] 33 25 30 80
email: Frelsens@den.salvationarmy.org; web site: www.frelsens-haer.dk

The work of The Salvation Army in Denmark commenced in Copenhagen in May 1887, pioneer officers being Major (later Lieut-Colonel) and Mrs Robert Perry.

Zone: Europe
Country included in the territory: Denmark
'The Salvation Army' in Danish: Frelsens Hær
Language in which the gospel is preached: Danish
Periodicals: *Mennesker & Tro*, *Kids Alive*, *Vision-Mission*, *Young Connection*

AN important event in the territory took place on 1 February 2006 when three lieutenants were commissioned as officers. In addition to serving as corps leaders for some years, the three new captains had also completed additional training in preparation for full officership.

In recent years The Salvation Army's social work in Denmark has been putting special focus on poorer families. So when the government published a report that showed increasing poverty and problems for homeless people and single-parent families, the Army received considerable media attention and appeared in the news on all major networks, especially up to Christmas.

The Army's critique of government policy was put at the top of the political agenda and nearly caused a vote of no confidence in the minister for social affairs.

Christmas aid to families set a new record and again the help was combined with various offers that can give children and parents happy experiences all year round – such as parties, camps and special events. These included free match tickets donated by professional football clubs in the five largest cities and a free trip to the famous Legoland, which opened specially the day before its official seasonal opening. Some 1,500 families who received Christmas help from the Army accepted this offer.

Wildersgade – The Salvation Army's welfare centre in the old part of Copenhagen – celebrated a well-attended 40-year jubilee. Another important celebration in the city was the centenary of its famous town hall. There were events all over the city and Salvationists were invited to feature in the celebratory concert at the town hall, acknowledging the Army's music as an important part of the city's life. Valby Band conducted by Erik Silfverberg and a vocal soloist participated in the concert.

Salvation Army ministry continued to advance in many places and the number of people attending meetings and activities during the year under review increased by four per cent. One of the many encouraging developments was the restarting of the corps band in Aalborg after several years.

Another highlight of the year was the visit in May of the New York Staff Band. The USA Eastern visitors played at an open-air concert in the centre of Copenhagen and presented a programme in a totally sold-out hall at the Temple Corps.

STATISTICS
Officers 75 (active 30 retired 45) **Employees** 230
Corps 33 **Outpost** 1 **Social Institutions** 16 **Welfare Centres** 6
Senior Soldiers 1,015 **Adherents** 219 **Junior Soldiers** 42

STAFF
Leadership Council: Maj Aud Berntsen; Col Ina Marvell; Maj Jens-Otto Nielsen, Maj Graham Owen, Maj Hannelise Tvedt
Sec for Programme: Maj Kirsten Owen
  Programme, Corps: Maj Aud Berntsen
  Programme, Social: Maj Hannelise Tvedt
Candidates: Capt Thomas Andersen

Editors: Mr Bent Dahl-Jensen (*Mennesker & Tro*) Major Kirsten Owen (*Vision-Mission*)
Finance: Mrs Annie Kristensen
Home League and Over-60s: Maj Fanny Worm
Missing Persons: Col Jørn Lauridsen
Missionary and Child Sponsorship: Maj Ruth Christensen
Music: Mr Erik Silfverberg
Property: Maj Terje Tvedt
Public Relations and Information Technology: Mr Lars Lydholm
Statistics: Maj Vilhelm Worm
Women's Ministries: Col Ina Marvell (TPWM)
Youth: Mrs Lykke Bendtsen

SOCIAL SERVICES
Head Office: Frederiksberg Allé 9, 1621 Copenhagen V; tel: 33 31 41 92; fax: 36 30 70 34

Clothing Industry (Recycling Centres)
6705 Esbjerg Ø, Ravnevej 2; tel: 75 14 24 22; fax: 75 14 00 47
5000 Odense C, Roersvej 33; tel: 66 11 25 21; fax: 66 19 05 21
9560 Hadsund, Mariagervej 3; tel: 98 57 42 48; fax: 98 57 38 72
4900 Nakskov, Narviksvej 15; tel: 54 95 12 05; fax: 54 95 12 04

Community Centres
9000 Aalborg, Skipper Clementsgade 11; tel: 98 11 50 62
1408 Copenhagen K, Wildersgade 66; tel: 32 54 44 10 (acc 80)
4900 Nakskov, Niels Nielsengade 6; tel: 54 95 30 06 (acc 60)

Day Nurseries
9900 Frederikshavn Humlebien, Knudensvej 1B; tel: 98 42 33 27 (acc 40)
2000 Frederiksberg, Melita, Mariendalsvej 4; tel: 38 87 01 48 (acc 58)
2500 Valby, Solsikken, Annexstræde 29; tel: 36 16 23 11 (acc 22)
2650 Hvidovre, Kastanjehuset, Idrætsvej 65A; tel: 36 78 40 21 (acc 33)
2650 Hvidovre, Solgården, Catherine Booths vej 22; tel: 36 78 07 71 (acc 100)
7500 Holstebro Solhøj, Skolegade 51; tel: 97 42 61 21 (acc 30)

Emergency Shelters for Families
2650 Hvidovre, Svendebjerggård, Catherine Booths vej 20; tel: 36 49 65 77 (acc 25)
1754 Copenhagen V, Den Åbne Dør, Hedebygade 30; tel: 33 24 91 03 (acc 15)

4700 Næstved, Østergade 13; tel: 55 77 22 70 (acc 6)

Eventide Nursing Centre
2200 Copenhagen N Aftensol, Lundtoftegade 5; tel: 35 30 55 00 (acc 43)

Social Advice Bureau and Goodwill Centre
Grundtvigsvej 17 st, 1864 Frederiksberg C; tel: 33 24 56 67

Project for Long-term Unemployed
Nørholmlejren, Oldenborrevej 2, 9000 Aalborg; tel: 98 34 18 10 (acc 10)

Rehabilitation Centre
Hørhuset, 2300 Copenhagen S, Hørhusvej 5; tel: 32 55 56 22 (acc 64)

Students Residence
2100 Copenhagen Ø, Helgesengade 25; tel: 35 37 74 32 (acc 41)

SOCIAL SERVICES (field administered)
Community Centres
2200 Copenhagen N, Kalejdoskop, Thorsgade 48 A; tel: 35 85 00 87
3000 Helsingør, Regnbuen Community Centre, Strandgade 60; tel: 49 21 10 06
4800 Nykøbing Falster, Jernbanegade 42, Community Centre and Corps activities; tel: 54 85 71 89
9560 Hadsund, Nørregade 10, Den Åbne Dør Community Centre; tel: 23 26 19 15

2500 Valby, Valby Langgade 83; tel: 36 45 67 67

7100 Vejle, Midtpunktet, Staldgårdsgade 4; tel: 75 82 78 38

Summer Camps
9000 Aalborg, Nørholmlejren, Oldenborrevej 2; tel: 98 34 18 10 (acc 50)
8700 Horsens, Hjarnø; tel: 75 68 32 24 (acc 25)
5450 Otterup, Rømhildsminde, Ferievej 11-13, Jørgensø; tel: 64 87 13 36

UNDER THQ
Holiday Home and Conference Centre:
Lillebælt, Nørre Allé 47, Strib, 5500
Middelfart; tel: 64 40 10 57; fax: 63 40 02 82 (acc 30)

Investigation Bureau: Frederiksberg Allé 9, 1621 Copenhagen V; tel: 33 31 41 92; Col Jørn Lauridsen

Radio Station: (Copenhagen area) Frederiksberg Allé 9, 1621 Copenhagen V; tel: 33 31 41 25 (studio)

Youth and Conference Centre: Baggersminde, Fælledvej 132, 2791 Dragør; tel: 32 53 70 18; fax: 32 53 70 98 (acc 80)

New Project
Community Centre: 2700 Brønshøj, Ruten 14; tel: 36 17 70 06

BABYSONG IS BOOMING

Begun in Scandinavia, BabySong reaches out into the community to parents of babies and toddlers. While their children enjoy songs, games and other activities, the parents assist their children in language development and interaction through music, at the same time building relationships with other parents and gaining parenting tips. This group operates at a Salvation Army corps in Finland.

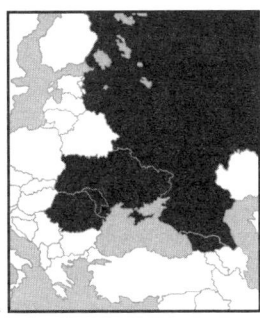

EASTERN EUROPE TERRITORY

Territorial leaders:
Commissioners Barry and Raemor Pobjie

Territorial Commander:
Commissioner Barry Pobjie (1 Oct 2002)

Chief Secretary:
Lieut-Colonel Alistair Herring (16 Sep 2006)

Territorial Headquarters: Krestiansky Tupik 16/1, Moscow

Postal address: Russian Federation, 109044 Moscow, Krestiansky Tupik 16/1

tel: [7] (495) 911 2600/2956; fax: [7] (495) 911 2753; email: Russia@eet.salvationarmy.org;
web site: www.thesalvationarmy.ru

Work was initiated in Russia in 1910 by Colonel Jens Povlsen of Denmark but circumstances necessitated his withdrawal after 18 months. Army operations then recommenced in St Petersburg in 1913 as an extension to the work in Finland. After the February 1917 revolution the work flourished, Russia became a distinct command and reinforcements arrived from Sweden. As a result of the October revolution they had, however, to be withdrawn at the end of 1918, leaving 40 Russian and Finnish officers to continue the work under extreme hardship until the Army was finally proscribed in 1923.

   Salvation Army activities were officially recommenced in July 1991, overseen by the Norway, Iceland and The Færoes Territory with the arrival of Lieut-Colonels John and Bjorg Bjartveit. It became a distinct command in November 1992. Work was extended to Ukraine (1993), Georgia (1993), Moldova (1994) and Romania (1999). On 1 June 2001 the command was redesignated the Eastern Europe Command. It was elevated to territory status on 1 March 2005.

Zone: Europe
Countries included in territory: Georgia, Moldova, Romania, Russian Federation, Ukraine
'The Salvation Army' in Georgian: Khsnis Armia; in Moldovan/Romanian: Armata Salvarii; in Russian: Armiya Spaseniya; in Ukrainian: Armiya Spasinnya
Languages in which the gospel is preached: Georgian, Moldovan, Romanian, Russian, Ukrainian
Periodicals: *Vestnik Spaseniya* (*The War Cry*), *The Officer* (both Russian)

THIRTEEN cadets were commissioned as officers in June 2005. The first-ever Romanian officer, Captain Roxana Cucu, was appointed back to Ploesti Corps in Romania, where she had served as a cadet. Twenty cadets of the Heralds of the Good News Session were welcomed and began their field-based flexible training. They attend residential courses in Moscow in two intakes and are being followed-up in their appointments by training institute staff and specially trained mentors.

   Unusually heavy rain led to extensive flooding in parts of Romania. Although this took place far from Bucharest, Salvationists managed to offer assistance to a number of families. Funding came from a local Muslim businessman, an Iraqi, who approached

The Salvation Army because he wanted to help those who were suffering in his adopted country.

'The Association The Salvation Army Christian Mission in Romania' was legally registered, bringing to an end a seven-year process to obtain legal registration in that country. The charter of the Centralised Religious Organisation of The Salvation Army in Russia was finally re-registered after a long and risky period of operating without legal registration.

The corps in Vladivostok was transferred from the Korea Territory to the Eastern Europe Territory. The event was marked by visits of the EET territorial leaders to Seoul and the Korea territorial leaders to Moscow. During a united ceremony in Vladivostok the new corps officers, Captains Vladimir and Alexandra Derugin, were installed. The move is significant, as it opens up the EET's borders to the East, incorporating all of Russia into the territory.

Ukraine was separated from the Ukraine/Moldova/Romania Division on 1 August and became a division in its own right. Major Marie Willermark arrived from Sweden on 19 January to be installed as the first Ukraine Divisional Commander.

The Partners in Mission scheme has been actively pursued. Several teams, including a dance group from Moldova, attended events in the USA Southern Territory. Service Teams from the USA Southern, Central and Western Territories visited EET extensively during the summer.

The first-ever Brengle Institute in the territory took place with (then) Commissioners Shaw and Helen Clifton as guest lecturers. A Battle School brought together young Salvationists from all countries in the territory.

The territory emphasised the focus on HIV/Aids by conducting seminars for officers and employees in Ukraine, Moldova and Georgia. The Territorial HIV/Aids Task Force Coordinator is also forming links with IHQ's facilitation team and with local network partners.

STATISTICS
Officers active 125 **Aux-Capts** 2 **Cadets** (1st Yr) 19 (2nd Yr) 9 **Employees** 319
Corps 59 **Outposts** 10 **Feeding Centres** 34 **Food Distribution Centres** 40 **Rehabilitation Centres** 2 **Seniors Centres** 2 **Social Centres** 22 **Vocational Training Centres** 2
Senior Soldiers 1,966 **Adherents** 1,061 **Junior Soldiers** 431

STAFF
Secretary for Russia Development: Maj Alexander Kharkov
Personnel: Comr Raemor Pobjie
Asst Sec for Personnel: Maj Peter Clarke
Prayer Ambassador: Capt Natalia Platonova
Territorial Sergeant Major: Yuri Gulanitsky
Social: Maj Michael Stannett
Youth: Maj Ruth Stannett
Candidates: Capt Marika Safarova
Training: Capt Anita Caldwell
Asst Training Principal: Capt Svetlana Sharov
Leadership Development: Mr Cliff Worthing
Pastoral Care: Capt Elena Shulyanski

Mission Development: Lt-Col Astrid Herring
League of Mercy: Maj Maria Kharkova
Women's Ministries: Capt Victoria Lalak
Finance: Mrs Flora Briones
Public Relations: Mr and Mrs Cliff and Simone Worthing
Audit & Asst Finance Officer: Capt Natalia Pismeniuk
Editorial: Mrs Simone Worthing

A villager from Vadu Rosca, Romania, turns to The Salvation Army for help after unusually heavy rain led to extensive flooding in parts of Romania. Although the floods occurred far from Bucharest, Salvationists were on the scene and assisted a number of families. Funding came from a local Muslim businessman, an Iraqi, who wanted to help those who were suffering in his adopted country.

Emergency Response: Mr Cliff Worthing
Projects Cordinators: Ms Kerry Ann Berrisford and Mr Neale Rudd

DIVISIONS
Russia: 105120 Russia, Moscow, Khlebnikov Pereulok, 7 bld, 2; tel: 495 678 03 51; fax: 495 678 91 60; Maj Alexander Kharkov

Moldova: Moldova, Chisinau, 2012, Armata Salvarii, PO Box 137, Str P. Movila #19, 2005; tel: [10] (37322) 235076; telefax: [10] (37322) 237972; Maj Jostein Nielsen

Ukraine: 01023 Kiev, 38, Shota Rustavely St, Suite 3; tel: 380 44 287 37 05; fax: 380 44 287 45 98; Maj Marie Willermark

REGIONS
Georgia: Megrelidze St. 16, Tbilisi, 0177 Georgia; tel: 995 (32) 39 9654, 39 9764; fax: 995 (32) 39 9619; Capt Giorgi Salarishvili

Romania: 722212 Bucharest, Sector 2, Str Maica Domnului Nr 2, Bl T58, Scara 1, Et 5, Ap 14; tel: [10] (4021) 211 11 99; email: willcundiff@aol.com Majs William and Sue Cundiff

INSTITUTE FOR OFFICER TRAINING
Russian Federation, 109044 Moscow, Krestiansky Tupik 16/1; tel: [7] (495) 278 0351; fax: [7] (495) 911 2753

SOCIAL SERVICE CENTRES
(Community outreach, HIV/Aids, alcohol, drugs, programmes for homeless)

Georgia
Didi Digomi:
Children's Centre: 35 Giorgi Brtzinsvale

Rustavi:
Youth Centre: Baratashvili St 26

Moldova
Chisinau:
Medical Clinic: Vadului Vodskaya, 100, 2nd Floor; tel: [10] (0422) 57-9325
Mobile Clinic; Project Shoes; Roma Project

Russia
Moscow:
Moscow, Khlebnikov pereulok 7, bld 2, Karl Larsson Centre

Rostov-on-Don:
The Bridge Programme, Lermontovskaya St 229; tel/fax: (8632) 48-2410; email: rostov_doncorps@mail.ru

St Petersburg
Littaini Prospect # 44b, 191104; tel: (812) 273-9297
Chaplaincy Centre: Usst Izhora Village
Medical Clinic
Feeding Programme
Food and Clothing Distribution
Rehabilitation Programme
Shoe Repair Workshop
Home Care Programme
Mobile Canteen: Novoribinskaya St 19

Ukraine
Kiev:
Rehabilitation Centre: Village Zdorovka, Vasilkovsky Region, Pushkinskaya Str #8

Corps-based Services
After-school Programmes; Homeless Children Outreach; Orphan Outreach; Shoe Repair Programme; Gardening Programmes; Deaf Ministry Programmes; Medical Programmes; Haircutting Programmes; Prison Ministry Programmes

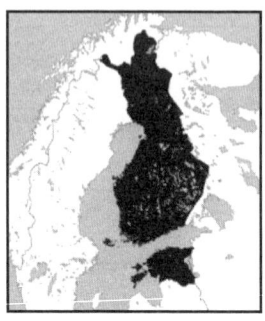

FINLAND AND ESTONIA TERRITORY

Territorial leaders:
Colonels André and Silvia Cox

Territorial Commander:
Colonel André Cox (11 Jul 2005)

Chief Secretary:
Lieut-Colonel Arja Laukkanen (1 Jun 2004)

Territorial Headquarters: Uudenmaankatu 40, 00120 Helsinki

Postal address: Post Box 161, 00121 Helsinki, Finland

Tel address: Pelastusarmeija; tel: [358] (09) 6812300; fax: [358] (09) 601131
email: finland@pelastusarmeija.fi; web site: www.pelastusarmeija.fi

Work in Finland was commenced on 8 November 1889 in Broholm's Riding School, Helsinki, by four aristocratic Finns – Captain and Mrs Constantin Boije with Lieutenants Hedvig von Haartman and Alva Forsius. Within six months Hedvig von Haartman was appointed leader of the work in the country.

Work in Estonia first commenced in 1927 and continued until 1940 when it was closed due to the Second World War. It recommenced in the autumn of 1995 when three Finnish officers were assigned to start the work in Tallinn.

Zone: Europe
Countries included in the territory: Estonia, Finland
'The Salvation Army' in Estonian: Päästearmee; in Finnish: Pelastusarmeija; in Swedish: Frälsningsarmén
Languages in which the gospel is preached: English, Estonian, Finnish, Russian, Swedish
Periodicals: *Krigsropet* (Swedish), *Nappis* (Finnish), *Sotahuuto* (Finnish)

'SHOWERS of Blessing' was the theme of congress meetings led by General John Larsson and Commissioner Freda Larsson in September 2005 and from the outset it was apparent that those present were eagerly anticipating the opportunity to gather around God's word and discover his will. Time and again the mercy seat was lined as people sought the Lord.

These inspirational days were a clear sign from God that his mission for The Salvation Army in Finland and Estonia remains unchanged.

After the congress it was time for the territory's leadership team to meet for its annual conference. Much thought, prayer and discussion centred around the situation within the territory and how to map out the way forward. As a result a first draft of a five-year strategic plan focusing on sustainability and renewal was developed.

The last weekend in October was a time of celebration in Estonia to mark the 10th anniversary of the re-opening of Salvation Army operations in that country. The territory welcomed Commissioners Lawrence R. and Nancy A. Moretz (USA Eastern) to lead the celebrations.

A highlight of this event was the enrolment of five new soldiers from Narva Corps. A history book tracing SA work in Estonia during the years 1927-40 and 1995-2005 was produced and printed in Estonian, Finnish and English.

A further celebration was held in Estonia in April 2006 when the corps project in the town of Võru was officially opened. A sizable number of people gathered to witness this happy event and Blackpool Citadel Band from the UK brought colour and sparkle to the festivities.

For the first time in Finland a Christmas charity concert was organised in support of the Christmas kettle collection. On the first Sunday in December 16 well-known Finnish artists gave their time and talent in support of the collection, which resulted in a 10 per cent increase on the previous year's total.

December also saw the beginning of a new centralised mail appeal to potential donors in an effort to build up a substantial donor database and a modern centralised fundraising system. This should help to provide much-needed financial resources to support many community and social programmes.

STATISTICS
Officers 160 (active 59 retired 101) **Cadets** 8 **Employees** 407

Corps 30 **Outposts** 15 **Goodwill Centres** 4 **Institutions** 28
Senior Soldiers 885 **Adherents** 82 **Junior Soldiers** 29

STAFF
Auxiliary League: Maj Antero Puotiniemi
Candidates: Maj Antero Puotiniemi
Cross-Cultural Mission and Evangelism:
Editor: Jan Jungner
Education: Maj Eija Kornilow
Field: Maj Marja Meras
Finance: Liisa Kaakinen
Home and Family: Maj Camilla Rahkonen
Information: Maj Antero Puotiniemi
Programme:
Property: Maj Pirjo Vallinsalo
Social: Maj Lasse Vallinsalo, Gun-Viv Glad-Jungner
Trade: Lt-Col Irma Salmi
Training: Maj Petter Kornilow
Women's Ministries: Col Silvia Cox (TPWM)
Youth: Lieut Kati Kivestö

SOCIAL SERVICES
Clothing Industry (Recycling Centres)
90580 Oulu, Ratamotie 22; tel: (08) 346713
33540 Tampere, Tursonkatu 3; tel: (03) 3640801
20300 Turku, Virusmäentie 65; tel: (02) 2315447
01260 Vantaa, Itäinen Valkoisenlähteentie 15; tel: (09) 8769572

Homes for Alcoholics
68600 Pietarsaari, Permontie 34; tel: (06) 7236766 (acc 15)
33100 Tampere, Tampereen Valtatie 4; tel: (03) 2235415 (acc 54)
20500 Turku, Hämeenkatu 18; tel: (02) 2329735 (acc 37)

Shelters for Men
15140 Lahti, Hämeenkatu 28; tel: (03) 7827539 (acc 29)
00530 Helsinki, Alppikatu 25; tel: (09) 7743130 (acc 234)
00550 Helsinki, Inarintie 8; tel: (09) 717377 (acc 34)
48100 Kotka, Porthaninkatu 24; tel: (05) 212837 (acc 32)
28120 Pori, Veturitallinkatu 3; tel: (02) 6333519 (acc 25)

Shelters for Women
00530 Helsinki, Papinkuja 1; tel: (09) 7533164 (acc 18)
00530 Helsinki, Castréninkatu 24-26 F 46 (acc 12)
15140 Lahti, Hämeenkatu 28 (acc 10)

Relief Bureaux
Alppikatu 25, 00530 Helsinki; tel: (09) 7532 597
Hämeenkatu 28 B, 15140 Lahti;
   tel: (03) 7823 671
Ratamotie 22, 90580 Oulu; tel: (08) 5564 472
Tursonkatu 3, 33540 Tampere;
   tel: (03) 2124 259
Virusmäentie 65, 20300 Turku;
   tel: (02) 2315 447

Community Centres
Alppikatu 25, 00530 Helsinki;
   tel: (09) 714 013
Permontie 34, 68600 Pietarsaari;
   tel: (06) 7236 766
Vanha Hämeentie 29, 20540 Turku

Social Care Service
00680 Helsinki
68600 Pietarsaari

Children's Day Care Centres
48100 Kotka, Korkeavuorenkatu 24;
   tel: (05) 2108600 (acc 36)
15140 Lahti, Hämeenkatu 28 A 5;
   tel: (03) 7832233 (acc 94)
90140 Oulu, Artturintie 27; tel: (08) 330706
   (acc 30)
06100 Porvoo, Joonaksentie 1;
   tel: (019) 580448 (acc 54)
28100 Pori, Mikonkatu 19; tel: (02) 6332474
   (acc 83)
33100 Tampere, Rongankatu 1;
   tel: (03) 2124648 (acc 29)
95420 Tornio, Putaankatu 2; tel: (016) 445156
   (acc 47)

Children's Home
06100 Porvoo, Aleksanterinkatu 24;
   tel: (019) 580443 (acc 10)
Eventide Homes
02710 Espoo, Viherlaaksonranta 19;
   tel: (09) 590167 (acc 60)
20740 Turku, Sigridinpolku; tel: (02) 2421238
   (acc 25)

Senior Citizens' Unit
00760 Helsinki, Puistolantie 6 (acc 75)

Goodwill Centre
00530 Helsinki, Alppikatu 25; tel: (09) 7532597

Summer Camp Centres
34300 Kuru Vanha Pappila, Tampere
   (acc 30)
03100 Nummela, Helsinki (acc 60)

Students' Hostel
40100 Jyväskylä, Ilmarisenkatu 2 E 86;
   tel: (014) 612 024 (acc 13)

**Care of Domestic Violence Victims
(Hedvig House)**
00530 Helsinki, Castréninkatu 24-26 F;
   tel: (09) 760 328

UNDER THQ
Petra Conference Centre
Pohjoinen Suotie 5, 02700 Kauniainen;
   tel: (09) 5053811; fax: (09) 5054770
   email: petrakur@saunalahti.fi; web site:
   www.pelastusarmeija.fi/petra/english.html

Youth and Conference Centre
Särkijärvi, Särkilammentie 45, 01120
   Västerskog; tel: (09) 8779972; fax: (09)
   8779069;
   email: sarkijku@saunalahti.fi; web site:
   ww.pelastusarmeija.fi/sarkijarvi/english/html

Youth Centre
Sovelontie 91, 33480 Ylöjärvi; tel: (03) 3491010

ESTONIA REGION
Kopli 8-14, 10412 Tallinn; tel: [372] 641 3330;
   fax: [372] 641 3331;
   Regional Leaders: Majs Derek and Helen
   Tyrrell
Corps 3 **Corps Project** 1
Hope House (Lootusemaja): Laevastiku 1a,
   10313 Tallinn; tel: [372] 656 1047 (acc 42)
Lasnamäe Youth and Children's Centre: Pae
   19, 11414 Tallinn; [372] 600 7753
   Camp: Ranna 24, Loksa; tel: [372] 603 1012
Second-Hand Shops: Kadri ja Villu Pood;
   Telliskivi 61, 10412 Tallinn

*Time and again the mercy seat was lined as people sought
the Lord . . . a clear sign from God that his mission for
The Salvation Army in Finland and Estonia remains unchanged*

FRANCE TERRITORY

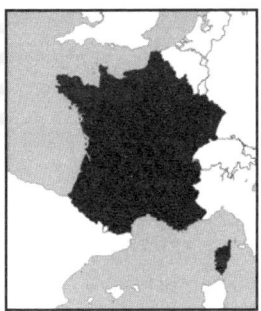

Territorial Commander:
Colonel Alain Duchêne (1 Nov 2006)
Chief Secretary:
Lieut-Colonel Joseph Lukau (1 Nov 2006)

**Territorial Headquarters: 60 rue des Frères Flavien
75976 Paris Cedex 20, France**

tel: [33] (1) 43 62 25 00; fax: [33] (1) 43 62 25 56; web site: www.armeedusalut.fr

Since 'La Maréchale' (eldest daughter of William and Catherine Booth) conducted the Army's first meeting in Paris on Sunday 13 March 1881, Salvationist influence has grown and remarkable social and spiritual results have been achieved. French officers commenced work in Algeria in 1934 and this work was maintained until 1970.

Zone: Europe
Country included in the territory: France
'The Salvation Army' in French: Armée du Salut
Languages in which the gospel is preached: French
Periodicals: *Avec Vous, Le Bulletin de la Ligue du Foyer, Le Fil, Le Magazine, L'Officier, Quand Même*

FIVE years after the creation of the Foundation (administrator of the social institutions) of The Salvation Army in France was a fitting time to take stock of the Army's development in the territory and to redefine the Foundation with regard to its relationship with the Congregation (ecclesiastical entity) in France and the international Salvation Army.

Leaders from the Congregation and the Foundation focused on the spiritual influence the Army can have on people accommodated in its social centres, bearing in mind the diversity of the residents and their problems.

Résidence Leirens, a home in the Alps for elderly people with learning difficulties, set up a programme to help the residents' development and to answer their questions about the meaning of their lives. An increase in the number of socially insecure people led the Foundation to extend soup distribution in Paris beyond the usual winter period.

To meet the needs of lonely people finding it difficult to live independently, the Foundation opened its first social services hotel. It provides individual accommodation within a semi-collective setting and puts the emphasis on friendliness and integration into society.

Keen to develop its activities to help the elderly socially insecure, the Foundation took over an old people's home with 145 places in the Loire region. In Belfort, an emergency centre was set up to respond better to the numerous practical problems of street people.

The Congregation's evangelistic activities are also developing. Sixty young people from the territory took part in the European Youth Congress in Prague (Czech Republic) and the Porteurs de Flambeau (Scouts) played an active part in the organisation of this event. A national coordinating board is encouraging and developing new activities and the exchange of ideas.

Since the territory no longer has divisions, a form of area coordination between corps has been set up, under the responsibility of an officer from one of the corps. This is a means of strengthening ties, sharing skills and promoting joint activities.

A training council has been set up to give a new orientation and dynamic to the In-Service Training Department. Its mission is to give up-to-date reports on the tailored training of candidates and cadets, to respond to requests from active officers and to establish training schemes in line with the overall project defined for the territory. Training courses are also offered to soldiers intending to assume responsibilities within their corps.

STATISTICS

Officers 179 (active 78 retired 101) **Employees** 1,660

Corps 29 **Outposts** 2 **Institutions** 43
Senior Soldiers 914 **Adherents** 168 **Recruits** 23
Junior Soldiers 65
Personnel serving outside territory Officers 10

THE SALVATION ARMY CONGREGATION

BOARD OF DIRECTORS
Col Alaine Duchêne, Maj Daniel Naud,
Maj Patrick Booth, Capt Philippe Schmitter,
Mr Alain Raoul

STAFF
Asst CS: Maj Patrick Booth
Action Espoir: Maj Kelly Pontsler (Territorial Co-ordinator)
Education and Prisons: Maj Jean-Paul Thoni
Field: Maj Daniel Naud
Associate Field Sec: Maj Eliane Naud
Finance: Mr Alain Raoul
Territorial Band: B/M Mrs Arielle Mangeard
Women's Ministries: Lt-Col Angelique Lukau (TPWM) Maj Margaret Booth (TSWM)

THE SALVATION ARMY FOUNDATION

BOARD OF DIRECTORS
President: Col Alain Duchêne
Secretary: Maj Daniel Naud
Treasurer: Mr Armand Laferrere
Members: Mr Jean Benet, Mrs Irène Debu-Carbonnier, Mr Bernard Westercamp

STAFF
Director General: Mr Alain Raoul
Asst Director General – Zone A: Mrs Michelle Samson
Asst Director General – Zone B: Mr Boris Antonoff
Asst Director General – Zone C: Mr Bernard Guilhou
Asst Director General – Zone D: Mrs Christine Le Roy Fiche
Asst Director General – Zone E: Mr Denis Lebaillif
Director of Communications: Mr Christophe Rousselot
Director of Finance: Mrs Martine Dumont
Missing Persons: Maj Anne-Marie Cabanes
Publications: Maj Robert Muller
Volunteers: Maj Dominique Glories

GOODWILL CENTRES
59140 Dunkerque: 1 rue de St Pol; tel: (03) 28 29 09 37
75003 Paris: Centre St Martin, 31 blvd St Martin; tel: (01) 40 27 80 07
75019 Paris: Maison du Partage, 32 rue Bouret; tel: (01) 53 38 41 30

RESIDENCES FOR RETIRED PERSONS

74560 Monnetier-Mornex: Résidence Leirens, Chemin St Georges; tel: (04) 50 31 23 12 (acc disabled 40)

75014 Paris: 9 bis, Villa Coeur-de-Vey; tel: (01) 45 43 38 75

93230 Romainville: 2 rue Vassou; tel: (01) 48 45 12 82

SUMMER COLONY FOR CHILDREN AND YOUTH CENTRE

30530 Chamborigaud: Chausse; tel/fax: (04) 66 61 47 08

SOCIAL SERVICES

* These centres include workshop facilities for the unemployed

Centres for Men

27380 Radepont: Château de Radepont; tel: (02) 32 49 03 82 (acc 73)

*76600 Le Havre: Le Phare, 191 rue de la Vallée; tel: (02) 35 24 22 11 (acc 280)

Annexe: (Atelier de récupération) 32 rue Gustave Nicolle (acc 100)

*59018 Lille Cedex: Les Moulins de l'Espoir, 48 rue de Valenciennes, BP 184; tel: (03) 20 52 69 09 (acc 124)

*69006 Lyon: La Cité de L'Armée du Salut, 131 ave Thiers; tel: (04) 78 52 60 80 (acc men 185 women 60)

*13003 Marseille: 190 rue Félix Pyat; tel: (04) 91 02 49 37 (acc 170)

57100 Thionville: 8 place de la République; tel: (03) 82 83 09 60

*68100 Mulhouse: Le Bon Foyer, 24 rue de L'Ile Napoléon; tel: (03) 89 44 43 56 (acc 60)

*75013 Paris: La Cité de Refuge, 12 rue Cantagrel; tel: (01) 53 61 82 00; including Visitation Dept, Labour Bureau and Clothing Distribution Centre (acc men 51 women 85)

Annexes: 75013 Paris: Centre Espoir, 39-43 rue du Chevaleret (Industrial Branch 'Help through Work' programme) (acc 203)

*76005 Rouen: 26 rue de Crosne; tel: (02) 35 70 38 00 (acc 50)

Annexe: 76150 Maromme, 36 rue Raymond Duflo; tel: (02) 35 76 02 27 (acc 15)

Centre for Women

30900 Nîmes: Les Glycines (home for battered wives), 33 rue de la Bienfaisance; tel: (04) 66 62 21 90 / 66 04 99 49 (acc 25)

75011 Paris: Le Palais de la Femme, 94 rue de Charonne; tel: (01) 46 59 30 00 (acc 644)

Centres for Men and Women

90000 Belfort: 3 rue de l'As de Carreau (acc 50)

74560 Monnetier-Mornex: Holiday Home, Les Hutins; tel: (04) 50 36 59 52 (acc 17)

75020 Paris: Résidence Albin Peyron, 60 rue des Frères Flavien, tel: (01) 48 97 54 50 (acc 400)

78100 St Germain en Laye: La Maison Verte, 14 rue de la Maison Verte; tel: (01) 39 73 29 39 (acc 40)

Centre for Families

94320 Thiais: Résidence Sociale, 7 bd de Stalingrad; tel: (01) 48 53 57 15

Children's Homes

35404 Saint-Malo Cedex:
La Maison des Garçons, 35 ave Eugene Herpin, BP 8; tel: (02) 99 40 21 97 (acc boys 18)

35404 Saint-Malo Cedex : Le Nid, 23 ave Paul Turpin, BP 21;tel: (02) 99 40 21 94 (acc 24)

Convalescent Centre

07800 La Voulte-sur-Rhône: Le Château de St Georges-les-Bains; tel: (04) 75 60 81 72 (acc 50)

Emergency Accommodation

75013 Centre d'accueil d'urgence, 12 rue Cantagrel; tel: (01) 53 61 82 00 (acc 42)

75013 Paris: Palais du Peuple, 29 rue des Cordelières; tel: (01) 43 37 93 61 (acc 220)

75011 Paris: Résidence Catherine Booth, 15 rue Crespin du Gast; tel: (01) 43 14 70 90 (acc 110)

Eventide Homes

60500 Chantilly: L'Arc-en-Ciel, 5 bd de la Libération; tel: (03) 44 57 00 33 (acc 35)

42028 Saint-Etienne Cedex 01 : La Sarrazinière, Allée Amilcare Cipriani, tel 04 77 62 17 92

47400 Tonneins: Le Soleil d'Automne, ave Blanche Peyron, Escoutet; tel: (05) 53 88 32 00 (acc 48)

Mother and Baby Home

75019 Paris: Centre Maternel des Lilas, 9 ave de la Porte des Lilas; tel: (01) 48 03 81 90 (acc mothers 36 babies 45)

Municipal Shelters

(managed by The Salvation Army)

90000 Belfort: Plate-forme d'urgence sociale, 7 rue Colbert; tel (03) 84 21 05 53

*51100 Reims: Le Nouvel Horizon, 10 rue Goïot;
tel: (03) 26 85 23 09 (acc 25)
Annex: 42 rue de Taissy; tel: (03) 26 05 12 08
('Help through Work' programme) (acc 75)

Rehabilitation Centre for Handicapped
45410 Artenay: Château d'Auvilliers;
tel: (02) 38 80 00 14 (acc 42)
93370 Montfermeil: MAS Le Grand Saule,
2 avenue des Tilleuls; tel: (01) 41 70 30 40

Training Centres for Children
67100 Strasbourg-Neudorf: Le Foyer du Jeune
Homme, 42 ave Jean Jaurès;
tel: (03) 88 84 16 50 (acc 42 boys)
Annex: Sora, Sce d'Adaptation en milieu
naturel
77270 Villeparisis: Domaine de Morfondé;
tel: (01) 60 26 61 61 (acc 95)
34091 Montpellier Cedex: Institut Nazareth,

13 rue de Nazareth, BP 24105;
tel: (0) 4 99 58 21 21; fax: (0) 4 99 58 21 12

Children's Day Care Centres
30000 Nîmes: Aire du Lycéen, 4/6 bd Victor
Hugo; tel: (04) 66 21 02 88
81200 Mazamet: Centre En Avant, 7 rue du Curé
Pous; tel/fax: (05) 63 61 12 30
43400 Le Chambon sur Lignon: Le Bivouac,
7 rue Neuve: tel: (04) 71 59 70 87
69007 Lyon: L'Arche de Noé, 5 rue Félissent;
tel (04) 78 58 29 66

Training Centres
68200 Mulhouse: Marie-Pascale Péan,
35 ave de Colmar; tel: (03) 89 42 14 77
(acc 26)
30000 Nîmes: La Villa Blanche Peyron, 122
Impasse Calmette; tel: (04) 66 04 99 40
(acc 18)

French Salvationists have open hearts for people of different nationalities and cultures. Below, the young people's sergeant-major of Paris Nation Corps clearly shows his care for a small African boy.

There are many people who offer to do voluntary work for The Salvation Army. In France the Army uses more than 1,000 volunteers for various kinds of duties. Above, a volunteer links up with the corps in Toulouse, where free breakfast is supplied for 60 to 80 people every morning.

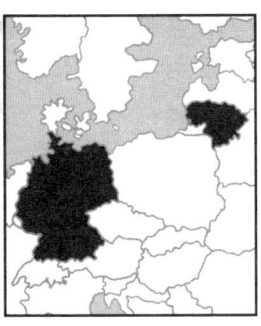

GERMANY AND LITHUANIA TERRITORY

Territorial leaders:
Colonels Horst and Helga Charlet

Territorial Commander:
Colonel Horst Charlet (12 Jun 2005)

Chief Secretary:
Lieut-Colonel Odd Berg (12 Jun 2005)

Territorial Headquarters: 50677 Köln, Salierring 23-27, Germany

tel: [49] (221) 20 8190; fax: [49] (221) 208 1957; email: NHQ@GER.salvationarmy.org;
web site: www.heilsarmee.de

Salvation Army work in Germany began in Stuttgart on 14 November 1886 through the persistent sale of the Swiss *Kriegsruf* by Staff-Captain Fritz Schaaf who, after being converted in New York, was stationed in Switzerland and could not resist the call to bring the message over the border into his fatherland.

The Salvation Army was first registered as a limited company in Berlin in 1897 and was recognised throughout Germany as a church and public corporation on 10 October 1967 by law in Nordrhein-Westfalen. It is recognised as a religious association with public rights in the states of Berlin, Hessen, Schleswig-Holstein and Baden-Württemberg.

Salvation Army work in Lithuania having begun in 1998, the Germany Territory was redesignated the Germany and Lithuania Territory in September 2005.

Zone: Europe
Countries included in the territory: Germany, Lithuania
'The Salvation Army' in German: Die Heilsarmee; in Lithuanian: Isganymo Armija
Language in which the gospel is preached: German, Lithuanian
Periodicals: *Danke, Der Kriegsruf, Heilsarmee-Forum*

A CHANGE of leadership saw Colonel Horst Charlet become the first German-born territorial commander for more than 70 years. Succeeding Commissioners Werner and Paula Frei, who retired from active service, Colonels Horst and Helga Charlet were installed by Commissioners Willem and Netty van der Harst (The Netherlands and Czech Republic), along with the new Chief Secretary (Lieut-Colonel Odd Berg) and Lieut-Colonel Grethe Berg.

In November 2005 International Headquarters gave official recognition of The Salvation Army's ministry in Lithuania, work having been first registered in that country in 1998. Things are going well but there are many needs in the country and more could be done if personnel and resources were available.

As well as the congregations which gather in the Army hall in Klaipeda there is a congregation of about 70 people at a rubbish dump, where meetings are held in the summertime. They are among the many poor people who live and work there, collecting things from the dump to sell in order to stay alive. Salvationists are regularly at the dump distributing provisions.

Young people's work featured strongly during '2005 – A Year for Children and Youth'. The name MCTurtle © was copyrighted during the year for a special work among children in Chemnitz. A large lorry, purpose-built with a stage, travelled around the suburbs attracting young people who eagerly watched as youth workers presented the gospel through drama, music, dance and words.

Young people in Klaipeda, Lithuania, rehearsed a musical titled *Friends* and performed it to a capacity audience. The musical was also transmitted via the internet.

In Naumburg, in former East Germany, the corps attracted around 600 visitors when it gave three performances of a Christmas musical. Also at Christmas 600 underprivileged, elderly and lonely people were guests of the corps in Hamburg for seasonal hospitality.

The media has shown considerable interest in The Salvation Army in Germany. One of the TV stations featured Kassel Corps and followed the corps leader during a whole week.

The Army in Germany and Lithuania entered 2006 with the strategy slogan *Beten, Planen, Handeln!* – which translates as 'Pray, Plan, Act!'

STATISTICS
Officers 159 (active 92 retired 67) **Cadets** 4 **Lieutenants** 7 **Employees** 730

Corps 48 **Outposts** 11 **Institutions** 41 **Senior Soldiers** 1,062 **Adherents** 413 **Junior Soldiers** 74

STAFF
Candidates and Training: Maj Marsha Bowles
Editor: Capt Alfred Preuß
Evangelisation and Field Programme:
Finance: Mr Hans Joachim Bode
  Asst Finance: Capt Hartmut Leisinger
Property: Mr Wilfried Otterbach
Public Relations and Fund-raising:
Social: Maj Frank Honsberg
Trade: Capt Elinor Lauer
Women's Ministries: Col Helga Charlet
  (TPWM) Lt-Col Grethe Berg (TSWM)
Youth: Maj David Bowles

DIVISIONS
East: 12159 Berlin, Fregestr 13/14;
  tel: (0)30-859 8890; fax: (0)30-859 889 99;
  email: DHQ_Ost@GER.salvationarmy.org;
  Maj Beat Rieder
North: 20359 Hamburg, Talstr 15;
  tel: (0)40-31 3405; fax: (0)40-317 2452;
  email: DHQ_Nord@GER.salvationarmy.org;
  Maj Rudolf Schollmeier
South: 70178 Stuttgart, Rotebühlstr 117;
  tel: (0)711-61 66 27; fax: (0)711-62 84 59;
  email: DHQ_Sued@GER.salvationarmy.org;
  Maj Fernanda van Houdt
West: 50858 Köln, Aachenerstr 1017-1019;
  tel: (0)221-48 63 04; fax: (0)221-48 82 88;
  email: DHQ_West@GER.salvationarmy.org;
  Maj Massimo Tursi

INVESTIGATION
Heckerstr 85, 34121 Kassel;
  tel: (0) 561 2889945; fax: (0) 561 2889946;
  email: Suchdienst@GER.salvationarmy.org;
  Lt-Col Erika Siebel

SENIOR CITIZENS' RESIDENCES
12159 Berlin, Dickhardtstr 52-53;
  tel: (0)30-8 51 57 90 (acc apts 42)
45127 Essen, Hoffnungsstr 23;
  tel: (0)201-22 47 71 (acc apts 25)
44623 Herne, Koppenbergshof 2;
  tel: (0)2323-2 22 47 (acc apts 5 flats 9)
50858 Köln, Rosenweg 1-5;
  tel: (0)221-280 8979 (acc apts 42)
68159 Mannheim, G3, 1 + 20;
  tel: (0)621-2 5361 (acc apts 31)
68165 Mannheim, Augartenstr 43, Haus Marie Engelhardt; tel: (0)621-44 27 28
  (acc apts 19)

75175 Pforzheim, Pflügerstr 37-43;
tel: (0)7231-6 56 14 (acc apts 30)

SOCIAL SERVICES
Counselling
79106 Freiburg, Lehenerstr 115;
tel: (0)761-89 44 92; fax (0)761-500 99 98;
email FreiburgSBW@GER.salvationarmy.org

20359 Hamburg, Counselling Centre, Talstr 11;
tel: (0)40-31 65 43

22117 Hamburg, Counselling for Alcoholics and
Rehabilitation Work, Oststeinbekerweg 2-4;
tel: (0)40-713 65 64; fax: (0)40-713 44 37;
email HamburgParkln@GER.salvationarmy.org

21073 Hamburg, Counselling for Homeless, Zur
Seehafenbrücke 20; tel: (0)40-309 53 60

Children's Day Nursery
12159 Berlin, Fregestr 13-14;
tel: (0)30-850 72920 (acc 30)

Drop-in Cafés
79098 Freiburg, Löwenstr 1;
tel: (0)761-38 54616; fax: (0)761-38 546 22

22453 Hamburg, Borsteler Chaussee 23;
tel: (0)40-514 314 33; fax: (0)40-514 314 14

90443 Nürnberg, Leonhardtstr 28;
tel: (0)911-28 73 156

Hostels
60314 Frankfurt, Windeckstr 58-60;
tel: (0)69-43 22 52 (acc 80)

73033 Göppingen, Markstr 58;
tel: (0)7161-7 42 17; fax: (0)7161-7 28 10
(acc 35)

37073 Göttingen, Untere Maschstr 13b;
tel: (0)551-4 24 84; fax: (0)551-5 31 14 22
(acc 30)

23552 Lübeck, Engelsgrube 62-64;
tel: (0)451-7 33 94; fax: (0)451-7 23 86
(acc 37)

80469 München, Pestalozzistr 36;
tel: (0)89-26 71 49; fax: (0)89-26 35 26
(acc 56+26)

70176 Stuttgart, Silberburgstr 139;
tel: (0)711-61 09 67/68; fax: (0)711-61 33 00
(acc 55)

65189 Wiesbaden, Schwarzenbergstr 7;
tel: (0)611-70 12 68; fax: (0)0611-71 40 21
(acc 191)

Nursing Homes
14163 Berlin, Goethestr 17-21;
tel: (0)30-3289000; fax: (0)30-32890022
(acc 51)

47805 Krefeld, Voltastr 50; tel: (0)2151-93 72 60;
fax: (0)2151-93 72626 (acc 65)

14532 Stahnsdorf, 'Florencehort', Potsdamer
Damm 12; tel: (0)3329-69 14 30;
fax: (0)3329-69 14 44 (acc 65)

Therapeutic Rehabilitation Institutions
14197 Berlin, Hanauerstr 63; tel: (0)30-8 20 08 40;
fax: (0)30-8 20 08 430 (acc 60)

22453 Hamburg, Borsteler Chaussee 23;
tel: (0)40-514 314 0; fax: (0)40-514 314 14
(acc 71)

34123 Kassel, Eisenacherstr 18;
tel: (0)561-570 35 90; fax: (0)561-570 359 22
(acc 80)

34123 Kassel-Lüderitzstr 13; tel: (0)561-40 46 78
(acc 8)

50825 Köln, Marienstr 116/118;
tel: (0)221-955 6090; fax: (0)221-5595 482
(acc 80)

90443 Nürnberg, Gostenhofer Hauptstr 47-49;
tel/fax: (0)911-28 730 (acc 239, including
therapeutic workshops and facilities for
alcoholics and elderly men)

Therapeutic Workshops
22453 Hamburg, Borsteler Chaussee 23;
tel: (0)40-514 314 35; fax: (0) 40-514 314 14

90443 Nürnberg, Leonhardstr 17-21;
tel: (0)911 28730

Women's Hostels
34134 Kassel-Niederzwehren, Am
Donarbrunnen 32; tel: (0)561-43113 (acc 7)

90443 Nürnberg, Gostenhofer Hauptstr 65;
tel: (0)911-272 3600 (acc 12)

65197 Wiesbaden, Königsteinerstr 24;
tel: (0)611-80 67 58; fax: (0)611-981 23 03
(acc 45)

CONFERENCE AND HOLIDAY CENTRE
24306 Plön, Seehof, Steinberg 3-4;
tel: (0)4522-5088200; fax: (0)4522-5088202;
email: seehof@heilsarmee.de
Conference and Holiday Home (acc 75 + 26)
Youth Camp (acc 50) Camping ground and
4 holiday chalets

LITHUANIA
Isganymo Armija, Tiltu 18, LT 91246 Klaipeda;
tel/fax: [00370] 46-310634;
email: klaipeda@isganymo-armija.org;
Capt Susanne Kettler-Riutkenen

GHANA TERRITORY

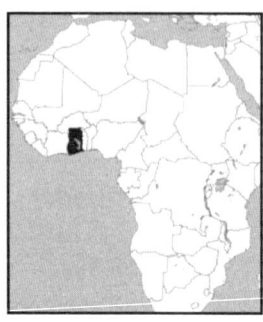

Territorial leaders:
Colonels Graeme and Anne Harding

Territorial Commander:
Colonel Graeme Harding (15 May 2003)

Chief Secretary:
Lieut-Colonel Peter Dali (1 Dec 2004)

Territorial Headquarters: PO Box CT 452 Cantonments, Accra, Ghana

tel: [233] (21) 776 971/763 403; fax: [233] (21) 772 695; email: saghana@gha.salvationarmy.org

Salvation Army operations began in Ghana in 1922 when Lieutenant King Hudson was commissioned to 'open fire' in his home town of Duakwa. Ensign and Mrs Charles Roberts were also appointed to pioneer work in Accra.

Zone: Africa
Country included in the territory: Ghana
'The Salvation Army' in Ga: Yiwalaheremo Asrafoi Le; in Fanti and Twi: Nkwagye Dom Asraafo; in Ewe: Agbexoxo Srafa Ha La
Languages in which the gospel is preached: Bassa, Builsa, Dangme, English, Ewe, Fante, Frafra, Ga, Gola, Grushia, Twi
Periodical: *Salvationist Newsletter*

IN response to the 2005 emphasis on young people, the territory convened a number of events which promoted mission to young people and youth capacity development. Five young people from the USA Eastern Territory, members of the Hands On Mission Team, spent seven weeks in Ghana taking part in youth and children's programmes in corps and societies, and assisting in various Salvation Army clinics. The team also participated in the territory's first Students Fellowship Convention.

In addition to the Americans' visit, the territory hosted 13 young people – from Kenya, South Africa, Mozambique, Nigeria, Liberia and Ghana itself – as part of the Frontier programme designed to enable young people to be trained for youth capacity development programmes.

With a view to territorial expansion, a Togolese officer was sent to Togo to explore the possibility of establishing Salvation Army work in that country. His findings indicate that prospects are good, having returned with a report of 123 converts being registered, 25 soldiers unexpectedly in place and, with the support of two local chiefs, a promise of land. With generally open borders away from main routes, the migration of existing soldiery to other areas is common.

Following the establishment of a

People Trafficking Task Force, under the Women's Ministries Department, the territory embarked on a programme of trafficking awareness. There has also been constructive dialogue with the Minister for Women and Children, leading to The Salvation Army's participation, with other stakeholders, in formulating a strategy to address issues related to the Human Trafficking Act (368) of 2005.

In the area of medical and social services, work related to HIV/Aids has been extended to include voluntary counselling and testing in communities beyond the immediate location of the territory's 11 clinics. Follow-up outreach service is also given.

Women's ministries have been extended through the inauguration of young women's fellowship groups, enabling older girls, from secondary school-age upwards, to have their own group. This innovation is proving beneficial for improving the work among the young women and girls in the Junior Home League.

A link has been established with Computers for Schools, a Canadian organisation which has provided refurbished computers for use in Salvation Army schools. This development has enlarged the scope of subjects taught and the facilities available, and there is agreement on a wider distribution to vocational training centres which operate under the umbrella of the Medical and Social Services Department.

Further assistance for schools has been supported by the Sweden One-Day project, through which three more schools have been built and handed over to the territory.

STATISTICS
Officers 238 (active 192 retired 46) **Cadets** 5 **Employees** 1,415
Corps 100 **Societies** 144 **Schools** 206 **Pupils** 19,482 **Clinics** 9 **Social Centres** 8 **Day Care Centres** 90
Senior Soldiers 16,671 **Junior Soldiers** 3,347

STAFF
Business Administration: Maj Samuel Amponsah
Communications and External Relations: Mr Kofi Sakyiamah
Editor: Capt Stephen Borbor
Extension Training: Maj Joseph Owusu-Mensah
Finance:
Medical, Social and Community Services: Maj Wendy Leavey
Personnel: Maj Mike Adu-Manu
Programme: Lt-Col William Gyimah
Projects and Child Sponsorship: Major Mavis Mackereth
Property: Maj Raymond Mackereth
Schools: Mr James B. Maison
Territorial Band: B/M Emmanuel Hackman
Trade: Capt Moses Turay
Training: Maj Magda Iversen
Women's Ministries: Col Anne Harding (TPWM) Lt-Col Jessica Dali (TSWM) Lt-Col Mary Gyimah (Women's Development & Training) Capt Mary Adu Gyan (TJHLS)
Youth and Candidates: Maj Isaac Danso

DIVISIONS
Accra: PO Box 166 Tema; tel: (022) 215 530; Maj Seth Appeateng
Akim Central: PO Box AS 283, Asamankese; tel: (081) 23 585; Maj Peter Oduro-Amoah
Ashanti Central: PO Box 15, Kumasi; tel/fax: (051) 240 16; Maj Samuel Baah
Ashanti North: c/o PO Box 14, Wiamoase, Ashanti; Maj Richmond Obeng-Appau
Central: PO Box 62, Agona Swedru; tel: (041) 20 285; Maj Godfried Oduro
Nkawkaw: PO Box 3, Nkawkaw; tel: (0842) 22 208; Maj Edward Addison
West Akim: PO Box 188, Akim Oda; tel: (0882) 2 305; Maj Isaac Danso

DISTRICTS

Brong Ahafo: PO Box 1454, Sunyani;
tel: (061) 23 513; Maj Edward Kyei
East Akim: PO Box KF 1218, Koforidua E/R;
tel: (081) 22 580; Maj Stephen Boadu
Northern: PO Box 233, Bolgatanga;
tel: (072) 22 030; Maj Ebenezer Danquah
Volta: PO Box 604, Ho, Volta Region;
Capt Rockson Oduro
Western: PO Box 178, Sekondi, C/R;
tel: (031) 23 763; Maj Seth Larbi

TRAINING COLLEGE

PO Box CE 11991, Tema; tel: (022) 306 252/
306 253

EXTENSION TRAINING CENTRE

PO Box CT 452, Cantonments, Accra;
tel: (021) 776 971; fax: (021) 772 695

CLINICS

Accra Urban Aid: PO Box CT 452,
Cantonments, Accra; tel: (021) 230 918
(acc incl maternity 11)
Accra Urban Aid Outreach: PO Box CT 452,
Cantonments, Accra; tel: (021) 246 764
(mobile outreach for street children)
Adaklu-Sofa: PO Box 604, Ho, V/R (acc incl
maternity 4)
Anum: PO Box 17, Senchi, E/R (acc incl
maternity 11)
Ba: PO Box 8, Ba, C/R (acc incl maternity 4)
Begoro: PO Box 10, Begoro, E/R (acc incl
maternity 10)

Duakwa: PO Box 2, Agona Duakwa, C/R
(acc incl maternity 30)
Wenchi: PO Box 5, Wenchi, Akim Oda
(acc incl maternity 8)
Wiamoase: PO Box 14, Wiamoase, Ashanti;
tel: (051) 32 613

EDUCATION

Sub-primary: 80
Primary schools: 89
Junior Secondary Schools: 35
Senior Secondary Schools: 2

SOCIAL WORK

Adaklu-Sofa Vocational Training Centre:
PO Box 604, Ho, V/R
Anidasofie Street Girls Training Centre:
PO Box CT 452, Cantonments, Accra;
tel: (021) 246 764
Begoro Rehabilitation Centre: PO Box 10,
Begoro, E/R
Child Care Training Centre: PO Box 8,
Ba, C/R
Community Rehabilitation Project:
PO Box 2, Agona Duakwa
Malnutrition Centre: PO Box 2, Agona
Duakwa, C/R
Rehabilitation Centre: PO Box 14, Wiamoase,
Ashanti
Voluntary Counselling and Testing Centre:
PO Box CT 452, Cantonments, Accra;
tel: (021) 776 971

Salvationists of Ashanti Central Division visit Kumasi Prison to hand over food, soap and other useful items for the prisoners. The chaplain expressed thanks to The Salvation Army on behalf of the director general and prison staff.

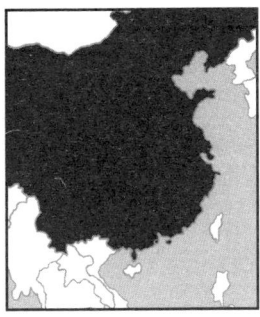

HONG KONG AND MACAU COMMAND

Officer Commanding:
Lieut-Colonel Alfred Tsang Hing-man
(1 Feb 2005)

General Secretary:
Lieut-Colonel Merv Rowland (1 Feb 2005)

Command Headquarters: 11 Wing Sing Lane, Yaumatei, Kowloon, Hong Kong

Postal address: PO Box 70129, Kowloon Central Post Office, Kowloon, Hong Kong

tel: [852] 2332 4531; fax: [852] 2771 6439; email: Hongkong@hkt.salvationarmy.org;

web site: www.salvation.org.hk

In March 1930, at a meeting held at Government House, Hong Kong, The Salvation Army was requested to undertake women's work in the crown colony, a work pioneered by Majors Dorothy Brazier and Doris Lemon. This work was directed from Peking until, in 1935, the South China Command was established in Canton to promote wide evangelistic and welfare operations. In 1939 Hong Kong became the Army's administrative centre. Later, the inclusion of the New Territories determined that the Command Headquarters move to Kowloon. Since 1951 the General of The Salvation Army has been recognised as a Corporation Sole. From 1993, disaster relief and community development projects have been carried out in mainland China. In 1999, a pioneer officer was appointed to the Special Administrative Region of Macau and Salvation Army work began there officially on 25 March 2000. In 2001, an officer was appointed to the North/North Eastern Project Office in Beijing.

Zone: South Pacific and East Asia
Regions included in the command: Hong Kong and Macau (Special Administrative Regions of the People's Republic of China) and Mainland China
'The Salvation Army' in Cantonese: Kau Sai Kwan; in Putonghua: Jiu Shi Jun
Languages in which the gospel is preached: Cantonese, English, Filipino, Putonghua
Periodicals: *Army Scene, The War Cry*

THE command's 75th anniversary was highlighted by the visit of General John Larsson and Commisssioner Freda Larsson. The year 2005 also marked 50 years of officer training, celebrated during commissioning weekend. Two cadets from mainland China were commissioned as officers and the mother of a newly commissioned captain received her third Fellowship of the Silver Star badge.

Congress activities included a youth rally with the General and a women's rally addressed by Commissioner Larsson. Sunday was a day of great blessing as Salvationists united for worship. Many responded publicly to the General's message. The afternoon was a 75th anniversary celebration, the theme 'From a Rich Past to a Brighter Future' giving corps and centres opportunity to participate in historical and cultural items.

Two encouraging visits with potential

119

for future support for The Salvation Army in Hong Kong and China were made by the General – to the Chief Executive of the Hong Kong Government and the Commissioner of the Ministry of Foreign Affairs.

The General officially opened a poolside restaurant where young people with disabilities are given training in food handling with a view to future employment. A civic dinner sponsored by the Salvation Army advisory board chairman honoured the General's visit.

At an event marking the end of '2005 – A Year for Children and Youth' the special guest from IHQ was Commissioner Judith Houghton (then Resource Coordinator for the Year for Children and Youth). Young people from corps, schools and social centres presented an exciting programme.

STATISTICS

Officers 53 (active 44 retired 9) **Cadets** (2nd Yr) 2 (1st Year) 3 **Employees** 2,299

Corps 19 **Outposts** 1 **Institutions** 20 **Schools** 7 **Kindergartens** 7 **Nursery Schools** 17 **Social Centres** 50 **Hotel** 1

Senior Soldiers 1,999 **Adherents** 40 **Junior Soldiers** 433

Personnel serving outside command Officers 4 Envoys 1

STAFF

Asst to General Secretary: Maj On Dieu Quang
China Development: Ms Puisi Chan
Community Relations: Maj Simon Tso Kam-shing
Corporate Administrator: Ms Hilda Lam
Editor/Literary: Maj David Ip Kam-yuen
Educational Services: Maj Jim Weymouth
Emergency Services Coordinators: Mr Dick Chan and Ms Karen Ng Wai-sze
Finance: Ms Idy Lam Mei-lan
Human Resources: Ms Eva Lau
Property: Envoy Daniel Hui Wah-lun
Social: Mrs Victoria Kwok Yuen Wai-yee
Trade: Ms Karen Ng Wai-sze

Training: Maj Marion Weymouth
Women's Ministries: Lt-Col Elaine Rowland (CPWM)
Youth and Candidates: Maj Tommy Chan Hi-wai

DIVISION

1/F, 6-8 Salvation Army St, Wanchai, HK; tel: 2591 4488; fax: 2332 3545; Maj Tony Ma Yeung-mo

TRAINING COLLEGE

6/F, 11 Wing Sing Lane, Yaumatei, Kln, PO Box 70129, Kowloon Central PO, Kln, HK; tel: 2783 2305; fax: 2332 9221; email: otc@tc.salvationarmy.org.hk

CHINA DEVELOPMENT

Hong Kong Head Office: tel: (852) 2783 2288; fax: (852) 2385 7823; Assistant: Major Yoo Mi-hae, tel: (852) 2359 9820
email: cdd@hkt.salvationarmy.org
North/Northeast Regional Project Office – China: D-102 Jin Mao Apartment, 2 Guang Hua Lane, Chao Yang District, Beijing 100020, China; tel: [86] (10) 6586 9331; fax: [86] (10) 6586 8382;
email: nnerpo@hkt.salvationarmy.org
Southwest Regional Project Office – China: 6D, Unit 1, Block 8, Northern District, Yin Hai Hot Spring Garden, 173 Guan Xing Rd, Guan Shang, Kunming 650200, Yunnan, China; tel: [86] (871) 7166 111; fax: [86] (871) 7155 222;
email: swrpo@hkt.salvationarmy.org
Xinghe Project Office – China: Rm 520, Xinghe Municipal Government Bldg, Xinghe, 013650 Inner Mongolia, China;
tel/fax: (86) 474 7212 010;
email: xho@hkt.salvationarmy.org

EDUCATIONAL SERVICES
Kindergartens

Chan Kwan Tung: G/F and 1/F, 11 Wing Sing Lane, Yaumatei, Kln; tel: 2384 7831; fax: 2388 5310 (acc 316; 2 sessions)
Fu Keung: Units 121-140, G/F, Fu Keung House, (Block 6), Tai Wo Hau Estate, NT; tel: 2614 4481; fax: 2439 0666 (acc 360; 2 sessions)
Hing Yan: G/F, Commercial Centre, Area 41, Hau Tak Estate, Tseung Kwan O, Kln; tel: 2706 6222; fax: 2704 9262 (acc 432; 2 sessions)
Ng Kwok Wai Memorial: 22-30 Hoi Shing Rd,

Clague Garden Estate, Tsuen Wan, NT;
tel: 2499 7639; fax: 2414 9214
(acc 360; 2 sessions)

Ping Tin: G/F, Ping Shing House, Ping Tin
Estate, Lam Tin, Kln; tel: 2775 5332;
fax: 2775 5412 (acc 270; 2 sessions) plus
Nursery (acc 28; 2 sessions)

Ping Tin Playgroup: G/F, Ping Shing House,
Ping Tin Estate, Lam Tin, Kln; tel: 2775 5332;
fax: 2775 5412 (acc 34; 2 sessions)

Tin Ka Ping: 15 Jat Min Chuen St, Shatin, NT;
tel: 2647 4227; fax: 2645 1869 (acc 674;
2 sessions)

Crèches 1 Month-2 Years

North Point: Podium Level 2, Healthy Village,
6 Healthy St Central North Point, HK;
tel: 2856 0892 (acc 28 full-day)

Pak Tin: G/F, Wing C, Fu Tin House, Pak Tin
Estate, Shamshuipo, Kln; tel: 2778 3588
(acc 16 full-day)

Nursery Schools 2-6 Years

Catherine Booth: 2/F, 11 Wing Sing Lane,
Yaumatei, Kln: tel: 2332 7963 (acc 110 full-day)

Hoi Fu: G/F, Wing B & C, Hoi Ning House,
Hoi Fu Court, Mongkok, Kln; tel: 2148 2477
(acc 112 full-day)

Jat Min: 1/F, 15 Jat Min Chuen St, Jat Min Chuen,
Shatin, NT; tel: 2647 4897 (acc 168 full-day)

Kam Tin: G/F 103 Kam Tin Rd, Yuen Long,
NT; tel: 2442 3606 (acc 100 full-day)

Lai Chi Kok: 1/F, Prosperity Court, 168 Lai Chi
Kok Rd, Mongkok, Kln; tel: 2787 5788 (acc
100 full-day)

Lei Muk Shue: G/F, Wing B & C, Yeung Shue
House, Lei Muk Shue Estate, Kwai Chung,
NT; tel: 2420 2491 (acc 112 full-day)

Lok Man: 1/F, Block H, Lok Man Sun Chuen,
Hunghom, Kln; tel: 2365 1994
(acc 145 full-day)

Ming Tak: G/F, Wing B & C, Hin Ming Court,
Tseung Kwan O, Kln; tel: 2623 7555
(acc 126 full-day)

North Point: Podium Level 2, Healthy Village,
6 Healthy St Central North Point, HK;
tel: 2856 0892 (acc 28 full-day)

Pak Tin: G/F, Wing C, Fu Tin House, Pak Tin
Estate, Shamshuipo, Kln; tel: 2778 3588
(acc 90 full-day)

Sam Shing: G/F, Adjacent to Moon Yu House,
Sam Shing Estate, Tuen Mun, NT;
tel: 2452 0032 (acc 100 full-day)

Tai Wo Hau: Unit 221-232 Fu Keung House,
Tai Wo Hau Estate, Tsuen Wan, NT;
tel: 2614 7662 (acc 126 full-day)

Tai Yuen: G/F, Tai Ling House, Tai Yuen
Estate, Tai Po, NT; tel: 2664 9725
(acc 100 full-day)

Tin Ping: G/F, Units 106-110, Wing B, Tin Hor
House, Tin Ping Estate, Sheung Shui, NT;
tel: 2671 9972 (acc 112 full-day)

Tsuen Wan: 1/F, Clague Garden Estate, 22 Hoi
Shing Rd, Tsuen Wan, NT;
tel: 2417 1400 (acc 182 full-day)

Wah Fu: 1/F-2/F, Wah Sang House, Wah Fu
Estate, HK; tel: 2551 6341 (acc 126 full-day)

Wo Che: G/F, Tak Wo House, Wo Che Estate,
Shatin, NT; tel: 2604 0428 (acc 168 full-day)

Primary Schools

Ann Wyllie Memorial: 100 Shing Tai Rd, Heng
Fa Chuen, HK; tel: 2558 2111; fax: 2898 4377
(acc 1,536; 2 sessions)

Lam Butt Chung Memorial: Yat Tung Estate,
Tung Chung, Lantau, NT;
tel: 2109 0328; fax: 2109 0223 (acc 960)

Sam Shing Chuen Lau Ng Ying: Sam Shing
Estate, Tuen Mun, NT; tel: 2458 8035;
fax: 2618 3171 (acc 792)

Tin Ka Ping: Pok Hong Estate, Shatin, NT;
tel: 2648 9283; fax: 2649 4305 (acc 768)

Secondary School

William Booth Secondary School, 100 Yuk Wah
St, Tsz Wan Shan, Kln; tel: 2326 9068;
fax: 2328 0052 (acc 1,120)

Special School

Shek Wu School, Area 8 Jockey Club Rd, Shek
Wu, Sheung Shui, NT; tel: 2670 0800;
fax: 2668 5353 (acc 200)

GUEST ACCOMMODATION

Booth Lodge, 7/F, 11 Wing Sing Lane,
Yaumatei, Kln; tel: (852) 2771 9266;
fax: (852) 2385 1140;
email: boothlodge@salvationarmy.org.hk

RECYCLING PROGRAMME

7/F Tat Ming Industrial Bldg, 44-52 Ta Chuen
Ping St, Kwai Chung, NT; tel: 2332 4433;
fax: 2332 4411; email: Recycling@hkt.salva-
tionarmy.org

Family Stores

Warehouse: 7/F Tat Ming Industrial Bldg, 44-52
Ta Chuen Ping St, Kwai Chung, NT;
tel: 2489 8833; fax: 2332 4411

Chuk Yuen Store: Shop S202, 3/F, Chuk Yuen
Shopping Centre, Chuk Yuen (South) Estate,
Wong Tai Sin, Kln; tel: 2320 0050

Kwun Tong Store: No 237, G/F, Hay Cheuk

Lau, Garden Estate, Kwun Tong, Kln;
tel: 2331 2577

Mongkok Store: Shop 1, G/F Xing Hua Ctr, 433
Shanghai St, Mongkok, Kln; tel: 3422 3205

Shek Wai Kok Store: Shop 331, Shek Wai Kok
Shopping Centre, Shek Wai Kok Estate, Tsuen
Wan, NT; tel: 2499 8981

Stanley Store: G/F, 98 Stanley Main St, HK;
tel: 3197 0070

Tai Hang Tung Store: G/F, 1 Lung Chu St, Tai
Hang Tung, Kln; tel: 2784 0689

Tin Hau Store: G/F, 29 Wing Hing St, Tin Hau,
HK; tel: 2887 5577

Wanchai Store: G/F, 31 Wood Rd, Wanchai,
HK; tel: 2572 2879

Yaumatei Store: G/F, 1A Cliff Rd, Yaumatei,
Kln; tel: 2332 4448

Yue Wan Store: Shop 29-30, Yue On House,
Yue Wan Estate, Chaiwan, HK; tel: 2558 8655

SOCIAL WORK
Camps
Bradbury: 6 Ming Fai Rd, Cheung Chau Island,
HK; tel: 2981 0358 (acc 108)

Ma Wan: Ma Wan Island, HK: tel: 2986 5244
(acc 40)

Children and Youth Centres
Chuk Yuen: 2-4F, Chuk Yuen Estate
Community Centre, Chuk Yuen (South)
Estate, Kln; tel: 2351 5321

Lung Hang: G/F, Sin Sum House, Lung Hang
Estate, Shatin, NT; tel: 2605 5569

Tai Wo Hau: 2-4F, Tai Wo Hau Estate
Community Centre, Tsuen Wan, NT;
tel: 2428 4581

Integrated Service for Young People
Chaiwan: Podium Level Market Bldg, Wan Tsui
Est, Chaiwan, HK; tel: 2898 9750

Tuen Mun: G/F, 13-24 Hing Ping House, Tai
Hing Est, Tuen Mun, NT; tel: 2461 4741

Tuen Mun East: 5/F Ancillary Facilities Block,
Fu Tai Estate, No 9 Tuen Kwai Rd, Tuen
Mun, NT; tel: 2467 7200

Tai Po: 2/F, Tai Man House, Tai Yuen Estate,
Tai Po, NT; tel: 2667 2913

Yaumatei: 1/F, Block 4, Prosperous Garden,
3 Public Square St, Kln; tel: 2770 8933

Community Development Projects
Ngau Tam Mei: Library, Yau Tam Mei School,
Yau Tam Mei Village, Yuen Long, NT;
tel: 2482 7175

Sam Mun Tsai: 31 Chim Uk Village, Shuen
Wan, Tai Po, NT; tel: 2660 9890

Urban Renewal Social Service Team
Tai Kok Tsui: G/F, Bedford Tower, 68-72
Bedford Rd, Tai Kok Tsui, Kln;
tel: 2391 6733

Shaukeiwan: Flat C, 15/F Eastern Commercial Ctr,
83 Nam On St, Shaukeiwan, HK;
tel: 2839 7142

Education and Development Centre
6 Salvation Army St, Wanchai, HK;
tel: 2572 6718

Youth Pre-employment Training Project
6 Salvation Army St, Wanchai, HK;
tel: 2771 6652

Tuen Mun Services for Young Night
Drifters
5/F Ancillary Facilities Block, Fu Tai Estate,
No 9 Tuen Kwai Rd, Tuen Mun, NT;
tel: 2467 7200

Integrated Services for Street Sleepers
1/F, GIC Bldg, 345A Shanghai St, Kln;
tel: 2710 8911

Hostels
Sunrise House: 323 Shun Ning Rd, Cheung Sha
Wan, Kln; tel: 2307 8001 (acc 310)

Yee On Hostel: Unit 111-116, 1/F, Hoi Yu
House, Hoi Fu Court, Mongkok, Kln;
tel: 2708 9553 (acc 40)

Day Care Centres for Senior Citizens
Bradbury: G/F, Wan Loi House, Wan Tau Tong
Estate, Tai Po Market, NT; tel: 2638 8880
(acc 44)

Chuk Yuen: 141-150 Podium Level, Chui Yuen
House, Chuk Yuen (South) Estate, Kln;
tel: 2326 6683 (acc 44)

Hoi Yu: G/F, Hoi Lam House, Hoi Fu Court,
2 Hoi Ting Rd, Mongkok, Kln; tel: 2148 1480
(acc 44)

Community Day Rehabilitation Service
Tak Tin: G/F, Tak Yan House, Tak Tin Estate,
Lam Tin; tel: 2177 7122

Shaukeiwan: 456 Shaukeiwan Rd, Shaukeiwan,
HK; tel: 2560 8123 (acc 40)

Community Day Rehabilitation and
Residential Service
Cheung Hong: 2/F & 3/F Hong Cheung Hse,

Cheung Hong Est, Tsing Yi, NT;
tel: 2432 1588

Integrated Home Care Service Teams
Kwun Tong: Unit 1-2, Wing B, G/F, Tak Lung
House, Tak Tin Estate, Lam Tin, Kln;
tel: 2340 0100
Sai Kung: 4/F, Po Kan House, Po Lam Estate,
Tseung Kwan O, Kln; tel: 2701 5828
Tai Po: 2/F, Tai Po Community Centre, Heung
Sze Wui St, Tai Po Market, NT;
tel: 2653 3941
Yau Tsim: 3/F, 11 Wing Sing Lane, Yaumatei,
Kln; tel: 2770 5266

Multi-service Centres for Senior Citizens
Tai Po: 2/F, Tai Po Community Centre, Heung
Sze Wui St, Tai Po Market, NT;
tel: 2653 6811
Yaumatei: 3/F, 11 Wing Sing Lane, Yaumatei,
Kln; tel: 2332 0005

Social Centres for Senior Citizens
Chuk Yuen: 1/F, Chuk Yuen Estate Community
Centre, Chuk Yuen (South) Estate, Kln;
tel: 2320 8032
Hoi Lam: 2/F, Hoi Yu House, Hoi Fu Court,
2 Hoi Ting Rd, Mongkok, Kln; tel: 2148 1481
Nam Tai: G/F, Nam Tai House, Nam Shan
Estate, Kln; tel: 2779 5983
Tai Wo Hau: 1/F, Tai Wo Hau Estate
Community Centre, Tai Wo Hau Estate,
Tsuen Wan, NT; tel: 2428 8563
Wah Fu: G/F, Wah Kin House, Wah Fu Estate,
HK; tel: 2550 9971

Senior Citizens Talent Advancement Project
Tung Tau Centre: Unit 1-3, G/F, Yat Tung
House, Tung Tau Estate, Kln; tel: 2340 0266
Kwun Tong Centre: 1/F, Flat A, Yee On Centre,
31 Yee On St, Kwun Tong, Kln;
tel: 2389 5568

Carer Service
3/F, 11 Wing Sing Lane, Yaumatei, Kln;
tel: 2782 2229

Family Support Networking Team
Shamshuipo: Flat B, 1/F, Kam Fai Bldg, 240-242
Aplui St, Shamshuipo, Kln; tel: 2390 9361

Residential Services for Boys
Wan Tsui Home for Boys: 115-128 G/F, Chak

Tsui House, Wan Tsui Estate, Chai Wan, HK;
tel: 2557 3290 (acc 46)
Yue Wan Boys' Hostel: 3-8 Yue Tai House, Yue
Wan Estate, Chaiwan, HK; tel: 2558 4048
(acc 15)

Children (Small Group Homes)
Tai Wo Hau: Fu Yin House, Wing K, Tai Wo
Hau Estate, Phase 4, Tsuen Wan, NT;
Home of Joy: Flat 214; tel: 2615 1709 (acc 8);
Home of Love: Flat 314; tel: 2615 1784 (acc 8)
Home of Peace: Flat 112; tel: 2615 1710 (acc 8)
Ping Tin: Ping Wong House, Ping Tin Estates,
Lam Tin, Kln;
Home of Faithfulness: Flat 103; tel: 2952 3691
(acc 8)
Home of Goodness: Flat 203; tel: 2952 3692
(acc 8)
Home of Kindness: Flat 303; tel: 2775 3542
(acc 8)

Residences for Senior Citizens
Bradbury Home of Loving Kindness: 16 Tung
Lo Wan Shan Rd, Tai Wai, Shatin, STTL 204,
NT; tel: 2601 5000 (acc 136)
Hoi Tai: 2/F, Hoi Tai House, Hoi Fu Court,
2 Hoi Ting Rd, Mongkok, Kln; tel: 2148 2000
(acc 131)
Lung Hang: 3&4/F, Wing Sam House, Lung Hang
Estate, Shatin, NT; tel: 2602 3696 (acc 155)
Nam Ming Haven for Women: G/F, Nam Ming
House, Nam Shan Estate, Tai Hang Tung, Kln;
tel: 2777 5484 (acc 38)
Nam Shan: 1&2/F, Nam Ming House, Nam Shan
Estate, Tai Hang Tung, Kln; tel: 2777 5102
(acc 150)
Po Lam: 4/F, Po Kan House, Po Lam Estate,
Tseung Kwan O, Kln; tel: 2701 5828 (acc 141)
Tak Tin: 2/F, Tak King House, Tak Tin Estate,
Lam Tin, Kln; tel: 2347 8183 (acc 81)
Kam Tin: 103 Kam Tin Rd, Yuen Long, NT;
tel: 2944 1369 (acc 150)

Warden Service in Sheltered Housing
Grace Apartments: Flat 3-95, Lotus Tower 4,
297 Ngau Tau Kok Rd, Kln; tel: 2763 6367
Kei Lok Apartments: Rm 225, Block 5,
Prosperous Garden, Public Square St,
Yaumatei, Kln; tel: 2782 6655

Integrated Service for Rehabilitation
Integrated Vocational Rehabilitation Service:
G/F, Heng Kong House, Heng On Estate,

Ma On Shan, NT; tel: 2640 0656 (acc 289)

On the Job Training Programme for People with Disabilities: G/F, Heng Sing Hse, Heng On Est, Ma On Shan, NT; tel: 2640 0656 (acc 48)

Sunnyway – On the Job Training Programme for Young People with Disabilities: G/F, Heng Sing Hse, Heng On Est, Ma On Shan, NT; tel: 2640 0656 (acc 30)

Heng On Hostel: G/F, Heng Shan House, Heng On Estate, Ma On Shan, NT; tel: 2640 0581 (acc 62)

Lai King Home (Training and Residential): 200-210 Lai King Hill Rd, Kwai Chung, NT; tel: 2744 1511 (acc 100)

Agency-based Occupational Therapy

Talent Shop: G/F, Heng Sing House, Heng On Estate, Ma On Shan, Shatin, NT; tel: 2633 7116

Share-Care Project – Family and Community

Support Service for Persons with Mental Handicaps: 200 Lai King Hill Rd, Kwai Chung, NT; tel: 2744 1511

Family Support Service for Persons with Autism: 6 Salvation Army St, Wanchai, HK; tel: 2893 2537

Social Enterprise

Shatin Park Kiosk: Kiosk no 4, Shatin Park, 2 Yuen Wo Road, Shatink, NT;

Shatin Family Store: Shop no 70-72, G/F Ming Yiu Lau, Jat Min Chuen, Shatin, NT; tel: 2636 6113

Poolside Restaurant: Restaurant Blk, G/F Ma On Shan Swimming Pool, On Chun St, Ma On Shan, NT; tel: 2633 0980

The WARM Project (Wheelchair & Assistive Device Re-engagement Movement): 1/F, Flat A, Yee On Centre, 31 Yee On St, Kwun Tong, Kln; tel: 2389 5568

Children from corps, schools and social centres in the Hong Kong and Macau Command give a drumming display during the closing ceremony for '2005 – A Year for Children and Youth'

INDIA NATIONAL

India is the Army's oldest mission field. Frederick St George de Latour Tucker, of the Indian Civil Service, read a copy of *The War Cry*, became a Salvationist and, as Major Tucker (later Commissioner Booth-Tucker), took the Indian name of Fakir Singh and commenced Army work in Bombay on 19 September 1882. The adoption of Indian food, dress, names and customs gave the pioneers ready access to the people, especially in the villages. In addition to evangelistic work, various social programmes were inaugurated for the relief of distress from famine, flood and epidemic. Educational facilities such as elementary, secondary and industrial schools, cottage industries and settlements, were provided for the depressed classes. Medical work originated in Nagercoil in 1893 when Harry Andrews set up a dispensary at the headquarters there. The medical work has grown from this. Work among the then Criminal Tribes began in 1908 at government invitation.

The Salvation Army is registered as a Guarantee Company under the Indian Companies Act 1913.

Several offices had been established in earlier years, including the Editorial and Literary Office and the Audit Office.

Since the establishment of the Health Services Advisory Council in 1986 a regionally based national secretariat has evolved to provide support to many aspects of Salvation Army work in India.

The Conference of Indian Leaders (COIL) established in 1989, meets annually to coordinate national Salvation Army affairs and give direction to the national secretariat.

Web site: www.salvationarmy.org/ind

THE SALVATION ARMY ASSOCIATION
Chairman: Comr P. D. Krupa Das

BUSINESS AND ADMINISTRATION OFFICE
'Balsam', TC-4/1962 Kowdiar PO,
Thiruvananthapuram 695 003, Kerala;
tel: (91) (471) 2316112/2316115;
fax: (91) (471) 2316112
email: indiabusinessadministration
@salvationarmy.org
Executive Secretary: Maj K. C. David

COMMUNICATIONS OFFICE
(including Editorial and Literary)
PO Box 8994, Dharamtala PO, Kolkata 700 013,
West Bengal; tel: (91) (33) 2245 5210/
2246 3140; fax: (91) (33) 2245 5210;
email: indiacommunications
@salvationarmy.org
Executive Secretary and Editor: Maj J.
Daniel Jebasingh-Raj, BA, MA, BTh, BD

HUMAN RESOURCES DEVELOPMENT OFFICE
Post Bag 1, Nanjundapuram PO, Coimbatore
641 036, Tamil Nadu;
tel: (91) (422) 231 9566/5593;
fax: (91) (422) 231 6153;
email: indiahumanresourcesdevelopment

@salvationarmy.org
Conference Centre: 'Surrenden', 15-18 Orange
Grove Rd, Coonoor 643 101, Nilgiris District,
Tamil Nadu; tel: (91) (423) 223 0242
Executive Secretary: Maj Wilfred Varughese

EDUCATION
Flat No A-404, Oberoi Gardens, Thakur Village,
Kandivili (East), Mumbai 400 101;
mobile: (91) (22) 9821 652 530;
fax: (91) (22) 2884 4340;
email: indianationaleducationalconsultant
@salvationarmy.org
Education Consultant: Lt-Col N. J.
Karunakara Rao, BSc, MSW, BGL, DHA

EMERGENCY SERVICES
Flat No A-404, Oberoi Gardens, Thakur Village,
Kandivili (East), Mumbai 400 101;
mobile: (91) (22) 9820 897 669;
fax: (91) (22) 2884 4340;
email: indianationalemergencyservicesconsultant
@salvationarmy.org
Consultant: Lt-Col N. J. Vijayalakshmi,
BA, BD

SOCIAL SERVICES
37 Lenin Sarani, Kolkata – 700013;
tel/fax: (91) (0) 33 2227 5780;
email: indiasocialdevelopment
@salvationarmy.org
Executive Secretary: Lt-Col Thumati
Vijayakumar

SALVATION ARMY HEALTH SERVICES ADVISORY COUNCIL

Post Bag 6 Ahmednagar-414 001, Maharashtra;
tel: (91) (241) 2321593;
fax: (91) (241) 2327756; email: sahsac@salvationarmy.org

Executive Secretary: Maj John Purshottam Macwan

WOMEN'S ADVISORY COUNCIL

Post Bag 1, Nanjundapuram PO, Coimbatore 641 036, Tamil Nadu; tel: (91) (422) 231 9566/5593; fax: (91) (422) 231 6153; email: indiawomensadvisorycouncil @salvationarmy.org

Executive Secretary: Maj Prema Wilfred Varughese, BA, BD

In the India Northern Territory, tin sheets to erect emergency shelters are distributed to victims of the Jammu and Kashmir earthquake

In the India South Western Territory, one of 75 new motorised boats supplied by The Salvation Army is handed over to a fisherman whose livelihood had been affected by the Indian Ocean tsunami

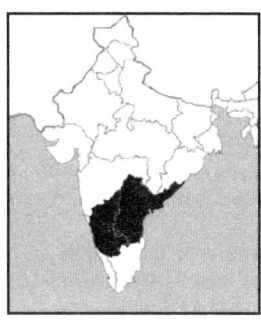

INDIA CENTRAL TERRITORY

Territorial leaders:
**Colonels M. Y. Emmanuel and
T. Regina Chandra Bai**

Territorial Commander:
Colonel M. Y. Emmanuel (1 Dec 2006)

Chief Secretary:
Lieut-Colonel Prema T. Rajan (1 May 2005)

**Territorial Headquarters: 31 (15) Ritherdon Road, Vepery,
Chennai 600 007**

Postal address: PO Box 453, Vepery, Chennai 600 007, India

Tel address: Salvation Chennai 600 007; tel: [91] (0044) 2532 3148; fax: [91] (0044) 2532 5987;
email: ICT_mail@ICT.salvationarmy.org; web site: www.salvationarmy.org/ind

The India Central Territory comprises three regions – North Tamil Nadu (Madras-Chennai), Karnataka and Andhra Pradesh. Salvation Army work commenced at Vijayawada in Andhra Pradesh in 1895 by Staff Captain Abdul Aziz, a person of Muslim background, with his friend Mahanada. Captain Abdul attended a revival meeting led by Captain Henry Bullard in 1884 at Bangalore and subsequently dedicated himself to be a Salvation Army officer. The territory was named the India Central Territory in 1992, with its headquarters at Madras (Chennai).

Zone: South Asia
States included in the territory: Andhra Pradesh, Karnataka, Tamil Nadu
'The Salvation Army' in Tamil: Ratchania Senai; in Telugu: Rakshana Sinyamu
Languages in which the gospel is preached: English, Tamil, Telugu
Periodicals: *Home League Magazine, Udyogasthudu, Yovana Veerudu, Yudha Dwani*

SALVATIONISTS moved swiftly in the provision of continued relief work following the Indian Ocean tsunami. Under its coastal rehabilitation projects the territory supplied food and nutrients for mothers and children, operated self-help programmes and organised the distribution of buffaloes, cooking stoves, boats, engines and fishing nets.

Housing projects were begun in a number of places, with plans for more than 300 houses to be built. In Nizampatinam, for example, 70 houses were constructed and handed over to the beneficiaries in February 2006 at a ceremony at which the Andhra Pradesh Transport Minister was chief guest. Each house is connected to the electricity supply and comprises a kitchen, living room and verandah. There is a separate toilet/bathroom.

The new development is called William Booth Nagar. The original suggestion of William Booth Colony was changed because nagar is a name which denotes a greater degree of civilisation – an important impression in the rehabilitation of the families who now live there. The 70 families are members of a tribal community which earned its living through catching canal fish and lived in slum conditions.

The land for the development was provided by the government. It was unreachable by road, so one of the first tasks was to build an access road through the jungle. An arch marks the beginning of the new road, giving a clear indication of the help The Salvation Army has provided. In the nagar itself, a borehole was dug 500 feet down to enable good drinking water to be provided.

In July 2005 student nurses and former students gathered to celebrate the silver jubilee of the school of nursing at Evangeline Booth Hospital, Nidubrolu. The territorial leaders were the chief guests, and visiting dignitaries including the Deputy Director for Nursing, Andhra Pradesh, and the District Medical and Health Officer participated. The territorial commander dedicated the new silver jubilee stage-cum-badminton court with its adjoining guest room, constructed with donations from students, alumni and well-wishers.

Nearly 1,000 young people gathered from all the territory's divisions, districts and institutions for a four-day youth congress in October 2005. Special guests Majors Merle and Dawn Heatwole (USA Central) were the source of wonderful blessings.

A successful series of home league rallies during February 2006 were held in 17 centres under the leadership of the TPWM, THLS and TLOMS. Gifts for the helping-hand scheme totalled 273,167 rupees (US$5,864), an increase of 34,037 rupees (US$730) on the previous year. Physically handicapped, sick and other needy people would be among the beneficiaries.

For the first time in the territory rallies for the Junior Home League were held (for young women aged 12 to 20). Held in all divisions and districts, the rallies attracted 1,339 delegates and resulted in 386 seekers, many of the young women accepting Christ in response to challenging messages given by the TPWM.

Salvationists give praise to God who has granted success in the territory's programmes and endeavours.

STATISTICS

Officers 681 (active 499 retired 182) **Cadets** (2nd Yr) 29 **Employees** 490
Corps 260 **Outposts** 128 **Societies** 142 **Institutions** 14 **Elementary Schools** 63 **Upper Primary Schools** 2 **English Medium Schools** 4 High Schools 2 **Junior College** 1 **Day Care Centres** 3 **Residential School** 1 **Clinic** 1 **Homes and Hostels** 13
Senior Soldiers 63,143 **Adherents** 6,270 **Junior Soldiers** 8,116

STAFF

Editor and Literary: Maj Samuel Rathan (supervising)
Education: Maj Samuel Rathan
Field: Maj Devarapalli Jayapaul, MA, BTS
Finance: Maj S. P. Abbulu, BCom
Human Resources Development: Capt Abraham Lincoln, MA, BTS, MDiv
Music and Creative Arts: Capt Prabathkumar, BCom
Outreach and Self-Support: Maj John Bhushanam, MA
Property and Projects: Maj K. Yesudas, BCom
Social: Maj M. Daniel Raju, MA
Trade: Capt I. D. Ebenezer, MA, BEd, BTS
Training: Capt John Williams, MA, BD (M Th)
Women's Ministries: Col T. Regina Chandra Bai (TPWM) Lt-Col Prema T. Rajan (TSWM)

Maj D. Yesudayamma (THLS) Maj S. Vimalakumari (TLOMS) Maj S. Pennimma (SAMF) Ananda Kumari (SOSS)
Youth and Sponsorship: Capt D. Daniel Raju, MA, DCE

DIVISIONS

Bapatla: Bapatla, Guntur District, 522 101; tel: (086432) 23931; Maj Cheeli Samuel

Chennai: 109 Gangadeeswara Koil St, Chennai 600 084; tel: (044) 2641 5021

Eluru: Adivarapupet, Eluru, West Godavari District, 534 005; tel: (08812) 237484

Gudivada: Krishna District, 521 301; tel: (08764) 243524; Maj Devadasi Joshi

Hyderabad: 6D Walker Town, Padmarao Nagar, Secunderabad, 500 025; tel: (040) 27502610; Maj Jupalli Zachariah, BA

Nellore: Dargamitta, Nellore, 524 003; tel: (0861) 2322 589; Maj Alladi Nathaniel

Tanuku: West Godavari District, 534 211; tel: (08819) 225366; Maj K. Y. Dhana Kumar, BCom

Tenali: Ithanagar, Tenali, Guntur District, 522 201; tel: (08644) 225949; Maj Elisha Rao Mocharla

Vijayawada: Near Gymkhana Club East side H. No 26-191/2, Ghandi Nagar, Vijayawada, 521 003; tel: (0866) 2575 168; Maj G.V. Ratnam

DISTRICTS

Divi: PO Nagayalanka, Krishna District, 521 120; tel: (08671) 274991; Maj M. Yesuratnam

Mandavalli: Station Rd, Mandavalli, Krishna Dt., 521 345; tel: (08677) 280503

Prakasam: Stuartpuram, Guntur District, 522 317; tel: (086432) 271131; Maj N. Jeevaratnam

Rajahmundry: Mallayapet, East Godavari District, 533 105; tel: (0883) 5579200; Maj K. Suvarna Raju

TRAINING COLLEGE

Dargamitta, Nellore, 524 003; tel: (0861) 2322687

HUMAN RESOURCES DEVELOPMENT

PB9, Nidubrolu, Guntur District 522 123; tel: (08643) 243447
Development Officer, Bapatla: Maj Suvarna Raju
Women's Development Officer, Nidubrolu: Capt Mani Kumari

EDUCATION
College (with hostel for boys and girls)
William Booth Junior College, Bapatla, Guntur District, 522 101; tel: (086432) 24259; Maj S. Jayananda Rao

High Schools (with hostels for boys and girls)
Bapatla, Guntur District, 522 101; tel: (086432) 24282; Correspondent: Maj M. P. Ch. Prasad (acc 300)
Girls' Hostel Superintendent: Maj P. Annamma
Stuartpuram, Prakasham District, 522 317; tel: (086432) 271131; Correspondent: Maj N. Jeevaratnam (acc 150)
SA Hostel: Stuartpuram; Maj K. J. Prakasha Rao

Upper Primary School
Dargamitta, Nellore, Nellore District

Elementary Schools (Telugu Medium)
Bapatla Division: Bethapudi, Chintayapalem, Gudipudi, Kattivaripalem, Mallolapalem, MR Nagar, Murukondapadu, Valluvaripalem, Perlipadu, Pasumarthivaripalem, Pedapalli, Parli Vadapalem, Yaramvaripalem, Yazali
Eluru Division: Bhogapuram, Dendulur, Gopavaram, Gandivarigudem, Kovvali, Musunur, Pathamupparru, Surappagudem, Velpucharla
Gudivada Division: Chinaparupudi, Edulamadalli, Guraza, Gajulapadu, Gudivada, Kodur, Kancharlapalem, Kornipadu, Mandavalli, Narasannapalem, Pedaparupudi, Ramapuram
Nellore Division: Alluru, Buchireddipalem, Chowkacherla, Iskapalli, Kakupalli, Kanapartipadu, Mudivarthi, Modegunta, North Mopur, Pallaprolu, Rebala
Tenali Division: Annavaram, Burripalem, Chukkapallivaripalem, Duggirala, Danthuluru, Emani, Ithanagar, Kollipara, Kattivaram, Nambur, Nelapadu
Prakasam District: Cherukuru, Stuartpuram

Primary Schools (English Medium)
The Haven, 21 Thiru Narayanaguru Rd, Choolai, Chennai 600 112; tel: (044) 2661 2784
Officer-in-Charge: Maj Ch. Solomon Raju, MA
Teachers' Colony, Vijayawada 500 008, Krishna District; tel: (0866) 2479854; Supt: Maj K. Samuel Raju
Hyderabad, 6D Walker Town, Padmarao Nagar PO, Secunderabad 500 025 (with day care centre); Correspondent: Maj J. Zachariah, BA
Nidubrolu; Headmistress: Maj Annamma Simon

Villivakkam and Chennai
Hosur-Karnataka

English Medium High School
Teachers' Colony, Vijayawada 500 008;
tel: (0866) 2479854; Correspondent:
Maj K. Samuel Raju

English Medium Matriculation School
The Haven, 21 Tiru Narayanaguru Rd, Choolai,
Chennai 600 112; tel: (044) 2661 2784;
Officer-in-Charge: Maj Ch. Solomon Raju, MA

Residential School
Tissot Sunrise School PB9 Bapatla, 522 101;
tel: (086432) 23336; Officer-in-Charge: Capt
T. Mark (acc 125)

Vocational Training Centre
Adivarpet, Eluru, West Godavari District, 534 005
(with boys' hostel); tel: (08812) 550070;
Officer-in-Charge: Maj Ch. Samuel

MEDICAL WORK
Evangeline Booth Hospital: Nidubrolu, Guntur
District, 522 123; tel: (08643) 2522124;
Administrator: Maj S. P. Simon, BA, ADHA
(acc 100)
Evangeline Booth Hospital (with home for the
aged), Bapatla, Guntur District, 522 101;
tel: (086432) 24134; Administrator: Maj B. G.
Prakasha Rao, BA (acc 75)
Clinic: Dindi, Nagayalanka PO, Nagayalanka
Mandal, Krishna District, 521 120

HIV/Aids Programme
Nidubrolu: Guntur District; Capt T. Raj Paul

SOCIAL WORK
Children's Homes and Hostels
Boys' Hostel, Mallayyapet, Rajahmundry;
tel: (0883) 2427926 (acc 40)

Boys' and Girls' Hostel: Stuartpuram, Bapatla
Mandal; tel: (08643) 71307 (acc 80, 8 girls)
Boys' Hostel, Virugambakkam, Chennai;
tel: (044) 23772723 (acc 80)
Boys' and Girls' Hostel, Nellore;
tel: (0861) 2340202 (acc 120)
Girls' Home and Old Age Home, Virugambakkam,
Chennai; tel: (044) 23770400 (acc 70)
Girls' Hostel, Adivarpet, Eluru;
tel: (08812) 226048 (acc 60)
Girls' Hostel, Nagayalanka; tel: (08671) 274512
(acc 24)
Girls' Hostel, Gudivada, Krishna District;
tel: (08674) 240739 (acc 25)
Girls' Hostel, 'Home of Peace', Tanuku;
tel: (08819) 229163 (acc 30)

Emergency Disaster Relief
Nidubrolu 522 124; tel: (08643) 244408;
Capt D. John Kumar

Working Women's Hostel
The Haven, 21 Thiru Narayanaguru Rd, Choolai,
Chennai 600 112; tel: (044) 2532 1789

Day Care Centre
21 Thiru Narayanaguru Rd, Choolai, Chennai
600 112; tel: (044) 2532 1789

Red Shield Guest House
15/31 Ritherdon Rd, Vepery, Chennai 600 007;
tel: (044) 2532 1821 (acc 60)

Waste Paper and Free Feeding Programmes
6D Walker Town, Secunderabad 500 025; A P
8 Perianna Maistry St, Periamet, Chennai-3;
tel: (044) 25610740

CONFERENCE AND TRAINING CENTRE
Vadarevu: Nr Chirala, Prakasam District

Nearly 1,000 young people gathered from all the territory's divisions, districts and institutions for a four-day youth congress . . . the source of wonderful blessings

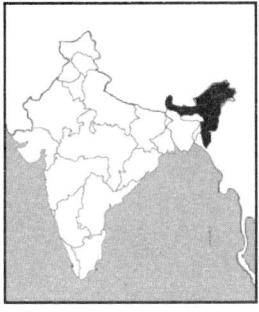

INDIA EASTERN TERRITORY

Territorial leaders:
**Colonels Jayapaul and
Yesudayamma Devarapalli**

Territorial Commander:
Colonel Jayapaul Devarapalli (1 Dec 2006)

Chief Secretary:
Lieut-Colonel Rohmingthanga (1 May 2005)

Territorial Headquarters: PO Box 5, Aizawl 796001, Mizoram, India

Tel address: 'Salvation Aizawl'; tel: [91] 389 2322290 (EPABX)/321864;
fax: [91] 389 2326123; email: IET_mail@IET.salvationarmy.org; web site: www.salvationarmy.org/ind

Work in the region commenced on 26 April 1917 when Lieutenant Kawlkhuma, the first Mizo officer commissioned in India, returned to start the Army work. He was then joined by a group of earnest believers who shared his vision of an 'Army like a church, very much in line with The Salvation Army'. India Eastern became a separate command on 1 June 1991 and became a territory in 1993.

Zone: South Asia
States included in the territory: Arunachal Pradesh, Assam, Manipur, Meghalaya, Mizoram, Nagaland, Sikkim, Tripura, West Bengal (part) and the Kingdom of Bhutan
'The Salvation Army' in Mizo: Chhandamna Sipai Pawl
Languages in which the gospel is preached: Adhibasi, Bengali, Bru, English, Hindi, Hmar, Manipuri (Meitei), Mizo, Nagamese, Nepali, Paite, Pali, Simte, Thadou, Vaiphai
Periodicals: *Sipai Tlangau* (Mizo *War Cry*), *The Officer* (Mizo), *Young Salvationist* (Mizo), *Chunnunpar* (Mizo Women's Ministries magazine)

THE territory announced 'The Year of Revival' as its focus and organised many campaign and revival meetings. As a result of extensive evangelism throughout the territory 1,664 new members were enrolled during this year. Assisted by senior soldiers, SAY (Salvation Army Youth) groups organised crusades and camps to restore backsliders, and these resulted in 301 being led to Jesus and brought back into the Salvation Army family.

Newly introduced prayer-and-fasting meetings in the territory are held twice a month at corps level and once a month at divisional level. Salvationists

and members of other churches, happy to join this prayer fellowship, are being spiritually strengthened as a result.

Central Division has established Prayer Mountain in Aizawl, where 10 prayer houses have been constructed through Salvationists' donations. Many soldiers go daily and spend time in prayer on the mountain; other church members are also using the location as a spiritual retreat.

Consultation on outreach ministry in the Himalaya region was held in Manipur Division under the leadership of International Secretary Commissioner Lalkiamlova.

Missionary officers working in that region shared their challenges and vision to strengthen the ongoing ministry. A strategy for evangelism in the region has been developed with the aim of establishing Salvation Army work in neighbouring countries Nepal and Bhutan.

A training course was held for nearly 300 outreach workers, including evangelist teachers, who carry out their ministry in remote non-Christian areas.

When more than 6,600 uniformed young Salvationists attended the territorial youth congress at Kolasib in October 2005, a march of witness was a spectacular event. Zonal leaders Commissioners Lalkiamlova and Lalhlimpuii led the congress, at the end of which 4,611 young people knelt the mercy seat to rededicate their lives to Christ and there were 49 commitments to officership.

Before the congress Commissioner Lalkiamlova addressed 80 youth workers and SAY council members on such matters as urbanisation and unemployment. Recommendations were accepted after much thoughtful discussion.

Thirteen cadets entered the training college and 27 applications were received from candidates for the next session.

The Women's Ministries Department from Central Division has provided a night shelter for women who are vulnerable and shunned by their families. A counselling group was formed to help change their lives and many of the women have since returned to their homes.

With assistance from International Heaquarters, the territory distributed blankets, mosquito nets, warm clothing, children's wear, candles and soap to 500 families living in refugee camps in Karbi Anglon.

STATISTICS

Officers 273 (active 218 retired 55) **Cadets** 13 **Employees** 250
Corps 207 **Societies/Outpost** 135 **Social Institutions** 12 **Schools 15**
Senior Soldiers 32,000 **Adherents** 736 **Junior Soldiers** 9,254

STAFF

Editor: Maj Vanlalfela
Property and Legal: Maj Kaizadinga
Field, Outreach and Community Health Action Network (CHAN): Maj Lalngaihawmi, MA
Finance: Capt Lalhmingliana, BA
Human Resources and Development: Maj Thanhlira
Projects and Sponsorship:
Public Relations and Communication: Maj Lalramhluna
Social: Maj Lianhlira
Trade: Maj Thanhlira
Training: Maj Vanlalthanga
Women's Ministries: Col Yesudayamma Devarapalli (TPWM) Lt-Col Lalkungi (TSWM and THLS) Maj Hmunropuii (SOSS) Maj Thanzuali (LOMS) Maj K. C. Ropari (SAMF) Capt Lalhlimpuii (WDO)
Youth and Candidates: Maj Laithanmawia

DIVISIONS

Cachar: Hospital Rd, Rangirkhari, PO Silchar, 788 005, Assam; tel: (03842) 220581; Maj Lalhriatpuia
Central: PO Aizawl, 796 001, Mizoram; tel: (0389) 2322393; Maj Jonathan Thanruma
Eastern: Keifang, PO Saitual, 796 262; tel: (389) 256227; Maj Lianthanga
Manipur: Salvation Rd, PO Churachanpur, 795 128, Manipur; tel: (3874) 233188; Maj Sangchhunga
Midland: Chhiahtlang, PO Serchhip, 796 181, Mizoram; tel: (3838) 225058; Maj Hrangngura
Northern: PO Darlawn, 796 111, Mizoram; tel: (389) 269228; Maj C. Dawngliana
Southern: PO Lunglei, 796 701, Mizoram;

tel: (95372) 2324027; Maj S. T. Dula
Western: PO Kolasib, 796 081, Mizoram;
tel: (3837) 220037; Maj S. Biakliana

DISTRICT
Tripura: Behliangchhip Zampui Hill, 799 269, Via
Dharmanagar, N Tripura; Maj K. Lalrinawma

TRAINING COLLEGE
Kolasib Vengthar, PO Kolasib, 796 081,
Mizoram; tel: (3837) 220466

UNDER THQ
Shillong: Eldorado, Nongrim Hills, Shillong,
Meghalaya; tel: (364) 2521527
Kohima: PO Box 292, Kohima, 797 001,
Nagaland; tel: (370) 222785
Namchi: Jorethang Rd, Namchi, 737 126, South
Sikkim; tel: (3595) 263208
Arunachal Pradesh: Dr Onik Moyong Complex,
Mimir Tinali, Pasighat, 791 102, East Siang
District, Arunachal Pradesh; tel: (368) 2225628
Kolkata: Liaison Office, SN Banerjee Rd,
Kolkatta; tel: (033) 22444713;
email: liaison_saiet@yahoo.co.in

EDUCATION
Special Residential Schools for the Physically Challenged
Mary Scott Home for the Blind: Kalimpong,
West Bengal; tel: (3552) 255252; email:
john_pachuau@yahoo.com (acc 80)
School for Deaf and Dumb Children: Darjeeling,
West Bengal; tel: (354) 2252332/2257645
email: sadeaf@sify.com (acc 50)

Higher Secondary Schools
Children's Training Higher Secondary School:
Churachandpur, Manipur; tel: (3874) 235097
Modern English Higher Secondary School:
Aizawl, Mizoram; tel: (389) 2323248

High Schools
Blue Mount: Behliangchhip, Zampui, Tripura
Booth Tucker Memorial School: Gahrodpunjee,
Cachar
Hermon Junior: Moreh, Manipur

Middle Schools
Children's Education School: Zezaw, Manipur
Children's Training School: Singngat, Manipur
Booth Tucker: Thingkangphai, Manipur
Hermon Junior: Moreh, Manipur
SA Middle School: Saikawt, Manipur
Willow Mount: Durtlang, Mizoram

Primary School
Integrated Primary School: Kolasib
Outreach Schools: 27

SOCIAL WORK
Home for Boys and Girls
Mary Scott Home for the Blind: Kalimpong,
W Bengal

Homes for Boys
Hostel for the Deaf and Dumb: Darjeeling,
W Bengal
Hostel for the Blind: Kolasib, Mizoram;
tel: (3837) 220236 (acc 25)
Enna In: Kolasib; tel: (3837) 221419 (acc 30)
Kawlkhuma Home: Lunglei; tel: (372) 224420
(acc 25)
Muanna In: Mualpui, Aizawl; tel: (389) 2320426
(acc 30)
Manipur Boys' Home: Mualvaiphei,
Churachandpur; tel: (3874) 235469 (acc 25)
Orphanage, Saiha: tel: (3835) 226140 (acc 15)
Silchar Home (acc 20)

Home for Girls
Hlimna In: Keifang, Mizoram; tel: (389) 2862278
(acc 65)

Motherless Babies' Homes
Aizawl: Tuikal 'A', Aizawl, Mizoram;
tel: (389) 2329868 (acc 35)
Manipur : Mualvaiphei, Churachandpur,
Manipur; tel: (3874) 235469 (acc 10)

HIV/AIDS PROGRAMME
Community Health Action Network (CHAN):
Kawlkhuma Bldg, Tuikal 'A', PO Box 5,
Aizawl 796001; tel: (389) 2320202/2327609;
fax: (389) 2326106;
email: chanaizawl@sancharnet.in

Community Caring Programme:
Churachandpur, Manipur; tel: (3874) 235469;
email: muanpuia_ccp@yahoo.co.in

CENTENARY PRESS
PO Box 5, Tuikal 'A', Aizawl, Mizoram;
tel: (389) 2329626

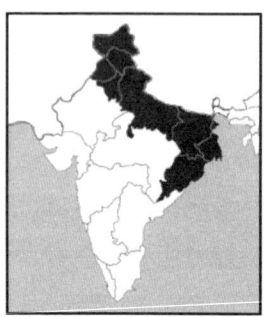

INDIA NORTHERN TERRITORY

Territorial leaders:
Colonels Kashinath and Kusam Lahase

Territorial Commander:
Colonel Kashinath Lahase (1 Jan 2006)

Chief Secretary:
Lieut-Colonel Paul Peter Christian
(1 Dec 2006)

**Territorial Headquarters: Flat No 103, Aashirwad Complex,
D-1, Green Park, New Delhi 110 016, India**

Tel address: Salvation New Delhi; tel: [91] (11) 2651 2394; fax: [91] (11) 2619 6296/2651 6912
email: INT_mail@INT.salvationarmy.org; web site: www.salvationarmy.org/ind

Shortly after arriving in India in 1882, Booth-Tucker visited major cities in northern India, including Allahabad, Delhi, Lucknow, Benares and Benares and Kolkata (Calcutta). Rural work was established later and operations were extended to Bihar and Orissa. The boundaries of the India Northern Territory have changed over the years; there have been headquarters in Gurdaspur, Bareilly, Lucknow, Benares and Kolkata and more recently Delhi. In 1947, part of the territory became Pakistan. The present territory was established on 1 June 1991.

Zone: South Asia
The territory is comprised of: the States of Bihar, Chattisgarh, Harayana, Himachal Pradesh, Jammu and Kashmir, Orissa, Punjab, Uttar Pradesh, Uttar Anchal, West Bengal, the Union Territories of Delhi, Chandigarh, and the Andaman and Nicobar Islands
'The Salvation Army' in Hindi, Punjabi and Urdu: Mukti Fauj
Languages in which the gospel is preached: Bengali, English, Hindi, Kui, Nepali, Oriya, Punjabi, Santhali, Tamil, Urdu
Periodicals: *Home League Quarterly* (Hindi and English), *Mukti Samachar* (Hindi and Punjabi), *The Officer* (Hindi)

AFTER an earthquake in Kashmir in October 2005 devastated people's hopes and property, a Salvation Army relief team visited the affected area and helped 800 families through the distribution of material for emergency shelters, rations and winter clothing.

In the Andaman and Nicobar Islands a children's park and community hall at Namunaghar and 80 permanent houses located in an area of South Andaman were dedicated by the territorial leaders during April 2006.

In Orissa and Punjab meetings were conducted weekly with the self-help groups of women living in villages below the poverty line. The women are being trained in savings and income-generation programmes, basic health issues, and learn about government schemes for poor women.

The opening of many new prayer halls and officers' quarters is enabling the Army's mission to progress, particularly in such places as Taran Taran, Pathankot and Kalayanpur where Salvationists had ministered for some years but no property had been available for permanent Salvation Army ownership. Rented accommodation proved a burden on financial resources but this issue has been solved by God's grace.

Mizoram Songsters were the special attraction at the annual congress held in Batala during October 2005. Most of the divisions enrolled new soldiers during soldiers' rallies held on Founders' Day (2 July) and on 19 September, the anniversary of Army work commencing in India.

Home league rallies were conducted by the TPWM and TSWM throughout the territory. Nearly 4,000 women attended; 1,291 of them knelt at the mercy seat; 57 senior and 61 junior home league members were enrolled.

At the commissioning 26 cadets received their officers' commissions from Commissioner Lalkiamlova (IS). Among a number of seminars and workshops, a 'Christian Discipleship' retreat focusing on personal growth in devotional life and holiness was attended by 20 delegates – officers, soldiers and candidates.

STATISTICS
Officers 397 (active 322 retired 75) **Cadets** 41 **Employees** 280
Corps 137 **Outposts** 358 **Societies** 830 **Institutions** 22 **Schools** 4 **College** 1
Senior Soldiers 53,642 **Adherents** 2,545 Junior **Soldiers** 9,958

STAFF
Church Growth: Maj Robin Kumar Sahu

Editor: Maj Manga Masih
Education: Capt Gurnam Masih
Field: Maj Edwin Masih
Finance: Maj Yesuvadiyan Manoharan
Human Resources: Maj Samir Patra
Property, Projects and Legal: Maj Tarsem Masih
Public Relations/Fund-raising: Maj Shafqat Masih
Social: Maj Dilip Singh
Training: Maj Rounki Lal
Women's Ministries: Col Kusum K.Lahase (TPWM) Lt-Col Anandiben Christian (TSWM)
Youth/Candidates: Maj Philip Nayak

DIVISIONS
In Punjab
Amritsar: 25 Krishna Nagar, Lawrence Rd, Amritsar 143 001, Punjab; Maj Peter Masih
Batala: Dera Baba Nanak Rd, Batala 143 505, Dist Gurdaspur, Punjab; tel: 01871-243038; Maj Prakash Masih
Beas: Ajeet Nagar, Beas, Amritsar 143 201, Punjab; tel: 01853-273834; Maj Gian Masih
Dera Baba Nanak: Dist Gurdaspur, PO Dera Baba Nanak 143 604, Punjab; tel: 01871-247262; Maj Bua Masih
Gurdaspur: Jail Rd, Dist Gurdaspur 143 521, Punjab; tel: 01874-220622; Maj Kashmir Masih

In Uttar Pradesh
Bareilly: 220 Civil Lines, Bareilly 243 001, UP; tel: 0581-2427081; Maj Yaqoob Masih
Moradabad: Kanth Rd, near Gandhi Ashram PAC, Moradabad 244 001; Maj Lazar Masih

In West Bengal
Kolkata: 37 Lenin Saranee, Kolkata 700 013; tel: 033-55101 591; fax: 033-22443 910; Capt Manuel Masih

DISTRICTS
Angul: Angul 759 122, Orissa; tel: 06764-232829; Maj Samuel Dass
Delhi: Surajpur Road, Firojpur, PO Dhamala Via Pinjore, Dist Panchkula, Haryana 134 102; tel: 01733-554946; Maj Makhan Masih
Simultala: Simultala 811 316, Dist Jamui, Bihar; Maj Chotka Hembrom

EXTENSION WORK
Mukerian: Rikhipura Mohalla, Dist Hoshiyarpur, Mukerian – 144 211, Punjab; tel: 01883-248733; Maj Sadiq Masih
Pathankot: Daulatpur Rd Prem Nagar, near FCI Godwan, Pathankot, Punjab; Maj Daniel Gill

Port Blair: Near Income Tax Office, Shadi Pur, Port Blair – 744106, Andaman Nicobar Islands; Capt Tarsem Masih

Taran Taran: Sandhu Ave, near Shota Kazi Kot Rd, Ward No 11, Taran Taran, Dist Amritsar, Punjab; Maj Tarsem Masih

TRAINING COLLEGE
Bareilly: 220 Civil Lines, Bareilly 243 001, UP; tel: 0581-2423304

MEDICAL WORK
Hospital
MacRobert Hospital: Dhariwal, Dist Gurdaspur 143 519, Punjab; tel: 01874-275152/275274; Administrator: Maj K. Y. Raj Kumar, BA (acc 50)

Clinics
Social Service Centre: 172 Acharya Jagdish Chandra Bose Rd, Kolkata 700 014; tel: 033-22840441

Community Health Centre: 192-A, Arjun Nager, New Delhi 110 029; tel: 011-2616 8895

EDUCATION
Senior Secondary School
Aliwal Rd, Batala 143 505, Dist Gurdaspur, Punjab; tel: 01871-242593; Lt-Col Kamla Prasad (acc 900)

Extension Branch
Gurdaspur School: The Salvation Army DHQ Compound, Jail Rd, Dist Gurdaspur, Punjab; tel: 01874-20622

English Medium Schools
Kanth Rd, opp Gandhi Ashram PAC, Moradabad 244 001, UP; tel: 0591-2417351/2429184; Capt Simon Peter (acc 400)

William Booth Memorial School: 220 Civil Lines, Bareilly 243001, UP; tel: 0581-2420 007; Maj Samuel R. Lal (acc 200)

College
Catherine Booth College for Girls: Aliwal Rd, Batala 143 505, Dist Gurdaspur, Punjab; tel: 01871-242593; Lt-Col Kamla Prasad (acc 300)

Non-residential Tailoring Units
Dera Baba Nanak: Dist Gurdaspur, Punjab Kancharapada, West Bengal

SOCIAL WORK
Homes for the Aged
Bareilly: 220 Civil Lines, Bareilly 243 001, UP; tel: 0581-2421432 (acc 20)

Dhariwal: MacRobert Hospital, Dhariwal,

Dist Gurdaspur 143 519, Punjab; tel: 01874-275152/275274 (acc 20)

Kolkata: 172 Acharya Jagadish Chandra Rd, Kolkata 700 014 (acc 15)

Homes for Boys
Angul: Angul 759 122, Orissa; tel: 06764-232829 (acc 10)

Batala: Aliwal Rd, Batala 143 505, Dist Gurdaspur (acc 60)

Kolkata: 37 Lenin Saranee, Kolkata 700 013; tel: 033-55124567 (acc 40)

Moradabad: Kanth Rd, Moradabad 244 001, UP; tel: 0591-2417351 (acc 40)

Paburia: At/PO-Paburia, Dist Kandhamal, 762 112 (Orissa); tel: 06847-264063 (acc 30)

Simultala: Simultala 811 316, Dist Jamui, Bihar (acc 43)

Homes for Girls
Angul: Angul 759 122, Orissa; tel: 06764-232829 (acc 40)

Bareilly: 220 Civil Lines, Bareilly 243 001, UP; tel: 0581-2421432 (acc 40)

Batala: Aliwal Rd, Batala 143505, Dist Gurdaspur (acc 60)

Behala: Hindustan Park, Behala, Kolkata 700034; tel: 033-24682692 (acc 120)

Gurdaspur: Jail Rd, Dist Gurdaspur 143 521, Punjab (acc 100)

HOSTELS
Blind (Men)
172 Acharya Jagdish Chandra Rd, Kolkata 700 014 (acc 30)

Working Men and Students
172 Acharya Jagdish Chandra Rd, Kolkata 700 014; tel: 033-2284 0441 (acc 200)

Young Women
Kolkata: 38 Lenin Saranee, Kolkata 700 013; tel: 033-2227 4281 (acc 50)

New Delhi: 192-A, Arjun Nager, New Delhi 110 029; tel: 011-26168895

RED SHIELD GUEST HOUSES
Kolkata: 2 Saddar St, Kolkata 700 016; tel: 033-2286 1659 (acc 80)

New Delhi: P-2 S Extension, Part II, New Delhi 110 049; tel: 011-2625 7310

WASTE PAPER DEPARTMENT
6 Malik Bldg, Chunamundi, Paharganj, New Delhi 110 055; tel: 011-2355 8433

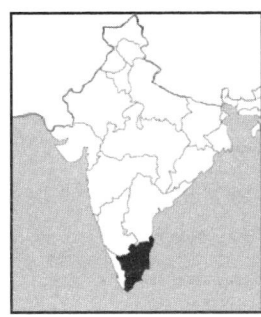

INDIA SOUTH EASTERN TERRITORY

Territorial leaders:
Commissioners M. C. and Susamma James

Territorial Commander:
Commissioner M. C. James (1 Dec 2006)

Chief Secretary:
Lieut-Colonel Bashir Masih (1 May 2005)

Territorial Headquarters: High Ground Road, Maharajanagar PO, Tirunelveli – 627 011, Tamil Nadu, India

Tel address: Salvation, Tirunelveli; tel: [91] (462) 2574331/2574313; fax: [91] (462) 2577152; email: ISE_mail@ISE.salvationarmy.org; web site: www.salvationarmy.org/ind

The Salvation Army commenced operations in south-east India on 27 May 1892 as a result of the vision received by Major Deva Sundaram at Medicine Hill, while praying and fasting with three officers when the persecution in Southern Tamil Nadu was at its height. On 1 October 1970 the Tamil-speaking part of the Southern India Territory became a separate entity as the Army experienced rapid growth.

Zone: South Asia
States included in the territory: Tamil Nadu, Pondicherry
'The Salvation Army' in Tamil: Ratchaniya Senai; in Malayalam: Raksha Sainyam
Languages in which the gospel is preached: English, Malayalam, Tamil
Periodicals: *Chiruveeran* (Tamil), *Home League Quarterly*, *Poresatham* (Tamil), *The Officer* (Tamil)

OPPORTUNITIES to serve others, win souls for Christ and establish Salvation Army mission in new areas opened up through the rehabilitation of families affected by the Indian Ocean tsunami. With financial support from overseas, the territory provided 160 new houses. In Kanyakumari, the district collector took part when the territorial commander conducted a dedication ceremony at the opening of newly constructed houses.

The TC also dedicated the dental unit at Catherine Booth Hospital which was fully renovated with air-conditioning facilities. Salvationists of the United Kingdom Territory donated an ultramodern dental chair and imaging equipment.

In response to the 'Way Forward' financing scheme, the territory continued its commitment to tithing and increased its giving to the International Self-Denial Fund and in territorial harvest festival offerings.

Made more aware of the scope and burden of mission, local officers were encouraged to participate in self-support systems. Wealthier corps are now supporting small corps, and territorial needs such as the training college, retired officers and local sponsorship projects are benefiting.

The territory's own finances now support 52 per cent of the territorial mission.

Some 225 self-help groups were created in the Community Health Development Project, with 3,500 women as members. While 400 HIV/Aids-affected people are being cared for, a new project to support children of HIV/Aids-affected parents has been introduced.

Helping-hand collections at home league rallies throughout the territory were given to help finance the construction of toilets, to purchase sewing machines for the skill-training of girls, and to support nursing and physically challenged students.

At the rural development vocational training centre in Chemparuthivilai training has been given in tailoring, embroidery, typing and computer skills. Women affected by the tsunami have received livelihood skills training. The vocational training centre for girls and women at Nagercoil and Aramboly's vocational training centre for young men who are physically challenged continue a vital ministry.

A sponsorship programme in Norway provided poor children with educational equipment while Canadian sponsors have helped more than 120 children continue their studies.

STATISTICS
Officers 608 (active 467 retired 141) **Cadets** (2nd Yr) 30 **Employees** 431
Corps 265 **Outposts** 111 **Societies** 87 **Schools** 21 **Institutions** 53
Senior Soldiers 45,074 **Adherents** 18,537 **Junior Soldiers** 5,094
Personnel serving outside territory Officers 20

STAFF
Community Health Development:
  Mr Benjamin Dhaya
Editor: Lt-Col Chelliah Rajamonickam
Education and Social: Maj Tharmar Alfred
Field: Maj Arulappan Paramadhas
Finance: Maj Jebamony Jayaseelan
Human Resources: Lt-Col Masilamony Ponniah
Projects: Maj Yacob Selvam
Property: Lt-Col Appavoo William
Public Relations: Maj Abraham Jeyasekhar
Supplies: Maj Sebagnanam James
Training: Maj Jeyaraj Samraj
Women's Ministries: Comr Susamma James
  (TPWM) Lt-Col Bachni Masih (TSWM)
  Lt-Col Thavamoni William (THLS)
  Maj Retnam (TLOMS)
Youth and Candidates: Capt Yesudian Ponnappan

DIVISIONS
Cape North: Azhagiapandipuram PO, 629 852
  tel: (04652) 281952; Maj Abel Bailis
Cape South: Vetturnimadam PO, Nagercoil 629
  003; tel: (04652) 272787; Maj Chelliah Moni
Kulasekharam: Kulasekharam PO, 629 161;
  tel: (04651) 279446; Maj Solomon Muthuraj
Marthandam: Marthandam PO, 629 165;
  tel: (04651) 272492; Maj Sundaram Motchakan
Palayamcottai: 28 Bell Amorses Colony,
  Palayamcottai 627 002; tel: (0462) 2573676;
  Maj Swaminathan Gnaniah
Radhapuram: Radhapuram PO, 627 111;
  tel: (04637) 254318; Maj Chelliah Swamidhas
Tenkasi: Tenkasi PO, 627 811;
  tel: (04633) 280774; Maj Devasundaram
  Samuel Raj
Thuckalay: Thuckalay PO, 629 175;
  tel: (04651) 252443; Maj Sam Devaraj
Valliyoor: Valliyoor PO, 627 117;
  tel: (04637) 221454; Maj Mark John Rose

DISTRICTS
Coimbatore: Daniel Ngr, K. Vadamaduai PO,
  641 017; tel: (0422) 2461277; Maj Yovan
  Dhason
Erode: 155 Amman Nager, Erode 638 002;
  tel: (0424) 2283909; Maj Prakasam David
Madurai: TPK Rd, Palanganatham PO, 625 003;
  tel: (0452) 2604169; Maj Asirvatham Devadhas
Trichy: New Town, Malakovil, Thiruvarumbur
  620 013; tel: (0431) 2556164; Maj Daniel
  Dhason
Tuticorin: 5/254 G, Caldwell Colony, Tuticorin
  628 008; tel: (0461) 2376841; Maj Yesudian
  Peter

A young woman is led to Christ while other Salvationists witness during an open-air meeting in Mulhouse, France

Above: Mercy seat counselling during the United Kingdom Territorial Congress

Top: A Portuguese group witnesses in an open-air meeting during the European Youth Congress in Prague, Czech Republic

Above and right: Young Salvationists on the streets of Helsinki, Finland, and downtown Buenos Aires, Argentina

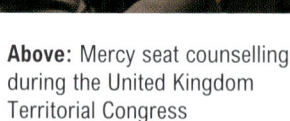

Above and below: On the march through the streets of San Francisco's Chinatown (USA Western Territory) and in Kangundo Division (Kenya Territory)

Left: UK Salvationists join the Make Poverty History march in Edinburgh

Above and right:
Witnessing in Congo
(Brazzaville) and
Cuba

Below: Young
Salvationists in
Japan travel in the
'Youth Caravan' to
take the gospel from
town to town

Pondicherry Extension Area: opp Mahatma
Dental College, Kamaraj Ngr, Goremedu
Check Post, Pondicherry 605 006;
tel: (0413) 2271933; Maj Arulanantham
Solomon

TRAINING COLLEGE
College Rd, Nagercoil 629 001;
tel: (04652) 231471

HUMAN RESOURCES DEVELOPMENT AND CONFERENCE CENTRE
Muttom, via Nagercoil 629 202;
tel: (04651) 238321

MEDICAL WORK
Catherine Booth Hospital: Nagercoil 629 001;
tel: (04652) 275516/7; fax: (04652) 275489;
Administrator: Maj Perinbanayagam
Suthananthadhas

COMMUNITY HEALTH AND DEVELOPMENT PROGRAMMES
Catherine Booth Hospital, Nagercoil 629 001
Women's Micro-credit and Health Programme
Community-based HIV/Aids Care and Support
Programmes
Reproductive and Child Health Programme
Community Health Centre
Voluntary Counselling and Testing Centre
cum STD Clinic Programme
Community Eye Health Programme
Director: Mr G. Benjamin Dhaya
tel: (04652) 272068

EDUCATION
Higher Secondary School (mixed)
Nagercoil 629003; tel: (04652) 272647;
Headmaster: Mr M. Kingsley, MSc, MEd

Matriculation Higher Secondary School (mixed)
Nagercoil; tel: (04652) 272534; Principal: Mr
Monickadhas, MA, BEd

Middle School (mixed)
Nambithoppu Middle School; Headmaster: Mr
Vethamuthu

Noble Memorial High School
Valliyoor; tel: (04637) 220380; Headmaster:
Mr A. Benjamin, MA, BEd

Village Primary Schools: 9

**Nursery and English Medium Primary
Schools:** 6

SOCIAL SERVICES
Hostels
Boys' Hostel: Nagercoil; tel: (04652) 272953
(acc 72)
Noble Memorial Boys' Hostel: Valliyoor;
tel: (04637) 221289 (acc 70)
Tucker Girls' Hostel: Nagercoil;
tel: (04652) 231293 (acc 135)
Girls' Hostel: Thuckalay;
tel: (04651) 252764 (acc 100)

Motherless Babies' Home
Palayamcottai, 627 002

Child Development Centres
Chemparuthivilai, Chemponvilai, Kadaigramam,
Madurai, Nagercoil, Pondicherry,
Radhapuram, Thuckalay, Valliyoor

**Vocational Training Centres for the
Physically Handicapped**
Men and Boys
Aramboly 629 003; tel: (04652) 263133

Women and Girls
Nagercoil 629 003; tel: (04652) 232348

**Rural Development and Vocational
Training Centre**
Chemparuthivilai 629 166; tel: (04651) 253292

Vocational Training Institute
Kilkothagiri Junction, 643 216 Nilgris

Industrial Training Institute
Aramboly; tel: (04652) 262198

Tailoring Institutes
Chemparuthivilai, Chemponvilai, Erode,
Kadaigramam, Katpady, Kiliancode,
Kulasekharam, Melacheval; Moolakarupatty,
Nettancode CDCs-Thuckalay,
Oppanayalpuramm, Osravilai, Radhapuram,
Palliyadi, Sambavarvadakarai, Trichy,
Tuticorin, Vadasery, Valliyoor, Vellachivilai

RETIRED OFFICERS' HOME
CB Hospital, Nagercoil 629 001

INDIA SOUTH WESTERN TERRITORY

Territorial leaders:
**Commissioners Chimanbhai and
Rahelbai Waghela**

Territorial Commander:
Commissioner Chimanbhai Waghela
(3 May 2003)

Chief Secretary:
Lieut-Colonel Samuel Charan (1 May 2005)

Territorial Headquarters: The Salvation Army, Kowdiar, Thiruvananthapuram, Kerala

Postal address: PO Box 802, Kowdiar, Thiruvananthapuram 695 003, Kerala State, India

Tel address: Salvation, Thiruvananthapuram; tel: [91] (471) 2314626/2723238; fax: [91] (471) 2318790; email: ISW_mail@ISW.salvationarmy.org; web site: www.salvationarmy.org/ind

Salvation Army work commenced in the old Travancore State on 18 March 1894 by Captain Yesudasen Sanjivi, who was a high-caste Brahmin before his conversion. His son, Colonel Donald A. Sanjivi, became the first territorial commander from Kerala. The work spread to other parts of the state through the dedication of pioneer officers, including Commissioner P. E. George. The India South Western Territory came into being on 1 October 1970 when the Southern India Territory divided into two. The territory has its headquarters at Thiruvananthapuram and comprises the entire Malayalam-speaking area known as Kerala State.

Zone: South Asia
State included in the territory: Kerala
'The Salvation Army' in Malayalam: Raksha Sainyam; in Tamil: Ratchania Senai
Languages in which the gospel is preached: English, Malayalam, Tamil
Periodicals: *Home League Quarterly* (Malayalam/English), *The Officer* (Malayalam), *Youdha Shabdam* (Malayalam), *Yuva Veeran* (Malayalam)

AS part of the rehabilitation programme after the Indian Ocean tsunami, 67 houses were built and given to people affected by the disaster. Later a further 53 houses were constructed. Financial help was given to carry out maintenance work on 80 partially damaged houses.

Also, 75 new motorised boats were supplied to help alleviate the loss of income experienced by many families whose livelihood depended on fishing. Financial help was made available for self-employment schemes, self-help groups were formed and medical help was arranged.

A trauma counselling seminar was held at Karunagappally, the tsunami-hit area in Kollam District. Delegates from India and Sri Lanka attended this inter-territory youth capacity development programme.

Other youth capacity development programmes were held in all divisions by the territory's HIV/Aids facilitation team. Young people were given training in checking the spread of HIV/Aids.

YES (Youth Experiencing Service) – a seven-member youth team from Australia – visited during September and October 2005. They participated in divisional youth camps, youth meetings and junior soldier rallies in many parts of the territory, where their leadership was inspirational.

The 'Christian Discipleship' holiness institute attracted 25 delegates from all over the territory. With its theme 'Growing in the Knowledge of God' (Colossians 1:10), the retreat's purpose was for delegates to develop a deeper awareness of Jesus and learn more about the disciplines which lead to Christian maturity.

'Heirs of the Kingdom' was the theme of a Youth Brengle Institute held to conclude 2005 as 'A Year for Children and Youth'. Based on Christ's Beatitudes, the Bible studies and other devotional sessions helped the 30 delegates to be more sensitive to the Holy Spirit empowering their Christian living. A few weeks later a youth leadership training programme served as part of the follow-up to the youth year.

Notable events confirmed that women's ministries are very much alive in the territory. Excellent attendances and exuberant participation were evident at all the divisional home league rallies; several junior home league rallies were also held. An absorbing one-day Bible camp was organised at Trivandrum Central Corps. Women's ministries seminars took place in various divisional centres, including a leadership seminar for divisional directors of women's ministries.

Ten cadets of the Visionaries Session were commissioned as officers and the territory was encouraged by the fact that 22 candidates, the biggest number in recent years, were waiting to enter officer-training in July 2006.

STATISTICS
Officers 705 (active 477 retired 228) **Cadets** (1st Yr) 22 **Employees** 174
Corps 333 **Societies** 35 **Outposts** 425 **Schools** 16 **Institutions** 20
Senior Soldiers 38,815 **Adherents** 15,804 **Junior Soldiers** 3,763
Personnel serving outside territory Officers 20

STAFF
Editor: Maj Davidson Daniel BA
Field: Maj K.P. Chacko
Finance: Maj K. C Peter
Human Resources Development: Maj D. Samuel
Property: Maj V. C. John
Public Relations: Maj S.Samuelkutty
Social: Maj John Suseelkumar
Training: Lt-Col P. T. Abraham
Women's Ministries: Comr Rahelbai Waghela (TPWM) Lt-Col Bimla Charan (TSWM) Maj Suseela Chacko (THLS) Maj Swarnamma Samuel (TLOMS) Maj M. V. Esther Davidson (SSFS)
Youth and Candidates: Maj D. Gnanadasan

DIVISIONS
Adoor: Adoor 691 523; tel: 04734-229648; Maj P. V. Stanly Babu
Cochin: Erumathala PO, Alwaye 683 105; tel: 0484-2638429; Maj C. S. Yohannan
Kangazha: Edayirikapuzha PO, Kangazha 686 541; tel: 0481-2494773; Maj P. Yohannan
Kattakada: Kattakada 695 572; tel: 0471-2290484; Maj Johns Samuel

Kottarakara: Kottarakara 691 506;
tel: 452650; Maj Rajan K. John

Malabar: Veliyamthode, Chandakunnu PO
Nilambur 679 342; tel: 2222824; Maj N. S.
George

Mavelikara: Thazhakara, Mavelikara 690 102;
tel: 2303284; Maj N. J. George

Nedumangadu: Nedumangadu 695 541;
tel: 2800352; Maj R. Christuraj

Neyyattinkara: Neyyattinkara 695 121;
tel: 2222916; Maj P. K. Philip

Peermade: Kuttikanam PO, Peermade 685 501;
tel: 232816; Maj T. J. Simon

Tiruvella: Tiruvella 689 101; tel: 2602657;
Maj K. M. Solomon

Thiruvananthapuram: Parambuconam,
Kowdiar PO, Thiruvananthapuram 695 003;
tel: 2433215; Maj M. Samuel

DISTRICTS

Kottayam: Pariyaram PO, Kottayam 686 018;
tel: 0481 2465652; Maj V. D. Samuel

Punalur: The Salvation Army, PPM PO, Punalur;
tel: 0475 2229218; Maj Sathiyaseelan

TRAINING COLLEGE

Kowdiar, Thiruvananthapuram 695 003;
tel: 2315313

MEDICAL WORK

Evangeline Booth General Hospital: Puthencruz
682 308; tel: Ernakulam 2731056;
Administrator: Capt Roy Joseph

Evangeline Booth Leprosarium: Puthencruz
682 308; tel: Ernakulam 2730054 (acc 200)

General Hospital: Kulathummel, Kattakada 695
572 Thiruvananthapuram Dist; tel: Kattakada
2290485; Hospital Sec: Maj P. S. Johnson
(acc 60)

Medical Centres:
Kanghaza 686 541, Edayappara;
tel: Kangazha 2494273 (acc 12)
Kowdiar, Thiruvananthapuram 695 003;
tel: 2723237

Community Health Centres: Valiyodu,
Bharathannoor, Panacode, Panniyodu

SCHOOLS

Higher Secondary School (mixed)
Thiruvananthapuram 695 003; tel: 2315488
(acc 1,371)

Primary Schools: 15 (acc 2,640)

SOCIAL WORK

Boys' Homes
Kangazha 686 541 (acc 30)

Kottarakara 691 506 (acc 30)
Kowdiar, Thiruvananthapuram 695 003
(acc 20)
Mavelikara 690 102 (acc 25)

Community Development Centres
North: Trikkakara – Cochin 682 021
South: Konchira, Thiruvananthapuram 695 607;
tel: 0472-2831540

Girls' Homes
Adoor 691 523 (acc 25)
Kowdiar, Thiruvananthapuram 695 003
(acc 24)
Nedumangad 695 541 (acc 30)
Peermade, Kuttikanam 685 501 (acc 30)
Trikkakara, Cochin 682 021 (acc 30)
Thiruvalla 689 101; tel: 0469-2831540
(acc 25)

**Vocational Training Centre for Physically
Handicapped Women**
Nedumangad 695 541 (acc 25)

Vocational Training Centre for Women
Nedumangad 695 541 (acc 25)

Young Men's Training Centres
Thazhakara, Mavelikara 690 102
Thiruvananthapuram 695 003

Printing Press
Kowdiar, Thiruvananthapuram 695 003

Computer Centre
Kowdiar, Thiruvananthapuram; tel: 2318524

Tailoring Centres
Adoor, Cochin, Kangazha, Kattakada,
Kottarakara, Malabar, Neyyattinkara,
Peermade

Young Women's Hostel (Goodwill Hostel)
Thiruvananthapuram 695 003; tel: 2319917
(acc 20)

Youth Centre
Kowdiar, Thiruvananthapuram 695 003

RED SHIELD GUEST HOUSES
Kowdiar, Thiruvananthapuram 695 003;
tel: 0471-2319926
Kovalam, Thiruvananthapuram; tel: 0471-3092283

RETIREMENT COTTAGES FOR
OFFICERS
Thiruvananthapuram (cottages 4)

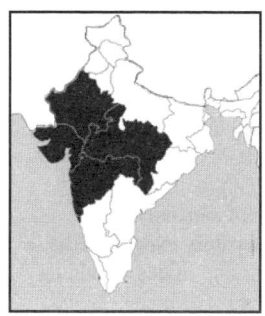

INDIA WESTERN TERRITORY

Territorial leaders:
Commissioners P. D. Krupa Das and P. Mary Rajakumari

Territorial Commander:
Commissioner P. D. Krupa Das (1 May 2005)

Chief Secretary:
Lieut-Colonel Sumant L. Parkhe (1 Dec 2006)

Territorial Headquarters: Sheikh Hafizuddin Marg, Byculla, Mumbai 400 008

Postal address: PO Box 4510, Mumbai 400 008, India

Tel address: Salvation Byculla Mumbai; tel: [91] (022) 2308 4705/2307 1140;

fax: [91] (022) 2309 9245;

email: IWT_mail@iwt.salvationarmy.org; web site: www.salvationarmy.org/ind

The Salvation Army began its work in Bombay (later Mumbai) in 1882 as a pioneer party led by Major Frederick Tucker and including Veerasoriya, a Sri Lankan convert, invaded India with the love and compassion of Jesus. Bombay (Mumbai) was the capital of Bombay Province, which included Gujarat and Maharashtra, and the first headquarters in India was in a rented building at Khatwadi. From these beginnings the work of God grew in Bombay Province. Various models of administration were tried for the work in Gujarat and Maharashtra until the India Western Territory was established in 1921.

Zone: South Asia

States included in the territory: Gujarat, Maharashtra, Madhya Pradesh, Rajasthan

'The Salvation Army' in Gujarati and Marathi: Muktifauj

Languages in which the gospel is preached: English, Gujarati, Hindi, Marathi, Tamil

Periodicals: *Home League Quarterly* (Gujarati and Marathi), *The Officer* (Gujarati and Marathi), *The War Cry* (Gujarati and Marathi), *The Young Soldier* (Gujarati and Marathi)

THE territorial theme for 2005 – 'Jesus is the Lord' – was emphasised as divisions launched their evangelistic campaigns. With it also being 'A Year for Children and Youth', more effort was made to attract children and young people to the Army.

Youth congresses were held in Gujarat and Maharashtra, where 300 and 350 young people attended the respective events. The word of God, preached by the territorial commander, helped them renew their commitment to God and the Army.

A mission team of five people from Singapore, Malaysia and Myanmar Territory – one of India Western's 'Partners in Mission' – visited in February 2006. The Singapore Central corps officer (Captain Andrew Dunkinson) ministered to young people at youth rallies in three divisions and a youth festival in Mumbai involved 115 young people. Captain Sheila Dunkinson led a special workshop for the cadets in Anand. The team's visit was a great spiritual inspiration, bringing a spirit of renewal among the territory's youth.

The territory is now well equipped to respond to sex trafficking. This includes rescuing minors and rehabilitating them, liaising with police and legal institutions to help stop sex trafficking, and working closely with prostitutes.

Some of the prostitutes are helped to find alternatives to the sex trade by being trained for self-employment or being referred to other organisations for rehabilitation. Some are also being reunited with their families and reintgrated into their communities.

Working in the red-light districts, Salvationists are helping to protect vulnerable children from the dangers of sex trafficking.

With the help of resources from the USA Southern Territory – another 'Partner in Mission' – special training was given to divisional commanders and staff from organisations in Mumbai to help local leaders respond to sex trafficking.

HIV/Aids education programmes implemented by the counselling clinic at Mumbai, the Emery Hospital (Anand) and Evangeline Booth Hospital (Ahmednagar) met with a good response. Locally, people are motivating their neighbourhood and community at large by caring for and supporting those living with HIV/Aids

and their families. Support is being given to the divisional coordination of local responses as corps learn from each other and build an integrated approach to HIV/Aids. Widows and women with HIV/Aids are being helped to cope financially.

When the territory experienced monsoon rains and floods, hundreds of people were made homeless and many children were orphaned, but The Salvation Army was on hand to help. Through generous donations from International Headquarters and 'partner' territories (USA Southern and Singapore, Malaysia and Myanmar) the Army assisted people regardless of creed and caste.

Salvationists acknowledge the work of the Holy Spirit in the territory and give the glory and honour to God.

STATISTICS

Officers 613 (active 394 retired 221) **Cadets** (1st Yr) 34 **Employees** 259
Corps 229 **Outposts** 290 **Institutions** 30 **Day Schools** 16
Senior Soldiers 31,136 **Adherents** 3,768 **Junior Soldiers** 8,923

STAFF

Editor: Maj B. P. Jadhav (Marathi)
Maj Punjalal U. Macwan (Gujarati)
Education: Maj Punjalal U. Macwan (Gujarati)
Field:
Human Resources: Maj Phulen Macwan (Gujarat) Maj D. K. Padale (Maharashtra)
Property and Development: Maj Vijay Dalvi (Maharashtra)
Property: Maj Jashwant Mahida (Gujarat)
Public Relations: Maj B. P. Jadhav
Social: Maj Punjalal U. Macwan (Gujarat)
Maj Suresh Pawar (Maharashtra)
Training: Maj Nicolas Damor (Gujarat);
Maj Ratnakar D. Kale (Maharashtra)
Women's Ministries: Comr P. Mary Rajakumari (TPWM) Lt-Col Nalini Parkhe (THLS)

Maj Ruth J. Mahida (LOMS-G) Maj Rajani V. Dalvi (LOMS-M) Maj S. Retnabai (SAMF-G) Maj Asha Kamble (SAMF-M) Maj Sheila Mandgule (SSF-M) Maj Margaret Macwan (SSF-G)

Youth: Maj Cornelius Christian (Gujarat) Maj Ashok Mandgule (Maharashtra)

DIVISIONS
Gujarat
Ahmedabad: Behrampura, Ahmedabad 380 022; tel: (079) 539 4258; Maj Jashwant T. Macwan (DYS to oversight)

Anand: Amul Dairy Rd, Anand 388 001; tel: (02692) 240638; Maj Kantilal K. Parmar, BA, BEd

Matar: Behind Civil Court, Matar District Kheda 387 530; tel: (02694) 285482; Maj David K. Sevak

Nadiad: Nadiad, District Kheda, 387 002; tel: (0268) 2558856; Maj Jashwant Soma Chauhan

Panchmahal: Dohad, Panchmahal, 389 151; tel: (02673) 221771; Maj Prabhudas J. Christian

Petlad: Sunav Rd, Post Petlad, District Kheda, 388 450; tel: (02679) 221527; Lt-Col Gideon Chhaganlal Chauhan

South Gujarat: Khambla Zampa, PO Vansda, 396 580District Navsari; Maj Natwarlal Macwan

Maharashtra
Ahmednagar: Fariabagh, Sholapur Rd, 414 001; tel: (022) 95241 358194; Capt Sanjay Wanjare

Mumbai: Sankli St, Byculla, Mumbai 400 008; tel: (022) 2301 3692; Maj Benjamin Gaikwad

Pathardi: Pathardi, District Ahmednagar, 414 102; tel: (02428) 223116; Maj Balu Borde

Pune: 19 Napier Rd, 411 040; tel: (022) 95206 363198; Maj Devdan Kasbe

Satara: Satara, District Satara 415 001; tel: (952162) 234006; Maj Benjamin Randive

Shevgaon: Shevgaon, District Ahmednagar, 414 502; tel: (952429) 223191; Maj Bhausaheb Magar

Shrirampur: District Ahmednagar, 413 709, Tal Shrirampur; tel: (95242) 226382

TRAINING COLLEGES
Gujarat: Anand 388 001, District Kheda, Amul Dairy Rd; tel: (02692) 254801

Maharashtra: Fariabagh, Ahmednagar 414 001; tel: (022) 95241 2355950

SCHOOLS
Boarding Schools (Boys and Girls)
William Booth Memorial Children's Home and Hostel: Anand 388 001, District Kheda, Gujarat; tel: (2692) 255580; Officer-in-Charge: Maj David Govind (acc 226)

William Booth Memorial Primary and High Schools, Farlabagh, District Ahmednagar, 414 001, Maharashtra; tel: (022) 95241 324267; Maj Ivor D. Salve (acc 513)

Day Schools
Anand: William Booth Memorial High School, Amul Dairy Rd; tel: (2692) 254901; Officer- in-Charge (Gujarat): Maj Samuel Parmar (acc 276)

English Medium Primary School: Maj Samuel Parmar (acc 260)

William Booth Primary School (acc 476)

Ashakiran: Primary School, Satara; under DHQ (acc 13)

Dynanjot: English Medium School, Vishrantwadi, 411 015; Capt P. Salve; tel: 95206 692761 (acc 25)

Muktipur: PO Bareja 382 425, District Ahmednabad; tel: 02718 233318 (acc 93)

Mumbai: Tucker English Medium School, Sankli St, Byculla, Mumbai 400 008; tel: (022) 307 7062 (acc 652)

Vadodara: English Medium School; Maj Purshottam D.

MEDICAL WORK
Emery Hospital: Anand, District Kaira, Gujarat; address: Amul Dairy Rd, 388 001; tel: (2692) 253737; Administrator: Maj Christopher Selvanath (acc 160)

Evangeline Booth Hospital: Ahmednagar 414 001, Maharashtra; tel: (022) 95241 2345059; Administrator: Maj Jayantilal G. Macwan; tel: (022) 95241 2325976 (acc 172)

Community-Based Aids Programme and Confidential Aids Counselling Clinic: Byculla, Mumbai; tel: (022) 309 3566 (incl Aruna Children's Programme and Asha Deep Tailoring Programme); Project Resources Officer: Maj Saresh Pawar;

HUMAN RESOURCES DEVELOPMENT CENTRES
Anand (Gujarat): Faujabad Comp, Ananda 388 001; Maj Phulen W. Macwan

Ahmednagar (Maharashtra): tel: (022) 95241
2358489; Maj David K. Padale

SOCIAL WORK
Farm Colony
Muktipur 382 425, Post Bareja, District
Ahmedabad; tel: (02718) 33318

Feeding Programme
Mumbai (Under King Edward Home)

Homes
Children:
Mumbai, Sion Rd, IOB Bldg, Sion (E)
400 022; tel: (022) 2409 4405 (acc 170)
Hope House, Pune: Gidney Park, Salisbury
Park Plot 41 No 554/2 Pune 411 037;
tel: 9529 24271728 (acc 50)

Elderly Men:
Mumbai 400 008, 122 Maulana Azad Rd,
Byculla; tel: (022) 23071346; (acc 50)

Industrial:
King Edward Home, 122 Maulana Azad Rd,
Byculla, Mumbai 400 008;
tel: (022) 2307 1346
Physically Handicapped Children:
Joyland, Anand 388 001, District Kheda,
Gujarat; tel: (02692) 51891 (acc 60)

Ray of Hope Home:
Vansda (under DHQ) (acc 60)

Hostels
Blind Working Men:
Ahmedabad: Locoshed, Rajpur-Hirpur,
Ahmedabad, Gujarat; tel: (079) 216 1217;
(acc 40)
Mumbai 400 008: Sankli St, Byculla;
tel: (022) 2305 1573 (acc 70)

Young Men:
Satara: c/o DHQ Satara; tel: (952162) 234006
(acc 30)

Young Women:
Anand: District Kheda, Gujarat;
tel: (02692) 254499 (acc 50)
Baroda: Nava Yard, Chhani Rd, Vadodara;
tel: (0265) 2775361
Mumbai 400 008: Concord House, Morland
Rd, Byculla; tel: (022) 2301 4219 (acc 63)
Pune: c/o DHQ, 19 Napier Rd, Pune 411 040
(acc 16)

RED SHIELD HOTEL
30 Mereweather Rd, Fort, Mumbai 400 039;
tel: (022) 2284 1824; fax: (022) 2282 4613
(acc 450)

When monsoon rains and floods hit the India Western Territory more than 2,100 people lost their lives, thousands of homes were destroyed and many children orphaned. The Salvation Army was swiftly on hand to put into action plans to feed up to 5,000 families from nearly 200 affected villages.

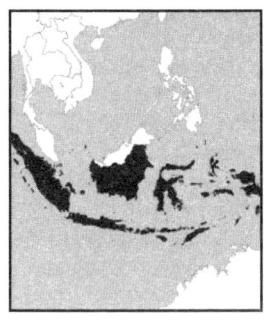

INDONESIA TERRITORY

Territorial leaders:
**Colonels Ribut Basuki and
Marie Kartodarsono**

Territorial Commander:
Colonel Ribut Basuki Kartodarsono
(1 Oct 2006)

Chief Secretary:
Lieut-Colonel Harold J. Ambitan
(1 Sep 2005)

Territorial Headquarters: Jalan Jawa 20, Bandung 40117

Postal address: Post Box 1640, Bandung 40016, Indonesia

Tel address: Salvation Bandung; tel: [62] (22) 4207029/4205056; fax: [62] (22) 423 6754;
web site: www.salvationarmy.or.id

The Army commenced in Indonesia (Java) in 1894. Operations were extended to Ambon, Bali, East Kalimantan, Sulawesi (Central, North and South), Sumatra (North and South) and East Nusa Tenggara, Aceh and Papua. A network of educational, medical and social services began.

Zone: South Pacific and East Asia
Country included in the territory: Indonesia
'The Salvation Army' in all Indonesian languages: Bala Keselamatan
Languages in which the gospel is preached: Indonesian with various dialects such as Batak, Daa, Dayak,
Javanese, Ledo, Makassarese, Moma, Niasnese, Tado and Uma

THE handover of 500 houses for the Indian Ocean tsunami victims at Meulaboh, Aceh, was completed and 227 more houses were being built, with Phase 2 of the construction scheduled for completion in September 2006. Trauma counselling, medical assistance, work among children, the provision of skilled training to women for income-generation, and community services were received enthusiastically and are greatly appreciated by the people.

Indonesia suffered further devastation when it was hit by another strong earthquake – in Yogyakarta, Central Java. The Compassion in Action team was quick to respond and ministered to victims at the disaster scene. This was another opportunity to show God's love through The Salvation Army's social, medical and other caring services.

July 2005 marked the 111th anniversary of The Salvation Army in Indonesia. This was celebrated in Semarang, Central Java (where the Army's work began), and in Central Sulawesi.

At the same time, celebrations were held to commemorate the 90th anniversary of William Booth Hospital in Semarang. In its early years an eye

147

hospital, it was developed into a general hospital to cater for the increasing number of people needing general medical treatment. The celebration was marked with thanksgiving and praise to God for his faithfulness in blessing the Army.

As a result of pioneering work in Nias Island, North Sumatera, and the funding by SAADO (Salvation Army Australia Development Office) the Teluk Dalam outpost, opened in 2003, was elevated to corps status.

Work in Nias is progressing rapidly, with the opening of additional outposts and health centres. The Salvation Army has established good relationships with the local government and its people since a devastating earthquake in March 2005.

A workshop on effective hospital business planning was provided for medical directors and administrators at Salvation Army hospitals, and for territorial headquarters leaders. The workshop was facilitated by professional consultants who, as a result of their input, will bring improvement to the territory's medical programme – a vital ministry to the people.

A Brengle Institute was held in Java and Bali Division for the officers' spiritual renewal. A combined institute also took place in Central Sulawesi for officers of the East Palu, West Palu and Kulawi Divisions. Majors Howard and Sheina Davis (Australia Southern) were the guest speakers and gave inspirational lectures on holy living.

During the year under review

70 outposts were elevated to corps status. Evangeline Booth Maternity Clinic was opened in Ambon and Catherine Booth Children's Home was built in Jakarta. A multiplication programme introduced in the territory has calculated that by 2010 soldiership will have doubled to 52,000; by 2015 corps will have doubled to 534; and by 2020, all institutions will be financially self-supporting.

STATISTICS

Officers 664 (active 550 retired 116) **Cadets** (1st Yr) 18 (2nd Yr) 28 **Employees** 1,615
Corps 267 **Outposts** 62 **Kindergartens** 7 **Primary Schools** 68 **Secondary Schools** 13 **High Schools** 5 **Technical High School** 1 **Hospitals** 6 **Theological University** 1 **Clinics** 18 **Academies for Nurses** 2 **Social Institutions** 22
Senior Soldiers 26,061 **Adherents** 15,710 **Junior Soldiers** 7,640
Officers serving outside oerritory 2

STAFF

Education: Maj Selly B. Poa
Field: Maj Selly B. Poa
Finance: Capt Yusak Tampai
Literature: Maj Habel Laua
Property and Legal: Maj Romeo Alip
Public Relations: Capt I. Nengah Wiarma
  Jl. Kramat Raya 55, Jakarta Pusat;
  tel: (021) 391 4518; fax: (021) 392 8636
Social: Maj Jones Kasaedja
Medical: Dr Pratiwi Kristianto, MM
Training: Maj Yavao Hondro
Women's Ministries: Col Marie Kartodarsono (TPWM), Lt-Col Deetje Ambitan (TSWM) Maj Anastasia Poa (THLS)
Youth and Candidates: Capt Marissa Mangela

DIVISIONS

Jawa and Bali: Jalan Dr Cipto 64b, Kelurahan Bugangan, Semarang 50126, Jateng; tel: (024) 355 1361; Lt-Col Pieter O. Siagian
Kulawi: Bala Keselamatan Post Office, Kulawi 94363, Sulteng; tel/fax: (0451) 811 017; Maj Philemon Ngkale
Palu Timur: Jalan Miangas 1, Kantor Pos Palu 94112; tel: (0451) 426 821;

fax: (0451) 425 846; Maj Lidia Simatupang

Palu Barat: Jalan Miangas 1-3, Palu 94112, Sulteng; mobile: 0816 4304498; Maj Winfrid Dalentang

Sulawesi Utara: Jalan A. Yani 15, Manado 95114; tel/fax: (0431) 864 052; Maj Henoch Nore

Sumatera Utara: Jl. Sei Kera 186 Medan 20232, Sumatera Utara; tel: (061) 4510284; Maj Dina Ismael

DISTRICTS

Kalimantan Timur: Maj Johanes Sayuti Maluku; Nusa Tenggara Timur; Sumatera Selatan

Palu Timur:
Parigi: Maj Nogerto Mariono
Tomini: Capt Leonard Togero
Napu Besoa: Maj Paris Tampu
Kalawara: under DHQ
Palolo: Capt I. Winfrid Dalentang

Palu Barat:
Bunggu:
Dombu: Maj Yosren Soekaryo
Pakawa:
Rowiga: under DHQ

Kulawi:
Lindu: Maj Benyamin Dama
Tobaku:
Kulawi: under DHQ
Kantewu: Maj Aman Mantaely
Gimpu: Lt-Col Mesak Losso
Karangana: Capt Bambang Supriyanto

Sumatera Utara:
Nias: Capt I. Nyoman Timonuli

TRAINING COLLEGE

Jalan Kramat Raya 55, Jakarta 10450, PO Box 3203, Jakarta 10002; tel: (021) 310 8148; fax: (021) 391 0410

EDUCATION

Jawa: 8 schools (acc 777)
Kalawara: 1 institute
Kalimantan Timur: 1 school (acc 42)
Sulawesi Selatan: 3 schools (acc 257)
Sulawesi Tengah: 79 schools (acc 6,539), 1 theological university (acc 60)
Sumatra Utara: 2 schools (acc 303)

MEDICAL WORK

General Hospitals (Jawa)

Bandung: Bungsu Hospital, jalan Veteran 6; tel: (022) 423 1550/1695; fax: (022) 423 1582; Director: Dr Pratiwi Kristianto (acc 49, poli-clinic attached)

Semarang: William Booth Hospital, Jalan Let. Jen. S. Parman 5 Semarang, 50232; tel: (024) 841 1800/844 8773; fax: (024) 844 8773; Capt Albert Sarimin (acc 100, eye and general clinic attached)

Surabaya: William Booth Hospital, Jalan Diponegoro 34; tel: (031) 561 4615/4616/ 5349; fax: (031) 567 1380; Capt Constantina Pattipeilohy (acc 200, maternity hospital and 3 poli-clinics attached)

Turen: Bokor Hospital, Jalan Jen A. Yani 89, Turen near Malang; tel: (0341) 824 453/002; fax: (0341) 823 878; Maj Edith Singara (acc 150, poli- and outpost clinics attached)

General Hospitals and Clinics (Sulawesi)

Palu: Woodward Hospital, Jalan L. H. Woodward 1, Kantor Pos Palu, Sulawesi Tengah; tel: (0451) 421 769/482 914/426 361; fax: (0451) 423 744; Maj Selviana Saptenno (acc 110)

Branch Hospitals

Ampera: under Woodward Hospital
Kulawi: Bethesda Hou Popakauria; Maj Veronika Bagania

Clinics

Ambon, East Kalimantan, Gimpu, Kamarora, Kantewu, Lembah Tongoa, Towulu

Sulawesi Utara: Kantor Pos Amurang, Kumelembuai, Makasili, Sulut

Maternity Hospital

Makassar, Sulawesi Selatan: Catherine Booth 'Mother and Child Hospital', Jalan Arif Rate 15 or Post Box 33; tel: (0411) 873 803/852 344; fax: (0411) 873 803; Maj Betty E. Widjaja (acc 53, poli-clinic attached)

Academies for Nurses' Training

Surabaya: under William Booth Hospital (acc 200)
Palu: under Woodward Hospital (acc 200)

SOCIAL INSTITUTIONS

Babies' and Toddlers' Home

Surabaya: Jalan Kombes Pol Durjat 10-12, Surabaya 60262; tel: (031) 534 1132; fax: (031) 532 2118 (acc 60)

Boys' Homes

Bandung: Jalan Dr Cipto 7; tel: (022) 423 0480 (acc 80)
Denpasar, Bali: Jalan Kebo Iwa No 29, Banjar

Liligundi, Ubung Kaja, Denpasar, Bali (acc 200)

Kalawara: Kantor Pos Palu, Sul Teng (acc 60)

Medan: Jalan K. L. Yos Sudarso 10, Lorong 1A; tel: (061) 661 3840 (acc 90)

Semarang: Jalan Musi Raya 2, Kel. Rejosari, Semarang 50125; tel: (024) 355 3287 (acc 80)

Surabaya: Jalan Gatotan 36; tel: (031) 352 2932 (acc 60)

Tompaso: Post Box 1100, Manado/Desa Liba, Kecamatan Tompaso 95693, Kab Minahasa; tel: (0431) 371 524 (acc 80)

Yogyakarta: Jalan Kenari 7, Miliran Post Box 1095; tel: (0274) 563598 (acc 32)

Children's Homes

Bandung: Jalan Jawa 18; tel: (022) 420 5549 (acc 90)

Denpasar: Jalan Hos Cokroaminoto 34; tel/fax: (0361) 426 484 (acc 60)

Jakarta: Catherine Booth Children's Home, Pondok Cabe (acc 100)

Malang: Jalan Panglima Sudirman 97; tel: (0341) 362 905 (acc 80)

Manado: Jalan Arnold Manonutu 501, Post Box 118; tel: (0431) 863 394 (acc 60)

Medan: Jalan Samanhudi 27; tel: (061) 414 2148 (acc 80)

Palu: Jalan Maluku 18, Palu 94112; tel: (0451) 424 586 (acc 80)

Centre for Homeless People

Semarang: Jalan Dr Cipto 64a, Kelurahan Bugangan, Semarang 50126, Jateng;

tel: (024) 771 0501/354 2536 (acc 100), dairy farm attached

Eventide Homes

Bandung: Jalan Jeruk 7; tel: (022) 727 1369 (acc 100)

Semarang: Jalan Musi Raya 4-6; tel: (024) 354 4855 (acc 60)

Turen: Jalan Achmad Yani 180; tel: (0341) 825 290 (acc 50)

Propeka (Social Services for School and Family Welfare)

Pulau Sicang: Kotak Pos 9, Belawan 20416, Sumatra Utara; tel: (061) 694 4003 (acc 500)

Sulawesi Tengah: Jalan Maluku 36, Palu 94112, Sul Teng; tel: (0451) 422 173 (acc 1,500)

Students' Hostels

Bandung: Jalan Dr Cipto 7; tel: (022) 423 0480 (acc 32)

Bandung: Jalan Jawa 18; tel: (022) 420 5549 (acc 32)

Medan: Jalan Samanhudi 27; tel: (061) 414 2148 (acc 30)

Surabaya: Jalan Gatotan 36; tel: (031) 352 2932 (acc 24)

Yogyakarta: Jalan Kenari 7, Miliran; tel: (0274) 563 598 (acc 8)

Transient House

Jalan Kramat Raya 55; tel: (021) 391 4518 (acc 18)

THQ GUEST HOUSES

Jalan Jawa 20; tel: (022) 420 7029 (acc 10)

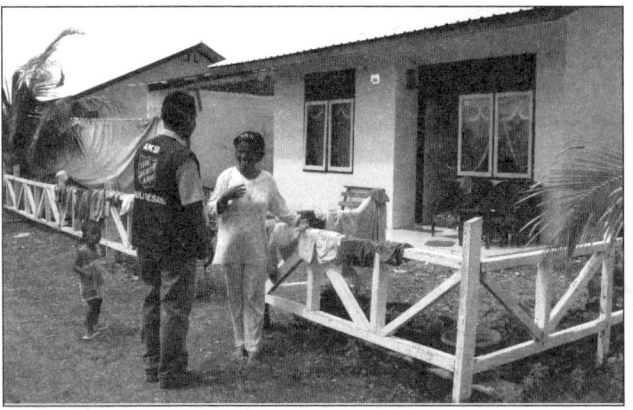

This woman was the happy recipient of one of 750 houses built by The Salvation Army in Indonesia during 2006 for tsunami victims in Meulaboh, Aceh

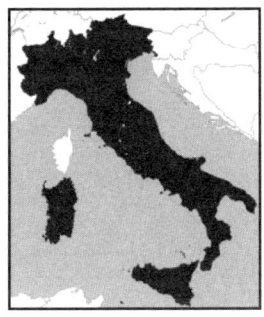

ITALY COMMAND

Command leaders:
Majors Massimo and E. Jane Paone

Officer Commanding:
Major Massimo Paone (1 Aug 2002)

Command Headquarters: Via degli Apuli 39, 00185 Rome, Italy

tel: [39] 06 4462614/06 4941089; fax: [39] 06 490078; email: Italy_Command@ity.salvationarmy.org
web site: www.esercitodellasalvezza.org

The Salvation Army flag was unfurled in Italy on 20 February 1887 by Major and Mrs James Vint and Lieutenant Fanny Hack, though subsequent difficulties necessitated withdrawal. In 1890 Fritz Malan (later lieut-colonel) began meetings in his native village in the Waldensian Valleys. In 1893 Army work was re-established.

In a decree of the President on 1 April 1965, The Salvation Army was recognised as a philanthropic organisation competent to acquire and hold properties and to receive donations and legacies.

Zone: Europe
Country included in the command: Italy
'The Salvation Army' in Italian: Esercito della Salvezza
Language in which the gospel is preached: Italian
Periodicals: *Il Bollettino dell' Unione Femminile, Il Grido di Guerra*

THE Salvation Army's holiday centre on the island of Ischia continues to be a place for spiritual renewal. In the summer of 2005 a women's retreat featured creative Bible studies on the theme 'There Was A Woman ...' while at the family camp more than 50 people of all ages appreciated studies on spiritual growth.

At Pentecost some 260 Salvationists and friends joined to celebrate 100 years of the Army's presence in Ariano Irpino. The centenary flag was passed on from the oldest soldier to the newest. The Mayor and Archbishop of Ariano, along with other Church representatives, attended the Sunday afternoon celebration.

After the commissioning of three new officers by Commissioner Thorleif Gulliksen (IS, Europe), Italian personnel were strengthened by another newly commissioned officer arriving from William Booth College in London.

An enthusiastic group of young people, representing most corps in Italy, attended the European Youth Congress in Prague (Czech Republic), where they were empowered by the Holy Spirit. Three of the delegates were enrolled as soldiers later in the year.

Refurbishment of the Rome Social Services Centre resulted in 34 new rooms to accommodate female guests. Regional and local council

The three newest captains in Italy are commissioned and ordained during a meeting in Rome Corps hall

representatives attending the opening ceremony expressed appreciation for the ministry at the centre.

During the 2006 Winter Olympics a More Than Gold team of evangelists worked with Salvationists of Turin Corps to share the gospel among huge crowds. The band played in one of the main city squares and the corps hall was open daily for refreshments.

More than 120 young people gathered in Rome for the National Youth Congress – the first for many years in the command. Greater New York Youth Band and Timbrelists (USA Eastern) and representatives from France and Spain were among the delegates and witnessed to interested onlookers during a Sunday afternoon concert in the city centre.

Guest speaker Major Sandra Ryan (Toronto 614 Corps, Canada) gave thought-provoking Bible messages. In the Sunday evening meeting 25 young people made decisions for Christ at the mercy seat.

Youth and children's work has been given particular emphasis, resulting in the enrolment of junior soldiers.

STATISTICS
Officers 49 (active 25 retired 24) **Lieutenants** 6 **Cadets** 2 **Employees** 10
Corps 17 **Outposts** 15 **Institutions** 7
Senior Soldiers 251 **Adherents** 83 **Junior Soldiers** 34
Personnel serving outside command Officers 2

STAFF
Women's Ministries (and Resources): Maj E. Jane Paone (CPWM)
Finance: Capt Patricia Pavoni
Family Tracing: Maj Angela Dentico
Youth/Candidates/Training: Capt Frederick Wong
Editor: Capt Debora Wong

SOCIAL WORK
Centre for the Homeless
Centro Virgilio Paglieri, Via degli Apuli 41, 00185 Roma; tel: 06 4451351; fax: 06 4456306 (acc 225)

Workers' Lodge
Villa Speranza, Contrada Serra 57a, 85100 Potenza; tel/fax: (0971) 51245 (acc 15)

Holiday Centres
Le Casermette, Via Pellice 4, 10060 Bobbio Pellice (To); tel/fax: (0121) 957728; web site: www.direzione@centrovacanze.it (acc 120)
Concordia, Via Casa di Majo 32-36, 80075 Forio d'Ischia (Na); tel: (081) 997324; fax: (081) 997576; email: concordia@esercitodellasalvezza.org (acc 65)
L'Uliveto, Via Stretta della Croce 20, 84030 Atena Lucana (Sa); tel/fax: (0975) 76321 (acc 70)

Guest Houses
Villa delle Rose, Via Aretina 91, 50136 Firenze; tel/fax: (055) 660445 (acc 13)
Foresteria, Via degli Apuli 41, 00185 Roma; tel/fax: 06 44 51 351; email: foresteriaroma@esercitodellasalvezza.org (acc 70)

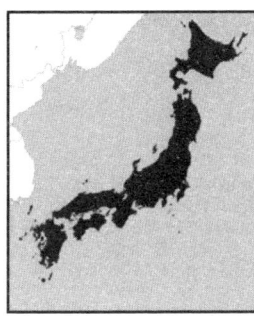

JAPAN TERRITORY

Territorial leaders:
Commissioners Makoto and Kaoru Yoshida

Territorial Commander:
Commissioner Makoto Yoshida (1 Jun 2006)

Chief Secretary:
Lieut-Colonel Naoshi Hiramoto (1 Mar 2004)

Territorial Headquarters: 17, 2-chome, Kanda Jimbocho, Chiyoda-ku, Tokyo 101-0051, Japan

tel: [81] (03) 3237 0881; fax: [81] (03) 3237 7676; web site: www.salvationarmy.or.jp/english/

In 1895 a small group of pioneer officers from Britain arrived in Japan at Yokohama to start operations. In spite of great difficulties, work was soon established.

Of several outstanding Japanese who were attracted to The Salvation Army, the most distinguished was Commissioner Gunpei Yamamuro OF, prominent evangelist and author, whose book *The Common People's Gospel* is now in its 527th printing.

Zone: South Pacific and East Asia
Country included in the territory: Japan
Languages in which the gospel is preached: Japanese, Korean
Periodicals: *Home League Quarterly, The Officer, The Sunday School Guide, Toki-no-Koe*

WITH vision and hope the Japan Territory celebrated '2005 – A Year for Children and Youth'. Various events were organised, focusing on the salvation and development of young people – one of the territory's most important and urgent issues.

The Youth Day, held divisionally in May, prepared the young people's hearts for the Territorial Youth Congress in August, led by General John Larsson and Commissioner Freda Larsson. Through Bible messages, fellowship and music the international leaders encouraged and inspired their congregations to live out their faith in today's society. Young Salvationists then responded to

this challenge in the 'Youth Caravan' during October. A group travelled to Hiroshima and, with the local corps members, organised and participated in outreach activities.

The focus on dedication and service continued in a 'Commitment' seminar held in March 2006 to coincide with the commissioning of the territory's new officer. Under the theme 'Serving God and People', delegates came together to learn more about Christian service by looking at Salvation Army work in various countries and listening to testimonies.

The highlight of the year was the Territorial Congress, led by the General and Commissioner Larsson following the Territorial Youth Congress. More than 800 people met from all parts of Japan, enjoying the reunion with other Salvationists and immersing themselves in God's word.

The territory rejoiced in the addition of new lieutenants, the first since the lieutenants system was introduced in Japan. The two women were sent to their appointments in July after receiving their initial training.

Two new buildings were erected to accommodate the changing needs of society. Kinshicho Building, on the site of Koto Corps, includes the corps premises, divisional headquarters and a second site of the Bazaar Men's Social Services Centre. Oasis House is a compound in which an annex of Sekoryo Children's Home, a shelter run by Fujinryo Women's Home and a care management centre for Grace Senior Citizens' Care Centre are situated.

Changes in government policies often require revisions in Army's social and medical work, but the territory is grateful that God is providing the ways and means to meet those challenges.

STATISTICS
Officers 187 (active 101 retired 86) **Cadets** (2nd Yr) 1 **Employees** 1,020
Corps 50 **Outposts** 9 **Institutions** 20 **Hospitals** 2
Senior Soldiers 3,056 **Adherents** 45 **Junior Soldiers** 90
Personnel serving outside territory Officers 2

STAFF
Business Administration: Maj Jiro Katsuchi
Editor: Sis Keiko Saito
Literary: Maj Kazumitsu Higuchi

Medical: Maj Naoko Harita, BA
Music: B/M Hajime Suzuki
Personnel: Maj Haruhisa Ota
Programme: Maj Kazumitsu Higuchi
Social: Maj Naoko Harita, BA
Staff Band: B/M Hajime Suzuki
Staff Songsters: S/L Mikako Ebara
Training: Maj Fumiko Kugo
Women's Ministries: Comr Kaoru Yoshida (TPWM) Lt-Col Seiko Hiramoto (TSWM)
Youth and Candidates: Maj Hiromi Ota

DIVISIONS
Hokkaido: Nishi 1-13-1, Minami-4-jo, Chuo-ku, Sapporo-shi 064-0804; tel: (011) 231 2805; fax: (011) 231 2825; Maj Tsukasa Yoshida
Kanto-Tohoku: 5 Yoriai-cho, Takasaki-shi, Gunma Ken 370-0822; tel: (027) 323 1337; fax: (027) 323 1334; Maj Masaru Yamanaka
Nishi Nihon: 3-6-20 Tenjinbashi, Kita-ku, Osaka-shi 530-0041; tel: (06) 6351 0084; fax: (06) 6351 0093; Maj Nobuhiro Hiramoto
Tokyo-Tokaido: 4-11-3 Taihei, Sumida-ku, Tokyo 130-0012; tel: (03) 5819 1460; fax: (03) 5819 1461; Maj Chieko Tanaka

TRAINING COLLEGE
1-39-5 Wada Suginami-ku, Tokyo 166-0012; tel: (03) 3381 9837

MEDICAL WORK
Booth Memorial Hospital: 1-40-5 Wada, Suginami-ku, Tokyo 166-0012; tel: (03) 3381 7236; fax: (03) 5385 0734 (acc hospital 179 hospice 20); Supt: Dr Kazuo Mukuno
Kiyose Hospital: 1-17-9 Takeoka, Kiyose-shi, Tokyo, 204-0023; tel: (0424) 91 1411/3; fax: (0424) 91 3900 (acc hospital 117 hospice 25); Supt: Dr Kunio Murakami

SOCIAL WORK
Men
Alcoholic Rehabilitation Centre
Jiseikan, 1-17-60 Takeoka, Kiyose-shi, Tokyo 204-0023; tel: (0424) 93 5374 (acc 50)
Rehabilitation Centre
2-21-2 Wada Suginami-ku, Tokyo 166-0012 tel: (03) 3384-9114 (acc 15)
Social Service Centre (Bazaar)
2-21-2 Wada Suginami-ku, Tokyo 166-0012; tel: (03) 3384 3769
Working Men's Homes
Jijokan, 2-17-10 Tsukishima, Chuo-ku, Tokyo 104-0052; tel: (03) 3531 3516 (acc 35)

Shibuya Corps Band (Japan) gives a street-level charity concert in support of the Hurricane Katrina disaster fund. Many passers-by stopped to listen to the music and, seeing photographs of Salvation Army relief work in the Gulf Coast area of America, gave generous donations.

Shinkokan, 87 Akagishita-machi, Shinjuku-ku, Tokyo 162-0803; tel: (03) 3269 4901 (acc 40)

Women's Homes
Fujinryo: 1-43-11 Wada Suginami-ku, Tokyo 166-0012; tel: (03) 3381 0992 (acc 40)
Shinseiryo: 4-11-14 Shibazaki-cho, Tachikawa-shi, Tokyo 190-0023; tel: (042) 522 2306 (acc 70)

Children's Homes
Aikoen: 1-3 Aoyama-cho, Kure-shi, Hiroshima 737-0023; tel: (0823) 21 6374 (acc 30)
Kibokan: 2-16-11, Nakahodzumi, Ibaraki-shi, Osaka 567-0034; tel: (0726) 23 3758 (acc 65)
Kiekoryo: 4-12-10 Kami Ikedai, Ota-ku, Tokyo 145-0064; tel: (03) 3729 0357 (acc 35)
Sekoryo: 2-21-1 Wada, Suginami-ku, Tokyo 166-0012; tel: (03) 3381 0545 (acc 50)
Toyohama-Gakuryo: 3082-5 Toyoshima, Toyohama-cho, Kure-shi, Hiroshima 734-0101; tel: (08466) 8 2029 (acc 60)

Day Nurseries
Kikusui Kamimachi Hoikuen: 2-52 Kikusui Kamimachi 3-jo, Shiroishi-ku, Sapporo-shi 003-0813; tel: (011) 821 2879 (acc 90)
Kure Hoikusho: 1-4 Aoyama-cho, Kure-shi 737-0023; tel: (0823) 21 4711 (acc 60)
Sano Hoikuen: 182 Asanuma-cho, Sano-shi 327-0831; tel: (0283) 22 4081 (acc 126)
Shiseikan Hoikuen: Nishi 7, Minami 3-jo, Chuo-ku, Sapporo-shi 060-0063;

tel: (011) 204 9560 (acc 120)
Soen Hoikusho: Nishi 14-1, Kita 5-jo, Chuo-ku, Sapporo-shi 060-0005; tel: (011) 221 6630 (acc 60)

Home for the Aged
Keisen Home: 1-17-61 Takeoka, Kiyose-shi, Tokyo 204-0023; tel: (0424) 93 5161/2 (acc 50)

Hostel
Kyoto Hostel: 37 Tokushoji-cho, Tominokoji-dori 4-jo Sagaru, Shimogyo-ku, Kyoto-shi 600-8051; tel: (075) 361 4690 (acc 16)

Senior Citizens' Housing and Care Centre
Grace: 1-40-15 Wada, Suginami-ku, Tokyo 166-0012; tel: (03) 3380 1248;
fax: (03) 3380 1206; Supt: Mrs Kazue Okubo (acc 100)

Care House
Izumi: 1-17-24 Takeoka, Kiyose-shi, Tokyo 204-0023; tel: (0424) 96 7575 (acc 32)

RETIRED OFFICERS' APARTMENTS
Olive House: 1-39-12 Wada, Suginami-ku, Tokyo 166-0012
Osaka Central Hall 5F: 3-6-20 Tenjinbashi, Kita-ku, Osaka 530-0041
Tokiwa House: 1-17-12 Takeoka, Kiyose-shi, Tokyo 204-0023

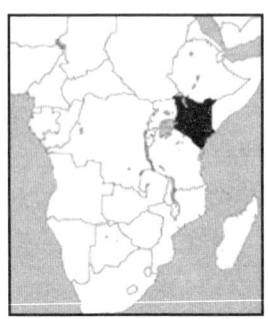

KENYA TERRITORY

Territorial Commander:
Commissioner Hezekiel Anzeze
(1 Feb 2002)

Chief Secretary:
Lieut-Colonel Kenneth G. Hodder
(1 Mar 2006)

Territorial Headquarters: Moi Avenue, Nairobi

Postal address: Box 40575, Nairobi, Kenya 00100 GPO

tel: [254] (020) 227541/2/9; fax: [254] (020) 342014; tel address: Salvation Nairobi

In 1896 three Salvationists went to Kenya to work on the building of a new railway and made their witness while based at the Taru Camp. The first official meetings were held in Nairobi in April 1921, led by Lieut-Colonel and Mrs James Allister Smith. The first cadets were trained in 1923. In 1931 the flag was unfurled in Mbale, Uganda, by Captain and Mrs Edward Osborne. On 1 November 2005 the East Africa Territory (which included the Uganda Region) was redesignated the Kenya Territory and Uganda was elevated to command status.

Zone: Africa
Country included in the territory: Kenya
'The Salvation Army' in Kiswahili: Jeshi La Wokovu
Languages in which the gospel is preached: English, Kiswahili and a number of tribal languages
Periodicals: *Sauti ya Vita* (English and Kiswahili)

AS the number of corps and soldiers in the territory increases, Salvationists are ever more conscious of those people who are yet to be reached for Christ. This passion for evangelism was evidenced in 2006 through adoption of the theme 'Win One Other', with Salvationists being challenged to 'duplicate' themselves spiritually in the life of another person.

Administratively, the territory's growth has been reflected in the creation of a new division and new districts. Also, the first public World Services Ingathering, held in Nairobi, brought the territory's efforts to support Salvation Army ministry around the world to a successful conclusion, with more funds being raised than ever before.

Property was identified for the construction of a new territorial headquarters, the first in almost 80 years. The purchase was made possible through generous gifts from territories and commands around the world, including the USA Eastern, Southern and Western Territories. But it would not have occurred without thousands of small gifts from individual officers, soldiers, junior soldiers and friends of the Army in Kenya, all of whom share a strong sense of ownership in the Movement.

Just as they consistently raise the majority of funds necessary to build new corps and outposts, Kenyan Salvationists have taken an active part in raising the funds for land upon which THQ can operate effectively in the future.

Plans were also fulfilled for the creation of the Territorial Band and Songsters, which premiered during the 2006 commissioning weekend. Thanks to generous gifts from the Kenya Trust, the Territorial Band played its first engagement with brand-new instruments.

Kenya was one of a number of countries that experienced a humanitarian crisis when the 'short' rains failed in the last few months of 2005. Food shortages became severe across many parts of Kenya, with some 2.5 million people directly affected. Large livestock losses were reported and rates of child malnutrition were also alarmingly high.

Nearly 3.5 million rural pastoral and farming people – including 500,000 schoolchildren – needed emergency assistance to sustain lives and protect livelihoods. The government launched an international appeal for humanitarian assistance and The Salvation Army was among those to respond.

As one component of its Sub-Saharan Africa famine relief work in Kenya, the International Emergency Services (IHQ) launched a 'Food for Fees' programme. Supplies of basic food commodities (maize, beans and oil) were delivered to secondary schools, guaranteeing that this group of vulnerable people received a substantial daily meal. In return, schools used the value of this gift-in-kind to offset fees for children whose families had lost herds and crops and were struggling to survive.

STATISTICS

Officers 985 (active 722 retired 263) **Cadets** 78 **Envoys in training** 22 **Lieutenants** 4 **Employees** 61
Corps 506 **Outposts** 1,208 **Pre-primary Schools** 342 **Primary Schools** 399 **Secondary Schools** 53 **Institutions** 43
Senior Soldiers 176,187 **Junior Soldiers** 175,445

STAFF

Audit: Maj Zakayo Kwendo
Business Administration: Maj James McDowell
Personnel: Maj Gabriel Kathuri
Programme: Maj Samuel Oklah
Projects: Marshall Currie
Property: Capt Harun Chepsiri
Public Relations: Maj David Simiyu
Social:
Trade:
Training: Maj Henry Nyaga
Women's Ministries: Lt-Col Jolene K. Hodder (TLWM)
Youth: Capt Kennedy Ombajo

DIVISIONS

Bungoma: PO Box 1106, Bungoma, Kenya; tel: 055-30589; Maj Enock Lufumbu
Eldoret: PO Box 125, Eldoret, Kenya; tel: 053-22266; Maj John Wafula
Embu: PO Box 74, Embu, Kenya; tel: 068-20107; Maj Francis Nganda
Kakamega: PO Box 660, Kakamega, Kenya; tel: 056-20344; Maj Edward Shavanga
Kangundo: PO Box 324, Kangundo, Kenya; tel: 044-21049; Maj Jackson Muasa
Kibwezi: PO Box 428, Sultan Hamud, Kenya; tel: 044-52200
Machakos: PO Box 160, Machakos, Kenya; tel: 044-21660; Lt-Col Julius Mukonga
Mbale: PO Box 80, Maragoli, Kenya; tel: 056-51076; Maj Tiras Mbaja
Musudzuu: PO Box 278, Seremi, Kenya; tel: 056-45055; Maj Martin Mboto

Nairobi: PO Box 31205, Nairobi, Kenya;
tel: 020-767208; Maj Naphas M'memi
Shigomere Bunyore: PO Box 125, Khwisero,
Kenya; tel: 056-20260; Maj Moses Shavanga
Tongaren: PO Box 127, Tongaren, Kenya;
Maj Johnstone Kathendu

DISTRICTS

Bunyore: PO Box 81, Bunyore, Kenya;
Maj Isaac Kivindyo
Coast: PO Box 98277, Mombasa, Kenya;
tel: 041-490629; Maj John Olewa
Elgon: PO Box 274, Malakisi, Kenya;
tel: 055-20443; Maj Boniface Munyekhe
Kisumu: PO Box 288, Kisumu, Kenya;
tel: 057-2025632; Maj Peter Mutuku
Kitale: PO Box 548, Kitale, Kenya;
tel: 054-30259
Kasikeu/Makueni: PO Box 428, Sultan Hamud,
Kenya; tel: 044-52200; Maj James Mukubwa
Kathiani: PO Box 2, Kathiani, Kenya
Meru: PO Box 465, Nkubu, Meru, Kenya;
tel: 064-51207; Capt Johnstone Wolayo
Migori: PO Box 59, Suna, Migori, Kenya;
Capt Jacob Olubwayo
Mwala: PO Box 19, Mwala, Kenya
Nakuru: PO Box 672, Nakuru, Kenya;
tel: 051-212455; Maj Nelson Miriti
Thika: PO Box 809, Thika, Kenya; tel: 067-22056
Turkana: PO Box 118-30500, Lodwar, Kenya;
tel: 054-21010; Capt Ibrahim Lorot
Yatta: PO Box 29 Kithimani, Kenya

TRAINING COLLEGE

PO Box 4467, Thika, Kenya; tel: 067-24149

CONFERENCE CENTRE

Park Rd, PO Box 40575, Nairobi, Kenya;
tel: 020-6762292

FARM

Avontour Estate, PO Box 274, Thika, Kenya

EDUCATIONAL WORK

SA Sponsored Primary Schools: 402

**SA Sponsored and Managed Secondary
Schools:** 51

Special Schools
Visually Handicapped
High School:
Thika: PO Box 704, Thika, Kenya;
tel: 067-22092 (acc 163)

Primary Schools:
Kibos: PO Box 77, Kisumu, Kenya;
tel: 057-43135 (acc 230)
Likoni: PO Box 96089, Mombasa, Kenya;
tel: 041-451101 (acc 120)
Thika: PO Box 80, Thika, Kenya;
tel: 067-21691 (acc 297)

Physically Disabled
Primary Schools:
Joyland: PO Box 1790, Kisumu, Kenya;
tel: 057-41864/50574 (acc 230)
Joytown: PO Box 326, Thika, Kenya;
tel: 067-21291 (acc 215)
Secondary School:
Joytown: PO Box 1370, Thika, Kenya;
tel: 067-22008 (acc 110)

Multi-Handicapped Special Units
Joytown: PO Box 326, Thika, Kenya;
tel: 067-21291 (acc 22)
Thika Primary School: PO Box 80, Thika,
Kenya; tel: 067-21691
Njoro Special School: PO Box 359, Njoro,
Kenya

SOCIAL SERVICES
Children's Homes
Kabete: PO Box 210-00606 Sarit Centre,
Nairobi, Kenya; tel: 020-442766
(acc 114)
Mombasa: PO Box 90531, Mombasa, Kenya;
tel: 041-224387 (acc 40)

Community Centre
Kibera: PO Box 21608, Nairobi, Kenya;
tel: 020-567064

Feeding Programme for Destitutes
Kisumu: PO Box 288, Kisumu, Kenya;
tel: 057-4151

Girls' Hostel
Nairobi: PO Box 31354, Nairobi, Kenya

Health Centre
Kolanya: PO Box 88, Malakisi, via Bungoma,
Kenya

Vocational Training Centres
Variety Village: PO Box 1472, Thika, Kenya;
tel: 067-21822
Nairobi Girls' Centre: PO Box 31304, Nairobi,
Kenya; tel: 020-766375 (acc 60)

Workshop
Kibos: PO Box 477, Kisumu, Kenya (acc 12)

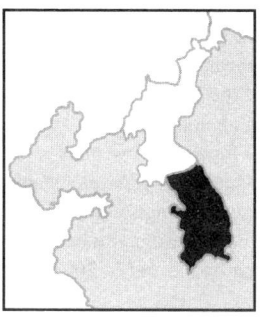

KOREA TERRITORY

**Commissioners Chun, Kwang-pyo
and Yoo, Sung-ja**

Territorial Commander:
Commissioner Chun, Kwang-pyo
(1 Jan 2005)

Chief Secretary:
Lieut-Colonel Park, Man-hee (1 Jan 2005)

**Territorial Headquarters: The Salvation Army Central Hall,
1-23 Chung dong, Choong Ku, Seoul 100-120**

Postal address: The Salvation Army, Central PO Box 1192, Seoul 100-611, Republic of Korea

tel: [82] (2) 720 9494; fax: [82] (2) 720 0496

email addresses: korea@kor.salvationarmy.org, sally@soback.kornet.net

web site: www.salvationarmy.or.kr

When the Founder visited Japan in 1907, he dispatched Commissioner George Scott Railton to survey prospects on the Korean peninsula. In October 1908 Colonel and Mrs Robert Hoggard (née Annie Johns) arrived with a group of officers to 'open fire' in Seoul. During the Korean conflict, which took place from 1950 to 1953, one Korean officer was martyred, one killed and two have been listed as missing.

Zone: South Pacific and East Asia
Country included in the territory: Republic of Korea
'The Salvation Army' in Korean sounds like: 'Koo Sei Goon'
Language in which the gospel is preached: Korean
Periodicals: *Home League Programme Helps*, *Loving Hands Sponsorship Magazine*, *The Officer*, *The War Cry*

WITH the international focus of 2005 on 'A Year for Children and Youth', the territory sought to revitalise its youth ministries. Three community centres catering for children were established, as well as four new study centres, and eight new youth programmes were commenced.

During a 'Power Camp for the N-Generation' 42 of the 630 young people who were present offered their lives for officership. The Bible Reading Retreat for Youth also took place.

Young people from the children's homes participated in a trip to North Korea's Mount Keumgang (the tour being offered to South Koreans by the Hyundai Asan Group, following official sanction by both governments). As well as being exposed to a culture similar to, yet different from, their own, they also gained a vision for mission to North Korea.

In celebration of the territory's 97th anniversary in October 2005, cultural events were held in each of the nine divisions. At a united rally for the Seoul Division and Seoul South Division the territorial commander enrolled 114 senior soldiers and junior soldiers, and 40 young people registered commitments to officership. During the rally in Chulla Division a special offering was taken for the Zimbabwe Territory.

During the year under review one corps and six social services centres were opened and 14 community programmes commenced. Plans are in hand for five new corps and seven social services centres during 2006.

Exploratory ministry is being undertaken, in conjunction with the Hong Kong and Macau Command, to establish an integrated programme in Yanbian, north-eastern China, focusing on the ethnic Korean population.

In December 2005, at World Cup Park in Seoul, the National Marathon Association held a 'Fundraising Marathon' for the Army's Christmas Kettle Appeal. Some 3,000 runners participated.

As well as the usual Christmas Kettle Appeal stands, two four-metre-high stands were set up as part of the 'Luminarie Festival' in downtown Seoul. The kettles were so popular they became a symbol of the festival, also encouraging a generous outpouring of financial support from the public.

The economic situation was difficult during 2005 but the Christmas Kettle Appeal recorded a 12.5 per cent increase. Territorial fundraising, with goods-in-kind, saw a 36 per cent increase on the previous year.

Marching towards the centenary celebration of the Korea Territory in 2008, a planning committee has been established to formulate a written history. The Sangamdong Development Project in Seoul is being steered toward assisting the territory to become self-supporting by the end of 2008.

STATISTICS

Officers 692 (active 556 retired 136) **Cadets** (1st Yr) 19 (2nd Yr) 21 **Employees** 564
Corps 239 **Outposts and Societies** 14 **Institutions** 35 **School** 1 **Child Day Care Centres** 6 **Corps Child Day Care Centres** 21 **Students' Study Centres** 26 **Counselling Centres** 6 **Sarangbang Centres** 3 **Special Service Vehicle Units** 3 **HIV/Aids Care and Prevention Team Units** 3 **Drop-in Centre for the Homeless** 1 **Self-Support Training Centres** 3 **Community Welfare Centres** 11
Senior Soldiers 39,913 **Adherents** 8,285 **Junior Soldiers** 6,148
Personnel serving outside territory Officers 19

STAFF

Sec for Personnel: Maj Lim, Hun-taek
Editor and Education Sec: Maj Lee, Choong-ho
Literary Sec: Maj Kim, Dong-jin
Overseas Service Bureau Director: Maj Kim, Dong-jin

Sec for Programme: Maj Lim, Young-sik
Church Growth: Capt Choi, Yung-mi
Social: Maj Kim, Nam-sun
Youth: Maj Kang, Jik-koo
Music Director: Capt Kim, Hai-du

Sec for Business: Maj, Park, Nai-hoon
Finance and Audit: Maj Kim, Young-tae, BA, MBA
Information Technology: Capt Lee, Hyun-hee
Property: Maj Lee, Ki-yong
Public Relations: Maj Ahn, Guhn-shik
Child Sponsorship: Maj Yang, Shin-kyung
Trade: Capt Kim, Sook-yung

Territorial Archivist: Lt-Col Kim, Joon-chul
Training: Maj Shin, Moon-ho
Women's Ministries: Comr Yoo, Sung-ja (TPWM) Lt-Col Kim, Keum-nyeo (TSWM) Maj Yeo, Keum-soo (THLS) Maj Chun, Soon-

ja (TLMS) Maj Pyo, Choon-yun (TSSS)
Maj Kil, Soon-boon (TSAMFS)

DIVISIONS

Choong Buk: 704 Doosan Hansol 1 cha
Apartments 101 dong, 447-15 Kaeshin
Dong, Heungduk Ku, Chung Ju, Choong
Book 361-746; tel: (043) 276 1634;
fax: (043) 263 6387; Maj Chun, Joon-hong
Choong Chung: 603 Oosung Apartments
126 dong, 640 Chunglim dong, Suh ku,
Taejon, Choong Nam Do 302-795;
tel: (042) 584 2891; fax: (042) 584 2892;
Maj Kim, Oon-ho
Choong Saw: 401 Hyundai Apartments
3-cha 302 dong, 388-2 Ssangyong dong,
Chonan, Choong Nam Do 330-091;
tel: (041) 572 0855; fax: (041) 578 0855;
Maj Pang, Kie-chang
Chulla: 375-21 Song San Dong, Chung Eup,
Chun Buk 580-200; tel: (063) 536 1190;
fax: (063) 536 1191; Maj Yang, Tae-soo
Kyung Buk: 1302 Kongjak Hanyang
Apartments 104 dong, Eupnae dong 1366-1,
Buk ku, Taegu 702-850; tel: (053) 322 3695;
fax: (053) 322 3694; Maj Choo, Seung-chan
Kyung Nam: 1306 Green Core Apartments
301 dong, 216 7 Manduk 3 dong, Buk ku,
Pusan, Kyung Sang Nam Do 616-782;
tel: (051) 337 0789; fax: (051) 337 2292;
Maj Park, Chong-duk
Seoul: The Salvation Army Office Building,
#705, Shinmoonro 1-ga, 58-1, Chongno gu,
Seoul 100-161; tel: (02) 720 9543;
fax: (02) 720 9546; Lt-Col Son, Myong-shik
Seoul South: 602, Soojung Hanyang Apartments
235-dong, 1086 Sanbon 3-dong, Danwon Ku,
Ansan, Kyunggi-do 425-765;
tel: (031) 413 7811; fax: (031) 413 7812;
Maj Kim, Kie-duk
Suh Hae: 301 Dongshin Apartments 204 dong,
Eupnae Dong 624-1, Sosan, Choong Nam
356-758; tel: (041) 667 2580;
fax: (041) 667 2576; Maj Kwon, Sung-dal

TRAINING COLLEGE

83-2 Chungang-dong, Kwachun, Kyunggi-do
427-010; tel: (02) 502 9505/2927;
fax: (02) 502 7160

CONFERENCE CENTRES

Ah Hyun Corps, Kangwondo (acc 300)
Taejon Central Corps, Taejon (acc 400)
Territorial Retreat and Conference Centre,
Paekhwa-san [Paekhwa Mountain] (acc 1,000)

RETIRED OFFICERS' RESIDENCE

'Victory Lodge' Silver Nursing Home (acc 50)

TERRITORIAL HERITAGE CENTRE

1st floor, The Salvation Army Central Hall,
1-23 Chung dong, Choong Ku, Seoul 100-120

THE SALVATION ARMY OFFICE BUILDING (THE SAOB)

Shinmoon ro 1-ga 58-1, Chong Ro Ku, Seoul
100-061

SOCIAL WORK
Bridge Centre (drop-in centre)
Seoul (acc 50)

Centres for the Handicapped
Kunsan: Catherine Centre for the Handicapped
(acc 60)
Kunsan: Day Care Centre for the Handicapped
Suwon: Support Centre for the Handicapped
(acc 8)

Children's Homes
Kunsan (acc 114), Seoul Broadview (acc 160),
Taegu (acc 61), Taejon No 1 (acc 50), Taejon
No 2 (acc 75)

Community Centres
Asan, Ansung, Booyuh, Boryung, Cheju,
Chilgok, Hapjung (Pyongtaek), Hong Eun,
Kang Buk, Mosan, Myung Chun, Najoo,
Nonsan, Seogwipo, Sosan, Suh San Suklim,
Tai An, Yoju, Yongwol

Corps Day Care Centres
Bahnyawol (acc 52), Boo Nam (acc 32), Chin
Chang (acc 32), Chin Ju [Cham Sarang]
(acc 38), Chun Kok (acc 39), Hap Duk (acc 49),
Kang Buk (acc 92), Kim Chon (acc 38),
Kwachun (acc 91), Masan [Moonwha] (acc 44),
Mil Yang [Catherine] (acc 40), Mindalae
(acc 57), Mosan (acc 51), Myung Chun
(acc 48), Nam Choong Ju (acc 27), Suh Taegu
(acc 80) Osan [Star] (acc 32), Sae Yung Chun
[Saetbyul], San Kok (acc 100), Shinchang
(acc 25), Sok Cho (acc 76), Song Tan (acc 40),
Suhdaemun (acc 52), Suh Taegu (acc 80), Suk
Lim (acc 52), Taegu (acc 81), Tong San
(acc 30), Wonju (acc 63), Yul Mok (acc 39),
Yung Deung Po (acc 47)

Counselling and Friendship Centres
Chonan (Counselling Centre for Women), Tong
Taegu, Taegu, Suh Taejon, Taejon, Tong
Taejon Tongbu

Korea Territory

Day Care Centres
Kang Buk (acc 97), Mindeullae (acc 50), Myung
Chun (acc 39), Seobu Sudaemun (acc 52),
Suh San Suklim Community Welfare (acc 52),
Taegu (acc 81)

HIV/Aids Care and Prevention Programme Units
Pusan Shelter Centre, Seoul

Naval Servicemen's Centre
Chin Hai

Oori Jip (transitional housing for those leaving children's homes)
Choongdong (Seoul Broadview Children's
Home) (acc 3), Chun Yun (acc 4),
Kunsan (acc 4), Taejon (acc 20)

Rest Centres
Ansung, Buyeo, Cheju, Hap Duk, Masan,
Mosan, Muloori, Najoo,Pang Nai,
SeogwipoSong Tan, Tai Kok, Wonju,
Yeoju

Sarangbang Centres (hostels for the homeless)
Buk Ah Hyun Dong (acc 30), Choong Chung
Ro (acc 130), Sudaemun (acc 50)

Self-Support Training Centres
Boryung, Nonsan, Taian

Senior Citizens' Services
Ansung Peace Village Nursing Home (acc 55),
Hongjae Dong Day Care Centre for the
Elderly (acc 20), Kwachun Home for the
Elderly (acc 50), Kwachun Nursing Home
(acc 30), Mooan 'Silver Centre', Namdong
House of Love (acc 20), Pusan Home for the
Elderly (acc 60), 'Victory Lodge' Silver
Nursing Home (acc 50), Wolsung Day Care
Centre for the Elderly (acc 9)

School
Inpyung Technical High School (acc 1,340)

Special Service and Relief Services
9 programmes, 3 vehicles

Students' Study Centres (and after-school programmes)
Ah Hyun, An Dong, An San, Baesan, Bang Hak,
Boo Jun, Boo Kok, Boo Nam, Buk Choon
Chun, Chang Yong, Chew Kok, Chin Chook,
Chin Hae, Chin Ju, Cheju, Chisan, Choong
Taegu, Choong Moo, Chuan, Chun An # 1,
Daiyun, Dan Chun, Dong du Chun, Doriwon,
Eonyak, Haeundae, Inchon, Kang Nam,
Kasuwon, Kie Sung, Kong Ju, Kunsan, Kwang
Chun, Mil Yang, Mooan, Nonsan, Oh Ka, On
Yang, Yusung, Pochun, Pyongtaek, Sae
Sungnam, Sam Sung, Sangloksoo, Seogwipo,
Shim Chon, Son Chi, Soyang, Sudaejon, Suh
Suwon, Suh Taegu Pisan 3-dong, Suh Chung
Ju, Sunglim, Sung Nam, Syn Heung, Syn
Pyung, Taechon, Taegu First, Taejon Central,
Tang Jin, Togo, Tomadong, Tonam, Tonghae,
Tong Kunsan, Tong Taechon, Uijungbu,
Uisung, Un Po, Wadong, Wolsung, Yang Kang,
Yea San, Yi Chon, Yi Won, Yong Chon, Yong
Dong, Yong Ho, Yongwol, Yul Mok, Yun Hie

Student Accommodation
Taejon (university students) (acc 25)

Vocational Training and Support Centres
Chung Daoon House, Taejon (30), Taejon (acc
women 30), Pusan Women's Home (acc 30)

Women's Homes
Chonan House of Hope (acc 10), Seoul (acc 35),
Taejon Women's Refuge Shelter (acc 55)

**Outside Seoul City Hall,
schoolchildren help Korea's
First Lady Kwon, Yang-suk
to launch The Salvation
Army's Christmas Kettle
Appeal as Territorial
Commander Commissioner
Chun, Kwang-pyo encour-
ages the public to give
generously to the appeal**

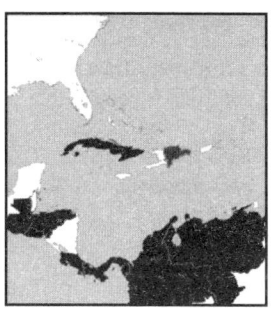

LATIN AMERICA NORTH TERRITORY

Territorial leaders:
Colonels Jorge and Adelina Ferreira

Territorial Commander:
Colonel Jorge Ferreira (1 Apr 2004)

Chief Secretary:
Major Zoilo Pardo (1 Jul 2006)

Territorial Headquarters: Avenida 11, Calle 20, San José, Costa Rica

Postal address: Apartado Postal 125-1005, Barrio México, San José, Costa Rica

tel: [506] 257-7535; fax: [506] 257-5291

email: LAN_Leadership@lan.salvationarmy.org@SAHUB; sallan@sol.racsa.co.cr;

web site: www.geocities.com/latin_america_north_territory/

The Army's work commenced in the Isthmus of Panama (1904), Costa Rica (1907), Cuba (1918), Venezuela (1972), Guatemala (1976), Colombia (1985), El Salvador (1989) and Honduras (2000).

Legal recognition was given to El Ejército de Salvación by the Republic of Panama (1946), Costa Rica (1975), Guatemala (1978), Colombia (1988), The Dominican Republic (1995), El Salvador (1996) and Honduras (2001). The territory was formed on 1 October 1976, then reformed on 1 September 1998, when Mexico became a command.

Zone: Americas and Caribbean

Countries included in the territory: Colombia, Costa Rica, Cuba, Dominican Republic, El Salvador, Guatemala, Honduras, Panama, Venezuela

'The Salvation Army' in Spanish: Ejército de Salvación

Languages in which the gospel is preached: English, Kacchikel, Spanish

Publications: *Voz de Salvación (Salvation Voice), Arco Iris de Ideas (Rainbow of Ideas)*

MANY contrasting situations are reflected in the countries that make up the territory. Nature is generous, giving forests, beaches, mountains, flowers and a diversity of animals. But at the same time hurricanes, earthquakes and volcanic eruptions bring cries of suffering from many people. There are natural resources and yet many people live in poverty.

The people are good, happy and very hospitable, but in some places there is violence and crime, alcoholism and drug addiction, juvenile gangs and guerrilla groups. Many children and youths are intelligent but some fall victim to abuse, sex-trade trafficking and prostitution.

In such situations The Salvation Army continues to minister, offering redemption, comfort and new life in Jesus Christ. At rehabilitation centres people have their broken lives restored. Education and training in life-skills are given to the children who attend the Army's schools, childcare classes

163

and feeding centres. Women attending home league courses benefit from helpful advice and receive practical skills.

Camps for women, men and youth, as well as divisional and corps events celebrating 'A Year for Children and Youth', have proved inspirational.

General John Larsson and Commissioner Freda Larsson visited the territory to lead two congresses, in Cuba and then in the Guatemala Division. At public meetings in Havana (Cuba) more than 800 people praised God with great enthusiasm and some 100 of them rededicated their lives to God's service. Many had travelled up to 20 hours from distant places, but their spiritual fervour never waned in spite of the fatigue.

In Guatemala the meetings included the commissioning, held for the first time outside the territorial centre of Costa Rica. Among the many people consecrating themselves to Christ were a number offering for full-time service as officers.

The territory's Salvationists have determined that they should be 'God's Army' – an army of salvation and holiness, that uses with passion any expression of evangelism, that has a strong biblical and doctrinal foundation, that encourages the participation of lay people, that values women's ministries, and that reforms society.

After these ideals for mission were presented and discussed at divisional symposiums, each division made their own resolutions and determined how best they could achieve their goals in building God's Kingdom. They did so inspired by a song that is popular in the territory: 'We will bring his glory to town and country, offering hope and the good news of salvation.'

STATISTICS

Officers 161 (active 149 retired 8) **Cadets** (1st Yr) 12 (2nd Yr) 3 **Employees** 186
Corps 57 **Outposts** 19 **Institutions** 8 **Schools** 21
Day Care Centres 15 **Children's Development Centres** 6 **Vocational Training Centres** 18 **Feeding Centres** 16 **Camps** 2
Senior Soldiers 2,465 **Adherents** 806 **Junior Soldiers** 1,208

STAFF

Business Administration: Maj Esteban Calvo
Personnel: Maj Ileana Calvo
Programme: Maj Eduardo Almendras

Editorial: Maj Víctor García
Education: Maj Víctor García
Finance: Capt Joan Cole
Projects/Sponsorship: Grettel Mejia
Training: Maj Angela García
Women's Ministries: Col Adelina Ferreira (TPWM) Maj Magali Pardo (TSWM)

DIVISIONS

Colombia: Apartado Aéreo 17756 Santa Fe de Bogotá, Colombia; tel: (571) 263 2633; fax: (571) 295 2921; email: crdiv_leadership@lan.salvatonarmy.org; web site: http/www.ejercitodesalvacion.com; Capt Odilio Fernández

Costa Rica: Apartado Postal 6227-1000, San José, Costa Rica; tel: (506) 221 8266; fax: (506) 223 0250; email: ejercito@racsa.co.cr; Maj Miguel Aguilera

Cuba: Calle 96 Nª 5513 entre 55 Y 57, Marianao CP 11400, Ciudad de la Habana, Cuba; tel: (53) 7260-2171; fax: (53) 7267-2537; email: ejdivcuba@enet.cu; Capt Orestes Linares

Guatemala: 2a Avenida 3-10, Sector A4 San Cristóbal 1, Zona 8 de Mixco, Guatemala; tel/fax: (502) 2478-4112/2443-2484; Capt Javier Obando

Panama: Apartado Postal 0843-01134, Via

Transistmica, Pueblo Nuevo, Halo Pintado-
Casa Nº 3, República de Panamá;
tel: (507) 261-8091;
email: Jorge_Mendez@lan.salvationarmy.org;
Maj Jorge Méndez

REGIONS

Dominican Republic: 18 Calle Mayagüez,
Ens, Ozama, Santo Domingo, Dominican
Republic; tel: (1809) 699-3818;
fax: (1809) 699-3830; Capt Gerardo Góchez

El Salvador: Apartado Postal No 7, Centro de
Gobierno, Calle 15 de Septiembre Nº 199 y
Nº 121 Barrio Candelaria, San Salvador;
tel: (503) 2280-3293; fax: (503) 2280-1805;
email: ejercito.salvacion@salnet.net;
Maj Max Mayorga

Project Honduras: Colonia El Hogar Bloque B
Casa Nº11 Tegucigalpa Apartadao Postal 6590,
Honduras; tel/fax: (504) 232-4927/235-9855;
email: edoban58@hotmail.com; Capt Eddy
Obando

Venezuela: Calle San Juan de Dios Melián,
Entre calle san Rafael y la Segunda de
Cabudare Riviera Departamento 1,
Cabudare-Barquisimento, Venezuela;
tel: (058) 251 261-6318;
email: Perdo_Jose_Lopez@yahoo.com;
Capt Perdo López

TRAINING COLLEGE

Calle Puente de Piedra, 1 km norte del Puente
de Piedra, Barrio Los Angeles, San Rafael
de Heredia, Costa Rica.
Postal address: Apartado 173-3015 San Rafael
de Heredia, Costa Rica; tel: (506) 262 0061;
fax: (506) 262 0733

SOCIAL SERVICES
INSTITUTIONS
Centres for Homeless
Costa Rica
Centro Modelo: Calle Naranjo, Concepción de
Tres Ríos, Provincia de Cartago;
tel: (506) 273-6307 (acc 80)
Refugio de Esperanza: Avenida 9 Zona Roja,
San José; tel: (506) 233-2059 (acc 30)

Disabled Centre
Costa Rica
Hogar Sustituto 'Tierra Prometida': Carretera
Interamericana 100 metros sur de Autos
Mundiales, Pérez Zeledón; tel: (506)771-2517
(acc13)

Residential Homes for the Elderly
Cuba
'William Booth': Calle 84 No 5525 e/55 y
Lindero, Mariano, CP 11400, Ciudad de la
Habana; tel: (537) 260-1118
Panama
Hogar Jackson: Avenida Amador Guerrero y
Calle 3 No 2014, Colón; tel: (507) 441-3371
(acc 30)

Residential Homes for Children
El Salvador
El Alba: Km 50, Carretera a la Herradura,
Caserio los Novios, Hacienda del Cauca;
tel: (503) 354-4430 (acc 20)
Panama
Hogar Dr Eno (Girls): Transistmica, Sabanitas,
Colón; tel: (507) 442-0371 (acc 20)
Venezuela
Hogar Nido Alegre: Calle 71 # 14 A63, Juana
de Avila, Apdo Postal 1464 Maracaibo 4001;
Estado de Zulia, Venezuela;
tel: (58-261) 798-3761 (acc 50)

SCHOOLS
Dominican Republic
Primary Schools
Cotui: 16 de Agosto Nº 98, Cotui, Sánchez
Ramírez; tel: (809) 585-3393 (acc 40)
Moca: Moca Republica Dominicana;
tel: (1809) 578-4792 (acc 20)
Tres Brazos: Calle Matadero Nº 70 (acc 20)

El Salvador
Kindergarten
Central Corps: Calle 15 Septiembre # 199 y
121, Barrio Candelaria, San Salvador;
tel: (503) 2280-1805 (acc 20)
Merliot Corps: Jardines del Volcán, Calle El
Jabali # 36, Ciudad Merliot, La Libertad;
tel: (503) 2278-8249 (acc 60)
Usulután Corps: 6a Avenida y 7a, Calle Oriente
31, Barrio El Calvario, Departamento de
Usulután; tel: (503) 2662-4428

Guatemala
Kindergarten
Escuintla Outpost: 3a Avenida 2-56, Zona 3,
Colonia Sebastopol; tel: (502) 7888-1559
(acc 100)
Satelite: Lote 5, Manzana 27, Proyecto 2, Ciudad
Satelite, Mixto; tel: (502) 484-3052 (acc 30)
Primary Schools
Central Corps: 15 Calle 8-29, Zona 1, Guatemala
City; tel: (502) 2232-2964 (acc75)

Chimaltenango: 7a Avenida y 1a Calle, Zona 1, Villas del Pilar; tel: (502) 7839-6585 (acc 150)

Mezquital: 4a Calle 3-99, Zona 12, Colonia Mezquital; tel: (502) 2479-8443 (acc 150)

Tecpán: Calle Tte Coronel Jack Waters, Barrio Poromá, Colonia Iximché; tel: (502) 7840-3020 (acc 300)

Tierra Nueva: Sector B-1, Manzana D, Lote 3, Colonia Tierra Nueva 11, Chinautla; tel: (502) 2484-1255 (acc 150)

Honduras

Avanzada de Tegucigalpa: Hospital Materno Infantil (Classroom 4); tel: (504) 232-4927

Avanzada San Pedro Sula: Hospital Mario Catarino Rivas (Classroom 2); tel: (504) 556-7238

Primary and Secondary Schools

Limón: Colegio Wm Booth, Centro Communal 'El Limón' Costadó Derecho, Zona 18; tel: (502) 2260-0723 (acc 395)

Maya: Colegio Nido Alegre Manzana 2, Lote 262, Zona 18, Colonia Maya; tel: (502) 2260-1519 (acc 150)

Panama
Kindergarten

Panamá Templo: Calle 25 y Avenida Cuba-Este; tel: (507) 262-2545 (acc 30)

Colón: Calle 14, Avenida Amador Guerrero 14201 Apartado 1163 Colón; tel: (507) 441-4570 (acc 50)

Kindergarten and School

Río Abajo: Calle 11y1/2, La Pulida, Río Abajo; tel: (507) 224-7480 (acc 40)

School for the Blind

Contact Panama DHQ address

DAY CARE CENTRES
Colombia

Armenia Outpost: Carrera 11 # 14-19 Barrio Guayaquil; tel: (576) 746-8591

San Cristóbal Sur, Bogotá: Calle 12 Sur # 11-71 Este, Barrio San Cristóbal Sur, Santa Fe de Bogotá; tel: (571) 333-0606/289-2672

Costa Rica

Central Corps: Avenida 16, Entre Calle 5 y 7 San José; tel: (506) 233-6850 (acc 35)

León XIII: Ciudadela León XIII, Detrás de la Escuela de León XIII, San José; tel: (506) 231-1786 (acc 80)

Limón Central: Av 4 entre Calles 7 y 9; tel: (506) 758-0657 (acc 75)

Pavas: Villa Esperanza de Pravas, Contiguo Al Instituto Nacional de Aprendizaje, San José; tel: (506) 231-1786 (acc 80)

El Salvador

Central Corps: Calle 15 Septiembre # 199 y # 121, Barrio Candelaria, San Salvador; tel: (503) 2280-1805 (acc 20)

Merliot Corps: Jardines del Volcán, Calle El Jabali # 36, Ciudad Merliot, La Libertad; tel: (503) 2278-8249 (acc 60)

Usulután Corps: 6a Avenida y 7a, Calle Oriente # 31, Barrio El Calvario Departamento de Usulután; tel: (503) 2662-4428

Guatemala

Central Corps: 15 Calle 8-39, Zona 1, Guatemala City; tel: (502) 232-2964 (acc 100)

Satelite: Lote 5, Manzana 27, Proyecto 2, Ciudad Satelite, Mixco; tel: (502) 484-3052 (acc 30)

Panama

Panamá Templo: Calle 25 Avenida Cuba-Este; tel: (507) 262-2545 (acc 20)

Colón: Avenida Amador Guerrero 14201, Apartado 1163; tel: (507) 441-4570 (acc 50)

Río Abajo: Calle 11y1/2 La Pulida; tel: (507) 224-7480 (acc 25)

Venezuela

Cuerpo San Luis: Barrio San Luis, San Francisco, Avenida 2 # 22-135, Estado Zulia, Venezuela.

CHILDREN'S DEVELOPMENT CENTRES
Colombia

Ibague, Tolima: Carrera 4ta Sur # 20A-34, Barrio Yuldaima, Apartado Aéreo 792; tel: (578) 260-8032

Itagui, Antioquía: Calle 55 # 58FF-12, Barrio Fátima, Apartado Aéreo 90267; tel: (094) 372-4118

Robledo, Medellín: Carrera 84B # 63-73, Barrio Robledo, Medellín, Antioquía; tel: (094) 234-8250

San Cristóbal Sur, Bogotá: Calle 12 Sur # 11-71 Este, Barrio San Cristóbal Sur, Santa Fe de Bogotá; tel: (571) 333-0606/289-2672

El Salvador

Calle 15 de Septiembre # 199 y # 121, Barrio Candelaria, San Salvador; tel: (503) 270-5273 (acc 246)

Usulután: 6a Avenida y 7a, Calle Oriente # 31, Barrio El Calvario, Departamento de Usulután; tel: (503) 662-4428 (acc120)

VOCATIONAL TRAINING CENTRES

Costa Rica

Centro Modelo: Carpentry and Pig Farming, Calle Naranjo, Concepción de Tres Ríos, Provincia de Cartago; tel: (506) 273-6307 (acc 80)

Computer Centres: 25 Julio Catalina Booth (acc 30)

Cuba

Cuerpo Central: Computer Centre, Calle 96 Nª 5513 entre 55 y 57, Marianao 11400, La Habana; tel: (53) 260-2171

Diezmero: Dressmaking, Calle 3ra Nª 25304 entre 2da y Martí Diezmero San Miguel del Padrón, CP 130000 Guevara, La Habana

El Salvador

Computer Centres: Central; Merliot; Usulután

Vocational Centre: Avanzada de Gualache

Dressmaking: Central

Guatemala

Carpentry: Limón, Tecpan

Computer Class: Chilaltenango, Limón, Mezquital, Satelite, Tecpan, Tierra Nueva, Satelite

Typing Class: Central, Satelite, Tecpan

Venezuela

Computer, Carpentry and Dressmaking Class: Calle 71 # 14 A63, Juana de Avila, Apdo Postal 1464, Maracaibo 4001; Estado de Zulia, Venezuela; tel: (0261) 798-3761 (acc 50)

FEEDING CENTRES

Colombia

Ibague, Tolima: Carrera 4ta Sur # 20A-34, Barrio Yuldaima, Apartado Aéreo 792; tel: (578) 260-8032

Itagui, Antioquía: Calle 55 # 58FF-12, Barrio Fátima, Apartado Aéreo 90267; tel: (574) 372-4118

Robledo, Medellín: Carrera 84B # 63-73, Barrio Robledo, Medellín, Antioquía; tel: (574) 234-8250

San Cristóbal Sur, Bogotá: Calle 12 Sur # 11-71 Este, Barrio San Cristóbal Sur, Santa Fe de Bogotá; tel: (571) 333-0606/298-2672

Costa Rica

Liberia: 500 mts Norte Estación de Bomberos 100 Este y 50 Norte, Barrio San Roque; tel: (506) 666-3603 (acc 100)

Limón 2000: Barrio Limón 2000 frente al Predio

El Aragón, Alameda # 4; tel: (506) 797-1602 (acc 30)

Nicoya: Escuela de San Martín 900 al Oeste, Barrio San Martín; tel: (506) 685-5531 (acc 100)

Sagrada Familia: Costado Este Escuela Carolina Dent, Barrio Sagrada Familia; tel (506) 227-5298 (acc 100)

Salitrillos: Salitrillos de Aserri, de las Prestaciones, 300 metros al sur; tel: (506) 230-4668 (acc 80)

San Isidro del General: Barrio Los Angeles, Apartado Postal 7-8000; tel: (506) 770-6756 (acc 150)

Santa Cruz: Barrio Tulita Sandino, 300 este del IDA Guanacaste; tel: (506) 680-0724 (acc 100)

25 de Julio: Hatillo Centro, detrás de las, Bodegas de Constenla, Colonia 25 de Julio; tel: (506) 227-8380 (acc 100)

Cuba

Central: Calle 96 Nª 5513 entre 19 y 21 Bejucal CP 32600, Habana

Panama

Colon: Avenida Amador Guerrero 14201, Apartado 1163; tel: (507) 441-4570 (acc 75)

Chilibre: Transistmica, Lote No 175 Chilibre; tel: (507) 216-2501 (acc 100)

Paraíso: 101 X Guyana St Paraíso; tel: (507) 232-4713

CAMPS

El Salvador

Km 50, Carretera a la Herradura, Caserio los Novios, Hacienda del Cauca; tel: (503) 2354-4530 (acc 150)

Tecpán: Calle Tte Coronel Jack Waters, Barrio Poromá, Colonia Iximché; tel: (502) 7840-3998 (acc 100)

At rehabilitation centres people have their broken lives restored. Education and training in life-skills are given to the children who attend the Army's schools, childcare classes and feeding centres

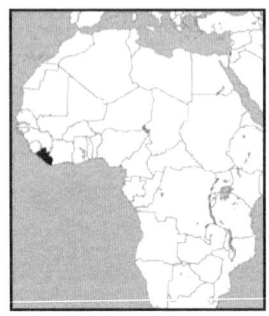

LIBERIA COMMAND

Command leaders:
Majors Robert and Hester Dixon

Officer Commanding:
Major Robert Dixon (4 Nov 2004)

General Secretary:
Major Romeo Alip (1 Oct 2006)

Command Headquarters: 17th Street, Sinkor, Monrovia

Postal address: PO Box 20/5792, Monrovia, Liberia

The Salvation Army opened fire in Liberia in May 1988 as part of the Ghana and Liberia Territory, with Major and Mrs Leonard Millar as pioneer officers. Progress was monitored by Ghana during the civil war, from May 1990. Liberia became a separate command on 1 January 1997.

Zone: Africa
Country included in the command: Liberia
Languages in which the gospel is preached: Bassa, English, Gola, Krahn, Pele

THE commissioning and ordination of the new captains of the Visionaries Session took place in July 2005 during the command congress led by the then Chief of the Staff Commissioner Israel L. Gaither and Commissioner Eva D. Gaither. Many people made public commitments to Christ.

In the first-ever command men's meeting the Chief of the Staff presented certificates to six men nominated by their various corps as 'man of the year'. Lemuel King of Monrovia City Corps was chosen as Command Man of the Year for 2005 and presented with a commemorative wooden plaque.

Thanks to the generosity of women in the New Jersey Division (USA Eastern) who helped finance the event, 500 women met together for the command's first holiday fellowship weekend, entitled 'African Queens – Vessels of Honour'. During the four days one of the women was crowned African Queen for the Liberia Command. The closing holiness meeting was a time of glorious praise to God.

The men's weekend retreat culminated in a visitation by the Holy Spirit, the mercy seat being lined with seekers.

In February 2006 all the command's women officers and female corps leaders met with the command president for women's ministries for a time of instruction, reflection and prayer. This was followed by the annual prayer and fasting retreat, which drew more than 100 women from every corner of the command.

168

Also in February nine members of the God's Soldiers Session from the USA spent 12 days assisting their session mates, command leaders Majors Robert and Hester Dixon, during their 25th year of service. They led open-air meetings, Bible studies, local officers' training sessions and music workshops, participated in work projects and visited displaced persons' camps.

Salvationists raise their hearts in praise to God for his unfailing love, protection and providential care.

STATISTICS

Officers 33 **Lieutenants** 8 **Aux-Capts** 2 **Envoys** 2 **Corps Leaders** 9 **Cadets** 5 **Employees** 320

Corps 21 **Outposts** 14 **District** 1 **Schools** 24 (pupils 5,642) **Commercial Institutes** 2 **Hostels/Homes** 2 **Child Day Care Centres** 18 **Clinics** 2 **Mobile Clinic** 1
Senior Soldiers 1,921 **Recruits** 320 **Adherents** 41 **Junior Soldiers** 359

STAFF

Women's Ministries: Maj Hester Dixon (CPWM) Maj Elizabeth Oduro (CSWM) Capt Etta Gaymo (LOMS)
Field: Capt Ben Gaymo
Finance: Mr Lawson Warbey
Property: Mr David Cooper-Bainda
Schools: Mr Ernest Suah
Trade: Mr Prince B. Siakeh
Training: Maj James Oduro
Youth: Capt Jonathan Walker
Candidates: Capt Willamena Walker

DISTRICT

Grand Bassa: contact Command HQ; Capt Anthony Sio

TIME FOR SCHOOL

Pupils at the Salvation Army school at Jos, Nigeria – one of 37 nursery and primary schools which serves children from all walks of life in that country

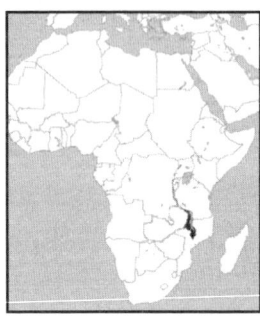

MALAWI COMMAND

Command leaders:
Lieut-Colonels David and Jean Burrows

Officer Commanding:
Lieut-Colonel David Burrows (1 Nov 2004)

Command Headquarters: PO Box 51140, Limbe, Malawi

tel: [265] 1 687105; fax: [265] 1 687031; email: MAL_Leadership@mal.salvationarmy.org

The Salvation Army began operations in Malawi on 13 November 1967 and was granted official government recognition on 2 October 1973. The Malawi Division was part of the Zimbabwe Territory until 1988, when it was integrated into the Zambia Command, which was given territorial status and became known as the Zambia and Malawi Territory. The Army's work in Malawi has grown and developed and on 1 October 2002 it became a separate region. Further growth and expansion of the work in Malawi resulted in the region being elevated to command status on 1 February 2004.

Zone: Africa
Country included in the command: Malawi
'The Salvation Army' in Chichewa: Nkhondo ya Chipulumutso
Languages in which the gospel is preached: Chichewa, English, Lomwe, Sena, Tumbuka

AS the Lord continues to bless Salvation Army ministry in Malawi, the command moves forward in faith with a vision for mission that encourages the empowerment of Salvationists at grass roots level.

A committee was formed to review strategy on corps growth, upgrading to corps status and policy on new openings. A revision of the divisional and district review process seeks to ensure credible and measurable goals while providing on-site training for leaders and officer personnel under their direction.

An in-service training director was appointed to implement specialised training events that seek to develop the capacities of officers, envoys,

corps leaders and local officers for future leadership at various levels of responsibility. The director is also working in collaboration with the education secretary on implementing a human resource development strategy and the officer appraisal system.

A further four cadets entered training, joining the God's Fellow Workers Session in the Zambia Territory, and a number of new inquirers have expressed an interest in officership. There has been a review of the candidates' process and a gradual implementation of increased educational standards. The development of plans for the command's own training college continues.

A successful youth celebration, held in July 2005 and attended by 450 young people of the command, was co-facilitated by a mission team from the USA Central Territory. Results include a renewed interest in corps cadet programmes, a fresh commitment to ministry among youth and children, and enquiries about officership.

STATISTICS

Officers 46 (active 42 retired 4) **Envoys** 12 **Cadets** (1st Yr) 4 **Employees** 97
Corps 37 **Outposts** 19 **Outreach Units** 40
Senior Soldiers 4,654 **Junior Soldiers** 756
Personnel serving outside command Officers 5

STAFF

Development Services: Mr Oswald Malunda
Education: Capt Alfred Banda
Finance: Maj George Nkhululu
Property: Maj George Nkhululu
Women's Ministries: Lt-Col Jean Burrows (CPWM)
Youth and Candidates: Capt Robert Mtengowalira

DIVISIONS

Blantyre: PO Box 51749, Limbe; tel: 01 655 901; Maj Gerald Chimimba
Phalombe: PO Box 99, Migowi; tel: 01 481 216; Maj Chatonda Theu

DISTRICTS

Central and North: PO Box 40058, Kanengo, Lilongwe; tel: 01 716 869; Capt Dyson Chifudzeni
Lower Shire: PO Box 35, Muona, Lower Shire: Capt Andson Namathanga

COMMUNITY DEVELOPMENT PROGRAMMES

Adult Literacy: Blantyre and Phalombe Divisions, Central and North and Lower Shire Districts
Community Counselling: Bangwe, Gooke, Migowi, Nguludi
Feeding/Food for Work: Bangwe, Blantyre, Migowi, Nguludi
HIV/Aids Home-based Care: Bangwe, Migowi, Nguludi, Nsanje
Orphans and Vulnerable Children: Blantyre and Phalombe Divisions, Central and North and Lower Shire Districts

SOCIAL SERVICES

Kayesa Youth Centre for Orphans and Vulnerable Children: Mchinji

Songsters offer their praise to God – African style

MEXICO TERRITORY

Territorial leaders:
Colonels Olin O. and Dianne Hogan

Territorial Commander:
Colonel Olin O. Hogan (1 Oct 2001)

Chief Secretary:
Major Josué Cerezo (1 Apr 2004)

**Territorial Headquarters: San Borja #1456, Colonia Vértiz Narvarte,
Delegación Benito Juárez, México 03600, DF**

Postal address: Apartado Postal 12-668, México 03020, DF

tel: [525] 5575-1042; 5559-5244/9625; fax: [525] 5575-3266

email: mexico@salvationarmy.org

In 1934, a group known as the Salvation Patrol was commenced in Mexico by Alejandro Guzmán. In October 1937, he was presented with a flag by General Evangeline Booth at the USA Southern Territory Congress in Atlanta, Georgia. The Salvation Patrol then became absorbed into the international Salvation Army, operating under the supervision of DHQ in Dallas, Texas, later becoming part of the Latin America North Territory. On 1 September 1998 it was made a command in its own right and, on 1 October 2001, it became a territory.

Zone: Americas and Caribbean
Country included in the territory: Mexico
'The Salvation Army' in Spanish: Ejército de Salvación
Language in which the gospel is preached: Spanish

THE year under review, ending with Commissioning 2006, was 'A Year of Prayer for Mexico'. Each officer participated in a weekly prayer time and each corps developed its own plan for praying – not just for The Salvation Army but for the country's concerns too. This proved to be a great blessing to Salvationists throughout the territory.

For many years the territory has dedicated the third Wednesday of every month to prayer. It has been a great help in strengthening officers' resolve to call on God with their needs, to thank him for his help and to learn to rest in him.

A continuing focus on growth and outreach into new areas has brought about the opening of 10 corps. Many officers caught the vision and opened outposts throughout the territory – in places as diverse as Rio Bravo Tamaulipas and Tapachula, Chiapas.

Salvationists were also encouraged to make further commitments to Christ and to lead people to the Saviour. As a result of this and other efforts, 201 senior soldiers were enrolled in 2005.

Spring campaign meetings conducted by cadets in two corps near the training college were well attended and many people were won to Christ. Monthly youth meetings in the Capital Division attracted attendances of 125 or more young people.

An attempt to alleviate the dire poverty of street children has been undertaken. Every week a group of Salvationists is reaching out to them, giving spiritual and material sustenance.

Training seminars for officers and soldiers have dealt with such topics as 'Pastoral Care and Leadership', 'Preaching and Worship', 'Self-Esteem' and 'Youth Ministries' (the last-named being conducted by a team from USA Eastern Territory).

Commissioning weekend events during May 2005 were times of much blessing as guest leaders Commissioners Lawrence and Nancy Moretz (USA Eastern) brought meaningful messages from God's word.

Mexico is growing in grace and hope, and the Church of Christ is strengthened by the many people who have found him as Saviour through The Salvation Army.

STATISTICS

Officers 153 (active 124 retired 29)
Lieutenants 9 **Cadets** (1st Yr) 5 (2nd Yr) 5
Employees 56
Corps 44 **Outposts** 15 **Institutions** 51
Senior Soldiers 1,382 **Adherents** 196 **Junior Soldiers** 829

STAFF

Education: Maj Douglas Danielson
Property: Maj James Hood
Social: Maj Sallyann Hood
Training: Maj Humberto García
Women's Ministries: Col Dianne C. Hogan (TPWM) Maj Ruth Cerezo (TSWM)
Youth and Candidates: Maj Guadalupe Galván

DIVISIONS

Capital: Alicante No 88, Colonia Álamos Delegación Benito Juárez, 03400 México, DF; Apartado Postal 25-408, México, DF 03421; tel: 5590-9220; fax: 5590-9603; Maj Douglas Danielson

Northwest: Tamborel 607, Colonia Santa Rosa, CP 31060; tel: (614) 1420-4002; Maj Ciro Velázquez

Río Bravo: Lombardo Toledano #2709, Colonia Alta Vista Sur, 64740 Monterrey, NL; Apartado Postal 1097, 64000 Monterrey, NL, México; tel: (81) 8359-5711; fax: (81) 8359-9115; Maj Facundo Vera

REGION

Southeast: Calle 103 No 506-A X 62, Colonia D. Moreno Cantón, Mérida, Yucatán; Maj Manuel Padilla

TRAINING COLLEGE

Calle Monte Albán #510, Colonia Independencia, México 03630, DF; tel: (55) 5672-7986; fax: (55) 5672-0608

CENTRE FOR CARE OF PERSONS IN TRANSITION

La Esperanza Centre: Labradores #85 Esquina con Imprenta, 15270, México, DF; tel: (55) 5789-1511, 5702-8033

CHILDREN'S CARE CENTRES

Ciudad Juárez, Chih: Ulises Irigoyen #1674 Colonia Chaveña, CP 32060; tel: (656) 1614-2828 (acc 25)

Chihuahua, Chih: Tamborel 601, Colonia Santa Rosa, CP 31050; tel: (614) 1420-4002 (acc 15)

Culiacán, Sinaloa: Cuauhtémoc #40 Sur, Colonia Las Vegas, Esquina Epitacio Osuna, Cerca de KZ4, CP 80090; tel: (66) 715-1043 (acc 100)

Matamoros, Tam: Calle Sonora #22 Esquina San Pedro, Colonia Esperanza, CP 87310; tel: (868) 810-1369 (acc 55)

Mexicali, BC: Avenida Aguascalientes #2300, Colonia Santa Clara; tel: (686) 53-11-94 (acc 50)

México, DF: Imprenta #225, Colonia Morelos, CP 15270; tel: (55) 5789-0554; fax: (55) 5702-3666 (acc 30)

Nuevo Laredo, Tam: Degollado #1217, CP 88000; tel: (867) 712-1455 (acc 10)

Reynosa, Tam: Allende #465 Poniente, CP 88500; tel: (899) 930-9028 (acc 50)

San Luis Potosí, SLP: Bolívar #1426 Barrio
San Miguelito, CP 78339; tel: (444) 815-4530
(acc 10)

Tampico, Tam: Avenida Central #501, Colonia
Moctezuma, CP 89250; tel: (833) 212-0365
(acc 15)

Tijuana, BC: Calle Aquiles Serdán #11585,
Colonia Libertad, CP 22300;
tel: (664) 683-2694 (acc 20)

Torreón, Coah: Calle 21, #373 Nte, CP 27000;
tel: (871) 7136-023 (acc 25)

Villahermosa, Tab: Calle Fco Sarabia #123,
Col Segunda del Águila, CP 86080;
tel: (993) 315-2694 (acc 25)

CHILDREN'S HOMES

Acapulco, Gro: Ave de los Cantiles #16,
Fraccionamiento Mozimba, CP 39460;
tel: (744) 446-0359 (acc 90)

Chihuahua, Chih: Tamborel #601, Colonia Santa
Rosa, CP 31050; tel: (614) 420-4002 (acc 50)

Coatzacoalcos, Ver: Gutiérrez Zamora #1120
Colonia Centro, CP 96400;
tel: (921) 214-5923 (acc 50)

Cuernavaca, Mor: Av Atlacomúlco, #124,
Col Acapantzingo, CP 62440;
tel: (777) 312-8207/ 8238 (acc 45)

Culiacán, Sin: Chuahutémoc #40 Sur, Colonia
Las Vegas, Esquina Epitacio Osuna, Cerca de
KZ4, CP 80090; tel: (667) 715-1043 (acc 25)

Guadalajara, Jal: Calzada Revolución
#2011, Sector Reforma, CP 44800;
tel: (33) 3635-4192 (acc 120)

Matamoros, Tam: Calle Sonora #22 Esquina
San Pedro, Colonia Esperanza, CP 87310;
tel: (868) 810-1369 (acc 55)

Mazatlán, Sin: Calle Ángel Flores s/n, Colonia
El Venadillo CP 82129; tel: (669) 980-7609
(acc 30)

Mérida, Yuc: Calle 103, #506 Ax 62, Col
Delio Moreno Cantón, CP 97268;
tel: (999) 928-5153 (acc 30)

México, DF: Ave Encino Grande #550,
Tetelpán, VAO, CP 17000;
tel: (55) 5585-0144 (acc 120)

Nuevo Laredo, Tam: Degollado 1217, CP 88000;
tel: (867) 712-1455 (acc 50)

Puebla, Pue: Calle 16 Sur #704 Col Analco
Centro, CP 72000; tel: (222) 242-6047
(acc 60)

Reynosa, Tam: Allende #465 Poniente, Colonia
Centro, CP 88500; tel: (899) 922-5463;
fax: (899) 930-9028 (acc 25)

Saltillo, Coah: Durazno #354, Colonia del Valle,
CP 25000; tel: (844) 436-2005 (acc 40)

San Luis Potosí, SLP: Bolívar #1426, Barrio San
Miguelito, CP 78339; tel: (444) 815-4530
(acc 30)

Tampico, Tam: Ave Central #501 Colonia
Moctezuma, CP 89250; tel: (833) 212-0365
(acc 55)

Torreón, Coah: Calle 21, #373 Nte, CP 27000;
tel: (871) 7136-023 (acc 50)

Veracruz, Ver: Revillagigedo #1507, Col
México, CP 91700; tel: (871) 7136-023
(acc 50)

Villahermosa, Tab: Calle Fco Sarabia #304,
Col Segunda del Águila, CP 86080;
tel: (993) 315-2694 (acc 50)

CLINIC AND DISPENSARY

México DF: Clínica de Salud Mental, Calle
Imprenta #221 Colonia Morelos, CP 15270;
tel: (55) 5794-1994

FEEDING CENTRES (SENIOR CITIZENS AND CHILDREN)

Alvarado, Ver: Ignacio Ramírez #87, CP 95250,
Apartado Postal 1; tel: (297) 973-2191 (acc 120)

Can Cún: Avenida Talleres entre 109 y 111
región 94, Manzana 80 Lote 28, Can Cún,
Quintana Roo; tel/fax: (998) 840-1074
(acc 30)

Culiacán, Sin: Chuahutémoc #40 Sur, Colonia
Las Vegas, Esquina Epitacio Osuna, Cerca de
KZ4, CP 80090; tel: (667) 715-1043 (acc 100)

Genaro Vázquez: Manzana Heroica Lote 13,
Colonia Genaro Vázquez, Monterrey, Nuevo
Leon (acc 100)

Mexicali, BC: Ave Aguascalientes #2300,
Colonia Santa Clara, CP 21110;
tel: (686) 553-1194 (acc 50)

México, DF (Corps #3): Norte 68 #3742,
Colonia M. de Río Blanco, CP 07880;
tel: (55) 5751-3598 (acc 40)

México, DF (Corps #6): Calle 12 No 68 Esquina
Avenida Pantitlan, Colonia Provenir, CP
57430, Netzahualcoyotl, Estado de México;
tel/fax: (55) 5200-1839 (acc 50)

Monclova, Coah: Benjamín Garza #1221,
Colonia Primero de Mayo, CP 25760;
tel: (866) 631-3502 (acc 110)

Monterrey, NL: Carvajal y de la Cueva #1716
Nte, Colonia Primero de Mayo, CP 64580;
tel: (81) 8375-0379 (acc 80)

Monterrey, NL: Manzana Heróica Lote 13, Col
Genaro Vázquez (acc 100)

Nogales, Sonora: Sierra Durango No 215,
Colonia Benit Juárez, CP 84016;
tel/fax: (631) 312-2708 (acc 20)

Puerto Vallarta: Sonora 232 Colonia Moseras,

A client at the mental health clinic run by The Salvation Army in the depressed Morelos district of Mexico City is welcomed by Major (Dr) Sallyann Hood, the clinic's director. Open six days a week, the clinic is supported by volunteer psychologists, a physiotherapist and university student interns.

Puerto Vallarta, Jalisco; tel: (322) 290-1587 (acc 50)

Sabinitas, NL: Calle Plutarco Elías Calles #401, Colonia 6 de Marzo, Guadalupe, NL 67160; tel: (81) 8299-5981 (acc 75)

Saltillo, Coah: Sosténes Rocha 17, Col Chamizal, CP 25180 (acc 80)

San Juan Ixhuatepec: Edo de México, Tenochtitlan #10, Administración San Juan Ixhuatepec, Tlanepantla, Edo de México, CP 54180; tel: (55) 5715-0649 (acc 80)

Tijuana, BC: Calle Aquiles Serdán #11585, Col Libertad, CP 22300, Apartado Postal 5-G; tel: (664) 683-2694 (acc 45)

Toluca, Edo de México: Calle San Fernando s/n, Cruce con Santa Teresa, Colonia San Jorge Pueblo Nuevo, Metepec, Edo de México 52140; tel: (722) 232-7945 (acc 40)

Xochitepec: Calle Hidalgo S/N esquina Jalisco, Colonia Lázaro Cárdenas, Xochitepec, Morelos 6279; tel/fax: (777) 361-3628 (acc 30)

FEEDING CENTRE (MEN)

Mexicali, BC: Ave Aguascalientes #2300, Colonia Santa Clara, CP 21110; tel: (686) 553-1194 (acc 50)

NIGHT SHELTERS (MEN)

Ciudad Juárez, Chih: Ulises Irigoyen #1674, Col Chaveña, CP 32060; tel: (656) 614-2828 (acc 70)

Mazatlán, Sin: Gutiérrez Nájera #514, CP 82000, Apartado Postal 142; tel: (669) 982-3453 (acc 10)

Mexicali, BC: Ave Aguascalientes #2300, Colonia Santa Clara, CP 21110; tel: (686) 553-1194 (acc 50)

México, DF: La Esperanza, Labradores #85, Esquina con Imprenta, Col Morelos, México 15270 DF; tel: (55) 5789-1511 (acc 125)

Monterrey, NL: Carvajal y de la Cueva #1716 Nte, Colonia Primero de Mayo, CP 64580; tel: (81) 8375-0379 (acc 80)

Piedras Negras, Coah: Victoria #805 Nte, Colonia Centro CP 26030; tel: (878) 782-2707 (acc 40)

Tijuana, BC: Calle Aquiles Serdán #11585, Col Libertad, CP 22300, Apartado Postal 5-G; tel: (664) 683-2694 (acc 30)

VOCATIONAL TRAINING CENTRE

México DF: Labradores #85 Esq. Con Imprenta, Colonia Morelos, CP 15270; tel: (55) 5789-1511

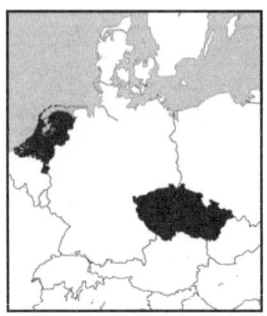

THE NETHERLANDS AND CZECH REPUBLIC TERRITORY

Territorial leaders:
Commissioners Willem and Netty van der Harst

Territorial Commander:
Commissioner Willem van der Harst
(1 Oct 2002)

Chief Secretary:
Lieut-Colonel Peter Dalziel (1 Oct 2002)

Territorial Headquarters: Spoordreef 10, 1315 GN Almere, The Netherlands

Tel address: Leger des Heils, Almere; tel: [31] (36) 5398111; fax: [31] (36) 5331458
email: ldhnl@legerdesheils.nl; web sites: www.legerdesheils.nl and www.armadaspasy.cz

Captain and Mrs Joseph K. Tyler, English officers, and Lieutenant Gerrit J. Govaars, a gifted Dutch teacher, commenced Army work in the Gerard Doustraat, Amsterdam, on 8 May 1887. Operations soon spread throughout the country and reached Indonesia (then The Netherlands East Indies) in 1894. Further advances were made in 1926 in Surinam and in 1927 in Curaçao.

Salvation Army operations in Czechoslovakia commenced in 1919, the pioneer being Colonel Karl Larsson. Evangelistic and social activities were maintained until suppressed in June 1950. After the opening of the central European borders, The Salvation Army's work was re-established and The Netherlands Territory was asked to take charge of the redevelopment. By the end of 1990 centres were reopened in Havirov, Prague, Brno and Ostrava and the work has grown steadily since then.

On 1 February 2002, the territory was renamed The Netherlands and Czech Republic Territory.

Zone: Europe
Countries included in the territory: Czech Republic, The Netherlands
'The Salvation Army' in Dutch: Leger des Heils; in Czech: Armáda Spásy
Languages in which the gospel is preached: Czech, Dutch
Periodicals: *Dag In Dag Uit*, *Heils-en Strijdzangen*, *InterCom*, *Strijdkreet*, *VoorWerk* (all Dutch), *Prapor Spásy* (Czech)

IT'S good to be wanted, to feel someone cares – this was the thought behind 'Combating Loneliness', the special emphasis across the united Salvation Army expression in The Netherlands. Corps and social services centres endeavour to meet the challenge of homelessness by providing facilities to make homeless people feel wanted. The Social Services Department particularly has been proactive in this direction, fulfilling its mission goals by offering practical and spiritual support to needy people in innovative ways.

After amendments to the country's

care system were announced, the Director of Social Services (Lieut-Colonel Ine Voorham) met the Minister of Finance, the State Secretary of Public Health, Welfare and Sport and the State Secretary of Social Services and Employment to discuss the consequences for vulnerable people. As a result a conference was held to attain comprehensive arrangements for clients who need long-term care.

In a recent campaign the Army launched a public education programme under the title 'We Believe' and social services representatives met government personnel with regard to changes in legislation that harm socially weak people.

Endeavouring to not only meet the spiritual and pastoral care of the Army's congregations but also provide training and education to all soldiers and local officers, courses have been organised to deal with theological and faith-related subjects, the art of preaching, pastoral care councils and many other topics. The Territorial Prayer Network adds inspirational support to the life of the territory.

It is always good to report new developments. Just a few years ago Terneuzen Corps struggled with a congregation of 15-20 people and little outreach. Now, with a new hall and the corps officer's consistent inspirational leadership, there is a regular congregation of some 80 people, a full programme of service to the community and outreach meetings in a nearby area.

In Zaandam, on the outskirts of Amsterdam, one of the drug addicts who attend the meetings designed a front reception area and so helped the corps develop a new facility for the community.

The work in the Czech Republic continues to advance in both its evangelical and community-based work. Two main events during the year raised The Salvation Army's profile: the hosting of the European Youth Congress, with General John Larsson and Commissioner Freda Larsson as special guests, was followed by the 15th anniversary of the re-opening of the work in the country. Those celebrations were led by Commissioners Wim and Netty van der Harst who, in 1990, had been part of the re-opening team and consolidated the Army's rebirth in the Czech Republic as leaders for six years.

STATISTICS
Officers 388 (active 162 retired 226) **Employees** 3,793
Corps 73 (99 local service centres) **Business Units** 17 (187 local service centres)
Senior Soldiers 5,108 **Adherents** 1,189 **Junior Soldiers** 640

STAFF
The Salvation Army Church
Field: Maj Johan C. J. van Vliet
Field Programme Support (incl Youth and Adult Ministries): Major Arie van Dijk
Candidates: Maj Wilhelm Omlo
Editor-in-Chief: Mr Rudi Tinga
Literary: Maj Johan B. K. Ringelberg
Education and Training: Maj Jeanne van Hal
Finance: Envoy Harm Slomp RA
Finance, Accommodation and

Dataprocessing: Mr Bert Barink
Music: Mr Roel van Kesteren
Officers' Affairs: Maj Wilhelm Omlo
Adult Ministries: see Field Programme Support
Women's Ministries: Comr Netty van der Harst (TPWM) Lt-Col Sylvia Dalziel (TSWM)
Youth: see Field Programme Support

DIVISIONS

Central: Piccolostraat 13, 1312 RC Almere;
tel: (36) 536 51 06; Maj Elsje Klarenbeek
North/East: Gein 27, 8032 BB Zwolle;
tel: (38) 452 67 13; fax: (38) 452 67 19;
Maj Hendrik van Pelt
South: Wittebrem 22, 3068 TM Rotterdam;
tel: (10) 4557921; Capt Johannes A. den Hollander

THE SALVATION ARMY MAIN FOUNDATION
Board of Administration
Chairman: Comr Willem van der Harst (TC)

Staff
Secretary: Lt-Col Peter Dalziel (CS)
Financial Sec: Envoy Harm Slomp RA
Managing Director: Envoy Jacobus F. Tinga

THE SALVATION ARMY SERVICES FOUNDATION
Board of Administration
Chairman: Comr Willem van der Harst (TC)
Vice-Chairman: Lt-Col Peter Dalziel (CS)
Official (non-voting) Sec: Envoy Harm Slomp RA (FS)
Members: Mr F. H. van der Woude; Mr G.L. Telling RA

Staff
Managing Director: Envoy Jacobus F. Tinga
Communications: Mr Robert C. van Boven
Domestic Affairs Staff/Personnel: Mr Arie M. Rietveld
Fund-Raising and Marketing: Mr Robert C. van Boven
Financial and Economics: Mr Peter van der Kist
Recycling: Mr Pieter Stigter
Sales and Supplies: Capt Robert Paul Fennema

RECYCLING SERVICES
Ettenseweg 6a, 4706 PB Roosendaal;
tel: (165) 376055; fax: (165) 376056
Depot: Hattem
Service Centres: Amsterdam, Dordrecht

SALES AND SUPPLIES
Spoordreef 10, 1315 GN Almere;
tel: (36) 539 82 08; fax: (36) 539 81 67

THE SALVATION ARMY FUND-RAISING FOUNDATION
Board of Administration
Chairman: Comr Willem van der Harst (TC)
Vice-Chairman: Lt-Col Peter Dalziel (CS)
Official (non-voting) Sec: Envoy Harm Slomp RA (FS)
Members: Mrs A. M. A. Bartels-Koene,
Mrs F. H. van Ham-Laning, Mr C. Hendriks,
Drs C. Bremmer, Mr J. de Widt

Staff
Managing Director: Envoy Jacobus F. Tinga

All activities of the Foundation are to be executed by The Salvation Army Services Foundation.

THE SALVATION ARMY FOUNDATION FOR WELFARE AND HEALTH CARE
Care for the homeless (total acc 3,615): night shelter (acc 649); day care (acc 772); 24-hour shelter (acc 1,254); young people (acc 195); supervised living (acc 745)
Substance misuse services (total acc 36): residential (acc 20); supervised living (acc 16)
Probation services (total capacity 792): ambulatory programmes (718); day training centres (acc 74)
Health care and care for the elderly (total capacity 1,361): permanent stay (acc 381); temporary stay (incl medical care of homeless) (acc 199); day care (acc 46); ambulatory programmes (incl home care) (490); supervised living (acc 245)
Custody care (total pupils 2,414)
Care for children and young people (total acc 386): residential care (acc 297); day care (acc 89)
Prevention and social rehabilitation services (total acc 746): ambulatory programmes (acc 458); work coaching (acc 214); day care (incl play groups) (acc 74)

Board of Administration
Chairman: Comr Willem van der Harst (TC)
Vice-Chairman: Lt-Col Peter Dalziel (CS)
Sec/Treasurer: Envoy Harm Slomp RA (FS)
Members: Mrs J. W. Immink, Envoy G. P. W. Jansen, Mr L. H. van den Heuvel, Mr H. N. Hagoort, Mr F. van der Heuvel

Staff
Managing Director: Lt-Col Christina A. Voorham
Deputy Director: Mr Hermanus M. van
Teijlingen
Administration and Information: Mr Johannes
C. van Voorst, Mr Aart Hulleman
Issue Managers: Mr Marinus A. J. Timmer,
Mr Josephus J. Sesink, Mr Jeroen
Hoogteijling CA
Controller: Mrs Monique Vernooij-Birkhoff
Main Office: Spoordreef 10, 1315 GN Almere;
tel: (36) 539 82 50; fax: (36) 534 07 10

**Probation Services Leger des Heils
Jeugdzorg & Reclassering**
Central Office: Nieuwegracht 94, 3512 LX
Utrecht; tel: (30) 232 64 70

**Centres for Living, Care and Welfare,
Northern Region**
Information: Kwinkenplein 10-A, 9712 GZ
Groningen; tel: (50) 317 26 70

**Centres for Living, Care and Welfare,
South-Western Region**
Information: Kromhout 110, 3311 RH
Dordrecht; tel: (78) 632 07 00

**Centres for Living, Care and Welfare,
Central Region**
Information: Jan van Eijklaan 2-6, 3723 BC
Bilthoven; tel: (30) 274 91 21

**Centres for Living, Care and Welfare,
Gelderland-East Province (incl
substance misuse services)**
Information: Wilmersdorf 9, 7327 AD Apeldoorn;
tel: (55) 53 80333

**Centres for Living, Care and Welfare,
Flevoland Province**
Information: Stationsoffice H, Stationsplein 5-13,
1315 KS Almere; tel: (36) 549 68 00

**Centres for Living, Care and Welfare,
Northern Holland**
Information: Mariettahof 25, 2033 WS Haarlem;
tel: (23) 553 39 33

Goodwill Centres, Amsterdam
Information: Rode Kruisstraat 24b, 1025 KN
Amsterdam; tel: (20) 630 11 11

Goodwill Work, The Hague
Information: St Barbaraweg 4, 2516 BT Den
Haag; tel: (70) 311 55 40

**Centre for Living, Care and Welfare
Twente/Achterhoek**
Information: Molenstraat 30, 7514 DJ Enschede;
tel: (53) 475 40 60

**Centre for Living, Care and Welfare
Limburg/Brabant**
Information: Mariastraat 13, 6211 EP Maastricht;
tel: (43) 350 33 84

**Centre for Living, Care and Welfare
Veluwe/IJsselstreek**
Information: Koekoeksweg 2C, 8084 M 't
Harde; tel: (525) 65 96 90

Centre for Social Services, Rotterdam
Information: Kooikerweg 28, 3069 WP
Rotterdam; tel: (10) 222 98 88

Child Care Centre, Utrecht/'t Gooi
UJL: Prins Frederiklaan 201, 3818 KC
Amersfoort; tel: (33) 467 80 70

Hotel and Conference Centre 'Belmont'
Goorsteeg 66, 6718 TB Ede; tel: (31) 848 23 65
(50 twin-bedded rooms, 14 conference
rooms acc varying from 12-375, during
summer 96 extra beds available, in tents
acc 160)

CZECH REPUBLIC

Officer-in-charge: Maj Pieter H. Dijkstra
(18 Jun 2003)

National Headquarters: Petrzilkova 2565/23,
158 00 Praha 5; tel/fax: (00420) 251 611 229;
email: info@armadaspasy.cz;
web site: www.armadaspasy.cz

STATISTICS
(not included in statistics of The Netherlands)
Officers 20 **Envoys** 4 **Cadets** (1st Yr) 2
Employees 335
Corps 8 **Community Centres** 15 **Institutions** 17
Senior Soldiers 80 **Adherents** 49 **Junior
Soldiers** 14

STAFF
Asst Leader: Maj Alida N. A. Dijkstra-Voorn
Asst to the Leaders: Pavla Vopeláková
**National Director for Institutional Social
Work:** Envoy Premek Kopecek
**Asst to National Director for Institutional
Social Work:** Envoy Marta Kopecková
Training: Maj Philippa Smale
Finance: Mrs Hana Kosová

CENTRES

Hostels for Men and Women and Night Shelters

Brno: Mlýnská 25, 602 00 Brno;
  tel: 543 212 530 (acc 136)
Krnov: Csl armády 837 bcd, 794 01 Krnov;
  tel: 554 612 296 (acc 85, includes mothers
  and children)
Opava: Nákladní 24, 746 01 Opava;
  tel: 553 712 984 (acc 48)
Prague: Tusarova 60, 170 00 Praha 7;
  tel: 220 184 000 (acc 220)

Hostels for Men and Night Shelters

Havírov: Hostel, Na spojce 2, 736 01 Havírov;
  tel: 596 810 197 (acc 35)
  Night Shelter, Pod Svahem 1, Havírov-
  Šumbark; tel: 596 881 007 (acc 24)
Karlovy Vary: Nákladní 7, 360 05 Karlovy Vary;
  tel: 353 569 267 (acc 45)
Ostrava: U Novych Válcoven 9, 709 00 Ostrava-
  Mariánské Hory; tel: 596 620 650 (acc 114)
Šumperk: Vikyrovicka 1495, Šumperk-Lu□e;
  tel: 583 224 634 (acc 35)

Homes for Mothers and Children

Havírov: Dvoráková 21/235, 736 01 Havírov; tel:

596 813 342 (acc 18 mothers plus children)
Krnov: Csl armády 837 bcd, 794 01 Krnov;
  tel: 554 612 296 (acc 85, includes hostel for
  men and women)
Ostrava: Gen Píky 25, Ostrava-Fifejdy 702 00;
  tel: 596 611 962 (acc women 30, mothers 10
  and 15-20 children)
Opava: Rybárská 86, 746 01 Opava;
  tel: 553 714 509 (acc mothers 11 children 33)

Alternative Punishment Programme

Opava: Nákladní 24, 746 01 Opava;
  tel: 553 712 984

Farm Rehabilitation Project

747 24 Strahovice 1; mobile: 737 215 396 (acc 4)

Elderly Persons Project

Ostrava-Kuncicky: Holvekova 38, 710 00
  Ostrava-Kuncicky; tel: 596 238 163 (acc 40)

Youth Centre

Brno-Bystrc: Kubickova 23, 635 00 Brno-Bystrc;
  tel: 546 221 756

Prison Work

Prague: Petr□ilkova 2565/23, 158 00 Praha 5;
  tel/fax: (00420) 737 215 427

Major Pieter Dijkstra (Officer-in-charge, Czech Republic) prays for Cadets Jan and Lenka Cholewa as he installs them as the corps officers for Havírov

NEW ZEALAND, FIJI AND TONGA TERRITORY

Territorial leaders:
Commissioners Garth and Merilyn McKenzie

Territorial Commander:
Commissioner Garth McKenzie
(1 June 2004)

Chief Secretary:
Colonel Robin Forsyth (1 June 2004)

Territorial Headquarters: 204 Cuba Street, Wellington, New Zealand

Postal address: PO Box 6015, Wellington 6001, New Zealand

tel: [64] (04) 384 5649; fax: [64] (04) 802 6258; web site: www.salvationarmy.org.nz

On 1 April 1883 Salvation Army activities were commenced at Dunedin by Captain George Pollard and Lieutenant Edward Wright. Social work began in 1884 with a home for ex-prisoners. Work was begun officially in Fiji on 14 November 1973 by Captain Brian and Mrs Beverley McStay, and in Tonga on 9 January 1986 by Captain Tifare and Mrs Rebecca Inia.

Zone: South Pacific and East Asia
Countries included in the territory: Fiji, New Zealand, Tonga
'The Salvation Army' in Maori: Te Ope Whakaora
Languages in which the gospel is preached: English, Fijian, Hindi, Korean, Maori, Rotuman, Samoan, Tongan and Vietnamese
Periodical: *War Cry*

THE 24-7 prayer initiative underpinned all that happened in the territory. Every corps took up the challenge to pray around the clock, and testimonies abounded of people coming to faith in Christ and others receiving a fresh anointing of the Holy Spirit's power.

The international Year for Children and Youth was celebrated with children's camps at which 143 young people gave their lives to Jesus. Youth struck a dynamic note at 'Livefire' youth councils, being clearly 'fired up' for their mission to present God's love to people.

The territory's first social justice conference titled 'Just Action' was coordinated by the Social Policy and Parliamentary Unit. The unit also released a report detailing strategies to assist low and modest income households into home ownership. It was well received by government and industry leaders.

A series of fact sheets released in the lead-up to the General Election helped voters explore key issues and was welcomed by Salvationists and Christians in other denominations.

Representative soldiers and officers

came together for planning workshops to produce a Territorial Strategic Mission Plan for 2006-2010. Delegates were urged to stay true to the Army's historical roots even as they took bold steps to become more mission-effective in the 21st century.

Determination to deliver more effectively on Salvation Army mission led to a shift in the direction of services for older people. In response to the government's 'Ageing in Place' strategy, encouraging people to remain at home in the community for as long as possible, the Army finalised the sale of its aged care centres. The Army will provide ongoing spiritual care for residents of those centres and is also broadening its work with aged and housebound people in the community.

A transfer of drug and alcohol treatment from Rotoroa Island, after 96 years, was another bold strategic decision that opened the way for new addiction services in two more cities in the greater Auckland region.

The territory is embracing the concept of integrated ministry, with smaller corps bringing together social service and church-based ministries to provide salvation for the whole person. Larger urban centres are moving towards a one-stop-shop concept that offers packages of Salvation Army care from one location. It is exciting to see formerly separated ministries working together in a more integrated fashion.

Tonga and Fiji continue to be fine examples of integrated mission.

Salvation Army health services provide medical support and educational resources in the Kingdom of Tonga. In Fiji, Salvationists are active in a diverse number of programmes, from sewing classes and home leagues to kindergartens and a farm project.

The year under review ended with the commissioning of 11 New Zealand cadets of the Visionaries Session. A further 22 continued their training – 10 from Fiji and Tonga (training in Fiji) and 12 in New Zealand.

STATISTICS
Officers 547 (active 359 retired 188) **Cadets** (1st Yr) 8 (2nd Yr) 22 **Employees** 2,491
Corps 93 **New Plants** 7 **Outposts** 3 **Mission Teams** 1 **Recovery Churches** 9 **Institutions** 65
Senior Soldiers 5,603 **Adherents** 1,610 **Junior Soldiers** 571
Personnel serving outside territory Officers 14 Layworkers 2

STAFF
External Relations: Maj Peter Thorp
Overseas Development Consultant: Mr Ian Frazer
Book Production: Maj Harold Hill
Moral and Social Issues Council: Maj Harold Hill
Social Policy and Parliamentary Unit: Maj Campbell Roberts

Business Administration: Capt Bruce Vyle
  Audit: Mr Graeme Tongs, CA, ACIS
  Finance: Capt Richard Morris, B Com, CA
  Information Technology: Mr Mark Bennett
  Property: Mr Ian McLaren, Dip Bus Studies
  Public Relations and Communications: Maj David Bennett
  Trade: Maj David Bateman, Dip Bus
  Planned Giving: Maj Sandra Mellsop

Personnel: Lt-Col Wilfred Arnold, BSoc S, MA (SW), CQSW
  Asst (Admin): Maj Margaret Ousey
  Asst (Pastoral Care): Lt-Col Margaret Arnold, RGON, BN, Grad Dip Soc Sci

Asst (Overseas Service): Capt Elaine Vyle, TTC
Human Resources: Mr Paul Geoghegan, BA Psych, Dip LEIR
Booth College of Mission:
  Principal: Maj Robert Donaldson, BSc, LTh
  School for Bible and Mission: Maj Garth Stevenson, BAgrSc, Dip Tchng
  Centre for Leadership Development: Maj Robert Donaldson, BSc, LTh
  Education Consultant and Registrar: Maj Kingsley Sampson, BA, MA Hons, BD, Dip Ed, Dip Tchng

Programme: Maj Alistair Herring
  Asst: Maj Astrid Herring
  Creative Ministries and National Youth Bandmaster: Mr Stephen Stein
  Youth and Candidates: Majs Lyndon and Bronwyn Buckingham
  SpiritSong: Vocal Leader Denise Hewitt
  Children's Ministries: Maj Allison Ross
Women's Ministries: Comr Merilyn McKenzie (TPWM) Col Shona Forsyth (TSWM/TS for Adult & Family Ministries)

DIVISIONS

Canterbury/North West: 71 Peterborough St, PO Box 25-207, Christchurch 8001; tel: (03) 377 0799; fax: (03) 377 3575; email: cnwdhq@nzf.salvationarmy.org; Maj Wayne Jellyman
Central: 204 Cuba St, PO Box 6421, Wellington 6001; tel: (04) 384 4713; fax: (04) 802 6267; email: cdhq@nzf.salvationarmy.org; Maj Graeme Reddish
Midland: 12 Vialou St, PO Box 500, Hamilton 2015; tel: (07) 839 2242; fax: (07) 839 2282; email: Midland_dhq@nzf.salvationarmy.org; Maj Lindsay Chisholm
Northern: 369 Queen St, PO Box 5035, Auckland 1001; tel: (09) 379 4150; fax: (09) 379 4152; email: ndhq@nzf.salvationarmy.org; Maj Ross Gower
Southern: 575 Princes St, PO Box 934, Dunedin; tel: (03) 474 1952; fax: (03) 474 1754; email: southern_dhq@nzf.salvationarmy.org; Maj Kevin Goldsack

FIJI DIVISION

Headquarters: PO Box 14412, Suva, Fiji; tel: [679] 331 5177; fax: [679] 330 3112
Divisional Commander: Maj Gordon Daly; email: dhq_fiji@nzf.salvationarmy.org
Corps 10 **Corps Plants** 2 **Outposts** 4
Community and Family Services: Eastern –

Grantham Rd, Suva; tel: (679) 337 2122
Community and Family Services: Western – 38 Sukanaivalu Rd, Lautoka; tel: (679) 664 5471
Family Care Centres:
Labasa: Sarwan Singh St, Nasea, Labasa; tel: (679) 881 1898 (acc 16)
Lautoka: 160 VM Pillai Rd, Rifle Range; tel: (679) 665 0952 (acc 16)
Suva: 21 Spring St, Toorak, Suva; tel: (679) 330 5518 (acc 18)
Court and Prison Officers:
Suva; tel: (679) 338 1347/331 5177
Lautoka; tel: (679) 665 0952/664 5471
Farm Project: Farm 80, Lomaivuna; tel: (679) 3300 127 ext 20
Girls' Home: Mahaffy Dr, Suva; tel: (679) 331 3318 (acc 20)
Raiwai Hostel: Hostel for young male tertiary students: Grantham Rd, Suva; tel: (679) 338 7438 (acc 20)
Red Shield House: Hostel for young females: 37 Moala St, Suva; tel: (679) 338 1347 (acc 8)
Sewing Skills Programmes:
Labasa: Lot 2 Batinikama, Siberia Rd; tel: (679) 881 4822
Lautoka: 38 Sukanaivalu Rd, Waiyavi; tel: (679) 666 3712
Suva: 50 MacGregor Rd, Suva; tel: (679) 3307 746 (acc 20)
Tiny Tots Kindergartens:
Ba: 6 Old Kings Rd, Yalalevu; tel: (679) 667 0155 (acc 15)
Labasa: Lot 2 Batinikama, Siberia Rd; tel: (679) 881 4822 (acc 15)
Lautoka: Waiyavi Centre, 38 Sukanaivalu Rd, Waiyavi; tel: (679) 666 3712 (acc 50)
Lomaivuna: Farm 80, Lomaivuna; tel: (679) 3300 127 ext 20 (acc 15)
Nadi: Lot 30-31, Goundar St, Nadi; tel: (679) 670 0405 (acc 15)
Suva Central: 56 MacGregor Rd, Suva; tel: (679) 330 7746 (acc 30)

School for Officer Training and Leadership Training
tel: (679) 330 7749; fax: (679) 330 7010; email: SFOT_FIJI@nzf.salvationarmy.org

TONGA REGION

Regional Headquarters: Westpac Bank of Tonga Building, Taufa'ahau Rd, PO Box 1035, Nuku'alofa, Tonga; tel: [676] 23-760, 27-835; fax: (676) 23760; email: satonga@kalianet.to
Regional Commander: Maj Rex Johnson
Corps 4 **Corps Plant** 1

Social Services Centre: Westpac Bank of Tonga
Building, Taufa'ahau Rd, Nuku'alofa, Tonga;
tel: [676] 23-760, 27-835
Court and Prison Work: Nuku'alofa
Addiction Programme: PO Box 1035,
Nuku'alofa; tel: (676) 23760;
email: satonga@kalianet.to
Kindergartens
Sopu, Nuku'alofa; tel: (676) 26370 (acc 30)
Kolvai; tel: (676) 23760 (acc 20)
Mobile Health Clinic
Popua Community

BOOTH COLLEGE OF MISSION (BCM)

**School for Officer Training (SFOT); Centre
for Leadership Development; School of
Bible and Mission:** 20 William Booth Grove,
Upper Hutt, PO Box 40-542, Upper Hutt;
tel: (04) 528 8628; fax: (04) 527 6900
Principal, BCM and SFOT: Maj Robert
Donaldson, BSc, LTh

FAMILY TRACING SERVICE

PO Box 6015, Wellington 6015;
tel: (04) 382 0710; fax: (04) 802 6257;
email: familytracing@nzf.salvationarmy.org

FARM

Jeff Memorial Farm, Kaiwera RD 2, Gore;
tel: (03) 205 3572

INDEPENDENT LIVING UNITS

Ashburton: Wilson Court, 251-255 Tancred St
(units 3)
Auckland: 353 Blockhouse Bay Rd (units 19)
Bell Block: 46 Murray St (units 10)
Blenheim: 35 George St (units 7)
Carterton: 204 High St South (units 8)
Christchurch: 794 Main North Rd, Belfast
(units 10)
Gisborne: Edward Murphy Village, 481
Aberdeen Rd (units 30)
Hamilton: Nawton Village, 57 Enfield St
(units 40)
Kapiti: 41 Bluegum Rd, Paraparaumu Beach
(units 18)
Mosgiel: Elmwood Retirement Village, 22
Elmwood Dr (units 30); 17 Cedar Cres
(units 30)
Oamaru: 9 Arthur St (units 12)
Papakura: 91 Clevedon Rd (units 6)
Wellington: Summerset Units, Newtown: 182a
Owen St (units 11); 210, 212, 214 Owen St
(units 3); 226 Owen St (units 9)

OFFICERS' ACCOMMODATION
(under THQ)

Auckland: 9 Willcott St (units 6); 6D Liston St,
Northcote (unit 1); 19 Splendour Cl, Henderson
(unit 1); 10 Sydenham Rd (unit 1)
Wellington: 176, 176a, 178, 178a Queens Dr
(units 4)

YOUTH CAMPS AND CONFERENCE
CENTRES

Blue Mountain Lodge Christian Adventure
Centre: RD 1, Owhango, National Park;
tel: (07) 892 2630;
web site: www.bluemountainlodge.co.nz

SOCIAL SERVICES (UNDER THQ)

Addiction and Supportive
Accommodation Services

National Office: Level 2, 369 Queen St, PO Box
7342, Wellesley St, Auckland 1;
tel: (09) 369 5143; fax: (09) 377 1249;
National Manager: Maj Lynette Hutson
email: lynette_hutson@nzf.salvationarmy.org

Bridge Programme: Community and
Residential Programmes
(Treatment of Alcohol and Drug Dependency)
Auckland Bridge Centre: PO Box 56-442,
7-15 Ewington Ave, Mt Eden, Auckland 1003;
tel: (09) 630 1491; fax: (09) 630 8395;
email: akbridge@xtra.co.nz (acc assessment 21,
treatment 16, day clients 7)
Manukau Bridge Centre: 16b Bakerfield Place,
PO Box 56 442, Manukau City;
tel: (09) 262 2332; fax: (09) 263 9325;
email: mkbridge@xtra.co.nz
Waitakere Bridge Centre: 17 James Laurie St,
PO Box 69 005, Glendene, Waitakere City;
tel: (09) 835 4069; fax: (09) 835 4690;
email: wkbridge@xtra.co.nz
Whangarei: Northland Bridge, PO Box 1746,
115 Bank St; tel: (09) 430 7500;
fax: (09) 430 7501
Christchurch: The Bridge Programme: PO Box
9070, Addington, 35 Collins St;
tel: (03) 338 4436; fax: (03) 338 4312 (acc 26)
Waikato: The Bridge Programme: 25 Thackeray
St, Hamilton; tel: (07) 839 6871;
fax: (07) 839 6872
Wellington: 22-26 Riddiford St, PO Box 6033,
Wellington; tel: (04) 389 6566;
fax: (04) 389 7110 (acc 24)
Dunedin: 44 Filleul St; tel: (03) 477 9853;
fax: (03) 477 1493 (acc 8)

Invercargill: 110 Leven St, PO Box 74;
  tel: (03) 218 3094;

Oasis Centres: Treatment Centres for Gambling
Auckland: PO Box 41-309, St Lukes, 726 New
  North Rd; tel: (09) 846 0660;
  fax: (09) 846 0440
Christchurch: PO Box 9070, 126 Bealey Ave;
  tel: (03) 365 9659; fax: (03) 365 7585;
  email: oasisch@xtra.co.nz
Dunedin: 44 Filleul St; tel: (03) 477 9852;
  fax: (03) 477 1493
Hamilton: 2nd Floor, Cecil House, Garden Pl;
  Postal address: 25 Thackeray St;
  tel: (07) 839 7053; fax: (07) 839 4428
Queenstown: 29 Camp St, PO Box 887,
  Queenstown; tel: (03) 442 5103;
  fax: (03) 442 9644
Wellington: 26 Riddiford St, PO Box 6033;
  tel: (04) 389 6566; fax: (04) 389 7110

Community Addictions Programme
Invercargill: Social Service Centre, PO Box 74,
  Cnr Gala and Leven Sts;
  tel/fax: (03) 218 3094
Kaitaia: PO Box 391, 100 Commerce St;
  tel: (09) 408 3362; fax: (09) 408 3365
Tauranga: PO Box 164, 375 Cameron Rd;
  tel: (07) 578 5505; fax: (07) 578 4536

Supportive Accommodation Services
Auckland: Epsom Lodge: PO Box 26-098,
  18 Margot St, Epsom, Auckland 3;
  tel: (09) 524 5675; fax: (09) 524 9604
  (acc men 90)
Christchurch: Addington Social Services Centre:
  PO Box 9057, 62 Poulson St, Addington,
  Christchurch 8002; tel: (03) 338 5154;
  fax: (03) 338 4390 (acc 90)
Invercargill: PO Box 74, Cnr Gala and Leven
  Sts; tel/fax: (03) 218 3094 (acc 35)
Temuka: Bramwell Booth House (Intellectual
  Disability): PO Box 57, Milford Rd;
  tel: (03) 615 9570; fax: (03) 615 9571 (acc 18)
Wellington: (Intellectual Disability) PO Box
  6033, 26 Riddiford St; tel: (04) 389 0594;
  fax: (04) 389 1130 (acc 12)

Mothercraft Centre
Bethany: 35 Dryden St, Grey Lynn, Auckland
  1002; tel: (09) 376 1324; fax: (09) 376 1307;
  web site: www.bethanycentre.org.nz
  (acc antenatal 14, mothers and babies 7) Day
  Programmes

Employment Plus
National Office: 204 Cuba St, PO Box 6015,
  Wellington 6001; tel: (04) 382 0714;
  fax: (04) 382 0711; toll free: 0800 437 587
  National Manager: Mr George Borthwick;
  email:
  g.borthwick@eplus.salvationarmy.org.nz
  National Mission Director: Maj Graham
  Rattray;
  email:
  graham_rattray@nzf.salvationarmy.org.nz
Finance Service Bureau: 12 Vialou St,
  PO Box 5347, Frankton, Hamilton;
  tel: (07) 834 3195; fax: (07) 834 3198

Regions
Central: 148 Manchester St, PO Box 569,
  Fielding; tel: (06) 323 9017; fax: (06) 323 9620;
  email: a.adams@eplus-salvationarmy.org.nz
Midland: 94 London St, PO Box 5139, Hamilton;
  tel: (07) 839 5034; fax: (07) 838 0376; email:
  k.reddish@eplus-salvationarmy.org.nz
Northern: 12 Kaka St, PO Box 1524, Whangarei;
  tel: (09) 438 4470; fax: (09) 438 6500; email:
  a.carrington@eplus-salvationarmy.org.nz
Southern: 148 Kaikorai Valley Rd, Kaikorai,
  PO Box 13-105, Green Island, Dunedin;
  tel: (03) 476 7111; fax: (03) 476 7188;
  email: d.ojala@eplus-salvationarmy.org.nz

Services for Older People
National Office: 204 Cuba St, PO Box 6015,
  Wellington 6001; tel: (04) 382 0742;
  fax: (04) 382 0711
  National Manager: Maj Alistair Herring
  email:
  alistair_herring@nzf.salvationarmy.org

Home Care
Business Centre: 71 Seddon Rd, PO Box 9417,
  Hamilton; tel: (07) 834 3967;
  fax: (07) 834 8156;
  email: homecare.hamilton@xtra.co.nz
Service Centres: Auckland (2), Hamilton,
  Paeroa, Tauranga

SOCIAL SERVICES (under DHQ)
Community Ministries
Aranui: 32 Portsmouth St; tel/fax: (03) 388 1072
Auckland City: PO Box 27-153, 691 Mt Albert
  Rd, Royal Oak; tel: (09) 625 7940;
  fax: (09) 625 6045
Blenheim: Cnrs George and Henry Sts, Blenheim;
  tel: (03) 578 0862; fax: (03) 578 0990
Christchurch: PO Box 1015, 32 Lichfield St;
  tel: (03) 366 8128; fax: (03) 366 8295

Dunedin: 44a Filluel St; tel: (03) 477 9852; fax: (03) 477 1493

Feilding: 124 Manchester St; tel: (06) 323 4718; email: feilding_corps@nzf.salvationarmy.org

Foxton: Avenue Rd; tel: (06) 363 8669; email: foxton_corps@nzf.salvationarmy.org

Gisborne: PO Box 1086, 389 Gladstone Rd; tel: (06) 868 9468; fax: (06) 868 1395; email: Gisborne_corps@nzf.salvationarmy.org

Gore: 21 Irwell St; tel: (03) 208 4443

Hamilton: The Nest, PO Box 8020, Cnr Ohaupo Rd and Kahikatea Dr; tel: (07) 843 4509; fax: (07) 843 3865; incl Mary Bryant Family Resource Centre, 24 Ohaupo Rd; tel: (07) 843 4509; email: jan_smithies@nzf.salvationarmy.org (acc 8)

Hastings: PO Box 999, Cnr Warren St and Ave Rd; tel: (06) 876 5771; fax (06)870 9331; email: hastings_corps@nzf.salvationarmy.org

Hornby: 23 Manurere St, Hornby, Christchurch 4; tel: (03) 349 6268; fax: (03) 349 6268

Hutt City: Cnr Kings Cres and Cornwall St, PO Box 30745, Lower Hutt; tel: (04) 570 0273; fax: (04) 570 0274; email: huttcity_cfs@nzf.salvationarmy.org web site: www.sacrossroads.org.nz

Invercargill: PO Box 252, Tay St; tel/fax: (03) 214 0223

Linwood: 177 Linwood Ave; tel: (03) 389 3723

Manukau City: PO Box 76-075, 16b Bakerfield Pl, Manukau City; tel: (09) 262 2332; fax: (09) 262 2333

Motueka: PO Box 85, Motueka; tel: (03) 528 9338; fax: (03) 528 9642

Napier: PO Box 3086, 56 Tait Dr; tel: (06) 844 4941; fax: (06) 844 8483: email: napier_corps@nzf.salvationarmy.org

Nelson: 57 Rutherford St, PO Box 22; tel: (03) 548 4807; fax: (03) 548 4810

North Shore City: 407 Glenfield Rd, Glenfield, Auckland, PO Box 40555, Glenfield; tel: (09) 441 2554; fax: (09) 441 7599

North Taranaki: PO Box 384, Cnr Powderham and Dawson Sts, New Plymouth; tel: (06) 758 9338; fax (06) 758 2325; email: northtaranaki_corps@nzf.salvationarmy.org

Palmerston North: 431 Church St, PO Box 869, Palmerston North; tel: (06) 358 7455; fax: (06) 358 2314; email: palmerstonnorth_cfs@nzf.salvationarmy.org

Porirua East: PO Box 53-025, Cnr Warspite Ave and Fantame St; tel: (04) 235 6266; fax: (04) 235 6482; email: porirua_cfs@nzf.salvationarmy.org

Queenstown: PO Box 887, Camp St; tel: (03) 442 5103; fax: (03) 442 9644

Rotorua: 1115 Haupapa St; tel: (07) 348 8113; fax: (07) 346 8075; email: rotorua_cfs@nzf.salvationarmy.org

Sydenham: 17 Southampton St; tel: (03) 331 7483; fax: (03) 332 8395

Tauranga: 375 Cameron Rd; tel: (07) 578 5505; fax: (07) 578 4536; email: tauranga_corps@nzf.salvationarmy.org

Timaru: 206 Wai-iti Rd, Timaru; tel/fax: (03) 684 7139

Tokoroa: PO Box 567; tel: (07) 886 9812; fax 886 9512; email: tokoroa_cfs@nzf.salvationarmy.org

Upper Hutt: 695 Fergusson Dr; tel: (04) 528 6745; email: upper_hutt_corps@nzf.salvationarmy.org

Wairarapa: PO Box 145 Carterton, 204-210 High St South, Carterton; tel: (06) 379 7176; fax: (06) 379 6109; email: wairarapa_cfs@nzf.salvationarmy.org

Waitakere City: PO Box 21-708 Henderson, 7-9 View Rd; tel: (09) 837 4471; fax: (09) 837 1246

Wellington: 26 Riddiford St, Newtown; tel: (04) 389 0594; fax: (04) 389 1130; Counselling Service: 26 Riddiford St, Newtown; tel: (04) 389 0594; fax: (04) 389 1130; email: wellington_cfs@nzf.salvationarmy.org Youth Services: 1 Ghuznee St; tel: (04) 384 6119; fax: (04) 384 6115

Whakatane: 79 Goulstone Rd; tel: (07) 308 2534; fax (07) 308 6923; email: salarmy.whakatane@xtra.co.nz

Early Childhood Education Centres

Gisborne: 'Noah's Young Ones': PO Box 1086, 389 Gladstone Rd, Gisborne; tel: (06) 868 9468; fax: (06) 868 1395 (roll 24)

Hamilton: The Nest Educare: PO Box 8020, Cnr Ohaupo Rd and Kahikatea Dr; tel: (07) 843 4066; fax: (07) 843 3865 (roll 50)

Masterton: Cecilia Whatman Early Childhood Education Centre: PO Box 145 Carterton, 132-140 Ngaumutawa Rd; tel: (06) 378 7316 (roll 50)

Upper Hutt: William Booth Educare: PO Box 40-542 Upper Hutt;

tel: (04) 528 8628 527 6929 (roll 25)

Waitakere: Kidz Matter 2US: PO Box 21-708, Henderson; tel: (09) 837 4471; fax: (09) 837 1246 (roll 25)

Wellington: Britomart ECEC: 126 Britomart St, Berhampore, Wellington 6002; tel: (04) 389 9781 (roll 28)

COURT AND PRISON SERVICE

Auckland: PO Box 27 153, Mt Roskill; tel: (09) 916 9267; fax: (09) 309 9751

Alexandra: 21 Aronui Rd; tel: (03) 448 9436

Blenheim: PO Box 417; tel: (03) 578 0862; fax: (03) 578 0990

Christchurch: PO Box 25 207; tel: (03) 377 0799; fax: (03) 377 3575

Dunedin: 44a Filleul St; tel: (03) 477 9852; fax: (03) 477 1493

Gore: 21 Irwell St; tel/fax: (03) 208 4443

Hamilton: tel: (07) 843 4509; fax (07) 843 3865

Invercargill: 14 Trent St; tel/fax: (03) 217 1131

North Shore: PO Box 40 034, Glenfield; tel: (09) 441 2554; fax (09) 441 7599

Manukau: fax: (09) 277 6396; mobile (027) 478 4429

Kaitaia: PO Box 391; tel: (09) 408 3362; fax (09) 408 3362

Lower Hutt/Upper Hutt: PO Box 31 363, Lower Hutt; tel: (04) 389 0594; fax: (04) 389 1130

Palmerston North: PO Box 869; tel/fax: (06) 353 3459

Porirua: PO Box 53 025, Porirua East; tel: (04) 914 3260; fax (04) 914 3262

Timaru: 206 Wai-iti Rd; tel/fax: (03) 684 7139

Waitakere: mobile (027 2430586

Wellington: PO Box 5094; tel: (04) 918 8063; fax (04) 918 8098

Westport: tel: (03) 789 8085; fax: (03) 789 8058

PAPUA NEW GUINEA'S CHIEF SCOUT

Major Sere Kala has become Chief Commissioner of the Scout Association of Papua New Guinea. A scout chaplain and member of the Association's National Executive for a number of years, he became an Officer of the Order of the British Empire (OBE) in the Queen's honours list for PNG released during Independence Day celebrations in September 2005. Major Kala is pictured with the Governor General of Papua New Guinea, Sir Paulias Matane.

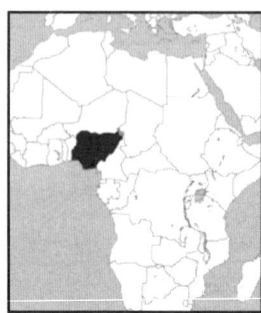

NIGERIA TERRITORY

Territorial leaders:
Commissioners Stuart and Hope Mungate

Territorial Commander:
Commissioner Stuart Mungate (1 Nov 2003)

Chief Secretary:
Lieut-Colonel Johnson Asoegwu
(1 Apr 2003)

Territorial Headquarters: 6 Shipeolu St, Igbobi, Shomolu, Lagos

Postal address: Box 3025, Shomolu, Lagos, Nigeria

Tel address: Salvation Army Lagos; tel/fax: [234] (1) 774 9125;
email: Nigeria@NIG.salvationarmy.org

Army operations began in Nigeria in 1920 when Lieut-Colonel and Mrs George H. Souter landed in Lagos, to be followed later by Staff-Captain and Mrs Charles Smith, with 10 West Indian officers.

Zone: Africa
Country included in the territory: Nigeria
'The Salvation Army' in Yoruba: Ogun Igbala Na; in Ibo: Igwe Agha Nzoputa; in Efik: Nka Erinyana; in Edo: Iyo Kuo Imienfan; in Urhobo: Ofovwi re Arhc Na; in Hausa: Soldiogi Cheta
Languages in which the gospel is preached: Edo, Efik/Ibibio, English, Hausa, Ibo, Ijaw, Calabari, Tiv, Urhobo, Yoruba
Periodicals: *Salvationist, The Shepherd, The War Cry*

THOUSANDS of Salvationists from across Nigeria gathered in Benin City to welcome General John Larsson and Commissioner Freda Larsson for a territorial congress that included a half-night of prayer and men's, women's and youth rallies. In the women's rally the World President for Women's Ministries (Commissioner Larsson) presented the President's Badge to nine women who had each won three new home league members.

After enrolling 61 senior and 16 junior soldiers the General challenged all Salvationists to rise in the power of the Holy Spirit and witness to the love of Christ. 'Reach out in love to all,' he said, 'flying on the Army's two wings of saving souls and serving suffering humanity.'

As a result of a visit to the President of Nigeria by the territorial leaders, The Salvation Army has been entrusted with running the National Agency for Poverty Alleviation programme in one of the country's states. The introduction of a Psychosocial Orphanage and Vulnerable Children programme has brought healing to many people. Widows who never knew the whereabouts of their children have been linked up with them; children who have never known affection have been showered with love.

With new initiatives, women's ministries help to spread the healing balm of Jesus to people feeling hurt and rejected, such as victims of child abuse and human trafficking. The addition of the new 'Grace' family programme is particularly benefiting widows. Young widows learn and gain support from those who have been walking the lonely road longer.

Family Week was conducted in all corps, societies and outpost to help strengthen families as the nucleus of church fellowships.

The Territorial Facilitating Team has travelled the country ministering to people living with HIV/Aids. A number of other NGOs are partnering with The Salvation Army in this work. An open door to minister to a Muslim community came when an imam invited the team to help train their people in HIV/Aids-related issues.

Many Salvationist students who had left the Campus Fellowship are returning. The influence of this programme is far-reaching as many occultists at schools throw away their idols and turn to Christ.

Music ministries also provide an avenue for witnessing. Non-Salvationists are identifying with this area of ministry and many have met Christ through the staff of the Music and Other Creative Arts Department.

STATISTICS
Officers 415 (active 330 retired 85) **Cadets** 8 **Employees** 400
Corps 170 **Societies and Outposts** 166 **Institutions** 17 **Schools** 37 **Clinics** 9

Senior Soldiers 26,391 **Adherents** 2,235 **Junior Soldiers** 8,800
Personnel serving outside territory Officers 2

STAFF
Business Administration: Maj Friday S. Ayanam
Community Programme: Maj Okokon M. Udo
Editor/Literary: Capt Ifenyinwa Olebunne
Extension Training Officer: Capt Michael Olatunde
Field Programme: Maj Festus Oloruntoba
Finance: Maj E. Lewanne Dudley
Personnel: Maj Cornelius K. Ajubiga
Prison Chaplain: Maj Benson Erhuwumnsee
Projects: Emmanuel Dorthe
Public Relations: Maj O. Mgbebuihe
Social: Maj Ebenezer O. Abayomi
　HIV/Aids: Maj G. Omokaro
Sponsorship: Capt Comfort Abayomi
Territorial Development Officer: Maj Glory Ayanam
Territorial Evangelist: Maj Silas Olebunne
Territorial Music Sec: David Nathaniel
Training: Maj Edwin Okorougo
Women's Ministries: Comr Hope Mungate (TPWM) Lt-Col Veronica Asoegwu (TSWM) Maj Caroline Ajubiga (THLS) Maj Mary Adejoro (TLOM)
Youth and Candidates: Capt Maurice Akpabio

DIVISIONS
Akwa Ibom Central: c/o Afia Nisit PA, via Uyo; Maj Etim A. Udo
Akwa Ibom East: PO Box 20, Ikot Ubo, via Eket; Maj Edet Essien
Akwa Ibom South West: c/o Abak PO Box 23, Abak; Capt Udoh Uwak
Akwa Ibom West: PO Box 47, Etinan; Maj Smart Umoh
Anambra East: Umuchu; Maj Stephen A. Uzoho
Anambra West: 5 Urenebo St, Housing Estate, PO Box 1168, Onitsha, Anambra State; Maj Chika Ezekwere
Ibadan: PO Box 261, Ibadan, Oyo State; Capt Michael Sijuade
Imo Central: based at Orogwe-Owerri; Maj Paul Onyekwere
Lagos: PO Box 2640, Surulere, Lagos State; Maj Joseph Akpan
Ondo/Ekiti: PO Box 51, Akure, Ondo State; Maj Michael Oyesanya

DISTRICTS
Abia: 2-8 Market Rd, PO Box 812, Aba, Abia State; Maj Simon Ekpendu

Badagry: PO Badagry, Lagos State; Maj Joseph Ogunde

Cross River: PO Box 11, Calabar, Cross River State; tel: (087) 220284; Maj Samuel Edung

Edo/Delta: PO Box 108, Benin City, Edo State; Maj Emmanuel Agazie

Egba: PO Box 46, Ado Odo, Ogun State; Maj Raphael Ogundahunsi

Imo North: PO Box 512, Akokwa; Capt Bramwell Anozie

Northern: PO Box 512, Jos, Plateau State; Capt Paul Dim

Rivers: PO Box 1161, Port Harcourt, Rivers State; Maj Patrick Orasibe

SECTIONS

Akwa Ibom South East: PO Box 25 Ikot Abasi; Maj Kennedy Inyang

Enugu/Ebonyi: Enugu, PO Box 1454, 4 Moorehouse St, Ogui, Enugu State; Maj Godspower Sampson

TRAINING COLLEGE

4 Shipeolu St, Shomolu, Igbobi, Lagos (PO Box 17); tel: (01) 774 9125

SOCIAL SERVICES

Corps-based Prison Ministry

Afaha Eket Corps Prison Work, Agbor Corps, Badagry Prison Work, Benin Central Prison Work, Ibadan Central Corps, Port Harcourt Corps Prison Team

THQ-based Prison Ministry

Badagry Prison, Ikoyi Prison, Kirikiri Maximum Security, Kirikiri Minimum Security, Kirikiri Women's Prison

HIV/Aids Action Centre and Voluntary Counselling and Testing Centre

11 Odunlami St, PO Box 125, Lagos

Medical Centres

Ado Odo Medical Centre: Ado Odo Corps, PO Box 46, Ado Odo, Ogun State (acc 2)

Gbethromy Training and Medical Centre: c/o Badagry PO, Badagry, Lagos State (acc 8)

Iyara Health Centre: c/o Ado Irele, Ondo State (acc 3)

Lagos Central Corps Clinic: 11 Odunlami St, PO Box 125, Lagos State (acc 2)

Nda Nsit Clinic/Maternity: Nda Nsit Corps, via Uyo, Akwa Idom State (acc 2)

Nkoro Corps Mobile Clinic: Nkoro Corps, via Boni PO Box, Rivers State (acc 4)

Ubrama Health Centre/Clinic: Ubrama PO Box Ahoada Alaga, Rivers State

Umucheke Corps Clinic: via Uruala PO, Ideato L/G. A., Imo State (acc 4)

Social Centres/Institutions/Programmes

Akai Children's Home: PO Box 1009, Eket, Akwa Ibom State (acc 35)

Benin Rehabilitation Centre: 20A First East Circular Rd, PO Box 108, Benin City, Edo State (acc 17)

Oji River Rehabilitation Centre: Oji River PO, via Enugu, Enugu State (acc 64)

Orphans/Vulnerable Centre/Orphans Psycho-Social Centre – Akai: PO Box 1009, Eket Akwa Ibom State

SCHOOLS

Nursery

Aba Corps, Agbor Corps, Akai Corps, Akokwa Corps, Amauzari Corps, Benin Corps, Ibughubu Corps, Ikot Inyang Eti, Ile Ife Corps, Ivue Corps, Jos Corps, Mpape Corps, Onitsha Corps, Osumenyi Corps, Somorika Corps, Suleja, Umucheke Corps, Umuchu Corps, Umudike Corps

Primary

Aba Corps, Akai, Amauzari Corps, Benin Corps, Ile Ife, Ikot Inyang Eti, Ivue Corps, Jos Corps, Mpape Corps, Onitsha Corps, Somorika Corps, Suleja

VOCATIONAL TRAINING CENTRES

Afia Nsit-Nsit VTC: Afia Nsit-Nsit Corps, PO Box 8, Afia Nsit Urua Nko, Akwa Ibom State (acc 8)

Abak Training Centre: Abak Corps, PO Box 23, Abak, Akwa Ibom State (acc 4)

Amauzari VTC: Amauzari Corps, via Owerri PO, Imo State (acc 4)

Enugu VTC: Enugu Corps, 4 Moorhouse St, PO Box 1454, Ogui, Enugu State (acc 6)

Ibesit Training Centre: Ibesit Corps, Anang PA, Ukanafun LGA, Akwa Ibom State (acc 3)

Ikot Okobo Training Centre: PO Box 493, Eket, Akwa Ibom State (acc 156)

Ilesha VTC: Ilesha Corps, PO Box 91, Ilesha, Oyo State (acc 30)

Ile-Ife VTC: Ile-Ife Corps, PO Box 113, Ile-Ife, Oyo State

Orogwe VTC: Orogwe Corps, via Owerri PO, Imo State (acc 235)

Supare VTC: Supare Corps, PMB 257, via Ikare Akoko, Ondo State (acc 30)

Umuogo VTC: Umuogo Corps, c/o Amuzu PA, via Owerri, Imo State (acc 8)

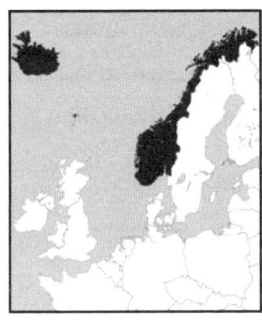

NORWAY, ICELAND AND THE FÆROES TERRITORY

Territorial Leaders:
Commissioners Carl and Gudrun Lydholm

Territorial Commander:
Commissioner Carl Lydholm (11 Jul 2005)

Chief Secretary:
Lieut-Colonel Erling Mæland (1 Sep 2005)

**Territorial Headquarters: Kommandør T I Øgrims plass 4,
0165 Oslo, Norway**

Postal address: Box 6866, St Olavs Plass, 0130 Oslo, Norway
Tel address: Frelses Oslo; tel: [47] 22 99 85 00; fax: [47] 22 20 84 49
email: hk@frelsesarmeen.no; web site: www.frelsesarmeen.no

Commissioners Hanna Ouchterlony and George Scott Railton with Staff-Captain and Mrs Albert Orsborn 'opened fire' in Oslo (Kristiania) on 22 January 1888. Work began in Iceland on 12 May 1895, pioneered by Adjutant Christian Eriksen, Captain Thorstein Davidsson and Lieutenant Lange, and spread to The Færoes in 1924.

Zone: Europe
Countries included in the territory: Iceland, Norway, The Færoes
'The Salvation Army' in Norwegian: Frelsesarmeen; in Icelandic: Hjälpraedisherinn; in Færoese: Frelsunarherurin
Languages in which the gospel is preached: Færoese, Icelandic, Norwegian
Periodicals: *Herópid* (Icelandic), *FAbU nytt*, *Krigsropet*, *Frelsesoffiseren* (Norwegian)

THE territorial theme 'To Be Together' was chosen for the international Year for Children and Youth, underlining the link between older and younger generations. The territorial congress highlighted this by bringing the children into all meetings for the first 20 minutes, when a doll theatre provided messages for the whole congregation.

This strong message of all generations belonging to each other and to the Army will have an impact in years to come as programmes are devised for the whole corps family.

The European Youth Congress in Prague (Czech Republic) was a time of spiritual renewal for delegates from the territory. Among these were 25 young people (a number of them newcomers to the Army) from Akureyri, a town of 17,000 people in the north of Iceland where every month 100-120 young people meet for a gospel concert by the corps's 35-strong gospel choir and one of its rock bands.

In July 2005 the Territorial Band

released a CD that became very popular with the public in Norway. One of the tracks, a song by Torgny Blørk/Leif Strand called 'My Heart is Yours', became number one in the pop chart and remained in first or second spot for 25 weeks.

The football team from the Army's drug and rehabilitation programme took part in the World Cup of street soccer in Edinburgh, Scotland. The event boosted the participants' self-esteem greatly. The drug and rehabilitation programme also started *Jobben* ('The Job'), an initiative for creating jobs in cooperation with local authorities and private firms.

'Fretex' (the Army's recycling programme that involves training vulnerable people for work) marked its centenary with a grand celebration. The importance of 'Fretex' in Norwegian society was made clear as the Prime Minister participated in the whole of a long evening of dinner and entertainment even though it was his last day in office (due to a change of government).

At the start of January 2006 the territory gathered in prayer for two weeks and the leaders met in conference to seek a mission/vision statement for the coming years: 'One Salvation Army – united in Christ, rooted in the word of God, together in prayer, and focused on the salvation and discipleship of all.'

STATISTICS

Officers 446 (active 191 retired 255) **Cadets** (2nd Yr) 6 **Employees** 1,633
Corps 116 **Outposts** 383 **Institutions** 37 (including slum posts) **Centre for Deaf and Blind** 1 **Industrial Centres/Second-hand Shops** 45
Senior Soldiers 5,930 **Adherents** 1,213 **Junior Soldiers** 191
Personnel serving outside territory Officers 16

STAFF

Sec for Business Administration: Maj Jan Risan
  Asst Sec for Business Administration: Maj Grete Mohn
Chief Accountant: Mr Egil Hognerud
Communication/Information/Marketing: Mr Andrew Hannevik
Missionary Projects: Maj Bernt Olaf Ørsnes
Personnel: Capt Lise O. Luther
Property: Mr Dag Tellefsen

Sec for Field Programme: Maj Clive Adams
  Asst Sec for Field Programme: Maj Inger Marit Nygård
Community: Maj Birgit T. Fosen
Music: Maj Jan Harald Hagen
Over 60s: Maj Leif-Erling Fagermo
Study: Mr Eiliv Herikstad
Territorial Band: B/M John Philip Hannevik
Youth: Maj Tone Gjeruldsen

Women's Ministries: Comr Gudrun Lydholm (TPWM) Lt-Col Signe Helene Mæland (TSWM)
Home and Family: Maj Marianne Adams

Sec for Social Services: Maj Elisabeth Henne
Administration: Mrs Guri Ingvaldsen
Alcohol and Drug Rehabilitation: Maj Hildegard A. Ørsnes
Children and Family Homes: Mrs Lindis Evja
Day Care Centres for Children: Maj Lisbeth Welander
Investigation: Maj Erling Levang
Welfare and Development: Maj Thorgeir Nybo
Work Rehabilitation and Recycling: Mr Thor Fjellvang

THQ

Candidates and Leader of TC/CS Secretariat: Maj Jan Peder Fosen
Editor: Mrs Hilde Dagfinrud Valen
Training: Maj Gro Merete Berg

DIVISIONS

Central: Borggt 2, PO Box 2869, Tøyen, 0608 Oslo; tel: 23 24 49 20; fax: 23 24 49 21; Maj Jan Øystein Knedal

Eastern: Kneika 11, PO Box 40, 3056
Solbergelva; tel: 32 87 12 90;
fax: 32 87 12 01; Maj Arne Undersrud
Midland: Knausv 12, Smeby, PO Box 3002,
2318 Hamar; tel: 62 52 21 83;
fax: 62 54 91 08; Maj Brith-Mari Heggelund
Northern: Bjørkvn 12, PO Box 8255 Jakobsli,
7458 Trondheim; tel: 73 57 14 20;
fax: 73 57 16 93; Maj Solfrid Bakken
North Norway: Skolegt 6, PO Box 177, 9252
Tromsø; tel: 77 68 83 70;
fax: 77 68 81 51; Maj Paul William Marti
Western: Kongsgt 50, PO Box 553, 4003
Stavanger; tel: 51 56 41 60; fax: 51 56 41 61;
Maj Per Arne Pettersen

TRAINING COLLEGE
1385 Asker: Brendsrudtoppen 40;
tel: 66 76 49 70; fax: 66 76 49 71

UNDER THQ
Jeløy Folk High School
1516 Moss: Nokiavn 30b, Folk High School;
tel: 69 91 10 70; fax: 69 91 10 80

Jeløy Conference Centre
1516 Moss: Nokiavn 30a; tel: 69 91 10 60;
fax: 69 91 10 65

ICELAND REGION
Gardastraeti 38, PO Box 372, IS 121 Reykjavik;
tel: [354] 552 0788; fax: [354] 562 0780; Maj
Anne Marie Reinholdtsen
Convalescent Home: Skólabraut 10, PO Box
115, IS-172 Seltjarnarnes; tel: [354] 561 2090;
fax: [354] 561 2089
Guest Home: PO Box 866, IS-121 Reykjavik;
tel: [354] 561 3203; fax: [354] 561 3315

THE FÆROES DISTRICT
(under THQ)
Torsgøta 19, PO Box 352, FO-110 Torshavn,
Færøyene; tel: (00298) 31 21 89;
fax: (00298) 31 41 89; Maj Samuel Jakon
Joensen
Hostel: FO-100 Torshavn, N Winthersgt 3;
tel: (00298) 31 73 93

SOCIAL SERVICES
Head Office: Kommandør T I Øgrims plass 4
0165 Oslo; tel: 22 99 85 00; fax: 22 99 85 84

Childrens' and Youths' Homes
3028 Drammen: Bolstadhagen 61;
tel: 32 20 45 80; fax: 32 20 45 81

1441 Drøbak: Nils Carlsensgt 31;
tel: 64 90 51 30; fax: 64 91 51 31
1540 Vestby: Soldammen, Svingen;
tel: 64 98 04 70; fax: 64 98 04 71
1112 Oslo: Nordstrandsvn 7; tel: 23 16 89 10;
fax: 22 29 20 85
2021 Skedsmokorset: Flesvigs vei 4;
tel: 63 87 44 19; fax: 63 87 41 77
4011 Stavanger: Vidarsgt 4; tel: 51 52 11 49;
fax: 51 52 66 31
7037 Trondheim: Øystein Møylas veg 20 B;
tel: 73 95 44 33, fax: 73 95 44 39

Day Care Centres for Children
1385 Asker: Brendsrudtoppen 60;tel: 66 78 74 86;
fax: 66 79 02 64
5011 Bergen: Skottegt 16; tel: 55 23 08 83;
fax: 55 23 47 45
1441 Drøbak: Nils Carlsensgt 31; tel: 64 93 15 09;
fax: 64 93 15 73
0664 Oslo: Regnbuevn 2C; tel: 23 03 93 30,
fax: 23 03 93 39

Family Centres
0487 Oslo: Kapellvn 61; tel: 22 09 86 20,
fax: 22 09 86 21
3023 Drammen: Home-Start Family Contact,
Landfalløya 78; tel: 32 83 39 93;
fax: 32 89 74 72

Nursing Homes
0661 Oslo: Ensjøtunet, Malerhaugvn 10b;
tel: 22 57 66 30; fax: 22 67 09 34

Old People's Welfare Centres
0650 Oslo: Borggt 2; tel: 22 67 47 85;
fax: 22 67 34 16
1516 Moss: Nokiaveien 30; tel: 69 27 50 94;
fax: 69 27 43 35
0661 Oslo: Malerhaugvn 10b; tel: 22 57 66 30;
fax: 22 67 09 34

Slum and Goodwill Centres
5808 Bergen: Ladegårdsgt 21;
tel: 55 56 34 70; fax: 55 56 34 71
3015 Drammen: Thornegt 1; tel: 32 83 38 12
0656 Oslo: Borggt. 2; tel: 23 03 74 494004

Hostels
5054 Bergen: Bjørnsonsgt 4; tel: 55 20 56 00;
fax: 55 20 56 01
8001 Bodø: Kongensgt 16; tel: 75 52 23 38;
fax: 75 52 23 39
5501 Haugesund: Sørhauggt 215;
tel: 52 72 77 01; fax: 52 72 35 30
0656 Oslo: Schweigaardsgt 70; tel: 23 24 39 00;
fax: 23 24 39 09
0561 Oslo: Heimen, Heimdalsgt 27 A;
tel: 23 21 09 60; fax: 22 68 00 98

0354 Oslo: Sporveisgt 33; tel: 22 95 73 50;
fax: 22 95 73 51

5812 Bergen: Bakkegt 7; tel: 55 30 22 85,
fax: 55 30 22 90

5415 Stord: Åkervikåsen 13; tel: 53 49 57 77;
fax: 53 49 57 72

5751 Odda, PO Box 206; tel: 53 64 70 50;
fax: 53 64 70 53

7041 Trondheim: Furulund, Lade Allè 84;
tel: 73 90 70 30; fax: 73 90 70 40

3111 Tønsberg: Farmannsvn 26; tel: 33 31 54
09; fax: 33 31 07 74

Rehabilitation Homes for Alcoholics/Drug Addicts

1900 Fetsund: The Door of Hope, Falldalsvn
411; tel: 63 88 79 60; fax: 63 88 79 61

4017 Stavanger: Auglendsdalen 64;
tel: 51 82 87 00; fax: 51 82 87 82

Day Care Centres (Alcoholics/Drug Addicts)

0187 Oslo: Urtegaten 16 A/C; tel: 23 03 66 80;
fax: 23 03 66 81

7012 Trondheim: Hvedingsveita 3;
tel: 73 52 09 00; fax: 73 51 03 97

6001 Ålesund: Solhøy, Giskegt 27;
tel/fax: 70 12 18 05

Health Clinic for Drug Addicts

0187 Oslo Urtegt 16 A/C; tel: 22 67 43 45

0650 Oslo Borggt 2, tel: 22 08 36 70

Prison Work

0666 Oslo, Ole Deviksv 20; tel: 23 06 92 35,
fax: 22 65 57 74

Home for Prisoners

0666 Oslo, Ole Deviksv 20; tel: 23 06 92 35;
fax: 22 65 57 74

Work Rehabilitation and Recycling Centres (FRETEX)

(including 45 second-hand shops)

5852 Bergen: Sandalsringen 3; tel: 55 92 59 00;
fax: 55 92 59 10

3036 Drammen: Kobbevikdalen 71;
tel: 32 20 83 50; fax: 32 20 83 51

3550 Gol: Sentrumsvn. 63; tel: 32 07 98 80;
fax: 32 07 98 81

9406 Harstad: Storgt 34; tel: 77 00 24 77;
fax: 77 00 24 71

7080 Heimdal: Heggstadmyra 2; tel: 72 59 59 15;
fax: 72 59 59 19

9900 Kirkenes: Pasvikvn 2; tel: 78 97 02 40;
fax: 78 97 02 41

2615 Lillehammer: Storgt 91; tel: 61 24 65 50;
fax: 61 24 65 51

0668 Oslo: Ole Deviksvei 20; tel: 23 06 92 00;
fax: 23 06 92 01

3735 Skien: Bedriftsvn 58; tel: 35 59 89 44;
fax: 35 59 57 44

4033 Stavanger: Midtgårdvn 22; tel: 51 95 13 00;
fax: 51 95 13 01

9018 Tromsø: Skattøravn 39; tel: 77 67 22 88;
fax: 77 67 22 87

6002 Ålesund: Korsegt 6; tel: 70 12 71 75;
fax: 70 12 71 75

Second-hand Shops:

Ålesund (2), Bergen (5), Bryne, Drammen (2),
Fredrikstad, Gol, Harstad, Haugesund,
Jørpeland, Kirkenes, Kristiansand, Levanger,
Lillehammer, Lillestrøm, Lyngdal, Molde,
Moss, Ølen, Oslo (5), Sandnes (2), Sandvika,
Sarpsborg, Skien , Stavanger (3), Tromsø,
Trondheim (5), Tønsberg, Voss; Art Galleri in
Bergen

The European Youth Congress in Prague (Czech Republic) was a time of spiritual renewal for delegates from the territory. Among these were 25 young people (a number of them newcomers to the Army) from Akureyri, a town of 17,000 people in the north of Iceland where every month 100-120 young people meet for a gospel concert by the corps's 35-strong gospel choir and one of its rock bands.

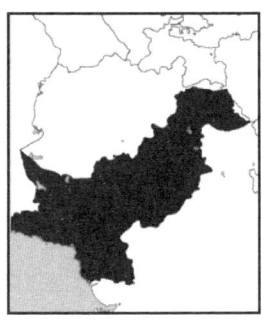

PAKISTAN TERRITORY

Territorial leaders:
Colonels Bo and Birgitte Brekke

Territorial Commander:
Colonel Bo Brekke (15 Sep 2006)

Chief Secretary:
Lieut-Colonel Emmanuel Paul (15 Sep 2006)

Territorial Headquarters: 35 Shahrah-e-Fatima Jinnah, Lahore

Postal address: PO Box 242, Lahore 54000, Pakistan

Tel address: Salvation Lahore; tel: [92] (42) 758 1644/756 9940; fax: [92] (42) 757 2699
email: pakistan@salvationarmy.org

The Salvation Army began work in Lahore in 1883 and was eventually incorporated under the Companies Act of 1913 on 9 October 1968.

Zone: South Asia
Country included in the territory: Pakistan
Languages in which the gospel is preached: English, Punjabi, Pashto, Urdu
Periodicals: *Home League Quarterly, The War Cry* (in Urdu)

A DEVASTATING earthquake registering 7.8 on the Richter scale shook northern Pakistan on 8 October 2005. The magnitude of destruction soon became apparent and the territory is eternally grateful for the ready response of so many people around the world, through the Emergency Services Office at International Headquarters.

With funding available within 48 hours, two large truck-loads of relief supplies were organised and taken to Abbotabad in the earthquake-stricken region. To ensure the safe arrival of the supplies and team of Salvation Army relief workers, the British High Commission provided security for the convoy.

The trucks contained enough supplies

to meet the immediate food and washing needs of 5,000 people (500 families). Each family received a food parcel containing, flour, water, milk powder, *dahl* (pulses), sugar, tea, washing powder and soap. Also on board were tents and blankets.

Salvationists distributed 1,700 tents, roofing iron and timber to construct 300 temporary shelters, sewing machines, blankets and school supplies. In partnership with the Pakistan military these were taken into the mountains for families who were determined to remain close to their family plots during the severe winter months.

Mountain tracks were sometimes impassable and it was often difficult to reach the villagers. Eventually, around 150,000 people were relocated from these communities into tent camps in Balakot and Manshera, although many chose to remain and see out the winter.

In regular consultation with government agencies, the territory is now committed to a long-term resettlement programme which includes the building of a school and community centre. A reconstruction office has been set up in Manshera.

The Salvation Army's work in prisons continues to be an excellent and much-valued ministry, the territorial advisory board having managed to get permission for Salvationists to have access to gaols. In Hyderabad the prison governor was so pleased with the work that he wrote his own letter of appreciation and established a regular programme for the district officer and the corps officers to maintain their ministry.

The miracle of God's grace continues to enable The Salvation Army to minister in the Islamic Republic of Pakistan.

STATISTICS
Officers 389 (active 299 retired 90) **Cadets** (2nd Yr) 22 **Candidates** (as corps leaders) 6 **Employees** 258
Corps 131 **Societies** 571 **Institutions** 7 **Schools** 3 **Training and Resource Centres** 5
Senior Soldiers 58,022 **Adherents** 12,406 **Junior Soldiers** 14,387

STAFF
Emergency Services: Capt MacDonald Chandi
Field:
Finance: Maj Britt Alhbin
Human Resources and Development: Capt Raja Azeem Zia
Projects: under Chief Secretary
Projects Officer:
Project Area Coordinators: Capt Emmanuel

Khurshid (Lahore) Capt Sabir Shaffi (Faisalabad)
Property: Maj Peter Scadden
Social: Maj Jeanette Scadden
Training: Maj Gloria Hammond
Women's Ministries: Col Birgitte Brekke (TPWM) Lt-Col Gulzar Emmanuel Paul (TSWM)
Youth: Maj Khuram Shahzada

DIVISIONS
Faisalabad: Jamilabad Jamia Salfia Rd, Faisalabad; tel: (411) 753586; Maj Samuel Tari
Islamabad: William Booth Village, Khana Kak (Majaraj Plaza) Iqbal Town, Islamabad; mobile: 0300 5244618; Maj Younis Joseph
Jaranwala: Water Works Rd, nr Telephone Exchange, Jaranwala; tel: (468) 312423; Lt-Col Morris John
Jhang: Yousaf Shah Rd, Jhang Saddar; tel: (471) 611589; Capt Michael Gabriel (Div Officer)
Karachi: 78 NI Lines, Frere St, Saddar, Karachi 74400; tel: (21) 225 4260; Maj Walter Emmanuel
Khanewal: Chak Shahana Rd, Khanewal 58150; tel: (692) 53860; Maj Samuel Barkat
Lahore: The Salvation Army, Bahar Colony, Kot Lakhpat, Lahore; tel: (42) 583 4568; Lt-Col Yusaf Ghulam
Sahiwal: Karbala Rd, Sahiwal; tel: (441) 66383; Maj Shafqat Masih (Div Officer)
Sheikhupura: 16 Civil Lines Rd, Qila, Sheikhupura; tel: (4931) 56521; Maj Salamat Masih

DISTRICT
Hyderabad: Bungalow No 9, 'E' Block, Unit No 11, Latifabad 11, Hyderabad; tel: (221) 813445; Capt Washington Daniel

TRAINING COLLEGE
Ali Bridge, Canal Bank Rd North, Tulspura, Lahore; tel: (42) 658 2450; email: sacollege@cyber.net.pk

LEADERSHIP TRAINING AND CONFERENCE CENTRE
Lahore: 35 Shahrah-e-Fatima Jinnah, PO Box 242, Lahore 54000; tel: (42) 758 1644 ext 338

SOCIAL SERVICES
Boarding Hostels
Boys
Jhang: Yousaf Shah Rd, Jhang Saddar; tel: (471) 624763 (acc 70)

Girls

Lahore: 35 Shahrah-e-Fatima Jinnah,
PO Box 242, Lahore 54000;
tel: (42) 756 9940 (acc 60)

Sheikhupura: 16 Civil Lines, Quilla,
Sheikhupura; tel: (56) 378 4378 (acc 50)

Children's Home

Karachi: Site Metroville, PO Box 10682,
Karachi 75700; tel: (21) 665 0513 (acc 50)

Lahore: Joyland, 90-B Block, Model Town,
Lahore; tel: (42) 585 0190 (acc 60)

EDUCATION

Schools

Azam Town Secondary School, Street 6, 100
Foot Rd, Azam Town, Karachi 75460; tel:
(21) 538 4223; Administrator: Capt Waseem
Asghar, BA, BEd

Shantinagar Educational Institute: Chak No
72/10-R, Shantinagar; tel: (692) 52985

Tibba Coaching Centre: Chak No 72/10-R,
Tibba, Shantinagar; tel: (692) 52985;
Administrator: Capt Yaqoob Sardar, BA, BEd

REHABILITATION CENTRES FOR DISABLED

Lahore: Manzil-e-Shifa, 35 Shahrah-e-Fatima
Jinnah, PO Box 242, Lahore 54000;
tel: (42) 756 9940

Karachi: Manzil-e-Umead, PO Box 10735,
Site Metroville, Karachi 75700;
tel: (21) 665 0434

**An earthquake victim in Pakistan takes
away his tent as *(below)* Captain
Macdonald Chandi and Major David
Wakefield oversee the distribution of
emergency shelter by the Pakistan military**

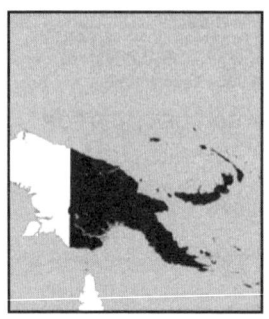

PAPUA NEW GUINEA TERRITORY

Territorial Commander:
Colonel Andrew Kalai (1 Jun 2005)

Chief Secretary:
Lieut-Colonel James Condon
(1 Sep 2004)

Territorial Headquarters: Angau Dr, Boroko, National Capital District

Postal address: PO Box 1323, Boroko, NCD, Papua New Guinea

tel: [675] 325-5522/5507; fax: [675] 323 3282; email: PNG Leadership@PNG.salvationarmy.org

The Salvation Army officially commenced in Papua New Guinea on 31 August 1956 and the first meeting was conducted on Sunday 21 October at the Royal Police Constabulary Barracks in Port Moresby. The first officers appointed to the work there were Major and Mrs Keith Baker and Lieutenant Ian Cutmore. On 4 July 1994, after 38 years as part of the Australia Eastern Territory, Papua New Guinea became an independent command and on 9 December 2000 was promoted to territory status.

Zone: South Pacific and East Asia
Country included in the territory: Papua New Guinea
Languages in which the gospel is preached: English, Hiri Motu, Pidgin and 30 local languages
Periodicals: *Tokaut*

ON 1 June 2005 the territory once more made an entry in Salvation Army history books with the appointment of the first national officers – Colonels Andrew and Julie Kalai – as Territorial Commander and Territorial President of Women's Ministries respectively. This was a very significant appointment in the Army's 49 years of operating in Papua New Guinea.

The territory was later shocked by the sudden promotion to Glory of Colonel Julie Kalai on 2 October 2006.

During '2005 – A Year for Children and Youth' a children's and youth mission worker was appointed in each division and region to improve and consolidate the territory's outreach to

children and youth. Crusades conducted by young Salvationists in settlement areas and villages across PNG resulted in many new decisions for Christ.

More than 700 delegates from across the country met in Lae to worship and enjoy fellowship together at the Territorial Youth Congress. The event coincided with a visit by the Mission Team from Australia Eastern Territory who led 'Feet First' training sessions in the two northern divisions prior to conducting missions in some of the villages.

Asked to devise a 'Year for Children and Youth' project, the Women's Ministries Department introduced playgroups to the territory. Women officers were trained in commencing a playgroup and within 10 months 18 groups had been set up. Families have been introduced to the Army through this new programme. Because of a lack of education in some areas, playgroups have incorporated literacy classes.

The territorial leaders have a vision for the development of new schools across the country and in April 2006 the TC opened a new primary school in Lae which will cater for 350 pupils. In Port Moresby, the national capital, a high school has been opened, initially accommodating 50 students but planning to expand with additional grades and students each year.

After many years without a new corps in Port Moresby, new fellowships now operate in Newtown and Morata; and as a result of Christmas outreach in a settlement area, meetings were begun at the Territorial Education and Training Centre. Within a few months that congregation grew to 100 people. This new fellowship particularly concentrates on ministering to widows and orphans of the HIV/Aid pandemic.

The then International Secretary and Zonal Secretary for Women's Ministries (Commissioners Makoto and Kaoru Yoshida) conducted the territorial review and visited North Coastal and North Eastern Divisions to see the Army's work at grass roots.

STATISTICS
Officers 178 (active 158 retired 20) **Cadets** (1st Yr) 13 (2nd Yr) 6 **Employees** 239

Corps 51 **Outposts** 61 **Institutions** 3 **Motels** 2 **Hostels** 2 **Schools** 5 **Health Centre** 1 **Health Sub Centres** 2 **Community Health Posts** 17 **Counselling Centres** 8
Senior Soldiers 5,411 **Adherents** 2,186 **Junior Soldiers** 1,320

STAFF
Business Adminstration: Maj Lilia Macayana, BSc (Com Acct)
Personnel: Capt Margaret McLeod, BEd, MTS
Programme: Maj Graeme McClimont, BA (Soc Welfare), BA (Behavioural Sc)
Education: Maj Jaime Macayana, BSc (Com Mgmt)
HIV/Aids Programme: Maj Araga Rawali
Leadership Development: Maj Lapu Rawali, BA
Property:
Public Relations:
SALT: Major Nani Memeto (acting)
Training: Maj Wayne Ennis, MA, BMin
Women's Ministries: Lt-Col Jan Condon (TSWM)
Youth: Capt Christian Goa

DIVISIONS
North Coastal: PO Box 667, Lae, Morobe Province; tel: 472 0905, fax: 472 0897; Maj Sere Kala
North Eastern: PO Box 343, Kainantu, Eastern Highlands Province; tel/fax: 737 1220; Maj Mais Kihi
South Eastern: Kwikila, Central Province; (mail to PO Box 1323, Boroko, NCD); Maj Rabona Rotona
South Western: PO Box 4227, Boroko, National Capital District; tel/fax: 321 6005; Capt Borley Yanderave
Gulf Regional Office: PO Box 132, Kerema, Gulf Province; tel: 648 1384; Maj Kabona Rotona
North-Western Regional Office: PO Box 365, Goroka, Eastern Highlands Province; tel: 732 1218; Capt David Temine

OFFICER TRAINING COLLEGE
PO Box 5355, Boroko, NCD; tel: 323 0553; fax: 325 6668

SALT CENTRE
PO Box 343, Kainantu, Eastern Highlands Province; tel: 737 1125

HOSTELS AND MOTELS
Goroka Motel: PO Box 365, Goroka, Eastern Highlands Province; tel/fax: 732 1218 (family units 2, double units 4, house 1)

'The Elphick' Motel: PO Box 637, Lae,
Morobe Province; tel: 472 2487;
fax: 472 7847 (acc double rooms 8)
Koki Hostel: PO Box 245, Port Moresby, NCD;
tel: 321 7683; fax: 321 7158 (acc family
units 65)
Koki Centennial House: (single women)
(acc double rooms 24)
Lae Hostel: PO Box 637, Lae, Morobe Province;
tel: 472 2487; fax: 472 7487 (acc family
rooms 71, single rooms 4, floor space
overnight 50)

SOCIAL PROGRAMME
Community Services
Courts and Prison Ministry, Missing Persons,
Welfare Feeding Projects
John Gill Juvenile Centre: PO Box 60, Badili,
NCD; tel: 320 0976 (acc 16)
Jim Jacobsen Centre: PO Box 901, Lae, Morobe
Province; tel: 472 6809

Development Services
Onamuga Development Project: Private Mail
Bag 3, Kainantu, Eastern Highlands Province

Education Services
Boroko FODE Centre (acc 300)

Boroko Primary School (acc 700)
Lae Primary School (acc 210)
SA High School (acc 50 – Grade 9 only)

Health Services
North Coastal: PO Box 667 Lae, Morobe Prov;
tel: 472 0905, fax 472 0897
Community Health Posts: Pongani, Waru
North Eastern: Private Mail Bag 3, Kainantu,
Eastern Highlands Province; tel: 737 1279
Onamuga Health Centre (acc 35)
Health Sub Centre: Misapi
Community Health Posts: Barokira, Kamila,
Kokopi, Kwongi, Norikori, Pitanka, Yauna
South Eastern: PO Box 1323, Boroko, NCD;
tel: 321 6000
Health Sub Centre: Boregaina (acc 10)
Community Health Posts: Dirinomu,
Kokorogoro, Kwaipo, Matairuka, Meirobu
South Western: PO Box 1323, Boroko, NCD;
tel: 321 6000
Community Health Posts: Ilavapari, Lapari,
Sogeri

Community Health Workers Training School
Private Mail Bag 3, Kainantu, Eastern Highlands
Province; tel: 737 1404 (acc 50)

The playgroup in Lae is one of 18 groups formed in Papua New Guinea within 10 months of the Women's Ministries Department launching them in the territory. Families have been introduced to The Salvation Army through this new programme. Because of a lack of education in some areas, playgroups have incorporated literacy classes.

THE PHILIPPINES TERRITORY

Territorial leaders:
Colonels Malcolm and Irene Induruwage

Territorial Commander:
Colonel Malcolm Induruwage (2 Apr 2006)

Chief Secretary:
Lieut-Colonel Graham Durston (1 May 2006)

**Territorial Headquarters: 1414 Leon Guinto Sr St,
Ermita, Manila 1000**

Postal address: PO Box 3830, Manila 1099, The Philippines

tel: [63] (2) 524 0086/88; fax: [63] (2) 521 6912; PR Dept: [63] (2) 536 3068

email: saphl1@phl.salvationarmy.org

The first Protestant preaching of the gospel in The Philippines was done by Major John Milsaps, a chaplain appointed to accompany US troops from San Francisco to Manila in July 1898. Major Milsaps conducted open-air and regular meetings and led many into a saving knowledge of Jesus Christ.

The advance of The Salvation Army in The Philippines came at the initiative of Filipinos who had been converted through contact with The Salvation Army in Hawaii, returned to their homeland and commenced meetings in Panay, Luzon, Cebu and Mindanao Islands during the period 1933-37. In June 1937 Colonel and Mrs Alfred Lindvall officially inaugurated this widespread work.

The Salvation Army Philippines was incorporated in 1963 as a religious and charitable corporation under Company Registration No 24211. The Salvation Army Social Services were incorporated in 1977 as a social welfare and development corporation under Company Registration No 73979 and The Salvation Army Educational Services was incorporated in 2001 as an educational corporation under Company Registration No A200009937.

Zone: South Pacific and East Asia
Country included in the territory: The Philippines
'The Salvation Army' in Filipino: Hukbo ng Kaligtasan; in Ilocano: Buyot ti Salakan
Languages in which the gospel is preached: Antiqueño (Kinaray-a), Bagobo, Bicolano, Cebuano, English, Hiligaynon (Ilonggo), Ilocano, Korean, Pangasinan, Filipino (Tagalog), T'boli, Waray
Periodicals: *Home League Programme Aids*, *The War Cry*

THE territory continued to widen the scope of women ministering to women and their families, working in collaboration with the Programme and Youth Departments with shared goals and interests. A resource manual produced by representatives of different departments offers teaching modules responding to the needs of families and communities.

At a residential workshop on environmental issues, 18 children aged eight to 14 learned how to recycle and to care for nature, animals and the environment. They called themselves the Echo Kids. It is planned to add a module on those subjects to the *Resources Manual for Women* and to introduce them into Junior Home League activities.

In preparation for the celebration of '2005 – A Year for Children and Youth' the Youth Department was directed by the Territorial Executive Conference to produce Sunday school material for the whole year. The group called Action Powerlink achieved this objective and materials were sent to all four divisions. Positive feedback has been received.

A succession of tropical depressions and typhoons devastated several provinces in The Philippines. The storms triggered flash floods and landslides that caused large numbers of injuries, deaths and displacements. Transportation and communication were severely damaged and took several days to restore. The territory, with help from the IHQ Emergency Services, responded to people's needs by providing relief, medical aid and rehabilitation work that is ongoing.

An intensified campaign in response to the Territorial Executive Conference resolution 'to recapture the spirit of Salvationism' gave rise to a programme thrust integral to corps growth. With the Bible as the basis, this 'Recapturing, Revitalising and Reclaiming' campaign helped the implementation team to formulate principles for continuing action.

The Corps Programme Secretary and the Training and Development Secretary visited the four divisions to promote the reinstituting of soldiers meetings in every corps. The purpose of these is to fit soldiers for the salvation war and make them readily responsive to Christ's commands. The book *Chosen To Be A Soldier* has become a requirement for all Salvationists to possess. Resource material supplementing the book has been developed for use in the soldiers meetings.

The development of a 'Process of Ministry' will assist corps officers and local officers to become active in evangelistic mission. The Army being raised up by God to reach out to the lost, the basic focus is not how many people are made soldiers – although that is very important – but how Christlike are would-be soldiers and how equipped they will become.

The territory believes that what evangelism is to the Church, aggressive Christianity is to the Army.

STATISTICS

Officers 231 (active 192 retired 39) **Cadets** (1st Yr) 5 (2nd Yr) **Envoys/Field Sergeants/ Lieutenants** 9 **Employees** 64
Corps 77 **Societies/Outposts/Outreaches/New Plants** 71 **Institutions** 2 **Social Centres** 23
Senior Soldiers 5,306 **Recruits** 2,348 **Adherents** 2,774 **Junior Soldiers** 1,268
Personnel serving outside territory Officers 6 Lay worker 1

STAFF

Sec for Business Administration:
Christian Bookstore: Mr Lemuel Aguirre
Finance: Capt Estelita Bautista
Information Technology: Mr Victor Benganan, Jr
Internal Auditor: Capt Jovita Padayao
Property Administrator: Alfredo Agpaoa Jr

Sec for Personnel Administration:
Maj Priscilla Nanlabi
Candidates and Silver Star: Capt Melinda Casidsid
Training and Development: Maj Elnora Urbien

Sec for Programme Administration:
Maj Leopoldo Posadass
Corps Programme: Maj Florante Parayno
Educational Services Coordinator: Maj Elnora Urbien
Projects: Capt Jocelyn Genabe
Sponsorships and Scholarship: Maj Evelyn Posadas
Youth and Children: Capt Quintin Casidsid
Gospel Arts Coordinator: Mr Nic Bagasol Jr
Editor/Literature:
Legal Consultant: Mr Paul Stephen Salegumba
THQ Chaplain/Asst to Administration:
Maj Florida Oalang
Training: Capt David Oalang

Women's Ministries: Col Irene Induruwage (TPWM) Lt-Col Rhondda Durston (TSWM) Capt Ruby Casimero (Family and Women's Development)

DIVISIONS

Central Philippines: 20 Senatorial Dr, Congressional Village, Project 8, Quezon City; tel: (02) 453 8208/929 6312; email: Central@phl.salvationarmy.org; Maj Virgilio Menia
Mindanao Island: 344 NLSA Rd, Purok Bayanihan, San Isidro, Lagao 9500 General Santos City; tel: (083) 553 5956; email: Mid@phl.salvationarmy.org; Maj Myline Joy Flores
Northern Luzon: Doña Loleng Subd Nancayasan, 293 Urdaneta, Pangasinan; tel: (075) 568 2310; email: Northern@phl.salvationarmy.org; Maj Edward Manulat
Visayas Islands: 731 M. J. Cuenco Ave, Cebu City; tel: (032) 416 7126; tel/fax: (032) 416 7346; email: Vid@phl.salvationarmy.org; Maj Ronaldo Banlasan

TRAINING COLLEGE

Pantay Rd, Sitio Bukal Brgy, Tandang Kutyo, Tanay, Rizal; tel: (02) 654 2909; fax: (02) 654 2895

UNDER THQ

Sponsorship/Scholarship Programme
Missing Persons/Family Tracing Service
Emergency Disaster Relief

SOCIAL SERVICES
Residential Social Centres
(Abused girls/children)
Bethany Home: 20 Senatorial Dr, Congressional Village, Project 8, Quezon City (acc 40)

(Street children)
Joyville Home: Pantay Rd, Sitio Bukal, Tanay, Rizal (acc 25)

Learning Centre
Asingan Educational Services Inc: Bautista St, Poblacion, 2439 Asingan, Pangasinan

Child Care Centres
Bagong Silang: Phase 78-81K6, Lot 3A, Package 3, Bagong Sitang Tala, Caloocan City
Bulalacao: Bulalacao, 5214 Oriental Mindoro
Caloocan: Cor Langaray, Dagat-dagatan Ave, Caloocan City
Cebu: 731 M. J. Cuenco Ave, 6000 Cebu City
Dagupan: Puelay District, 2400 Dagupan City
Dasmarinas: Blk 11, Lot 6, San Antonio de Padua II, Area E, DBB, Dasmarinas, Cavite
Davao: Blk 14, Lot 10, Kingfisher St, RPJ Village II, Seaside Subd, Matina Aplaya, Matina, 8000 Davao City
General Santos: 344 NLSA Rd, Purok Bayanihan, San Isidro, Lagao, 9500 General Santos City
Hermoza: Barrio Hermoza, 2523 Bayambang, Pangasinan
Iloilo: Arroyo St, 5000 La Paz, Iloilo City
Laoag: 50 Buttong, 2900 Laoag City, Ilocos Norte
Legazpi: 332 San Roque, Governor St, San Roque, Legazpi City
Mariveles: Porto del Sur, National Rd, 2105 Mariveles, Bataan
Olongapo: Camia St, Sta Rita, 2200 Olongapo City
Quezon City 1: 115 Batanes St, San Isidro Gals, Quezon City
Quezon City 2: 20 Senatorial Dr, Congressional Village, Project 8, Quezon City
Signal Village: Daisy St, Zone 6, Signal Village, Taguig, Metro Manila
Sta Barbara: 20 Poblacion Norte, 2419 Sta Barbara, Pangasinan
Tondo: 18215 Velasquez St, 1012 Tondo, Manila
Upper Katalikanan: Poblacion 8, Midsayap, 9410 North Cotabato

Nutrition, Feeding and Day Care
Dasmarinas: Blk 11, Lot 6, San Antonio de Padua II Area E, DBB, Dasmarinas, Cavite
Davao: Blk 14, Lot 10, Kingfisher St, RPJ Village II, Seaside Subd, Matina Aplaya, Matina, 8000 Davao City

General Santos: 344 NLSA Rd, Purok Bayanihan, San Isidro, Lagao 9500 General Santos City

Iligan: Purok-5A Tambo, 9200 Iligan City, Lanao del Norte

Iloilo: Arroyo St, 5000 La Paz, Iloilo City

Makati: 3493 Honda St, Pinagkaisahan, 1200 Makati City

Manila Central: 1414 Leon Guinto Sr, St 1000 Ermita, Manila

Midsayap: c/o Mrs Patricia Berte, Poblacion 8, Midsayap 9410 North Cotabato

Pavia: c/o La Paz Corps, Arroyo St, La Paz, Iloilo City

Signal Village: Daisy St, Zone 6, Signal Village, Taguig, Metro Manila

Tanay: Damaso Reyes St, Interior, Libis 1080 Tanay, Rizal

Dormitories for Students and Working Women

Bacolod: Lacson/Rosario St, 6100 Bacolod City, Negros Occidental (acc 25)

Baguio: 35-37 P. Guevarra St, Aurora Hill, 2600 Baguio City (acc 50)

Lapu-Lapu: Gun-ob, Lapu-lapu City (acc 12)

Makati: 3493 Honda St, Pinagkaishan, 1200 Makati City (acc 12)

Quezon City 1: 67 Batanes St, Galas, Quezon City (acc 12)

San Jose Antigue: Carretas St, 5700 San Jose, Antigue

San Jose Mindoro: 3090 Roxas St, Doña Consuelo Subd, 5100 San Jose, Occidental Mindoro (acc 12)

Programmes for Minorities

Bamban: c/o San Jose Corps, 3090 Roxas St, Doña Consuelo Subd, Occidental Mindoro

Bulalacao: Bulalacao, 5214 Oriental Mindoro

Lake Sebu: T'boli Village, Lake Sebu

Wali: Bo Wali, Maitum, Saranggani Province

Skills Training

Bayanihan: William Booth Bayanihan Village, Casia Bankal, Bayanihan, 6015 Lapu-lapu, Cebu City

Lapu-lapu: Gun-ob 6015, Lapu-lapu City

Livelihood

Ansiray Fishcages: Ansiray, 5100 San Jose, Occidental Mindoro

Bamban Carabao Raising: 3090 Roxas St, Doña Consuelo Subd, 511 San Jose, Occidental Mindoro

Bella Luz Cooperative Store: Brgy Bella Luz, 3318 San Mateo, Isabela

Cabayaoasan Agricultural Cooperative: Cabayaoasan, 2413 Mangatarem, Pangasinon

Camangaan Agricultural Cooperative: Bo Camangaan, Rosales, 2442 Pangasinon

Lake Sebu Tinalak Weaving: 9512 Poblacion, Lake Sebu, South Cotabato

Lebe Fishing Boat: Bo Lebe, 9514 Kiamba, Saranggani Province

Lopez Quezon Carabao Raising: Abines St, Talolong Lopez, Quezon

Lourdes Carabao Raising: Barangay Lourdes, Lopez, Quezon

Pahanocoy Tricycad: Florence Ville Subd, Pahanocoy, 6100 Bacolod City

Pandanan Salt Making: Bo Pandanan, 5702 Patnongon, Antigue

Agricultural Assistance

Nasukob Agricultural Loan: Nasukob 5214 Bulalacao

Santa Agricultural Loan: Mabibila Sur, Santa, Ilocos Sur

Wali: Bo Wali, Maitum, Saranggani Province

Micro-Enterprise Credit Projects

Almacen: Barangay Almacen, 2111 Hermoza, Bataan

Ansiray: 5100 San Jose, Occidental Mindoro

Badipa: Bayaoas, Urdaneta, Pangasinan

Bautista: Nibaliw Norte 2424 Bautista, Pangasinan

Bulalacao: Bulalacao 5214, Oriental Mindoro

Cacutud: 34-B Misael St, Diamond Subd, Balibago, Angeles City

Cebu Central: 731 M. J. Cuenco Ave, Cebon City 6000

Dagupan: Puelay District, 2400 Dagupan City

General Santos: 344 NLSA Rd, Purok Bayanihan, San Isidoro, Lagao 9500 General Santos City

Iligan: Purok 5A Tambo, 9200 Iligan City, Lanao del Norte

Lake Sebu: 4512 Poblacion, Lake Sebu, South Cotabato

Legaspi: Governor St, 332 San Roque Legaspi City

Liloan: Catherine Booth Development Center, Tayud, Liloan, 6002 Cebu City

Magsaysay: Burgos St, Magsaysay, Occidental Mindoro

Malingao: Bo Malingao, Tubod, 9202 Lanao del Norte

Manila Central: 1414 Leon Guinto Sr, St 1000 Ermita, Manila

Mariveles: Porto del Sur, National Rd, 2105 Mariveles, Bataan

Merville: 128 Sitio Malaya, Brgy Merville, Paranaque City

Nasukob: Nasukob 5214 Bulalacao, Oriental Mindoro

Orani: 163 Calero St, Orani, 2112 Bataan

Ozamis: Carmen Annex, 7200 Ozamis City

Pasay: 511 Inocencio St, Pasay City

Sampaloc: Sitio, Hinadiongan, Sampaloc, Tanay, Rizal 1080

San Jose Mindoro: 3090 Roxas St, Doña Consuelo Subd, 511 San Jose, Occidental Mindoro

Signal Village: Daisy St, Zone 6, Signal Village, Taguig, Metro Manila

Sta Ana: 2439 Asingan, Pangasinan

Wali: Wali, Maiturn, 9515 Saranggani Province

Water Systems

Bulalacao: Bulalacao 5214 Oriental Mindoro

Camangaan: Bo Carmangaan, Rosales 2442, Pangasinon

Lipsong: Bulalacao 5214, Oriental Mindoro

Lourdes: Barangay Lourdes, Lopez, Quezon

Mariveles: Porto del Sur, National Rd, 2105 Mariveles, Bataan

Palili: c/o The Salvation Army, 163 Calero St, Orani 2112 Bataan

Sampaloc: Sitio, Hinadiongan Sampalac Tanay, Rizal 1080

HEALTH

Barangay Health Workers in Rural Corps Botica sa Barangay

Cabayaosan Corps: Cabayaosan, Mangatarem Pangasinan

San Jose Occidental Mindoro: 3090 Roxas St,

Doña Consuelo Subd, San Jose Occidental Mindoro

HIV/Aids Programmes

Bella Luz: Brgy Bella Luz, 3318 San Mateo, Isabela

Bulalacao: Bulalacao, 5214 Oriental Mindoro

Cebu: 731 MJ Cuenco Ave, Cebu City

Dagupan: Puelay District 2400 Dagupan City

Diffun: Bonifacio, Purok 5, 3401 Diffun, Quirino Province

General Santos: 344 NLSA Rd, Purok Bayanihan, San Isidro, Lagao, 9500 General Santos City

Lake Sebu: 4512 Poblacion, Lake Sebu, South Cotabato

Laoag: 50 Buttong, 2900 Laoag City, Ilocos Norte

Lebe: Bo. Lebe, 9514 Kiamba, Saranggani Province

Nasukob: Nasukob 5214 Bulalacao Oriental Mindoro

Pandanan: Bo. Pandanan, Patnongon, Antique

Santiago: Purok 3, Brgy Rosario, 3311 Santiago City

Sinamar: Sinamar Norte, 3318 San Mateo, Isabela

Tondo: Cnr Inocencio and Velasquez Sts, Tondo, Manila

Villa Ros: Purok 4, Villa Ros Bagabag, Nueva Viscaya

Wali: Barrio Wali Maitum, Saranggani Province

Housing Project

Lopez, Quezon: Abines St, Talolong, Lopez, Quezo

Girls and youth leaders from the Northern Luzon Division meet for the launch of Teenstuff, a new group commenced in The Philippines Territory for teenage girls

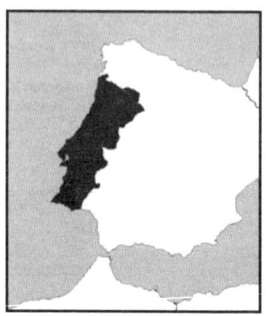

PORTUGAL COMMAND

Command leaders:
Majors Alberto and Maria Serém

Officer Commanding:
Major Alberto Serém (1 Sep 2006)

Command Headquarters: Rua Dr Silva Teles, 16, 1050-080 Lisboa
Postal address: Apartado 14109, 1064-002 Lisboa, Portugal
tel: [351] (21) 780 2930; fax: [351] (21) 780 2940;
email: Portugal Command@POR.salvationarmy.org

On 25 July 1971, official recognition was given to the first corps established in Portugal. The work was started in the northern city of Porto by a group of evangelical Christians. On 28 January 1972, Major and Mrs Carl S. Eliasen arrived in Lisbon to start work there and to supervise the existing activities.

On 4 July 1974 The Salvation Army was recognised by the Ministry of Justice as a religious and philanthropic organisation. All social activities are incorporated in Centro Social do Exército de Salvação which was constituted in Portugal on 26 March 1981 (Public Utility Register 16/82 dated 10 March 1982).

Zone: Europe
Country included in the command: Portugal
'The Salvation Army' in Portuguese: Exército de Salvação
Language in which the gospel is preached: Portuguese

THE highlight of the year under review was the entry into training of four cadets. Two are training at William Booth College in London and the others in Brazil. The command gives thanks to God that young Salvationists in Portugal are responding to Christ's call to full-time ministry.

On 26 March 2006 The Salvation Army's social services celebrated 25 years of legal constitution in Portugal with a service of thanksgiving and a concert for clients and Salvationists. Letters of recognition of the social services' good work were received from city and local councils.

New senior and junior soldiers have been enrolled. Spiritual ministry in prisons and hospitals has been developed and is making progress. Some prisoners have been converted and one has expressed a desire to become a recruit.

Much fundraising in Portugal and by supporters in other countries took place to enable 13 delegates to attend the European Youth Congress in Prague (Czech Republic). It was a time of great blessing for the young people.

Outreach in locations new to Salvation Army work is being explored from two of the command's missions. Thousands of leaflets about

Children at an after-school club in Lisbon enjoy a game with the Salvation Army captain

The Salvation Army and hundreds of New Testaments have been distributed. A selection of Christian literature is regularly displayed on a rack outside one mission's hall and the most frequently replaced item is the New Testament. Salvationists in Portugal thank God that people are hungry for the bread of life.

STATISTICS
Officers active 12 **Lieutenants** 3 **Employees** 114
Mission Areas with Corps 5 **Institutions** 7
Senior Soldiers 74 **Adherents** 48 **Junior Soldiers** 17
Personnel serving outside command Officers 6

STAFF
Public Relations: Maj Pedro Neves
Social: Dr Sandra Martins Lopes
Women's Ministries: Maj Maria José Serém (CPWM)

SOCIAL SERVICES
Children's Home
Centro Acolhimento Novo Mundo,
Ave Desidério Cambournac 14, 2710-553
Sintra; tel: 219 244 239; fax: 219 249 688
(acc 14)

Clothing and Food Distribution Centre
Rua Escola do Exército, 11-B, 1150-143 Lisboa;
tel: 213 528 137; fax: 213 160 732

Thrift Shop
Chelas: Rua Rui de Sousa, Lote 65 A-Loja C,
1900-802 Lisboa

Day Centres for the Elderly and Home Help Services
Colares: Av dos Bombeiro Voluntários, Várzea
de Colares, 2705-180 Sintra; tel: 219 288 450;
fax: 219 288 458
Lisboa: Rua Capitão Roby 19, Picheleira,
1900-111 Lisboa; tel: 218 409 108;
fax: 218 409 112
Porto: Av Vasco da Gama, 645, Loja 1,
Ramalde, 4100-491 Porto; tel: 226 172 769;
fax: 226 171 120

Eventide Homes
Nosso Lar: Av dos Bombeiros Voluntários,
Várzea de Colares, 2705-180 Colares;
tel: 219 288 450; fax: 219 288 458 (acc 45)
Marinel: Rua das Marinhas, 13, Tomadia, Praia
das Maçãs, 2705-313 Colares;
tel: 219 288 480; fax: 219 288 481 (acc 45)

Night Shelter for the Homeless
Rua da Manutenção, Xabregas, 1900-318
Lisboa; tel: 218 680 908; fax: 218 680 913
(acc 75)

HOLIDAY AND CONFERENCE CENTRE
Vivenda Boa Nova, Rua do Vinagre 9, 2705-354
Colares; tel: 219 291 718 (Holiday bookings
to CHQ)

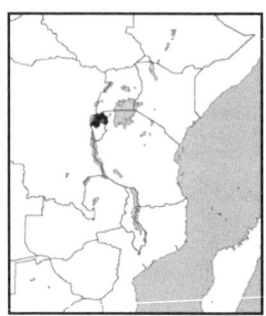

RWANDA REGION

Regional leaders:
Majors Joash and Florence Malabi

Regional Commander:
Major Joash Malabi (1 Nov 2004)

Regional Headquarters: Plot 204, Kimihurura Mutekano
Zone 0057, Kigali

Postal address: PO Box 812, Kigali, Rwanda

tel: [250] 587639; fax: [250] 511812; email: Rwanda@rwa.salvationarmy.org

As a result of civil war and genocide in Rwanda, The Salvation Army became actively involved in relief work in September 1994. Operations were concentrated in Kayenzi Commune, part of the Gitarama Prefecture. Following mission work by officers from Zaïre, Uganda and Tanzania in 1995, officers were appointed from Congo (Brazzaville) to develop corps and mission work in Kayenzi Commune. Kayenzi Corps officially began its ministry on 5 November 1995.

Zone: Africa
Country included in the region: Rwanda
The Salvation Army in Kinyarwanda: Ingabo Z'Agakiza
Languages in which the gospel is preached: English, French, Kinyarwanda

TEN Rwandan delegates counted it a great privilege to participate in the All-Africa Congress in Harare (Zimbabwe) during August 2005. Excited to be part of the larger Salvation Army, they returned home with a new vision for the Army in their country – 'Rwanda for Christ'.

For the first time in the region's history six young people from the country attended the African Youth Summit in Congo (Brazzaville), where they considered strategies in youth leadership and the Army's mission in central Africa.

As part of the 'Frontier' programme, which focuses on youth development and leadership potential, Rwanda hosted seven young people from six other African countries who formed a support team for community outreach and mission. Rwandan young people were stimulated and are putting into practice experiences shared during the time spent with their counterparts.

Work was officially started in Kigali city and Rutobwe with the opening of outposts. On completion of their training, eight lieutenants were appointed to corps postings.

A $9,000 donation from Canada and Bermuda Territory paid for supplies of beans and maize flour given to 1,800 families. Another feeding programme enabled 1,200 starving children to be fed during November

The seven cadets who have been welcomed into Rwanda's first training session

Women join in worship during the World Day of Prayer in Kigali

and December. At Christmas the Women Ministries Department distributed 1,040 parcels to children and provided clothing to 1,240 old people.

At the start of 2006 a training session began in Rwanda for the first time. When seven cadets were welcomed in a meeting at Kayenzi Corps the 425 people present had good reason to praise the Lord.

STATISTICS
Officers 10 **Lieutenants** 8 **Cadets** 7 **Employees** 28
Corps 4 **Societies** 1 **Outposts** 5 **Pre-School Facility** 1 (acc 80)
Senior Soldiers 823 **Adherents** 233 **Junior Soldiers** 588

STAFF
Women's Ministries: Maj Florence Malabi (RPWM)
Regional Sec: Maj Daniel Moukoko
Finance: Maj Daniel Moukoko
Projects: Maj Arschette Moukoko

SINGAPORE, MALAYSIA AND MYANMAR TERRITORY

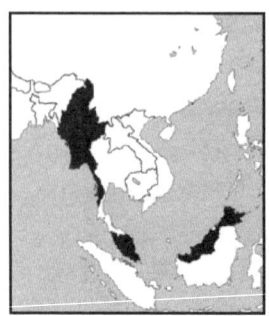

Territorial leaders:
Colonels David and Grace Bringans

Territorial Commander:
Colonel David Bringans (1 Mar 2003)

Chief Secretary:
Lieut-Colonel Gillian Downer (1 Nov 2000)

Territorial Headquarters: 20 Bishan St 22, Singapore 579768

Postal address: Ang Mo Kio Central, PO Box 640, Singapore 915605

tel: [65] 6555 0188; fax: [65] 6552 8542; web site: www.salvationarmy.org.sg

In May 1935 Salvation Army work began in Singapore. It spread to Penang (1938), Melaka and Ipoh (1940), Kuching (Sarawak) (1950), Kuala Lumpur (1966) and Kota Kinabalu (Sabah) (1996).

'The General of The Salvation Army' is a 'corporation sole' by The Salvation Army Ordinance 1939 in the Straits Settlements; by The Salvation Army (Incorporation) Ordinance 1956 in the Federation of Malaya; and by the Missionary Societies Order 1957 in the Colony of Sarawak.

Adjutant Taran Das (Reuben Moss), who was attached to the Lahore headquarters in India, was appointed to open the work in Burma (now Myanmar) by Commissioner Booth Tucker in January 1915. Myanmar Salvationists have, since 1966, developed their witness and service despite the restriction on reinforcements from overseas. In 1994 Myanmar was joined to the Singapore and Malaysia Command. The command was elevated to territory status on 1 March 2005.

Zone: South Pacific and East Asia

Countries included in the territory: Malaysia, Myanmar, Singapore

'The Salvation Army' in Chinese: (Mandarin) Chiu Shi Chen, (Cantonese) Kau Shai Kwan, (Amoy, Hokkien) Kiu Se Kun; Bahasa: Bala Keselamatan; Myanmar: Kae Tin Chin Tat; Tamil: Retchania Senai

Languages in which the gospel is preached: Burmese, Chin (Mizo, Zahau, Dai), Chinese (Amoy, Cantonese, Hokkien, Mandarin), English, Bahasa, Malay, Tamil, Telegu

Periodical: *The War Cry*

JUST over a year after celebrating the recognition of territorial status, Salvationists in Singapore, Malaysia and Myanmar continue to rejoice as new and exciting expansion provides further evident of God's goodness.

In Singapore the Peacehaven Nursing Home celebrated five years of ministry, and Bishan Chinese Corps and Eratchippu Corps (Tamil) opened new facilities. Eighty local officers and prospective local officers met for the Covenant Keepers Conference. One hundred young people from Singapore and Malaysia took part in an exciting youth camp at which 22 of them offered their lives for officership. The Heavenly Calling

Retreat was attended by 45 delegates, including 16 young people.

The territorial commander ordained and commissioned the four cadets of the Visionaries Session as officers; 38 new soldiers were enrolled.

For one day in December the 34 Starbucks outlets offered free beverages to the public for a donation to Salvation Army work. These donations, with the 1:1 matching grant by South East Community Development Council and collections throughout the month by corps and centres, helped raise S$294,536 (US$186,323) for the Christmas Kettle Appeal.

Highlights in Malaysia included the enrolment of 43 soldiers, three Tamil congregations becoming four with the opening of Rawang Outpost, and more than 200 people from Singapore and Malaysia attending a successful Tamil camp with guest leader Lieut-Colonel Prima Rajan (India Central Territory).

A remodelled corps facility and community kindergarten in Kuala Lumpur was opened and dedicated to the glory of God by the TC, as was the new building housing the Public Relations and Community Services Office for Kuala Lumpur and the Malaysian Liaison Office.

In Myanmar Region four cadets of the Heralds of the Good News Session were welcomed into the school for officer training in Yangon; new training staff and additional regional headquarters staff were installed by the TC. A new flag was presented to Tun Aung Nyunt (a former Buddhist monk now a committed Salvationist) and his wife, Nyaung Hauk Din, as they began another corps plant at Myingyan, near Mandalay.

More than 700 people gathered with territorial and regional leaders for silver jubilee celebrations marking 25 years of Salvation Army work in Upper Myanmar. Mizo pioneer Salvationists were honoured and present-day Salvationists rejoiced as 43 new soldiers were enrolled by the TC. A further 104 soldiers were enrolled in the region during the year.

The territory continues to move forward under its theme of 'Vision for Mission = Passion for People'.

STATISTICS

Officers 115 (active 112 retired 12) **Lieutenants** 4 **Cadets** 11 **Employees** 726
Corps 50 **Outposts** 12 **Institutions** 16 **School** 1 **Kindergarten** 2 **Day Care Centres** 18
Senior Soldiers 2,247 **Adherents** 420 **Junior Soldiers** 547

STAFF

Editor: Col Grace Bringans
Finance: Mdm Koh Guek Eng
Human Resources: Mrs Toh-Chia Lai Ying
Programme: Maj Bob Lee, BD
Property: Mr John Ng
Public Relations: Mr Gregory Lee
Projects: Lt-Col Gillian Downer
Training: Maj Ruth Pascoe
Women's Ministries: Col Grace Bringans (TPWM)
Youth and Candidates: Maj Andy Lim

SCHOOL FOR OFFICER TRAINING (SINGAPORE AND MALAYSIA)

500 Upper Bukit Timah Rd, Singapore 678106; tel: 6349 5333

Children's Homes

Gracehaven: 3 Lorong Napiri (off Yio Chu Kang Rd), Singapore 547528; tel: 6488 1510 (acc 160)

The Haven: 350 Pasir Panjang Rd, Singapore 118692; tel: 6774 9588/9 (acc 50)

Day Care Centres for Children

Ang Mo Kio Child Care Centre: Blk 610 Ang Mo Kio Ave 4, #01-1227 Singapore 560610; tel: 6452 4862 (acc 89)

Bukit Batok East Child Care Centre: Blk 247 Bukit Batok East Ave 5, #01-86 Singapore 650247; tel: 6562 4976 (acc 73)

Bukit Batok West Child Care Centre: Blk 415 Bukit Batok West Ave 5, #01-264 Singapore 650415; tel: 6567 2050 (acc 91)

Bukit Panjang Child Care Centre: Blk 402 Fajar Rd, #01-217 Singapore 670402; tel: 6760 2624 (acc 82)

Bukit Panjang Family Service Centre: Blk 404 Fajar Rd, #01-267 Singapore 670404; tel: 6763 0837 (acc 98)

Pasir Ris Child Care Centre: Blk 427 Pasir Ris Dr 6, #01-43 Singapore 510427; tel: 6582 0286 (acc 76)

Tampines Child Care Centre: Blk 159 Tampines St 12, #01-95 Singapore 521159; tel: 6785 2976 (acc 90)

Day Care Centres for the Elderly

Bedok Multiservice Centre for the Elderly: Blk 121, #01-161 Bedok North Rd, Singapore 460121; tel: 6445 1630 (acc 65)

Bedok Rehabilitation Centre: Blk 121, #01-163 Bedok North Rd, Singapore 460121; tel: 6445 1630 (acc 35)

Family Support Services

Blk 42, Beo Cresc, #01-95 Singapore 160042; tel: 6273 7207

Hostels

Foreign Students' Hostel: 500 Upper Bukit Timah Rd, Singapore 678106; tel: 6349 5344 (acc 80)

Young Women's Hostel: The Haven, 350 Pasir Panjang Rd, Singapore 118692; tel: 6774 9588/9 (acc 10)

Peacehaven Nurses' Hostel: 9 Upper Changi Rd North, Singapore 507706; tel: 6546 5678 (acc 100)

Nursing Home

Peacehaven Nursing Home: 9 Upper Changi Rd North, Singapore 507706; tel: 6546 5678 (acc 339)

Prison Support Services

7 Upper Changi Rd North, Singapore 507705; tel 6546 7788 ext 4052

Red Shield Industries

309 Upper Serangoon Rd, Singapore 347693; tel: 6288 5438

Youth Development Centre

Blk 65 Kallang Bahru, #01-305 Singapore 330065; tel: 6291 6303; under Territorial Youth Dept

Corps Community Services

Balestier Corps and Community Services: 48 Martaban Rd, Singapore 328664; tel: 6253 1433

Changi Corps and Community Centre: 7 Upper Changi Rd North, Singapore 507705; tel: 6546 5827

EAST MALAYSIA REGION

Boys' Home

Kuching Boys' Home: Jalan Ban Hock, 93100, Kuching, PO Box 547, 93700 Kuching, Sarawak, Malaysia; tel: (082) 24 2623 (acc 35)

Children's Home

Kuching Children's Home: 138 Jalan Upland, 93200 Kuching, PO Box 106, 93700 Kuching, Sarawak, Malaysia; tel: (082) 24 8234 (acc 60)

Day Care Centres

Kuching Kindergarten: Sekama Rd 93300, Kuching Sarawak, Malaysia, PO Box 44, 93700 Kuching Sarawak, Malaysia; tel: (082) 333981 (acc 120)

Rainbow Centre: 588B Lucky Garden, Tanjong Batu Rd, 97000, Bintulu Sarawak, PO Box 1701, 97010 Bintulu Sarawak, Malaysia; tel: (086) 313842 (acc 35)

Corps Community Services

Bintulu Corps and Community Services: Lot 216, 2nd Floor BDA Shophouse, 16 Jalan Tanjong Batu, 97000 Bintulu; tel: (086) 315 843

Kota Kinabalu Corps and Community Services: 20-2 Block A Inanam Business Ctr, Batu 6, Jalan Tuaran, 88450 Kota Kinabalu, Sabah, PO Box 14234, 88848 Kota Kinabalu, Sabah, Malaysia; tel: (088) 433766

Kuching Corps and Community Services: Jalan Ban Hock, 93100 Kuching, Sarawak, Malaysia; tel: (082) 242623

WEST MALAYSIA REGION

Boys' Homes

Ipoh Boys' Home: 4367 Jalan Tambun, 31400 Ipoh, PO Box 221, 30720 Ipoh, Perak, Malaysia; tel: [60] (05) 545 7819 (acc 60)

Lighthouse Boys' Home: 346-G Taman Yong Pak Kian, Ujong Pasir 75050 Melaka, Malaysia; tel: (06) 283 2101 (acc 25)

Centre for Special Children
Hopehaven Centre for Special Children: 321 Jalan Parameswara, 75000 Melaka, Malaysia; tel: [60] (06) 283 2101 (acc 100)

Children's Homes
Ipoh Children's Home: 255 Kampar Rd, 30250 Ipoh, Perak, Malaysia; tel: (05) 254 9767; fax: (05) 242 9630 (acc 50)
Penang Children's Home: 8A Logan Rd, 10400 Penang, Malaysia; tel: (04) 227 0162 (acc 58)
Lighthouse Children's Home: 321 Jalan Parameswara, 75000 Melaka, Malaysia; tel: (06) 283 2101 (acc 35)

Day Care Centres for Children
Batang Melaka Day Care Centre: J7702 Main Rd, 77500 Batang Melaka, Malaysia; tel: (06) 446 1601 (acc 80)
Kuala Lumpur Kindergarten: 1 Lingkungan Hujan, Overseas Union Garden 58200 KL, Malaysia; tel: (03) 7782 4766 (acc 100)
Little Lambs Day Care Centre for Needy Children: 321 Jalan Parameswara, 75000 Melaka, Malaysia; tel: (06) 283 2101 (acc 20)

Homes for the Aged
Joyhaven Home for the Elderly: 1 Jalan 12/17, Seksyen 12, 46200 Petaling Jaya, Selangor, Malaysia; tel: (03) 7958 6257 (acc 25)
Perak Home for the Aged: Jalan Bersatu, Jelapang, 30020 Ipoh, Perak, Malaysia; tel: (05) 526 2108 (acc 55)

Red Shield Industries
No 30, Jalan TPP 1/12, Taman Perindustrian Puchong Batu 12, Jalan Puchong, 47100 Puchong, Selangor Darul Ehsan, Malaysia; tel: (03) 8061 4757

Rehabilitation Centre
Chang T'en Men's Shelter, 46 Kg Bandar Hilir,

Bandar, Melaka, Malaysia; tel: (06) 283 2101 (acc 20)

Corps Community Services
Batang Melaka Corps and Community Services: J7702 Main Rd, Batang Malaka, 77500 Selander, Melaka West Malaysia; tel: (06) 4461601
Puchong Community Services: 26-1 Jalan Puteri 4/2, Bandar Puteri 47100, Puchong, Selangor, Malaysia; tel: (03) 8061 4929
Melaka Corps and Community Services: 321 Jalan Parameswara, 75000 Melaka, Malaysia; tel: (06) 283 1203

MYANMAR REGION
Headquarters: 176-178 Anawrahta St, Botahtaung, East Yangon 11161, Myanmar; Postal address: GPO Box 394, Yangon, Myanmar; tel: [95] (1) 294267/293307; fax: [95] (1) 298067
Regional Officer: Maj James Aaron

DISTRICTS
Tahan: District Office: D-group, Tahan, Kalemyo; tel: [95] (73) 21396
Tamu: District Office: Kanan Corps, Kanan Township

SCHOOL FOR OFFICER TRAINING (MYANMAR)
50 Byaing Ye O Zin St, Tarmway, Yangon; tel: [95] (1) 543694

Boys' Home
406 Banyadala Rd, Tarmway, Yangon, Myanmar (acc 50)

Children's Home
50 Bago Rd, Pyu, Myanmar (acc 50)

Girls' Home
50 Byaing Ye O Zin St, Tarmway, Yangon, Myanmar (acc 50)

Tuition Programme
Bago

Corps Day Care Centre
Tarmway

Salvationists in Singapore, Malaysia and Myanmar continue to rejoice as new and exciting expansion provides further evidence of God's goodness

SOUTH AMERICA EAST TERRITORY

Territorial leaders:
Colonels Nestor and Rebecca Nuesch

Territorial Commander:
Colonel Nestor Nuesch (1 Dec 2006)

Chief Secretary:
Lieut-Colonel Luis E. Castillo (1 Apr 2004)

Territorial Headquarters: Avda. Rivadavia 3257 (C1203AAE), Buenos Aires, Argentina

Postal address: Casilla de Correos 2240 (C1000WAW) Buenos Aires, Argentina

Cables: Salvación Buenos Aires; tel/fax: [54] (11) 4864-9321/9348/9491/1075;
email: ejersaljefatura@SAE.salvationarmy.org;
web site: www.ejercitodesalvacion.org.ar

Four officers, who knew no Spanish, established The Salvation Army in Buenos Aires in 1890. Operations spread to other South American nations, of which Paraguay (1910), Uruguay (1890) and Argentina now comprise the South America East Territory.

The Salvation Army was recognised as a juridical person in Argentina by the Government Decree of 26 February 1914 (No A 54/909); in Uruguay by the Ministry of the Interior on 17 January 1917 (No 366537); and in Paraguay by Presidential Decree of 28 May 1928 (No 30217).

Zone: Americas and Caribbean
Countries included in the territory: Argentina, Paraguay, Uruguay
'The Salvation Army' in Spanish: Ejército de Salvación
Language in which the gospel is preached: Spanish, Korean, Guaraní
Periodicals: *El Cruzado*, *El Oficial*, *El Salvacionista*, *El Mensajero* (Women's Ministries magazine)

IT was natural that during '2005 – A Year for Children and Youth' there would be an emphasis on children's and youth work in the territory. The greater part of this ministry has been done far from the bright lights of public attention in corps and outposts very often situated in deprived and depraved areas where poverty and criminality is the order of the day.

In addition to evangelistic work with children, many centres have run feeding programmes. But it has been a general policy not simply to hand out food parcels or provide cooked meals without linking this service to some sort of educational programme. Social workers, nutritional advisers and other experts in relevant matters have presented seminars and lectures to children and parents, aimed at helping them to cope better with their difficult situations.

The big event of the year was the

Territorial Youth Congress held in Villa Giardina near Córdoba. Some 450 young people from the three countries that make up the territory met from Thursday to Sunday to celebrate their life in Christ, deepen their faith and renew their commitment as disciples of the risen Saviour. Workshops on a variety of subjects proved beneficial.

Special guests were Captains Shane and Pauline Gruer-Caulfield, Canadian officers serving in Spain, whose teaching and messages challenged the young people profoundly. Many decisions, including offers for full-time service as officers, were made.

A visit by Pendel Brass (USA Eastern Territory) to Buenos Aires touched the lives of many people in this great metropolis. Carrying out practical work such as painting and repairing Quilmes Children's Home in the daytime, the musicians engaged in musical activities during the evenings and weekends – witnessing, teaching and inspiring.

An important feature of the annual programme for the past 11 years has been the Territorial Institute of Music, which has a significant effect in the territory, spiritually and musically. Thanks to financial support from partners in mission and many others, 160 young people met for this important event in Buenos Aires.

The Latin American College for Officers, under the leadership of Commissioners Siegfried and Inger Lise Clausen, was attended by 30 delegates from the Latin American territories, Spain and the North American territories.

STATISTICS
Officers 150 (active 119 retired 31) **Cadets** 8 **Employees** 113
Corps 41 **Outposts** 20 **Institutions** 41
Senior Soldiers 1,457 **Adherents** 645 **Junior Soldiers** 553

STAFF
Programme/Public Relations: Maj Raúl Bernao
Editorial: Maj Hugo D. Gutiérrez
Education and Training: Maj Ricardo Bouzigues
Music and Gospel Arts: S/L Omar Pérez
Social: Capt Eduardo Baigorria
Youth and Candidates: Maj Wendy Johnstone

Business: Maj Lidia Saavedra
Finance: Sergio Cerezo (Accountant) – in charge
Legal: Susana Barros – in charge
Property: Rolando Ramírez – in charge
Projects/Sponsorship/Missing Persons: Claudia Franchetti
Coordinator Thrift Store Programmes: Lt-Col Jorge Páez

Women's Ministries: Col Rebecca Nuesch (TPWM) Lt-Col Aída Castillo (TSWM) Maj Lidia Bernao (TLOMS) Lt-Col Evangelina Luriaud (SSF)

DIVISIONS
Buenos Aires: Avda Rivadavia 3257 – Piso 2 (C1203AAE), Buenos Aires, Argentina; tel: (011) 4861 1930/9499; Maj Pablo Nicolasa
Central Argentina: Urquiza 2142, (S2000AOD) Rosario Pcia. de Santa Fe, Argentina; tel/fax: (0341) 425 6739; Maj Carlos Bembhy
Uruguay: Hocquart 1886, (11800) Montevideo, Uruguay; tel: (598) (2) 409 7581; Maj Bartolo Aguirre

DISTRICTS
Paraguay and Northeast Argentina: Dr Hassler y MacArthur 4402, Casilla 92, Asunción, Paraguay; tel/fax: 595 (21) 608 584; Maj Danton Moya
Southern Argentina: Moreno 763 (B8000FWO) Bahía Blanca, Pcia. de Buenos Aires; tel/fax: (0291) 4533 642; Maj Dorcila Soza

EDUCATION CENTRE AND TRAINING COLLEGE

Avda. Tte Gral. Donato Álvarez 465/67, (C1406BOC) Buenos Aires; tel/fax: (011) 4631 4815

COMMUNITY AND DAY CARE CENTRES

Argentina
Pellegrini 376, (E3200AMF) Concordia (Entre Ríos); tel: (0345) 421 1751 (acc 30)

Uruguay
Sarandí 1573, (60,000) Paysandú; tel: (72) 22709 (acc 30)

CONFERENCE CENTRES AND YOUTH CAMP

Argentina
Parque General Jorge L. Carpenter, Avda. Benavídez, (Paraguay y Uruguay) (1619) Benavídez, Pcia. de Buenos Aires; tel: (03488) 458644
'Betel', Arruabarrena 1659, (X5174GKG) Huerta Grande, Córdoba; tel: (03548) 423747
Parque El Oasis, Ruta 14 Km. 7 Camino Público a Rosario – Zona Rural (Santa Fe); tel: (0341) 495 0003

Uruguay
Centro para Campamentos 'El Renuevo', Ruta 1 de Playa Fomento s/n, Colonia Valdense, Colonia

SOCIAL SERVICES

Counselling and Labour Exchange
Loria 190, (C1173ACD) Buenos Aires; tel: (011) 4865 0074

Boys' Home
Uruguay
J. M. Blanes 62, (50,000) Salto; tel: (732) 32740 (acc 30)

Children's Homes (mixed)
Argentina
Monroe 1166, (B1878IPP) Quilmes, Pcia. de Buenos Aires; tel: (011) 4253 0623 (acc 32)

Paraguay
Dr Hassler y MacArthur, Asunción; tel: [595] (21) 600 291 (acc 60)

Eventide Homes
Argentina
Calle Mitre, 54 No 2749, (1650) Villa Maipú, San Martín, Pcia. de Buenos Aires; tel: (011) 4753 4117 (acc 54)
Primera Junta 750 (B1878IPP) Quilmes, Pcia. de Buenos Aires; tel: (011) 4254 5897 (acc 37)

Uruguay
Avda Agraciada 3567, (11800) Montevideo; tel: (2) 308 5227/309 5385 (acc 75)

Industrial Homes
Argentina
Avda Sáenz 580, (C1437DNS) Buenos Aires; tel: (011) 4911 7561/0781/7585
Amenábar 581, (S2000OQK) Rosario; tel: (0341) 482 0155
O'Brien 1272/84, (C1137ABD) Buenos Aires; tel: (011) 4305 5021
Salta 3197, Barrio San Javier, (H3500BOF) Resistencia; tel: (03722) 464 151

Night Shelters
Argentina (Men)
Brown 1725, (S2000AOD) Rosario, Pcia. de Santa Fe; tel: (0341) 425 0861 (acc 20)
Copahué 2032, (C1288ABB) Buenos Aires; tel: (011) 4301 1503 (acc 75)
Godoy Cruz 352, (M5500GOQ) Mendoza, Pcia. de Mendoza; tel: (0261) 4204998 (acc 24)
Maza 2258 (C1240ADV) Buenos Aires; tel: (011) 4912 0843 (acc 86)

(Women and Children)
José I. Rucci 1231, (B1822CJY) Valentín Alsina, Pcia. de Buenos Aires; tel: (011) 4228 4328 (acc 32)
O'Brien 1272, (C1137ABD) Buenos Aires; tel: (011) 4304 8753 (acc 40)

Students' Homes
Argentina
Bat de Junín 2921, (S3000ASQ) Santa Fe; tel: (0342) 452 0563 (acc 28)
Calle 4, No 711, (1900) La Plata, Pcia. de Buenos Aires; tel: (0221) 483 6152 (acc 15)
Félix Frías 434/6, (X5000AHJ) Córdoba; tel: (0351) 423 3228 (acc 15)
San Martín 964, (U9100BET) Trelew, (Chubut); tel: (02965) 433 125 (acc 34)

Women's Residence
Argentina
Esparza 93, (C1171ACA) Buenos Aires; tel: (011) 4861 3119 (acc 50)

Primary School
EEGB No 1027 'Federico Held', Barrio ULM, (3730) Charata, Pcia. del Chaco; tel: (03731) 421 292

Medical Clinic
Héroes de la Independencia y Vietnam, Villa Laurelty, San Lorenzo, Paraguay; tel: [595] 21 577 082

SOUTH AMERICA WEST TERRITORY

Chief Secretary in Charge:
Lieut-Colonel Susan McMillan
(1 Oct 2006)

Territorial Headquarters: Avda. España 46, Santiago, Chile

Postal address: Casilla 3225, Santiago 1, Chile

Tel address: Salvación Santiago Chile; tel: [56] (2) 671 8237/695 7005; fax: [56] (2) 698 5560
email: southamericawest@salvationarmy.org

Salvation Army operations were commenced in Chile soon after the arrival of Brigadier and Mrs William T. Bonnet to Valparaíso on 1 October 1909. The first corps was opened in Santiago on 28 November, with Captain David Arn and Lieutenant Alfred Danielson as officers. Adjutant and Mrs David Thomas, with Lieutenant Zacarías Ribeiro, pioneered in Peru in March 1910. The work in Bolivia, started in December 1920, was planned by Brigadier Chas Hauswirth and established by Adjutant and Mrs Oscar E. Ahlm. Quito saw the Army's arrival in Ecuador on 30 October 1985 under the command of Captain and Mrs Eliseo Flores Morales.

Zone: Americas and Caribbean
Countries included in the territory: Bolivia, Chile, Ecuador, Peru
'The Salvation Army' in Aymara: Ejercitunaca Salvaciananaca; in Quechua: Ejercituman Salvacionman; in Spanish: Ejército de Salvación
Languages in which the gospel is preached: Aymara, Quechua, Spanish
Publications: *El Grito de Guerra* (*The War Cry*), *El Trebol* (Women's Ministries annual magazine and programme aids)

DURING the latter part of 2005 the territory continued to emphasise its work among children and youth, in keeping with the international theme. Youth task forces, set up with youth representation as well as corps officers to plan and oversee youth-related activities, proved to be useful tools and continue to provide advice and assistance to divisional youth secretaries.

The Territorial Task Force reviewed and updated manuals for work among young people.

'Conquering New Territory' was the territorial theme for 2005 and as a result of focusing on specific communities two outposts were opened and another was elevated to corps status.

The Territorial Strategic Plan began to be implemented in 2006. For the next five years the territorial focus will be on God's word, and the annual themes all commence with the words: 'Because Your Word…'. The first of these was 'Because Your Word … Challenges Me to Serve You'.

Leadership training seminars and courses included 'Integrated Mission for Youth' (Argentina); 'Health Programmes' (Uruguay); the Zonal Soldiers School (Brazil); and 'Human Trafficking' (Ecuador), which included parents, children and adolescents, and community leaders.

A train-the-trainers seminar – 'Servant Leadership' – for officers and lay people from the four countries within the territory was led by members of the International Personnel Department (IHQ).

Twenty-four officers received scholarships to take the 'Wesleyan Distinctives' course presented by William and Catherine Booth College (Canada). The territory also participated with WCBC in a feasibility study for distance learning. The first phase gave encouraging signs that officers' education would be improved by this means, and the territory continues working with WCBC to develop this opportunity.

Leaders of the 2006 Territorial Music Camp were Bandmaster John Philip and Sigrun Hannevik from Oslo (Norway). Their musical expertise coupled with a deep Christian faith brought excellent results, musically and spiritually.

Executive officers councils were particularly blessed by the participation of Commissioner Linda Bond (International Secretary for Spiritual Life Development and International External Relations), her Bible studies and messages being the source of much inspiration.

STATISTICS

Officers 278 (active 249 retired 29) **Cadets** (1st Yr) 6 (2nd Yr) 14 **Employees** 912
Corps 83 **Outposts and Pioneer Works** 16 **Schools** 14 **After School/Community Centres** 34 **Hospital** 1 **Kindergartens** 21 **Institutions** 22
Senior Soldiers 3,841 **Adherents** 513 **Junior Soldiers** 1,947

STAFF

Business Administration: Maj María de Alarcón
Personnel: Maj David Alarcón
Programme: Maj Antonio Arguedas
Women's Ministries: Maj Lilian de Arguedas (TSWM)
Education: Lt-Col Luis Aguilera
Schools: Maj Elizabeth de Negrete
Finance and Legal: Maj María de Alarcón
Public Relations and Property: Maj María Flores
Social and Sponsorship: Capt Paulina de Márquez
Strategic Planning: Maj Eliseo Flores
Trade: Capt Manuel Márquez
Literary and Editor, _The War Cry_: Maj Lilian de Arguedas
Training: Lt-Col Luis Aguilera

DIVISIONS

Bolivia Altiplano: Calle Cañada Strongest 1888, Zona San Pedro, Casilla 926, La Paz, Bolivia; tel: 591 (2) 249-1560; fax: 591 (2) 248-5948; Maj Eliseo Flores
Bolivia Central: Calle Rico Toro 773 Zona Queru, Casilla 3594, Cochabamba; tel: 591 (4) 4454281 - 4454337; fax: 591 (4) 411-5887; Maj Franklin Abasto
Chile Central: Agustinas 3020, Casilla 3225, Santiago 1; tel/fax: 56 (2) 681-4992/681-5277; Maj Cecilia Bahamonde
Chile South: Av Caupolicán 990, Casilla 1064, Temuco; tel: 56 (45) 215-850; fax: 56 (2) 271-425; Maj Juan Carlos Alarcón
Ecuador: Tomás Chariove 149-144 y Manuel Valdivieso, El Pinar, Casilla 17.10.7179, Quito; tel/fax: 593 (2) 243-5422/244-7829; Maj Jaime Herrera
Peru: Calle Zaragoza 215, Pueblo Libre, Lima 21, Apartado 690, Lima 100; tel: 51 (1) 261-4576; fax: 51 (1) 261-4694; Maj Alex Nesterenko

DISTRICT

Chile North: Sucre 866, Casilla 310, Antofagasta; tel: 56 (55) 280-668; fax: 56 (55) 224-094; Maj Luis Cisternas

TRAINING COLLEGE

Escuela de Cadetes: Coronel Souper 4564,
Santiago, Chile; tel: 56 (2) 776-2425/
776-0865; fax: 56 (2) 779-9187

BIBLE INSTITUTE

Aymara: Prolongación Illampu 188, Zona San
Pedro, La Paz, Bolivia; tel: 591 (2) 231-1189
(acc 20)

SALVATION ARMY CAMP GROUNDS
Bolivia

Chaparé, Chimoré: Población Chimoré, Chaparé
Eben-Ezer: Los Yungas, Puente Villa,
Comunidad Tarila, Provincia Nor Yungas

Chile

El Complejo Angostura: Panamericana Sur Km
55; tel: 591 (2) 825-0398

EDUCATIONAL WORK
SCHOOLS
Bolivia

Lindgren: Murillo 434, Barrio Central Viacha,
La Paz; tel/fax: 591 (2) 280-0404 (acc 200)
Villa Cosmos: Uraciri Patica 2064, Barrio
Cosmos 79, Unidad Vecinal C (acc 175)
William Booth: Sucre 909, Oruro;
tel/fax: 591 (2) 280-0404 (acc 800)

Chile

Arica: Av Rancha Rayada 3839, Población 11 de
Septiembre, Arica; tel/fax: 56 (58) 211-100
(acc 678)
Calama: Aníbal Pinto 2121, Calama;
tel/fax: 56 (55) 311-316/345-802 (acc 1,155)
Catalina Booth: Irene Frei 2875, Villa
Esmeralda, Calama; tel/fax: 56 (55) 312-608
(acc 800)
Naciones Unidas: Séptimo de Línea 148,
Población Libertad, Puerto Montt;
tel/fax: 56 (65) 254-047/251-918, 56 (2)
6431875 (acc 1,320)
Pudahuel: Mapocho 9047, comuna de Pudahuel,
Casilla 3225, Santiago (acc 176)
William Booth: Zenteno 1015, Osorno;
tel: 56 (64) 247-449; tel/fax: 56 (64) 233-141
(acc 720)

Peru

Eduardo Palací: Av Progreso 1032, Urb San
Gregorio, Vitarte; tel/fax: 51 (1) 356-0297
(acc 500)
Miguel Grau: Av 29 de Diciembre 127, Trujillo;
tel/fax: 51 (44) 255-571 (acc 320)

Ecuador

Cayambe: Calle H 1 393 Morales, Urbanización
Las Orquídeas, Casilla 1710-7179 Cayambe;
tel: 593 (2) 211-0196 (acc 300)

Pre-Primary Schools
Chile

El Bosque: Las Vizcachas 858, Población Las
Acacias, El Bosque, Santiago;
tel: 56 (2) 529-4242 (acc 45)
Refugio Feliz: Calle Mapocho 9047, Comuna de
Pudahuel, Casilla 3225, Santiago;
tel: 56 (2) 644-6175 (acc 90)

MEDICAL WORK
Bolivia

Harry Williams Hospital: Av Suecia 1038-1058,
Zona Huayra K'assa, Casilla 4099,
Cochabamba; tel: 591 (4) 422-7778;
fax: 591 (4) 423-1601 (acc 27)
Community Extension Programme: Av Suecia
1083, Zona Huayra K'assa, Casilla 542,
Cochabamba; tel: 591 (4) 423-2195
Mobile Clinic: Av Suecia 1038-1058, Zona
Huayra K'assa, Casilla 4099, Cochabamba;
tel: 591 (4) 422-7778; fax: 591 (4) 423-1601

Ecuador

Dental Clinic, Quito Sur: Calle Apuela #321 y
Malimpia, Santa Rita, Casilla 17.107179;
tel: 593 (2) 284-5529
Integral Health Centre, Esmeraldas: Calles
Uruguay y Ecuador, Barrio Las Américas,
Casilla Esm. 08.01.73, Esmeraldas;
tel: 593 (6) 710-439
Community Health Programme (Rural Areas):
Pimampiro

SOCIAL WORK
Social Welfare Office

Chile Central: Herrera 151, Santiago;
tel: 56 (2) 681-4992

Men's Shelters
Bolivia

La Paz: Calle Prolongación Illampu 188, Zona
San Pedro, La Paz, Casilla 926, La Paz;
tel: 591 (2) 231-1189 (acc 100)

Chile

Antofagasta: Calle Prat 1045, Casilla 917
Antofagasta; tel: 56 (55) 223-847 (acc 50)
Iquique: Calle Esmeralda 862, Casilla 134
Iquique; tel: 56 (57) 421-325 (acc 40)
Valparaíso: Calle Villagrán 9, Casilla 1887
Valparasio; tel: 56 (32) 214-946 (acc 170)

Peru

Callao: Calle Colón 138/142, Apartado 139
Callao; tel: 51 (1) 429-3128 (acc 62)

Transit Houses
Chile

Santiago (for girls): Calle Zenteno 1499, Santiago,
Casilla 3225, Santiago; tel: 56 (2) 554-1767
(acc 16)

Pregnant Teens Refuge
Ecuador

Manta: Avda 201 entre calles 116 y 117,
Barrio La Pas, Casilla 13-05-149;
tel: 593 (5) 292-0147 (acc 40)

Student Residence Halls
Bolivia

'Tte-Coronel Rosa de Nery' (girls): Calle Lanza
S-0555, Casilla 3198, Cochabamba;
tel: 591 (4) 422-7123, 591 (4) 422-4191 (acc 40)
'Remedios Asín' (girls): Cañada Strongest
#1878, Casilla 926, La Paz;
tel: 591 (2) 222-1993 (acc 55)
Dr María J. Saavedra, Villa 8 de Diciembre:
Calle Rosendo Gutiérrez 120, Barrio Alto
Sopocachi, Casilla 926, La Paz;
tel: 591 (2) 221-0483 (acc 10)

Chile

Antofagasta (boys): Calle Sucre 866, Casilla
917, Antofagasta; tel: 56 (55) 284-763
(acc 30)
Santiago (boys): Calle Santiago Concha 1333,
Casilla 3225, Santiago 21;
tel: 56 (2) 555-3406 (acc 24)

Peru

Lima (girls): Jirón Huancayo 245, Apartado 690,
Lima 100; tel: 51 (1) 433-8747 (acc 28)
San Martín: Jirón Amoraca 212, Distrito Morales
Tarapoto, San Martín, Casilla 88, Tarapoto,
San Martín; tel: 51 (94) 527-540 (acc 20)

Children's Homes
Bolivia

Evangelina Booth Girls' Home: Francisco
Viedma 1054, Villa Montenegro, Casilla 542,
Cochabamba; tel: 591 (4) 424-1560 (acc 40)
Oscar Ahlm's Boys' Home: Km 19 Carretera a
Oruro/Camino a Comunidad Thiomogo, San
Jorge, Vinto Casilla 542, Cochabamba;
tel: 591 (4) 4485098 (acc 45)
Remedios Asin Boys' Home: Calle Murillo
436, Barrio Central Viacha, Casilla 15084,
La Paz; tel/fax: 591 (2) 280-0404 (acc 70)

Chile

El Broquel Girls' Home: 12 Poniente 8390,
La Granja, Casilla 3225, Santiago 1;
tel/fax: 56 (2) 541-6079 (acc 40)
El Redil Boys' Home: Calle Arzobispo
Valdivieso 410, Llo Lleo, Casilla 61, Llo
Lleo; tel: 56 (35) 282-054 (acc 60)
Los Copihues Girls' Home: Calle Los Sauces
0202, Población Las Quilas, Temuco, Casilla
1064, Temuco; tel: 56 (45) 234-028 (acc 60)
Helmuth Hühner Boys' Home: Av Arturo
Allessandri 6342, Lo Valledor, Pedro Aguirre
Cerda, Casilla 3225, Santiago 1;
tel: 56 (2) 521-5575 (acc 69)

Eventide Home
Chile

Otoño Dorado: Av La Florida 9995, La Florida;
tel: 56 (2) 287-5280; tel/fax: 56 (2) 287-1869
(acc 49)

Day Care Centres for the Aged
Chile

Los Lagos: Berlín 818, Población Los Lagos,
Angol; tel: 56 (459) 712-583 (acc 20)

Ecuador

Cayambe: Calle Montalvo 220 Cayambe; tel:
593 (2) 236-1273 (acc 60)

Day Nurseries/Kindergartens
Bolivia

Catalina Booth: Lanza S-0555, Cochabamba;
tel: 591 (4) 422-7123 (acc 150)
Mi Casita: Calle j. Mostajo s/n, Zona El
Temporal, Cochabamba; tel: 591 (4) 445-0809
(acc 70)
Wawassninchej: Av. Suecia 1083 Zona Huayra
K'assa, Cochabamba; tel 591 (4) 422-4808
(acc 50)
Nueva Vida: Uv 133, Barrio Santa Fe de
Palmáosla, Manzana 28, Casa 2, Zona Sur
Santa Cruz; tel: 591 (3) 356-9760 (acc 100)
Refugio de Amor: Villa 8 de Diciembre, Calle
Rosendo Gutiérrez 120, Barrio Alto
Sopocachi, Casilla 926, La Paz (acc 50)

Chile

Faro de Angeles: Calle Santa Martha 443, Cerro
Playa Ancha, Valparaíso; tel: 56 (2) 281-160
(acc 100)
Catalina Booth: Hipólito Salas 760, Concepción;
tel: 56 (41) 230-447 (acc 60)
La Estrellita: Maipú 284, Maipú;
tel: 56 (2) 531-2638 (acc 55)
Lautarito: Castro 5179, Población Lautaro,

Antofagasta; tel: 56 (55) 269-548 (acc 70)

Neptuno: Los Aromos 833, Lo Prado, Santiago; tel: 56 (2) 773-5154 (acc 60)

Nido Alegre: Calle Santa Petronila 1048, Quinta Normal, Casilla 3225, Santiago 21; tel: 56 (2) 773-8554 (acc 96)

Puente Alto: Santo Domingo 90, Comuna Pte Alto, Casilla 3225, Santiago; tel: 56 (2) 775-1166 (acc 75)

'Gotitas': Avda Carlos Condell 1535, Los Salares, Casilla 436, Copiapó; tel: 56 (52) 216099

Rayito de Luz: Picarte 1894, Valdivia; tel/fax: 56 (63) 214-404 (acc 120)

Rayitos de Sol: Av Brasil 73, Casilla 3225, Santiago 21; tel: 56 (2) 699-3595; fax: 56 (2) 688-4755 (acc 100)

Refugio Feliz: Calle Andes, esq. Calle María Ignacia 973, Villa Manuel Acevedo, Comuna Pudahuel, Casilla 3225, Santiago 21; tel: 56 (2) 644-6175 (acc 90)

Ecuador

Arca de Noe: Avda 201, entre calles 116 y 117, Barrio La Paz, Casilla 13-05-149, Manta; tel: 593 (5) 292-0147 (acc 60)

Gotitas de Miel: Montalvo 124 y Panamá, Casilla 1710.1120, Quito; tel: 593 (2) 258-1081/228-4776 (acc 100)

La Colmena: Calle Pomasqui 955 y Pedro Andrade, La Colmena, Casilla 1710.7179, Quito; tel: 593 (2) 236-1273 (acc 60)

Mi Casita: Apuela 321 y Malimpia, Santa Rita, Casilla 17.1071.79, Quito; tel: 593 (2) 236-1273 (acc 40)

'Mi Pequeño Redil': Urbanización Sierra Hermosa, Calle 5, lotes 237-239, Quito; tel: 593 (2) 282-6835

Nueva Esperanza: Av Martha de Roldós km 5 ½, Casilla 09.01.10478, Guayaquil; tel: 593 (4) 225-6012; fax: 593 (4) 225-8482 (acc 40)

Pedacito de Cielo: Calles Uruguay y Ecuador, Barrio Las Américas, Casilla Esm. 08.01.73, Esmeraldas; tel: 593 (6) 710-439 (acc 50)

Food Aid Programme
Chile

Ancud: Oscar Bonilla 2, Calle 4, Casa 721, Ancud; tel: 56 (65) 622-045 (acc 80)

Peru

Chiclayo: PP.JJ. Sto. Toribio de Mogrovejo, MZ 'I' Lote 6 (neighbour); tel: 51 (74) 208-216 (neighbour) (acc 100)

Tacna: Av Los Pintores 575, Urb. Las Begonias, 'Cono Sur Este', Apartado 806, Tacna; tel: 51 (54) 700-612 (acc 80)

'El Porvenir': Calle Synneva Vestheim 583, Cacerío El Porvenir, Provincia Rioja, Dpto San Martín; tel: 51 (94) 520-368 (community phone)

Community Day Centres/School-Age Day Care Centres (attached to corps/ouposts)
Bolivia

Achachicala: Av Ramos Gavilán 2050, Zona Achachicala, Casilla 926, La Paz; tel: 591 (2) 230-5719 (acc 291)

Batallón Colorados: Calle Batallón Colorados 114, Barrio Municipal, Casilla 347, Sucre; tel: 591 (4) 645-4905 (acc 60)

Corqueamaya: Cantón Huayna Potosí, Provincia Los Andes, Casilla 926, La Paz; tel: 591 (7) 125-0326 (acc 70)

El Tejar: Calle Juan Gutiérrez Paniagua 703, Zona Alto Tejar, Casilla 926, La Paz; tel: 591 (2) 236-2850 (acc 100)

El Temporal: Calle J. Mostajo s/n Zona El Temporal, Cochabamba; tel: 591 (4) 445009 (acc 70)

'El Vergel' Nutritional Programme: Población Chimoré, Chaparé (acc 40)

Huayra K'assa: Av Suecia 1083, Zona Huayra K'assa, Casilla 542, Cochabamba; tel: 591 (42) 423-2195 (acc 50)

La Chimba: Av Cañada Cochabamba 2572, Zona La Chimba, Casilla 542, Cochabamba; tel: 591 (4) 428-3079 (acc 80)

Lacaya: Cantón Lacaya, Provincia Los Andes, Casilla 926, La Paz; tel: 591 (7) 195-3041 (acc 75)

Pacata: Calle 2, No 372, Zona Villa Barrientos, Casilla 542, Cochabamba; tel: 591 (4) 429-8278 (acc 35)

Parotani: Calle Coronel Ferrel 732, Comunidad de Parotani, Provincia de Quillacollo, Casilla 542, Cochabamba; tel: 591 (4) 426-3682 (acc 60)

Pockonas: Cornelio Durán 302, Barrio Pockonas, Casilla 347, Sucre; tel: 591 (4) 646-2201 (acc 50)

Potosí: Calle Lidio Ustarez 846, Barrio San Martín, Casilla 215, Potosí (acc 30)

Primero de Mayo: Callen 12, no 50, Barrio Sucre, Casilla 4819, Santa Cruz; tel: 591 (3) 349-9969 (acc 50)

Tarija: Calle Primero de Mayo 4711, Esq Calle Murillo, Casilla 1123, Tarija; tel: 591 (4) 663-2022 (acc 50)

Tiahuanacu: Calle Gral. José Balliván 377, Provincia Ingavi, Casilla 926, La Paz; tel: 591 (7) 190-3756 (acc 100)

Villa Cosmos: Calle Uraciri Patica 2064,

Captains Martha and Luis Lema are the first officers to be commissioned from the Quichua people of Ecuador

Barrio Cosmos 79, Unidad Vecinal 'C', Casilla 926, La Paz (acc 300)

Villa Fátima: Calle Mururata 1251, Barrio Villa La Merced, Casilla 926, La Paz; tel: 591 (2) 221-0483 (acc 80)

Viacha: Calle Murillo 434, Barrio Central Viacha, Casilla 926, La Paz; tel: 591 (2) 280-0127 (acc 240)

Zona Este de Oruro: Pasaje Arica 485, Casilla 86, Oruro; tel: 591 (2) 528-1868 (acc 300)

Chile
Antuhue: Av Presidente Ibáñez s/n, Población Antuhue, Casilla 277, Puerto Montt; tel: 56 (65) 286-236 (acc 140)

Hualpencillo: Av Alemania 3510, Hualpencillo, Talcahuano, Casilla 1171, Concepción; tel/fax: 56 (41) 434-410 (acc 150)

Las Acacias: Las Vizcachas 858, Población Las Acacias, El Bosque; tel: 56 (2) 529-4242 (acc 50)

Nueva Extremadura: Batallón Chacabuco, 03524,

Población Santiago de Nueva Extremadura, La Pintana, Santiago; tel: 56 (2) 542-4523 (acc 40)

Puente Alto: Calle Santo Domingo 90, Comuna de Puente Alto, Casilla 3225, Santiago 21; tel: 56 (2) 850-3331 (acc 75)

Ecuador
El Rancho: Manzana 44, Lote 801, 802 Rancho Alto, Casilla 7110.7179, Quito (acc 120)

Gotitas de Miel: Montalvo 124 y Panamá, Casilla 1710.1120, Quito; tel: 593 (2) 258-1081/228-4776 (acc 50)

Nido Alegre: Calle Pomasqui 955 y calle Pedro Andrade, La Colmena, Casilla 1710.7179, Quito; tel: 593 (2) 236-1273 (acc 130)

Mi Casita: Apuela 321 y Malimpia, Santa Rita, Casilla 17.1071.79, Quito; tel: 593 (2) 284-5529 (acc 120)

Nueva Esperanza: Av Martha de Roldós km 5½ Casilla 09.01.10478, Guayaquil; tel: 593 (4) 225-6012; fax: 593 (4) 225-8482 (acc 140)

Peru
Buenos Aires: Jirón César Vallejo 358, Zona Buenos Aires, Apartado 759, Trujillo; tel: 51 (44) 285-506 (acc 50)

La Esperanza: Calle Los Olivos 745, Distrito La Esperanza, Apartado 759, Trujillo; tel: 51 (44) 271-887 (acc 40)

San Martín de Porras: Jirón Arequipa 4084, Distrito San Martín de Porras, Apartado 690, Lima 100; tel: 51 (1) 572-1413 (acc 40)

Tacna: Av Los Pintores 575, Urb. Las Begonias, Cono Sur Este, Apartado 806, Tacna; tel: 51 (54) 700-612 (acc 80)

Vitarte: Av Progreso 1032, Urb. San Gregorio, Vitarte, Apartado 690, Lima 100; tel: 51 (1) 356-0297 (acc 80)

Workshop
Ecuador
Tailoring Workshop and Sewing Centre: Talle de Costura SPS, Quito, Calle Apuela #321 y Malimpia, Santa Rita, Casilla 17.107179; tel: 593 (2) 284-5529

For the next five years the territorial focus will be on God's word, and the annual themes all commence with the words: 'Because Your Word…'. The first of these was 'Because Your Word … Challenges Me to Serve You'.

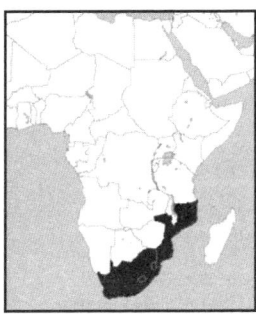

SOUTHERN AFRICA TERRITORY

Territorial leaders:
Commissioners Trevor and Memory Tuck

Territorial Commander:
Commissioner Trevor Tuck (1 Jun 2005)

Chief Secretary:
Lieut-Colonel Hezekiel N. Mavundla
(20 Dec 2004)

**Territorial Headquarters: 119-121 Rissik Street,
Wanderers' View, Johannesburg 2001**

Postal address: PO Box 1018, Johannesburg 2000, South Africa

Tel address: Salvation Braamfontein; tel: [27] (011) 718 6700; fax: [27] (011) 718 6790;
email: CS_SouthernAfrica@SAF.salvationarmy.org; web site: www.salvationarmy.co.za

On 4 March 1883 Major and Mrs Francis Simmonds with Lieutenant Alice Teager 'opened fire' in Cape Town. Other officers were sent to the island of St Helena in 1886 to consolidate work commenced (in 1884) by Salvationist 'Bluejackets'. Social services began in 1886. The Army's first organised ministry among the African people was established in 1888 in Natal and, in 1891, in Zululand. Evangelistic effort in Mozambique, pioneered in 1916 by African converts, was officially recognised in 1923.

Zone: Africa

Countries included in the territory: Lesotho, Mozambique, St Helena, South Africa, Swaziland

'The Salvation Army' in Afrikaans: Die Heilsleër; in IsiXhosa: Umkhosi wo Sindiso; in IsiZulu: Impi yo Sindiso; in Portuguese: Exército de Salvação; in SeSotho: Mokhosi oa Poloko; in SiPedi: Mogosi wa Pholoso; in Tshivenda: Mbi ya u Tshidza; in Tsonga: Nyi Moi Yoponisa

Languages in which the gospel is preached: Afrikaans, English, Portuguese, SeSotho, Shangaan, SiPedi, Tsonga, Tswana, Tshivenda, IsiXhosa, IsiZulu

Periodicals: *Echoes of Mercy, Home League Highlights, Home League Resource Manual, Outer Circle Newsletter, SAMF Newsletter, The Reporter, The War Cry*

THE territory has seen a time of consolidation and expansion of its programmes. This was especially so in the response to HIV/Aids ministry, much progress being experienced in the *Matsoho A Thuso* ('Helping Hand') programme with its emphasis on abstinence and faithfulness. More than 2,550 home-based carers have been trained and 23,000 learners have been provided with life-skills training dealing primarily with issues of sexuality and morality.

A new project was put into operation in Soweto, based at the Carl Sithole Centre. A programme of voluntary counselling and testing and anti-retroviral treatment support will operate closely with the Chris Hani Baragwanath Hospital's Perinatal HIV Research Unit. People from all parts of Soweto and beyond will be able to receive pre- and post-testing counselling, HIV testing, CD4 blood tests and medical attention.

According to Captain (Dr) Felicia Christians, the clinic coordinator and resident doctor, the facility will encourage voluntary counselling and testing as part of an overall HIV/Aids prevention campaign.

The territory continued to be extensively involved with the World Feeding Programme in Lesotho. It also released Captain David Widdowson to join the IHQ Emergency Services team that worked in India in the aftermath of the devastating December 2004 tsunami in that region.

It has also been a time of leadership change, with Commissioners William and Lydia Mabena entering retirement and being replaced by national officers, Commissioners Trevor and Memory Tuck. The new territorial leaders have cast a vision encapsulated in the focus 'Together with Christ in Mission', which will be the territory's emphasis for the next three years.

To introduce this theme and plan the way forward, three Mission Conferences were held early in 2006 to ensure that every leader will have input.

STATISTICS

Officers 328 (active 220 retired 108) **Aux-Captains** 8 **Lieutenants** 11 **Cadets** 10 **Employees** 537
Corps 235 **Corps Plants, Societies and Outposts** 96 **Mission Team** 1 **Schools** 2 **Hospitals** 2 **Institutions** 26 **Day Care Centres** 18 **Goodwill Centres** 7 **Recycling Stores** 4 **Nursery Schools** 3
Senior Soldiers 26,154 **Adherents** 3,020 **Junior Soldiers** 5,412

STAFF

Business Administration: Maj Timothy Mabaso, BA
Child Sponsorship: Maj Diann Jones
Community Relations and Development: Maj Keith Conrad
Ecumenical: Maj Paul Kontsi
Editor: Maj Eva Marseille
Education: Maj Mercy Mahlangu, BA
Family Health: Maj Lenah Jwili
Family Tracing: Lt-Col Veronica Trollip
Finance: Maj Gerrit Marseille
Health Services: Capt Dr Felicia Christians, MBChB (UCT), MCFP (SA), MPH, MFam Med (UCT)
HIV/Aids Ministries: Maj Lenah Jwili
Information Technology: Capt Jonathan Payne
Personnel: Maj William Langa
Programme: Maj Barry Schwartz
Property: Maj Andrew Moholoagae
Trade: Mrs Helen Tuck
Training: Maj Alistair Venter ThA, BTh (S Afr) Capt Mario Nhacuba (Mozambique)
  Candidates: Maj Alistair Venter ThA, BTh
Women's Ministries: Comr Memory Tuck (TPWM) Lt-Col Mirriam B. Mavundla (TSWM) Maj Flemah Mabaso (LOM/SAMF)
Youth: Capt Stephen Malins

REGION

Mozambique: Ave Armando Tivane 849, Maputo, Mozambique;
  tel: [258] 1 487 422/423; fax: [258] 1 487 408; Maj Amaro Pereira

DIVISIONS

Central: PO Box 756, Rosettenville, Johannesburg 2130; tel: (011) 435-0267; fax: (011) 435-2835; Maj Albert Shekwa
Eastern Cape: PO Box 35086, Newton Park, Port Elizabeth 6055; tel: (041) 585-5363; fax: (041) 586-3521; Maj Daniel Kasuso
Eastern Kwa Zulu/Natal: PO Box 1267, Eshowe 3815; tel: (035) 474-1132; fax: (035) 474-1132
Mid Kwa Zulu/Natal: PO Box 100061, Scottsville, Pietermaritzburg 3209; tel: (033) 386-3881; fax: (033) 386-8019; Maj Jabulani Khoza
Mpumalanga/Swaziland: PO Box 1571, Nelspruit 1200; tel/fax: (013) 741-2869; Maj Ivy Mntambo
Northern: PO Box 3549, Louis Trichardt 0920; tel/fax: (015) 963-6145; Maj Johannes Raselalome

Northern Kwa Zulu/Natal: PO Box 923, Vryheid 3100; tel: (034) 982-3113; fax: (034) 983-2882; Maj Bennie Harms

South East: PO Box 1473, Kokstad 4700; Mount Frere; tel/fax: (039) 255-0134; Maj Lazarus Mohibidu

Western Cape: PO Box 13079, Mowbray, Cape Town 7705; tel: (021) 689-8915; fax: (021) 689-3023; Maj Lyndsay Rowe

St Helena: The Salvation Army, Jamestown, Island of St Helena, South Atlantic Ocean; tel: 09 (290) 2703; fax: 09 (290) 2052

COLLEGES FOR OFFICER TRAINING

PO Box 32902, Braamfontein 2017, South Africa; tel: (011) 718 6762

Rua Hospital de Bagamoio 1360 (Post Box) CP 4099, Maputo, Mozambique; tel: [258] 01 470206

DAY CARE CENTRES FOR PRE-SCHOOL CHILDREN

Central: Benoni, Eldorado Park, Galashewe, Katlehong, Lethlabile, Mangaung

Mpumalanga/Swaziland: Barberton, Emangweni, Pienaar

Mid Kwa Zulu/Natal: Hammarsdale, Imbali, Kwa Mashu, Umlazi

Northern: Messina

Northern Kwa Zulu/Natal: Ezakheni, Madadeni, Mondlo, Ulundi, Vryheid

Western Cape: Bonteheuwel, Mitchells Plein, Manenburg

DAY CARE CENTRES FOR SENIOR CITIZENS

Central: Benoni, Kimberley, Krugersdorp, Pretoria, Vereeniging

Eastern Cape: East London, Port Elizabeth

Mid Kwa Zulu/Natal: Pietermaritzburg

Western Cape: Goodwood

GOODWILL CENTRES

Benoni West 1503: Benoni Goodwill Centre, PO Box 17299

East London, Vincent 5217: Hind House, PO Box 13012

Kimberley 8300: Kimberley Goodwill Centre, PO Box 1691

Krugersdorp 1740: Family Mission Centre, PO Box 351

Pietermaritzburg, Scottsville 3209: Hope Goodwill House, PO Box 100-213

Vereeniging 1930: Sally Ann Cottage, PO Box 2090

HEALTH SERVICES

Booth Hospital: 32 Prince St, Oranjezicht, Cape Town 8001; tel: (021) 465-4896/46 (acc 84)

Mountain View Hospital: PO Salvation 3110, via Vryheid, Natal; tel: (034) 967-1544 (acc 88)

Mountain View Community Care Clinics: Ombimbini, Gumtree, Mahlahleni, Squwbezi, Mooiplaas, Mvusi (c/o DHQ Mount Frere), Barkerville (c/o DHQ Mount Frere)

Msunduza Community and Primary Health Care Centre and Mbuluzi Clinic: Box 2543, Mbabane, Swaziland; tel: (268) 404-5243

RETIRED OFFICERS RESIDENCES

Doonside 4135: Sunset Lodge, 10 Worldsview Cl, Worldsview

Emmarentia 2029: Emmarentia Flats, PO Box 85214, Johannesburg; tel: (011) 646-2126

Orlando 1804: Ephraim Zulu Flats, PO Box 49; tel: (011) 982-1084

SOCIAL SERVICES

Crèches

Bridgman Crèche: PO Box 62, Kwa Xuma 1868; 88, 3b White City, Jabavu 1856; tel: (011) 982-5574 (acc 140)

Carl Sithole Crèche: Carl Sithole Centre, PO Box 180, Orlando 1804; tel: (011) 986-7417 (acc 40)

Children's Homes

Bethany: Carl Sithole Centre, Klipspruit, PO Box 180, Orlando 1804; tel: (011) 986-7417 (acc children 6-18 yrs 110)

Bethesda: Zodwa's House, Carl Sithole Centre, PO Box 180, Orlando 1804, Soweto (acc children 2-6 yrs 32)

Ethembeni (Place of Hope): 63 Sherwell St, Doornfontein, Johannesburg 2094; tel: (011) 402-8101 (acc children 0-3 yrs 60)

Firlands: Fourth Ave, PO Box 44291, Linden 2104; tel: (011) 782-5556/7 (acc children 3-18 yrs 60)

Joseph Baynes House: 89 Trelawney Rd, Pentrich, PO Box 212275, Oribi 3205, Natal; tel: (033) 386-2266 (acc children 0-18 yrs 72)

Strathyre: Eleventh Ave, Dewetshof, PO Box 28240, Kensington 2101, Johannesburg; tel: (011) 615-7327/7344 (acc children 3-18 yrs 50)

Community Programme

Thusanong/Osizweni: Home-based Community Care and Counselling Programme, Carl Sithole Centre, Klipspruit, Soweto, PO Box 180, Orlando 1804; tel: (011) 986-7417

Street Children's Home

Musawenkosi: PO Box 14794, Madadeni
Township 2951 (acc boys 7-18 yrs 16)

Eventide Homes (men)

Beth Rogelim: Cape Town 8005, 22 Alfred St;
tel: (021) 425-2138 (acc 52)

Eventide Home (women)

The Haven: Stellenbosch 7599, PO Box 402;
tel: (021) 889-5031 (acc 18)

Eventide Homes (men and women)

Emmarentia: Johannesburg, PO Box 85214,
Emmarentia 2029, 113 Komatie Rd;
tel: (011) 646-2126 (acc 40)
Ephraim Zulu Senior Citizen Centre: Orlando
1804, PO Box 49; tel: (011) 982-1084 (acc 100)
Salisbury House: East London, 19 Rhodes St,
PO Box 18380; tel: (011) 722-4454
Sunset Lodge: Doonside, 4135, 10 World's
View Cl, PO Box 53, World's View, 4125,
South Coast, Natal; tel: (031) 903-3139 (acc 76)
Thembela: Durban 4001, 68 Montpelier Place;
tel: (031) 321-6360 (acc 53)

Homes for Abused Women

Cape Town 8000: Care Haven, PO Box
38186, Gates Ville 7766;
tel: (021) 638-5511; fax: (031) 637-0226;
email: careaid@iafrica.co.za
(acc 18 women 60 children)
Durban: Family Care, PO Box 47122,
Greyville 4023; tel: (031) 309-1395
(acc 45)
Port Elizabeth: Haven of Hope Home,
PO Box 2304, North End 6056;
tel: (041) 373-4317 (acc 32)
Pretoria: Beth Shan, PO Box 19713, Pretoria
West 0117 (acc 15 women)

Men's Homes

Bloemfontein Men's Home: 23 Fountain St,
Bloemfontein 9301; tel: (051) 447-2626
(acc 28)
Beth Rogelim: 22 Alfred St, Cape Town
8005; tel: (021) 425-2138 (acc 100)
Durban Men's Home: 150 Berea Rd, Durban
4001; tel: (031) 201-7922/2404 (acc 66)

Rehabilitation Centres

Hesketh King Treatment Centre: PO Box 5,
Elsenburg 7607, Cape; tel: (021) 884-4600
(acc 60)
Mountain Lodge: PO Box 168, Magaliesburg
2805 (acc 60)

Social Centres

Durban Family Care Centre: PO Box 47122,
Greyville, Durban 4023; tel: (031) 309-1395
(acc 70)
Haven of Hope Home: PO Box 2304, North
End, Durban 6056; tel: (041) 373-4317
(acc 60)
Johannesburg Social Services: Simmonds St Ext,
Johannesburg 2001; tel: (011) 832-1227;
fax: (011) 833-6259 (acc 56)
Pretoria Family Care Centre: PO Box 19713,
Pretoria West 0117; tel: (012) 327-3005
(acc 80)

SCHOOLS

Bethany Combined School: Carl Sithole Centre,
PO Box 180, Orlando 1804;
tel: (011) 986-7417
Mathunjwa High School: PO Box 923, Vryheid
3100
William Booth Primary School: Mountain View,
PO Salvation 3110; tel: (034) 967-1533

YOUTH TRAINING CENTRE

Mission House, 162 High St, Rosettenville,
2130; tel/fax: (011) 435-1822

**During a visit to the Southern Africa Territory,
General Clifton meets one of the many
children who attend the Carl Sithole Centre**

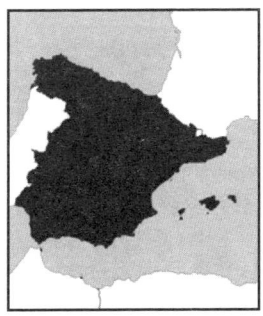

SPAIN COMMAND

Command leaders:
Majors F. Bradford and Heidi Bailey

Officer Commanding:
Major F. Bradford Bailey (1 Aug 2005)

Command Headquarters: Hermosilla 126 Lc 1, 28028 Madrid

Postal address: Ejército de Salvación, c/ Hermosilla, 126 Local 1, 28028 Madrid, Spain

tel: [34] 91 356 6644; fax: [34] 91 361 4782; email: Spain_Command@SPA.salvationarmy.org

Following the appointment of Captain and Mrs Enrique Rey to La Coruña on Ascension Day 1971, it was announced on 24 December 1971 that The Salvation Army had been granted the status of a Legal Person, enjoying full legal rights in the country and permitted to carry on its work without let or hindrance.

Zone: Europe
Country and autonomous communities included in the territory: Canary Islands, Mallorca, Spain
'The Salvation Army' in Spanish: Ejército de Salvación
Languages in which the gospel is preached: English (Mallorca, Denia), Filipino, Spanish

THE command is purposefully involved in renewing its passion for the lost, and longs to fulfill William Booth's vision of 'getting saved, keeping saved and getting somebody else saved'.

Aiming to develop powerful and practical expressions of faith, corps are challenged to strengthen their ties to social service ministries, resulting in a more seamless organisation and integrated ministry to all people.

From the first soldier's enrolment in La Coruña, birthplace of The Salvation Army in Spain 35 years ago, to the nearly 400 enrolments that have followed, officers and soldiers alike remain fervent in their desire to fulfill the Great Commission to make disciples, despite the country's

cultural, religious and financial challenges.

With a renewed sense of commitment to integrated mission, the command is focused on 'Building an Army' that is Committed to the Content of the Word; Committed to Caring for Each Other; Committed to Communion Together; Committed to Connecting With Others; Committed To Communicating the Message.

Salvationists praise God for the vibrant ministry in the new Philippine outpost in Barcelona, where two soldiers are leading the work in English.

It is also encouraging to know that more than 50 young people and adults are undertaking recruits classes for soldiership, as such a commitment to

Students in the brass class rehearse during a music school in Spain. Held during the summer of 2005, it was the command's first music camp and included a youth chorus. More than 50 young people attended.

the Lord and the Army has always been a slow and difficult process in Spain.

The Salvation Army in Spain advances, claiming God's promise: 'The Lord will indeed give what is good, and our land will yield its harvest' (Psalm 85:12 *New International Version*).

STATISTICS

Officers 29 (active 27 retired 2) **Employees** 22
Corps 10 **Outposts** 6 **Institution** 1
Senior Soldiers 341 **Adherents** 64 **Junior Soldiers** 83
Personnel serving outside command Officers 5

STAFF

Women's Ministries: Maj Heidi Bailey (CPWM)
Business Administration: Maj Ambrosio Aycón
Programme and Evangelism: Maj Juan José Arias
  Asst Programme and Evangelism Officer: Maj Belinda Arias
Accountant: Fausta Gonzales
Evangelical Training: Capts Shane and Pauline Gruer-Caulfield
Projects: Maj Heidi Bailey

SOCIAL SERVICES

Food and/or Clothing Distribution Centres
Alicante 03002: Avda de Denia 45, B°5 PB Dcha, Edif Montreal (known as 'La Pirámide)
Barcelona 08024: c/ del Rubí 18
Denia, Alicante 03700: c/ San José 14 B
La Coruña 15010: c/ Francisco Añón 9
Las Palmas 35014: Plaza de los Ruiseñores, Local 8 alto, Miller Bajo
Madrid 28028: c/ Hermosilla, 126, Local 4
Madrid 28038: Avda Rafael Alberti, 18 Bis
Mallorca 07015: Cala Mayor, Avda Joan Miró 285
Tenerife 38006: c/ Marisol Marín 10
Valdemoro-Madrid 28340: c/Bretón de los Herreros 10

Emergency Feeding Kitchens
Alicante 03700: 45, B°5 PB Dcha, Edif Montreal (known as 'La Pirámide)
Barcelona 08024: c/ del Rubí 18
La Coruña 15010: c/ Francisco Añón 9

Thrift Shops 8

Eventide Home (men and women)
Finca El Apostolado, Vereda del Alquitón 9, Arganda del Rey, Madrid 28500 (acc 35)

CONFERENCE, RETREAT AND HOLIDAY CENTRE

Camp Sarón, Partida Torre Carrals 64, 03700 Denia, Alicante; tel: 96 578 2152; fax: 96 643 1206; web site: www.campsaron.com (acc 61)

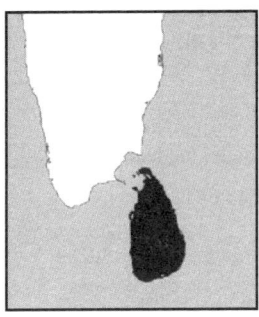

SRI LANKA TERRITORY

Territorial leaders:
Colonels Lalzamlova and Nemkhanching

Territorial Commander:
Colonel Lalzamlova (1 Jun 2006)

Chief Secretary:
Lieut-Colonel Edward Daniel (1 May 2004)

Territorial Headquarters: 53 Sir James Peiris Mawatha, Colombo 2

Postal address: PO Box 193, Colombo, Sri Lanka

tel address: Salvation Colombo; tel: [94] (11) 2324660/2332159; fax: [94] (11) 2436065;
email: Sri_Leadership@sri.salvationarmy.org; web site: www.sri.salvationarmy.org

Salvation Army work began in Ceylon (now Sri Lanka) on 26 January 1883 under the leadership of Captain William Gladwin. 'The General of The Salvation Army' is a corporation Sole by Ordinance No 11 of 1924.

Zone: South Asia
Country included in the territory: Sri Lanka
'The Salvation Army' in Sinhala: Galavime Hamudava; in Tamil: Ratchaniya Senai
Languages in which the gospel is preached: English, Sinhala, Tamil
Periodical: *Yudha Handa*

THE key to the development of The Salvation Army's mission in Sri Lanka being leadership among its people, the Leadership Development Department was set up in January 2006. Its purpose is to identify, invest, equip, cultivate and develop Salvationists in their capacities for leadership.

Children's and youth workers were busy in 2005 – the Year for Children and Youth – conducting several territorial events. These included the Vacation Bible School, Music School, Teenagers Camp, a corps cadet weekend, and a youth camp and rally. In April 2006, workshops for youth leaders and worship leaders were held. All these events were attended by

more than 1,200 young people.

In partnership with the Territorial Emergency and Disaster Response Services, officers from the International Emergency Services, IHQ, conducted training workshops on 'Disaster Preparedness' and 'Community Capacity Development'. These were designed to train officers to set up emergency response teams in their own localities.

In a busy year for the Property Department, construction and renovation projects were a major part of the workload. A new home for elderly women at Rajagiriya was completed. On the eastern side of the island it was satisfying to complete the renovation of the Ampara compound. This included doubling the size of the church, enabling use of the pre-school space and improving its playground equipment.

The department also began to investigate various development options for the Army's main sites in order to generate income that will help the territory finance its mission. With the help of the IHQ Enterprise Secretary the department aims to see these ideas become reality.

Through the ongoing tsunami reconstruction programme in Jaffna, Kalutara, Hikkaduwa and Galle the Army has built more than 500 new houses and repaired almost 100, assisted hundreds of small businesses in recovering their livelihoods, established mobile clinic services and set up a tsunami alerting system in Galle for the families affected by the disaster in December 2004.

Cadets on campaign from the training college had the opportunity to visit Jaffna in spite of continuing conflict in the country.

Under the direction of Commissioners Ivan and Heather Lang (Australia Southern), officers, cadets and workers met for a retreat at Negombo. With 137 officers and 36 children present, it was thought to be the first retreat

that the territory's officers had shared with their children. Many delegates experienced spiritual renewal, bringing hope for the Army's future in Sri Lanka under the theme 'Mission Possible'.

STATISTICS

Officers 147 (active 99 retired 48) **Cadets** 9 **Employees** 156

Corps 44 **Outpost** 1 **Corps Plants** 7 **Social Homes** 7 **Hostels** 7 **Community Centres** 5 **Day Care Centres** 7 **Health Centres** 3 **Conference Centres** 2

Senior Soldiers 3,472 **Adherents** 816 **Junior Soldiers** 476

Personnel serving outside territory Officers 2

STAFF

Candidates: Capt Rohini Hettiarachchi
Community Development: Maj Noel Lapeña
Community Relations and Resource Development: Envoy Simon Wong
Editorial: Maj Anura Vithana
Field, Community Services, Evangelism and Ecumenical Relations: Maj P. Anthony Fernando
Finance: Mrs Mattie Louise Brandon
HIV/Aids Programme: Mrs Swarna De Silva
Information Technology: Miss Coojanie Heendeniya
Leadership Development: Maj Chandralatha Jayaratnasingham
Projects: Maj Colleen Marshall
Property: Maj Ian Marshall
Social Services and Sponsorship: Maj Marilou Lapeña
Training: Maj Nihal Hettiarachchi
Tsunami Resconstruction Programme: Maj Packianathan Jayaratnasingham
Women's Ministries: Col Nemkhanching (TPWM) Lt-Col Lalitha Daniel (TSWM)
Youth: Maj A. Newton Fernando

Through the ongoing tsunami reconstruction programme . . . the Army has built more than 500 new houses and repaired almost 100, assisted hundreds of small businesses in recovering their livelihoods, established mobile clinic services and set up a tsunami alerting system

DIVISIONS

Rambukkana: Mawanella Rd, Rambukkana;
tel: (035) 2265179; email: salrambu@sltnet.lk;
Maj Sarukkalige Chandrasiri

Western: 53 Sir James Peiris Mawatha,
Colombo 2; tel: (11) 2324660 ext 270;
Maj Alister Philip

DISTRICTS

Kandy: 26 Srimath Bennet Soysa Veediya,
Kandy; tel: (08) 2234804

Northern: Kandy Rd, Kaithady, Jaffna;
mobile: 0777 218762; Maj Newton Jacob

SECTIONS

Eastern: 135 Trincomalee St, Batticaloa;
tel: (065) 2224558; fax: (065) 2224768 (AST
Link Communication & Agency Post Office –
Batticaloa); Capt M. Puvanendran

Southern: 231 Galle Rd, Kalutara North;
tel: (034) 2226303; Capt Ranjith Senaratne

TRAINING COLLEGE

77 Ananda Rajakaruna Mawatha, Colombo 10;
tel: (11) 2686116; email: lankatg@sltnet.lk

SOCIAL SERVICES

Children's Homes

Batticoloa Girls' Home: 135 Trincomalee St,
Batticaloa; tel: (065) 2224558 (acc 16)

Dehiwela Girls' Home: 12 School Ave,
Dehiwela; tel: 2717049 (acc 50)

Kaithady Children's Home & Centre: Kandy Rd,
Kaithady, Jaffna; tel: (mob) 0777 218762
(acc boys 16 girls 22 remandees 10)

Rajagiriya Boys' Home: Obeysekerapura,
Rajagiriya; tel: 2862301 (acc 30)

Sunshine House: 127 E. W. Perera Mawatha,
Colombo 10 (acc remandees 34)

Swedlanka Boys' Home: South Pallansena Jaya
Mawatha, Kochchikade; tel: (031) 2277964
(acc 25)

The Haven: 127, E. W. Perera Mawatha,
Colombo 10; tel: 2695275 (acc babies 10
children 10)

Hostels

Dehiwela Eventide Home for Women: 8 School
Ave, Dehiwela; tel: 2728542 (acc 34)

Hope House Home for Employed Disabled Men:
11 Sir James Peiris Mawatha, Colombo 2;
tel: (11) 2324660 ext 200 (acc 12)

Ladies' Hostel (1): 18 Sri Saugathodaya
Mawatha, Colombo 2; tel: (11) 2544004 (acc 82)

Ladies' Hostel (2): 30 Union Pl, Colombo 2:
tel: (11) 2421318 (acc 78)

Rawathawatte Hostel for Women: 14 Charles Pl,

Rawathawatte, Moratuwa; tel: 4213018
(acc working girls 28)

Rajagiriya Hostels & William Fleming Memorial
Shelter for Destitutes: 1700 Cotta Rd,
Rajagiriya; tel: 2885947 (acc men 8 women 6
destitute men 12 destitute women 6 working
girls 24)

The Haven: 127 E. W. Perera Mawatha, Colombo
10; tel: 2695275 (acc unwed mothers 14
elderly women 10 rehabilitation 10)

Community Centres

Dias Place: 16, Dias Place, Colombo 11;
tel: 2423912

Hope House: 11 Sir James Peiris Mawatha,
Colombo 2; tel: (11) 2324660 ext 200

Matale: 147 Trincomalee St, Matale;
tel: (066) 2230844

Rambukkana: Mawanella Rd, Rambukkana;
tel: (035) 2265179

Weerasooriya Centre: 88 Weerasooriya Watta,
Patuwatha, Dodanduwa; tel: (091) 2277146

Child Day Care Centres

Amparai: Main Rd, Amparai; tel: (063) 2223779

Kudagama: Kudagama, Dombemada

Hewadiwela: Hewadiwela; tel: (035) 2266785

Madampe: Madampe (NWP); tel: (032) 2247285

Talampitiya: Mahagama, Kohilagedera,
Talampitiya; tel: (037) 2238278

Wattegama: 34 Nuwaratenne Rd, Wattegama;
tel: (060) 2803319

HEALTH SERVICES

Colombo:

Physiotherapy Unit; tel (11) 2324660 ext 204

HIV/Aids Community Counselling Programme,
53 Sir James Peiris Mawatha, Colombo 2;
tel: (11) 2324660 ext 208

Counselling and Counselling Training Centre

TSUNAMI RECONSTRUCTION PROGRAMMES

Hikkaduwa, Southern Section: Weerasooriya
Conference Centre, Weerasooriya Watte,
Pathuwatha, Dodanduwa-Hikkaduwa;
tel: 091-2277146; Mr Christopher Needham

Jaffna, Northern District: 77 Rasavinthottam,
off Kandy Rd, Jaffna; tel/fax: 021 2225745;
Maj Newton Jacob

CONFERENCE CENTRES

Rambukkana Conference Centre for Camp:
Mawanella Rd, Rambukkana;
tel: (035) 2265179

Weerasooriya Conference Centre: Weerasooriya
Watta, Patuwatha, Dodanduwa;
tel: (091) 2277146

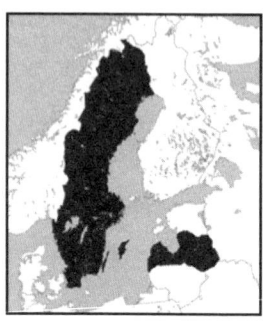

SWEDEN AND LATVIA TERRITORY

Territorial leaders:
Commissioners Victor and Roslyn Poke

Territorial Commander:
Commissioner Victor Poke (1 Nov 2006)

Chief Secretary:
Lieut-Colonel Kristina Frisk (1 Aug 2006)

Territorial Headquarters: Östermalmsgatan 71, Stockholm, Sweden

Postal address: Box 5090, SE 102 42 Stockholm, Sweden

Tel address: Frälsnings Stockholm; tel: [46] (08) 562 282 00; fax: [46] (08) 562 283 91; email: fralsningsarmen@fralsningsarmen.se; web site: www.fralsningsarmen.se

Commissioner Hanna Ouchterlony, inspired by the first Army meeting held on Swedish soil in Värnamo in 1878 led by the young Chief of the Staff, Bramwell Booth, began Salvation Army work in a Stockholm theatre on 28 December 1882. The first women's home and a men's shelter were opened in 1890. Work among deaf and blind people was inaugurated in 1895. The Salvation Army was re-established in Latvia on 18 November 1990 and on 23 January 1991 The Salvation Army in Latvia became a juridical person. On 15 November 1994 the General decided that the Sweden Territory should be called the Sweden and Latvia Territory.

Zone: Europe
Countries included in the territory: Latvia, Sweden
'The Salvation Army' in Swedish: Frälsningsarmén; in Latvian: Pestīšanas Armija
Languages in which the gospel is preached: Latvian, Russian, Swedish
Periodicals: *FA-musikant*, *Stridsropet*, *William*

DURING 2005 the territory began an intensive process of reflection on the questions of identity and mission: What are we? What are we not? In October the executive council spent three days together to think, discuss and pray about these questions based on the text 'Seek the peace and prosperity of the city to which I have sent you' (Jeremiah 29:7 – paraphrased).

This is an ongoing procedure and during 2006 literature, including eye-catching posters, was sent to every Army centre in the territory on the subject. As part of the same project, steps were taken at corps level to strengthen the working relationship between field and social work. This proved beneficial to the territory's overall mission.

At the beginning of May 2005 the territory's Roots Conference was held in Örebro. Around 500 people of all ages enrolled for the event devoted to worship, with delegates coming from Latvia, Norway and the USA. The programme included seminars and the sharing of information.

In September, International Headquarters held an Integrated Mission European Conference in Stockholm. Dr Ian Campbell and Mrs Alison Rader Campbell were the leaders, bringing with them an international team. In addition, 18 delegates from within Europe registered for a most enlightening and challenging time. During the conference the delegates visited local people, interacting in their daily lives.

The Christmas programme was launched as early as October when a Christmas CD was released. The purpose of the CD was not only to raise money for the Christmas appeal – to help children in crisis situations – but also to bring the full message of the season to its listeners.

The territory decided to give an annual prize to someone from outside The Salvation Army who has rendered services in keeping with the Army's fundamental ideas and principles. The award was named The Hanna Prize, after Commissioner Hanna Ouchterlony, the territory's pioneer.

Early in January 2006, 150 young people and leaders gathered on the island of Gotland for a conference entitled 'No Compromise'. The guest speaker was Captain Danielle Strickland (Canada and Bermuda Territory). The Youth Department has launched a website for young people at www.blodocheld.se

In Riga, Latvia, a public welcome took place for the six cadets of the Proclaimers of the Good News Session. During the meeting four lieutenants who will begin the distance-learning programme were acknowledged.

STATISTICS

Officers 450 (active 199 retired 251) **Cadets** (2nd Yr) 3 **Employees** 1,255
Corps 166 **Outposts** 51 **Goodwill Centres** 36 **Institutions** 22 **Hotels/Guest Homes** 2 **Centres for Deaf and Blind** 7 **Community and Family Services** 16
Senior Soldiers 5,719 **Adherents** 680 **Junior Soldiers** 236
Personnel serving outside territory Officers 8

STAFF

Sec for Business Administration: Maj Bert Åberg
Finance: Capt Elisabeth Beckman
Audit: Maj Birgitta Kjellqvist
Information Technology: Mr Edi Rieder
Legacies: Lt-Col Ing-Britt Hansson
Personnel: Mrs Eva Malmberg
Property: Mr Per Olof Beckman

Sec for Communications: Comr Roslyn Poke
External Relations: Mr Anders Östman
Schools and Exhibitions: Maj Bo Albinsson
Editor: Maj Eva Kleman
Fundraising: Mr Mats Wiberg
Child Sponsorship: Mrs Anna-Carin Wiberg Löw
Mission/Development: Mr Christian Lerne
Marketing: Jan Kempe

Asst Sec for Field/Programme: Maj Kenneth Nordenberg
Candidates: Maj Mona Stockman
Music: Mr Lars-Otto Ljungholm
Trade: Mrs Kerstin Fridberger
Training: Maj Johnny Kleman
Youth: Maj Kjell Karlsten

Sec for Social Services: Maj Britt-Marie Alm
Asst Sec for Social Services: Maj Kenneth Karlsson
Children and Families: Maj Kenneth Karlsson
Community and Families: Maj Ingelise Linck, Maj Roger Blomberg
Disabled and Multicultural Ministry: Maj Roger Blomberg
Rehabilitation: Capt Sonja Blomberg

Women's Ministries: Comr Roslyn Poke (TPWM) Maj Ingrid Albinsson (TH&FS)

DIVISIONS

Göteborg: Järntorgsgatan 8, 413 01 Göteborg;

tel: (031) 10 29 40; fax: (031) 10 29 43;
Maj Kjell Olausson
Jönköping: V. Storgatan 21, 3 tr, PO Box 295,
551 14 Jönköping; tel: (036) 16 31 60;
fax: (036)12 83 65; Col Kehs David Löfgren
Örebro: Kungsgatan 24, 702 24 Örebro;
tel: (019) 14 29 48; fax: (019) 611 47 41;
Maj Per-Olof Larsson
Umeå: Bölevägen 17A, 904 31 Umeå;
tel: (090) 13 50 47; fax: (090) 13 81 77;
Maj Christian Paulsson

TRAINING COLLEGE

Frälsningsarméns Bibel och Officersinstitutesz,
Ågestagården, Bonäsvägen, 123 52 Farsta;
tel: (08) 562 281 50; fax: (08) 562 281 70

CONFERENCE CENTRE/GUEST HOME

Smålandsgården, Örserum, 563 91 Gränna;
tel: (0390) 300 14; fax: (0390) 304 17 (acc 67)

PEOPLE'S HIGH SCHOOLS

Ågesta Folkhögskola: Bonäsvägen 5,
123 52 Farsta; tel: (08) 562 281 00;
fax: (08) (08) 562 281 20
Älvsjö Branch: Älvsjö Gårdsväg 9,
125 30 Älvsjö; tel: (08) 647 52 77;
fax: (08) 556 233 15

SOCIAL SERVICES

Head Office: Östermalmsgatan 71, PO Box
5090, 102 42 Stockholm; tel: (08) 562 282 00;
fax: (08) 562 283 98

Family Tracing Service: PO Box 5090, 102 42
Stockholm; tel: (08) 562 283 75;
fax: (08) 562 283 98

Training, Development, Research Institute:
'FA Institut', Ormingeplan 2, PO Box 2143,
132 02 Saltsjö-Boo; tel: (08) 747 12 15;
fax: (08) 747 12 55
Conference Centre/Guest Home:
'Lännerstahemmet', Djurgårdsvägen 7, 132 46
Saltsjö-Boo; tel: (08) 715 11 58;
fax: (08) 747 11 76

Work Among Alcoholics
Treatment Centre for Substance Abusers
'Kurön', 178 92 Adelsö; tel: (08) 560 518 80;
fax: (08) 560 514 05 (acc 63)

Rehabilitation Centres
Göteborg: 'Nylösegården', Skaragatan 3,
415 01 Göteborg; tel: (031) 25 59 59;
fax: (031) 21 99 86 (acc 20)

Göteborg: 'Lilla Bommen', S:t Eriksgatan 4,
411 05 Göteborg; tel: (031) 60 45 56;
fax: (031) 711 83 67 (acc 63)
Lund: 'Piletorp', Snickarevägen 6,
227 31 Lund; tel: (046) 211 23 05;
fax: (046) 13 79 04
Stockholm: 'Värtahemmet', Kolargatan 2;
115 42 Stockholm; tel: (08) 545 835 00;
fax: (08) 545 835 07 (acc 42)
Stockholm Tyresö: 'Källan', Wättingegårdsväg
1, 135 40 Tyresö; tel: (08) 448 73 50;
fax: (08) 448 73 59 (acc 20)
Sundsvall: 'Klippangården', Fredsgatan 38,
852 38 Sundsvall; tel: (060) 17 31 74;
fax: (060) 17 52 10 (acc 16)
Uppsala: 'Sagahemmet', Storgatan 2 A, 753 31
Uppsala; tel: (018) 10 08 01;
fax: (018) 12 12 39 (acc 26)
Västerås: 'Furan', Skogsduvevägen 11, 724 70
Västerås; tel: (021) 30 27 21;
fax: (021) 30 27 18 (acc 21)
Örebro: 'Gnistan', Bruksgatan 13, 702 20
Örebro; tel: (019) 32 38 40;
fax: (019) 32 37 72 (acc 11)

Night Shelters
Lund: 'Piletorp', Snickarevägen 6, 227 31
Lund; tel: (046) 211 23 05; fax: (046) 13 79
04 (acc 7)
Stockholm: 'Midsommarkransen',
Midsommarslingan 1-3, 126 32 Hägersten;
tel: (08) 19 13 30; fax: (08) 744 20 78 (acc
27)
Uppsala: 'Sagahemmet', Storgatan 2 A, 753 31
Uppsala; tel: (018) 10 08 01;
fax: (018) 12 12 39 (acc 10)
Örebro: 'Gnistan', Bruksgatan 13, 702 20
Örebro; tel: (019) 32 38 40; fax: (019) 32 37 72
(acc 10)

Sheltered Workshops
'Frälsningsarméns Snickeri', Kolargatan 2;
115 42 Stockholm; tel: (08) 664 25 30;
fax: (08) 664 03 60 (acc 28)

Drop-in Centre
Stockholm: Bergsundsstrand 51, 117 38
Stockholm; tel: (08) 34 85 98;
fax: (08) 31 97 85

Harbour Light Corps
'Fyrbåkskåren', S:t Eriksgatan 4, 411 05
Göteborg; tel: (031) 19 82 18

Advisory Service
Uppsala: 'Brobygget', S:t Persgatan 20,
753 20 Uppsala; tel: (018) 71 05 44;
fax: (018) 14 84 59

This woman is one of many people benefiting from a Salvation Army project to supply water to communities in China

Top left: HIV/Aids health education given to a class in China

Above: Biogas stoves supplied to families in China

Left and below: Communities in Myanmar and Ghana value these Salvation Army water projects

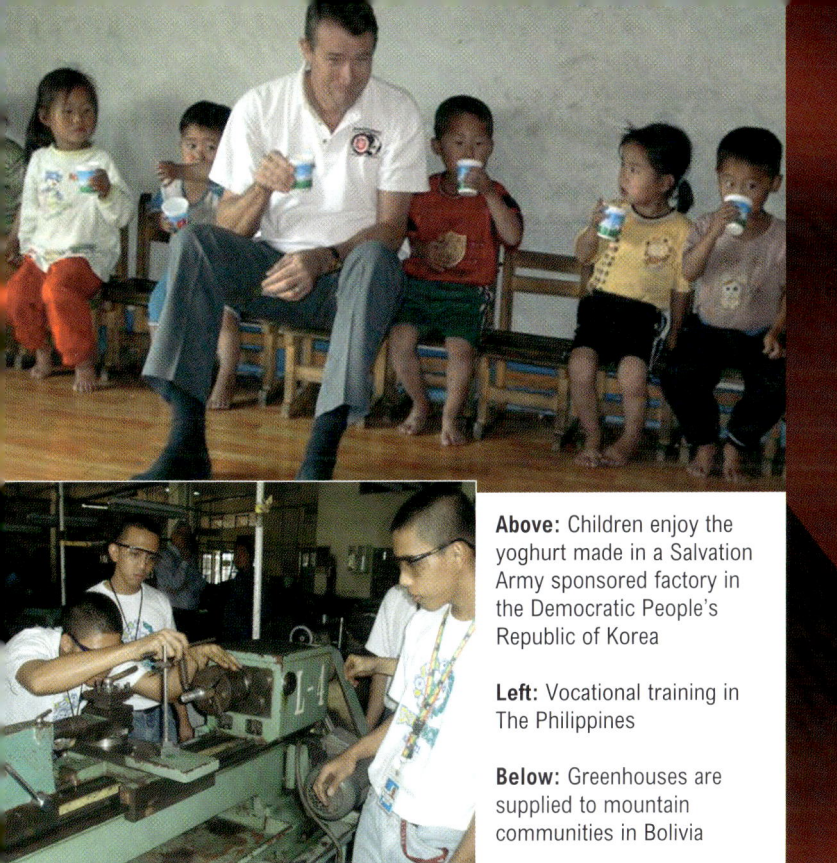

Above: Children enjoy the yoghurt made in a Salvation Army sponsored factory in the Democratic People's Republic of Korea

Left: Vocational training in The Philippines

Below: Greenhouses are supplied to mountain communities in Bolivia

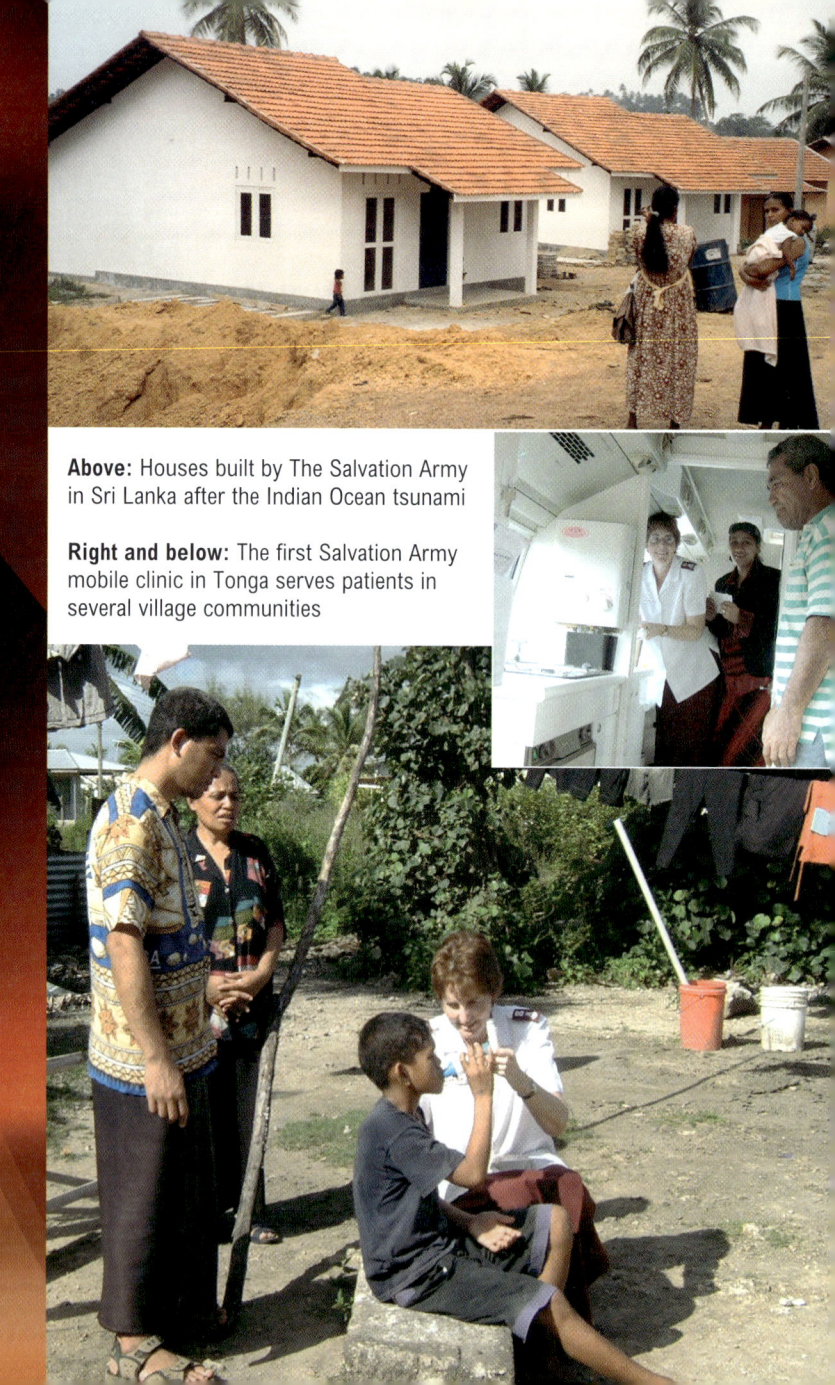

Above: Houses built by The Salvation Army in Sri Lanka after the Indian Ocean tsunami

Right and below: The first Salvation Army mobile clinic in Tonga serves patients in several village communities

Work Among Children and Families

Pre-Schools

Jönköping: 'Vårsol', Von Platensgatan 10,
553 13 Jönköping; tel: (036) 71 15 02;
fax: (036) 71 21 90 (acc 17)
Umeå: 'Krubban', Måttgränd 74, 906 24
Umeå; tel: (090) 18 05 90;
fax: (090) 18 27 88 (acc 18)
Västra Frölunda: 'Morgonsol', Poppelgatan 11;
PO Box 5003, 426 05 Västra Frölunda;
tel/fax: (013) 29 10 29 (acc 34)

School and Treatment Centre for Adolescents

'Sundsgården', 179 96 Svartsjö;
tel: (08) 560 428 21; fax: (08) 560 425 00
(acc 27)

Treatment Centre for Families

'FAM-Huset', Hagvägen 1, 513 32 Fristad;
tel: (033) 21 01 62; fax: (033) 21 01 63
(acc adults 8, babies 8)

Emergency Diagnostic and Short-term Treatment Centre

'Vårsol', Von Platensgatan 10, 553 13
Jönköping; tel: (036) 16 74 58;
fax: (036) 71 21 90 (acc 6)

Group Homes for Adolescents

Jönköping: 'Vårsols Ungdomsboende', V:a
Storgatan 21, 553 15 Jönköping;
tel: (036) 17 32 75; fax: (036) 17 32 74 (acc
6)
Stockholm: 'Locus', Grev Turegatan 66, 114 38
Stockholm; tel: (08) 667 21 82;
fax: (08) 667 21 87 (acc 14)

Family Centre with Advisory Service

'Vårsols Familjecenter', V:a Storgatan 21, 553
15 Jönköping; tel: (036) 17 32 72;
fax: (036) 17 32 74

Vacation Centres for Children

Gävle: 'Rörberg', Hedesundavägen 89, 818 91
Valbo; tel: (026) 330 19 (acc 15)
Luleå: Sunderbyvägen 323, 954 42 Södra
Sunderbyn; tel: (0920) 26 57 25 (acc 15)
Malmö: Klockarevägen 20, 236 36 Höllviken;
tel: (040) 45 05 24 (acc 15)

Work Among Families and Elderly People

Centre for Elderly People

'Dalen', Storgatan 14, 571 31 Nässjö;
tel: (0380) 188 11 (acc 20)

Community and Family Services

Gävle: Hedesundavägen 89, 818 91 Valbo;
tel/fax: (026) 330 28
Göteborg: Brämareg 7, 417 04 Göteborg;
tel: (031) 23 80 00
Göteborg: S. Allégatan 9, 413 01 Göteborg;
tel: (031) 711 36 27
Halmstad: Snöstorpsv 52, PO Box 4065, 300 04
Halmstad; tel: (035) 10 53 48;
fax: (035) 15 72 05
Helsingborg: Fågelsångsgatan 12, PO Box 1232,
251 12 Helsingborg; tel: (042) 21 06 44
Jönköping: V:a Storgatan 21, 553 15 Jönköping;
tel: (036) 71 42 67
Linköping: Badhusgatan 6 A, 582 22 Linköping;
tel: (013) 12 14 12
Luleå: Köpmangatan 52a, 9972 34 Luleå;
tel: (0920) 188 75
Malmö: Hyregatan 3 C, PO Box 171 58, 200 10
Malmö; tel: (040) 30 25 18;
fax: (040) 23 12 88
Norrköping: Vattengatan 5, 602 20 Norrköping;
tel: (011) 12 22 28; fax: (011) 12 53 19
Ronneby/Karlshamn: Strandgatan 10, 372 30
Ronneby; tel: (0457) 107 59
Stockholm: 'Elisabetgården', Observatoriegatan
4, 113 29 Stockholm; tel: (08) 30 49 80;
fax: (08) 34 71 37
Umeå: Sveagatan 3 B, 903 27 Umeå;
tel: (090) 13 76 16
Uppsala: S:t Persgatan 20, 753 20 Uppsala;
tel: (018) 71 05 44; fax: (018) 14 84 59
Västerås: Hantverkargatan 3, PO Box 430,
721 08 Västerås; tel: (021) 14 65 78;
fax: (021) 13 88 50
Örebro: Kungsgatan 24, 702 24 Örebro;
tel/fax: (019) 18 74 32

Drop-in Centres

Göteborg: Brämareg 7, 417 04 Göteborg;
tel: (031) 23 80 00
Göteborg: S Allégatan 9, 413 01 Göteborg;
tel: (031) 711 36 27
Uppsala: S:t Persgatan 20, 753 20 Uppsala;
tel: (018) 71 05 44; fax: (018) 14 84 59
Visby: 'Krukmakarens Hus', Mellangatan 21,
621 56 Visby; tel: (0498) 21 12 24
Västerås: Hantverkargatan 3, PO Box 430,
721 08 Västerås; tel: (021) 14 65 78;
fax: (021) 13 88 50

Recreation Centres for Elderly People

Malmö: 'Furubo', Klockarevägen 22, 236 36
Höllviken; tel: (040) 45 39 13
Norrköping: 'Ro', Rovägen 2, 610 24
Vikbolandet; tel: (0125) 500 56

Work Among Disabled People and Multicultural Ministries

Deaf and Blind People
Göteborg: S Allég 9, 413 01 Göteborg;
  tel: (031) 51 54 79
Luleå: Åkerbärsstigen 11, 974 52 Luleå
Malmö: Hyregatan 3 A, 211 21 Malmö;
  tel: (040) 611 78 57
Stockholm: Observatoriegatan 4, 113 29
  Stockholm; tel: (08) 31 22 53
Umeå: Sveagatan 3 B, 903 27 Umeå;
  tel: (090) 17 84 02
Örebro: Kungsgatan 24, 702 24 Örebro;
Örnsköldsvik: Postbox 280, 891 26
  Örnsköldsvik; tel: (0660) 163 66

Computerised Workplace for Multi-Handicapped People
'Refugen', Ågestagården, Bonäsvägen, 123 52
  Farsta; tel: (08) 562 281 40;
  fax: (08) 562 281 42

Multicultural Ministries
'Akalla', Sibeliusgången 6, 164 73 Kista;
  tel: (08) 750 62 16; fax: (08) 751 71 61

Second-hand Shops
Head office: Stensätravägen 3B, 127 39
  Skärholmen; tel: (08) 563 169 50;
  fax: (08) 563 169 60
Shops: Borås, Eskilstuna, Göteborg (2),
Halmstad, Helsingborg, Jönköping (2),
Kristinehamn, Linköping, Malmö (2), Motala,
Norrköping, Skellefteå, Stockholm (5), Umeå,
Uppsala (2), Västerås, Örebro

LATVIA REGION (UNDER THQ)
Regional Headquarters: Bruninieku iela 10A,
LV 1001 Riga; tel: [371] 731 00 37;
fax: [371] 731 52 66;
email: info@pestisanasarmija.lv;
web site: www.pestisanasarmija.lv
Regional Commander: Maj Göran Larsson

STATISTICS
Officers 8 (active 7 retired 1) **Envoys** 5
  Employees 134
Corps 6 **Outposts** 5 **Institutions** 4

SOCIAL SERVICES
Leontine Gorkša Childrens' Home: Agenskalna
  iela 3, LV 1007 Riga; tel: [371] 760 17 00
Maternity and Child Health Centre: Bruninieku
  iela 10A, LV 1001 Riga; tel: [371] 727 13 84
'Patverums' Day Centre for Children at Risk:
  Bruninieku iela 10 A, LV 1001 Riga;
  tel: [371] 731 14 63
Skangale School Home: Liepa pag, Césu rajons,
  LV 4128 Liepa; tel: [371] 410 22 20;
  fax: [371] 410 22 21

A scene from the nationwide TV broadcast which promoted The Salvation Army's Christmas campaign in Switzerland *(see page 238)*

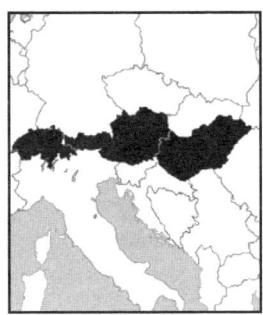

SWITZERLAND, AUSTRIA AND HUNGARY TERRITORY

Territorial leaders:
Commissioners Edouard and Françoise Braun

Territorial Commander:
Commissioner Edouard Braun (1 Nov 2004)

Chief Secretary:
Colonel Ines Adler (1 Apr 2000)

Territorial Headquarters: Laupenstrasse 5, Bern, Switzerland

Postal address: Die Heilsarmee, Postfach 6575, 3001 Bern, Switzerland

Tel address: Heilsarmee Bern; tel: [41] (31) 388 05 91; fax: [41] (31) 388 05 95;

email: info@swi.salvationarmy.org

web sites: www.heilsarmee.ch; www.armeedusalut.ch; www.salvationarmy.ch

On 10 December 1882 Salvation Army operations were commenced in the Salle de la Réformation, Geneva, by the Maréchale, Catherine Booth, and Colonel Arthur S. Clibborn. Bitter opposition was encountered but now the Army is recognised as an evangelical and social force throughout the Confederation. The Salvation Army's constitution consists of Foundation Salvation Army Switzerland; Cooperative Salvation Army Social Organisation; Salvation Army Immo Ltd.

Work first commenced in Austria on 27 May 1927 in Vienna. Unofficial meetings had been held earlier, but the official opening was conducted by Lieut-Commissioner Bruno Friedrich and Captain Lydia Saak was the officer-in-charge. 'Verein der Heilsarmee' was legally recognised by the Austrian Federal Ministry on 8 May 1952.

The Salvation Army's operations in Hungary were commenced on 24 April 1924 by Colonel Rothstein with two German women-officers. The evangelistic and social activities were maintained until suppressed in 1950. After the opening of the central European borders, The Salvation Army was officially re-established on 3 November 1990 by General Eva Burrows.

Zone: Europe

Countries included in the territory: Austria, Hungary, Switzerland

'The Salvation Army' in German: Die Heilsarmee; in French: Armée du Salut; in Hungarian: Az Üdvhadsereg; in Spanish: Ejército de Salvación

Languages in which the gospel is preached: French, German, Hungarian, Spanish

Periodicals: *Espoir* (French), *Dialog* (German), *Dialogue* (French), *IN* (French and German), *Just 4 U* (French), *Trialog* (German), *Klecks* (German)

THE Salvation Army in Switzerland welcomed two important visitors during 2005. The Federal President made an unannounced visit to an emergency shelter in Geneva, but everyone was prepared for General John Larsson's visit for the Ascension Day congress in Zurich. The day's motto 'Together We're Strong' underlined the interdependence between young and old and the unity between social and evangelistic work.

Badges made from pieces of rope, symbolising a strong connection, were produced by residents of a Salvation Army home.

In a humorous TV slot, broadcast nationwide in connection with the Christmas campaign, the interaction between young and old was a central theme. A Salvationist next to a collecting kettle tried unsuccessfully to attract attention with his singing. Some young people were performing a hip-hop dance nearby and the Salvationist accepted their invitation to try a few steps – to the delight of the young people and spectators.

A Salvation Army that approaches people and is prepared to adapt its methods is the image the territory seeks to project.

Highlights of the year included the opening of a corps in Canton Wallis (Sierre); the commissioning of 12 officers, eight of them from Hungary; and the participation of 228 Swiss and 11 Hungarian young people at the European Youth Congress in Prague (Czech Republic).

The European School for Officer Training in Basle became a training college for the territory again, but continues to offer facilities for the training of cadets from other territories and commands.

When storms brought destruction and suffering in the Bernese Oberland, Salvationists from the small Interlaken Corps were immediately at the scene offering support with exemplary commitment to the emergency workers. They were thanked by the authorities

and Swiss military for the way they demonstrated belief in action.

Despite the country's slow economic revival, people still threatened by poverty are the elderly, families and single parents. They are being helped by the increasing number of corps that are distributing free food.

STATISTICS
Officers 432 (active 207 retired 225) **Lieutenants** 7 **Cadets** (1st Yr) 4 (2nd Yr) 4 (3rd Yr) 4 **Employees** 1,359
Corps 73 **Outposts** 20 **Institutions** 48 **Thrift Stores** 27
Senior Soldiers 3,256 **Adherents** 746 **Junior Soldiers** 428
Personnel serving outside territory Officers 17 Layworkers 2

STAFF
Dept of Evangelisation: Lt-Col Franz Boschung
Society and Family: Comr Françoise Braun (TPWM) Lt-Col Hanny Boschung (TSWM) Maj Christianne Winkler (Coordinator for women's groups)
Regional Officer Hungary: Maj Ruth Tschopp
City Commander Vienna: Maj Hans-Marcel Leber
Music and Gospel Arts: Sgt Phillip Manger
Youth: Capts Thomas and Barbara Bösch

Dept of Social Work: Sgt Erhard Meyner
Social French Part: Mr Michel Bonjour
Social German Part:
Prison Work: Maj Samuel Winkler
Family Tracing: Maj Neil Bannister
Refugees: Mr Jakob Amstutz
Thrift Stores: Mr David Küenzi

Dept of Personnel: Maj Marianne Meyner
Candidates: Maj Daniela Zurbrügg
Training: Maj Hervé Cachelin
Personnel Administration: Sgt Christian Hefti

Dept of Finance and Business Administration: Sgt Philip Bates
Finance + Controlling Evangelisation: Maj Peter Zurbrügg
Finance + Controlling THQ: Sgt Kenneth Hofer
Finance + Controlling Social: Mr Michael Lippuner
Property: Mr Marc Hendry

Mission & Development: Sgt Markus
Muntwiler

Dept of Communication: Sgt Pierre Reift
Editor-in-Chief and Publishing: Sgt Pierre Reift
Fundraising: Mr Bernhard Stegmayer
Museum & Archives: Maj Heidi Scheurer
Trade Shop: Mrs Hanni Butler

DIVISIONS

Basel: Breisacherstrasse 45, 4057 Basel;
tel: (061) 691 11 50; fax: (061) 691 12 59;
Maj Hans Knecht
Bern: Gartenstrasse 8, 3007 Bern;
tel: (031) 380 75 45; fax: (031) 380 75 42;
Maj Walter Bommeli
Division Romande: Rue de l'Ecluse 16, 2000
Neuchâtel; tel: (032) 729 20 81; Maj Jacques
Donzé
Ost-Division: Eidmattstrasse 16, 8032 Zürich;
tel: (044) 383 69 70; fax: (044) 383 52 48;
Maj Fritz Schmid

SCHOOL FOR OFFICER TRAINING

4012 Basel, Habsburgerstrasse 15, Postfach 410,
CH-4012 Basel; tel: (061) 387 91 11;
fax: (061) 381 77 63

SOCIAL WORK

Social Services Advice Bureaux

4053 Basel: Frobenstrasse 18; tel: (061) 272 00
07; fax: (061) 273 29 00
3007 Bern: Gartenstrasse 8; tel: (031) 380 75 40;
fax: (031) 380 75 42
2503 Biel-Bienne: Oberer Quai 12;
tel: (032) 322 53 66; fax: (032) 322 60 64
1018 Lausanne: Rue de la Borde 22;
tel: (021) 646 46 10
8400 Winterthur: CASA, Wartstrasse 9;
tel: 052 202 77 80
8026 Zürich: Müllerstrasse 87;
tel/fax: (044) 298 90 60
8032 Zürich: Eidmattstrasse 16; tel: 044 422 79 00

Adult Rehabilitation Centres

1201 Genève: Centre-Espoir, Rue Jean-Dassier
10; tel: (022) 338 22 00; fax: (022) 338 22 01
(acc 109)
3098 Köniz: Buchseegut, Buchseeweg 15;
tel: (031) 970 63 63; fax: (031) 970 63 64
(acc 44) (with gardening and workshop)
1003 Lausanne: Avenue Ruchonnet 49;
tel: (021) 310 40 40; fax: (021) 310 40 42
(acc 23)
1005 Lausanne: La Résidence, Place du Vallon 1a;
tel: (021) 320 48 55; fax: (021) 310 39 34
(acc 38)

5022 Rombach (Aarau): Obstgarten,
Bibersteinstrasse 54; tel: (062) 839 80 80;
fax: (062) 839 80 89 (acc 34)
2024 St-Aubin: Le Devens, Socio-medical Home;
tel: (032) 836 27 29; fax: (032) 836 27 28
(acc 34)
9205 Waldkirch: Hasenberg; tel: (071) 434 61 61;
fax: (071) 434 61 71 (acc 44) (agriculture and
workshop)

Community Centres

1200 Genève: rue J.J.-de-Sellon 3, Destino
(coffee bar); tel/fax: (022) 740 19 30
8032 Zürich: Eidmattstrasse 16, Eidmattegge;
tel: (044) 383 16 96
8001 Zürich: Schoffelgasse 13, Gelber Stern; tel:
(044) 252 35 22
8005 Zürich: Luisenstrasse 23, Open Heart;
tel: (044) 272 85 20

Emergency Shelters

1201 Genève: Accueil de Nuit, Chemin Galiffe 4;
tel: (022) 338 22 00; fax: (022) 338 22 01
(acc 40)
1005 Lausanne: La Marmotte, Place du Vallon 1a;
tel: (021) 320 48 55; fax: (021) 310 39 34
(acc 28)

Holiday Flats

3715 Adelboden: Chalet Bethel;
tel: (033) 673 21 62 (acc 20)
9650 Nesslau: Oberfeld 371, Bühl;
tel: (071) 994 19 58 (acc 5-7)

Homes for the Aged

3013 Bern: Lorrainehof, Lorrainestrasse 34;
tel: (031) 330 16 16; fax: (031) 330 16 00
(acc 52 + 10 flats) (health care)
1814 La Tour-de-Peilz: Le Phare-Elim, Avenue
de la Paix 11; tel: (021) 977 33 33;
fax: (021) 977 33 90 (acc 44) (health care)
1201 Genève: Résidence Amitié (health care),
Rue Baudit 1; tel: (022) 919 95 95;
fax: (022) 740 30 15 (acc 52) (health care)
2000 Neuchâtel: Le Foyer, Rue de l'Ecluse 18;
tel: (032) 729 20 20 (acc 30) (health care)

Homes for Children

8344 Bäretswil: Sunnemätteli Home for
Handicapped Children; Wirzwil;
tel: (044) 939 11 88; fax (044) 979 10 45
(acc 16)
4054 Basel: Kinderheim Holee, Holeestrasse 62;
tel: (061) 301 24 50; fax: (061) 301 24 44
(acc 23)
8932 Mettmenstetten: Kinderheim Paradies;

tel: (044) 768 58 00; fax: (044) 768 58 19 (acc 23)

3110 Münsingen: Kinderwohnheim Sonnhalde, Standweg 7; tel: (031) 721 08 06; fax: (031) 721 42 72 (acc 24)

Day Care Centres

1224 Chêne-Bougeries (Genève): La Maternelle, Chemin Jules-Cougnard 5; tel/fax: (022) 349 50 54 (acc 45)

8280 Kreuzlingen: Kindertagesheim Sonnenschein, Alpenrosenstrasse 8; tel: (071) 672 62 82 (acc 20)

2024 St-Aubin: La Bergerie, Rue de la Poste 5a; tel: (032) 835 39 55; fax: (032) 835 39 56 (acc 19)

8008 Zürich: Neumünsterallee 17; tel: 044 383 47 00 (acc 46)

Hostels for Men

4058 Basel: Rheinblick, Rheingasse 80; tel/fax: (061) 681 21 30 (acc 48)

8004 Zürich: Dienerstrasse 76; tel: (044) 298 90 80; fax: (044) 242 41 71 (acc 26)

8005 Zürich: Geroldstrasse 27; tel: (043) 204 10 20; fax: (043) 445 70 21 (acc 25)

Hostels for Men and Women

3006 Bern: Passantenheim, Muristrasse 6; tel: (031) 351 80 27; fax: (031) 351 46 97 (acc 43)

2503 Biel: Haus am Quai, Oberer Quai 12; tel: (032) 322 68 38; fax: (032) 322 60 64 (acc 24)

3600 Thun: Passantenheim, Waisenhausstrasse 26; tel: (033) 222 69 20 (acc 15)

8400 Winterthur: Wartstrasse 40-42; tel: (052) 212 64 75 (acc 30)

8026 Zürich: Molkenstrasse 6; tel: (044) 298 90 00; fax: (044) 242 38 97 (acc 86)

Hostel for Women

4058 Basel: Frauenwohnheim Rheinblick, Alemannengasse 7; tel: (061) 681 34 70; fax: (061) 681 34 72 (acc 37)

Young Women's Residence

4059 Basel: Schlössli, Eichhornstrasse 21; tel: (061) 335 31 10; fax: (061) 335 31 29 (acc 12)

Refugee Work

Main office: 3008 Bern, Effingerstrasse 67; tel: (031) 380 18 80; fax: (031) 398 04 28 (9 centres 4 coordination offices)

Social Flats

3007 Bern: Begleitetes Wohnen, Gartenstrasse 8; tel: (031) 380 75 41; fax: (031) 380 75 42 (38 flats)

HOTELS

4055 Basel: Bed and Breakfast, Habsburgerstrasse 15; tel: (061) 387 91 11; fax: (061) 381 77 63

1204 Genève: Bel' Espérance, Rue de la Vallée 1; tel: (022) 818 37 37; fax: (022) 818 37 73 (65 beds 40 rooms)

3852 Ringgenberg: Guesthouse, Vordorf 264; tel: (033) 822 70 25; fax: (033) 822 70 74 (24 beds 12 rooms)

YOUTH CENTRES

Under THQ

3715 Adelboden (acc 75)

Under DHQ

Basel: 4462 Rickenbach, Waldegg (acc 100)

Division Romande: 1451 Les Rasses (acc 150)

Zürich: 8712 Stäfa (acc 55)

AUSTRIA

City Command: Maj Hans-Marcel Leber

AT-1020 Vienna Salztor-Zentrum, Grosse Schiffgasse 3; tel: [43] (1) 214 48 30; fax: [43] (1) 214 48 30 55

Hostel for Men

AT-1020 Vienna: Salztor-Zentrum, Grosse Schiffgasse 3; tel: [43] (1) 214 48 30; fax: [43] (1) 214 48 30 55 (acc men 60, sheltered housing 42, external flats 21)

HUNGARY REGION

Regional Headquarters: Bajnok utca 25, HU-1063 Budapest VI, Hungary; tel/fax: [36] (1) 332 3324; Maj Ruth Tschopp

Hostel for Men

'Új Remenység Háza', HU-1086 Budapest VIII, Dobozi utca 29; tel/fax: [36] (1) 314 2775 / 303 9318 (acc 98)

Hostel for Women

'A Válaszút Háza', HU-1171 Budapest XVII, Lemberg utca 38-42; tel/fax: [36] (1) 259 1095 (acc 24)

Refuge for Maltreated Women and Children

'Fény Hazá', IV utca 16, HU-1172 Budapest XVII; tel/fax: [36] (1) 332 33 24 (acc mothers with children 5)

TAIWAN REGION

Regional Commander:
Major Fona Ling (1 Jul 2005)

Regional Headquarters: 273/3F Tun Hwa South Road, Section 2, Da-an District, Taipei 106

Postal address: PO Box 44-100, Taipei, Taiwan

tel: [886] (02) 2738 1079/1171; fax: [886] (02) 2738 5422; email: taiwan@taw.salvationarmy.org

Pioneered in 1928 by Colonel Yasowo Segawa, work in Taiwan was curtailed by the Second World War. Following initiatives by American servicemen Leslie Lovestead and Robert McEaneney, the work was officially re-established in October 1965 by Colonel and Mrs George Lancashire. Formerly linked with Hong Kong, it became a separate region on 1 January 1997.

Zone: South Pacific and East Asia
Country included in the region: Taiwan
'The Salvation Army' in Taiwanese (Hokkien): Kiu Se Kuen; in Mandarin: Chiu Shih Chun
Languages in which the gospel is preached: English, Hakka, Mandarin, Taiwanese (Hokkien)
Periodicals: *Taiwan Regional News*

THE Puli Youth Services Centre serves as a home for teenagers who have been placed in care by the courts. It is a two-year programme. However, because of family problems some of the young people may not return home so a halfway house – Joshua Home – was established. Here the young people are living together with a teacher and being given opportunities to work and become independent.

There was disappointment and discouragement when service contracts for the Yunlin County Youth Centre and the Changhua Children's Centre expired and the government did not allow further

extensions. However, thanks to support from International Headquarters a bid will be made for a new site so that these programmes can continue.

Six Service Corps members from the USA Western Territory visited the region for six weeks, serving in a number of corps, assisting with youth programmes and helping to run a summer camp. Nearly 200 people met to worship together at the Regional Easter Camp – the first such gathering for many years.

Heavy rainfall from the typhoons that passed through Taiwan caused floods, landslides and destruction of roads and farms. The typhoons also destroyed the reservoir's water system so, even with all the rain, there has been a very low water supply.

Through struggles and difficulties, God's hand is at work. There is always a blessing in the storm.

STATISTICS

Officers 15 (active 13 retired 2) **Cadets** (1st Yr) 1 (2nd Yr) 2
Corps 5 **Outreach Centre** 1 **Social Services Centres** 4
Senior Soldiers 191 **Adherents** 128 **Junior Soldiers** 41

STAFF

Women's Ministries: Maj Fona Ling, Chan Suet-fong (RPWM)
Youth and Social: Capt Sara Tam Mei-sun

SOCIAL SERVICES

Homeless
Taipei Homeless Caring Centre: c/o 1/F, No 42, Lane 65, Chin Si St., Taipei 103

Youth
Puli Youth Services Centre: No 302-1, Chung San Rd, Sec 1, Puli Town, Nantou County 545 (acc 40)
Puli Youth Hostel for Boys: Joshua Home, 4/F Room 2, No 15 Lane 261, Zhong Hwa Rd, Puli Town, Nantou County 545

COMMUNITY SERVICES

Puli Community Development Centre: c/o No 62-1, Shueitou Rd, Puli Town, Nantou County 545

CHILDREN REALLY MATTER

Children gather for Sunday school *(below)* at an outpost in Mendoza, Argentina, while a young girl *(right)* receives love and attention at a day centre in Rayito de Luz, Paraguay. Much of the children's and youth work in the South America East Territory is carried out in corps and outposts very often situated in deprived areas affected by poverty and criminality *(see pages 214-216)*.

TANZANIA COMMAND

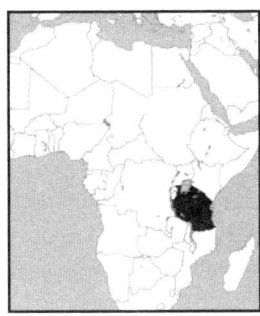

Command leaders:
Lieut-Colonels Malcolm and Valerie Forster

Officer Commanding:
Lieut-Colonel Malcolm Forster (1 Nov 2004)

General Secretary:
Major Stephen Chepkurui (1 Aug 2004)

Command Headquarters: Kilwa Road, Dar es Salaam

Postal address: PO Box 1273, Dar es Salaam, Tanzania

tel/fax: [255] (22) 2850468/2850542; email: Malcolm_Forster@TNZ.salvationarmy.org;

web site: www.salvationarmy.org/tnz/www.tnz.nsf

Adjutant and Mrs Francis Dare began the work in Tabora, Tanzania (formerly known as Tanganyika), in November 1933, as part of the East Africa Territory. In 1950, at the request for assistance from the Colonial Governor, the Army set up Mgulani Camp, where the Tanzania Headquarters is now located. Tanzania became a separate command on 1 October 1998.

Zone: Africa
Country included in the command: Tanzania
'The Salvation Army' in Kiswahili: Jeshi la Wokovu
Languages in which the gospel is preached: Kiswahili and various tribal languages

LIVING the life of holiness in the power of the Holy Spirit continues to be the command's emphasis as God's people in Tanzania become more aware of the Spirit's ministry and power. He is especially moving among the youth.

This was very much evidenced at the first-ever Ministry School for Youth held during 2005 as part of the 'Year for Children and Youth' celebrations. Young people shared in worship, prayer and Bible study, and benefited from workshops on HIV/Aids, mission and evangelism, and training skills.

Times of grace and power were also experienced at three other 'firsts'.

The command's women's rally highlighted the home league theme – 'Being the Woman God Wants You To Be' – and featured powerful and challenging testimony. At a month-long 'Flexible Training' seminar 18 corps leaders received theoretical and practical training as part of their ongoing development, and the command's first training seminar for YPSMs was held.

The commissioning of 10 cadets of the Visionaries Session as officers was led by (the then) Chief of the Staff Commissioner Israel L. Gaither and Commissioner Eva D. Gaither. A few months later the command was delighted to welcome 13 cadets into

243

the God's Fellow Workers Session –
six married couples and the first
single cadet to be trained in the
command.

Work with orphans and vulnerable
children (Mama Mkubwa) has been
strengthened and expanded due to
monies received from USAID. Many
more communities, some in remote
areas, are being helped through this
programme.

Salvationists in Tanzania go on
praying: 'Show your power, O Lord,
our God!'

STATISTICS
Officers 115 (active 107 retired 8) **Cadets** 13
Employees 155
Corps 61 **Outposts** 68 **Schools** 2 **Day Care**
Centres 17 **Vocational Institutes** 1 **Hostel** 1
Senior Soldiers 4,122 **Junior Soldiers** 2,195
Personnel serving outside command Officers 8

STAFF
Education: Maj Lynda Levis
Field: Maj Frazer Chalwe
Finance: Mr Colin Foster (Administrator)
Projects Officer: Mr Frederick Urembo
Property: Maj Frazer Chalwe
Social Services: Mr Frederick Urembo
Sponsorship: Mrs Ann Foster
Training Principal: Maj Herman Mbakaya
Women's Ministries: Lt-Col Valerie Forster
(CPWM) Maj Grace Chepkurui (CSWM)
Maj Rhodina Chalwe (LOMS/SAMF)
Youth and Candidates: Maj Joy Paxton

DIVISIONS
Mbeya: PO Box 1214, Mbeya;
tel: (025) 2560009; Maj Casman
Chinyemba
Tarime: PO Box 37, Tarime;
tel: (028) 2690095; Maj Hubert Ngoy

DISTRICTS
Coastal: PO Box 7622, Dar es Salaam;
tel: (022) 2860365; Maj Isaac Pepete
Mwanza: PO Box 11267, Mwanza;
tel: (028) 40123; Maj Yohana Msongwe

Serengeti: PO Box 28, Mugumu;
tel: (028) 2621434; Maj Daniel Simwali

TRAINING COLLEGE
PO Box 1273, Dar es Salaam

AGRICULTURE DEVELOPMENT PROGRAMME
PO Box 1273, Dar es Salaam

EDUCATIONAL WORK
Primary School for the Physically Handicapped
Matumaini Shule ya Walemavu, PO Box 1273,
Dar es Salaam; tel: (022) 2851861 (acc 175)

Secondary School
Itundu School, PO Box 2994, Mbeya

SOCIAL SERVICES
Community-Based Rehabilitation/Inclusive
Education: Dar es Salaam, Mbeya, Tabora
HIV/Aids Community Counselling Services:
Coastal, Mbeya, Mwanza, Serengeti, Tarime
Kwetu Counselling and Psycho-Social Support
Services: PO Box 1273, Dar es Salaam
Mbagala Girls' Home: PO Box 1273,
Dar es Salaam
Mgulani Hostel and Conference Centre:
PO Box 1273, Dar es Salaam;
tel: (022) 2851467 (acc 110)
Vocational Training Workshop: PO Box 1273,
Dar es Salaam
Water & Sanitation Services: Serengeti and
Tarime

WOMEN'S COMMUNITY DEVELOPMENT PROGRAMMES
Mbeya, Mwanza, Serengeti, Tabora, Tarime

**A secretarial college is run by The Salvation
Army in Shukrani, Tanzania**

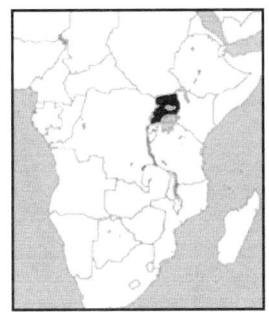

UGANDA COMMAND

Command leaders:
Majors Godfrey and Diane Payne

Officer Commanding:
Major Godfrey Payne (1 Nov 2005)

Command Headquarters: Plot 78-82 Lugogo Bypass, Kampala

Postal address: PO Box 11776, Kampala, Uganda

tel: [256] 41 533901; Kampala mobile: [256] 782 855556;
email: UGA_Leadership@uga.salvationarmy.org

The Army opened fire in Uganda in 1931 when Captain and Mrs Edward Osborne unfurled the flag in Mbale, as part of the East Africa Territory. Uganda became a separate command on 1 November 2005.

Zone: Africa
Country included in the command: Uganda
'The Salvation Army' in Kiswahili: Jeshi La Wokovu; in Kiganda: Eje Liobulokozi
Languages in which the gospel is preached: English, Kiswahili, Kiganda and a number of tribal languages

AT the end of 2005 Uganda became an independent command after 74 years as a 'daughter' region of the East Africa Territory. Sunday 11 December was the day of the inauguration event.

Hundreds of Salvationists converged on the municipal stadium in Mbale, the site of The Salvation Army opening fire in Uganda in 1931. The ceremony was attended by the International Secretary for Africa (Commissioner Amos Makina) and senior officers from the new Kenya Territory.

The year under review saw the start of a five-year programme to educate and assist families and communities suffering from the ongoing effects of HIV/Aids. This included an income-generation scheme for women.

The work first commenced in north Uganda by International Emergency Services (IHQ) has continued with funding from UNICEF, extending to 11 camps in the Lira District. The project seeks to assist the government in providing emergency education relief through the construction and repair of classrooms, and the introduction in many camps of a programme for under-fives.

At the start of 2006 the command's capacity to expand and develop was enhanced by the formation of a division and two districts.

The command is continually grateful to the numerous people who support its work as well as the many faithful officers and soldiers who sometimes struggle against great odds to keep faith and hope alive.

Uganda

Commissioner Amos Makina (International Secretary for Africa, IHQ) takes the salute at a march past preceding the inauguration of the Uganda Command

STATISTICS
Officers 53 (active 51 retired 2) **Employees** 78
Corps 23 **Outposts** 44 **Outreach Centres** 2
   Pre-primary School 1 **Primary Schools** 10
   Institutions 3
Senior Soldiers 3,509 **Junior Soldiers** 2,959

STAFF
Finance: Maj Samuel Wamugoda
Social Services: Maj Rachel Tickner
Women's Ministries: Maj Diane Payne
   (CPWM)

DIVISION
Eastern: PO Box 168, Tororo; Maj Moses
   Wandulu

DISTRICTS
Central-West: PO Box 73, Kigumba via
   Masindi; tel: 046-523672; Maj Joseph
   Wandulu
Southern: PO Box 2012, Busia; tel: 043-
   251296; Maj Eliud Nabiswa

SOCIAL SERVICES
Children's Home
Tororo: PO Box 48, Tororo, Uganda;
   tel: 045-45244 (acc 51)

Community Centre
Kampala: PO Box 11776, Kampala, Uganda;
   tel: 041-532517

Home for Physically Impaired Children
Kampala: PO Box 1186, Kampala, Uganda;
   tel: 041-542409 (acc 30)

PROJECTS
**Emergency Outreach to Internally
   Displaced People**
PO Box 13, Lira; tel: 047-320873

**Emergency Support for Early Childhood
   Development**
PO Box 1227, Gulu; tel: 047-135828

SAU-OVC Programme
HIV/Aids Education for Orphans and Vulnerable
   Children: PO Box 11776, Kampala;
   tel: 041-533113

WORTH Programme
Income Generation for Women: PO Box 2214,
   Mbale; tel: 045-79295

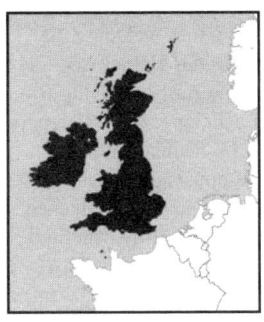

UNITED KINGDOM TERRITORY WITH THE REPUBLIC OF IRELAND

Territorial leaders:
Commissioners John and Elizabeth Matear

Territorial Commander:
Commissioner John Matear (2 Apr 2006)

Chief Secretary:
Lieut-Colonel William Cochrane
(1 Aug 2006)

Territorial Headquarters: 101 Newington Causeway, London SE1 6BN, UK

tel: [44] 20 7367 4500; email: thq@salvationarmy.org.uk
web site: www.salvationarmy.org.uk

The foundation of the territory dates from the earliest formation of The Salvation Army prior to the adoption of that title in 1878 when the Founder, William Booth, took charge of a mission to the East End of London in July 1865. Certain UK corps were first established as Christian Mission stations.

Throughout the Army's history its work in this geographical area has been organised in a variety of forms and territories but before 1990 these were all part of International Headquarters administration. However, on 1 November 1990 a restructuring occurred so that now the United Kingdom Territory is separate from International Headquarters and under a single command similar to that of the Army's other territories.

Zone: Europe
Countries included in the territory: Channel Islands, Isle of Man, Republic of Ireland, United Kingdom of Great Britain and Northern Ireland
Languages in which the gospel is preached: English, Korean, Urdu, Welsh
Periodicals: *Kids Alive!*, *Salvationist*, *The War Cry*

THE Salvation Army matches prayer with practice. Public perception has often put action first, but it would be nothing without its foundation in faith. Hence the territory's slogan 'Belief in Action'.

However, among Salvationists in the UK and Ireland there has been renewed emphasis on practical prayer. Many corps have taken up the challenge to spend days, nights, even weeks in continuous prayer, using imaginative means to involve whole worshipping communities in intercession. The results are beginning to show, not always in spectacular fashion but in a steady strengthening of resolve and a clearer sense of mission.

Some statistics suggest things that are little short of spectacular. For example, a report of October 2005 indicated an overall increase of 54 per cent in attendances at children's and youth programmes. Traditional Sunday schools have been supplemented with new-style children's clubs, often with highly inventive names. Investment in the youth programme ALOVE – 'The Salvation Army for a new generation' – saw more than 200 youth congregations run by young people for young people. Many of them attended the territorial youth rally 'Devotion'.

Corps programmes are often 'doing church differently', responding to communities in culturally relevant ways. Elsewhere there was consolidation, as in the merger of two centres in Kirkcaldy. There was groundbreaking work in social centres, too, such as in Sunderland and Bradford, while the Red Shield Services opened a centre on the Falkland Islands.

When London suffered fatal bomb attacks in July 2005, Salvation Army emergency support was quickly on hand. The situation activated for the first time a city-wide emergencies plan, for which Major Muriel McClenahan had been seconded to the government department responsible. Subsequently the major was appointed an OBE in the New Year Honours List of 2006. Another Salvationist was honoured when Derek Foster, an MP for 26 years, entered the House of Lords in 2005.

The Army continued to speak up for those affected by problem gambling, and was influential in limiting the number of 'super-casinos' planned in the UK. It also made its voice heard on issues including the Racial and Religious Hatred Act, the Equality Act, the Assisted Dying Bill and human trafficking. Its 2005 report *A Home For All* challenged the Government's housing policies.

Public recognition was heightened when The Salvation Army benefited from *The Times* newspaper's most successful charity appeal at Christmas 2005, as well as the seventh 'Pass the Parcel' appeal with Superdrug stores and ITV's *This Morning* programme. Less conventionally, *Soup Kitchen*, a book of recipes from celebrity chefs, raised funds for the Army's work among the homeless.

The Army featured in significant national and local events, such as the Make Poverty History campaign in June 2005, and Liberation Day in Jersey the same month. It was represented at the national Tsunami Memorial Service in May 2005, both for its help to the bereaved in the UK and for UK personnel who were part of the Army's emergency team in South Asia.

The territorial congress took Acts 2:42 as its theme text, emphasising teaching, fellowship, prayer and worship in a Christ-centred community. Other annual events of 2005 included the Roots Convention, the Gospel Arts Concert celebrating the 25th anniversary of the International Staff Songsters, the New Horizons holiday fellowship week and the Royal Albert Hall Carol Concert.

Two UK Salvationists were admitted to the Order of the Founder. Composer Lieut-Colonel Ray Steadman-Allen's work is known the world over, and his classic book *Colour and Texture in the Brass Band Score* has been reprinted. Commissioner (Dr) Harry Williams served as a Salvation Army doctor and surgeon in India for 30 years, then became an international leader, helping set up medical relief work in many countries.

Another UK Salvationist to be recognised by the territory was Robin Bryant, who retired in 2005 after more than 28 years as the Army's official photographer.

At the 16th High Council in January 2006, Territorial Commander Commissioner Shaw Clifton was elected as the next General.

THE SALVATION ARMY TRUSTEE COMPANY
Registered Office: 101 Newington Causeway, London SE1 6BN

THE SALVATION ARMY (REPUBLIC OF IRELAND)
Registered Office: PO Box 2098, Dublin 1, Republic of Ireland

STATISTICS
Officers 2,764 (active 1,392 retired 1,372) **Cadets** (1st Yr) 30 (2nd Yr) 35 **Employees** 5,059 **Corps** 692 **Outreach Centres** 29 **Outreach Units** 8 **Outposts** 25 **Social Service Centres** 105 **Red Shield Clubs** 23 **Mobile Units for Servicemen** 9 **Senior Soldiers** 34,652 **Adherents** 10,558 **Junior Soldiers** 5,968 **Personnel serving outside territory** Officers 107 Layworkers 12

STAFF
Women's Ministries: Comr Elizabeth Matear (TPWM) Lt-Col Beryl Burridge (TSWM)
TC's Representative in Scotland: Comr Keith Banks
TC's Associate Representative in Scotland: Comr Pauline Banks
Asst Chief Sec: Lt-Col Roland Sewell (Special Services)

Asst Chief Sec: Maj Joan Parker
Executive Sec to Territorial Leadership: Maj Clifford Ashworth
International Staff Band: B/M Stephen Cobb
International Staff Songsters: S/L Mrs Dorothy Nancekievill

Sec for Business Administration: Maj John Wainwright
Asst Sec for Business Administration (Risk and Research): Mr David Rice
Asst Sec for Business Administration (Business Operations): Maj Margaret Stredwick
Company Sec: Maj Alan Read
Finance: Maj David Hinton
Internal Audit: Mr Andrew Michell
Property: Mr Mark Johnston-Wood
Strategic Information: Dr David Clayden
SAGIC: Mr John Mott
Trade: Mr Trevor Caffull

Sec for Communications: Lt-Col Royston Bartlett
Editor-in-Chief and Publishing Sec: Maj Christine Clement
Editors: Maj Nigel Bovey (*The War Cry*), Capt Dean Pallant (*Salvationist*), Mr Justin Reeves (*Kids Alive!*); Maj David Dalziel (Literary Editor)
Head of Media: Cathy Le Feuvre
International Heritage Centre and Schools and Colleges Information Service: Director: Maj Stephen Grinsted
Marketing and Fundraising: Mr Julius Wolff-Ingham

Sec for Personnel: Maj Mike Parker
Asst Sec for Personnel: Maj George Pilkington
Asst Sec for Personnel (Development): Maj Sylvia Hinton
Human Resources (Employees): Miss Irene Lovely
Child Protection: Mr Dean Juster
Overseas Services Sec: Maj Elizabeth Burns
Pastoral Care Unit: Maj Ray Bates
Retired Officers' Sec: Maj Ruth Downey

Sec for Programme: Lt-Col Keith Burridge
International Development: Mr Duncan Parker
Evangelism: Capt Norman Ord
Adult and Family Ministries: Maj Janice Williams
Children's and Youth Ministries: Maj Roger Batt
ALOVE: Mr Russell Rook
Church Growth and Planned Giving: Capt Christine Ord

Music Ministries: Mr Stephen Cobb
Family Tracing: Maj Mike Sebbage
Social Services: Maj Ian Harris (Director)
Maj Jane Cowell (Deputy Director)
Research and Development:
Dr Mike Emberson, BEM, MSc, PhD
Compliance and Monitoring: Maj Paul Hardy
Red Shield Defence and Emergency Services:
Maj Malcolm Watkins
Special Events: Mr Melvin Hart

WILLIAM BOOTH COLLEGE

Denmark Hill, London SE5 8BQ;
tel: (020) 7326 2700; fax: (020) 7326 2750
Principal: Maj Melvyn Jones
Associate Principal: Maj Kath Jones
Directors of School for Officer Training:
Training Programme: Maj Karen Shakespeare
Spiritual Programme: Capt Gordon Cotterill
**Director of School for In-Service Training
and Development:** Maj Judith Payne
Territorial Candidates Director: Maj Neil
Webb
Business Services Director: Maj David
Shakespeare

INTERNATIONAL HERITAGE CENTRE AND SCHOOLS AND COLLEGES INFORMATION CENTRE

(including The William Booth Birthplace
Museum, Nottingham)
Denmark Hill, London SE5 8BQ;
tel: (020) 7737 3327; fax: (020) 7737 4127;
email: heritage@salvationarmy.org.uk
Director: Maj Stephen Grinsted
Archivist: Mr Gordon Taylor, BSc (Est Man)

SCOTLAND SECRETARIAT

12a Dryden Rd, Loanhead, Midlothian EH20 9LZ;
tel: (0131) 440 9100; fax: (0131) 440 9111;
Scotland Sec: Maj Robert McIntyre

DIVISIONS

Anglia: 2 Barton Way, Norwich NR1 1DL;
tel: (01603) 724 400; fax: (01603) 724 411;
Maj Alan Burns
Central North: 80 Eccles New Rd, Salford,
Gtr Manchester M5 4DU;
tel: (0161) 743 3900; fax: (0161) 743 3911;
Lt-Col John Hassard
Central South: 16c Cowley Rd, Uxbridge,
Middx UB8 2LT; tel: (01895) 208800;
fax: (01895) 208811; Maj Christine Bailey
East Midlands: Paisley Grove, Chilwell
Meadows Business Park, Nottingham NG9

6DJ; tel: (0115) 983 5000; fax: (0115) 983
5011; Maj Jonathan Roberts
East Scotland: 12a Dryden Rd, Loanhead,
Midlothian EH20 9LZ; tel: (0131) 440 9100;
fax: (0131) 440 9111; Maj Robert McIntyre
Ireland: 12 Station Mews, Sydenham, Belfast
BT4 1TL; tel: (028) 9067 5000;
fax: (028) 9067 5011; Maj David Jackson
London Central: 2nd Floor, 33/35 Kings
Exchange, Tileyard Road, London, N7 9AH;
tel: (020) 7619 6100; fax: (020) 7619 6111;
Maj Ray Irving
London North-East: Maldon Rd, Hatfield
Peverel, Chelmsford, Essex CM3 2HL;
tel: (01245) 383 000; fax: (01245) 383 011;
Maj Michael Highton
London South-East: 1 East Court, Enterprise
Rd, Maidstone, Kent ME15 6JF;
tel: (01622) 775000; fax: (01622) 775011;
Maj Anthony Cotterill
North Scotland: Deer Rd, Woodside, Aberdeen
AB24 2BL; tel: (01224) 496000;
fax: (01224) 496011; Maj Martin Hill
North-Western: 16 Faraday Rd, Wavertree
Technology Park, Liverpool L13 1EH;
tel: (0151) 252 6100; fax: (0151) 252 6111;
Maj Marion Drew
Northern: Balliol Business Park West,
Newcastle-upon-Tyne NE12 8EW;
tel: (0191) 238 1800; fax: (0191) 238 1811;
Maj Melvin Fincham
South and Mid Wales: East Moors Rd, Ocean
Park, Cardiff CF24 5SA; tel: (029) 2044 0600;
fax: (029) 2044 0611; Maj Peter Moran
South-Western: 6 Marlborough Court,
Manaton Close, Matford Business Park,
Exeter, Devon EX2 8PF;
tel: (01392) 822100; fax: (01392) 822111;
Maj Clifford Bradbury
Southern: 6-8 Little Park Farm Rd,
Segensworth, Fareham, Hants PO15 5TD;
tel: (01489) 566800; fax: (01489) 566811;
Maj Ian Barr
West Midlands: 102 Unett St North, Hockley,
Birmingham B19 3BZ; tel: (0121) 507 8500;
fax: (0121) 507 8511; Maj Samuel Edgar
West Scotland: 4 Buchanan Court,
Cumbernauld Rd, Stepps, Glasgow G33 6HZ;
tel: (0141) 779 5000; fax: (0141) 779 5011;
Maj Ivor Telfer
Yorkshire: 1 Cadman Court, Hanley Rd,
Morley, Leeds LS27 0RX; tel: (0113) 281
0100; fax: (0113) 281 0111; Maj William
Heeley

United Kingdom Territory with the Republic of Ireland

CONFERENCE CENTRES

Carfax: Bath BA2 4BS; tel: (01225) 462089

St Christopher's (small): 15 Sea Rd, Westgate-on-Sea; tel: (01843) 831875

Sunbury Court (incl Recreation Centre and Log Cabin): Sunbury-on-Thames, Middlesex TW16 5PL; tel: (01932) 782196

CONFERENCE AND YOUTH CENTRE

Sunbury Court, Log Cabin and Recreational Centre: Sunbury-on-Thames, Middlesex TW16 5PL; tel: (01932) 782196

SELF-CATERING ACCOMMODATION

Caldew House: Sebergham; tel: (01225) 462089 (large house)

Hulham Cottage: Exmouth; tel: (01225) 462089 (2 flats)

Larkstone Villas: Ilfracombe; tel: (020) 7367 4654 (2 flats)

St Christopher's (small): 15 Sea Rd, Westgate-on-Sea; tel: (01843) 831875

Sunbury Court, Log Cabin and Recreational Centre: Sunbury-on-Thames, Middlesex TW16 5PL; tel: (01932) 782196

FAMILY TRACING SERVICE

101 Newington Causeway, London SE1 6BN; tel: (020) 7367 4747; fax: (020) 7367 4723

FARM

Hadleigh: Castle Lane, Hadleigh, Benfleet, Essex; tel: (01702) 558550

HOTELS

Bath: Carfax Hotel, Gt Pulteney St, Bath BA2 4BS; tel: (01225) 462089

Bournemouth: Cliff House, 13 Belle Vue Rd, Bournemouth, Dorset BH6 3DA; tel: (01202) 424701 (office); (01202) 425852 (guests)

Westgate-on-Sea: St Christopher's, 15 Sea Rd, Westgate-on-Sea; tel: (01843) 831875

INSURANCE CORPORATION

The Salvation Army General Insurance Corporation Ltd, Faith House, 23-24 Lovat Lane, London EC3R 8EB; tel: 0845 634 0260; fax: 0845 634 0263

PASTORAL CARE UNIT

Administration and Seminar Centre, including Trauma Care Programme: 432 Forest Rd, Walthamstow, London E17 4PY; tel: (020) 8509 1803; fax: (020) 8520 3755; Director: Maj Ray Bates

Pastoral Support Officers

Helpline: tel: (020) 8509 1803; After office hours tel: 07711 148537

London Central, London North-East, London South-East, Southern, South-West England and UKT Personnel Overseas: tel: (01279) 417673

North-West, Central North, West Midlands and Wales: tel: (01282) 697378

Northern, Yorkshire, East Midlands and Anglia: tel: (0113) 253 7205

Scotland and Ireland: tel: (01506) 854474

Counselling Services: 1 Water Lane, Stratford, London E15 4LU; tel: (020) 8536 5480; fax: (020) 8536 5489; Maj Philip Packman

TRADE (SP&S LTD)

1 Tiverton St, London SE1 6NT; tel: (020) 7367 4500/6580 mail order; fax: (020) 7367 6589

TRADING (THE SA TRADING CO LTD)

66-78 Denington Rd, Denington Industrial Estate, Wellingborough, Northants NN8 2QH

Textile Recycling Division: tel: (01933) 441086; fax: (01933) 445449; email: TA102@dial.pipex.com

Charity Shops Division: tel: (01933) 441807; fax: (01933) 442942; email: cpsatco@compuserve.com

SOCIAL SERVICES DEPARTMENT

Centres for Elderly People

Bath: Smallcombe House, Bathwick Hill, Avon BA2 6EJ; tel: (01225) 465694; fax: (01225) 465769 (acc men and women 31, sheltered flat 1)

Buxton: The Hawthorns, Burlington Rd, Derbyshire SK17 9AR; tel: (01298) 23700; public call box: (01298) 24955; fax: (01298) 73624 (acc 34)

Coventry: Youell Court, Skipworth Rd, Binley CV3 2XA; tel (024) 76561300; fax: (024) 76561306 (acc 40)

Edinburgh:
Davidson House, 266 Colinton Rd, EH14 1DT; tel: (0131) 441 2117 (acc 40)

Eagle Lodge, 488/1 Ferry Rd, EH5 2DL; tel: (0131) 551 1611; fax: (0131) 552 5673 (acc 32)

Glasgow: Eva Burrows Centre, Clyde Place, Halfway, Cambuslang G72 7QT; tel: (0141) 646 1461 (acc 32, day centre 24)

Hassocks: Villa Adastra, 79 Keymer Rd,

W Sussex BN6 8QH; tel: (01273) 842184 (office); (01273) 845299 (residents) (acc 40, day centre 20)

Holywood: The Sir Samuel Kelly Memorial Home, 39 Bangor Rd, Holywood, Co Down BT18 0NE; tel: (028) 9042 2293; fax: (028) 9042 7361 (acc 40)

London:

Alver Bank, 17 West Rd, Clapham, SW4 7DL; tel: (020) 7627 8061 (office); (020) 7428 1119 (residents) (acc 27)

Glebe Court, 2 Blackheath Rise, Lewisham, SE13 7PN; tel: (020) 8297 0637 (office); (020) 8463 0508 (residents); fax: (020) 8852 7298 (acc 42)

Rookstone, Lawrie Park Cres, Sydenham, SE26 6HH; tel: (020) 8778 0317 (office); (020) 8778 0314 (residents); fax: (020) 8778 5822 (acc 32)

Nottingham: Notintone House, Sneinton Rd, NG2 4QL; tel: (0115) 950 3788; public call box: (0115) 950 2060 (acc 40)

Prestwich: Holt House, Headlands Dr, Hilton Lane, Gtr Manchester M25 9YF; tel: (0161) 773 0220 (office); (0161) 798 5860 (residents); fax: (0161) 798 6428 (acc 32)

Sandridge: Lyndon, 2 High St, Sandridge, Nr St Albans, Herts AL4 9DH; tel: (01727) 851050 (acc 32)

Southend-on-Sea: Bradbury Home, 2 Roots Hall Dr, Essex SS2 6DA; tel: (01702) 435838 (acc 34)

Tunbridge Wells: Sunset Lodge, Pembury Rd, Kent TN2 3QT; tel: (01892) 530861 (office); (01892) 533769 (residents) (acc 27)

Weston-super-Mare: Dewdown House, 64 Beach Rd, Avon BS23 4BE; tel: (01934) 417125 (acc 40)

Centres for Families (Residential)
Belfast:

Glen Alva, 19 Cliftonville Rd, BT14 6JN; tel: (028) 9035 1185 (acc family units 20 max 77 residents)

Thorndale Parenting Assessment/Family Centre, Duncairn Ave, Antrim Rd, BT14 6BP; tel: (028) 9035 1900 (acc family units 34 single bedsits 4 max 125 residents)

Leeds: Mount Cross, 139 Broad Lane, Bramley, LS13 2JP; tel: (0113) 257 0810 (acc flats 28 max 78 residents)

Portsmouth: Catherine Booth House, 1 Aylward St, PO1 3PH; tel: (023) 9273 7226 (acc family units 15 max 40 residents)

Refuge from Domestic Violence (women with children)
Birmingham: Shepherd's Green House; address and telephone confidential; contact via West Midlands DHQ (acc 16 families, 4 single women)

Centres for People with Learning Difficulties
Kilbirnie: George Steven Centre, Craigton Rd, Kilbirnie, Ayrshire KA25 6LJ

Plymouth: Mayflower, Courtfield Rd, Devon PL3 5BB; tel: (01752) 660302 (acc residential 15, day care 15)

Stoke: Lovatt Court, Lovatt St, Stoke-on-Trent ST4 7RL; tel: (01782) 415621

Centres for the Single Homeless
Belfast:

Centenary House, 2 Victoria St, BT1 3GE; tel: (02890) 320320 (acc direct access 79)

Calder Fountain (attached to Centenary House) (registered care 28, resettlement 12)

Birmingham: Wm Booth Lane, W Midlands B4 6HA; tel: (0121) 236 6554; (0121) 236 7135 (office) (acc 74)

Blackburn: Bramwell House, Heaton St, Lancs BB2 2EF; tel: (01254) 677338 (acc 54)

Bolton: Gilead House, Duke St, BL1 2LU; tel: (01204) 394499 (acc 67 + 3 flats)

Bradford: Lawley House, 371 Leeds Rd, West Yorks BD3 9NG; tel: (01274) 731221 (acc direct access 51 resettlement 12)

Braintree: New Direction Centre, David Blackwell House, 25-27 Bocking End, Essex CM7 9HB; tel: (01376) 553373 (acc 14)

Bristol: Little George St, BS2 9EL; tel: (0117) 955 2821 (acc 79)

Cardiff: Ty Gobaith, 240 Bute St, South Glamorgan CF1 5TY; tel: (029) 2048 0187 (acc 66)

Cardiff: Northlands, 202 North Rd, Cardiff CF4 3XP; tel: (029) 2061 9077 (acc 26)

Coventry: 1 Lincoln St, West Midlands CV1 4JN; tel: (024) 7625 1477 (acc 97)

Darlington: Tom Raine Court, Coburg St, DL1 1SB; tel: (01325) 489242 (acc 37)

Dublin: Granby Centre, 9-10 Granby Row, Dublin 1, Eire; tel: [353] (1) 872 5500 (acc units 106)

Dundee: Strathmore Lodge, 31 Ward Rd, DD1 1NG; tel: (01382) 225448 (acc 45 + 11 resettlement flats)

Edinburgh:
Ashbrook, 492 Ferry Rd, EH5 2DL;
  tel: (0131) 552 5705 (acc 24)
The Pleasance, EH8 9UE; tel: (0131) 556 3957
  (acc 45)
Glasgow:
Hope House, 14 Clyde St, G1 5JH;
  tel: (0141) 552 0537 (acc 89)
Wallace of Campsie House, 30 East Campbell St,
  G1 5DT; tel: (0141) 552 4301;
  fax: (0141) 552 5910 (acc 52)
William Hunter House, 70 Oxford St, G5 9EP;
  tel: (0141) 429 5201 (acc 43)
Grimsby: Brighowgate, South Humberside
  DN32 0QW; tel: (01472) 242648 (acc 46)
Hull: William Booth House, 2 Hessle Rd, HU1
  2QQ; tel: (01482) 225521 (acc 113)
Huntingdon: Kings Ripton Court, Kings
  Ripton Rd, PE17 2NZ; tel: (01480) 423800
  (acc 36)
Inverness: Huntly House, 1-2 Huntly Pl, IV3
  6HA; tel: (01463) 234123 (acc 27); includes
  Huntly House Resettlement Project;
  tel: (01463) 234123
Ipswich: Lyndon House, 107 Fore St, Suffolk
  IP4 1LS; tel: (01473) 251070 (acc 39)
Isle of Man: David Gray House, 6 Drury Tce,
  Douglas, IM2 3HY; tel: (01624) 662814 (acc 4)
Leamington Spa: Eden Villa, 13 Charlotte
  Street, Leamington Spa CV31 3EB;
  tel: (01926) 450708
Leeds: Spring Grove, 139 Broad Lane, Bramley,
  LS13 2JP; tel: (0113) 257 7552 (acc 6)
Liverpool:
Ann Fowler House, Fraser St, L3 8JX;
  tel: (0151) 207 3815 (acc 38)
Darbyshire House, 380 Prescot Rd, Liverpool
  L13 3DA; tel: (0151) 228 0925 (acc 45)
London:
David Barker House, Blackfriars Rd, SE1
  (acc 40)
Booth House, 153-157 Whitechapel Rd, E1 1DF;
  tel: (020) 7247 3401 (acc 150)
Cambria House, 37 Hunter St, WC1;
  tel: (020) 7837 1654 (acc 45)
Edith Road, 10-12 Edith Rd, Hammersmith,
  W14; tel: (020) 7603 1692 (acc 25)
Edward Alsop Court, 18 Great Peter St,
  Westminster, SW1 2BT; tel: (020) 7233 0296
  (acc 108)
Hopetown, 60 Old Montague St, Whitechapel,
  E1 5LF; tel: (020) 7377 6429 (acc 107)
Riverside House, 20 Garford St, West India
  Dock Rd, E14 8JG; tel: (020) 7987 1520
  (acc 60)

Manchester: 1 Wilmott St, Chorlton-on-
  Medlock, M15 6BD; tel: (0161) 236 7537
  (acc 113)
Newcastle upon Tyne:
39 City Rd, NE1 2BR; tel: (0191) 233 9150
  (acc 66)
Cedar House, Denmark St, Byker, Newcastle
  upon Tyne, NE6 2UH; tel: (0191) 224 1509
  (acc direct access 18, resettlement flats 6)
Nottingham:
Sneinton House, 2 Boston St, NG1 1ED;
  tel: (0115) 950 4364 (acc 70)
Acorn Lodge, Campbell St (acc 12)
Perth: 16 Skinnergate, PH1 5JH;
  tel: (01738) 624360 (acc 36)
Plymouth: Devonport House and Zion House,
  Park Ave, PL1 4BA; tel: (01752) 562170/
  564545 (acc 80)
Reading: Willow House, Willow St, Berks
  RG1 6BD; tel: (0118) 959 0681 (acc 38)
Rochdale: Providence House, High St, Lancs
  OL12 0NT; tel: (01706) 645151 (acc 73)
St Helens: Salisbury House, Parr St, Lancs
  WA9 1JU; tel: (01744) 744800 (acc 68)
Salford: James St (off Oldfield Rd), Gtr
  Manchester M3 5HP; tel: (0161) 831 7020/
  7040 (acc 38)
Sheffield: 161 Fitzwilliam St; Office and Postal
  Address: 126 Charter Row, S1 4HY;
  tel: (0114) 272 5158 (acc 51)
Skegness: Witham Lodge, Alexandra Rd,
  PE25 3TL; tel: (01754) 899151 (acc 30)
Southampton: Mountbatten Centre, 57 Oxford St,
  Hants SO14 3DL; tel: (023) 8033 3508/
  8063 7259
Stoke-on-Trent: Vale St, Staffs ST4 7RN;
  tel: (01782) 744374 (acc 64 + 4 training flats)
Sunderland: Swan Lodge, High St East,
  SR1 2AU; tel: (0191) 565 5411 (acc 50)
Swindon: Davis House, Turl St, Wilts SN1 1EF;
  tel: (01793) 531107/8/9 (acc 121)
Warrington: James Lee House, Brick St,
  Howley, Cheshire WA1 2PD;
  tel: (01925) 636496 (acc 54)

Children's Homes/Centres (Residential)
Dublin:
Lefroy Night Light, 12-14 Eden Quay, Dublin 1,
  Eire; tel: [353] (1) 874 3762 (acc 8 overnight
  emergency beds)
Lefroy Support Flats, 12-14 Eden Quay,
  Dublin 1, Eire; tel: [353] (1) 874 3762 (acc 7)
Leeds: Spring Grove, 139 Broad Lane, Bramley,
  LS13 2JP; tel: (0113) 257 7552 (acc 6 female
  care leavers)

London: The Haven, Springfield Rd, SE26 6HG; tel: (020) 8659 4033/4 (acc 18)

Day Care for Children

Leeds: Copper Beech Day Nursery, 137 Broad Lane, Bramley, LS13 2JP; tel: (0113) 256 5820 (registered for 62)

There are a further 7 Day Nurseries, 27 Preschools/Playgroups, 4 Crèches and 14 Out of School Clubs attached to centres and corps

Domiciliary Care (elderly)

Community Care Service (Angus): 24 West High St, Forfar, DD8 1BA; tel: (01307) 469393

Drop In Centres

Edinburgh: 77 Bread St, EH3 9AH; tel: (0131) 228 5351

Glasgow: Laurieston Centre, 39 South Portland Steeet, G5 9JL; tel: (0141) 429 6533

London: 97 Rochester Row, SW1P 1LJ; tel: (020) 7233 9862

Norwich: Pottergate Arc, 28 Pottergate, NR2 1DX; tel: (01603) 663496

Southampton: H2O Project, 57 Oxford Street, SO14 3DL; tel: (023) 8022 4632

Employment Training Centres

Hadleigh: Castle Ave, Castle Lane, Hadleigh, Benfleet, Essex SS7 2AS; tel: (01702) 552963

Norwich: Employment 2000, Calvert St; tel: (01603) 761175

Night Shelter

Dublin: Cedar House, Marlborough Pl, Dublin 2, Eire; tel: [353] (1) 873 1241 (acc 50)

Outreach Teams

Bristol: Little George St, BS2 9EL; tel: (0117) 955 2821

Cardiff: Bus Project, Ty Gobaith, 240 Bute St, S Glam CF1 5TY; tel: (029) 2048 0187

London: Faith House, 11 Argyle St, King's Cross, WC1H 8EJ; tel: (020) 7837 5149

York: Homeless Prevention/Resettlement, Gillygate, YO31 7EA; tel: (01904) 630470

Prison Ministries

Prison Ministries Officer, 101 Newington Causeway, London SE1 6BN; tel: (020) 7367 4866

Probation Hostel

Isle of Man: David Gray House, 6 Drury Tce, Douglas, IM2 3HY; tel: (01624) 662814 (acc 9)

Red Shield Services

UKT HQ: 101 Newington Causeway, London SE1 6BN; tel: (020) 7367 4851

HQ Germany: SAHQ/CVWW, Block 1, NAAFI Complex, BFPO 15; tel: [49] (5221) 24627

Sheltered Housing

London: Alver Bank, 17 West Rd, Clapham, SW4 7DL; tel: (020) 7627 8061 (acc single 6, double 2)

Tunbridge Wells:
Charles Court, Pembury Rd, TN2 3QQ; tel: (01892) 547439 (acc single 9, double 8)

Addiction Service

Bristol: Bridge Project, Little George St, BS2 9EL; tel: (0117) 955 2821 (acc 32)

Cardiff: Bridge Project, Ty Gobiath, 240 Bute St, CF1 5TY; tel: (029) 2048 0187 (acc 15)

Greenock: Fewster House, 10 Terrace Rd, Greenock, Renfrewshire PA15 1DJ; tel: (01475) 721572 (acc 39)

Highworth: Gloucester House, 6 High St, Swindon, Wilts SN6 7AG; tel: (01793) 762365 (acc 12, Halfway House 3, day programme 4)

London: Greig House Addiction Services, 20 Garford St, West India Dock Rd, E14 8JG; tel: (020) 7987 5658 (acc 25)

Stirling: Harm Reduction Service, SA Hall, Drip Road, FK8 1RA

Biomedical Services

Biomedical Support Services are provided across Social Work disciplines in partnership with the University of Kent, Canterbury

The Salvation Army matches prayer with practice. Public perception has often put action first, but it would be nothing without its foundation in faith. Hence the territory's slogan 'Belief in Action'.

THE UNITED STATES OF AMERICA

National leaders:
Commissioners Israel L. and Eva D. Gaither

National Commander:
Commissioner Israel L. Gaither (1 May 2006)

National Chief Secretary:
Lieut-Colonel Barry C. Swanson (1 Jul 2006)

**National Headquarters: 615 Slaters Lane,PO Box 269,
Alexandria, VA 22313-0269, USA**

tel: [1] (703) 684 5500; fax: [1] (703) 684 3478
web site: www.salvationarmyusa.org

The Salvation Army began its ministry in the United States in October 1879. Lieutenant Eliza Shirley left England to join her parents who had migrated to America earlier in search of work. She held meetings that were so successful that General William Booth sent Commissioner George Scott Railton and seven women officers to the United States in March 1880 to formalise the effort. Their initial street meeting was held on the dockside at Battery Park in New York City the day they arrived.

In only three years, operations had expanded into California, Connecticut, Indiana, Kentucky, Maryland, Massachusetts, Michigan, Missouri, New Jersey, New York, Ohio and Pennsylvania. Family services, youth services, elderly services and disaster services are among the many programmes offered in local communities throughout the United States, in Puerto Rico, the Virgin Islands, the Marshall Islands and Guam.

The National Headquarters was incorporated as a religious and charitable corporation in the State of New Jersey in 1982 as 'The Salvation Army National Corporation' and is qualified to conduct its affairs in the Commonwealth of Virginia.

Zone: Americas and Caribbean
Periodicals: *The War Cry*, *Word & Deed – A Journal of Theology and Ministry*, *Women's Ministries Resources*, *Young Salvationist*

IN 2005 'Doing the Most Good' became The Salvation Army's new branding promise to the USA public.

More than two dozen non-profit organisations attended the North American Disaster Training Conference in May, which saw the launch of the first set of disaster training courses written specifically to enhance the response skills of Salvation Army officers, staff and volunteers.

The August 2005 issue of *NonProfit Times*, a national business publication, featured the then National Commander

(Commissioner W. Todd Bassett) in its annual Power and Influence Top 50 and named the Army as the most recognisable name in religious social service.

Hurricane Katrina, which devastated New Orleans and areas of the Gulf Coast, made a previously unequalled demand on Salvation Army personnel, who were on the scene immediately with food, shelter, clothing and cash for incidentals. In the recovery phase, Salvation Army caseworkers are still addressing the needs of those affected.

The National Commander toured the area by helicopter with President George W. Bush and America's donors confirmed their faith in the Army by entrusting an unprecedented $370 million to the Army's largest-ever service response to a natural disaster in the USA.

The Trafficking Victims Protection Reauthorization Act of 2005, mandating the first national survey of the commercial sex industry in the USA, was passed by the House of Representatives and Senate. The National Initiative Against Sexual Trafficking staff advocated the passage of this bill and the national leaders were at the White House for its signing by President Bush.

NATIONAL STATISTICS
(incorporating all USA territories)
Officers 5,409 (active 3,553 retired 1,856)
Cadets (1st Yr) 122 (2nd Yr) 134 **Employees** 60,619

Corps 1,286 **Outposts** 32 **Institutions** 743
Senior Soldiers 84,620 **Adherents** 17,034
Junior Soldiers 27,893

STATISTICS (NATIONAL HEADQUARTERS)
Officers (active) 26 **Employees** 61

STAFF
Women's Ministries: Comr Eva D. Gaither (NPWM) Lt-Col E. Sue Swanson (NSWM) (NRVAVS); fax: (703) 684 5511
Asst Nat Chief Sec: Maj Sandra Defibaugh
Nat Treasurer and Nat Sec for Business Administration: Lt-Col John Falin
Nat Sec for Personnel: Lt-Col Judy Falin
Nat Sec for Programme: Maj Gary Miller; fax: (703) 519 5880
Nat Social Services Sec: Maj Ronald Foreman fax: (703) 519 5889
Nat Community Relations and Development Sec: Maj George Hood; fax: (703) 684 5538
Nat Editor-in-Chief and Literary Sec: Maj Edward Forster; fax: (703) 684 5539
Nat Consultant on Christian Education: Maj Dorothy Hitzka; fax: (703) 519 5880
Salvation Army World Service Office (SAWSO): Lt-Col Daniel L. Starrett, jr; fax: (703) 684 5536

ARCHIVES AND RESEARCH CENTRE
Email: Archives@usn.salvationarmy.org

Not long after becoming USA national leaders, Commissioners Israel L. and Eva D. Gaither are received by President George W. Bush in the Oval Office at the White House

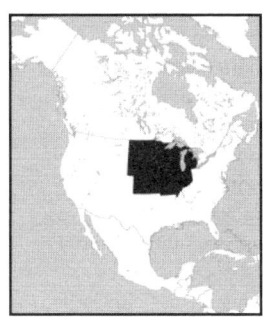

USA CENTRAL TERRITORY

Territorial leaders:
Commissioners Kenneth and Joy Baillie

Territorial Commander:
Commissioner Kenneth Baillie (13 Nov 2002)

Chief Secretary:
Lieut-Colonel Paul R. Seiler (1 Jul 2006)

Territorial Headquarters: 10 W Algonquin Rd, Des Plaines, IL 60016-6006, USA

tel: [1] (847) 294-2000; fax: [1] (847) 294-2295; web site: www.usc.salvationarmy.org

The Salvation Army was incorporated as a religious and charitable corporation in the State of Illinois in 1913 as 'The Salvation Army' and is qualified to conduct its affairs in all of the states of the territory.

Zone: Americas and Caribbean
USA states included in the territory: Illinois, Indiana, Iowa, Kansas, Michigan, Minnesota, Missouri, Nebraska, North Dakota, South Dakota, Wisconsin
'The Salvation Army' in Spanish: Ejército de Salvación; in Swedish: Frälsningsarmén
Languages in which the gospel is preached: English, Korean, Laotian, Russian, Spanish, Swedish
Periodical: *Central Connection*

REFLECTING the territorial emphasis of delving deeper into God's word and putting into action its transforming truths, the territory's outreach increased, with more divisions and corps sending mission teams overseas than ever before and child sponsorship reaching a record high.

The territory's Partners in Mission relationships were enriched through exchange visits with India Central and South America West. The Philippines received editorial support for its women's ministries and Sunday school materials.

The territory helped sponsor the first All-Africa Congress and sent representatives. Territorial personnel in overseas appointments reached its highest peak in more than a decade (27 in 10 countries) and 29 young people served on summer mission teams domestically and in Ecuador, Malawi and Ukraine. Two interns served in Chile.

Discipleship Training courses were ordered by nearly a third of the corps and were translated into Spanish and shared with territories around the world. A territorial translation committee was created to help the territory's nearly two dozen Hispanic corps and ministries.

Supporting the international Year

for Children and Youth, special emphasis was placed on youth programming. Held in conjunction with commissioning, YouthQuake 6.05 featured speakers from the Canada and Bermuda Territory's War College to shake up 3,200 delegates, 500 of whom joined the 'Be a Hero' campaign. A new territorial merit award, the Silver Crest, was introduced for girls who are both sunbeams and junior soldiers.

The college for officer training commissioned 39 officers in one of its largest and most ethnically diverse sessions and later welcomed 30 cadets of the Heralds of the Good News Session.

Several corps and institutional facilities were dedicated or renovated. The process for selecting locations for Ray and Joan Kroc Corps Community Centres continued.

The vision of Korean officers who started a Korean corps in Chicago, Illinois, came to fruition with a new building and name: The Salvation Army Mayfair Community Church. Metropolitan Division highlighted Chicago's cultural diversity at its 'Mosaic of Praise'.

Disaster relief efforts centred on the Gulf Coast hurricanes (every division assisted evacuees), tornadoes in Wisconsin and Indiana, a Midwestern heatwave and continuing aid for victims of the Indian Ocean tsunami. Indiana Division received a $1 million corporate grant for emergency services.

SATERN (Salvation Army Team Emergency Radio Network) reached a record membership of more than 3,200 ham radio operators.

In support of his administration's homeless relief grant, President George W. Bush toured a Salvation Army shelter in Minnesota. The Access House Safe Haven, Kansas City, Missouri, won the territorial award for best social services programme and Springfield Corps, Illinois, received a state award for helping its shelter residents find employment.

Central Music Institute featured The Netherlands Territorial Music Director and hosted several international students, while Central Bible and Leadership Institute inspired and equipped nearly 600 delegates. The fifth territorial worship arts retreat focused on transformational worship, drawing delegates from other USA territories and Canada. The first territorial men's ministries conference took place.

STATISTICS

Officers 1,219 (active 762 retired 457) **Cadets** (1st Yr) 27 (2nd Yr) 28 **Employees** 12,184
Corps 269 **Institutions** 134
Senior Soldiers 19,192 **Adherents** 3,383 **Junior Soldiers** 5,282
Personnel serving outside territory Officers 27

STAFF

Personnel: Lt-Col Harry Brocksieck
Programme: Maj Charles R. McCarty
Business: Lt-Col Mickey L. McLaren
Adult Rehabilitation Centres: Maj Graham Allan
Audit: Maj David Clark
Candidates: Majs Andrew S. and Cheryl Miller
Community Relations and Development: Majs Ralph and Susan Bukiewicz
Corps Mission and Adult Ministries: Maj Russell Sjogren
Evangelism and Corps Growth: Maj Jan Sjogren

Finance: Maj Robert Doliber
Information Technology: Mr Ronald E. Shoults
Legal and Legacy: Maj Donald L. Lenz
Music and Gospel Arts: B/M William
F. Himes Jr, OF
Officer Resource and Development:
Lt-Col Barbara Brocksieck
Pastoral Care Officers: Majors Larry and
Margo Thorson
Property: Maj David Corliss
Resource Connection Dept: Mr Robert Jones
Risk Management: Maj Norman R. Nonnweiler
Social Services: Maj Richard E. Vander Weele
Training: Maj Jeffrey Smith
Women's Ministries: Comr Joy Baillie (TPWM)
Lt-Col Carol Seiler (TSWM) Maj Mary
Corliss (TCCMS/TMFS)
Youth: Majs Robert and Collette Webster

DIVISIONS

Eastern Michigan: 16130 Northland Dr,
Southfield, MI 48075-5218;
tel: (248) 443-5500; Maj Norman S. Marshall
Heartland: 401 NE Adams St, Peoria,
IL 61603-4201; tel: (309) 655-7220;
Maj Merle Heatwole
Indiana: 3100 N Meridian St, Indianapolis,
IN 46208-4718; tel: (317) 937-7000;
Maj Richard Amick
Kansas and Western Missouri: 3637
Broadway, Kansas City, MO 64111-2503;
tel: (816) 756-1455; Lt-Col Theodore J. Dalberg
Metropolitan: 5040 N Pulaski Rd, Chicago, IL
60630-2788; tel: (773) 725-1100;
Lt-Col David E. Grindle
Midland: 1130 Hampton Ave, St Louis, MO
63139-3147; tel: (314) 646-3000;
Maj Dennis L. R. Strissel
Northern: 2445 Prior Ave, Roseville, MN
55113-2714; tel: (651) 746-3400; Maj Daniel
Sjogren
Western: 3612 Cuming St, Omaha,
NE 68131-1900; tel: (402) 898-5900;
Lt-Col William Harfoot
Western Michigan and Northern Indiana:
1215 E Fulton, Grand Rapids, MI 49503-
3849; tel: (616) 459-3433; Maj James Nauta
Wisconsin and Upper Michigan: 11315 W
Watertown Plank Rd, Wauwatosa, WI
53226-0019; tel: (414) 302-4300; Maj Robert
E. Thomson, jr

COLLEGE FOR OFFICER TRAINING

700 W Brompton Ave, Chicago, IL 60657-1831;
tel: (773) 524-2000

SOCIAL SERVICES
Adult Rehabilitation Centres

Chicago (Central), IL 506 N Des Plaines St;
tel: (312) 738-4367 (acc 200)
Chicago (North Side), IL 60614: 2258 N
Clybourn Ave; tel: (773) 477-1771 (acc 135)
Davenport, IA 52806: 4001 N Brady St;
tel: (563) 323-2748 (acc 80)
Des Moines, IA 50309-4897: 133 E Second St;
tel: (515) 243-4277 (acc 58)
Flint, MI 48506: 2200 N Dort Highway;
tel: (810) 234-2678 (acc 122)
Fort Wayne, IN 46802: 427 W Washington Blvd;
tel: (260) 424-1655 (acc 55)
Gary, IN 46402: 1351 W Eleventh Ave;
tel: (219) 882-9377 (acc 98)
Grand Rapids, MI 49507-1601: 1491 S Division
Ave; tel: (616) 452-3133 (acc 110)
Indianapolis, IN 46203-3915: 711 E Washington
St; tel: (317) 638-6585 (acc 97)
Kansas City, MO 64106: 1315 E 10th St;
tel: (816) 421-5434 (acc 140)
Milwaukee, WI 53202-5999: 324 N Jackson St;
tel: (414) 276-4316 (acc 93)
Minneapolis, MN 55401-1039: 900 N Fourth St;
tel: (612) 332-5855 (acc 125)
Omaha, NE 68105-2642: 2551 Dodge St;
tel: (402) 342-4135 (acc 95)
Rockford, IL 61104-7385: 1706 Eighteenth Ave;
tel: (815) 397-0440 (acc 80)
Romulus, MI 48174-4205: 5931 Middlebelt;
tel: (734) 729-3939 (acc 111)
St Louis, MO 63108-3211: 3949 Forest Park
Blvd; tel: (314) 535-0057 (acc 102)
South Bend, IN 46601-2226: 510-18 S Main St;
tel: (574) 288-2539 (acc 52)
Southeast, MI: (acc 311)
South Campus: 1627 W Fort St, Detroit,
MI 48216; tel: (313) 965-7760;
toll-free: (866) GIVE-TOO
North Campus: 118 W Lawrence, Pontiac,
MI 48341; tel: (248) 338-9601
Springfield, IL 62703-1003: 221 N 11th St;
tel: (217) 528-7573 (acc 84)
Waukegan, IL 60085-6511: 431 S Genesee St;
tel: (847) 662-7730 (acc 100)

UNDER DIVISIONS
Emergency Lodges

Alton, IL 62002: 525 Alby
Ann Arbor, MI 48108: 3660 Packard Rd
Appleton, WI 54914: 124 E North St
Belleville, IL 62226: 4102 W Main St
Benton Harbor, MI 49022: 645 Pipestone St
Bloomington, IL 61701: 212 N Roosevelt
Champaign, IL 61820: 119-123 E Univ Ave

'Mosaic of Praise' highlights the Metropolitan Division's cultural diversity

Chicago, IL 60640: 800 W Lawrence
Columbia, MO 65203: 602 N Ann St
Davenport, IA 52803-5101: 301-307 W 6th St
Decatur, IL 62525: 229 W Main St
Detroit, MI 48208-2517: 3737 Lawton
Grand Island, NE 68801-5828; 818 W 3rd St
Grand Rapids, MI 49503: 143 Lakeside Dr SE
Hillsboro, IL 62049: Box 356
Hutchinson, KS 67504-0310: 200 S Main
Independence, MO 64050-2664: 14704
    E Truman Rd
Indianapolis, IN 46204: 540 N Alabama St
Iron Mountain, MI 49801: 114 W Brown St
Jefferson City, MO 65101: 907 Jefferson St
Kankakee, IL 60901: 148 N Harrison
Kankakee, IL 60901: 541 E Court Ave
Kansas City, KS 66102: 1201½ Minnesota
LaCrosse, WI 54601: 223 N 8th St
Lafayette, IN 47904-1934: 1110 Union St
Lawrence, KS 66044: 946 New Hampshire St
Madison, WI 53703: E 630 Washington Ave E
Mandan, ND 58554: 100 6th Ave SE
Mankato, MN 56001-2338: 700 S Riverfront Dr
Milwaukee, WI 53205: 1730 N 7th St
Monroe, MI 48161: 815 E 1st St
O'Fallon, MO 63366-2938: 1 William Booth Dr
Olathe, KS 66061: 400-402 E Santa Fe
Omaha, NE 68131: 3612 Cuming St
Peoria, IL 61603: 417 NE Adams St
Peoria, IL 61603; 414 NE Jefferson St
Quincy, IL 62301: 400 Broadway
Rockford, IL 61104: 1706 18th Ave E

St Cloud, MN 56304: 619 E St Germain St
St Joseph, MO 64501: 618 S 6th St
St Louis, MO 63132: 10740 W Page Ave
St Louis, MO 63108: 3744 Lindell Blvd
Sheboygan, WI 53081: 710 Pennsylvania Ave
Sioux Falls, SD 57103-0128: 800 N Cliff Ave
Somerset, WI 54025: 203 Church Hill Rd
Springfield, IL 62702: 530 N 6th
Springfield, MO 65802: 1707 W Chestnut
    Expwy
Warren, MI 48091: 24140 Mound Rd
Waterloo, IA 50703: 218 Logan Ave
Waterloo, IA 50703: 229 Logan Ave
Waterloo, IA 50703: 603 S Hanchett Rd
Waukesha, WI 53188: 445 Madison St
Wichita, KS 67202-2010: 350 N Market

Senior Citizens' Residences
Chicago, IL 60607: 1500 W Madison
Columbus, IN 47201: 300 Gladstone Ave
Grandview, MO 64030: 6111 E 129th St
Indianapolis, IN 46254-2738: 4390 N High
    School Rd
Kansas City, KS 66112: 1331 N 75th St
Minneapolis, MN 55403-2116: 1421 Yale Pl
Oak Creek, WI 53154: 150 W Centennial Dr
Oak Creek, WI 53154: 180 W Centennial Dr
Omaha, NE 68131: 923 38th St
St Louis, MO 63118: 3133 Iowa St

Harbour-Light Centres
Chicago, IL 60607: 1515 W Monroe St;
    tel: (312) 421-5753

Clinton Township, MI 48043: 42590 Stepnitz
Detroit, MI 48201: 3737 Lawton;
  tel. (313) 361-6136
Indianapolis, IN 46222: 2400 N Tibbs Ave;
  tel: (317) 972-1450
Minneapolis, MN 55403: 1010 Currie;
  tel: (612) 338-0113
Monroe, MI 48161: 3580 S Custer
St Louis, MO 63188: 3010 Washington Ave

Substance Abuse Centres

Detroit, MI 48216: 3737 Humboldt
Grand Rapids, MI 49503: 72 Sheldon Blvd SE:
  tel: (616) 742-0351
Kansas City, KS 66101: 1200 N 7th St;
  tel: (913) 342-5500
Kansas City, MO 101 W. Linwood;
  tel: (816) 756-2769
Kansas City, KS 66102: 1203 Minnesota Ave;
  tel: (913) 281-5060
Kansas City, KS 66102: 1019 Waterway Dr;
  tel: (913) 342-2173

Transitional Housing

Appleton, WI 54914: 105 S Badger Ave
Brainerd, MN 56401: 208 S 5th St
Champaign, IL 61820: 502 N Prospect
Clinton Township MI 48036-3161: 42590
  Stepnitz Dr
Duluth, MN 55806: 215 S 27th Ave W
Grand Forks, ND 58203: 1600 Univ Ave
Green Bay, WI 54301: 626 Union Ct
Jefferson City, MO 65101: 907 Jefferson St
Joplin, MO 64801: 320 E 8th St
Kansas City, MO 64111: 101 W Linwood Blvd
Kansas City, MO 64127: 6935 Bell Rd
Lawrence, KS 66044: 946 New Hampshire
Minneapolis, MN 55403: 1010 Currie
New Albany, IN 47151: 2300 Green
  Valley Rd
Omaha, NE 68131: 3612 Cuming St
Rochester, MN 55906: 20 First Ave NE
Rockford, IL 61104: 416 S Madison
Steven's Point, WI 54481: 824 Fremont
St Louis, MO 63118: 2740 Arsenal
Sioux Falls, SD 57103-0128; 800 N Cliff Ave
Springfield, MO 65802: 10740 W Chestnut Expwy
Waterloo, IA 50703: 149 Argyle St
Wausau, WI 54401-4630: 113 S Second St
Wichita, KS 67202-2010: 350 Market

Child Day Care

Benton Harbor, MI 49023: 1840 Union St
Bloomington, IN 47404-3966: 111 N Rogers St
Chicago, IL 60607: 1515 W Monroe

Columbia, MO 65203: 1108 W Ash
DeKalb, IL 60115-0442: 830 Grove St
Emporia, KS 66801: 327 Constitution St
Fond du Lac, WI 54936: 237 N Macy St
Kansas City, KS 66117: 500 N 7th St
Kansas City, MO 64111: 500 W 39th St
Kokomo, IN 46902: 1105 S Waugh St
Lansing, MI 48901-4176: 525 N Pennsylvania Ave
Leavenworth, KS 66048: 600 Walnut
Madison, WI 53703: 630 Washington Ave
Menasha, WI 54911: 1525 Appleton Rd
Mishawaka, IN 46544: 1026 Dodge Ave
Oak Creek, WI 53154: 8853 S Howell Ave
Olathe, KS 66051: 420 E Santa Fe
Omaha, NE 68131: 3612 Cuming St
Pekin, IL 61554: 243 Derby St
Peoria, IL 61603: 210 Spalding Ave
Plymouth, MI 48170: 9451 S Main St
Rockford, IL 61101: 210 N Kilburn
Rockford, IL 61104: 220 S Madison
Royal Oak, MI 48073: 3015 N Main St
Saginaw, MI 48602: 2030 N Carolina St
St Louis, MO 63118: 3740 Marine Ave
St Paul, MN 55102: 401 W 7th St
Sheboygan, WI 53081: 1116 Huron St
Topeka, KS 66601: 1320 E 6th St
Traverse City, MI 49685-0063: 1239 Barlow St

Emergency Diagnostic and Short-term Treatment Centre

Edwin Denby Memorial Children's Home:
  20775 Pembroke Ave, Detroit, MI 48219;
  tel: (313) 537-2130 (acc 40)
Wilcox Residential Programs: North Platte,
  NE 69101-2268, 1121 W 18th St;
  tel: (308) 534-4164

Youth Group Homes

North Platte, NE 69101-2258: 1121 W 18th St
Omaha, NE 68131-1998: 3612 Cuming St

Emergency Shelter Care of Children

Kansas City, MO 64111: 101 W Linwood Blvd
North Platte, NE 69101: 704 S Welch Ave
Oak Park, IL 60302-1713: 924 N Austin
Omaha, NE 68131: 3612 Cuming St
St Paul, MN 55108-2542: 1471 Como Ave W
Wichita, KS 67202-2010: 350 N Market

Head Start Programmes

Chicago, IL 60651: 4255 W Division
Chicago, IL 60612: 20 S Campbell
Chicago, IL 60644: 500 S Central
Chicago, IL 60620: 9211 S Justine
Chicago, IL 60651: 1345 N Karlov
Chicago, IL 60607: 1 N Ogden
Chicago, IL 60621: 845 W 69th St

Omaha, NE 68131-1998: 3216 Cuming St
Saginaw, MI 48602: 2030 N Carolina St

**Homes (each of the following have
facilities for unmarried mothers)**
Detroit, MI 48219-1398: 20775 Pembroke Ave
Grand Rapids, MI 49503: 1215 E Fulton St;
    tel: (616) 459-9468 (Kindred homes)
Omaha, NE 68131-1998: 3612 Cuming St

Latchkey Programmes
DeKalb, IL 60115-0442: Camp 'I can do it'
DeKalb, IL 60115-0442: 830 Grove St
Evanston, IL 60201-4414: 1403 Sherman Ave
Gary-Merrillville, IN 46408-4420: 4800
    Harrison St
Huntingdon, IN 46750: 1424 E Market St
Huron, SD 57350: 237 Illinois St SW
Indianapolis, IN 46203-1944: 1337 Shelby St
Kokomo, IN 46902: 1101 S Waugh
Jacksonville, IL 62650: 331 W Douglas St
Minneapolis, MN 55411: 3000 W Broadway
Newton, IA 50208: 301 N 2nd Ave E
North Platte, NE 69101: 421 E 6th St
Omaha, NE 68131: 3612 Cuming St
Pekin, IL 61554: 243 Derby St
Royal Oak, MI 48073: 3015 N Main Sts
Springfield, MO 65802: 1707 W Chestnut Expway
St Louis, MO 63113: 2618 N Euclid Ave
St Louis, MO 63143: 7701-15 Rannells Ave
Wyandotte, MI 49192-3498: 1258 Biddle Ave

Residential Services for Mentally Ill
Omaha, NE 68131: 3612 Cuming St
Permanent and/or Supportive Housing
Coon Rapids, MN 55433: 10347 Ibis Ave
Jefferson City, MO 65101: 907 Jefferson St
Joplin, MO 64801: 320 E 8th St
Lansing, MI 48912: 525 N Pennsylvania
Minneapolis, MN 55403: 53 Glenwood Ave
St Louis, MO 63103: 205 N 18th St
St Paul, MN 55108: 1471 Como Ave W

Foster Care
St Louis, MO 63132: 10740 Page
Wichita, KS 67202: Kock Center, 350 N Marat

Medical/Dental Clinics
Grand Rapids, MI 49503: 1215 E Fulton St
Minneapolis, MN 55403: 1010 Currie St
Rochester, MN 55906: 20 1st Ave NE
Sheboygan, WI 53081: 710 Pennsylvania Ave

UNDER THQ
Conference Centre: 10 W Algonquin, Des
    Plaines, IL 60016-6006

*In addition, a number of fresh-air camps,
youth centres, community centres, red shield
clubs, day nurseries, family service and
emergency relief bureaux are attached to
corps and divisions.*

A survivor is consoled by a Salvationist as she looks out on the scene of devastation after a tornado hit Evansville, Indiana, killing 22 people. Emergency services personnel in the USA Central Territory were on the scene within hours of the tornado striking.

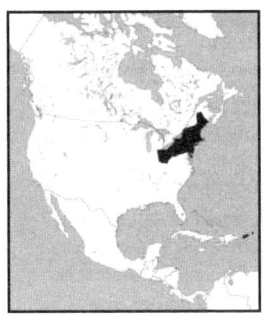

USA EASTERN TERRITORY

Territorial leaders:
Commissioners Lawrence R. and Nancy A. Moretz

Territorial Commander:
Commissioner Lawrence R. Moretz
(13 Nov 2002)

Chief Secretary:
Colonel Larry Bosh (1 Jul 2006)

Territorial Headquarters: 440 West Nyack Road, PO Box C-635, West Nyack, New York 10994-1739, USA

tel: [1] (845) 620-7200; fax: [1] (845) 620-7756; web site: www.salvationarmy-usaeast.org

Zone: Americas and Caribbean
USA states included in the territory: Connecticut, Delaware, Kentucky, Maine, Massachusetts, New Hampshire, New Jersey, New York, Ohio, Pennsylvania, Rhode Island, Vermont
Other countries included in the territory: Puerto Rico, Virgin Islands
'The Salvation Army' in Korean: Koo Sei Kun; in Norwegian: Frelsesarmeen; in Spanish: Ejército de Salvación; in Swedish: Frälsningsarmén
Languages in which the gospel is preached: Creole, English, Korean, Laotian, Portuguese, Russian, Spanish, Swedish
Periodicals: *¡Buenas Noticias!* (Spanish), *Cristianos en Marcha* (Spanish), *Good News*, *Priority!*, *Ven a Cristo Hoy* (Spanish)

THE devastating effects of Hurricane Katrina along the Gulf Coast in August 2005 brought the vision of Territorial Commander Commissioner Lawrence R. Moretz into sharp focus. Before the storm hit, he wrote:

'I see a territory *united* in the proclamation of the gospel, *convinced* of the holistic mission of the Army, *attentive* to the guidance of the Holy Spirit, *responsive* to the needs of the people, *trained* and *skilled* in mission and ministry, *embracing* new forms of service and corps models, *growing* in numerical strength, *planning* to work efficiently and effectively,

demonstrating God's love in active service, *developing* new resources – human and financial, *valuing* each other as members of God's family and co-labourers in the ministry of reconciliation, *reaching out* to find new converts and making them disciples of Jesus as members of The Salvation Army, *affirming* the call of God for new officer candidates, *evangelising* the lost for Christ with a new, aggressive plan for soul-saving and disciple-making, and *worshiping* God as Father, Jesus as King, and the Holy Spirit as Comforter.'

Seventy-one of the territory's

officers and 195 volunteers and employees implemented that vision by assisting in Louisiana, Mississippi and Texas.

With Katrina as backdrop, major initiatives took on new meaning. When the TC led the public welcome of 39 Heralds of Good News cadets everyone's thoughts were on the loss of life sustained during the storm, which reminded them of the ongoing social ills requiring the cadets' message of hope. 'Amazing things can happen when God calls a herald to speak for him,' said guest preacher (then Chief of the Staff) Commissioner Israel L. Gaither.

Delegates to the Territorial Social Services Conference, several of whom would soon comfort storm victims, listened as speakers and workshop leaders shared stories and strategies on how to strengthen the 'patchwork family' of those who have suffered physical, mental and sexual abuse and provide them with freedom, friends and restored faith.

Youth attending the 'On the Edge' weekend in New York City 'submerged' themselves in urban ministry as speakers reflected on the work of Army pioneers, and members of the Territorial Arts Ministry Team learned more than acting, dancing and singing at the annual Conservatory as they focused their attention on orphanages in Nigeria with a 'Be a Hero' fund-raising campaign designed to raise $50,000.

During the opening camp meetings at Old Orchard Beach, Maine,

Commissioner Moretz said, 'We have had a dream and vision, and tonight we have an answer to prayer,' as he presented the newly formed Eastern Territory Songsters. His vision remained strong throughout the year with an emphasis on evangelism which resulted in record numbers of junior soldiers being enrolled. The vision was also strengthened by initiatives promoting the teaching of holiness.

STATISTICS

Officers 1,730 (active 1,132 retired 598) **Cadets** 90 **Employees** 11,946
Corps 406 **Outposts** 4 **Institutions** 144
Senior Soldiers 20,637 **Adherents** 7,426 **Junior Soldiers** 8,342
Personnel serving outside territory Officers 29 Layworker 1

STAFF

Personnel: Maj Mark W. Tillsley
Programme: Maj Richard J. Munn
Business: Maj Warren A. Smith
Asst Chief Sec: Lt-Col Tito E. Paredes
Territorial Ambassadors for Evangelism: Lt-Cols Howard and Patricia Burr
Territorial Ambassadors for Holiness: Majs David and Jean Antill
Territorial Ambassador for Prayer/Spiritual Formation: Maj Janet M. Munn
ARC Commander: Lt-Col Timothy Raines
Audit: Maj John Cramer
Community Relations/Development: Maj Karla Clark
Education: Maj Edward Russell
Finance: Maj James W. Reynolds
Information Technology: Mr Paul Kelly
Legal: Maj Thomas V. Mack
Literary: Linda D. Johnson
Mission and Culture: Maj William R. Groff
Music: B/M Ronald Waiksnoris
  New York Staff Band: B/M Ronald Waiksnoris
  Territorial Songsters: S/L William Rollins
Officers' Services/Records: Maj Peter H. Stritzinger
Pastoral Care and Spiritual Special: Lt-Col R. Eugene Pigford

Property/Mission Expansion: Maj Hubert S. Steele III

Risk Management: Mr Samuel C. Bennett

Social Services: Maj John Cheydleur

Supplies/Purchasing: Maj Frank Klemanski

Training: Maj Stephen Banfield

Women's Ministries: Comr Nancy A. Moretz (TPWM) Lt-Col Gillian Bosh (TSWM) Maj Sharon Tillsley (TMFS) Maj Eva Geddes (TCCM, TWAS) Lt-Col Susan Gregg (OCS)

Youth and Candidates: Maj Ivan Rock

DIVISIONS

Eastern Pennsylvania and Delaware: 701 N Broad St, Philadelphia, PA 19123; tel: (215) 787-2800; Lt-Col William R. Carlson

Empire State: 200 Twin Oaks Dr, PO Box 148, Syracuse, NY 13206-0148; tel: (315) 434-1300; Maj Donald W. Lance

Greater New York: 120 West 14th St, New York, NY 10011-7393; tel: (212) 337-7200; Maj Guy Klemanski

Massachusetts: 147 Berkeley St, Boston, MA 02116-5197; tel: (617) 542-5420; Lt-Col Fred Van Brunt

New Jersey: 4 Gary Rd, Union, NJ 07083-5598; tel: (908) 851-9300; Maj Donald Berry

Northeast Ohio: 2507 E 22nd St, 44115-3202, PO Box 5847, Cleveland, OH 44101-0847; tel: (216) 861-8185; Lt-Col William H. LaMarr

Northern New England: 297 Cumberland Ave, PO Box 3647, Portland, ME 04104; tel: (207) 774-6304; Maj David E. Kelly

Puerto Rico and Virgin Islands: 306 Ave De La Constitución 00901-2235, PO Box 71523, San Juan PR, 00936-8623; tel: (787) 999-7000; Capt Ricardo J. Fernandez

Southern New England: 855 Asylum Ave, PO Box 628, Hartford, CT 06142-0628; tel: (860) 543-8400; Maj William A. Bamford III

Southwest Ohio and Northeast Kentucky: 114 E Central Parkway, PO Box 596, Cincinnati, OH 45201; tel: (513) 762-5600; Maj Kenneth W. Maynor

Western Pennsylvania: 424 Third Ave, Pittsburgh, PA 15219; tel: (412) 394-4800; Maj Robert J. Reel

SCHOOL FOR OFFICER TRAINING

201 Lafayette Ave, Suffern, NY 10901-4798; tel: (845) 357-3501; Training Principal: Maj Stephen Banfield

THE SALVATION ARMY RETIREMENT COMMUNITY

1400 Webb St, Asbury Park, NJ 07712; tel: (732) 775-2200; Maj Jean Booth (Administrator) (acc 35)

SOCIAL SERVICES

Adult Rehabilitation Centres

*(*Includes facilities for women)*

ARC Commander: Lt-Col Timothy Raines

Akron, OH 44311: 1006 Grant St, PO Box 1743; tel: (330) 773-3331 (acc 83)

Albany, NY 12206: 452 Clinton Ave, PO Box 66389; tel: (518) 465-2416 (acc 90)

Altoona, PA 16602: 200 7th Ave, PO Box 1405, 16603 (mail); tel: (814) 946-3645 (acc 39)

Binghamton, NY 13904: 3-5 Griswold St; tel: (607) 723-5381 (acc 62)

*Boston (Saugus), MA 01906: 209 Broadway Rte 1; tel: (781) 231-0803 (acc 125)

Bridgeport CT 06607: 1313 Connecticut Ave; tel: (203) 367-8621 (acc 50)

Brockton, MA 02401: 281 N Main St; tel: (508) 586-1187 (acc 56)

Bronx, NY 10457: 4133 Park Ave; tel: (718) 583-3500 (acc 108)

Brooklyn, NY 11217: 62 Hanson Pl; tel: (718) 622-7166 (acc 136)

Buffalo, NY 14217-2587: 1080 Military Rd, PO Box 36, 14217-0036; tel: (716) 875-2533 (acc 90)

Cincinnati, OH 45212: 2250 Park Ave, PO Box 12546, Norwood, OH 45212-0546; tel: (513) 351-3457 (acc 175)

Cleveland, OH 44103: 5005 Euclid Ave; tel: (216) 881-2625 (acc 159)

Columbus, OH 43215: 570 S Front St; tel: (614) 221-4269 (acc 85)

*Dayton, OH 45402: 913 S Patterson Blvd; tel: (937) 461-2769 (acc 74)

Erie, PA 16501: 1209 Sassafras St, PO Box 6176, 16512; tel: (814) 456-4237 (acc 50)

*Harrisburg, PA 17110-3650: Vartan Way, PO Box 17106-0095 (mail); tel: (717) 541-0203 (acc 62)

*Hartford, CT 06132: 333 Homestead Ave, PO Box 320440; tel: (860) 527-8106 (acc 110)

Hempstead, NY 11550: 194 Front St; tel: (516) 481-7600 (acc 100)

Jersey City, NJ 07302: 248 Erie St; tel: (201) 653-3071 (acc 75)

Mount Vernon, NY 10550: 745 S Third Ave; tel: (914) 664-0800 (acc 80)

Newark, NJ 07101: 65 Pennington St, PO Box 815; tel: (973) 589-0370 (acc 135)

New Haven, CT 06511: 301 George St, PO Box 1413, 06506; tel: (203) 865-0511 (acc 45)

*New York, NY 10036: 535 W 48th St; tel: (212) 757-7745 (acc 140)

Paterson, NJ 07505: 31 Van Houten St, PO Box 1976, 07509; tel: (973) 742-1126 (acc 89)

*Philadelphia, PA 19128: 4555 Pechin St; tel: (215) 483-3340 (acc 138)

Pittsburgh, PA 15203: 44 S 9th St; tel: (412) 481-7900 (acc 127)

Portland, ME 04101: 30 Warren Ave, PO Box 1298, 04104; tel: (207) 878-8555 (acc 45)

Poughkeepsie, NY 12601: 570 Main St; tel: (845) 471-1730 (acc 50)

*Providence, RI 02906: 201 Pitman St; tel: (401) 421-5270 (acc 127)

*Rochester, NY 14611: 745 West Ave; tel: (585) 235-2769 (acc 135)

San Juan, PR 00903: ARC, Fernández Juncos Ave, Cnr of Valdés, Puerta de Tierra, PO Box 13814, 00908; tel: (787) 722-3301 (acc 36)

Scranton, PA 18505: 610 S Washington Ave, PO Box 3064; tel: (570) 346-0007 (acc 62)

Springfield, MA 01104: 285 Liberty St, PO Box 1569, 01101-1569 (mail); tel: (413) 785-1921 (acc 70)

Staten Island, NY 10304: 2053 Clove Rd, PO Box 050169, 10305 (mail); tel: (718) 442-3080 (acc 39)

*Syracuse, NY 13224: 2433 Erie Blvd East; tel: (315) 445-0520 (acc 100)

Toledo, OH 43602: 27 Moorish Ave, PO Box 355, 43697; tel: (419) 241-8231 (acc 60)

Trenton, NJ 08638: 436 Mulberry St, PO Box 5011; tel: (609) 599-9803 (acc 86)

Wilkes-Barre, PA 18702: 739 Sans Souci Parkway, PO Box 728, 18703-0728; tel: (570) 823-4191 (acc 52)

*Wilmington, DE 19801: 107 S Market St; tel: (302) 654-8808 (acc 81)

*Worcester, MA 01603: 72 Cambridge St; tel: (508) 799-0520 (acc 115)

ATTACHED TO DIVISIONS
Adult Day Care

Buffalo, NY 14202: Golden Age Center, 950 Main St; tel: (716) 888-9800 (acc 300)

Carlisle, PA 17013: 20 East Pomfret St, PO Box 309; tel: (717) 249-1411

Cincinnati, OH 45210: 131 E 12th St; tel: (513) 762-5693 (acc 25)

Lancaster, OH 43130: 228 Hubert Ave; tel: (740) 687-1921 (acc 50)

Newport, KY 41072: 340 West 10th St,

PO Box 271; tel: (859) 291-8107 (acc 25)

Quincy, MA 02169-6932: 6 Baxter St; tel: (617) 472-2345 (acc 27)

Springfield, MA 01105: 170 Pearl St, PO Box 971, 01101-0971; tel: (413) 733-1518 (acc 30)

Syracuse, NY 13202: 749 S Warren St; tel: (315) 479-1313

Extended In-home Service for the Elderly

Syracuse, NY 13202: 749 S Warren St; tel: (315) 479-1300

Adult Rehabilitation and Correctional Services

Buffalo, NY 14202: STRIVE Program at Gowanda, 960 Main St; tel: (716) 883-9800

Day Care Centres

Akron, OH 44303: Child Development Center, 135 Hall St; tel: (330) 762-8177 (acc 64)

Beaver Falls, PA 15010-0010: 416 16th St, PO Box 11; tel: (724) 847-9007 (acc 64)

Boston, MA 02118: 1500 Washington St, PO Box 180127; tel: (617) 536-5260 (acc 52)

Boston, MA 02124: 26 Wales St; tel: (617) 436-2480 (acc 78)

Bronx, NY 10451: 425 E 159th St; tel: (718) 742-2346 (acc 45)

Bronx, NY 10457: 2121 Washington Ave; tel: (718) 563-1530

Brooklyn, NY 11212: Day Care Center, 280 Riverdale Ave; tel: (718) 922-7661 (acc 459)

Brooklyn, NY 11212: Brooklyn Family Day Care, 20 Sutter Ave; tel: (718) 735-7286 (acc 115)

Brooklyn, NY 11216: 110 Kosciusko St; tel: (718) 857-7264 (acc 30)

Brooklyn, NY 11221: 1151 Bushwick Ave; tel: (718) 455-0100 (acc 55)

Brooklyn, NY 11231: Family Day Care, 80 Lorraine St; tel: (718) 834-8755 (acc 105)

Cambridge, MA 02139: 402 Massachusetts Ave, PO Box 647; tel: (617) 547-3400 (acc 28)

Cincinnati, OH 45202: 3501 Warsaw Ave; tel: (513) 251-1451 (acc 112)

Cleveland, OH 44103: 6010 Hough Ave; tel: (216) 432-0505 (acc 98)

Danbury, CT 06813-0826: 15 Foster St, PO Box 826; tel: (203) 792-7505 (acc 30)

Darby, PA 19023: 22 N Ninth St; tel: (610) 583-7202 (acc 25)

Hartford, CT 06105: 121 Sigourney St; tel: (860) 543-8488 (acc 69)

Hempstead, NY 11550: 65 Atlantic Ave; tel: (516) 485-4980 (acc 60)

Jersey City, NJ 07034: 562 Bergen Ave, PO Box 4237, Bergen Station; tel: (201) 435-7355 (acc 70)

Lexington, KY 40508: 736 W Main St;
tel: (859) 252-7709 (acc 80)

Meriden, CT 06450-0234: 23 St Casimir Dr, PO
Box 234; tel: (203) 235-6532 (acc 27)

Morristown, NJ 07960: 95 Spring St, PO Box
9150; tel: (973) 538-0543 (acc 95)

New York, NY 10034: 3732 10th Ave;
tel: (212) 569-4300

Philadelphia (Germantown), PA 19133: 2601
North 11th St; tel: (215) 225-2700 (acc 131)

Pittsburgh (East Liberty), PA 15206: 6017 Broad
St; tel: (412) 361-3614 (acc 55)

Providence, RI 02905: 20 Miner St;
tel: (401) 781-7238 (acc infant, pre-school
and kindergarten 110)

Rochester, NY 14614: State Street Day Care
Center, 100 State St; tel: (585) 263-3103

Syracuse, NY 13202: Cab Horse Commons, 677
S Salina St; tel: (315) 479-1305

Syracuse, NY 13202: 749 S Warren St;
tel: (315) 479-1334

Syracuse, NY 13202: University United
Methodist Church Day Care, 324 University
Ave; tel: (315) 426-1231

Syracuse, NY 13202: South Salina Street
Infant Care Center, 667 S Salina St;
tel: (315) 479-1329

Syracuse, NY 13207: Elmwood Day Care
Center, 1640 S Ave; tel: (315) 478-3460

Syracuse, NY 13202: School Age Day Care,
749 S Warren St; tel: (315) 475-1688

Wilmington, DE 19899: 107 W 4th St;
tel: (302) 472-0712 (acc 110)

Family Centres

Newark, NJ 07102: Newark Area Services
Kinship Care, 45 Central Ave;
tel: (973) 623-5959

Development Disabilities Services

Brooklyn, NY 11220: Centennial House,
426 56th St; tel: (718) 492-4415 (acc 9)

Brooklyn, NY 11237: Decade House,
315 Covert St; tel: (718) 417-1583 (acc 10)

Brooklyn, NY 11212: Millennium House,
13 Pulaski St; tel: (718) 222-0736

Glendale, NY 11385: Glendale House,
71-29 70th St; tel: (718) 381-7329 (acc 10)

New York, NY 10011: Family Care, 132 West
14th St; tel: (212) 807-6100

Philadelphia, PA 19123: Developmental
Disabilities Program, 701 N Broad St,
Administrative Offices; tel: (215) 787-2804
(community homes 46 acc 100)

South Ozone Park, NY 11420: Hope House,
115-37 133rd St; tel: (718) 322-1616 (acc 9)

Springfield, OH 45501: Hand-in-Hand,
15 S Plum St; tel: (937) 322-3434

The enrolment of 12 junior soldiers, 22 senior soldiers and five transferred senior soldiers during Easter Sunday meetings at New Brunswick Corps, New Jersey Division

St Albans, NY 11412: Pioneer House, 104-14
186th St; tel: (718) 264-8350 (acc 12)

Evangeline Residences

New York, NY 10011: 123 W 13th St (Markle
Memorial Residence); tel: (212) 242-2400;
fax: (212) 229-2801 (acc 286)
New York, NY 10003: 18 Gramercy Park S
(Parkside Residence); tel: (212) 677-6200;
fax: (212) 677-0640 (acc 293)
New York, NY 10016: 145 E 39th St
(Ten Eyck-Troughton Memorial Residence);
tel: (212) 490-5990; fax: (212) 697-2934
(acc 333)

Family Counselling

Boston, MA 02118: Family Service Bureau,
1500 Washington St; tel: (617) 236-7233;
fax: (617) 236-0123
Bronx, NY 10458: Bronx Belmont Center for
Families, 601 Crescent Ave;
tel: (718) 329-5410
Bronx, NY 10453: Morris Heights Center
for Families, 7 W Burnside Ave;
tel: (718) 561-3190; fax: (718) 561-3856
Brooklyn, NY 11206: Bushwick Center for
Families, 815 Broadway; tel: (718) 302-6921
Brooklyn, NY 11207: Williamsburg Center for
Families, 295 Division St;
tel: (718) 782-4587
Buffalo, NY 14202: Emergency Family
Assistance, PINS Prevention Services,
Hispanic Family Service, Family Court
Visitation Program, Spouse Abuse Education
Workshop, 960 Main St; tel: (716) 883-9800
Cincinnati, OH 45210: Cincinnati Family
Service Bureau, 131 E 12th;
tel: (513) 762-5660
Covington, KY 41014: N Kentucky Family
Service Bureau, 1806 Scott Blvd;
tel: (859) 261-0835
Newport, KY 41072: N Kentucky Family
Service Bureau, 340 W 10th St;
tel: (859) 491-5180
Rochester, NY 14604-4310: Rochester
Emergency Family Assistance, 70 Liberty
Pole Way, PO Box 41210; tel: (716) 987-9540
Syracuse, NY 13202: Family Services, 749
S Warren St; tel: (315) 479-1324
Syracuse, NY 13207: Family Place Visitation
Center, 350 Rich St; tel: (315) 474-2931

Foster Home Services

Allentown, PA 18102: Foster Care In-Home
Placement Services, Adoption Services and
Administrative Services, 344 N 7th St;
tel: (610) 821-7706

Brooklyn, NY 11207: Bushwick Homes for
Children, 815 Broadway; tel: (718) 302-6921
Jamaica, NY 11432: Jamaica Homes for
Children: 90-23 161st St, Rm 401;
tel: (718) 558-4486; fax: (718) 558-5799
Mineola, NY 11501: Nassau Therapeutic
Program: 85 Willis Ave; tel: (516) 746-1484;
fax: (516) 746-1488
New York, NY 10011: 132 W 14th St;
tel: (212) 807-6100; fax: (212) 366-9044
Syracuse, NY 13207: Friendship House,
3624 Midland Ave; tel: (315) 378-0088
Syracuse, NY 13202: Hearts & Homes Post
Adoption Services, 677 S Salina St;
tel: (315) 479-1369

Group Homes for Adolescents

Bronx, NY 10451: Glover House, 301 E 162nd St;
tel: (718) 992-4020 (acc men 12)
Bronx, NY 10469: North Bronx Group Home,
1268 Adee Ave; tel: (718) 515-6600
(acc men 12)
Brooklyn, NY 11207: Brooklyn Group Home,
117 Pennsylvania Ave; tel: (718) 485-9133
(acc men 12)
Buffalo, NY 14202: Family Court Visitation
Program and PINS Prevention Services,
158 N Pearl St; tel: (716) 883-9800
Fall River, MA 02720: Grace House/Gentle
Arms of Jesus Teen Living Center, 429
Winter St; tel: (508) 324-4558 (acc 15)
Lefrak City, NY 11368: Lefrak City Group
Home, 96-04 57th Ave, Apt 3K;
tel: (718) 271-8318 (acc women 10)
Manhattan, NY 10027: Manhattan West Group
Home, 136 West 127th St; tel: (212) 678-6121
(acc men 12)
Manhattan, NY 10031: Manhattan East Group
Home, 241 East 116th St; tel: (212) 534-5455
(acc men 12)
New York, NY 10030: Convent House, 474 W
143rd St; tel: (212) 368-6835 (acc women 12)
New York, NY 10003: East Village Residence,
1 E 3rd St; tel: (212) 228-8306;
fax: (212) 253-1708 (acc 32)
New York, NY 10027: Lenox House, 131 West
132nd St; tel: (212) 334-1394 (acc men 12)

Harbour Light Centres

Boston, MA 02118: 407-409 Shawmut Ave,
PO Box 180130; tel: (617) 536-7469
(acc 87)
Cleveland, OH 44115-2376: Harbor Light
Complex, 1710 Prospect Ave;
tel: (216) 781-3773 (acc 124)

Pittsburgh, PA 15233: 865 W North Ave;
tel: (412) 231-0500 (acc 50)

Hotels, Lodges, Emergency Homes

Akron, OH 44302: Booth Manor Emergency
Lodge, 216 S Maple St; tel: (330) 762-8481
(acc 40

Allentown, PA 18102: Hospitality House,
344 N 7th St; tel: (610) 432-0128 (acc 65)

Bellaire, OH 43906: 315 37th St;
tel: (740) 676-6810 (acc 20)

Boston, MA 02119: Roxbury Emergency Shelter
for Families, 23 Vernon St;
tel: (617) 427-6700 (acc 19)

Brooklyn, NY 11207: Bushwick Family
Residence, 1675 Broadway; tel: (718) 574-2701
(acc families 87)

Brooklyn, NY 11201: Brooklyn Drop-in Center,
39-41 Bond St; tel: (718) 935-0439 (acc 75)

Brooklyn, NY 11203: Kingsboro Men's Shelter,
681 Clarkson Ave; tel: (718) 363-7738
(acc 80)

Bronx, NY 10456: Franklin Women's Shelter
and Referral, 1122 Franklin Ave;
tel: (718) 842-9827 (acc 200)

Buffalo, NY 14202: 960 Main St, Emergency
Family Shelter; tel: (716) 884-4798 (acc 96)

Cambridge, MA 02139-0008: Day Drop-in
Shelter for Men and Women, 402 Mass Ave,
PO Box 390647; tel: (617) 547-3400 (acc 200)
Night shelter for men (acc 50)

Carlisle, PA 17013: Stuart House (Women's
Transitional Housing), 125-127 S Hanover St;
tel: (717) 249-1411 (acc 41)

Carlisle, PA 17013: Genesis House (Men's
Emergency Housing), 24 E Pomfret St;
tel: (717) 249-1411

Chester, PA 19013: Stepping Stone Program,
151 W 15th St; tel: (610) 874-0423 (acc 35)

Cincinnati, OH 45210: Emergency Shelter,
131 E 12th St; tel: (513) 762-5655 (acc 20)

Cleveland, OH 44115: Zelma George Family
Shelter, 1710 Prospect Ave;
tel: (216) 641-3712 (acc 110)

Concord, NH 03301: McKenna House (adult
shelter), 100 S Fruit St; tel: (603) 228-3505
(acc 29)

Dayton, OH 45402: Women and Children's
Homeless Shelter, 138 S Wilkinson St;
tel: (937) 228-8241 (acc 27)

Dayton, OH 45402: Men's Homeless Shelter,
624 S Main St; tel: (937) 228-8210 (acc 55)

East Northport, NY 11731: Northport Veterans
Residence, PO Box 300; tel: (631) 262-0601

East Stroudsburg, PA 18301: 226 Washington St;
tel: (570) 421-3050

Elizabeth, NJ 07201: 1018 E Grand St;
tel: (908) 352-2886 (acc 45)

Elmira, NY 14902: 414 Lake St, PO Box 293;
tel: (607) 732-0314 (24-hour Domestic
Violence Hotline); Victims of domestic
violence safe house (acc 15)

Elmira, NY 14901: Our House, 401-403
Division St; tel: (607) 734-0032 (acc 20)

Hartford, CT 06105: 225 S Marshall St;
tel: (860) 543-8430 (Youth Shelter) (acc 14);
tel: (860) 543-8423 (Family Shelter) (acc 27)

Jamestown, NY 14702: ANEW Center Shelter
for Domestic Violence, Residential/Non
Residential Program, PO Box 368;
tel: (716) 483-0830; 24-hour Hotline
tel: (800) 252-8748

Johnstown, PA 15901: Emergency Shelter;
tel: (814) 539-3110 (acc 24)

Laconia, NH 03801: The Carey House, 6 Spring
St; tel: (603) 528-8086 (acc 30)

Lexington, KY 40508: Families, 736 W Main St;
tel: (859) 252-7706 (acc 129)

Lock Haven, PA 17745: Horizon House,
330 E Main St; tel: (570) 748-2406 (acc 18)

Montclair, NJ 07042-2776: 68 N Fullerton Ave;
tel: (973) 744-8666 (acc 18)

Morristown, NJ 07960: 95 Spring St;
tel: (973) 538-0997 (acc women 8)

Newark, OH 43055: 250 E Main St;
tel: (740) 345-3289 (acc 18)

New Britain, CT 06050: 78 Franklin Sq;
tel: (860) 225-8491 (acc 25)

New York, NY 10022: Homeward Bound, 221
E 52nd St; tel: (212) 758-4689

Norristown, PA 19404: 533 Swede St;
tel: (610) 275-9225 (acc 41)

Northport, NY 11768-0039: Northport Veterans'
Residence, 79 Middleville Rd, Bldg 11, PO
Box 300 (mail); tel: (631) 262-0601 (acc 87)

Perth Amboy, NJ 08862-0613: 433 State St;
tel: (732) 826-7040 (acc men 40) (seasonal)

Philadelphia, PA 19107: Eliza Shirley House,
1320 Arch St; tel: (215) 568-5111 (acc 125)

Philadelphia, PA 19123: Red Shield Family
Residence, 715 N Broad St;
tel: (215) 787-2887 (acc 100)

Pittsburgh, PA 15219: Family Crisis Center, 424
Third Ave; tel: (412) 394-4819 (acc 40)

Pottstown, PA 19464: Lessig-Booth Family
Residence, 137 King St; tel: (610) 327-0836
(acc 32)

Queens (Jamaica), NY 11435: Briarwood

Family Residence, 80-20 134th St;
tel: (718) 268-3395 (acc 91)

Queens Outreach Project, 90-23 161st St (street
effort, not building bound); tel: (718) 523-3366

Queens (Long Island City), NY 11101: Borden
Avenue Veterans' Residence, 21-10 Borden
Ave; tel: (718) 784-5690 (acc 410)

Rochester, NY 14604-4310: Men's Emergency
Shelter, Booth Haven, 70 Liberty Pole Way,
PO Box 41210; tel: (585) 987-9500 (acc 39)

Rochester, NY 14604-4310: Women's Shelter,
Hope House, 100 West Ave, PO Box 41210;
tel: (585) 697-3430 (acc 19)

Rochester, NY 14604-4310: Safe Haven
Emergency Shelter, 70 Liberty Pole Way,
PO Box 21210; tel: (585) 987-9540 (acc 16)

San Juan, PR 00903: Homeless Shelter, Proyecto
Esperanza, Fernández Juncos, Cnr Valdés;
tel: (787) 722-2370

Schenectady, NY 12305: Evangeline Booth
Home and Women's Shelter, 168 Lafayette St;
tel: (518) 370-0276

Syracuse, NY: Parenting Center, 667 S Salina St;
tel: (315) 479-1329

Syracuse, NY 13202: Emergency Lodge, 749
S Warren St; tel: (315) 479-1332

Trenton, NJ 08601: Homeless Drop In Center,
575 E State St; tel: (609) 599-9373

Waterbury, CT 06720: 74 Central Ave;
tel: (203) 756-1718 (acc 29)

Waterbury, CT 06720: Youth Shelter, 140
Willow St; tel: (203) 756-3651 (acc 14)

West Chester, PA 19380: Railton House, 101
E Market St; tel: (610) 696-7434 (acc 18)

Wilkes Barre, PA 18701: Kirby Family House,
35 S Pennsylvania Ave; tel: (570) 824-8380
(acc 50)

Wilmington, DE 19899: Booth Social Service
Center, 104 W 5th St; tel: (302) 472-0764
(acc 52)

Wooster, OH 44691: 24-Hour Open Door
Emergency Shelter, 459 S Market St Family
Life Center; tel: (330) 264-4704 (acc 56)

Zanesville, OH 43701: 515 Putnam Ave;
tel: (740) 454-8953 (acc 35)

Homeless Youth and Runaways

Binghamton, NY 13901: Open Door
Emergency Shelter, 127-131 Washington St;
tel: (607) 722-0164

Rochester, NY 14604-1210: Genesis House,
35 Ardmore St, PO Box 41210;
tel: (585) 235-2600 (acc 14)

Syracuse, NY 13205: Barnabas House, 1912
S Salina St; tel: (315) 459-1157 (acc 8)

Syracuse, NY 13205: Booth House and Host
Home, 264 Furman St; tel: (315) 471-7628
(acc 8)

Transitional Housing Programme

Arlington, MA 02474-6597: Wellington House,
8 Wellington St (Single Resident Occupancy)
(Under supervision of Cambridge, MA,
Corps); tel: (617) 547-3400 (acc 20)

Buffalo, NY 14202: 984 Main St;
tel: (716) 884-4798

Cincinnati, OH 45210: (families with children)
19 and 21 E 15th St; tel: (513) 762-5660

Cleveland, OH 44103: Willson Tower, 1919 E
55th St; tel: (216) 923-0000 (acc 70)

Cleveland, OH 44115: Pass Program, 1710
Prospect Ave; tel: (216) 619-4727 (acc 91)

Cleveland, OH 44115: Project Share, 2501 E.
22nd St; tel: (216) 623-7492 (acc 38)

Lancaster, PA 17603: 131 South Queen St;
tel: (717) 397-7565 (acc 21)

Philadelphia, PA 19103: Mid-City Apartments,
2025 Chestnut St; tel: (215) 569-9160
(acc 60)

Philadelphia, PA 19131: Bridge House, 4050
Conshohocken Ave; tel: (215) 473-3166 (acc 24)

Philadelphia, PA 19147: Reed House, 1320 S
32nd St; tel: (215) 755-6789 (acc 66)

Syracuse, NY 13205: Transitional Family
Apartments, 1482 S State St;
tel: (315) 479-1330

Syracuse, NY 13205: Transitional Living Project
Apartments (youth), 1941 S Salina St

Syracuse, NY 13205: Women's Shelter, 1704 S
Salina St; tel: (315) 472-0947

Youth Service and Emergency Shelter

Hartford, CT: Youth Shelter Co-ed, 225
Marshall St; tel: (860) 543-8430

Syracuse, NY 13205: Barnabas, 1941 S Salina
St; tel: (315) 475-9744

Senior Citizens' Residences

Cincinnati, OH 45224: Booth Residence for the
Elderly and Handicapped, 6000 Townvista;
tel: (513) 242-4482 (acc 150)

New York, NY 10025: Williams Residence, 720
West End Ave; tel: (212) 316-6000;
fax: (212) 280-0410 (acc 367)

Philadelphia, PA 19139: Booth Manor, 5522
Arch St; tel: (215) 471-0500 (acc 50)

Philadelphia, PA 19131: Ivy Residence, 4051
Ford Rd; tel: (215) 871-3303 (acc 75)

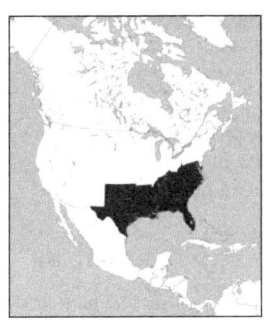

USA SOUTHERN TERRITORY

Territorial leaders:
Commissioners Maxwell and Lenora Feener

Territorial Commander:
Commissioner Maxwell Feener (1 Jul 2006)

Chief Secretary:
Lieut-Colonel David Jeffrey (1 Jul 2006)

Territorial Headquarters: 1424 Northeast Expressway, Atlanta, GA 30329-2088, USA

Tel address: Salvation, Atlanta; tel: [1] (404) 728 1300; fax: [1] (404) 728 1392;
web site: www.salvationarmysouth.org

The Salvation Army was incorporated as a religious and charitable corporation in the State of Georgia in 1927 as 'The Salvation Army' and is qualified to conduct all its affairs in all of the states of the territory.

Zone: Americas and Caribbean
USA states included in the territory: Alabama, Arkansas, Florida, Georgia, Kentucky, Louisiana, Maryland, Mississippi, North Carolina, Oklahoma, South Carolina, Tennessee, Texas, Virginia, West Virginia, District of Columbia
Languages in which the gospel is preached: English, Haitian-Creole, Korean, Laotian, Spanish, Vietnamese
Periodical: *Southern Spirit*

THE territory celebrated as a family in the summer of 2005 with a territorial family conference titled 'Our Journey Home with Jesus – a true Southern homecoming'. This reminded those present that the apostle Paul, in his letter to the Corinthian church, described the Church as the Body of Christ – one family, all the members different, each making his or her contribution. Delegates considered how that family is held together and given meaning and purpose by faith, hope and love - love being the greatest.

General John Larsson and Commissioner Freda Larsson were guest leaders at the three-day conference. The final gathering included the ordination and commissioning of the Preparers of the Way Session of cadets.

The 2005 hurricane season began early with the Florida, Alabama-Louisiana-Mississippi and Texas Divisions utilising every resource available to bring immediate relief to victims of several violent storms. Many other divisions subsequently become involved in sending personnel to the scene of Hurricane Katrina and providing assistance to survivors who migrated to other cities over a 30-state area.

No one could have predicted the destruction caused by Katrina when it made landfall on 29 August. A 362-mile stretch of Gulf coastline was totally devastated, more than 1,300 people died and over one million were displaced. The Salvation Army suffered the loss of buildings along the coast, and in New Orleans, Louisiana, the Centre of Hope became a refuge for more than 300 survivors of the levee breaks which caused widespread flooding and toxic pollution throughout most of the city.

Majors Richard and Fay Brittle, area commanders in New Orleans, remained with this diverse group. Some were residents of the centre but the majority were people rescued as they floated by on anything that would keep them from drowning.

'The youngest was a six-week-old baby, the oldest an 88-year-old woman wearing nothing but a housecoat and carried in by her son,' said Major Richard Brittle. 'Because we were without electricity, the heat was stifling, so we broke open the windows for ventilation and prayed to God for rescue. Our prayers were answered [three days later] when helicopters came and airlifted everyone off the roof of the four-storey building.'

The major went on: 'We worked all morning to get everyone up a ladder and on to the roof to be rescued – women and children first, followed by the men. Fay and I were last to leave. The helicopter dropped us on the I-10 bridge among thousands of other survivors. I saw the Army's canteen in the distance and said to my wife, "We're going to be alright now."'

STATISTICS

Officers 1,405 (active 949 retired 456) **Cadets** (1st Yr) 40 (2nd Yr) 41 **Employees** 15,425
Corps 347 **Societies/Outposts** 8 **Institutions** 367
Senior Soldiers 27,399 **Adherents** 2,810 **Junior Soldiers** 8,037
Personnel serving outside territory Officers 21 Layworker 1

STAFF

Personnel: Lt-Col Donald Faulkner
Programme: Lt-Col Charles White
Business: Lt-Col H. Alfred Ward
Adult Rehabilitation Centres Command: Maj Larry White
Audit: Maj Eugene Broome
Community Relations and Development: Maj John Jordan
Education: Maj Michael Reagan
Evangelism and Adult Ministries: Maj John White
Employee Relations: Mrs Brenda Klaas
Finance: Lt-Col David Mothershed
Legal: Lt-Col William Goodier
Multicultural Ministries: Maj Fernando R. Martinez
Music: Dr Richard E. Holz
Officers' Health Services: Maj Carol Clemons
Property: Mr Robert L. Taylor
Retired Officers: Maj Hilda Howell
Social Services: Mr Kevin Tompson-Hooper
Supplies and Purchasing: Maj Robert Bagley
Training: Maj Kenneth Luyk
Women's Ministries: Comr Lenora Feener (TPWM) Lt-Col Barbara Jeffrey (TSWM) Lt-Col Marian Faulkner (LOMS/Outreach) Lt-Col Mary Ward (TWAS)
Youth/Candidates: Maj W. Edward Hobgood

DIVISIONS

Alabama-Louisiana-Mississippi: 1450 Riverside Dr, PO Box 4857, 39296-4857, Jackson, MS 39202; tel: (601) 969 7560; fax: (601) 969-9077; Maj Dalton Cunningham
Arkansas and Oklahoma: 5101 N Pennsylvania

Ave, PO Box 12600, 73157, Oklahoma City, OK 73112; tel: (405) 840 0735; fax: (405) 840 0460; Maj Henry Gonzalez

Florida: 5631 Van Dyke Rd, Lutz, FL 33558, PO Box 270848, 33688-0848, Tampa, FL 33618; tel: (813) 962 6611; fax: (813) 962 4098; Maj R. Steven Hedgren

Georgia: 1000 Center Pl, NW, PO Box 930188, 30003 Norcross, GA 30003; tel: (770) 441-6200; fax: (770) 441-6214; Maj William Mockabee

Kentucky and Tennessee: 214-216 W Chestnut St, Box 2229, 40201-2229, Louisville, KY 40202; tel: (502) 583 5391; fax: (502) 625 1199; Maj Willis Howell

Maryland and West Virginia: 814 Light St, Baltimore, MD 21230; tel: (410) 347 9944; fax: (410) 539 7747; Maj Mark Bell

National Capital and Virginia: 2626 Pennsylvania Ave NW, PO Box 18658, Washington, DC 20037; tel: (202) 756 2600; fax: (202) 756 2660; Lt-Col William L. Crabson

North and South Carolina: 501 Archdale Dr, Box 241808, 28224-1808, Charlotte, NC 28217-4237; tel: (704) 522 4970; fax: (704) 522 4980; Maj Vernon Jewett

Texas: 6500 Harry Hines Blvd, PO Box 36607, 75235, Dallas, TX 75235; tel: (214) 956 6000; fax: (214) 956 9436; Maj Kenneth Johnson

SCHOOL FOR OFFICER TRAINING

1032 Metropolitan Pkwy, SW Atlanta, GA 30310; tel: (404) 753 4166; fax: (404) 753 3709

ATTACHED TO DIVISIONS
Alcoholic Rehabilitation

Dallas, TX 75235: 5302 Harry Hines Blvd (acc 90)

Fort Worth, TX 76103: 1855 E Lancaster (women only, acc 13)

Mobile, AL 36604: 1009 Dauphin St (acc 30)

Child Care Centres

Annapolis, MD 21403: 351 Hilltop Lane (acc 80)
Austin, TX 78701: 501 E 8th St (acc 28)
Austin, TX 78767: 4523 Tannehill Hill (acc 26)
Bradenton, FL 34205: 1720 11th St W (acc 99)
Clearwater, FL 34625: 1625 N Belcher Rd (acc 70)
Charlotte, NC 28206: 534 Spratt St (acc 25)
Charlottesville, VA 22901 (acc 25)
Dallas, TX 75235: 5302 Harry Hines Blvd (acc 24)
Decatur, AL 36604: 100 Austinville Rd SW
Fairfax, VA 22030: 4915 Ox Rd (acc 110)

Fort Worth, TX 76106: 3023 NW 24th St (acc 98)
Freeport, TX 77541-2620: 1618 Ave J (acc 85)
Gulfport, MS 39501: 2009 24th Ave (acc 5)
Hialeah, FL 33014: 7450 W 4th Ave (acc 147)
Irving, TX 75061: 250 E Grauwyler (acc 62)
Jacksonville, FL 32202: 318 N Ocean (acc 125)
Lakeland, FL 33801: 835 N Kentucky (acc 45)
Louisville, KY 40203: 237 E Breckenridge (acc 42)
Lynchburg, VA 24501: 2215 Park Ave (acc 40)
Memphis, TN 38105: 696 Jackson Ave (acc 60)
Miami Sunset, FL 33243-1327: 8445 SW, 72nd St (acc 161)
Midland, TX 79703: 3500 Park Ave (acc 125)
Naples, FL 34104: 3180 Esley Ave (acc 53)
Nashville, TN 37207: 631 Dickerson Rd (acc 37)
New Orleans, LA 70125: 4530 S Claiborne Ave (acc 50)
Ponca City, OK 74601: 711 S 3rd (acc 49)
Princeton, WV 24740: 300 Princeton Ave (acc 102)
Salisbury, MD 21804: 415 Oak St (acc 52)
San Antonio (Southside), TX 78211: 1034 Fenfield Ave (acc 92)
Winston-Salem, NC 27101: 1255 N Trade St (acc 10)

Children's Residential Care

Birmingham, AL 35212: Youth Emergency Services, 6001 Crestwood Blvd (acc 33)
St Petersburg, FL 33733: Sallie House Emergency Shelter, PO Drawer 10909

Family Resident Programme

Alexandria, VA 22301: 2525 Mt Vernon Ave (acc 40)
Amarillo, TX 79105: 400 S Harrison (acc 15)
Arlington, TX 76013: 711 W Border (acc 30)
Atlanta, GA 30310: 464 Luckie St (acc 50)
Austin, TX 78701: 501 E 8th St (acc 60)
Austin, TX 78767: 4523 Tannehill Ln (Women & Children Shelter) (acc 26)
Baltimore, MD 21030: 1114 N Calvert St (acc 75)
Beaumont, TX 77701: 1078 McFadden (acc 10)
Cambridge, MD 21613: 200 Washington St (acc 10)
Charlottesville, VA: 207 Ridge St NW (acc 36)
Chattanooga, TN 37403: 800 N McCallie Ave (acc 72)
Clearwater, FL 33756: 1527 East Druid, (acc 38)
Corpus Christi, TX 78401: 513 Josephine (acc 28)
Dallas, TX 75235-5302: Harry Hines Blvd (acc 30)
Dalton, GA 30720: 1101 Chattanooga Rd (acc 14)
Denton, TX 76201: 1508 McKinney St (acc 30)
Ft Myers, FL 33901: 2163 Stella St (acc 28)

Fort Worth, TX 76103: 1855 E Lancaster Ave (acc 62)

Hagerstown, MD 21740: 534 W Franklin St (acc 30)

Harrisonburg, VA 22802: 185 Ashby Ave (acc 42)

Hollywood, FL 33020: 1960 Sherman St (acc 140)

Houston, TX 77004: 1603 McGowen (acc 42)

Lakeland, FL 33801: 835 N Kentucky Ave (acc 45)

Louisville, KY 40203: 209 E Breckinridge (acc 35)

Louisville, KY 40203: 213 E Breckinridge (acc 18)

Lynchburg, VA 24501: 2215 Park Ave (acc 22)

Memphis, TN 38105: 696 Jackson Ave (acc 120)

Naples, FL 34104: 3180 Estey Dr (acc 55)

Nashville, TN 37207-5608: 631 N 1st St (acc 53)

Newport News, VA 23607: 1003 28th St (acc 40)

Norfolk, VA 23220: 2097 Military Highway, Chesapeake (acc 65)

Ocala, FL 34475: 320 NW 1st Ave (acc 24)

Orlando, FL 32804: 400 W Colonial Dr (acc 22)

Panama City, FL 32401: 1824 W 15th St (acc 48)

Parkersburg, WV 24740: 534-570 Fifth St (acc 32)

Pensacola, FL 32505: 1310 North S St (acc 24)

Richmond, VA 23220: 2 W Grace St (acc 52)

San Antonio, TX 78212: Hope Center (acc 300)

Sarasota, FL 34236: 1400 10th St (acc 19)

Tampa, FL 33602: 1603 N Florida (acc 43)

Texarkana, TX 71854: 316 Hazel (acc 46)

Tyler, TX 75701: 717 N Spring St

Washington, DC 20009: 1434 Harvard St NW (acc 60)

Wheeling, WV 26003: 140 16th St (acc 32)

Williamsburg, VA 7131: Merrimac Trail (acc 17)

Harbour Light Centres

Atlanta, GA 30313: 400 Luckie St (acc 250)

Houston, TX 77009: 2407 N Main St (acc 308)

Washington, DC 20002: 2100 New York Ave, NE (acc 207)

Senior Citizens' Centres

Arlington, TX 76013: 712 W Abrams (acc 68)

Beaumont, MS 1502: Bolton Ave

Birmingham, '614 Birmingham' AL 35203: 2410 8th Ave N

Brooklyn, MS: Carnes Rd

Dallas Cedar Crest, TX 75203: 1007 Hutchins Rd

Dallas Oak Cliff, TX 75208: 1617 W Jefferson Blvd

Dallas Pleasant Grove, TX 75217-0728: 8341 Elam Rd

Ft Worth, TX 76106: 3023 NW 24th St

Houston Aldine/Westfield, TX 77093: 2600 Aldine Westfield

Houston Pasadena, TX 77506: 45/6 Irvington Blvd

Houston Temple, TX 77009: 4516 Irvington Blvd

Jacksonville, FL 32202: 17 E Church St

Lufkin, TX 75904: 305 Shands

Montgomery, AL 36107: 900 Bell St

Oklahoma City, OK 73129: 311 SW 5th St (includes 5 drop-in centres)

Orange, TX 77630: 2515 N 3rd St

San Antonio Citadel, TX 78201: 2810 W Ashby Pl

San Antonio Hope Center, TX 78212: 521 W Elmira

Sarasota, FL 34230: 1701 S Tuttle

Shreveport, LA 71163: 200 E Stoner

St Petersburg, FL 33713: 3800 9th Ave N

Washington (Sherman Ave), DC 20010: 3335 Sherman Ave NW

Washington (Southeast), DC 20003: 1211 G St SE

Senior Citizens' Residences

Atlanta, GA 31106: Wm Booth Towers, 1125 Ponce de Leon Ave NE (acc 99)

Charlotte, NC 28202-1618: Wm Booth Gardens Apts, 421 North Poplar St (acc 130)

Cumberland, MD 21502-0282: Wm Booth Tower, 220 Somerville Ave (acc 113)

Fort Worth, TX 76119-5813: Catherine Booth Friendship House, 1901 E Seminary Dr (acc 157)

Houston, TX 77009: Wm Booth Garden Apts, 808 Frawley (acc 62)

Ocala, FL 34470: Evangeline Booth Garden Apts, 2921 NE 14th St (acc 64)

Orlando, FL 32801: Wm Booth Towers, 633 Lake Dot Circle (acc 168)

Orlando, FL 32801: Catherine Booth Towers, 625 Lake Dot Circle (acc 125)

Pasadena, TX 77502: Evangeline Booth, 2627 Cherrybrook Ln. (acc 62)

San Antonio, TX 78201-5397: Wm Booth Gardens Apts, 2710 W Ashby Pl (acc 95)

Tyler, TX 75701: Wm Booth Gardens Apts, 601 Golden Rd (acc 132)

Waco, TX 76708-1141: Wm Booth Gardens Apts, 4200 North 19th (acc 120)

Waco, TX 75708-1141: Catherine Booth, North 19th (acc 75)

Service Centres

Alexander City, AL 35010: 823 Cherokee Rd

Americus, GA 31709: 609 E Lamar St

Andalusia, AL 36420: (Covington County) 220 S Cotton St

Bainbridge, GA 31717: 600 Scott St

Bay City, TX 77404: 1911 7th St

Borger, TX 79007-4252: 404-414 N
Whittenburg St
Bogalusa, LA 70427: 400 Georgia Ave
Brownwood, TX 76801: 405 Lakeway
Bushnell, FL 33513: 870 N Main Street
Carrollton, GA 30117: 115 Lake Carroll Blvd
Carthage, MS 39051: 610 Hwy 16 West, Suite A
Cleburne, TX 76031: 607 S Main
Columbia, MD 21045 (Howard County):
PO Box 2877
Copperas Cove, TX 76522: 458 Town Square
Shopping Center
Corinth, MS 38835: 2200 Lackey Dr
Covington, GA 30014: 5193 Washington St
Culpeper, VA 22701: 14300 Achievement Dr
Douglas, GA 31533: 110 S Gaskin Ave
Dublin, GA 31021: 1617 Telfair St
Elberton, GA 30635: 262 N McIntosh St
Elizabethtown, KY 42701: 1006 N Mulberry
Enterprise, AL 366331: (Coffee County) 1919-B
E Park Ave
Fort Payne, AL 35967: (Dekalb County)
450 Gault Ave N
Frankline, VA, 23851: 50l N Main St
Fulton, MS 38843: 414 E Main St
Glen Burnie, MD 21061: 511 S Crain Hwy
Gonzales, LA 70737: 218 Bayou Narcisse
Guntersville, AL 35976: (Marshall County)
1336 Gunter Ave
Houma, LA 71270: 1414 E Tunnel Blvd.
Houston, MS 38851: 114 Washington St
Jackson, GA 30233 (Jackson/Butts County):
178 N Benton St
Jasper, AL 35502: (Walker County) 207 20th St E
Kaufman, TX 75142: 305 W Fair
Lenoir, NC 28645: 309 Main St NW
Lewisville, TX 75067: 206 W Main St
McComb, MS 39648: 604 S. Magnolia Street
McDonouch, GA 30253: 401 Race Track Rd
McGehee, AR 71670: (Desha County) 202 N 2nd
Milledgeville, GA 31061: 931 N Jefferson St
Morganton, NC 28655: 224 Summit St
Natchez, MS 39120: 175 Hwy 61 S
New Braunfels, TX 78130: 373 B Landa St
Newnan, GA 30264: 670 Jefferson St
Oneonta, AL 35121: (Blount County) 333
Valley Rd
Opelika, AL 36801: (Lee County) 720 Columbus
Pkwy
Oxford, MS 38655: 1015 N Lamar St
Ozark, AL 36360: (Dale County) 154 E Broad St
Pontotoc, MS 38863: 187 Hwy 15 N
Putnam County, WV 25177: 720 North Winfield
Rd, St Albans, WV
Sallisaw, OK: 301 N 6th St, Fort Smith,
AR 72901

Scottsboro, AL 35768: (Jackson County) 1501
W Willow St
Spencer, WV 25276: (Roane County)
145 Main St
Starksville, MS 39759: 501 Hwy 12 W
St Albans, WV 25177: (Putnam County)
720 N Winfield Rd
St Mary's, GA 31558: 1909 Osborne Rd
Sylacauga, AL 35150: (Taledega South) 100 E
Third St
Talladega, AL 35160: (Taledega North) 215 E
Battle St
Tarpon Springs, FL 34689: 209 S Pinellas Ave
Thomasville, AL 36784: 118 Wilson Ave W
Troy, AL 36081: 70 A Court St
Vidalia, GA 30475: 204 Jackson St
Warrenton, VA 20186: 26 S Third St
Wellsburg, WV 26070: 491 Commerce St
Westminster, MD 21157: 300 Hahn Rd
Winchester, VA 22604: 300 Fort Collier Rd

Spouse House Shelters
Cocoa, FL: 919 W Peachtree (acc 16)
Panama City, FL 32401: 1824 W 15th St (acc 12)
Port Richey, FL 34673: PO Box 5517 (Hudson,
FL) (acc 32)
Roanoke, VA: 815 Salem Ave (acc 40)
Thomasville, GA 31792: 207 South St (acc 8)
Warner Robins, GA 31093: 305 Green St
(acc 15)

SOCIAL SERVICES
Adult Rehabilitation Centres (including industrial stores)
Alexandria, VA 22312: Northern Virginia
Center, 6528 Little River Turnpike (acc 120)
Atlanta, GA 30318-5726: 740 Marietta St, NW
(acc 144)
Austin, TX 78745: 4216 S Congress (acc 118)
Baltimore, MD 21230: 2700 W Patapsco Ave
(acc 108)
Birmingham, AL 35234: 1401 F. L.
Shuttlesworth Dr (acc 103)
Charlotte, NC 28204: 1023 Central Ave
(acc 118)
Dallas, TX 75235-7213: 5554 Harry Hines Blvd
(acc 127)
Fort Lauderdale, FL 33312-1597: 1901 W
Broward Blvd (acc 99)
Fort Worth, TX 76111-2996: 2901 NE 28th St
(acc 109)
Houston, TX 77007-6113: 1015 Hemphill St
(acc 167)
Hyattsville, MD 20781: (Washington, DC, &
Suburban Maryland Center) 3304 Kenilworth
Ave (acc 151)

Jacksonville, FL 32246: 10900 Beach Blvd (acc 121)

Memphis, TN 38103-1954: 130 N Danny Thomas Blvd (acc 87)

Miami, FL 33127-4981: 2236 NW Miami Court (acc 133)

Nashville, TN 37213-1102: 140 N 1st St (acc 86)

Oklahoma City, OK 73106-2409: 2041 NW 7th St (acc 81)

Orlando, FL 32808-7927: 3955 W Colonial Dr (acc 104)

Richmond, VA 23220-1199: 2601 Hermitage Rd (acc 81)

San Antonio, TX 78204: 1324 S Flores St (acc 110)

St Petersburg, FL 33709-1597: Suncoast Area Center, 5885 66th St N (acc 108)

Tampa, FL 33613-2205: 13815 N Salvation Army Ln (acc 125)

Tulsa, OK 74106-5163: 601-611 N Main St (acc 86)

Virginia Beach, VA 23462: Hampton Roads Center, 5560 Virginia Beach Blvd (acc 123)

In addition, 11 fresh-air camps and 304 community centres, boys'/girls' clubs are attached to the divisions.

A mother and child receive assistance at one of the USA Southern Territory's Hurricane Katrina distribution centres

Hundred of other victims of the Hurricane Katrina disaster line up for food handed out from a fleet of Salvation Army emergency vehicles

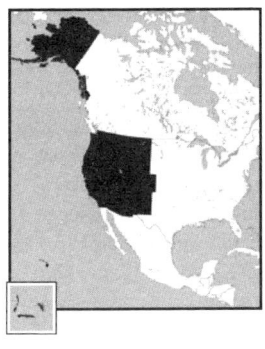

USA WESTERN TERRITORY

Territorial leaders:
Commissioners Philip W. and Patricia L. Swyers

Territorial Commander:
Commissioner Philip W. Swyers
(1 Jan 2005)

Chief Secretary:
Lieut-Colonel Donald C. Bell (1 Jul 2002)

Territorial Headquarters: 180 E Ocean Boulevard, PO Box 22646 (90801-5646), Long Beach, California 90802-4709, USA

Tel: [1] (562) 436-7000; fax: [1] (562) 491-8891; web site: www.usw.salvationarmy.org

The Salvation Army was incorporated as a religious and charitable corporation in the State of California in 1914 as 'The Salvation Army' and is qualified, along with its several affiliated separate corporations, to conduct its affairs in all of the States of the territory.

Zone: Americas and Caribbean
USA states included in the territory: Alaska, Arizona, California, Colorado, Hawaii, Idaho, Montana, Nevada, New Mexico, Oregon, Utah, Washington, Wyoming, Texas (El Paso County), Guam (US Territory)
Other countries included in territory: Republic of the Marshall Islands, Federated States of Micronesia
'The Salvation Army' in Cantonese: Kau Shai Kwan; in Japanese: Kyu-sei-gun; in Mandarin (Kuoyo): Chiu Shi Chuen; in Spanish: Ejército de Salvación
Languages in which the gospel is preached: Cantonese, Chamarro, Chuukese, English, Haida, Hmong, Ilocano, Japanese, Kolrae, Korean, Laotian, Mandarin, Marshallese, Pohnpeian, Portuguese, Spanish, Tagalog, Tlingit, Tsimpshean, Visayan
Periodicals: *Caring*, *New Frontier*, *Nuevas Fronteras* (Spanish)

BUILDING on the solid groundwork of its six strategic priorities, the territory has added new goals for the next five years. It aims to maintain financially sound divisions led by bold, committed officers who are supported by enthusiastic soldiers – all working to expand God's Kingdom in a culturally diverse territory.

During '2005 – A Year for Children and Youth', and into 2006, the territory continued its commitment to youth work. Plans were announced

for a Battle School dedicated to training and inspiring youth; the Youth Department also announced a campaign titled 'Six In '06', aiming for every Sunday school to increase its attendance by six.

Of the more than 150 delegates attending a 'Life Service' conference held at the college for officer training, 69 responded to the call to officership and 31 committed themselves to service as local officers.

Sites for new Ray and Joan Kroc

Corps Community Centres were identified in Salem, Oregon; San Francisco Tenderloin, California; Kapolei, Hawaii; Coeur d'Alene, Idaho; Long Beach, California; and Phoenix South Mountain, Arizona.

The West sharpened its global vision with an expanded World Missions website, and a team from Santa Clara Grace Korean Corps in California travelled, for the third consecutive year, to Senegal on a 10-day Moslem Mission.

In acknowledgement of the territory's cultural diversity, the Territorial Music Department changed its name to the Music and Worship Development Department and announced a new music and gospel arts programme, including a territorial band, youth band, youth chorus and songsters, and worship arts and music leaders' retreats.

During commissioning weekend the 16 cadets of the Preparers of the Way Session were ordained and commissioned as officers and six auxiliary-captains were elevated to full captaincy. Highlights were a music and arts festival titled 'Kids Live 2005' and the third annual Latino Rally, which drew a congregation of nearly 1,000. Later in the year the training college welcomed 14 new cadets to the Heralds of the Good News Session, almost all with prior ministry experience.

When Hurricanes Katrina and Rita struck the Gulf Coast, the territory responded immediately by dispatching personnel to the scene and assisting the many displaced people who were relocated to the West.

At the 28th annual Western Music Institute, 124 delegates and 47 faculty members were challenged to take on the full armour of God. The Western Youth Institute provided 142 delegates with a challenging week during which they were invited to join 'The Uprising' by living a revolutionary Christian life.

For the new year the territorial commander outlined goals designed to guide the territory in 'Doing the Most Good'. These include 50 new cadets, financial solvency, capital and Red Shield campaigns, Kroc centres and cultural diversity.

The territory's Information Technology Department was named by *InformationWeek* magazine as one of the USA's most innovative IT organisations.

STATISTICS

Officers 1,016 (active 674 retired 342) **Cadets** 27 **Employees** 9,396

Corps 264 **Outposts** 19 **Institutions** 234

Senior Soldiers 16,833 **Adherents** 3,182 **Junior Soldiers** 5,932

Personnel serving outside territory Officers 34 Lay Personnel 2

STAFF

Personnel: Maj Ralph E. Hood
Business: Lt-Col Kurt Burger
Programme: Lt-Col Terry W. Griffin
ARC Command: Maj Ron Strickland
Audit Dept: Maj Walter Fuge
Candidates and Recruitment: Maj Nancy Dihle
Community Care Ministries: Maj Ivy Hood
Community Relations/Development:
Maj Cynthia Foley
Corps Ministries and Spiritual Formation:
Lt-Col Linda L. Griffin
Education: Maj Linda Manhardt
Finance: Maj Victor A. Leslie

Gift Services: Ms Kathleen Durazo
Human Resources: Ms Margaret (Miki) Webb
Information Technology: Mr Clarence White
Legal: Mr Michael Woodruff
Music: Mr Neil Smith
Officer Services: Capt Rhonda Lloyd
Officer Care and Development: Maj William
Nottle
Property: Capt Robert S. Lloyd
Risk Management: Mr John McCarthy
Senior Housing Management: Mrs Susan
Lawrence
Social Services: Mr Gordon A. Bingham
Training: Maj Donald Hostetler
Women's Ministries: Comr Patricia L. Swyers
(TPWM) Lt-Col Debora K. Bell (TSWM)
World Missions: Maj Theodore Mahr
Youth: Capt Kyle Smith

DIVISIONS

Alaska: 143 E 9th Ave, Anchorage, AK
99501-3618 (Box 101459, 99510-1459);
tel: (907) 276-2515; Maj Douglas Tollerud
Cascade: 1785 NE Sandy Blvd, Portland,
OR 97232-2872 (Box 8798, 97208-8798);
tel: (503) 234-0825; Maj Robert L. Rudd
Del Oro: 3755 N Freeway Blvd, Sacramento,
CA 95834-1926 (Box 348000, 95834-8000);
tel: (916) 563-3700; Maj Eda M. Hokom
Golden State: 832 Folsom St, San Francisco,
CA 94107-1123 (Box 193465, 94119-3465);
tel: (415) 553-3500; Maj Joe E. Posillico
Hawaiian and Pacific Islands: 2950 Manoa
Rd, Honolulu, HI 96822-1798 (Box 620,
96809-0620); tel: (808) 988-2136; Maj David
E. Hudson
Intermountain: 1370 Pennsylvania St, Denver,
CO 80203-2475 (Box 2369, 80201-2369);
tel: (303) 861-4833; Lt-Col Raymond L.
Peacock
Northwest: 111 Queen Anne Ave N, Seattle,
WA 98109-4955 (Box 9219, 98109-0200);
tel: (206) 281-4600; Lt-Col Harold F.
Brodin
Sierra Del Mar: 2320 5th Ave, San Diego,
CA 92101-1679 (Box 122688, 92112-2688);
tel: (619) 231-6000; Lt-Col Douglas O'Brien
Southern California: 900 W James M Wood
Blvd, Los Angeles, CA 90015-1356 (Box
15899 Del Valle Station 90015-0899);
tel: (213) 896-9160; Lt-Col Paul E.
Bollwahn
Southwest: 2707 E Van Buren St, Phoenix,
AZ 85008-6039 (Box 52177, 85072-2177);
tel: (602) 267-4100; Lt-Col Don R. Mowery

COLLEGE FOR OFFICER TRAINING

30840 Hawthorne Blvd, Rancho Palos Verdes,
CA 90275-5301; tel: (310) 377-0481;
fax: (310) 541-4469

SOCIAL SERVICES

Adult Rehabilitation Centres (Men)

Anaheim, CA 92805: 1300 S Lewis St;
tel: (714) 758-0414 (acc 147)
Bakersfield, CA 93301: 200 19th St;
tel: (661) 325-8626 (acc 58)
Canoga Park, CA 91304: 21375 Roscoe Blvd;
tel: (818) 883-6321 (acc 52)
Carpinteria, CA 93013: 6410 Cindy Lane, PO
Box 780, 93014; tel: (805) 684-6999 (acc 85)
Colorado Springs, CO 80903: 505 S Weber St,
PO Box 1385, 80901; tel: (719) 473-6161
(acc 65)
Denver, CO 80216: 4751 Broadway;
tel: (303) 294-0827 (acc 96)
Fresno, CA 93721: 804 S Parallel Ave, PO Box
12967, 93779; tel: (559) 490-7020 (acc 91)
Honolulu, HI 96817: 322 Sumner St;
tel: (808) 522-8400 (acc 75)
Long Beach, CA 90813: 1370 Alamitos Ave;
tel: (562) 218-2351 (acc 94)
Lytton, CA 95448: 200 Lytton Springs Rd,
Healdsburg, PO Box 668, Healdsburg, 95448;
tel: (707) 433-3334 (acc 95)
Oakland, CA 94607: 601 Webster St, PO Box
24054, 94623; tel: (510) 451-4514 (acc 130)
Pasadena, CA 91105: 56 W Del Mar Blvd;
tel: (626) 795-8075 (acc 107)
Phoenix, AZ 85004: 1625 S Central Ave;
tel: (602) 256-4500 (acc 92)
Portland, OR 97214: 139 SE Martin Luther King
Jr Blvd; tel: (503) 235-4192 (acc 72)
Riverside County, CA 92570: 24201 Orange
Ave, Perris, PO Box 278, Perris 92572;
tel: (951) 940-5790 (acc 125)
Sacramento, CA 95814: 1615 D St, PO Box
2948, 95812; tel: (916) 441-5267 (acc 86)
San Bernardino, CA 92408: 363 S Doolittle Rd;
tel: (909) 889-9605 (acc 77)
San Diego, CA 92101: 1335 Broadway;
tel: (619) 239-4037 (acc 104)
San Francisco, CA 94110: 1500 Valencia St;
tel: (415) 643-8000 (acc 112)
San Jose, CA 95126: 702 W Taylor St;
tel: (408) 298-7600 (acc 103)
Santa Monica, CA 90404: 1665 10th St;
tel: (310) 450-7235 (acc 95)
Seattle, WA 98134: 1000 4th Ave S;
tel: (206) 587-0503 (acc 100)
Stockton, CA 95205: 1247 S Wilson Way;
tel: (209) 466-3871 (acc 84)

Tucson, AZ 85713: 2717 S 6th Ave;
tel: (520) 624-1741 (acc 85)

Adult Rehabilitation Centres (Women)

Anaheim, CA 92805: 1300 S Lewis St;
tel: (714) 758-0414 (acc 28)

Arcadia, CA 91007: Pasadena Women's
Program, 180 W Huntington Dr;
tel: (626) 795-8075 (acc 14)

Arvada, CO 80002: Cottonwood, 13455 W 58th
Ave; tel: (303) 456-0520 (acc 24)

Fresno, CA 93704: Rosecrest, 745 E Andrews
St; tel: (559) 490-7020 (acc 14)

Pasadena, CA 91107: Oakcrest Women's
Program, 180 W Huntington Dr;
tel: (626) 795-8075 (acc 13)

Phoenix, AZ 85003: Lyncrest Manor, 344 W
Lynwood St (acc 12)

San Diego, CA 92123: Door of Hope, 2799
Health Center Dr; tel: (619) 239-4037 ext 354
(acc 15)

San Francisco, CA 94116: Pinehurst Lodge,
2685 30th Ave; tel: (415) 681-1262 (acc 26)

Seattle, WA 98102: The Marion-Farrell House,
422 11th Ave E; tel: (206) 587-0503 (acc 14)

UNDER DIVISIONS

Clinics

Fairbanks, AK 99701: Dental Care Access
Program, 723 27th Ave; tel: (907) 452-3103

Kalispell, MT 59901: 110 Bountiful Drive;
tel: (406) 257-4357

Lodi, CA 95240: 525 W Lockeford St;
tel: (209) 367-9560

Oxnard/Port Hueneme, CA: 622 W Wooley Rd;
tel: (805) 483-9235

Portland, OR 97204: Homeless Infirmary
Program (HIP), 30 SW 2nd Ave;
tel: (503) 239-1259

Reno, NV 89512: 1931 Sutro St;
tel: (775) 688-4555

Family Services

Anchorage, AK 99503: McKinnell Family
Services, 4611 Gambell St; tel: (907) 277-2593

Denver, CO 80205: Denver Family Services,
2201 Stout St; tel: (303) 295-3366

Honolulu, HI 96817: Honolulu Family Services
Offices, 420 Waiakamilo Rd, Unit 108;
tel: (808) 845-2544

Lodi, CA 95240: Hope Harbor Family Service
Center, 622 N Sacramento St;
tel: (209) 367-9560

Los Angeles, CA 90015-1352: Los Angeles
Family Service, 832 W James M. Wood Blvd;
tel: (213) 438-0933

Marysville, CA 95901: Family Services, 410 J St;
tel: (530) 634-6060

Phoenix, AZ 85034-2177: Family Service Center,
2702 E Washington; tel: (602) 267-4122

Sacramento, CA 95814: Family Service Center,
1200 North B St; tel: (916) 442-0303

Santa Rosa, CA 95404: Family Service Office,
160 Montgomery Ave; tel: (707) 542-0998

Seattle, WA 98101-1923: Emergency Family
Assistance, 1101 Pike St; tel: (206) 447-9944

Tiyan, Guam: Family Services Center, 613-615
E Sunset Blvd; tel: (671) 477-3528

Adult Care Centres

Anchorage, AK 99508: 3350 E 20th Ave,
Serendipity Adult Day Services;
tel: (907) 279-0501 (acc 35)

Centralia, WA 98531: Evangeline Booth Adult
Care Program, PO Box 488;
tel: (360) 736-4339 (acc 40)

Henderson, NV 89015: 830 E Lake Mead Dr,
Box 91300, 89009; tel: (702) 565-9578
(acc 49)

Honolulu, HI 96817: 296 N Vineyard Blvd;
tel: (808) 521-6551 (acc 57)

San Pedro, CA 90731-2351: 138 S Bandini;
tel: (310) 832-7228 (acc 30)

Torrance, CA 90503: 4223 Emerald St;
tel: (310) 370-4515 (acc 40)

Alcoholic and Drug Rehabilitation Services

Albuquerque, NM 87102: 400 John St SE,
Box 27690, 87125-7690; tel: (505) 242-3112
(acc 28)

Anchorage, AK 99503: Adult Rehabilitation
Program, 660 E 48th Ave; tel: (907) 562-5408
(acc 61)

Anchorage, AK 99503-7317: Box 190567,
99519-0567, Clitheroe Center, Point
Woronzoff; tel: (907) 276-2898 (acc 61)

Guam, GU 96910: Lighthouse Recovery Center,
440 E Marine Dr, PO Box 23038, GMF
GU 96921, E Agana; tel: (671) 477-7671

Honolulu, HI 96816-4500: Women's Way/
Family Treatment Services, 845 22nd Ave;
tel: (808) 732-2802 (acc 41)

Honolulu, HI 96817: Addiction Treatment
Services, 3624 Waokanaka St;
tel: (808) 595-6371 (acc 80)

Honolulu, HI 96822-1757: Therapeutic Living,
2950 Manoa Rd, #A; tel: (808) 988-1786

Los Angeles, CA 90073: The Haven-Victory
Place, 11301 Wilshire Blvd, Bldg 212;
tel: (310) 478-3711 ext 48761 (acc 200)

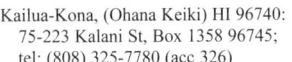

USA Western Territory

Child Day Care Centres

Aiea (Leeward-Ohana Keiki), HI 96701: 98-612 Moanalua Loop; tel: (808) 487-1636 (acc 57)

Aurora, CO 80011: 802 Quari Ct, Box 31739, 80041-0739; tel: (303) 366-7585 (acc 123)

Boise, ID Booth, 83702: 1617 N 24th, Box 1216 83701; tel: (208) 343-3571 (acc 15)

Bozeman, MT 59715: 32 S Rouse, Box 1307, 59771-1307; tel: (406) 586-5813 (acc 14)

Colorado Springs, CO 80903-4023: Children's Development Center, 709 S Sierra Madre; tel: (719) 578-9190 (acc 30)

Denver, CO 80205-4547: Denver Red Shield Child Day Care (acc 163); Denver Red Shield Tutor Program, 2915 High St; tel: (303) 295-2108 (acc 250)

Denver, CO 80219-1859: Denver Citadel Tutor Program, PO Box 280750, 80228-0750, 4505 W Alameda Ave; tel: (303) 922-4540 (acc 15)

Globe, AZ 85501: Box 1743, 85502, 161 E Cedar St; tel: (928) 425-4011 (acc 20)

Greeley, CO 80632: Day Care Center, 1119 6th St, Box 87, 80632; tel: (970) 346-1661 (acc 45

Helena, MT 59601: Pure Gold Christian Day Care, 1330 Hudson; tel: (406) 442-8244 (acc 150)

Honolulu, (FTS-Kula Kokua), HI 96816: 845 22nd Ave; tel: (808) 732-2802 (acc 24)

Honolulu, (Kauluwela-Ohana Keiki) HI 96817: 296 N Vineyard Blvd; tel: (808) 521-6551 (acc 75)

Honolulu, (Leeward-Ohana Keiki) HI 96701: 98-612 Moanalua Loop; tel: (808) 487-1636 (acc 60)

Kailua-Kona, (Ohana Keiki) HI 96740: 75-223 Kalani St, Box 1358 96745; tel: (808) 325-7780 (acc 326)

Los Angeles, CA 90026: Alegria Day/After-School Care, 2737 Sunset Blvd; tel: (323) 454-4200 (acc 76)

Los Angeles, CA 90021: 836 Stanford Ave; tel: (213) 623-9022 (acc 200)

Los Angeles, CA 90025: Bessie Pregerson Childcare, Westwood Transitional Village, 1401 S Sepulveda Blvd; tel: (310) 477-9539 (acc 64)

Los Angeles, CA 90001: South Los Angeles, 7655 Central Ave; tel: (323) 277-0732 (acc 62)

Modesto, CA 95354, 625 'I' St, PO Box 1663 (mail), 95353; tel: (209) 342-5220 (acc 60)

Monterey, CA 93942: PO Box 1884 (mail), 1491 Contra Costa, Seaside, 93955; tel: (831) 899-4915 (acc 105)

Oakland, CA Box 510, 94604: Booth Memorial, 2794 Garden St; tel: (510) 535-5088 (acc 63)

Phoenix, AZ 85008: 2707 E Van Buren St; tel: (602) 267-4138 (acc 33)

Pomona, CA 91767: Box 2562, 91769, 490 E Laverne Ave; tel: (909) 623-1579 (acc 115)

Portland, OR 97296: 2640 NW Alexandra Ave; tel: (503) 239-1248 (acc 18)

Riverside, CA 92501: 3695 1st St; tel: (909) 784-4495 (acc 104)

Sacramento, CA 95817-1923: 2550 Alhambra Blvd; tel: (916) 451-4230 (acc 45)

San Diego, CA 92123: Door of Hope, 2799 Health Center Dr; tel: (858) 279-1100 (acc 108)

San Francisco, CA 94103: 407 9th St; tel: (415) 503-3000 (acc 31)

Santa Barbara, CA 93111: Day Care and After-School Latchkey Program, Box 6190, 93160-6190, 4849 Hollister Ave; tel: (805) 683-3724 (acc 93)

Santa Fe Springs, CA 90606: Infant/Pre-School and After-School Care, 12000 E Washington Blvd; tel: (310) 696-7175 (acc 28)

Seattle, WA 98103: Little People Day Care, 9501 Greenwood Ave N Box 30638, 98103-0638; tel: (206) 782-3142 (acc 65)

Tacoma, WA 98405: Joyful Noise Child Care, 1100 S Puget Sound Ave; tel: (253) 752-1661 (acc 47)

Mount Crags Chorus performs at the Southern California Music Camp in USA Western Territory

Torrance, CA 90503: 4223 Emerald St;
tel: (310) 370-4514 (acc 60)

Tustin, CA 92680: 10200 Pioneer Rd;
tel: (714) 918-0659 (acc 75)

Correctional Services Offices

Los Angeles, CA 90015-1356: 900 W James M.
Wood Blvd, Box 15899, Del Valle Station
90015-0899; tel: (213) 896-9185

Portland, OR 97232: 1785 NE Sandy Blvd;
tel: (503) 239-1229

Emergency Shelters, Hospitality Houses

Anchorage, AK 99508: Booth Memorial, 3600 E
20th Ave; tel: (907) 279-0522 (acc 5)

Anchorage, AK 99501: Eagle Crest Transitional
Housing, 438 E 9th Ave; tel: (907) 276-5913
(acc 76)

Anchorage, AK 99501: McKinnell Res 546
E 15th Ave; tel: (907) 276-1609 (acc 35)

Anchorage, AK 99508: Cares for Kids (Crisis
Nursery), 3600 E. 20th Ave;
tel: (907) 276-8511 (acc 15)

Bell, CA 90201: 5600 Rickenbacker;
tel: (323) 263-1206 (acc 474)

Boise, ID 83702: 1617 N 24th St;
tel: (208) 343-3571 (acc 24)

Cheyenne, WY 82001: Sally's House 1920
Seymour St, PO Box 385, 82003 (mail);
tel: (307) 634-2769 (acc 6)

Colorado Springs, CO 80909: Bridge House,
2641 E Yampa St; tel: (719) 227-8773
(acc 7)

Colorado Springs, CO 80909-4037: 2649 E
Yampa St, Freshstart Transitional Family
Housing; tel: (719) 227-8773 (acc 61)

Colorado Springs, CO 80903-4023: R.J.
Montgomery New Hope Center, 709 S Sierra
Madre; tel: (719) 578-9190 (acc 200)

Denver, CO 80216: Crossroads Center, 1901
29th St; tel: (303) 298-1028 (acc 294)

Denver, CO 80221-4115: Denver New Hope
(Lambuth) Family Center, 2741 N Federal
Blvd; tel: (303) 477-3758 (acc 84)

El Paso, TX 79905: Box 10756-79997, 4300 E
Paisano Dr; tel: (915) 544-9811 (acc 136)

Fresno, CA 93711-3705: Gablecrest Women's
Transitional Home, 1107 West Shaw;
tel: (559) 226-6110 (acc 52)

Glendale, CA 91204-2053: Nancy Painter Home,
320 W Windsor Rd; tel: (213) 245-2424
(acc 19)

Grand Junction, CO 81502: Women's and Family
Shelter, 915 Grand Ave, PO Box 578-0578
81501 (mail); tel: (907) 242-3343 (acc 10)

Hilo, HI 96720: Interim Home for Youth, Box
5085; tel: (808) 935-4411 (acc 18)

Honolulu, HI 96816: FTS-Supportive Living,
845 22nd Ave; tel: (808) 732-2802 (acc 24)

Kahului, HI 96732-2256: 45 Kamehameha St;
tel: (808) 877-3042

Kailua-Kona, HI 96740: Interim Home-Youth
Shelter, 74-5045 Huaala St, PO Box 5085,
Hilo, HI 96720; tel: (808) 935-4411 (acc 8)

Kodiak, AK 99615-6511: Kodiak, Beachcombers
Transitional Housing, 1855 Mission Rd;
tel: (907) 486-8740

Las Vegas, NV 89030: Safehaven-Shelter, 31 W
Owens Ave; tel: (702) 639-0277 (acc 22)

Las Vegas, NV 89030: Pathways, 37 W Owens
Ave; tel: (702) 639-0277 (acc 42)

Las Vegas, NV 89030: Lied Transitional
Housing, 45 W Owens Ave;
tel: (702) 642-7252 (acc 70)

Las Vegas, NV 89030: Emergency Lodge,
47 W Owens Ave; tel: (702) 639-0277
(acc 167)

Las Vegas, NV 89030: PATH, 47 W Owens
Ave; tel: (702) 639-0277 (acc 34)

Lodi, CA 95240-2128: Hope Harbor Family
Service Center, 622 N Sacramento St;
tel: (209) 367-9560 (acc 81)

Long Beach, CA 90810: The Village at
Callebrio, 2260 Williams St;
tel: (562) 388-7600 (acc 135)

Los Angeles, CA 90007: Harmony Hall, 3107 S
Grand Ave; tel: (213) 748-0391 (acc 60)

Los Angeles, CA 90073: Naomi House (for
women veterans), Exodus Lodge (for mentally
ill), The Haven, 11301 Wilshire Blvd, Bldg
212, Los Angeles; tel: (310) 478-3711 ext
48761 (acc 100)

Los Angeles, CA 90013: Safe Harbor, 721 E
5th St; tel: (213) 622-5253 (90013) (acc 56)

Los Angeles, CA 90015: Alegria (HIV/Aids
housing), 2737 Sunset Blvd; tel: (323) 263-1206
(acc 195)

Los Angeles, CA 90028: The Way In (teen
counselling), 5941 Hollywood Blvd,
Box 38668, 90038-0668; tel: (213) 468-8666
(acc 26)

Los Angeles, CA 90025-3477: Westwood
Transitional Housing, 1401 S Sepulveda Blvd;
tel: (310) 477-9539 (acc 64)

Marysville, CA 95901-5629: The Depot Family
Shelter, 408 J St; tel: (530) 742-0892 (acc 58)

Marysville, CA 95901, Transitional Living
Facility, 5906 B Riverside Dr;
tel: (530) 743-5017 (acc 40)

WELCOME
ALL AFRICA CONGRESS
Africa
for
Christ
2005
ZIMBABWE

Some of the 7,000-strong congregation meeting at the National Sports Stadium in Harare, Zimbabwe, for the All-Africa Congress

Top: Seekers respond to the Bible message from General John Larsson (inset)

Above left: The Vice President Zimbabwe, Her Excellency Joyc< T. Mujuru, with the acting Mayc of Harare, both Salvationists

Above: Soweto Songsters (Southern Africa Territory)

Left: Flags at the opening ceremony

Top: Congo (Brazzaville) Timbrelists

Above: Dancers from Rwanda
Left: Not too old to dance!

Below: Some of the Southern Africa delegates

From top: Marching through Prague, Czech Republic; in worship and praise; a Bible study group; Eastern Europe delegates from (left to right) Romania, Moldova and Georgia

Medford, OR 97501-4630: 1065 Crews Rd;
tel: (541) 773-7005 (acc 43)

Nampa, ID 83651: 1412 4th St, South;
tel: (208) 461-3733 (acc 54)

Oakland, CA 94601: Family Emergency Shelter,
2794 Garden St, Box 510, 94604 (mail);
tel: (510) 437-9437 (acc 65)

Olympia, WA 98501: Hans K. Lemcke Lodge,
808 5th Ave SE, 98501; tel: (360) 352-8596
(acc 86)

Petaluma, CA 94975: PATH - Petaluma Area
Transitional Housing, PO Box 750684;
tel: (707) 769-0716

Phoenix, AZ 85008: Kaiser Family Center, 2707
E Van Buren, Elim House, PO Box 52177,
85072; tel: (602) 267-4122 (acc 114)

Portland, OR 97296: Women's Shelter, 2640
NW Alexandra Ave; tel: (503) 239-1248
(acc 10)

Portland, OR 97208: Women and Children's
Family Violence Center, PO Box 2398;
tel: (503) 239-1254 (acc 53)

Sacramento, CA 95814-0603: Emergency
Shelter, 1200 N 'B' St; tel: (916) 442-0331
(acc 132)

Salem, OR 97303:
1901 Front St NE; tel: (503) 585-6688 (acc 83);
105 River St NE; tel: (503) 391-1523 (acc 6);
1960 Water St NE; tel: (503) 566-7267 (acc 10)

San Bernardino, CA 92410: Box 991, 92402,
845 W Kingman St; tel: (909) 885-0353
(acc 60)

San Diego, CA 92101: Family Development
Center, 730 'F' St, Box 122688, 92112;
tel: (619) 231-6030 (acc 60)

San Diego, CA 92101: STEPS, 825 7th Ave;
tel: (619) 699-2223 (acc 30)

San Francisco, CA 94103: SF Harbor House,
407 9th St; tel: (415) 503-3000 (acc 66)

San Jose, CA 95112: Santa Clara Hospitality
House, 405 N 4th St, Box 2-D, 95109-0004
(mail); tel: (408) 282-1175 (acc 79)

Santa Ana, CA 92701: 818 E 3rd St;
tel: (714) 542-9576 (acc 52)

Santa Barbara, CA 93101: 423 Chapala St;
tel: (805) 962-6281 (acc 40)

Santa Fe Springs, CA: Transitional Living Center
12000 E Washington Blvd, 90606, Box 2009,
90610; tel: (562) 696-9562 (acc 116)

Santa Rosa, CA 95404-6610: Transitional Living
Program, 1059 2nd St; tel: (707) 535-4271
(acc 5)

Seaside, CA 93955: Casa De Las Palmas
Transitional Housing, 535 Palm Ave; Box

18842, 93942-1884 (mail);
tel: (831) 392-1762 (acc 36)

Seattle, WA 98102: Women's Shelter
(Emergency Financial Assistance), 1101 Pike
St, PO Box 20128; tel: (206) 447-9944
(acc 20)

Seattle, WA: Catherine Booth House (Shelter for
Abused Women), Box 20128, 98102;
tel: (206) 324-4943 (acc 17)

Seattle, WA 98134: William Booth Center –
Emergency Shelter and Transitional Shelter/
Living, 811 S Maynard; tel: (206) 621-0145
(acc 183)

Seattle, WA 98136: Hickman House (Women),
5600 Fauntleroy Way SW, Box 20128, 98102;
tel: (206) 932-5341 (acc 35)

Spokane, WA 99201: Box 9108, 99209-9108,
SAFE Center, 1403 W Broadway;
tel: (509) 325-6814 (acc 68)

Spokane, WA 99201: Sally's House (Foster Care
Home), Box 9108, 99209-9108, 222
E Indiana; tel: (509) 325-6826 (acc 14)

Spokane, WA 99207-2335: Transitional
Housing, 127 E Nora Ave; tel: (509) 326-7288
(acc 96)

Tacoma, WA 98405: Jarvie Family/Women
Emergency Shelter, 1521 6th Ave, Box 1254,
98401-1254; tel: (253) 627-3962 (acc 72)

Tucson, AZ 85705: 1021 N 11th Ave;
tel: (520) 622-5411 (acc 91)

Ventura, CA 93001-2703: 155 S Oak St;
tel: (805) 648-5032 (acc 51)

Watsonville, CA 95076-5048: Supportive
Housing Program for Women, 232 Union St;
tel: (831) 763-0131 (acc 60)

Whittier, CA 90602: 7926 Pickering Ave, PO
Box 954, 90608; tel: (562) 698-8348
(acc 17)

Harbour Light Centres

Denver, CO 80205: Denver Harbor Light, 2136
Champa St; tel: (303) 296-2456 (acc 80)

Los Angeles, CA 90013: Box 791, 90053-0791.
809 E Fifth St; tel: (213) 626-4786
(acc 195)

Portland, OR 97204: Box 5635, 97228-5635,
30 SW 2nd St; tel: (503) 239-1259
(acc 143)

San Francisco, CA 94103-4405: 1275 Harrison
St; tel: (415) 503-3000 (acc 124)

Residential Youth Care and Family
Service Centres

Anchorage, AK 99508: Booth Memorial Youth
& Family Services, 3600 E 20th Ave;
tel: (907) 279-0522 (acc 15)

Boise, ID 83702: Family Day Care Center,
Box 1216, 83701, 1617 N 24th St;
tel: (208) 343-3571 (acc 15)

Portland, OR 97210: Box 10027, 2640 NW
Alexandra Ave; tel: (503) 239-1248 (acc 33)

San Diego, CA 92123: DOH Haven, Transitional
Living Center, 2799 Health Center Dr;
tel: (858) 279-1100

Adult Rehabilitation Programs (Men)

Albuquerque, NM 87102: Box 27690, 87125-
7690, 400 John St SE; tel: (505) 242-3112
(acc 36)

Anchorage, AK 99503: 660 E 48th Ave;
tel: (907) 562-5408 (acc 61)

Chico, CA 95973: 13434 Browns Valley Dr;
tel: (530) 342-2199

Grand Junction, CO 81502: Box 578, 81502,
903 Grand Ave; tel: (970) 242-8632 (acc 32)

North Las Vegas, NV 89030: Box 30096, 211
Judson St; tel: (702) 649-2374 (acc 118)

Reno, NV 89502-1119: 835 E Second St;
tel: (775) 688-4570 (acc 66)

Reno, NV 89512-1605: 2300 Valley Rd;
tel: (775) 688-4559

Salt Lake City, UT 84102-2030: 252 South 500
East; tel: (801) 323-5817 (acc 51)

Adult Rehabilitation Programs (Women)

Grand Junction, CO 81502: Adult Rehabilitation
Program – Women's Residence, 915 Grand
Ave, PO Box 578-0578 81501 (mail);
tel: (907) 242-8632 (acc 10)

Las Vegas, NV 89030: 39 W Owens;
tel: (702) 649-1469 (acc 42)

Senior Citizens' Housing

Albuquerque, NM: Silvercrest, 4400 Pan Am
Fwy NE, 87107; tel: (505) 883-1068
(acc 55)

Broomfield, CO 80020-1876: Silvercrest 1110 E
10th Ave; tel: (303) 464-1994 (acc 85)

Capitola, CA 95010-2761: Silvercrest Senior
Citizens' Residence, 750 Bay Ave;
tel: (831) 464-6435 (acc 114)

Chula Vista, CA: Silvercrest, 636 3rd Ave,
91910; tel: (619) 427-4991 (acc 73)

Colorado Springs, CO 80909-7507: Silvercrest I,
904 Yuma St; tel: (719) 475-2045 (acc 50)

Colorado Springs, CO 80909-5097: Silvercrest II,
824 Yuma St; tel: (719) 389-0329 (acc 50)

Denver, CO 80219-1859: Silvercrest, 4595 W
Alameda; tel: (303) 922-2924 (acc 66)

Denver, CO 80221-2234: West Adams
Silvercrest, 2821 W 65th Pl, PO Box 211008
(mail); tel: (303) 657-1088 (acc 32)

El Cajon, CA 92020: Silvercrest, 175 S Anza St;
tel: (619) 593-1077 (acc 73)

El Paso, TX 79903: Silvercrest, 3926 Bliss Ave,
PO Box 10756 (mail); tel: (915) 566-0840
(acc 25)

El Sobrante, CA 94803-1859: Silvercrest,
4630 Appian Way; tel: (510) 758-1518
(acc 85)

Escondido, CA 92026: Silvercrest, 1301 Las
Villas Way; tel: (760) 741-4106 (acc 75)

Eureka, CA 95501-1264: Silvercrest, 2141
Tydd St; tel: (707) 445-3141 (acc 152)

Fresno, CA 93721-1041: Silvercrest, 1824
Fulton St; tel: (559) 237-9111 (acc 158)

Glendale, CA 92104: Silvercrest, 323 W
Garfield; tel: (818) 543-0211 (acc 150)

Hollywood, CA 90028: Silvercrest, 5940 Carlos
Ave; tel: (323) 460-4335 (acc 140)

Lake View Terrace, CA 91354: Silvercrest,
11850 Foothill Blvd; tel: (818) 896-7580

Los Angeles, CA 90006: Silvercrest, 947 S
Hoover St; tel: (213) 387-7278 (acc 89)

Mesa, AZ 85201: Silvercrest, 255 E 6th St;
tel: (480) 649-9117 (acc 81)

Missoula, MT 59801: Silvercrest, 1550 S 2nd W;
tel: (406) 541-0464 (acc 50)

N Las Vegas, NV 89030: Silvercrest, 2801
Equador Ct; tel: (702) 643-0293 (acc 60)

Oceanside, CA 92056: Silvercrest, 3839 Lake
Blvd; tel: (760) 940-0267 (acc 67)

Pasadena, CA 91106: Silvercrest, 975 E Union
St; tel: (626) 432-6678 (acc 72)

Phoenix, AZ 85003: Silvercrest, 613 N 4th Ave;
tel: (602) 251-2000 (acc 125)

Portland, OR 97232: Silvercrest, 1865 NE Davis;
tel: (503) 236-2320 (acc 78)

Puyallup, WA 98373: Silvercrest, 4103
9th St SW; tel: (253) 841-0785 (acc 40)

Redondo Beach, CA 90277: Mindeman
Senior Residence, 125 W Beryl St;
tel: (310) 318-2827/0582 (acc 46)

Reno, NV 89512-2448: Silvercrest, 1690
Wedekind Rd; tel: (775) 322-2050 (acc 59)

Riverside, CA 92501: Silvercrest, 3003 Orange;
tel: (909) 276-0173 (acc 72)

San Diego, CA 92101: Silvercrest, 727 E St;
tel: (619) 699-7272 (acc 122)

San Francisco, CA 94133-3844: SF Chinatown
Senior Citizens' Residence, 1450 Powell St;
tel: (415) 781-8545 (acc 8)

San Francisco, CA 94107-1132: Silvercrest,
133 Shipley St; tel: (415) 543-5381
(acc 345)

An officer brings some moments of delight to young victims of Hurricane Katrina whose family had set up home in an emergency shelter. When Hurricane Katrina struck the Gulf Coast, the USA Western Territory immediately sent personnel to the scene and assisted the many displaced people who were relocated to the West.

Santa Fe Springs, CA 90670: Silvercrest, 12015 Lakeland Rd; tel: (562) 946-7717 (acc 21)

Santa Monica, CA 90401: Silvercrest, 1530 5th St; tel: (310) 393-5336 (acc 122)

Santa Rosa, CA 95404-6601: Silvercrest, 1050 Third St ; tel: (707) 544-6766 (acc 187)

Seattle, WA 98103, Silvercrest, 9543 Greenwood Ave N; tel: (206) 706-0855 (acc 75)

Stockton, CA 95202-2645: Silvercrest, 123 N Stanislaus St; tel: (209) 463-4960 (acc 82)

Tulare, CA 93274: 350 North 'L' St; tel: (559) 688-0704

Turlock, CA 95380: Silvercrest, 865 Lander Ave; Box 116, 95380-5815 (mail); tel: (209) 669-8863 (acc 85)

Ventura, CA 93004: Silvercrest, 750 Petit Ave; tel: (805) 647-0110 (acc 73)

Wahiawa, HI 96786: Silvercrest Residence, 520 Pine St; tel: (808) 622-2785 (acc 159)

Senior Citizens' Nutrition Centres

Anchorage, AK 99518-1112: Older Alaskans Program (OAP), 401 International Airport Rd, Ste #19; tel: (907) 349-0613

Denver, CO 80205-4547: Denver Red Shield, 2915 High St; (tel): (303) 295-2107

Denver, CO 80221-0395: West Adams, 2821 W 65th Pl; tel: (303) 428-6430

Fresno, CA 93712-1041: 1824 Fulton St; tel: (559) 233-0139

Modesto, CA 95354-2225: 625 'I' St; tel: (209) 577-4068

Modesto, CA 95358-8803: 1649 Las Vegas St; tel: (209) 538-7111

Oakland, CA 94607: 379 12th St; tel: (510) 834-1089

Phoenix, AZ: Laura Danieli Senior Activity Center, 613 N 4th Ave; tel: (602) 251-2005

Portland, OR 97232-2822: Rose Centre – Senior Citizens Program, 211 NE 18th Ave; tel: (503) 239-1221

Salinas, CA 93906-1519: 2460 N Main St; tel: (831) 443-9655

San Diego, CA 92101-1679: Senior Citizens Program (9 Locations), 2320 5th Ave; tel: (619) 843-9451

San Francisco, CA 94107-1125: Senior Citizens Meal Program, 850 Harrison St; tel: (415) 777-5350

San Jose, CA 95112: 359 N 4th St; tel: (408) 282-1165

Tulare, CA 93274-4131: 314 E San Joaquin Ave; tel: (559) 687-2520

Turlock, CA 95380-5815: 893 Lander Ave; tel: (209) 667-6091

Watsonville, CA 95076-5203: 29-A Bishop St; tel: (831) 724-0948

In addition there are 15 fresh-air camps and 32 youth community centres attached to divisions, as well as 617 service units in the territory

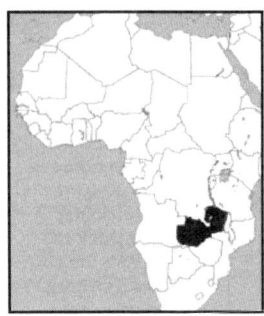

ZAMBIA TERRITORY

Territorial Commander:
Commissioner Vinece Chigariro
(1 Aug 2004)

Chief Secretary:
Lieut-Colonel Grey Miyoba (1 May 2005)

Territorial Headquarters: 685A Cairo Road, Lusaka

Postal address: PO Box 34352, Lusaka 10101, Zambia

tel: [260] 1 238291/228327; fax: [260] 1 226784; email: sathq@coppernet.zm

In 1922 emigrants from villages on the north bank of the Zambezi River working in a mica mine near Urungwe were converted. They carried home the message of salvation to their chief, and established meeting places in their villages. Two years later, Commandant Kunzwi Shava and Lieutenant Paul Shumba were appointed to command the new opening. The Zambia Division in the Rhodesia Territory became the Zambia Command in 1966. In 1988, the Malawi Division was transferred from the Zimbabwe Territory to form the new Zambia and Malawi Territory. The Zambia and Malawi Territory became the Zambia Territory on 1 October 2002 when Malawi became an independent region.

Zone: Africa
Country included in the territory: Zambia
Languages in which the gospel is preached: Chibemba, Chinyanja, Chitonga, English, Lozi

THE Salvation Army was recognised by the government and other Christian organisations in the country when the Vice President of Zambia (the Hon Lupando Mwape) was among thousands of Christians who attended an interdenominational service to mark the World Day of Prayer at Lusaka's Cathedral of the Holy Cross. The event was hosted by The Salvation Army.

Further government recognition of the Army's work came after the country was hit by heavy rains and most areas were affected by floods. Among the worst hit parts was Kazungula, where many people were left homeless. Territorial Commander Colonel Vinece Chigariro, with other officers, drove to the disaster area and distributed hundreds of blankets to flood victims.

The TC met with the Minister of Southern Province (the Hon Alice Simango), who expressed heartfelt thanks on behalf of the government. 'I am humbled and overjoyed by what The Salvation Army is doing in Southern Province,' she told Colonel Chigariro.

The Army's work in the province includes a hospital and a school in Chikankata, HIV/Aids programmes, and food distribution among HIV/Aids patients at Livingstone General Hospital.

Two babies were born during the TC's visit to the displaced persons camp and both received clothing supplied through the Women's Ministries Department.

More than 300 delegates from all the territory's divisions and districts attended the All-Africa Congress held in Harare (Zimbabwe) during August 2005 and presided over by General John Larsson. Many made a public response to the General's Bible message with its challenge from Christ to 'Come unto me' and 'Go into the world'.

Zonal leaders Commissioners Amos and Rosemary Makina (IHQ) visited during October and November 2005 for a territorial review and the commissioning of the Visionaries Session. This was also attended by the Malawi Command leaders (Lieut-Colonels David and Jean Burrows) as four Malawians were among the 23 new officers.

The highlight of Good Friday and Easter Sunday 2006 was the TC's visit to the Lower Gwembe Valley Section. Colonel Chigariro was the first territorial leader to visit this remote area and during the meetings many people found Christ as their personal saviour. The Roman Catholic church closed so that members could join the Salvationists for the Easter service.

STATISTICS
Officers 214 (active 196 retired 18) Cadets 24 (Zambia 20 Malawi 4) Employees 349
Corps 90 Societies 69 Outposts 87 New Openings 86 Hospital 1 High School 1 Old People's Home 1 Farm 1

Senior Soldiers 20,471 Adherents 1,008 Junior Soldiers 4,319
Personnel serving outside territory Officers 4

STAFF
Sec for Personnel: Maj Elisha Mankomba
Sec for Programme: Maj Vincent K. Milambo
Sec for Business Administration:
  Maj Davidson Varhgese
Audit: Maj Bislon Hanunka
Community Development and Social Services:
  Capt Beryl Pierce
Extension Training: Maj Ireen Hacamba
Finance: Capt Donald Hangoma
Property: Capt Emmanuel Manyepa
Micro-Credit: Maj Melody Hanunka
Projects: Capt Kennedy Mizinga
Sponsorship: Capt Patricia Hangoma
Territorial Band: B/M John Chinyemba
Territorial Songsters: S/L Jericho Milambo
Trade: Medah Manyepa
Training: Maj Joster Chenda
Women's Ministries: Comr Vinece Chigariro (TPWM) Lt-Col Leniah Miyoba (Asst TPWM) Maj Saraphina Milambo (TSWM,) Capt M. Chikondo (TJHLS) Maj Alice Mankomba (TLOMS, SAMF)
Youth and Candidates: Capt Henry Shiridzinodya

TRAINING COLLEGE
PO Box 34352, Lusaka, 10101; tel: (01) 261755; email: saotc@zamnet.zm

DIVISIONS
Lusaka North West: PO Box 33934, Lusaka; Maj Francis Nyambalo
Lusaka South East: PO Box 34352, Lusaka; tel: (01) 221960; Maj Bernard Chisengele
Mapangazya: P Bag S2, Mazabuka; Maj Bexter Magaya
Mazabuka: PO Box 670017, Mazabuka; tel: (032) 30420; Maj Metson Chilyabanyama

DISTRICTS
Copperbelt: PO Box 70075, Ndola; tel: (02) 680302; Capt Last Siamoya
Siavonga: PO Box 59, Siavonga; tel: (01) 511362; Capt Bryson Sitwala
Zambia Southern: PO Box 630537, Choma; Maj Adeck Mwiinga

SECTION (reporting to THQ)
Eastern: PO Box 510199, Chipata; tel: (097) 881828; Capt James Gitangita

CHIKANKATA MISSION
P Bag S2, Mazabuka
Mission Director: Maj Christopher Mabuto

CHIKANKATA HEALTH SERVICES
P Bag S2, Mazabuka; tel: (01) 222060;
email: administration@chikankata.com
Chief Medical Officer: Dr Trevor Kaile, BSc,
MBChB
Doctor: Elsa B'jorkqvist
Manager/Administration: Mr Richard
Bradbury, MSc
**Manager/Aids Management Training
Services:** Mr Ben Njobvu, Dip Ed
**Manager/Community Health and
Development:** Mr Charles Mang'ombe,
DipCME
Manager/Nursing Education: Ms Clemmy
Sooka, BSc, RN, RM
Hospital Chaplain: Maj Anna Mabuto
Nursing Officer: Mrs Mirriam Kalenga

Medical Clinics (under Chikankata)
Chaanga, Chikombola, Nadezwe, Nameembo,
Syanyolo

Youth Project (under Chikankata)
Chikombola

CHIKANKATA HIGH SCHOOL
P Bag S1, Mazabuka; tel: (01) 220820;
email: bhachitapika@chikankata.com
Headmaster: Mr Oscar Mwanza
Deputy Head: Mr Edson Matonka
Chaplain and Business Manager:
Matron: Capt Catherine Mukoboto

OLD PEOPLE'S HOME AND VOCATIONAL TRAINING CENTRE
Mitanda Home for the Aged: PO Box 250096,

Kansenshi, Ndola; tel: (02) 680460; email:
mitanda@coppernet.zm
Administrators: Majs Richard and Eunice
Mweemba
Nursing Officer: Capt Jennifer Muleya

PRE-SCHOOL GROUPS
Chikankata; Chikanzaya; Chipapa; Chipata;
Chitumbi; Choma; Dundu; George; Hapwaya;
Ibbwe Munyama; John Laing; Kakole;
Kalomo; Kanyama; Kawama; Kazungula;
Lusaka Citadel; Maamba; Magoye; Mitchel;
Mukwela; Mumbwa; Ngangula; Njomona;
Nkonkola; Peters; Siavonga; Sikoongo;
Sinazongwe; Situmbeko

COMMUNITY SCHOOLS
Chipata (Lusaka), Choma, George, John Laing,
Kanyama, Kawama, Luanshya

COMMUNITY WORK
Agriculture Projects: Chikankata, Chitumbi,
Dundu, Hamabuya, Malala, Ngamgula
Feeding Programme: Lusitu
Fish Farming Projects: Kanyama, George
Health Centres: George, John Laing, Kanyama
HIV/Aids Training, Counselling: Chikankata,
THQ
Micro-Credit Projects:
    Lusaka North West: Matero, George, Kabwe
    Lusaka South East: Chelstone, Chawama
    Mapangazya: Chikankata, Chitumbi
    Mazabuka: Kaleya, Njomona
    Copperbelt: Chimwemwe, Kabushi
    Siavonga: Chirundu, Lusitu, Mitchell, Sivonga

FARM (income-generating)
PO Box 250096, Kansenshi, Ndola;
tel: (02) 680460

Hosha-playing Salvationists on the march past at the All-Africa Congress held in Harare (Zimbabwe) – more than 300 delegates attended from the Zambia Command

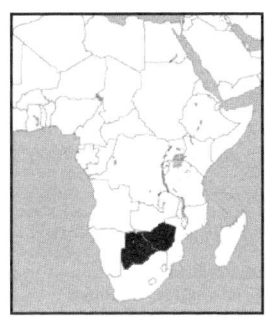

ZIMBABWE TERRITORY

Territorial leaders:
Commissioners Stanslous and Jannet Mutewera

Territorial Commander:
Commissioner Stanslous Mutewera
(1 Jul 2004)

Chief Secretary:
Lieut-Colonel Robert Ward (1 Aug 2002)

Territorial Headquarters: 45 Josiah Chinamano Avenue, Harare

Postal address: PO Box 14, Harare, Zimbabwe

tel: [263] (4) 736666/7/8, 250107/8; fax: [263] (4) 726658; tel address: Salvation Harare; email: ZIMTHQ@zim.salvationarmy.org; web site: www.salvationarmy.org/www_zim.nsf

A pioneer party, led by Major and Mrs Pascoe, set out from Kimberley, South Africa, on 5 May 1891 in a wagon drawn by 18 oxen, arriving in Fort Salisbury on 18 November. The then Rhodesia became a separate territory on 1 May 1931. Work spread to Botswana where The Salvation Army was officially recognised in 1997.

Zone: Africa
Countries included in the territory: Botswana, Zimbabwe
'The Salvation Army' in Ndebele: Impi yo Sindiso; in Shona: Hondo yo Ruponiso
Languages in which the gospel is preached: Chitonga, English, Ndebele, Shona, Tswana
Periodicals: *Zimbabwe Salvationist, ZEST* (women's magazine)

FACED with four-figure annual inflation, the continuing onslaught of HIV/Aids and shortages of basic commodities and services, the territorial executive chose the theme 'Seek God's Face, Make A Difference' as the key message for the territory.

Zimbabwe hosted the first All-Africa Congress conducted by General John Larsson and then Chief of the Staff Commissioner Israel L. Gaither. More than 14,000 Salvationists joined in the final meeting, completing five days of great blessing and inspiration.

The Territorial Youth Planning Committee gave oversight to the Year for Children and Youth, and will continue to ensure that such events as the Youth Ambassador initiatives, corps cadet camps and sports ministries thrive. A youth associate position was added to the Youth Department to stimulate youth programmes at community level.

The Salvation Army Officers' Children Association (SAOCA) was given priority during the year, gathering in five different areas to consider concerns and ideas. Discussion led to planning a first-ever Territorial SAOCA Congress for 2007.

Five months after the Visionaries

Session was commissioned 40 cadets of the God's Fellow Workers Session were welcomed to the training college. The different venue for the welcome meetings – Bulawayo – provided a special memory for the cadets and the southern region.

Outreach was emphasised by the Women's Ministries Department during two territorial workshops for women leaders and soldiers in the Medical Fellowship and League of Mercy. Three-day divisional reviews of women's ministries were held to build stronger divisional teams and to set clear plans for future mission.

Salvationists continued to display amazing generosity in achieving the highest total yet for the Territorial Thanksgiving Ingathering. Most remarkable, however, was the almost US$100,000 collected for the International Self-Denial Appeal – the highest total yet, despite the harsh economic climate.

The territory received the title deeds for the Horseshoe Sports Complex, a 20-acre site with buildings donated for Salvation Army work in this rural setting. Three farms were also donated to the territory. Several corps buildings and officers' quarters were opened.

A new Shona songbook was published, much to the delight of soldiers and boarding school students who had been waiting enthusiastically for its arrival. Zimbabwe's first Territorial Band was inaugurated.

Using questionaires and a facilitated workshop, a divisional task force reviewed the effectiveness of the size of Central Mashonaland Division (20,000 soldiers). The proposal to split the division into three new geographical entities was accepted by THQ and IHQ, effective 1 August 2006.

STATISTICS

Officers 578 (active 467 retired 111) **Cadets** 38 **Employees** 1,430

Corps 401 **Societies** 214 **Outposts** 179 **Institutions/Social Centres** 7 **Hospitals** 2 **Schools – Pre-Schools** 51 **Primary** 37 **Secondary** 18 **Vocational Training** 7

Senior Soldiers 121,000 **Adherents** 3,571 **Recruits** 10,687 **Junior Soldiers** 47,129

Personnel serving outside territory Officers 7

STAFF

Sec for Business: Maj Innocent Kwenda
Sec for Personnel: Lt-Col Henry Mhasvi
Sec for Programme: Maj Benjamin Mnyampi
Audit: Maj Clever Kamambo
Development Services: Capt Criswell Chizengaya
Education: Capt Christopher Pamacheche
Extension Training: Mrs Rochelle McAlister
Finance: Maj Francis Nyakusamwa
HIV/Aids Coordinator: Maj Norma Kwenda
Human Resources Development: Maj Shiellah Rutanhira
Information Technology: Capt Timothy Johnson
Property: Capt Edmore Zinyowera
Public Relations: Capt Anderson Chipiro
Social: Maj Nicholas Chigwaza
Sponsorship: Capt Lindani Nikisi
Statistics: Maj Daphne Kamambo
Territorial Bandmaster: B/M M. Mtombeni
Territorial Songster Leader: S/L K. E. Mushababiri
Trade: Capt Florence Pamacheche
Training: Maj Eleckson Rutanhira
Women's Ministries: Comr Jannet Mutewera (TPWM) Lt-Col Marguerite Ward (TSWM) Maj Grace Mnyampi (TLOMS) Lt-Col Evan Mhasvi (THLS)
Youth/Candidates: Capt Absolom Makanga

DIVISIONS

Bindura: PO Box 197, Bindura; tel: (071) 6689; Maj Frederick Masango
Chiweshe: PO Box 98, Glendale; tel: (077) 214524; Maj Dubayi Ncube
Greater Harare: PO Box 1496, Harare; tel: (04) 747359; Maj Sydney Mabhiza

Guruve: c/o Box 150, Guruve; tel: (058) 505; Maj Edwin Jeremiah

Harare Eastern: PO Box 26, Zengeza; tel: (070) 22639; Maj Trustmore Muzorori

Hurungwe: PO Box 269, Karoi; tel: (064) 629229; Maj Dominic Nkomo

Kadoma: PO Box 271, Kadoma; tel: (068) 23338; Maj Isaac Mhembere

Makonde: PO Box 33, Chinhoyi; tel: (067) 2107; Maj Joel Sundika

Masvingo: PO Box 314, Masvingo; tel: (039) 63308; Maj Samuel Mkami

Matebeleland: PO Box 227 FM, Famona, Bulawayo; tel: (09) 46934; Capt Sipho Mbangwa

Midlands: PO Box 624, Kwekwe; tel: (055) 3992; Maj Michael Bridge

Mupfure: PO Box 39, Mt Darwin; tel: (076) 529; Maj Jonathan Yafele

Semukwe: PO Box Maphisa Township, Maphisa; tel: (082) 396; Maj Final Mubaiwa

DISTRICTS

Manicaland: PO Box DV8, Dangamvura, Mutare; tel: (020) 30014; Maj Funny Nyereyemhuka

Murehwa: PO Box 268, Murehwa; tel: (078) 2455; Maj Lovemore Chidhakwa

AREAS

Harare Central: c/o Highfield Temple; Stand # 3300, Old Highfield; tel: 663 159; Area Coordinator: Capt Onai Jera

Harare West: c/o Dzivarasekwa Corps, PO Box 37, Dzivarasekwa; tel: (04) 216 293; Area Coordinator: Maj Tineyi Mambo

Hwange: PO Box 130, Dete; tel: 018 237; Area Coordinator: tel: (04) 216 293

TRAINING COLLEGE

PO Box CR95, Cranborne; tel: (04) 742298; fax: (04) 742575

MASIYE TRAINING CAMP

PO Box AC800 Bulawayo; tel: (09) 60727 CAMP tel/fax: (0838) 228; tel: (0838) 222 & 261; emails: info@masiye.com (camp), info@byo.masiye.com (town office); Ezekiel Mafusire (Director)

EDUCATION: BOARDING SCHOOLS

Bradley Secondary School: P Bag 909 Bindura; tel: (071) 3421; Maj Isiah Motsi (Administrator), Mrs Phoebe Moyo, BSc, Grd CE (Headmistress) (acc 516)

Howard High School: PO Box 230, Howard; tel: (0758) 45921; Maj Langton Zimpingani, BA (Administrator), Mr Shelton Kaungwa, BSc, Grad CE (Headmaster) (acc 908)

Mazowe High School: P Bag 211A, Harare; tel: (075) 25603; Capt Reuben Muchaurawa, BA (Administrator), Mr Thomson Katanda, BEd, Grad CE (Headmaster) (acc 670)

Usher Secondary School: P Bag P5271, Bulawayo; tel: (083) 2904; Capt Lovemore Meda (Administrator), Mrs Idah Moyo, BA, Grd CE (Headmistress) (acc 560)

MEDICAL

Athol Evans Hospital Home: Chiremba Rd, Queensdale, PO Box CR70, Cranborne; tel: (04) 572121; email: aec.sec@zol.co.zw; Maj Gordon Howard, MZIPR (Administrator), Maj Katherine Howard, SRN (Matron) (acc 164)

Bumhudzo Hospital Home: St Mary's Township, PO Box ZG 48, Zengeza, Harare; tel: (070) 24911; Maj Spiwe Chirandu (Administrator/Matron); 'C' scheme hospital home (acc 55); 'B' scheme residential (acc 55)

Howard Hospital: PO Box 190, Glendale; tel: (0758) 2433; emails: howard.hospital@africaonline.co.zw, pthistle@healthnet.zw; Mrs Zungu (Matron), Dr Paul Thistle (CMO) (acc 144)

Tshelanyemba Hospital: PO Tshelanyemba, Maphisa; tel: (082) 254; email: tshelanyemba.hosp@healthnet.zw; Capt Bigboy Nkomo (Administrator), Maj (Dr) Dawn Howse, MD (CMO) (acc 103)

SOCIAL SERVICES

Bulawayo

Enterprise House: Josiah Tongogara St/12th Ave, PO Box 3208; tel: (09) 60012; Maj Judith Nemhara (Administrator) (acc men 65)

Ralstein Home: Masotsha Ndhlovu Ave; tel: (09) 61972; Capt Obediah Nharara (Asst Officer) (acc mixed 30)

Harare

Braeside Social Complex: General Booth Rd, Braeside, PO Box CR66, Cranborne; tel: (04) 742001; Maj Elias Siyawareva (Administrator) (acc women 20, men 64)

Arcadia Girls' Hostel: Jampies St, Arcadia; tel: (04) 770082; Capt Susan Marere (Administrator) (acc 28)

Howard

Weaving and Dressmaking School: PO Howard; tel: (0758) 45921; Maj Beauty Zimpingani (Supervisor)

Officers on Active Service

Based on information received by 31 August 2006

1. The following list contains the names of all active officers with the rank of lieut-colonel and above, and other officers holding certain designated appointments.

2a. The place and date in parenthesis immediately following the name denote the place from which the officer entered Army service and the year of service commencement. Officers commissioned prior to 1 January 1973 have their active service dated from the conclusion of the first year of training. After 1 January 1973 active service begins at the date of commissioning following a two-year session of training.

b. Details of married women officers' entry to active service are shown separately, including maiden name. If a wife was trained separately from her husband the word *and* joins the two entries, but if trained together the word *with* joins them.

c. At the end of each entry of married officers a joint record of their service in other countries is given. Where applicable this includes countries each served in individually before marriage.

3. Where an officer is serving in a territory/command other than his/her own this is indicated by including the territory/command of origin after the corps from which he/she entered training. In all other instances the information given implies that the officer is serving in his/her home territory.

4. Details of appointments (where not given in this section) may be ascertained under the territorial or departmental headings.

5. A key to abbreviations is given on pages 342-343.

A

ABASTO, Franklin (Central Oruro, 1983); Maj, S Am W. b 25 Mar 47, and
ABASTO, Gladys (née Bustos) (Concepción, 1983) m 1984; Maj, S Am W. b 24 Apr 53.

ABAYOMI, Ebenezer (Ife Ife, 1988); Maj, Nig. b 4 Apr 60, and
ABAYOMI, Comfort (Ife Ife, 1990); Maj, Nig. b 12 Dec 63.

ABBOTT, Wilbert (Musgrave Harbour, NF, 1970); Maj, Can. b 30 Dec 48, and
ABBOTT, Bertha (née Pretty) (St John's, NF, 1970) m 1972; Maj, Can. b 1 Feb 51.

ABBULU, Sankurati Pedda (Achanta, 1978); Maj, Ind C. b 2 Jan 50, with
ABBULU, Vimala (née Kumari) m 1970; Maj, Ind C. b 10 Dec 53. Served in Tanz.

ÅBERG, Bert (Malmö 1, 1973); Maj, Swdn. b 14 Jan 51.

ABRAHAM, Lincoln Maddu (Guduru, 1991); Capt, Ind C. b 12 Sep 64, with
MERCY, Manjula m 1988; Capt, Ind C. b 22 May 66.

ABRAHAM, Puthenparambil T. (Karimala, 1972); Lt-Col, Ind SW. b 17 Feb 48, and
ABRAHAM, Mariamma (Central Adoor, 1975) m 1975; Lt-Col, Ind SW. b 30 Mar 52.

ADAMS, Clive (Claremont, S Afr, 1983); Maj, Nor. b 1 May 57. BTh, and
ADAMS, Marianne (née Jokobsen) (Oslo 3, 1985) m 1985; Maj, Nor. b 2 Oct 60. Served

in S Afr, UK and at IHQ.

ADDISON, Edward (Swedru, 1981); Maj, Gha. b 24 Jan 54. Ww Lt Margaret, pG 1983, and
ADDISON, Mercy (née Simpson) (Swedru, 1985) m 1985; Maj, Gha. b 4 Nov 60.

ADLER, Ines (Birsfelden, 1969); Col, CS, Switz. b 30 Sep 43.

ADU-MANU, Mike (Jamasi, 1987); Maj, Gha. b 10 Apr 48, with
ADU-MANU, Theresa (née Asante Pinamang) m 1970; Maj, Gha. b 1 Apr 48.

AGUILERA, Luis (Concepción, 1967); Lt-Col, S Am W. b 14 Aug 47, and
AGUILERA, Maria (née Caceres Morales) (Central Santiago, 1968) m 1969; Lt-Col, S Am W. b 31 Jan 45. Served in Sp and Mex.

AGUILERA, Miguel (Lo Valledor, S Am W, 1978); Maj, L Am N. b 9 Jul 55, and
AGUILERA, Angélica (née Cortes) (Lo Valledor, S Am W, 1978) m 1979; Maj, L Am N. b 11 Sep 58. Served in S Am W and Sp.

AGUIRRE, Bartolo (Salto, 1972); Maj, S Am E. b 4 May 45, with
AGUIRRE, Violeta (née Silveira) m 1969; Maj, S Am E. b 28 Oct 48.

AINSWORTH, Rodney (Mitchelton, 1973); Maj, Aus E. b 26 Nov 49, and
AINSWORTH, Leonie (née Matthews) (Woonona, 1976) m 1976; Maj, Aus E. b 6 Dec 53.

AJUBIGA, Cornelius Kemakolam (Umudim, 1974); Maj, Nig. b 26 Jun 48, with
AJUBIGA, Caroline m 1971; Maj, Nig. b 29 Nov 53.

AKPAN, Joseph (Calabar, 1980); Maj, Nig. b 30 Sep 58, with
AKPAN, Patience m 1978; Maj, Nig. b 15 May 62.

AKPAN, Mfon Jaktor (Igbobi, Nig, 1969); Comr, TC, Con (Braz). b 21 Jul 49, and
AKPAN, Ime Johnnie (née Udo) (Ikot Udobia, Nig, 1974) m 1974; Comr, TPWM, Con (Braz). b 9 Nov 53. Served in Nig.

ALARCÓN, David (Punta Arenas, 1980); Maj, S Am W. b 24 Jun 56, and
ALARCÓN, María (née Arredondo) (Rancagua, 1980) m 1982; Maj. S Am W. b 3 Mar 55.

ALARCÓN, Juan Carlos (Punta Arenas, 1972); Maj, S Am W. b 25 Jan 51, and
ALARCÓN, Nancy (née Muñoz) (Punta Arenas, 1971) m 1973; Maj, S Am W. b 17 Sep 52. Served in USA E.

ALHBIN, Britt Gunborg (Höganäs, Swdn, 1966); Maj, Pak. b 1 May 41. Served in Swdn and Indon.

ALIP, Romeo (Manila Central, Phil, 1978); Maj, GS, Lib. b 2 Jan 49. BSc (Architecture), and
ALIP, Evelyn (née Kilong-Kilong) (Cebu Central, Phil, 1977) m 1979; Maj, Lib. b 1 Jul 55. Served in Phil and Indon.

ALLAN, Graham (Kokomo, IN, 1975); Maj, USA C. b 24 Feb 49. BA (Counselling/Bus Admin), and
ALLAN, Vickie (née Hardebeck) (Kokomo, IN, 1975); Maj, USA C. b 26 Jan 50.

ALLEMAND, Carolyn (née Olckers) (Cape Town Citadel, S Afr, 1980); Lt-Col, UK. b 4 Oct 55. Served in S Afr, at IHQ and in S Am E. m 1989; Lt-Col Gustave, ret 2006.

ALLEY, Kelvin (Belconnen, 1987); Maj, Aus E. b 3 Apr 54. BA (Pub Adm), BDiv, with
ALLEY, Julie (née Stewart) m 1975; Maj, Aus E. b 17 Jun 56.

ALM, Britt-Marie (Hisingskåren, Göteborg, 1970); Maj, Swdn. b 28 Dec 45.

ALMENDRAS, Eduardo Lagos (Puento Alto, S Am W, 1975); Maj, L Am N. b 3 Aug 51, with
ALMENDRAS, Dalia Rosa Porras (née Diaz) m 1974; Maj, L Am N. b 23 Dec 48. Served in S Am W and Aus S.

AMBITAN, Harold (Manado 1, 1973); Lt-Col, CS, Indon. b 9 May 49, and
AMBITAN, Deetje (née Malawah) (Bandung, 1972) m 1975; Lt-Col, TSWM, Indon. b 8 Jun 49.

AMICK, Richard (Hutchinson, KS, 1978); Maj, USA C. b 24 Nov 54. BA (Bus Admin), and
AMICK, Vicki (née Anderson) (Grand Haven, MI, 1978) m 1979; Maj, USA C. b 29 Jun 55.

AMPONSAH, Samuel (Wamfie 1987); Maj, Gha. b 30 Sep 59, with
AMPONSAH, Hagar (née Kissiwa) m 1985; Maj, Gha. b 9 Jul 62. Served at IHQ.

ANZEZE, Hezekiel (Naliava, 1980); Comr, TC, Ken. b 15 Mar 49. Ww Comr Clerah, pG 2005.

APPEATENG, Seth (Manso, 1989); Maj, Gha. b 9 Jun 62, with
APPEATENG, Janet (née Nkansah) m 1987; Maj, Gha. b 12 Dec 67.

ARGUEDAS, Antonio (Callao, 1974); Maj, S Am W. b 9 Sep 53, and
ARGUEDAS, Lilian (née Sánchez) (Lima Central, 1981) m 1981; Maj, S Am W. b 24 Nov 58.

ARNOLD, Wilfred D. (Hamilton, 1973); Lt-Col, NZ. b 22 May 45. BSoc Sc, MA (Soc Work), CQSW, with
ARNOLD, Margaret Dawn (née Fitness) m 1966; Lt-Col, NZ. b 6 Jul 45. BN, RGON, Grad Dip Soc Sc. Served in Aus S and Sing.

ASOEGWU, Johnson O. (Usumenyi, 1971); Lt-Col, CS, Nig. b 2 Aug 47, with
ASOEGWU, Veronica (née Okezue) m 1966; Lt-Col, TSWM, Nig. b 28 Feb 49. Served in Zimb.

ASPERSCHLAGER, Gary C. (Orange, NJ, 1976); Lt-Col, USA E. b 20 Apr 46. BS (Biol), MA (Div), and
ASPERSCHLAGER, Pearl A. (née Samson) (White Plains, NY, 1973) m 1976; Lt-Col, USA E. b 20 Aug 46. BA (Ed).

AYANAM, Friday S. (Akai, 1988); Maj, Nig. b 2 Oct 64, and
AYANAM, Glory (Ndikpo-Atang); Capt, Nig. b 28 Apr 64.

B

BAAH, Samuel (Duakwa, 1987); Maj, Gha. b 13 Mar 63, with
BAAH, Theresa (née Kumi) m 1984; Maj, Gha. b 10 Sep 64.

BABU, P. V. Stanly (Chevalloor, 1983); Maj, Ind SW. b 28 Nov 55, and
BABU, Nirmala (Kanniyakuzhy, 1986) m 1986; Maj, Ind SW. b 14 Mar 63.

BAHAMONDE, Cecilia (Lo Vial, 1983); Maj, S Am W. b 23 Mar 63.

BAIGORRIA, Eduardo (Córdoba, 1989); Capt, S Am E. b 2 Mar 65, and

BAIGORRIA, Andrea (née Racelis) m 1989; Capt, S Am E. b 6 Sep 69.

BAILEY, Christine (Barking, 1975); Maj, UK. b 15 Apr 49. BA (Hons) (Soc Sci – Pol), PGCE. Served in S Am E.

BAILEY, Fredrick Bradford (Kansas City (Westport Temple), MO, USA C, 1982); Maj, OC, Sp. b 4 May 58. BS (Soc Wrk), with **BAILEY, Heidi Juliette** (née Chandler) m 1978; Maj, CPWM, Sp. b 17 Jul 54. Served in USA C and S Am W.

BAILIS, Abel (Chenkody, 1980); Maj, Ind SE. b 20 Feb 53, and **BAILIS, J. Abaranam** (Chadayanvillai, 1972) m 1980; Maj, Ind SE. b 23 Aug 48.

BAILLIE, Kenneth (Warren, USA E, 1966); Comr, TC, USA C. b 3 Nov 42. BA (Soc), with **BAILLIE, Joy M.** (née Gabrielsen) m 1962; Comr, TPWM, USA C. b 30 May 41. BA (Biochem). Served in Can, USA E and E Eur (OC/CPWO).

BAKEMBA, Prosper (Mabenga, 1982); Maj, Con (Braz). b 21 Oct 49, with **BAKEMBA, Monique** (née Mafoua) m 1980; Maj, Con (Braz). b 28 Jun 52.

BAKER, Gary (Nundah, 1976); Maj, Aus E. b 23 Sep 48. ThA, with **BAKER, Judith** (née Wells) m 1969; Maj, Aus E. b 3 June 49.

BAKKEN, Solfrid (née Kristensen) (Tromsø, 1971); Maj, Nor. b 11 May 52.

BAMANABIO, Eugène (Mfilou, 1990); Maj, Con (Braz). b 10 Jul 62, with **BAMANABIO, Brigitte** (née Locko Oumba) m 1988; Maj, Con (Braz). b 13 Dec 63. Served in Rw.

BAMFORD, William A. III (Quincy, MA, 1989); Maj, USA E. b 11 Jun 57. BS (Pharm), MS (Org Ldrshp), with **BAMFORD, G. Lorraine** (née Brown) m 1980; Maj, USA E. b 25 Jul 53. BA (Mod Langs).

BANFIELD, Stephen (Quincy, MA, 1978); Maj, USA E. b 17 Mar 53. BA (Psych), with **BANFIELD, Janet Mae** (née Anderson) m 1976; Maj, USA E. b 27 Apr 55.

BANKS, Keith (Wokingham, 1963); Comr, UK. b 5 Nov 42, and **BANKS, Pauline** (née Jane) (Stowmarket, 1964) m 1965; Comr, UK. b 3 Feb 44. Served in PNG (OC/CPWO), Jpn (CS/TSWO) and at IHQ (IS Int Per/Int Statistician).

BANLASAN, Ronaldo (Davao, 1990); Maj, Phil. b 21 May 61, and **BANLASAN, Theresita** (née Mangalisan) (La Paz, 1983) m 1990; Maj, Phil. b 29 Jul 59.

BARKAT, Samuel (Thal, 1973); Maj, Pak. b 7 Aug 51, with **SAMUEL, Margaret** m 1971; Maj, Pak. b 7 Aug 52.

BARNARD, Rodney (Norwood, 1982); Maj, Aus S. b 7 Apr 49, with **BARNARD, Jennifer** (née Rowe) Maj, Aus S. b 5 Nov 50. Served in UK.

BARR, John M. (Ian) (Saltcoats, 1972); Maj, UK. b 10 Aug 50. BD (Hons), MA Cert Ed, and **BARR, Christine** (née Hawkins) (Newport Maindee, 1972) m 1974; Maj, UK. b 23 May 49. BSc (Hons), MA. Served at IHQ.

BARTLETT, Royston R. (Croydon Citadel, 1971); Lt-Col, UK. b 28 May 44. Dip Mgt, MCIMgt. Served in UK, Swdn (CS) and at IHQ.

BAUTISTA, David (Asingan, 1996); Capt, Phil. b 12 May 61. BSc (Industrial Ed), and **BAUTISTA, Estelita** (née Baquirin) (Asingan, 1994) m 1996; Capt, Phil. b 12 Nov 62. BS (Comm).

BELL, Donald C. (Spokane, WA, 1978); Lt-Col, CS, USA W. b 12 Oct 49. BA (Econ), JD (Law), and **BELL, Debora K.** (née Perry) (Hobbs, NM, 1977) m 1979; Lt-Col, TSWM, USA W. b 6 Feb 56. Served at USA Nat.

BELL, Mark (Hagerstown, MD, 1977); Maj, USA S. b 27 Mar 51, with **BELL, Alice** (née Armendariz) m 1975; Maj, USA S. b 26 Sep 54.

BEMBHY, Carlos A. (Caballito, 1972); Maj, S Am E. b 5 Sep 51, and **BEMBHY, Isabel Ines** (née Mamchur) (Tres Arroyos, 1968) m 1973; Maj, S Am E. b 10 Jun 48.

BENGTSSON, Anita (Ystad, 1963); Lt-Col, Swdn. b 7 Jul 42. Served in Den (CS).

BERG, Odd (Harstad, Nor, 1969); Lt-Col, CS, Ger. b 4 Mar 47. Cand Theol, and **BERG, Grethe Karin** (née Knetten) (Nor, 1969) m 1971; Lt-Col, TSWM, Ger. b 12 May 48. Served in Nor, UK and Den.

BERNAO, Raúl (Trelew, 1983); Maj, S Am E. b 11 Oct 61, and **BERNAO, Lidia** (née Lopez) (Santiago del Estero, 1981) m 1984; Maj, S Am E. b 20 Feb 59.

BERRY, Donald E. (Kearny, NJ, 1976); Maj, USA E. b 9 Jun 49, with **BERRY, Vicki** (née Van Nort) m 1970; Maj, USA E. b 15 Jan 50. BA (Engl), MA (Strategic Comms & Ldrshp)

BHUSHANAM, S. John (Perlipadu, 1977); Maj, Ind C. b 1 Jun 45, with
BHUSHANAM, Pennimma m 1971; Maj, Ind C. b 26 May 52.

BIAKLIANA, S. (Hnahthial, 1981); Maj, Ind E. b 15 Feb 56, and
BIAKMAWII (Dolchera, 1982) m 1982; Maj, Ind E. b 10 Aug 62.

BIYENGA, Nzeza Simon (Kinshasa 4, 1968); Maj, Con (Kin). b 1 Jan 46, with
BIYENGA, Emilie (née Kinduelo) m 1966; Maj, Con (Kin). b 1 Jan 50.

BLACKMAN, William (St James, Winnipeg, MB, 1973); Maj, Can. b 12 Dec 44, with
BLACKMAN, Winifred (née Deacon) m 1969; Maj, Can. b 10 Dec 45. BA.

BOLLWAHN, Paul E. (Danville, IL, USA C, 1967); Lt-Col, USA W. b 20 Aug 42. BS, MSW (Admin), ACSW, CSW, CSWM, with
BOLLWAHN, Ronda G. (née Harvey) m 1965; Lt-Col, USA W. b 6 May 44. BS, MA (Admin). Served in USA C and at USA Nat.

BOMMELI, Walter Daniel (Freienstein ZH, 1974); Maj, Switz. b 25 May 50, and
BOMMELI, Hanny (née Eugster) (Heiden, 1974) m 1975; Maj, Switz. b 11 May 49. Served in Ger.

BOND, Eric (St Catharines, ON, 1987); Maj, Can. b 24 Dec 46. BA (Teachers Cert), with
BOND, Donna (née Williams) m 1968; Maj, Can. b 10 Mar 49.

BOND, Linda (St James, Winnipeg, Can, 1968); Comr, IHQ. b 22 Jun 46. BRelig Ed. Served in UK, Can (CS) and USA W (TC).

BONE, Cilla (South Croydon, UK, 1971); Maj, Aus S. b 24 Jul 49. Served in UK, at IHQ and in Aus E.

BONNAR, Kenneth (Scarborough, ON, 1974); Maj, Can. b 13 Oct 40. BA (Teachers Cert), with
BONNAR, Glennice (née Gray) m 1965; Maj, Can. b 13 Apr 44. Served in HK, Sing and Zam.

BOOTH, Patrick (Paris-Central, 1989); Maj, Asst CS, Frce. b 12 Jan 55, with
BOOTH, Margaret (née Miaglia) m 1983; Maj, TSWM, Frce. b 31 July 61. Served in UK

BORDE, Balu Ramji (Jalgoon, 1969); Maj, Ind W. b 6 May 48, with
BORDE, Kanchanmala m 1970; Maj, Ind W. b 1 Jun 48.

BOSCHUNG, Franz (Basle 2, 1977); Lt-Col, Switz. b 21 Sep 49, with
BOSCHUNG, Hanny (née Abderhalden)

m 1971; Lt-Col, Switz. b 7 Apr 50. Served in Con (Braz).

BOSH, Larry (Mansfield, OH, 1966); Lt-Col, CS, USA E. b 9 Jun 46. BS (Acct), MBA, and
BOSH, Gillian (née Reid) (Akron Citadel, OH, 1960) m 1967; Lt-Col, TSWM, USA E. b 4 Dec 40. Served at IHQ and USA Nat (Nat CS/NSWM, NRVAVS).

BOUZIGUES, Ricardo (Colegiales, 1976); Maj, S Am E. b 12 Sep 52. MA (Practical Theol), and
BOUZIGUES, Sonia (née Alvez) (Cordoba, 1979) m 1979; Maj, S Am E. b 12 Nov 54.

BRADBURY, Clifford (Southsea, 1966); Maj, UK. b 17 Aug 45, and
BRADBURY, Jean (née Curtis) (Dorchester, 1965) m 1968; Maj, UK. b 2 Feb 45.

BRAUN, Edouard (Vevey, Frce, 1968); Comr, TC, Switz. b 16 Aug 42, with
BRAUN, Françoise (née Volet) m 1966; Comr, TPWM, Switz. b 8 Dec 43. Served in Frce (TC/TPWM).

BREKKE, Bo (Oslo 3, Nor, 1980); Col, TC, Pak. b 9 May 57, and
BREKKE, Birgitte (née Nielsen) (Copenhagen Temple, Den, 1980) m 1980; Col, TPWM, Pak. b 17 Sep 54. SRN. Served in Den, Nor, Sri Lan, Ban (OC/CPWO), UK and E Eur (CS/Sec Mission Development).

BRIDGE, Michael (Umtali, 1974); Maj, Zimb. b 4 Sep 47, and
BRIDGE, Enlettah (née Madure) (Kwekwe, 1977); Maj, Zimb. b 2 Dec 55.

BRINGANS, David (Albion, Aus E, 1970); Col, TC, Sing. b 25 May 47, with
BRINGANS, Grace (née Palmer) m 1968; Col, TPWM, Sing. b 21 Sep 46. Served in NZ, HK, Sing (GS/CSWO), Vietnam and Tai (RC/RPWM).

BROCKSIECK, Harry (Quincy, IL, 1964); Lt-Col, USA C. b 30 Apr 43. BS (Human Resources Mgmt), MS (Psych/Counselling), and
BROCKSIECK, Barbara (née Cooke) (Decatur, IL, 1964) m 1965; Lt-Col, USA C. b 12 Oct 40. BS (Ed). Served in E Eur.

BRODIN, Harold F. (Aberdeen, WA, 1964); Lt-Col, USA W. b 30 May 42, with
BRODIN, Joann (née Thompson) m 1962; Lt-Col, USA W. b 13 Aug 42.

BROWN, Rosemarie (Kingston Central, 1978); Maj, Carib. b 17 Oct 57. BA (Theol).

BUEYA, Nsoki Joseph (Kavwaya, 1981); Maj, Con (Kin). b 12 Jul 48, with
BUEYA, Germaine (née Nkenda Mbuku)

m 1978; Maj, Con (Kin). b 10 Jun 52.

BULLOCK, Mary (Hucknall, 1980); Maj, UK. b 26 Oct 46. BA(Hons) French, Dip Applied Social Studies

BURGER, Kurt (Los Angeles Congress Hall, CA, 1972); Lt-Col, USA W. b 26 Aug 46. BS (Bus Admin), BA (Psych), MBA (Bus Admin), Cert CPA, and
BURGER, Alicia (née Pedersen) (San Bernardino, CA, 1976) m 1988; Lt-Col, USA W. b 6 Jul 46.

BURN, Margaret (née Cain) (Lincoln Citadel, 1966); Lt-Col, UK. b 12 Nov 46.

BURNS, Alan (Harlow, 1976); Maj, UK. b 1 May 54. BSc, BSc (Hons), MA (Evang), and
BURNS, Alison (née Hitchin) (Regent Hall, 1979) m 1981; Maj, UK. b 8 Oct 52. Served at IHQ.

BURR, W. Howard (Lexington, KY, 1973); Lt-Col, USA E. b 8 Nov 47. BA (Psych), MS (Ed Admin), with
BURR, Patricia (née Stigleman) m 1970; Lt-Col, USA E. b 29 Jun 51.

BURRIDGE, Keith (Ealing, 1967); Lt-Col, UK. b 21 Jun 44. MBE, with
BURRIDGE, Beryl (née Brown) m 1965; Lt-Col, UK. b 11 Nov 44.

BURROWS, David J. (Skipton, UK, 1970); Lt-Col, OC, Mal. b 30 Apr 47. SRN, and
BURROWS, Jean A. (née List) (Ware, UK, 1970) m 1972; Lt-Col, CPWM, Mal. b 19 Mar 48. SRN, SCM. Served in Pak, at IHQ and in Tanz (OC/CPWM).

BURTON, Joan (Goole, UK, 1978); Maj, Brz. b 5 Jul 55. Served in UK.

BUSROE, Ronald (Danville, KY, USA S, 1978); Maj, Carib. b 5 Dec 51. BA (Hist), with
BUSROE, Carol (née Jay) m 1974; Maj, Carib. b 9 Jan 53. BSc (Maths). Served in USA S.

C

CACHELIN, Hervé (Biel, 1979); Maj, Switz. b 16 Feb 57, and
CACHELIN, Deborah (née Cullingworth) (Catford, UK, 1981) m 1983; Maj, Switz. b 2 Jul 57. Served in Aus E and UK.

CAIRNS, Philip (Campsie, 1982); Maj, Aus E. b 5 Feb 51. Dip Mus, MTh, with
CAIRNS, Janice (née Manson) m 1972; Maj, Aus E. b 7 Oct 48.

CALDWELL, Bradley Joseph (Shreveport, LA, USA S, 1993); Capt, E Eur. b 31 Aug 64. BA (Phil), with
CALDWELL, Anita Maye (née Howard)

m 1989; Capt, E Eur. b 1 Dec 64. Served in USA S.

CALVO, Esteban (Concepcion de Rios, 1987); Maj, L Am N. b 23 Jan 63, and
CALVO, Ileana (née Jimenez) (Concepcion de Rios, 1986) m 1989; Maj, L Am N. b 5 Jun 66.

CANNING, Donald William (Miami Citadel, FL, 1974); Lt-Col, USA S. b 28 Jan 43, with
CANNING, Constance Jean (née Osborne) m 1966; Lt-Col, USA S. b 20 Sep 46.

CANNING, Joan (Moncton, NB, Can, 1983); Maj, IHQ. b 27 Sep 62. BA (Bib and Theol Studies). Served in Can.

CARLSON, William (Staten Island Port Richmond, NY, 1971); Lt-Col, USA E. b 9 Jan 48. BA (Soc Studies), and
CARLSON, Marcella (née Brewer) (Staten Island Port Richmond, NY, 1971) m 1971; Lt-Col, USA E. b 18 Sep 49.

CASTILLO, Luis (Antofagasta, S Am W, 1977); Lt-Col, CS, S Am E. b 7 Jan 48, and
CASTILLO, Aída (Quinta Normal, 1968) m 1972; Lt-Col, TSWM, S Am E. b 5 Nov 49. Served in S Am W (CS/TSWM) and Mex (CS/TSWM).

CASTOR, Onal (Aquin, Carib, 1979); Lt-Col, CS, Con (Kin). b 20 Jul 55, and
CASTOR, Edmane (née Montoban) (Duverger, Carib, 1980) m 1980; Lt-Col, TSWM, Con (Kin). b 1 Oct 57. Served in Carib and USA S.

CEREZO, Josué (Monterrey, 1985); Maj, CS, Mex. b 16 May 57. BS, with
CEREZO, Ruth (née Garcia) m 1983. Maj, TSWM, Mex. b 22 Oct 60. BA SocWk. Served in L Am N.

CHACKO, K. P. (Cherukole East, 1979); Maj, Ind SW. b 17 Apr 49. BA, with
CHACKO, Suseela (née Achamma) m 1974; Maj, Ind SW. b 22 Apr 47. BA.

CHAGAS, Edgar (São Paulo Central, 1988); Maj, Brz. b 24 Feb 58. MA (Sc), with
CHAGAS, Sara (née Parker) m 1982; Maj, Brz. b 26 Aug 60. BA (Psychol).

CHAMP, James (Chatham, ON, 1975); Maj, Can. b 29 Mar 52. BRE, and
CHAMP, Barbara (née Allington) (Earlscourt, ON, 1975) m 1976; Maj, Can. b 26 Jul 47. Served in UK.

CHANDRASIRI, Sarukkalige (Gonapinuwela, 1980); Maj, Sri Lan, b 9 Sep 53, and
CHANDRASIRI, Rohini (née Horathalge) (Siyambalangamuwa, 1968) m 1979; Maj, Sri Lan. b 7 Oct 50.

CHARAN, Samuel (Rampur, Ind N, 1978); Lt-Col, CS, Ind E. b 1 Apr 53, with

CHARAN, Bimla Wati (née Bimla Wati)
m 1974; Lt-Col, TSWM, Ind E. Served in Ind N.
CHARLET, Horst (Berlin-Neukölln, 1969);
Col, TC, Ger. b 1 May 46. DipSW, Dip Soc
Pedagogue, with
    CHARLET, Helga (née Werner); Col, TPWM,
    Ger. b 18 Oct 48. Served in Ger (CS/TSWM)
CHAUHAN, Gideon Chhaganlal (Bhalej,
1968); Lt-Col, Ind W. b 20 Mar 47, and
    CHAUHAN, Ushaben (Keripur, 1973) m 1973;
    Lt-Col, Ind W. b 28 Apr 52.
CHAUHAN, Jashwant Soma (Tarapur, 1979);
Maj, Ind W. b 20 Feb 52, with
    CHAUHAN, Indiraben m 1976; Maj, Ind W.
    b 8 Jun 56.
CHENDA, Joster (Matero, 1981); Maj, Zam.
b 10 Jun 57, and
    CHENDA, Christine (née Chingala) (Libala,
    1983) m 1983; Maj, Zam. b 3 Mar 62.
CHEPKURUI, Stephen (Cheptais, Ken, 1982);
Maj, GS, Tanz. b 22 Feb 58, and
    CHEPKURUI, Grace (née Madolio) (Vigeze,
    Ken, 1980) m 1985; Maj, CSWM, Tanz.
    b 15 May 55. Served in E Afr.
CHEYDLEUR, John Reeves (Philadelphia
Northeast, PA, 1983); Maj, USA E.
b 11 Mar 44. BA (Psych), MA (Counselling/
Psych), PhD (Org Psych), with
    CHEYDLEUR, Judith Ann (née Kunkle)
    m 1965; Maj, USA E. b 27 Jul 39. BA (Psych/
    Soc), MA (Writing).
CHIGARIRO, Vinece (Gunguwe, Zimb, 1975);
Comr, TC, Zam. b 7 Mar 54. Served in Zimb
and Tanz (GS).
CHIGWAZA, Nicholas (Harare Citadel, 1970);
Maj, Zimb. b 9 Feb 48. DipSW, and
    CHIGWAZA, Tendai (née M'loyie)
    (Tadzembwa, 1975) m 1975; Maj, Zimb.
    b 5 Sep 55.
CHILYABANYAMA, Metson (Chitumbi,
1987); Maj, Zam. b 30 Oct 55, with
    CHILYABANYAMA, Rosemary (née
    Mboozi) m 1982; Maj, Zam. b 8 Aug 61.
CHISENGELE, Bernard (Monze, 1983); Maj,
Zam. b 1 Jan 51, and
    CHISENGELE, Dorothy (née Mweemba)
    (Kaumba, 1985) m 1985; Maj, Zam. b 14 Nov 59.
CHISHOLM, Lindsay (Timaru, 1980); Maj,
NZ. b 2 Jan 45, with
    CHISHOLM, Raewyn (née Smith) m 1967;
    Maj, NZ. b 29 Sep 47.
CHOO, Seung-chan (Yung Deung Po, 1980);
Maj, Kor. b 15 Jun 50, with
    LEE, Ok-hee m 1978; Maj, Kor. b 2 Aug 54.
CHRISTIAN, Paul Peter (Bhalej, Ind W, 1978);

Lt-Col, CS, Ind N. b 22 Sep 48, and
    CHRISTIAN, Anandiben (née Kalidas)
    (Ghoghawada, Ind W, 1980) m 1980; Lt-Col,
    TSWM, Ind N. b 12 Jul 57.
CHRISTIAN, Prabhudas Jetha (Sinhuj, 1978);
Maj, Ind W. b 23 Jan 52, and
    CHRISTIAN, Persis (née Zumal) (Jhalod,
    1978) m 1978; Maj, Ind W. b 5 Apr 48.
CHRISTURAJ, Rajamani (Elappara, 1983);
Maj, Ind SW. b 27 Dec 61, with
    MATHEW, Mary m 1983; Maj, Ind SW.
    b 11 May 59.
CHUN, Joon-hung (Yong Dong, 1978); Maj,
Kor. b 20 Jun 48, with
    SHIN, Myung-ja m 1976; Maj, Kor.
    b 28 Sep 49.
CHUN, Kwang-Pyo (Duk Am, 1971); Comr,
TC, Kor. b 15 Sep 41, with
    YOO, Sung-Ja m 1969; Comr, TPWM, Kor.
    b 11 Jan 41.
CLIFTON, Shaw (Edmonton, UK, 1973);
General (see page 26), with
    CLIFTON, Helen (née Ashman) m 1967;
    Comr, World President of Women's Ministries,
    IHQ. b 4 May 48. BA (Eng Lang/Lit) (Hons),
    PGCE. Served at IHQ, in Zimb, USA E,
    Pak (TC/TPWO), NZ (TC/TPWM) and UK
    (TC/TPWM).
CLINCH, Ronald (Launceston, 1986); Maj,
Aus S. b 6 Sep 54, with
    CLINCH Robyn (née Mole) m 1982; Maj,
    Aus S. b 8 Nov 60.
COCHRANE, William (Barrhead, 1975);
Lt-Col, CS, UK. b 7 Sep 54.
COLE, Joan (Limón, 1995); Capt, L Am N.
b 8 May 70.
CONDON, James (Shoalhaven, Aus E, 1971);
Lt-Col, CS, PNG. b 29 Nov 49, and
    CONDON, Jan (née Vickery) (Uralla, Aus E,
    1971) m 1972; Lt-Col, TSWM, PNG.
    b 27 Jan 47. Served in Aus E and UK.
COPPLE, Donald (Flin Flon, MB, 1963);
Lt-Col, Can. b 10 Apr 42, and
    COPPLE, Ann (née Cairns) (Pt St Charles,
    QC, 1962) m 1965; Lt-Col, Can. b 15 Jul 42.
COTTERILL, Anthony (Regent Hall, 1984);
Maj, UK. b 9 Dec 57. BA (Hons), with
    COTTERILL, Gillian (née Rushforth) m 1979;
    Maj, UK. b 15 Sep 57. SRN.
COTTERILL, Jennifer (Broken Hill, 1968);
Maj, Aus E. b 7 Nov 48.
COWLING, Alison (Macleans, Aus E, 1978);
Maj, IHQ. b 10 Feb 50. Served in Aus E.
COX, André (Geneva 1, Switz, 1979); Col,
TC, Fin. b 12 Jul 54, with

COX, Silvia (née Volet) m 1976; Col, TPWM, Fin. b 18 Nov 55. Served in Switz and Zimb.

CRABSON, William L. (Baltimore Temple, MD, 1965); Lt-Col, USA S. b 27 Sep 42, with **CRABSON, LaVerne Jeanette** (née Doyle) m 1962; Lt-Col, USA S. b 20 Apr 42.

CUNNINGHAM, James Dalton (Gastona, NC, 1974); Maj, USA S. b 15 Feb 52, with **CUNNINGHAM, Wanda** (née Ammons) m 1971; Maj, USA S. b 14 Jul 52.

D

DADDOW, Allan (Adelaide Congress Hall, 1978); Maj, Aus S. b 4 Jan 44, with **DADDOW, Lorraine** (née Andrew) m 1965; Maj, Aus S. b 21 Sep 45.

DALBERG, Theodore J. (Omaha Citadel, NE, 1967); Lt-Col, USA C. b 9 Feb 42, with **DALBERG, Nancy** (née Foubister) m 1963; Lt-Col, USA C. b 16 Jul 44.

DALENTANG, Winfrid (Turen, 1990); Maj, Indon. b 18 Dec 59, with **DALENTANG, Yani Sudiyaningsih** m 1980; Maj, Indon. b 1 Jun 61.

DALI, Peter (Ebushibungo, Ken, 1978); Lt-Col, CS, Gha. b 2 Mar 52, and **DALI, Jessica** (née Kavere) (Masigolo, Ken, 1978) m 1979; Lt-Col, TSWM, Gha. b 25 Dec 55. Served in Ken and at IHQ.

DALY, Gordon (Wellington South, 1977); Maj, NZ. b 5 Mar 54, and **DALY, Susan** (née Crump) (Te Aroha, 1976) m 1977; Maj, NZ. b 22 Oct 54. Served in Carib and S Am W.

DALZIEL, Peter (Malvern, Aus S, 1964); Lt-Col, CS, Neth. b 13 Jul 42. MCMI, and **DALZIEL, Sylvia** (née Gair) (West Rainton, UK, 1964) m 1967; Lt-Col, TSWM, Neth. b 21 Sep 44. NNEB, CTh. Served in UK, S Afr, Aus E and at IHQ.

DAMOR, Nicolas Maganlal (Jalpa, 1979); Maj, Ind W. b 1 Jun 55, and **DAMOR, Flora** (née David) (Dilsar, 1980) m 1980; Maj, Ind W. b 26 Apr 58.

DANIEL, Edward (Meesalai, 1977); Lt-Col, CS, Sri Lan. b 18 Mar 56, and **DANIEL, Lalitha** (née Ranchagodage) (Colombo Central, 1981) m 1981; Lt-Col, TSWM, Sri Lan. b 1 Oct 53.

DANIELS, Frank (Katanning, 1967); Maj, Aus S. b 10 Apr 47, and **DANIELS, Yvonne** (née Knapp) (Melbourne City Temple, 1972) m 1972; Maj, Aus S. b 4 Oct 47.

DANIELSON, Douglas (El Paso, TX, USA W, 1987); Maj, Mex. b 19 Aug 58. BSc (Computer Sci), with **DANIELSON, Rhode** (née Doria) m 1983; Maj, Mex. b 29 Jul 59. BSEd, MA (Maths). Served in USA W, S Am E, Carib and L Am N (CS/TSWM).

DAVID, K. C. (Puthuchira, Ind SW, 1978); Maj, Ind Nat. b 5 Jan 53. BA, and **DAVID, Gracy** (née Marykutty) (Thevalapuram, Ind SW, 1981) m 1981; Maj, Ind Nat. b 12 Nov 55. Served in Ind SW.

DAVIS, Trevor (Northampton Central, 1966); Lt-Col, UK. b 20 May 44. FTCL. Served in NZ and at IHQ. m 1968; Lt-Col Margaret, ret 2006.

DAWNGLIANA, C. (Chhilngchip, 1981); Maj, Ind E. b 1 Oct 55, and **MANTHANGI, H.** (Champhai, 1982) m 1982; Maj, Ind E. b 20 Sep 61.

DEN HOLLANDER, John A. (Treebeek, 1990); Capt, Neth. b 21 Nov 56, with **DEN HOLLANDER, Annetje C.** (née Poppema) m 1978; Capt, Neth. b 4 May 57.

DE SÁ, Tomas (Suzano, 1972); Lt-Col, Brz. b 30 Nov 50, and **DE SÁ, Rute** (née Almeida) (Alegrete, 1971) m 1975; Lt-Col, Brz. b 27 Nov 50. Served in USA C and Port (OC/CPWO).

DEVARAPALLI, Jayapaul (M. R. Nagaram, Ind C, 1974); Col, TC, Ind E. b 25 Dec 47. MA, BTS, with **DEVARAPALLI, Yesudayamma** m 1971; Col, TPWM, Ind E. b 21 Nov 54. Served in Ind C.

DEVASUNDARAM, Samuel Raj (Vadasery, 1974); Maj, Ind SE. b 21 Sep 54, and **DEVASUNDARAM, Kanagamony** (Brahmapuram, 1978) m 1978; Maj, Ind SE. b 5 Feb 52.

DIANDAGA, Frédéric (Nzoko, 1988); Maj, Con (Braz). b 26 May 55, and **DIANDAGA, Claudia** (née Bayekoula) (Ouenze, 1990) m 1990; Capt, Con (Braz). b 29 Oct 66.

DIANTEZULWA, Makani Sébastien (Kingudi, 1977); Maj, Con (Kin). b 16 Apr 48, with **DIANTEZULWA, Martine** (née Diatubaka Nyambudi) m 1975; Maj, Con (Kin). b 1 Nov 56.

DIKALEMBOLOVANGA, Eugène Nsona Lendo (Matadi, 1983); Maj, Con (Kin). b 30 Apr 52. BMgmt & Econ Sci, with **DIKALEMBOLOVANGA, Odile Nzuzi Simbi** (née Simbi Luasa) m 1980; Maj, Con

(Kin). b 2 Mar 58. Served at IHQ (SALT Afr).

DIXON, Robert (Philadelphia Germantown, USA E, 1981); Maj, OC, Lib. b 20 Mar 49, with
DIXON, Hester (née Burgess) m 1967; Maj, CPWM, Lib. b 20 Nov 49. Served in USA E.

DOLIBER, Robert (Champaign, IL, 1978); Maj, USA C. b 15 Jul 54, BS (Bus Adm), MBA, and
DOLIBER, Rae (née Briggs) (Champaign, IL, 1982); Maj, USA C. b 5 Jun 58.

DOLLÉ, Ursula (Bern 1, 1969); Lt-Col, Switz. b 8 Jun 43.

DONALDSON, Robert (Dunedin South 1987); Maj, NZ. b 8 Jul 61. BSc, LTh, with
DONALDSON, Janine (née Hamilton) m 1983, Maj, NZ. b 23 Sep 62. Served in Zam.

DONZÉ, Jacques (St. Aubin, 1988); Maj, Switz. b 16 Feb 64, with
DONZÉ, Claude-Evelyne (née Roth) m 1983; Maj, Switz. b 5 Feb 63. Served in Belg.

DOWNER, Gillian (Great Yarmouth, UK, 1977); Lt-Col, CS, Sing. b 18 Mar 54. Served in UK, Phil, Vietnam, HK and Tai.

DREW, Marion (Boscombe, 1979); Maj, UK. b 12 Jan 49. BA (French & Law) Dip Inst Linguists. Served at ICO.

DUCHÊNE, Alain (Paris Montparnasse, 1971); Col, TC, Frce. b 1 Jan 45. Served at ESFOT and in Frce (CS). m 1972; Lt-Col Suzette, ret 2002.

DUDLEY, E. Lewanne (Becon, NY, USA E, 1982); Maj, Nig. b 13 Sep 52. Served in USA E.

DULA, Sangthang T. (Diakkawn 1986); Maj, Ind E. b 2 Jul 63. B Th, MA (Mission), MTh (Missiology), DMiss, with
MALSAWMI m 1984; Maj, Ind E. b 10 Jun 59.

DUNSTER, Robin (Dulwich Hill Temple, Aus E, 1970); Comr, CoS, IHQ. b 12 Jan 44. SRN, SCM, RPN, RMN, IPPF (Ed). Served in Aus E, Zimb (CS), Con (Kin) (TC) and Phil (TC).

DUNWOODIE, Joan (Bromley, UK, 1969); Lt-Col, IHQ. b 2 May 45. Teach Cert, DipTh. Served in UK, Zai, S Afr and Con (Braz) (CS).

DURSTON, Graham (Maryborough, Aus E, 1970); Lt-Col, CS, Phil. b 12 Nov 43. BDiv (Hons), MTh, Grad Cert Management (AGSM) with
DURSTON, Rhondda (née Rees) m 1966; Lt-Col, TSWM, Phil. b 11 Dec 45. L Th (MCD), B Admin Lead (UNE). Served in Aus E and Aus S.

DYALL, John (Regent Hall, UK, 1978); Lt-Col, IHQ. b 6 Jun 42. Served in UK, Thailand, Zam, HK, Hun and Pak (CS).

E

EDGAR, Samuel (Londonderry 1969); Maj, UK. b 26 Feb 49. Served in Ger.

EGGER, Paulette (Vallorbe, 1977); Maj, Switz. b 22 Nov 55.

ELIASEN, Anna Riitta (née Hamalainen) (Erie Central, PA, 1974); Lt-Col, USA E. b 11 Aug 45. BA (Org Mgmt). Ww Lt-Col Samuel E., pG 1997. Served in UK, Brz, S Am E, Sp and Fin (CS).

ELIASEN, Torben (Bosque, 1983); Lt-Col, CS, Brz. b 28 Nov 60, and
ELIASEN, Deise Calor (née de Souza) (Rio Comprido, 1985) m 1985; Lt-Col, Brz. b 22 Feb 66. BA (Journalism).

EMMANUEL, Muthu Yesudhason (Neduvaazhy, Ind SE, 1974); Col, TC, Ind C. b 8 May 51, and
REGINA, Chandra Bai (Valliyoor, Ind SE, 1978) m 1978; Col, TPWM, Ind C. b 3 Mar 55. Served in Ind SE, Ind N (CS/TSWM) and Ind E (TC/TPWM).

EMMANUEL, Walter (Green Town, 1983); Maj, Pak. b 7 Jul 57, with
EMMANUEL, Mussaraf (née Ullah) m 1981; Maj, Pak. b 1 Dec 65.

ENNIS, Wayne (Ringwood, Aus S, 1968); Maj, PNG. b 16 Aug 45. MA, BMin, and
ENNIS, Jeanette (née Deacon) (Ringwood, Aus S. 1967); m 1969; Maj, PNG. b 15 Nov 44. Served in Aus S and Sing.

ESSIEN, Edet (Ikot Ebo, 1974); Maj, Nig. b 28 Apr 48, with
ESSIEN, Comfort Maj, Nig. b 25 Mar 53.

EXBRAYAT, Christian (Le Chambon s/Lignon, Frce, 1968); Maj, OC, Belg. b 11 Oct 46, and
EXBRAYAT, Joëlle (née Welleman) (Lille, Frce, 1972) m 1973; Maj, CPWM, Belg. b 27 Jul 48. Served in Frce.

EZEKWERE, Chika Boniface (Umuchu, 1978); Maj, Nig. b 1 Jan 49, with
EZEKWERE, Virginia Ete m 1976; Maj, Nig. b 1 Jan 54.

F

FALIN, John (Albany, GA, USA S, 1966); Lt-Col, USA Nat. b 9 Apr 42. AS (Bus Admin), BA, BS (Psych), and
FALIN, Judy (née Pegram) (Greensboro, NC, USA S, 1966) m 1967; Lt-Col, USA Nat. b 5 Jan 45. Served in USA S.

FARTHING, Peter (Dundas Outpost, 1978); Maj, Aus E. b 8 Mar 51. BSoc Studies (Hons), DMin, and
FARTHING, Kerrie (née Gale) (Wollongong,

1978) m 1978; Maj, Aus E. b 31 Aug 52.
Served at IHQ.

FAULKNER, Donald S. (Norfolk, VA, 1977);
Lt-Col, USA S. b 12 Jan 43. BSc, with
FAULKNER, Marian L. (née Horstemeyer)
m 1965; Lt-Col, USA S. b 21 Feb 44.

FEENER, Maxwell (Port Leamington, NF, Can,
1966); Comr, TC, USA S. b 5 Jul 45, with
FEENER, Lenora (née Tippett) m 1967;
Comr, TPWM, USA S. b 26 Dec 45. Served
in Can, S Afr (CS/TSWM) and USA S (CS/
TSWM).

FERGUSON, Lester (Nassau, 1988); Maj,
Carib. b 1 Sep 65. BA (Bib and Theol),
MA (Christian Education), and
FERGUSON, Beverley (née Armstrong)
(Bridgetown Central, 1999) m 1999; Capt,
Carib. b 12 Dec 64.

FERNANDEZ, Odilio (Diezmero, 1996); Capt,
L Am N. b 8 Aug 63, with
FERNANDEZ, Ivis (née Diaz) m 1987; Capt,
L Am N. b 7 May 70.

FERNANDEZ, Ricardo J. (Caparra Temple, PR,
1996); Capt, USA E. b 3 Jun 60, with
FERNANDEZ, Mirtha N. (née Benitez)
m 1979; Capt, USA E. b 4 Jan 57.

FERNANDO, P. Anthony (Moratumulla, 1975);
Maj, Sri Lan. b 5 Oct 47, with
FERNANDO, Freeda Esther (née Fernando)
m 1971; Maj, Sri Lan. b 7 Feb 53.

FERREIRA, Jorge (Cordoba, 1972); Col,
TC, L Am N. b 24 Jun 53, and
FERREIRA, Adelina (née Solorza) (Lauis,
1974) m 1979; Col, TPWM, L Am N.
b 19 Sep 55. Served in S Am E (CS/TSWM).

FINCHAM, Melvin (Croydon Citadel, 1981);
Maj, UK. b 20 May 56, and
FINCHAM, Suzanne (née Kenny) (Stockport
Citadel, 1981) m 1981; Maj, UK. b 19 Jan 59.

FINGER, Raymond (Hawthorn, 1974); Maj,
Aus S. b 11 Jul 51, and
FINGER, Aylene (née Rinaldi) (Maylands,
1974) m 1976; Maj, Aus S. b 17 Apr 53.

FLINTOFF, Ethne (Dunedin North, NZ, 1971);
Lt-Col, OC, Ban. b 11 Nov 46. RN, RM.
Served in NZ, Ind W, Ind N and Pak.

FLORES, Eliseo (Cochabamba, 1977); Maj,
S Am W. b 28 Jul 56, and
FLORES, Remedios (née Gutiérrez) (Oruro,
1977) m 1978; Maj, S Am W. b 6 Apr 55.

FLORES, Myline Joy (Lebe, 1988); Maj, Phil.
b 2 May 63. BMin.

FORSTER, Malcolm (St Helier, UK, 1971);
Lt-Col, OC, Tanz. b 26 Mar 51, and
FORSTER, Valerie (née Jupp) (Croydon

Citadel, UK, 1978) m 1979; Lt-Col, CPWM,
Tanz. b 5 Jun 55. Served in UK, at IHQ, in
S Afr, Zam & Mal, Gha & Lib, and Mal (OC/
CPWM).

FORSYTH, Robin W. (Edinburgh Gorgie, UK,
1968); Col, CS, NZ. b 30 Aug 46, with
FORSYTH, Shona (née Leslie) m 1966; Col,
TSWM, NZ. b 25 Mar 48. Served in Aus S,
Mex, UK and L Am N (TC/TPWM).

FRANCIS, William (Paterson, NJ, USA E, 1973);
Comr, IS Am and Carib, IHQ. b 5 Mar 44.
BA (Mus/Hist), MDiv, Hon DD, with
FRANCIS, Marilyn (née Burroughs)
m 1965; Comr, SWM Am and Carib, IHQ.
b 3 Feb 43. BA (Mus), MA. Served in USA E
(CS/TSWM).

FRANS, Roy (Surabaya, Indon, 1977); Comr,
IS SPEA, IHQ. b 30 Oct 50, and
FRANS, Arda (née Haurissa) (Jakarta 1,
Indon, 1978) m 1978; Comr, SWM SPEA,
IHQ. b 10 May 44. Served in Indon, Aus E,
Sing, Ban and Sri Lan (TC/TPWM).

FREDERIKSEN, Miriam (née Larsson) (Paris
Central, Frce, 1962); Lt-Col, IHQ. b 15 May 43.
Served in Den and Nor (CS).

FRISK, Kristina M. (née Larsson) (Örebro 1,
1965); Lt-Col, CS, Swdn. b 22 May 45.
m 1977; Lt-Col Anders, ret 2004.

G

GAIKWAD, Benjamin Yacob (Bodhegaon,
1974); Maj, Ind W. b 3 Oct 48, and
GAIKWAD, Sudina P. (née Makasare)
(Bodhegaon, 1975) m 1975; Maj, Ind W.
b 23 Oct 57.

GAINES, Jerry (San Francisco Citadel, CA,
USA W, 1966); Lt-Col, USA E. b 29 Sep 41.
BA/MBA (Bus Admin), and
GAINES, Jeanine (née Wheeler) (Albuquerque,
NM, USA W, 1962) m 1967; Lt-Col, USA E.
b 7 May 40. Served in USA W and L Am N.

GAITHER, Israel L. (New Castle, PA, USA E,
1964); Comr, Nat Comm, USA Nat.
b 27 Oct 44. Hon LHD, and
GAITHER, Eva D. (née Shue) (Sydney, OH,
USA E, 1964) m 1967; Comr, NPWM, USA
Nat. b 9 Sep 43. Served in USA E (CS/TSWO),
S Afr (TC/ TPWO), USA E (TC/TPWM) and
at IHQ (CoS/WSWM).

GARCIA, Ángela (née Sanguinetti) (Lima
Central, S Am W, 1982); Maj, L Am N.
b 15 Oct 53. m 1983; Maj Victor. Served in
S Am W and USA C.

GARCÍA, Humberto (Monterrey, 1990); Maj,
Mex. b 19 Jan 57. LLM, with

GARCÍA, Leticia (née Castañeda) m 1981; Maj, Mex. b 9 Mar 59. BA (Primary Ed).

GEORGE, N. S. (Vayala-Adoor, 1980); Maj, Ind SW. b 19 Mar 50, and
GEORGE, A. Annamma m 1983; Maj, Ind SW.

GHULAM, Yusaf (Shantinagar, 1975); Lt-Col, Pak. b 4 Jan 55, and
GHULAM, Rebecca (née Charn Masih) (Shantinagar, 1975) m 1976; Lt-Col, Pak. b 6 May 56.

GNANIAH, Swaminathan (Thikkurichi, 1973) Maj, Ind SE. b 10 Jul 47, and
GNANIAH, Retnamony (Manalikarai, 1977) m 1977; Maj, Ind SE. b 20Aug 1954.

GOLDSACK, Kevin John (Palmerston North, 1970); Maj, NZ. b 5 Feb 42, with
GOLDSACK, Merilyn Judith (née Hopwood); Maj, NZ. b 27 Feb 43. Served in Aus E.

GONZALEZ, Henry (Orange, TX, 1967); Maj, USA S. b 18 Aug 46. BS (Sociol), and
GONZALEZ, Mary Dorris (née McCollum) (Meridian, MS, 1967) m 1969; Maj, USA S. b 13 Sep 48.

GOODIER, William (Washington Southeast, DC, 1969); Lt-Col, USA S. b 27 Feb 42, with
GOODIER, Mary Lee (née Cunningham) m 1963; Lt-Col, USA S. b 10 Jan 42. Served in Carib.

GOWER, Ross Richardson (Christchurch City, 1980); Maj, NZ. b 15 Dec 50, with
GOWER, Annette Veronica (née Knight) m 1972; Maj, NZ. Served in UK.

GRAHAM, Keith Livingston (Bluefields, 1967); Maj, Carib. b 23 Dec 47, and
GRAHAM, Molvie (née James) (St John's, 1968) m 1970; Maj, Carib. b 13 Dec 46.

GREEN, Lynette (née Marion) (Bendigo, Aus S, 1965); Lt-Col, Aus E. b 30 Mar 44. Ww Maj Frederick, pG 1998. Served in Aus S, E Afr and Port (OC).

GRIFFIN, Stanley (St John's, 1979); Maj, Carib. b 20 Feb 54, and
GRIFFIN, Hazel (née Whyte) (St John's, 1980) m 1981; Maj, Carib. b 23 Sep 57. Served in L Am N.

GRIFFIN, Terry W. (Seattle Temple, WA, 1970); Lt-Col, USA W. b 2 Nov 46. BA (Bib Lit), MA (Relig), with
GRIFFIN, Linda (née Bawden) m 1967; Lt-Col, USA W. b 28 Aug 46.

GRINDLE, David E. (Detroit Brightmoor, MI, 1966); Lt-Col, USA C. b 5 Mar 44, with
GRINDLE, Sherry (née McNabb) m 1964; Lt-Col, USA C. b 25 Jul 45.

GULLIKSEN, Thorleif R. (Haugesund, 1967); Comr, Nor. b 26 Apr 40, with
GULLIKSEN, Olaug (née Henriksen) m 1962; Comr, Nor. b 25 Jan 38. Served in Neth (TC/TPWO) and at IHQ (IS/SWM Eur).

GYIMAH, William (Wiamoase, 1976); Lt-Col, Gha. b 31 Dec 47, with
GYIMAH, Mary (née Pokuaa) m 1974; Lt-Col, Gha. b 14 Aug 48. Served in Gha & Lib.

H

HAMILTON, Ian E. (Clayton, 1971); Lt-Col, Aus E. b 8 Jun 47, with
HAMILTON, Marilyn (née Rawiller) m 1968; Lt-Col, Aus E. b 6 Aug 48. Served in Aus S.

HAMMOND, Gloria (Winnipeg Citadel, MB, Can, 1980); Maj, Pak. b 7 Nov 56. BA (Hist), M Th. Served in Can and Sri Lan.

HANGOMA, Donald (Munali, 1995); Capt, Zam. b 15 Jan 70, and
HANGOMA, Patricia (née Michelo) (1993); Capt, Zam. b 19 Mar 70.

HANSSON, Ing-Britt (née Wilson) (Jönköping, 1962) Lt-Col, Swdn. b 16 Sep 42. m 1965; Lt-Col Hans, ret 2001.

HARDING, Graeme (Lewisham, UK, 1963); Col, TC, Gha. b 13 Jan 42. Dip Soc, and
HARDING, Anne (née Lewis) (Exeter Temple, UK, 1963) m 1965; Col, TPWM, Gha. b 3 Nov 40. SRN, SCM. Served in UK, SAfr, Zimb, Gha & Lib (CS/TSWO) and at IHQ.

HARFOOT, William (Detroit Brightmoor, MI, 1977); Lt-Col, USA C. b 6 Sep 48. BS, MA, with
HARFOOT, Susan (née Stange) m 1969; Lt-Col, USA C. b 21 Oct 48. Associate of Arts.

HARITA, Naoko (Shibuya, 1968); Maj, Jpn. b 19 Jul 43. BA (Sociol).

HARMS, Bennie (Johannesburg City, 1974); Maj, S Afr. b 15 Apr 52, with
HARMS, Jennifer (née Hall) m 1972; Maj, S Afr. b 21 Oct 48. Served in Zimb.

HARRIS, Ian W. (Penge, 1989); Maj, UK. b 1 Sep 56. MA, Dip Soc Work, with
HARRIS, Jean (née Foster) m 1979; Maj, UK. b 31 Jul 56.

HARTVEIT, Jørg Walter (Langesund, 1971); Lt-Col, Nor. b 22 Jun 47. m 1971; Lt-Col Rigmor, ret 2006.

HAUGHTON, Devon (Port Antonio, 1981); Maj, Carib. b 22 Jul 59, and
HAUGHTON, Verona Beverly (née Henry) (Havendale, 1976) m 1982; Maj,

HEATWOLE, Merle D. (Milwaukee Citadel, WI, 1984); Maj, USA C. b 7 Jan 60. BS (Maths), with
HEATWOLE, Dawn Idell (née Lewis) m 1981; Maj, USA C. b 26 Nov 62.

HEDGREN, R. Steven (Chicago Mont Clare, IL, 1978); Maj, USA S. b 7 Mar 50. BS (Bus Admin), with
HEDGREN, Judith Ann (née White) m 1975; Maj, USA S. b 14 Feb 49. Served in USA C.

HEELEY, William (Rock Ferry, 1974); Maj, UK. b 6 May 48, and
HEELEY, Gillian (née Lacey) (Rock Ferry, 1975) m 1975; Maj, UK. b 18 Apr 52.

HEGGELUND, Brith-Mari (Harstad, 1972); Maj, Nor. b 22 Jul 49.

HENNE, Ingrid Elisabeth (Bergen 1, 1982); Maj, Nor. b 6 Sep 52.

HERRERA, Jaime (Hualpencillo, 1981); Maj, S Am W; b 27 Jul 59, and
HERRERA, Zaida (née Lopizic) (Santiago Central, 1983) m 1983; Maj, S Am W; b 12 Feb 58. Served in Braz.

HERRING, Alistair Chapman (Wellington City, NZ, 1975); Lt-Col, CS, E Eur. b 4 Mar 51. DipSW, with
HERRING, Verna Astrid (née Weggery) m 1971; Lt-Col, E Eur. b 29 Oct 51. Served in NZ

HETTIARACHCHI, Nihal (Colombo, 1985); Maj, Sri Lan. b 20 Jun 64, and
HETTIARACHCHI, Rohini Swarnalatha (née Wettamuni) (Colombo Central, 1994) m 1994; Capt, Sri Lan. b 18 Oct 64.

HIGHTON, Michael (Hinckley, 1985); Maj, UK. b 27 May 53, with
HIGHTON, Lynn (née Edwards) m 1975; Maj, UK. b 10 Mar 53.

HIGUCHI, Kazumitsu (Nagoya, 1976); Maj, Jpn. b 9 Apr 51, and
HIGUCHI, Aiko (née Kutomi) (Shibuya, 1979) m 1982; Maj, Jpn. b 25 Sep 53.

HILL, Martin (Northampton Central, 1984); Maj, UK. b 3 Jul 55. BA (Hons) (Soc Sci), MTh Ap Th.

HINTON, David (Blackheath, 1975); Maj, UK. b 28 Oct 53, and
HINTON, Sylvia (née Brooks) (Bedlington, 1975) m 1977; Maj, UK. b 2 Dec 53.

HIRAMOTO, Naoshi (Ueno, 1971); Lt-Col, CS, Jpn. b 24 Oct 46. BA (Law), and
HIRAMOTO, Seiko (née Kobayashi)

(Kyobashi, 1968) m 1973; Lt-Col, TSWM, Jpn. b 7 Oct 43. BA (Eng Lit).

HIRAMOTO, Nobuhiro (Ueno, 1979); Maj, Jpn. b 28 Dec 51. BA (Chinese Lit), and
HIRAMOTO, Yasuko (née Kinoshita) (Ueno, 1979) m 1979; Maj, Jpn. b 7 Dec 51.

HISCOCK, David G. (Corner Brook Citadel, NF, 1965); Lt-Col, Can. b 11 May 45, and
HISCOCK, Margaret (née Brown) (Bay Roberts, NF, 1966) m 1967; Lt-Col, Can. b 27 Mar 45. BA.

HODDER, Kenneth G. (Pasadena Tabernacle, CA, USA W, 1988); Lt-Col, CS, Ken. b 16 Jun 58. BA (Hist), JD (Law), with
HODDER, Jolene (née Lloyd) m 1982; Lt-Col, TLWM, Ken. b 30 Jul 63. BA (Home Econ). Served in USA W and USA S.

HODGE, John (Wollongong, 1972); Lt-Col. Aus E. b 27 Aug 45. Dip Teach, MBA, BA (Relig Studies and Ed). Ww Lt Marie, pG 1974. Served in PNG, and
HODGE, Pamela (née Henry) (Bankstown, 1972) m 1975; Lt-Col. Aus E. b 29 Oct 49. Served in Carib (CS/TSWO), Phil (TC/TPWO) and NZ.

HOGAN, Olin O. (Aberdeen, WA, USA W, 1962); Col, TC, Mex. b 23 Sep 41. BA (Bus Admin), MA (Bible and Theol), and
HOGAN, Dianne C. (née Cagle) (Seattle Temple, WA, USA W, 1963) m 1964; Col, TPWM, Mex. b 10 Dec 43. Served in USA W.

HOKOM, Eda M. (Caldwell, ID, 1974); Maj, USA W. b 19 Mar 48. BA (Soc Sci), BS (Relig Ed). Served in PNG.

HOLLEY, Brian (Granville, 1966); Maj, Aus E. b 20 Nov 43. BAL, Th C, and
HOLLEY, Glenys (née Kingston) (Dulwich Hill Temple, 1967) m 1968; Maj, Aus E. b 30 Oct 42.

HONDRO, Yavao (Medan 11, 1980); Maj, Indon. b 31 Jan 56. BPub Admin, and
HONDRO, Mariana (née Pohan) (Medan 11, 1982) m 1982; Maj, Indon. b 19 Jul 60.

HONSBERG, Frank (Cologne, 1987); Maj, Ger. b 24 Jan 63. Grad Bus Mgmt, with
HONSBERG, Stefanie (née Gossens) m 1985; Maj, Ger. b 17 Dec 65.

HOOD, Brian (Bundaberg, 1974); Lt-Col, Aus S. b 23 Mar 44, with
HOOD, Elaine (née Toft) m 1970; Lt-Col, Aus S. b 19 Apr 51. Served in Aus E and PNG.

HOOD, George (Hamilton, OH, USA W, 1983); Maj, USA Nat. b 31 Jan 47. BS (Mgmt), MS (Mgmt), and

HOOD, Donna J. (née Morrison) (Newport, KY, USA W, 1984) m 1969; Maj, USA Nat. b 25 Oct 47. BS. Served in USA E and USA W.

HOOD, James (San Diego Citadel, CA, USA W, 1977); Maj, Mex. b 27 Oct 46. BS (Agric Eng), MS (Civil Eng), with **HOOD, Sallyann** (née Carpenter) m 1971; Maj, Mex. b 12 Nov 45. BA (Pre-med Zoology), MD Ob/Gyn. Served in USA W and Ind SE.

HOOD, Ralph E. (Fresno, CA, 1966); Maj, USA W. b 13 Jul 42. BA (Bus Admin), BS (Relig Ed), and **HOOD, Ivy** (née Hill) (Rockford West, IL, 1964) m 1967; Maj, USA W. b 20 Jun 41. Served in USA C.

HOSTETLER, Donald D. (Cincinnati Citadel, OH, 1971); Maj, USA W. b 2 Jan 49. BA (Soc), MA (Public Admin), with **HOSTETLER, Arvilla J.** (née Marcum) m 1969; Maj, USA W. b 14 Aug 50.

HOUGHTON, Raymond (Woodhouse, UK, 1967); Comr, TC, Carib. b 12 Apr 44. MCMI, with **HOUGHTON, Judith** (née Jones) m 1965; Comr, TPWM, Carib. b 15 Nov 45. Served in UK (CS/TSWO) and at IHQ (IS to CoS/Mission Resources Sec).

HOWELL, Willis (Hyattsville, MD, 1985); Maj, USA S. b 3 Mar 56, with **HOWELL, Barbara** (née Leidy) m 1978; Maj, USA S. b 3 Apr 57.

HRANGNGURA (Hnahthial, 1981); Maj, Ind E. b 16 Jan 52, with **BIAKSAILOVI** (Hnahthial) m 1953; Maj, Ind E, b 9 Apr 53.

HUDSON, David E. (Portland Tabernacle, OR, 1975); Maj, USA W. b 28 Jun 54. BS (Bus Mgmt), and **HUDSON, Sharon** (née Smith) (Santa Ana, CA, 1975) m 1976; Maj, USA W. b 14 Jun 52.

HUGHES, Alex (Paisley West, 1960); Comr, UK. b 29 Jan 42, and **HUGHES, Ingeborg** (née Clausen) (Catford, 1964) m 1971; Comr, UK. b 2 Jan 42. Served in L Am N, S Am E (CS/THLS and TC/TPWO), S Am W (TC/TPWO), at IHQ (IS/SWO Am and Carib) and in UK (TC/TPWM).

HULSMAN, Everdina (Nijverdal, 1975); Lt-Col, Neth. b 21 Dec 47.

HUNTER, Barbara (née Booth) (Tucson, AZ, USA W, 1967); Lt-Col, USA E. b 17 Mar 47. BS (Org Mgmt). Ww Lt-Col William, pG 2001. Served in USA W and Rus (GS/CSWO).

I

INDURUWAGE, Malcolm (Colombo Central, Sri Lan, 1977); Col, TC, Phil. b 24 Sep 50, and **INDURUWAGE, Irene** (née Horathalge) (Colombo Central, Sri Lan, 1977) m 1977; Col, TPWM, Phil. b 29 Nov 55. Served in Sri Lan and Phil (CS/TSWM).

IRVING, Ray (Shiremoor, 1989); Maj, UK. b 20 Apr 51. MVA, MCMI, and **IRVING, Angela** (née Richards) (Torquay, 1972) m 1989; Maj, UK. b 12 Feb 51.

ISMAEL, Dina (Bandung 1, 1990); Maj, Indon. b 19 Jan 60.

IVERSEN, Magda (Stavanger, Nor, 1971); Maj, Gha. b 19 Aug 44. BA(Relig), SRN. Served in Nor and Zam.

J

JACKSON, David (Romford, 1976); Maj, UK. b 10 Nov 52. Served at IHQ.

JACKSON, Ghulam (Shantinagar, 1972); Maj, Pak. b 27 Jan 46. BA, BEd, with **JACKSON, Joycline** (née Inayat) m 1968; Maj, Pak. b 18 Apr 46.

JAMES, M. C. (Monkotta, Ind SW, 1979); Comr, TC, Ind SE. b 20 Oct 54. MA Soc, and **JAMES, L. Susamma** (Pothencode, Ind SW, 1983) m 1983; Comr, TPWM, Ind SE. b 1 Mar 61. Served in Ind C (TC/TPWM).

JAYARATNASINGHAM, Packianathan (Jaffna, 1973); Maj, Sri Lan. b 4 Nov 52, and **JAYARATNASINGHAM, Delankage Chandralatha** (née Delankage) (Siyambalangamua, 1979) m 1980; Maj, Sri Lan. b 28 Oct 59. Served at IHQ.

JAYASEELAN, Jebamony (Maharajaduram 1982); Maj, Ind SE. b 20 May 57, and **JAYASEELAN, Gnanaselvi** (née Masih) (1985); Maj, Ind SE. b 30 Dec 57.

JEBASINGH-RAJ, J. Daniel (Booth Tucker Hall, Nagercoil, Ind SE, 1987); Maj, Ind Nat. b 10 Jun 61. BA (Eng), MA (Social), BTh, BD, with **JEBASINGH-RAJ, T. Rajam** (Kuzhikalai, Ind SE, 1992) m 1992; Capt, Ind Nat. b 12 Mar 64; BA (English), MA (History), BTh PM. Served in Ind SE.

JEFFREY, David (Morgantown, WV, 1973); Lt-Col, CS, USA S. b 2 Aug 51, and **JEFFREY, Barbara** (née Garris) (Morgantown, WV, 1966) m 1969; Lt-Col, TSWM, USA S. b 1 Jan 46.

JEFFREY, John (Port Pirie, 1970); Lt-Col, CS, Aus S. b 8 Nov 42, with

JEFFREY, Judith (née Standen) m 1966; Lt-Col, TSWM, Aus S. b 15 Mar 48.

JELLYMAN, Wayne (Napier, 1980); Maj, NZ. b 21 Feb 53. DipT, and
JELLYMAN, Joanne (née Beale) (Sydenham, 1978) m 1980; Maj, NZ. b 29 Jul 53.

JEREMIAH, Edwin (Mupfure, 1990); Maj, Zimb. b 30 Jun 60, with
JEREMIAH, Tambudzai (née Kabaya) m 1979; Maj, Zimb. b 10 Feb 62.

JEWETT, Vernon Wayne (Atlanta Temple, GA, 1980); Maj, USA S. b 11 Dec 47. BA, MA, with
JEWETT, Martha Gaye (née Brewer) m 1975; Maj, USA S. b 22 Oct 52. BA.

JOHN, Morris (Rancho Lines, 1975); Lt-Col, Pak. b 1 Jan 53, with
JOHN, Salma (née Feroz) m 1974; Lt-Col, Pak. b 1 Jan 56.

JOHN, Rajan K. (Parayankerry, 1979); Maj, Ind SW. b 26 Mar 52, with
JOHN, Susamma m 1977; Maj, Ind SW. b 17 Oct 52.

JOHN ROSE, Mark (Muttakaud, 1970); Maj, Ind SE. b 14 Oct 46, and
ROSE, Jebamoney (née Masih) (Thuckalay, 1973) m 1973; Maj, Ind SE. b 15 Sep 49. Served in Ind C.

JOHNSON, Kenneth (Charlotte Temple, NC, 1984); Maj, USA S. b 10 Aug 56. BS (Bus Mgmt), with
JOHNSON, Paula (née Salmon) m 1981; Maj, USA S. b 23 Nov 62.

JOHNSON, Paulose (Pallickal, 1969); Lt-Col, Ind SW. b 24 Feb 46, and
JOHNSON, Thankamma (Mulakuzha, 1971) m 1971; Lt-Col, Ind SW. b 3 May 49.

JONAS, Dewhurst (St John's, 1982); Maj, Carib. b 20 May 56, and
JONAS, Vevene (née Gordon) (Rae Town, 1980) m 1983; Maj, Carib. b 1 Jun 57.

JONES, David (Andover, 1968); Lt-Col, UK. b 21 Nov 41. m 1965; Lt-Col Valerie, ret 2006.

JONES, Melvyn (Hoxton, 1976); Maj, UK. b 21 Nov 51. MA (Nat Sci), with
JONES, Kathleen (née Hall) m 1974; Maj, UK. b 15 Mar 51. SRN, SCM.

JOSEPH, Younis (Kamalia, 1979); Maj, Pak. b 12 Dec 54, with
YOUNIS, Margaret (née Gabrial) m 1978; Maj, Pak. b 5 Dec 57.

JOSHI, Devadasi (Musunuru, 1981); Maj, Ind C. b 1 Oct 54, with
JOSHI, Leelamani m 1977; Maj, Ind C. b 1 Jun 53.

JUNG, Verônica (Cachoeira Paulista, 1984); Maj, Brz. b 15 Sep 59.

K

KALA, Sere (Koki, 1990); Maj, PNG. b 1 Jul 58, with
KALA, Hanua (née Malaga) m 1979; Maj, PNG. b 10 Sep 59.

KALAI, Andrew (Koki, 1981); Col, TC, PNG. b 18 Jan 56. BA (Psychology). Ww Capt Napa, pG 1994, Ww Col Julie, pG 2006. Served in UK.

KALE, Ratnakar Dinkar (Ahmednagar Central, 1977); Maj, Ind W. b 1 Jul 53, and
KALE, Leela (née Magar) (Byculla, 1981) m 1981; Maj, Ind W. b 1 Mar 60.

KANIS, Jacob (Kampen, 1968); Lt-Col, Neth. b 12 Oct 46, and
KANIS, Wijna (née Arends) (Kampen, 1968) m 1969; Lt-Col, Neth. b 21 Apr 47.

KARTODARSONO, Ribut (Surakarta, 1975); Col, TC, Indon. b 13 Dec 49. BA (Relig Ed), MA (Relig Ed & Public Societies), and
KARTODARSONO, Marie (née Ticoalu) (Bandung 3, 1975) m 1979; Col, TPWM, Indon. b 30 Nov 52. Served in Indon (CS/TSWM) and UK.

KARUNAKARA RAO, N. J. (Madras Central, Ind C, 1976) Lt-Col, Ind Nat. b 3 Apr 48. Dip Hosp Admin, MA (Soc Work), BSc (Bot), with
VIJAYALAKSHMI, N. J. m 1973; Lt-Col, Ind Nat. b 9 Jul 55. BA (Eng Lit), BD. Served in Ind SE, Ind C, Sri Lan (CS/TSWO) and Ind W (CS/TSWO).

KASAEDJA, Jones (Kulawi, 1982); Maj, Indon. b 22 Jun 68, and
KASAEDJA, Mariyam (née Barani) (Salupone, 1982) m 1989; Maj, Indon. b 10 Oct 1954.

KASBE, Devdan Laxman (Ahmednagar Central, 1970); Maj, Ind W. b 9 Feb 49, and
KASBE, Maria B. (née Devhe) (Dapodi, 1972) m 1972; Maj, Ind W. b 16 Oct 52.

KATHENDU, Johnstone Njeru (Siakago, 1988); Maj, Ken. b 22 Jun 63, with
KATHENDU, Nancy (née Turi) m 1984; Maj, Ken. b 26 Feb 64.

KATSUCHI, Jiro (Hamamatsu, 1984); Maj, Jpn. b 3 May 49, and
KATSUCHI, Keiko (née Munemori) (Nagoya, 1969) m 1986; Maj, Jpn. b 30 Jun 47.

KELLY, David E. (Cincinnati, OH, 1980);

Maj, USA E. b 30 Nov 59. AS (Bus Adm), MA (Ldrshp & Min), and **KELLY, Naomi R.** (née Foster) (Tonawanda, NY, 1977) m 1981; Maj, USA E. b 14 Sep 56. BA (Org Mgmt).

KHARKOV, Alexander (Moscow Central, 1993); Maj, E Eur. b 31 Jan 58, with **KHARKOV, Maria** (née Seleverstova) m 1979; Maj, E Eur. b 30 Nov 49.

KHOZA, Jabulani (Mbabane, 1985); Maj, S Afr. b 8 Jun 62, and **KHOZA, Fikile** (née Mkhize) (Ezakheni, 1986) m 1986; Maj, S Afr. b 28 Aug 66.

KIHI, Mais (Kainantu, 1988); Maj, PNG. b 9 Sep 1956, with **KIHI, Paula** (née Anton) m 1980; Maj, PNG. b 18 Mar 63.

KIM, Kie-duk (Yong Dong, 1971); Maj, Kor. b 21 May 42, with **PARK, Chung-ja** m 1966; Maj, Kor. b 10 Dec 42.

KIM, Nam-sun (Ah Hyun, 1983); Maj, Kor. b 11 Sep 54.

KIM, Oon-ho (Eum Am, 1979); Maj, Kor. b 31 Jan 52, with **LEE, Ok-kyung** m 1977; Maj, Kor. b 9 Jun 53.

KIM, Young-tae (Chin Chook, 1986); Maj, Kor. b 23 Mar 56. BAdmin, MBA, with **PYO, Choon-yun** m 1977; Maj, Kor. b 29 Jul 53.

KING, Charles (New Barnet, UK, 1975); Maj, IHQ. b 29 Nov 48. Served in UK.

KJELLGREN, Hasse (Östra Kåren, Swdn, 1971); Comr, IS Eur, IHQ. b 1 Nov 45. BSc, and **KJELLGREN, Christina** (née Forssell) (Hisingskaren, Swdn, 1971) m 1971; Comr, SWM Eur, IHQ. b 21 May 47. Served in S Am E (TC/TPWO), Switz (TC/TPWM) and Swdn (TC/TPWM).

KLARENBEEK, Elsje (Amsterdam Zuid, 1979); Maj, Neth. b 2 Jun 52.

KLEMAN, Johnny (Boras, 1982); Maj, Swdn. b 29 Jul 59.

KLEMANSKI, Guy (Lewiston-Auburn, ME, 1970); Maj, USA E. b 21 Nov 50, and **KLEMANSKI, Henrietta** (née Wallace) (Cleveland, West Side, OH, 1970) m 1972; Maj, USA E. b 27 Jul 47.

KNAGGS, James (Philadelphia Roxborough, PA, USA E, 1976); Comr, TC, Aus S. b 5 Dec 50. MPS (Urban Min), with **KNAGGS, Carolyn** (née Lance) m 1972; Comr, TPWM, Aus S. b 19 Sep 51. Served

in USA E (CS/TSWM).

KNAPP, Jocelyn (Camberwell, 1969); Lt-Col, Aus S. b 7 Apr 44. Served in Aus E.

KNECHT, Hans (Wetzikon, 1968); Maj, Switz. b 17 Jan 43, and **KNECHT, Heidi** (née Weidmann) (Bulach, 1968) m 1969; Maj, Switz. b 13 Jul 43.

KNEDAL, Jan Øystein (Templet, Oslo, 1974); Maj, Nor. b 25 Aug 52, and **KNEDAL, Brit** (née Kolloen) (Templet, Oslo, 1976) m 1978; Maj, Nor. b 27 Apr 58

KORNILOW, Petter (Parkano, 1981); Maj, Fin. b 21 Aug 53, and **KORNILOW, Eija Hellevi** (née Astikainen) (Tampere Kaleva, 1981) m a1981; Maj, Fin. b 28 Jun 56.

KROMMENHOEK, Dick (Amsterdam Congress Hall, Neth, 1983); Col, IHQ. b 18 Jun 52. MA (Music), with **KROMMENHOEK, Vibeke** (née Schou Larsen) m 1978; Col, IHQ. b 27 Nov 56. MA (Th). Served in Neth, Den (TC/TPWM) and Frce (TC/TPWM).

KRUPA DAS, P. D. (Leprosy Hospital, Madras, Ind C, 1972); Comr, TC, Ind W. b 15 Apr 48. BCom, MCom, and **RAJAKUMARI, P. Mary** (New Colony, Bapatla, Ind C, 1978) m 1978; Comr, TPWM, Ind W. MA (Engl), MA (Hist). Served in Ind C, at HIQ, at Ind Cent Off, in Ind W (CS/THLS), Ind N (TC/TPWM) and Ind SE (TC/TPWM).

KUGO, Toshinori (Takasaki, 1965); Maj, Jpn. b 29 Jun 43, and **KUGO, Fumiko** (née Minato) (Tenma, 1964) m 1969; Maj, Jpn. b 22 Mar 43.

KUNTAM, Yesudhana Kumar (Khajipalem, Bapatla, 1980); Maj, Ind C. b 21 Sep 1957. BCom, with **KUNTAM, Yesamma** (née Dasari) m 1978; Maj, Ind C. b 18 May 1961.

KWENDA, Innocent Peter (Mutondo, 1976); Maj, Zimb. b 10 Apr 57, and **KWENDA, Norma** (née Nyawo) (Dombwe-Makonde, 1977) m 1977; Maj, Zimb. b 10 Jul 55.

KWON, Sung-dal (Son Chi, 1977); Maj, Kor. b 17 Apr 47, with **KIM, Moon-ok** (Son Chi, 1977) m 1973; Maj, Kor. b 29 Oct 53.

L

LAHASE, Kashinath V. (Chapadgaon, Ind W, 1972); Col, TC, Ind N. b 1 Nov 49, with **LAHASE, Kusum K.** m 1970; Col, TPWM,

Ind N. b 7 Jun 49. Served in Ind W, Ind SW and Ind N (CS/TSWM).

LAL, Rounki (Amritsar, 1972); Maj, Ind N. b 15 May 48, with
LAL, Agnes m 1968; Maj, Ind N. b 3 Feb 50.

LALBULLIANA (Darlawn, Ind E, 1987); Maj, Ken. b 20 Sep 64, and
LALBULLIANA, Lalnunhlui (Thingsulthliah, Ind E, 1990) m 1990; Maj, Ken. b 12 Dec 65. Served in Ind E.

LALHMINGLIANA (Chaltlang, 1994); Capt, Ind E. b 29 Sep 71. BA (Hons) (Hist), and
LALHLIMPUII (Bethel, 1994) m 1994; Capt, Ind E. b 28 Oct 71. Served at IHQ.

LALHRIATPUIA (Republic 1982); Maj, Ind E. b 1 Jun 62, and
LALCHHUANMAWII (Temple, 1985) m 1986; Maj, Ind E. b 18 Sep 64.

LALKIAMLOVA (Kahrawt, 1971); Comr, IS S Asia, IHQ. b 7 Mar 49. BA, and
LALHLIMPUII (Saitual, 1973) m 1973; Comr, SWM S Asia, IHQ. b 25 Sep 53. Served in Ind E, Ind SW (CS/TSWO) and Ind C (TPWM).

LALNGAIHAWMI (Central 1978); Maj, Ind E. b 1 Jan 54. MA.

LALZAMLOVA (Tuinu, Ind E, 1986); Col, TC, Sri Lan. b 20 May 62. BA, with
NEMKHANCHING (Nu-i) m 1984; Col, TPWM, Sri Lan. b 23 Feb 63. Served in Ind E and Ind N.

LAMARR, William (Yonkers Citadel, NY, 1967); Lt-Col, USA E. b 8 Apr 45, and
LAMARR, Judy (née Lowers) (East Liverpool, OH, 1962) m 1968; Lt-Col, USA E. b 14 Sep 41. LPN (Nursing)

LANCE, Donald W. (Philadelphia Roxborough, PA, 1980); Maj, USA E. b 7 Feb 53. BA (Business), and
LANCE, Renee (née Hewlett) (Scranton, PA, 2002) m 2003; Capt, USA E. b Jun 53. RN (Nursing).

LANGA, William (Witbank, 1977); Maj, S Afr. b 15 Jul 49, with
LANGA, Thalitha (née Themba); Maj, S Afr. b 1 Sep 50.

LAPEÑA, Marilou (née Hercer) (Quezon City 1, Phil) m 1987; Maj, Sri Lan. b 26 Sep 61. Served in Phil.

LARSSON, Per-Olof (Orebro 1, 1978); Maj, Swdn. b 7 Dec 51, and
LARSSON, Karin (née Blomberg) (Dala-Jarna, 1977) m 1978; Maj, Swdn. b 5 Jun 50.

LAUA, Abner (Palu, 1968); Lt-Col, Indon. b 8 Mar 45, and

LAUA, Mina (née Hohoy) (Surabaya Kulawi, 1972) m 1972; Lt-Col, Indon. b 14 Dec 46.

LAUKKANEN, Arja (Turku 2, 1975); Lt-Col, CS, Fin. b 29 Apr 46.

LAWS, Peter (Wauchope, 1973); Maj, Aus E. b 23 Oct 1950. BAL, MBA, with
LAWS, Jan (née Cook) m 1970; Maj. Aus E. b 18 Jun 50.

LEAVEY, Wendy (Street, UK, 1980); Maj, Gha. b 17 Feb 53. SRN, SCM. Served in UK.

LECOCQ, Noélie (Quaregnon, 1973); Maj, GS, Belg. b 29 Feb 48.

LEE, Kong Chew (Bob) (Balestier, 1983); Maj, Sing. b 8 Oct 57. BDiv, and
LEE, Teoh Gim Leng (Wendy) (Penang, 1983) m 1982; Maj, Sing. b 24 Aug 57.

LEE, Sang-hyung (Chung Eup, 1973); Lt-Col, Kor. b 11 Dec 41, with
KIM, Kyung-soon (Chung Eup, 1973) m 1971; Lt-Col, Kor. b 28 Nov 49. Served in USA W.

LESLIE, Victor A. (Port-of-Spain, Carib, 1980); Maj, USA W. b 5 Nov 56. BA (Mgmt), MA (Relig Studies), Cert (Chem Dependence), JD (Law), MBA (Mgmt), and
LESLIE, Rose-Marie (née Campbell) (Lucea, Carib, 1977) m 1980; Maj, USA W. b 15 Aug 57. BS (Soc Work), AS (Nursing), RN (Nursing), BS (Nursing), Cert (Public Health Nurse). Served in Carib.

LIANHLIRA (Ratu, 1979); Maj, Ind E. b 28 Apr 51, with
THANZUALI m 1975; Maj, Ind E. b 20 Jan 57.

LIANTHANGA (Darlawn, 1974); Maj, Ind E. b 1 Mar 50, and
RINGLIANI (Darlawn, 1974) m 1975; Maj, Ind E. b 10 Jan 52.

LIM, Hun-taek (Kunsan, 1979); Maj, Kor. b 28 Feb 50; with
CHUN, Soon-ja m 1977; Maj, Kor. b 15 Aug 50. Served in Aus S.

LIM, Young-shik (Shin An, 1975); Maj, Kor. b 26 Jun 49, with
YEO, Keum-soo m 1972; Maj, Kor. b 6 Dec 50.

LINARES, Orestes (Camaguey, 1997); Capt, L Am N. b 13 Aug 60, with
LINARES, Sandra (née Fernández) m 1986; Capt, L Am N. b 26 Jun 63.

LING, Fona (née Chan) (Lok Man, HK, 1973); Maj, RC/RPWM, Tai. b 29 Jun 53. Ww Maj James, pG 2001. Served in HK and Aus E.

LINGARD, George (Toowoomba, 1971); Maj, Aus E. b 31 Jan 41, and
LINGARD, Beryl (née Pamenter) (Toowoomba, 1972) m 1972; Maj, Aus E. b 2 Oct 44.

LÖFGREN, Kehs David (Norrköping, 1968); Col, Swdn. b 8 Nov 45, and
LÖFGREN, Edith (née Sjöström) (Borlänge, 1974) m 1977; Col, Swdn. b 2 Mar 51. Served in UK and Nor (CS/TSWO).

LOSSO, Mesak (Jakarta 2, 1968); Lt-Col, Indon. b 12 Nov 45, and
LOSSO, Mona (née Warani) (Turen, 1971) m 1972; Lt-Col, Indon. b 13 Jun 44.

LOUBAKI, Urbain (Bakongo, 1992); Capt, Con (Braz). b 20 Dec 64, with
LOUBAKI, Judith (née Bikouta) m 1989; Maj, Con (Braz). b 16 Apr 68.

LOUKOULA, Cécile (Ouenzé, 1990); Maj, Con (Braz). b 30 Aug 56.

LUDIAZO, Jean Bakidi (Salle Centrale, Kinshasa, 1971); Comr, TC, Con (Kin). b 19 Nov 45, with
LUDIAZO, Véronique (née Lusieboko Lutatabio) m 1970; Comr, TPWM, Con (Kin). b 26 Sep 53. Served in Con and Can.

LUFUMBU, Enock (Londiani, Nakuru, 1982); Maj, Ken. b 10 Feb 52, with
LUFUMBU, Beatrice (née Kageha) m 1978; Maj, Ken. b 22 Feb 57.

LUKAU, Mangiengie Joseph (Kimbanseke 1, Con (Kin), 1977); Lt-Col, CS, Frce. b 18 Sep 53, with
LUKAU, Angélique (née Makiese) m 1975; Lt-Col, TPWM, Frce. b 1 Sep 54. Served in Con (Kin).

LUYK, Kenneth Edwin (Columbus, GA, 1985); Maj, USA S. b 2 Oct 55. MA (Relig), with
LUYK, Dawn Marie (née Busby) m 1981; Maj, USA S. b 5 Jun 60. BA (Chrstn Min).

LYDHOLM, Carl A. S. (Gartnergade, Den, 1966); Comr, TC, Nor. b 14 Nov 45, and
LYDHOLM, Gudrun (née Arskog) (Odense, Den, 1967) m 1967; Comr, TPWM, Nor. b 5 Aug 47. MTh. Served in Den, UK, Rus/CIS (GS/CSWM) and Fin (TC/TPWM).

M

MA, Tony Yeung-mo (Tai Hang Tung, 1985); Maj, HK. b 20 Oct 55, and
MA, Elen Yi-lung (née Lu) (Tainang, 1981) m 1985; Maj, HK. b 4 Nov 52.

MABANZA, Alexandre (Makaka, 1975); Maj, Con (Braz). b 15 Dec 50, with
MABANZA, Madeleine (née Mantseka) m 1972; Maj, Con (Braz). b 24 Jan 54.

MABASO, Timothy John (Witbank, 1988); Maj, S Afr. b 10 Jun 57. BA (Bus Admin), with
MABASO, Flemah Ntombizakithi (née Zulu) m 1983; Maj, S Afr. b 16 Dec 57.

MABHIZA, Sydney (Dzumbunu, 1976); Maj, Zimb. b 12 Dec 46, with
MABHIZA, Gladys (née Mahowa) m 1974; Maj, Zimb. b 12 Jun 54.

MABUTO, Christopher (Chaanga, 1979); Maj, Zam. b 1 Feb 54, with
MABUTO, Annah (née Hamayobe) m 1974; Maj, Zam. b 25 Feb 58.

MACAYANA, Jaime (Hermosa, Phil, 1977); Maj, PNG. b 12 Dec 52. BS (Com Mgmt), and
MACAYANA, Lilia (née Agustin) (Manila Central, Phil, 1978) m 1978; Maj, PNG. b 13 Sep 52. BS (Com Acct). Served in Phil and at IHQ.

MACMILLAN, M. Christine (North York, 1975); Comr, TC/TPWM, Can. b 9 Oct 47. Served in UK, Aus E and PNG (TC).

MACWAN, John Purshottam (Alindra, Ind W, 1969); Maj, Ind Nat. b 1 Feb 48, and
MACWAN, Miriam (née Peter) (Bhalej, Ind W, 1974) m 1974; Maj, Ind W. b 13 Oct 55. Served in Ind W.

MACWAN, Natwarlal M. (Ghoghawada, 1969); Maj, Ind W. b 23 Jan 46, and
MACWAN, Savitaben (Sundha-Vansol, 1983) m 1976; Maj, Ind W. b 1 Jun 56.

MACWAN, Phulen W. (Poona, 1981); Maj, Ind W. b 21 Apr 51.

McCARTY, Charles R. (Terre Haute, IN, 1967); Maj, USA C. b 1 Jan 44. BS (Psych), with
McCARTY, Janet (née Walker) m 1964; Maj, USA C. b 6 Mar 45.

McCLIMONT, Graeme (Brighton, Aus S, 1977); Maj, PNG. b 29 Jan 48. BA (Soc Welfare), BA (Behavioural Sc), with
McCLIMONT, Helen (née Clee) m 1969; Maj, PNG. b 1 Dec 49. Served in Aus S and UK.

McDOWELL, James (Wilwaukee, WI, USA C, 1981); Maj, Ken. b 2 May 58, with
McDOWELL, Valerie (née Welch) m 1982; Maj, Ken. b 25 Mar 58. Served in USA C.

McINTYRE, Robert George (New City Road, 1967); Maj, UK. b 15 Oct 44, and
McINTYRE, Isobel (née Laird) (Partick Temple, 1969) m 1969; Maj, UK. b 23 Sep 48.

McKENZIE, Garth (Wellington City, 1975); Comr, TC, NZ. b 19 Feb 44, with
McKENZIE, Merilyn (née Probert) m 1968; Comr, TPWM, NZ. b 20 Jul 46. Served in Aus S.

McKENZIE, Sydney (Havendale, 1970); Lt-Col, Carib. b 24 Dec 47, and
McKENZIE, Trypheme (née Forrest) (Bluefields, 1971) m 1973; Lt-Col, Carib. b 14 Jan 50.

McLAREN, Mickey L. (Midland, MI, 1970); Lt-Col, USA C. b 13 Oct 44. BA (Bus Admin), with
McLAREN, June C. (née Monroe) m 1964; Lt-Col, USA C. b 11 Jun 42. Served in Gha.

McLEOD, Margaret (Medicine Hat, Can, 1994); Capt, PNG. b 29 Apr 63. BEd, MTS. Served in Can.

McMILLAN, Susan (Montreal Citadel, Can, 1979); Lt-Col, CS, S Am W. b 20 Oct 54. BAS, MBA, CGA. Served in Can, Mex & Central Am and S Am E.

MAELAND, Erling Dag (Bryne, 1964); Lt-Col, CS, Nor. b 9 Oct 43, and
MAELAND, Signe Helene (née Paulsen) (Bryne, 1964) m 1965; Lt-Col, TSWM, Nor. b 12 Jun 45. Served in UK and at IHQ.

MAGAR, Bhausaheb J. (Dahiphal, 1977); Maj, Ind W. b 2 Jun 53, and
MAGAR, Pushpa (née Gajbhiv) (Dahiphal, 1978) m 1979; Maj, Ind W. b 2 Jun 54.

MAGAYA, Bexter (Chitumbi, 1981); Maj, Zam. b 29 Jan 56, with
MAGAYA, Jessie (née Milambo) m 1979; Maj, Zam. b 20 Sep 63.

MAKINA, Amos (Gwelo, Zimb, 1971); Comr, IS Afr, IHQ. b 28 Jun 47, and
MAKINA, Rosemary (née Chinjiri) (Mutonda, Zimb, 1973) m 1973; Comr, SWM Afr, IHQ. b 8 Aug 52. Served in Gha and Zimb (TC/TPWM).

MALABI, Joash (Mulatiwa, Ken, 1984); Maj, RC, Rw. b 17 May 55, and
MALABI, Florence (née Mutindi) (Webuye, Ken, 1988) m 1988; Maj, RPWM, Rw. b 26 Jun 64. Served in E Afr.

MANKOMBA, Elisha (Choma, 1989); Maj, Zam. b 22 Mar 53, with
MANKOMBA, Alice (née Mutinta) m 1983; Maj, Zam. b 4 Jun 64.

MANOHARAN, Yesuvadiyan (Nantikuzhy, Ind SE, 1987); Maj, Ind N. b 14 May 64, and
MANOHARAN, Vethamony (Ettamadai, Ind SE, 1987) m 1987; Maj, Ind N. b 20 Mar 64. Served in Ind SE.

MANULAT, Edward (San Jose Antique, 1983); Maj, Phil. b 1 Dec 59, and
MANULAT, Arlene (née Nicor) (Pandanan, 1984) m 1984; Maj, Phil. b 10 Aug 59.

MARQUEZ, Manuel (La Esperanza, 1995); Capt, S Am W. b 12 Feb 71, and
MARQUEZ, Paulina (née Condori) (Viacha, 1987) m 1997; Capt, S Am W. b 2 Mar 64.

MARSHALL, Norman Stephen (Chicago Mont Clare, IL, 1978); Maj, USA C. b 17 Jun 45.

BA (Sociol), MS (Human Services Admin), MA (Org Devpt), with
MARSHALL, Diane Bernice (née Hedgren) m 1974; Maj, USA C. b 30 Sep 47. BS (Ed).

MARTI, Paul William (Templet, Oslo, 1980), Maj, Nor. b 24 Jan 61, and
MARTI, Margaret Saue (née Saue) (Voss, 1980) m 1983, Maj, Nor. b 29 Aug 58. Served in Switz.

MARTIN, Larry R. (Edmonton Northside, AB, 1978); Maj, Can. b 31 Jul 1950, BA, MA, MTS, and
MARTIN, Velma (née Ginn) (Edmonton Northside, AB, 1978) m 1972; Maj, Can. b 4 Oct 50. Served in UK.

MARVELL, Michael (Westminster, UK, 1961); Col, TC, Den. b 26 Nov 40. BA (Hons), and
MARVELL, Ina E. (née Nissen) (Gartnergade, 1961) m 1965; Col, TPWM, Den. b 1 Oct 35. Served in UK, Den (CS/TSWO), at IHQ and in Swdn (CS/TSWM).

MASANGO, Frederick (Mangula, 1971); Maj, Zimb. b 24 Jul 49, and
MASANGO, Rosemary (née Handiria) (Karambazungu, 1981) m 1981; Maj, Zimb. b 13 Feb 56.

MASIH, Bashir (Talwandi, Ind N, 1969); Lt-Col, CS, Ind SE. b 10 Apr 48, and
MASIH, Bachini (Gurdaspur, Ind N, 1972) m 1972; Lt-Col, TSWM, Ind SE. b 24 Nov 50. Served in Ind N and Ind C (CS/TSWM).

MASIH, Bua (Bhandal, 1967); Maj, Ind N. b 3 Mar 47, and
MASIH, Marriam Bua (Bhandal, 1968) m 1968; Maj, Ind N. b 5 Nov 46.

MASIH, Edwin (Bareilly, 1979); Maj, Ind N. b 6 Oct 57, and
MASIH, Sumita (Gurdaspur, 1983) m 1983; Maj, Ind N. b 9 Oct 63.

MASIH, Gian (Jalalabad, 1972); Maj, Ind N. b 1 Oct 50, and
MASIH, Salima (Barnala, 1972) m 1978; Maj, Ind N. b 1 Dec 54.

MASIH, Joginder (Bhoper, Ind N, 1982); Maj, GS, Ban. b 13 Jul 58, with
MASIH, Shanti m 1980; Maj, CSWM, Ban. b 15 May 59. Served in Ind N.

MASIH, Kashmir (Khushadpur, 1990); Capt, Ind N. b 1 Mar 63, with
MASIH, Veena m 1987; Capt, Ind N. b 1 Sep 66.

MASIH, Lazar (Rampur, 1974); Maj, Ind N. b 20 May 52, with
MASIH, Sharbati (née Sharbati) m 1969; Maj, Ind N. b 15 Jun 53.

MASIH, Manuel (Amritsar, 1994); Capt, Ind N. b 1 Apr 64, with
MASIH, Anita m 1991; Capt, Ind N. b 22 Apr 62.

MASIH, Peter (Daburjie, Amritsar, 1968); Maj, Ind N. b 23 Oct 48, and
MASIH, Darmi (Bakhatpur, 1966) m 1968; Maj, Ind N. b 15 Nov 46.

MASIH, Prakash (Khunda, 1984); Maj, Ind N. b 10 Mar 58, with
MASIH, Mariam m 1981; Maj, Ind N. b 2 Apr 62.

MASIH, Salamat (Shantinagar, 1989); Maj, Pak. b 12 Aug 64, with
SALAMAT, Grace (née Sardar) m 1987; Capt, Pak. b 18 Apr 64.

MASIH, Shafqat (Rehimabad, Sheikhupu, 1981); Maj, Pak. b 30 Oct 48, with
SHAFQAT, Parveen (née Sardar) m 1979; Maj, Pak. b 26 Jun 51.

MASIH, Yaqoob (Chamroua, 1986); Maj, Ind N. b 6 Jun 62, with
MASIH, Sumitra m 1980; Maj, Ind N. b 6 Jan 63.

MASON, Raphael (Mandeville, 1967); Lt-Col, CS, Carib. b 7 Jul 47, and
MASON, Winsome (née De Lisser) (Montego Bay, 1967) m 1969; Lt-Col, TSWM, Carib. b 19 Feb 49. Served in USA E.

MASSIÉLÉ, Antoine (Yaya, 1982); Maj, Con (Braz). b 20 Feb 53, with
MASSIÉLÉ, Marianne (née Ngoli) m 1978; Maj, Con (Braz). b 2 Jan 50.

MATA, Mayisilwa Jean-Baptiste (Kisenso, 1983); Maj, Con (Kin). b 21 Oct 51, with
MATA, Marie (née Mundele Kisokama) m 1981; Maj, Con (Kin). b 22 Mar 58.

MATEAR, John (Whifflet, 1978); Comr, TC, UK. b 26 Apr 47, and
MATEAR, Elizabeth (née Kowbus) (Greenock Citadel, 1977) m 1978; Comr, TPWM, UK. b 16 Aug 52. Dip Youth, Commun and Soc Work, Emp Law. Served in UK and Carib (TC/TPWM).

MATTHEWS, Ward (Atlanta Temple, USA S, 1984); Maj, Carib. b 27 Jul 60. BS, and
MATTHEWS, Michele (née Matthews) (Tampa, FL, USA S) m 1999; Capt, Carib. b 1 Feb 67, BA Soc Services/Psychology, BS Nursing. Served in USA S.

MATONDO, Isidore Mayunga (Boma, 1989); Maj, Con (Kin). b 6 Jul 56, with
MATONDO, Lily Nlandu (née Luzoladio) m 1987; Maj, Con (Kin). b 7 Dec 62.

MAVOUNA, Nkouka François (Nzoko, 1988);

Maj, Con (Braz). b 15 Mar 60, with
MAVOUNA, Louise (née Matondo) m 1986; Maj, Con (Braz). b 11 Dec 62.

MAVUNDLA, Ntandane Hezekiel (Barberton, 1970); Lt-Col, CS, S Afr. b 19 Jan 47, and
MAVUNDLA, Busisiwe Mirriam (née Maphanga) (Barberton, 1970) m 1970; Lt-Col, TSWM, S Afr. b 2 Aug 52.

MAXWELL, Wayne (Canberra City Temple, 1984); Maj, Aus E. b 31 May 58. BMin, with
MAXWELL, Robyn (née Alley) m 1980; Maj, Aus E. b 14 Feb 60.

MAYNOR, Kenneth (Cleveland South, OH, 1980); Maj, USA E. b 1 Feb 59. BS (Org Mgmt), with
MAYNOR, Cheryl Ann (née Staaf) m 1977; Maj, USA E. b 27 Sep 58. BS (Church Mgmt).

MBAJA, Tiras Atulo (Kibera, 1986); Maj, Ken. b 13 Jul 54, with
MBAJA, Mebo (née Mukiza) m 1983; Maj, Ken. b 25 Mar 60.

MBALA, Lubaki Sébastien (Kifuma, 1987); Maj, Con (Kin). b 23 Jun 58, and
MBALA, Godette Mboyo (née Moseka) (Kintambo, 1987) m 1988; Maj, Con (Kin). b 26 Sep 62.

MBANGWA, Sipho (Bulawayo, 1995); Capt, Zimb. b 5 Jun 67, and
MBANGWA, Nyarai (née Matambanadzo) (Tshabalala, 1997) m 1997; Capt, Zimb. b 1 Nov 74.

MBOTO, Martin Mathias (Chambai, Tanz, 1972); Maj, Ken. b 1950, with
MBOTO, Grace (née Mulengeka) m 1970; Maj, Ken. b 1952.

MENDES, Marcio (Belo Horizonte, 1980); Maj, Brz. b 24 Feb 57, and
MENDES, Jurema (née Mazzini) (Quarai, 1979) m 1981; Maj, Brz. b 4 Aug 57. BA (Ed).

MENDEZ, Jorge (El Faro, 1988); Maj, L Am N. b 5 Oct 51, with
MENDEZ, Idali (née Jiminez) m 1973; Maj, L Am N. b 24 Aug 52.

MERAS, Marja (Turku 2, 1977); Maj, Fin. b 6 Sep 49.

MEYNER, Marianne (née Stettler) (Basle 2, 1983); Maj, Switz. b 14 Apr 57, with
MEYNER, Urs m 1978; Maj, Switz. b 30 Jan 51.

MHASVI, Henry (Kandeya, 1973); Lt-Col, Zimb. b 6 Dec 49, and
MHASVI, Evan (née Mhizha) (Shirichena, 1977) m 1977; Lt-Col, Zimb. b 1 Feb 55. Served in Zam.

MHEMBERE, Isaac (Mukwenya 1989); Maj, Zimb. b 5 May 69, and
MHEMBERE, Charity (née Muchapondwa) (Muchapondwa, 1990) m 1991; Maj, Zimb. b 2 Jan 67.

MILLER, Gary (Youngstown Citadel, OH, USA E, 1962); Maj, USA Nat. b 24 May 42. BGS (General Studies), and
MILLER, Cheryl (née Harvey) (Wilmington, DE, USA E, 1966) m 1966; Maj, USA Nat. b 31 Jan 45. Served in USA E.

MIYOBA, Grey (Chitumbi, 1975); Lt-Col, CS, Zam. b 14 Mar 54, and
MIYOBA, Leniah (née Mweemba) (Chitumbi, 1977) m 1977; Lt-Col, Asst TPWM, Zam. b 5 Jan 56. Served in USA W.

MKAMI, Samuel Chacha (Kitagutiti, Tan, 1988); Maj, Zimb. b 16 Apr 65, with
MKAMI, Mary Rega (née Kibera) m 1985; Maj, Zimb. b 20 Jul 66. Served in Tanz.

M'MEMI, Naphas (Sabatia, 1984); Maj, Ken. b 10 Aug 56, with
M'MEMI, Grace (née Kasaya); Maj, Ken. b 28 Aug 58.

MNTAMBO, Ivy (née Ngwenya) (Soweto Central, 1982); Maj, S Afr. b 13 Sep 57.

MNYAMPI, Benjamin Amosi (Dar-es-salaam, Tan, 1986); Maj, Zimb. b 1 Mar 54, with
MNYAMPI, Grace Sage m 1984; Maj, Zimb. b 3 Jun 63. Served in Tanz.

MOCHARLA, Elisha Rao (Anganna Gudem, 1970); Maj, Ind C. b 29 Sep 49. BTS, with
MOCHARLA, Prema Mani (née Ganta) m 1969; Maj, Ind C. b 8 Aug 51.

MOCKABEE, William (Anniston, AL, 1975); Maj, USA S. b 1 Nov 54, and
MOCKABEE, Debra (née Salmon) (Oklahoma City, OK, 1976) m 1976; Maj, USA S. b 9 Sep 54.

MOHIBIDU, Lazarus (Mangaung, 1976); Maj, S Afr. b 7 Nov 52.

MONI, Chelliah (Oyaravillai, 1976); Maj, Ind SE. b 18 May 55. MA, and
MONI, Mallika (Alady, 1978) m 1978; Maj, Ind SE. b 6 Mar 57.

MORAN, Peter (Bradford West Bowling, 1979); Maj, UK. b 11 Feb 51, with
MORAN, Sandra (née Clapham) m 1971; Maj, UK. b 16 Jul 49.

MORETZ, Lawrence R. (Sunbury, PA, 1964); Comr, TC, USA E. b 22 Jul 43, and
MORETZ, Nancy A. (née Burke) (Kingston, NY, 1964) m 1965; Comr, TPWM, USA E. b 29 Nov 44. Served in S Am W (TC/TPWO) and USA C (TC/TPWM).

MORIASI, Stephen (Keng'uso, Ken, 1984); Maj, IHQ. b 7 Jun 60, and
MORIASI, Rose Mmbaga (née Onchari) (Embago, Ken, 1988) m 1990; Maj, IHQ. Served in E Afr.

MORRIS, Richard (Glenfield 1994); Capt, NZ. b 18 Mar 61. BCom, with
MORRIS, Jennifer (née Walker); m 1989; Capt, NZ. b 20 Feb 67.

MORROW, Danny R. (Canton, OH, 1962); Lt-Col, USA S. b 22 Feb 40, and
MORROW, Esther R. (née Pritchard) (Youngstown, OH, 1962) m 1962; Lt-Col, USA S. b 3 Apr 42.

MOTCHAKAN, Sundaram (Aramboly, 1974); Maj, Ind SE. b 17 Mar 50, and
MOTCHAKAN, Selvabai (Kaliyancaud, 1974) m 1975; Maj, Ind SE. b 2 May 50.

MOTHERSHED, David (Tampa, FL, 1977); Lt-Col, USA S. b 17 Oct 41, with
MOTHERSHED, Martha (née Suarez) m 1961; Lt-Col, USA S. b 5 Mar 41.

MOULTON, Jean (née Pittman) (Kitchener, ON, 1970); Maj, Can. b 30 Mar 46.

MOULTON, Raymond E. (Wychwood, ON, 1967); Lt-Col, Can. b 26 Oct 42. BA, with
MOULTON, Marilyn K. (née Petley) m 1963; Lt-Col, Can. b 5 Dec 41. Served in USA W.

MOWERY, Don R. (Salt Lake City, UT, 1969); Lt-Col, USA W. b 29 Aug 44. Cert Alcohol and Drugs, with
MOWERY, Jan (née Dempsey) m 1961; Lt-Col, USA W. b 7 Oct 42.

MUASA, Jackson (Kivaku, 1980); Maj, Ken. b 9 Jan 56, and
MUASA, Ciennah (née Mwandi) (Kee, 1980) m 1982; Maj, Ken. b 10 Oct 57.

MUBAIWA, Final (Nyarukunda, 1990); Maj, Zimb. b 29 June 60, with
MUBAIWA, Pfumisai (née Ngwenya) m 1988; Maj, Zimb. b 12 May 69.

MUKONGA, Julius (Kwa Kyambu, 1978); Lt-Col, Ken. b 10 Mar 53, with
MUKONGA, Phyllis (née Mumbua) m 1976; Lt-Col, Ken. b 28 Mar 57.

MUNGATE, Stuart (Mabvuku, Zimb, 1970); Comr, TC, Nig. b 15 Nov 46. BA, Grad Cert Ed, Dip Bus Admin, and
MUNGATE, Hope (née Musvosvi) (Mucherengi, Zimb, 1974) m 1974; Comr, TPWM, Nig. b 23 Mar 53. Dip Journ. Served in Zimb and Con (Kin) (CS/TSWM).

MUNN, Richard (Lexington, KY, 1987); Maj, USA E. b 16 Jan 56. BA (Ed), MDiv

310

(Theol), DM (Chrstn Ldrshp), with
MUNN, Janet (née White) m 1980; Maj,
USA E. b 22 Oct 60. BA (Psych/Spanish),
MA (Ldrshp &Min).

MUTEWERA, Stanslous (Sinoia, 1970); Comr,
TC, Zimb. b 25 Dec 47, and
MUTEWERA, Jannet (née Zinyemba)
(Tsatse, 1973) m 1973; Comr, TPWM, Zimb.
b 11 Nov 52. Served in UK.

MUTHURAJ, Solomon (Perumpazhanchy,
1967); Maj, Ind SE. b 7 May 48, and
MUTHURAJ, Gracemony (Chemparuthivillai,
1971) m 1972; Maj, Ind SE. b 23 Jul 43.

MUZORORI, Trustmore (Alaska Mine, 1987);
Maj, Zimb. b 4 Mar 66. BA (Eng and Comm
Studies), and
MUZORORI, Wendy (née Kunze) (Mutukwa,
1989) m 1989; Maj, Zimb. b 16 Feb 68.

N

NANGI, Masamba Henri (Kinzadi, 1979); Maj,
Con (Kin). b 21 May 53, with
NANGI, Josephine (née Nsimba Babinga);
Maj, Con (Kin). b 30 Dec 53.

NANLABI, Priscilla (San Jose, 1980); Maj,
Phil. b 15 Nov 58.

NATHANIEL, Alladi (Bhogapuram, 1980);
Maj, Ind C. b 9 Dec 52. BA, with
NATHANIEL, Rajeswari (née Yesu) m 1971;
Maj, Ind C. b 6 Jul 55.

NAUD, Daniel (Paris-Montparnasse, 1979);
Maj, Frce. b 8 Mar 54, and
NAUD, Eliane (née Volet) (Strasbourg, 1980)
m 1980; Maj, Frce. b 3 Apr 60. Served in Belg.

NAUTA, James (Grand Rapids Heritage Hill,
MI, 1989); Maj, USA C. b 18 Apr 44. BA
(Psych), MSW, with
NAUTA, Janice B. (née Rager) m 1964; Maj,
USA C. b 28 Jul 42.

NCUBE, Dubayi (Ndola, 1972); Maj, Zimb.
b 8 Jun 52, and
NCUBE, Orlipha (née Ndlovu) (Mpopoma,
1976) m 1976; Maj, Zimb. b 25 Dec 54.

NESTERENKO, Alex (Vitarte, 1986); Maj,
S Am W. b 13 Dec 63, and
NESTERENKO, Luz (née Henríquez)
(Santiago Central, 1990) m 1991; Capt,
S Am W. b 10 May 67. Served in Rus/CIS.

NGANDA, Francis (Kanzalu, 1978); Maj,
Ken. b 11 Jan 52, with
NGANDA, Lucy (née Njioka) m 1976;
Maj, Ken. b 8 Apr 59.

NGKALE, Pilemon (Palu, 1978); Maj, Indon.
b 10 Jul 54, and
NGKALE, Christien (née Kapoh)

(Jakarta 2, 1979) m 1982; Maj, Indon.
b 25 Dec 52.

NICOLASA, Pablo (Buenos Aires Central,
1989); Maj, S Am E. b 20 Feb 61, with
NICOLASA, Estela (née Ocampo) m 1984;
Maj, S Am E. b 4 Jul 60.

NIELSEN, Jostein (Stavanger, Nor, 1980);
Maj, E Eur. b 2 Jul 56, and
NIELSEN, Magna (née Våje) (Arendal, Nor,
1987) m 1978; Maj, E Eur. b 23 Sep 57.
Served in Nor.

NKANU, Bintoma Norbert (Kavwaya, 1981);
Maj, Con (Kin). b 29 Jun 54, with
NKANU, Héléne (née Makuiza Lutonadio)
m 1978; Maj, Con (Kin). b 18 Nov 61.

NKOMO, Dominic (Hwange, 1986); Maj, Zimb.
b 24 Oct 59. Ww Maj Sitabile, pG 2005.

NLABU, Nzolameso Ferdinand (Kingudi,
1971); Lt-Col, Con (Kin); b 10 Aug 48, with
NLABU, Hélène (née Kingondi) m 1968;
Lt-Col, Con (Kin). b 1 Mar 49.

NORE, Henoch (Kalawara, 1977); Maj, Indon.
b 17 Aug 50, and
NORE, Agustina (née Warani) (Malang,
1974); Maj, Indon. b 25 Jan 51.

NSUMBU, Mambueni Emmanuel (Kingudi,
1981); Maj, Con (Kin). b 14 Aug 52, with
NSUMBU, Clémentine (née Mbimbu Bamba)
m 1978; Maj, Con (Kin). b 10 Jun 59.

NUESCH, Nestor (New York Temple, NY,
USA E, 1977); Col, TC, S Am E. b 1 Dec 49.
BA (Bus Admin), MBA, and
NUESCH, Rebecca (née Brewer) (Ithaca, NY,
USA E, 1977) m 1977; Col, TPWM, S Am E.
b 17 Jan 55. Served in USA E.

NYAGA, Henry Njagi (Kagaari, 1986); Maj,
Ken. b 21 Feb 54, with
NYAGA, Catherine (née Njoki) m 1984;
Maj, Ken. b 3 Sep 59.

NYAKUSAMWA, Francis (Karoi, 1986);
Maj, Zimb. b 31 May 59. Dip Church
Mgmt/Admin, Dip Bus Admin/Mgmt, Dip
Bus Mgmt/Com, with
NYAKUSAMWA, Juliet (née Marufu) m 1984;
Maj, Zimb. b 19 Mar 58.

NYAMBALO, Francis (Migowi, Mal, 1982);
Maj, Zam. b 15 Mar 50, with
NYAMBALO, Jamiya (née Khumani) m 1980;
Maj, Zam. b 14 Aug 56. Served in Mal.

O

OALANG, David (Sta Barbara, 1995); Capt,
Phil. b 20 Feb 66, and
OALANG, Elsa (Quezon City 1, 1988); Maj,
Phil. b 25 May 62. BSc (Mass Comm)

OBANDO, Javier (Central , Costa Rica, 1991); Capt, L Am N. b 2 Mar 66, with
OBANDO, Maria Eugenia (née Venegas) m 1988; Capt, L Am N. b 21 Apr 65.

OBENG-APPAU, Richmond (Suame, 1989); Maj, Gha. b 1 Nov 61, with
OBENG-APPAU, Dora (née Kwane) m 1986; Maj, Gha. b 26 Jun 60.

O'BRIEN, Douglas G. (San Francisco Citadel, 1976); Lt-Col, USA W. b 1 Aug 49. BA (Speech), MA (Relig), and
O'BRIEN, Diane (née Lillicrap) (Staines, UK, 1975) m 1988; Lt-Col, USA W. b 8 Nov 50. FTCL, GTCL. Served in UK.

ØDEGAARD, B. Donald (Oslo 3, Nor, 1966); Comr, IS Prog Res, IHQ. b 18 Dec 40. Cand Mag, and
ØDEGAARD, Berit (née Gjersøe) (Tønsberg, Nor, 1964) m 1967; Comr, IHQ. b 27 Sep 44. SRN. Served in Zimb, S Afr, Nig (TC/TPWO), E Afr (TC/TPWO) and Nor (TC/TPWM).

ODURO, Godfried, (Kyekyewere, 1981); Maj, Gha. b 17 Jul 54, with
ODURO, Felicia (née Obeng) m 1978; Maj, Gha. b 25 Jun 60.

ODURO-AMOAH, Peter (Achiase, 1989); Maj, Gha. b 26 Aug 58, with
ODURO-AMOAH, Grace (née Fosua) m 1984; Maj, Gha. b 11 Feb 64.

OKLAH, Samuel (Accra Newtown, Gha, 1983); Maj, Ken. b 5 Mar 58, with
OKLAH, Philomina (née Addo) (Tema, Gha, 1985) m 1985; Maj, Ken. b 21 Dec 65. Served in Gha.

OKOROUGO, Edwin Rapurnchukwu (Amesi, 1982); Maj, Nig. b 2 Aug 49. BA (Relig Studies), MA (Eth and Phil), with
OKOROUGO, Agnes (née Nwokekwe) m 1978; Maj, Nig. b 5 Apr 52.

OLAUSSON, Kjell Edor (Hisingskår, 1978); Maj, Swdn. n 12 Nov 56, and
OLAUSSON, Gunilla (née Lind) (Helsingborg, 1986) m 1986; Maj, Swdn. b 23 Aug 60.

OLORUNTOBA, Festus (Supare, 1976); Maj, Nig. b 7 Jul 55, and
OLORUNTOBA, Gloria (Egbe, 1986) m 1986; Maj, Nig. b 8 Mar 61.

ONYEKWERE, Paul I. (Umuogo, 1984); Maj, Nig. b 27 Jul 58, with
ONYEKWERE, Edinah P.; Maj, Nig. b 29 Oct 61.

OTA, Haruhisa (Hamamatsu, 1973); Maj, Jpn. b 30 Jan 50, and
OTA, Hiromi (née Nakatsugawa) (Hamamatsu, 1973) m 1976; Maj, Jpn. b 21 Jun 48.

OWEN, Graham (Nuneaton, UK, 1977); Maj, CS, Den. b 8 Jul 53, and
OWEN, Kirsten (née Jacobsen) (Copenhagen Temple, 1977) m 1978; Maj, Den. b 2 May 56. Served in UK.

OYESANYA, Michael (Iperu, 1984); Maj, Nig. b 17 May 61, and
OYESANYA, Roseline (Iperu, 1988) m 1988; Maj, Nig. b 21 Jun 65.

P

PADALE, David Keru (Kapurwadi, 1969); Maj, Ind W. b 1 Jun 47, and
PADALE, Roshanjohn (née Sable) (Padali, 1974) m 1974; Maj, Ind W. b 6 Oct 56.

PAEZ, Jorge O. (Bahía Blanca, 1961); Lt-Col, S Am E. b 19 May 41, and
PAEZ, Azucena (née Berenguer) (La Unión, 1968) m 1973; Lt-Col, S Am E. b 1 Dec 45.

PANG, Kie-chang (Yung Chun, 1975); Maj, Kor. b 7 Oct 44, and
PARK, Keum-ja (Ah Hyun, 1973) m 1975; Maj, Kor. b 16 Mar 44.

PAONE, Massimo (Naples, 1977); Maj, OC, It. b 8 Jun 52, and
PAONE, Elizabeth Jane (née Moir) (Nunhead, UK, 1982) m 1982; Maj, CPWM, It. b 17 Dec 58. BA (Hons). Served in UK and Frce.

PARAMADHAS, Arulappan (Elanthiady, 1972); Maj, Ind SE. b 11 May 54, and
PARAMADHAS, S. Retnam (Changaneri, 1974) m 1976; Maj, Ind SE. b 30 May 51.

PARAYNO, Florante (Sta Barbara, 1985); Maj, Phil. b 17 Apr 59, and
PARAYNO, Maria Cerlina (née Montemayor) (Pasig, 1983) m 1986; Maj, Phil. b 15 Aug 61.

PARDO, Zoilo B. (Santa Ana, CA, USA W, 1989); Maj, CS, L Am N. b 9 Dec 53. BA (Acct), with
PARDO, Magali (née Pacheco) m 1980; Maj, TSWM, L Am N. b 20 Apr 56. BA (Gen Ed) BA (Acct). Served in USA W and Mex.

PAREDES, Tito E. (La Paz, S Am W, 1976); Lt-Col, USA E. b 14 Aug 54, and
PAREDES, Martha (née Nery) (Cochabamba, S Am W, 1976) m 1977; Lt-Col, USA E. b 3 Jun 54. Served in S Am W and L Am N (CS/TSWM).

PARK, Chong-duk (Pupyung, 1977); Maj, Kor. b 22 May 50, with
YOON, Eun-sook m 1975; Maj, Kor. b 23 Oct 50.

PARK, Man-hee (Chung Ju, 1975); Lt-Col, CS, Kor. b 11 Aug 47, with

KIM, Keum-nyeo m 1973; Lt-Col, TSWM, Kor. b 5 Feb 51.

PARK, Nai-hoon (Syn Heung, 1978); Maj, Kor. b 23 Oct 46, with
KIL, Soon-boon m 1971; Maj, Kor. b 26 Nov 49.

PARKER, Michael (Hucknall, 1977); Maj, UK. b 28 Jul 50, with
PARKER, Joan (née Brailsford) m 1971; Maj, UK. b 16 Jan 52. Served at IHQ.

PARKHE, Sumant Lazarus (Marathi Central, 1969); Lt-Col, CS, Ind W. b 11 Apr 47, and
PARKHE, Nalini Sadanan (née Makasare) (1974) m 1974; Lt-Col, TSWM, Ind W. b 5 May 54.

PARMAR, Hanokh (Virsad, 1979); Lt-Col, Ind W. b 6 Apr 57, and
PARMAR, Vinaben (née Mavjibhai) (Vasad, 1981) m 1981; Lt-Col, Ind W. b 30 May 59. Served in Ind N.

PARMAR, Kantilal K. (Ode, 1983); Maj, Ind W. b 1 Jun 53. BA, BEd, and
PARMAR, Eunice K. (née Gaikwad) (Mohmedwadi, 1977) m 1983; Maj, Ind W. b 30 Oct 52.

PASCOE, Zillah Ruth (Whangarei, NZ, 1970); Maj, Sing. b 20 Sep 47. Served in NZ.

PATRA, Samir (Calcutta Central, 1985); Maj, Ind N. b 6 Aug 57, with
PATRA, Sita m 1983; Maj, Ind N. b 5 Apr 65.

PAUL, Emmanuel (Longawal, 1969); Lt-Col, CS, Pak. b 18 Aug 47, with
EMMANUEL, Gulzar (née Nawab) m 1966; Lt-Col, TSWM, Pak. b 27 Apr 43.

PAULSSON, Christian (Centrumkåren, Stockholm, 1984); Maj, Swdn. b 28 Jun 64, and
PAULSSON, Anna-Lena (née Wiklund) (Arvidsjaur/Malmberget, 1984); m 1986; Maj, Swdn. b 18 Aug 63.

PAWAR, Suresh S. (Ahmednagar EBH, 1981); Maj, Ind W. b 10 Feb 60, and
PAWAR, Martha (née Shirsath) (Ahmednagar Central, 1981) m 1981; Maj, Ind W. b 17 Nov 63.

PAYNE, Goff (Godfrey) (Tunbridge Wells, UK, 1980); Maj, OC, Uga. b 15 Oct 51, with
PAYNE, Diane (née Harris) m 1975; Maj, CPWM, Uga. b 28 Dec 52. Served in UK and E Afr.

PEACOCK, Raymond L. (Denver Citadel, CO, 1963); Lt-Col, USA W. b 9 Mar 42. BA (Soc), MSW (Soc Prog Admin), and
PEACOCK, Carolyn Bea (née Irby) (Portland Harbour Light, 1968) m 1969; Lt-Col, USA W. b 7 Aug 47. Served at USA Nat.

PEARCE, Lynette J. (Parkes, Aus E, 1972); Comr, IS Int Per, IHQ. b 13 Jan 45. BA. Served in Aus E and at ICO.

PEDDLE, Brian (Dildo/New Harbour, NF, 1977); Maj, Can. b 8 Aug 57, and
PEDDLE, Rosalie (née Rowe) (Carbonear, NF, 1976) m 1978; Maj, Can. b 17 Jan 56.

PETER, K. C. (Amarakunnu, 1980); Maj, Ind SW. b 15 Apr 48. BSc, with
PETER, K. J. Annamma; Maj, Ind SW. b 4 Feb 51.

PETTERSEN, Per Arne (Sarpsborg, 1969); Maj, Nor. b 20 Mar 47, and
PETTERSEN, Lillian (née Madsø) (Namsos, 1969) m 1971; Maj, Nor. b 5 Jun 45.

PHILIP, Alister (Colombo Central, 1988); Maj, Sri Lan. b 11 Oct 61, and
PHILIP, Nilanthi (née Fernando) (Moratumulla, 1987) m 1989; Maj, Sri Lan. b 24 May 67.

PHILIP, P. K. (Thottamon, 1975); Maj, Ind SW. b 12 Dec 48, and
PHILIP, Rachel (Kottarakara Central, 1980) m 1979; Maj, Ind SW. b 10 Nov 54.

PIERCE, Beryl Joyce (née Fuges) (Anacortes, WA, USA W, 1974); Capt, Zam. b 21 Feb 51. Served in USA W.

PIGFORD, Raymond E. (Wellsville, NY, 1970); Lt-Col, USA E. b 26 Jun 44. BA (Sci), MA (Ed Admin), with
PIGFORD, Edith Helen (née Waldron) m 1966; Lt-Col, USA E. b 12 May 45. BA (Chr Ed and Fr). Served in Can.

PITTA, Samuel Rathan (Mandavalli, 1974); Maj, Ind C. b 3 May 51, with
PITTA, Ananda Kumari; Maj, Ind C. b 1 Oct 57.

POA, Selly Barak (Jakarta, 1979); Maj, Indon. b 25 Sep 55, and
POA, Anastasia (née Djoko Slamet) (Surakarta 2, 1984) m 1985; Maj, Indon. b 29 Jun 1962.

POBJIE, Barry R. (Paddington, Aus E, 1965); Comr, TC, E Eur. b 25 Jan 45. Ww Capt Ruth, pG 1978. Served in PNG, and
POBJIE, Raemor (née Wilson) (Port Kembla, Aus E, 1971) m 1980; Comr, TPWM, E Eur. b 22 Sep 48. Served in NZ and Aus E.

POKE, Victor (Burnie, Aus S, 1968); Comr, TC, Swdn. b 8 Jan 46, and
POKE, Roslyn (née Pengilly) (Maylands, Aus S, 1968) m 1970; Comr, TPWM, Swdn. b 20 Jun 45. Served in Aus S and UK (CS/TSWM).

PONNIAH, Masilamony (Periavilai, 1969); Lt-Col, Ind SE. b 2 Jun 49, and
SATHIYABAMA (Layam, 1974) m 1974; Lt-Col, Ind W. b 14 Apr 56. Served in Ind W.

POSADAS, Leopoldo (Dagupan City, 1981); Maj, Phil. b 18 Aug 58, and
POSADAS, Evelyn (née Felix) (Hermoza, 1982) m 1982; Maj, Phil. b 2 Aug 57. Served in Ban.

POSILLICO, Joseph E. (Los Angeles Lincoln Heights, CA, 1972); Maj, USA W. b 29 Dec 50, and
POSILLICO, Shawn L. (née Patrick) (San Francisco, CA, 1984) m 1988; Maj, USA W. b 3 Aug 57. BS (Bus Econ).

PRITCHETT, Wayne (Deer Lake, NF, 1970); Lt-Col, Can. b 13 Aug 46. BA, BEd, MTh, and
PRITCHETT, Myra (née Rice) (Roberts Arm, NF, 1969) m 1972; Lt-Col, Can. b 19 Jun 50. BA, MTh.

PULULU, Pepe Célestin (Makala 1, 1985); Maj, Con (Kin). b 15 Oct 52, with
PULULU, Véronique (née Lukombo Nkenge) m 1978; Maj, Con (Kin). b 4 Dec 57.

R

RAINES, Timothy (Mt Vernon, NY, 1971); Lt-Col, USA E. b 30 Dec 47. BS (Org Mgmt), and
RAINES, Lynda Lou (née Swingle) (Zanesville, OH, 1969) m 1969; Lt-Col, USA E. b 23 Aug 48. BS (Org Mgmt).

RAJAMONICKAM, Chelliah (Elanthaiady, 1967); Lt-Col, Ind SE. b 18 Jan 47, and
MARTHAL (Vellachivilai, 1970) m 1970; Lt-Col, Ind SE. b 20 May 44.

RAJAN, Prema T. (Bombay Central, Ind W, 1974); Lt-Col, CS, Ind C. b 19 Feb 47. Served in Ind W, at IHQ and in Ind SE (CS).

RAJU, M. Daniel (M. R. Nagaram, 1984); Maj, Ind C. b 20 Jun 54. MA (Econ), with
RAJU, Rachel (née Kondamudi) m 1982; Maj, Ind C. b 15 Jun 62. Served at IHQ.

RANDIVE, Benjamin B. (Shevgaon, 1981); Maj, Ind W. b 11 Jan 60, and
RANDIVE, Ratan S. (née Teldune) (Shenegaon Central, 1981) m 1981; Maj, Ind W. b 17 Aug 62.

RASELALOME, Johannes (Seshego, 1982); Maj, S Afr. b 3 May 60, and
RASELALOME, Veliswa Atalanta (née Mehu) (Tshoxa, 1982) m 1985; Maj, S Afr. b 16 Jul 62.

RATCLIFF, Robert (Vancouver, 1967); Maj, Can. b 24 Jan 42, with

RATCLIFF, Shirley (née Hutchinson) m 1962; Maj, Can. b 21 Jan 42.

RATNAM, Guddam Venkata (Guraza, 1973); Maj, Ind C. b 5 Apr 49, with
RATNAM, Gaddam Rajakumari m 1969; Maj, Ind C. b 15 Mar 52.

RAWALI, Lapu (Koki, 1983); Maj, PNG. b 27 Jul 54. BA, with
RAWALI, Araga (née Heroha) m 1974; Maj, PNG. b 19 Apr 55.

REDDISH, Graeme John (Thames, 1974); Maj, NZ. b 28 Aug 49. Ww Maj Nola, pG 2002, and
REDDISH, Wynne (née Jellyman) (Miramar, 1982) m 2005; Maj, NZ. b 22 Apr 57.

REEL, Robert J. (Wilkes-Barre, PA, 1970); Maj, USA E. b 28 Dec 44. BA (Org Mgmt), with
REEL, Lynette M. (née Hufford) m 1964; Maj, USA E. b 2 Sep 45. BA (Org Mgmt).

REES, John (Ipswich, 1974); Maj, Aus E. b 29 Jun 47, with
REES, Narelle (née Lehmann) m 1969; Maj, Aus E. b 27 Jun 48.

REFSTIE, Peder R. (Mandal, Nor, 1965); Comr, TC, Brz. b 13 Jul 43, and
REFSTIE, Janet M. (née Dex) (Bedford, UK, 1966) m 1969; Comr, TPWM, Brz. b 7 Jul 43. Served in UK, S Am W, Port, Nor, Sp (OC/ CPWM), at IHQ and in S Am E (TC/TPWM).

REYNDERS, Gilbert (Pittsburgh Temple, PA, 1973); Lt-Col, USA E. b 15 Oct 49. BA (Pol Sci), and
REYNDERS, Warna L. (née Newton) (Kearny, NJ, 1974) m 1974; Lt-Col, USA E. b 24 Oct 51.

REYNOLDS, James (Canton Citadel, OH, 1976); Maj, USA E. b 2 Jun 48. BS (HRM), with
REYNOLDS, Blanche Louise (née Labus) m 1972; Maj, USA E. b 16 Jun 50.

RICE, Sandra (Roberts Arm, NF, 1980); Maj, Can. b 16 Feb 58. BEd, BA, MA (Theol Studies).

RICHARDSON, Alfred (Mount Dennis, ON, 1967); Maj, Can. b 5 Dec 44, with
RICHARDSON, Ethel (née Howell) m 1964; Maj, Can. b 2 Apr 43.

RIEDER, Beat (Basle 1, Switz, 1989); Maj, Ger. b 8 Oct 58, and
RIEDER, Annette (née Pell) (Cologne, 1986) m 1989; Maj, Ger. b 9 May 64. Served in Switz and Can.

RISAN, Jan (Stavanger, 1990); Maj, Nor. b 28 Mar 63, with

RISAN, Kjersti Håland m 1982; Maj, Nor.
b 30 May 63.
ROBERTS, Jonathan (Leicester Central, 1986);
Maj, UK. b 20 Feb 62. BA (Hons) (Econ),
BA (Hons) (Theol), and
ROBERTS, Jayne (née Melling) (Southend
Citadel, 1985) m 1986; Maj, UK. b 23 Apr 58.
BA (Hons) (Eng).
ROBERTS, William A. (Detroit Citadel, MI,
USA C, 1971); Comr, IS Bus Admin, IHQ.
b 26 Feb 46. BS, MA, with
ROBERTS, Nancy Louise (née Overly)
m 1968; Comr, IHQ. b 27 Oct 43. BS, MA.
Served in USA C and S Am E (TC/TPWM).
ROHMINGTHANGA (Kawrthah, 1974);
Lt-Col, CS, Ind E. b 20 Nov 46, with
LALKUNGI m 1967; Lt-Col, TSWM, Ind E.
b 6 Oct 51.
ROTONA, Rabona (Boregaina, 1979); Maj,
PNG. b 1 Jan 52, with
ROTONA, Gabi m 1978; Maj, PNG. b 1 Jan 57.
ROWE, Dennis (Norwood, 1982); Maj, Aus S.
b 25 Jun 48, and
ROWE, Patricia (née Muir) (Woodville
Gardens, 1950) m 1972; Maj, Aus S.
b 18 Mar 48. Served in HK and Tai.
ROWE, Lindsay (Chance Cove, NF, Can,
1973); Maj, S Afr. b 21 Sep 51. BA(hon),
M Div, and
ROWE, Lynette (née Hutt) (Winterton, NF,
Can, 1971) m 1974; Maj, S Afr. b 13 Feb 52.
Served in Can and Carib.
ROWE, Raymond (Chance Cove, NF, 1968);
Maj, Can. b 3 Nov 47, and
ROWE, Audrey (née Knee) (Corner Brook,
NF, 1968) m 1970; Maj, Can. b 30 Jul 44.
ROWLAND, Mervyn (Granville, Aus E, 1967);
Lt-Col, GS, HK. b 11 Jul 43. BAL, Grad Dip
(Conflict Resolution), and
ROWLAND, Elaine (née Holley) (Granville,
Aus E, 1968) m 1968; Lt-Col, CPWM, HK.
b 11 Oct 46. BAL. Served in Aus E.
RUDD, Robert L. (Portland Tabernacle, OR,
1986); Maj, USA W. b 16 Apr 47, with
RUDD, Mariam (née Rhoades) m 1968;
Maj, USA W. b 8 Jul 47.
RUTANHIRA, Elackson (Dubugwani, 1988);
Maj, Zimb. b 27 Jul 62. Dip (Gen Mgmt),
with
RUTANHIRA, Shiellah (née Jakaza) m 1986;
Maj, Zimb. b 6 Oct 68.

S

SAAVEDRA, Lidia (Tucumán, 1979), Maj,
S Am E. b 9 May 49.

SAKAMESSO, Jean-Aléxis (Ouenze, 1979);
Maj, Con (Braz). b 25 May 50, with
SAKAMESSO, Pauline (née Louya) m 1976;
Maj, Con (Braz). b 19 Jan 56.
SALMI, Irma (née Määttä) (Oulu, 1968);
Lt-Col, Fin. b 26 Aug 45. m 1969; Lt-Col Ahti,
ret 2004.
SAM DEVARAJ, Appavoo (Palayamcottai,
1976); Maj, Ind SE. b 23 Jun 51. BA, MA
(Public Admin), and
DEVARAJ, Kanagaretnam (Anducodu,
1975) m 1977; Maj, Ind SE. b 19 Oct 51.
SAMRAJ, Jeyaraj (Booth Tucker Hall,
Nagercoil, 1982); Maj, Ind SE. b 14 Aug 58.
MA (Sociol), and
SAMRAJ, Jessi Thayammal (Gnaniahpuram,
1986) m 1986; Maj, Ind SE. b 21 Oct 63.
MusB. Served at Ind Nat.
SAMUEL, Cheeli (Vinjaram, 1967); Maj,
Ind C. b 17 Jul 47, and
SAMUEL, Devakaruna (née Bathula)
(Kovalli, 1968) m 1969; Maj, Ind C.
b 11 Jan 51.
SAMUEL, Daniel (Kaduvapoke, 1970); Maj,
Ind SW. b 25 Dec 46, and
SAMUEL, Swarnamma (Chruvaloor, 1975)
m 1975; Maj, Ind SW. b 24 Jan 48.
SAMUEL, Johns (Central, Trivandrum, 1984);
Maj, Ind SW. b 22 May 53. BSc, and
JOHNS, Annamma (Panackavayal, 1987)
m 1987; Maj, Ind SW. b 3 May 1961.
SAMUEL, M. (Central, Kottarakara, 1974);
Maj, Ind SW. b 15 Dec 51, and
SAMUEL, K. Thankamma (Ommanoor,
1977) m 1976; Maj, Ind SW. b 15 Oct 53.
SANCHEZ, Oscar (Lima Central, S Am W,
1982); Maj, Brz. b 21 Nov 56, and
SANCHEZ, Ana Rosa (née Limache) (Huayra
K'assa, S Am W, 1985) m 1987; Maj, Brz.
b 12 Jun 60. Served in Sp, S Am W and
USA W.
SANGCHHUNGA (Ratu, 1974); Maj, Ind E.
b 15 Mar 52, and
VANLALAUVI (Ngopa, 1975) m 1975; Maj,
Ind E. b 10 Jun 55.
SAVAGE, Peter J. (Linwood, 1969); Lt-Col, NZ.
b 21 Oct 42. CFRE, with
SAVAGE, Raeline J. (née Allan) m 1966;
Lt-Col, NZ. b 29 Dec 46. BMus.
SCHMID, Fritz (Adelboden/Thun, 1980); Maj,
Switz. b 20 Nov 53, and
SCHMID, Margrit (née Dössegger) (Seon,
1981) m 1981; Maj, Switz. b 4 Dec 52.
SCHOLLMEIER, Rudolf (Mannheim, 1968);
Maj, Ger. b 9 Nov 43, and

SCHOLLMEIER, Christine (née Harvey) (Cologne, 1968) m 1970; Maj, Ger. b 31 Jul 48.
SCHWARTZ, Barry Richard (Goodwood, 1973); Maj, S Afr. b 17 Apr 48, with
SCHWARTZ, Anja Jacoba (née Kamminga) m 1967; Maj, S Afr. b 28 Jul 48.
SEILER, Paul R. (Hollywood Tabernacle, CA, USA W, 1981); Lt-Col, CS, USA C. b 23 May 51. MBA, BS (Bus Admin), with
SEILER, Carol (née Sturgess) m 1978; Lt-Col, TSWM, USA C. b 6 Apr 52. RN, BS (Nursing), MPH. Served in USA W.
SERÈM, Alberto (Lisbon Central, 1985); Maj, OC, Port. b 27 Nov 56, and
SERÈM, Maria José (née Leitão) (Picheleira, 1977) m 1980; Maj, CPWM, Port. b 13 Dec 52. Served in UK and It.
SEVAK, David Keshav (Sokhada, 1981); Maj, Ind W. b 15 Nov 50, and
SEVAK, Vimalaben (Bharoda, 1983) m 1983; Maj, Ind W. b 5 Jun 63.
SEWELL, Roland (Buckingham, 1976); Lt-Col, UK. b 26 Dec 44. MBE, BSc (Hons) (Eng), CEng, MICE, with
SEWELL, Dawn (née Towle) m 1967; Lt-Col, UK. b 25 Dec 46. RN. Served in Zam, Nig (CS/TSWM) and at IHQ.
SEYMOUR, Geanette (Belmore, 1973); Lt-Col, CS, Aus E. b 20 Feb 50. BA (Soc Work).
SHAVANGA, Edward Alumasa (Matunda, 1982); Maj, Ken. b 9 Mar 58, with
SHAVANGA, Florence (née Vulehi) m 1979; Maj, Ken. b 11 Oct 60.
SHAVANGA, Moses (Musudzuu, 1984); Maj, Ken. b 10 Jun 57, with
SHAVANGA, Gladys (née Sharia) m 1982; Maj, Ken. b 18 Mar 61. Served in Tanz.
SHEKWA, Albert Zondiwe (Emangweni, 1974); Maj, S Afr. b 12 Mar 51, and
SHEKWA, Peggy (née Maimela) (Louis Trichardt, 1974) m 1974; Maj, S Afr. b 3 Jun 54.
SHEPHERD, Glen (Winnipeg Citadel, 1981); Col, CS, Can. b 7 Feb 48. BA, MA (Econ-Sociol), with
SHEPHERD, Eleanor (née Pitcher) m 1969; Col, TSWM, Can. b 4 Mar 47. BA (Econ-Sociol). Served in Frce (TC/TPWM) and at IHQ.
SHIN, Moon-ho (Yang Chung, 1973); Maj, Kor. b 1 May 44, with
CHO, In-sook m 1970; Maj, Kor. b 12 Aug 47.
SIAGIAN, Pieter (Solo, 1973); Lt-Col, Indon. b 5 May 45, and
SIAGIAN, Sukarsih (née Sosromihardjo)

(Turen, 1972) m 1975; Lt-Col, Indon. b 2 Aug 49.
SIJUADE, Michael A. (Ife Ife, 1992); Capt, Nig. b 13 Jun 64, with
SIJUADE, Comfort m 1990; Capt, Nig. b 11 Nov 67.
SIMON, T. J. (Perumpetty, 1977); Maj, Ind SW. b 15 Nov 52, with
SIMON, Ammini, m 1979; Maj, Ind SW. b 1 Feb 60.
SINGH, Dilip (Simultala, 1990); Maj, Ind N. b 4 Nov 68, and
SINGH, Nivedita (née Christian) (Fatapukur, 1992) m 1992; Capt, Ind N. b 14 Sep 71.
SJOGREN, Daniel (St Paul (Temple), MN, 1972); Maj, USA C. b 12 Nov 51, and
SJOGREN, Rebecca (née Nefzger) (Hibbing, MN, 1973) m 1973; Maj, USA C. b 11 Jun 53.
SMITH, Jeffrey (Flint Citadel, MI, 1986); Maj, USA C. b 19 Jan 54. BA (Bible), MRE, with
SMITH, Dorothy R. (née Kumpula) m 1974; Maj, USA C. b 22 Oct 54. BA (Psychol/ Sociol), MA (Pastoral Counselling).
SMITH, Peter (Malvern, UK, 1980); Maj, IHQ. b 6 Sep 43. Solicitor of the Supreme Court. Served in UK.
SMITH, Ronald (Wallsend, 1961); Lt-Col, UK. b 8 Mar 42. m 1964; Lt-Col Janette, ret 2004.
SMITH, Warren A. (Bethlehem, PA, 1961); Maj, USA E. b 30 Apr 41. BA (Bus Admin), MPA, and
SMITH, Diana Elaine (née Small) (Bethlehem, PA, 1962) m 1963; Maj, USA E. b 19 Feb 43.
SOLOMON, K. M. (Oramana, 1978); Maj, Ind SW. b 3 Jun 55, and
SOLOMON, P. K. Elizabeth (1982) m 1982; Maj, Ind SW. b 5 Nov 56.
SON, Myong-shik (Masan, 1975); Lt-Col, Kor. b 15 Jun 41, with
CHUNG, Yang-soon m 1969; Lt-Col, Kor. b 27 Sep 48.
SONDA, Jean-Pierre (Mahita, 1990); Maj, Con (Braz). b 28 Nov 56, with
SONDA, Jeannette (née Ndoudi) m 1988; Maj, Con (Braz). b 25 Jan 67.
SOUTHWELL, Ian (Fairfield, Aus S, 1968); Lt-Col, IHQ. b 19 Jun 42. BSc, BEd. Served in Zam, Phil, Aus S, Kor (CS) and HK (OC). m 1967; Lt-Col Sonja, ret 2006.
SOUZA, Maruilson (Petrolina, 1987); Maj, Brz. b 6 May 64. BA(Acct), MBA, BA (Theol), MA (Theol), with
SOUZA, Francisca m 1982; Maj, Brz. b 15 Oct 66.

SPILLER, Lyndon S. (Springvale, 1970); Lt-Col, Aus S. b 26 May 45, with **SPILLER, Julie** (née King) m 1968; Lt-Col, Aus S. b 7 Aug 47. Served in Aus S, Pak, Zam, Gha (CS/TSWO) and E Afr (CS/TSWM).

STAITE, John A. (Subiaco, Aus S, 1967); Lt-Col, Aus E. b 17 Apr 42, with **STAITE, Helen** (née Hewitson) m 1962; Lt-Col, Aus E. b 3 Jan 42. Served in Aus S.

STARRETT, Daniel L. (Roswell, NM, USA W, 1973); Lt-Col, USA Nat. b 1 Jun 52. BS (Appl Bus & Mgmt), MBA, and **STARRETT, Helen** (née Laverty) (San José, CA, USA W, 1973) m 1974; Lt-Col, USA Nat. b 20 Jul 48. Served in USA W and at IHQ.

STERLING, David (Tottenham Citadel, UK, 1975); Maj, IHQ (SALT Afr). b 11 Mar 49. BA (Eng) (Hons), and **STERLING, Brenda** (née Turner) (Tottenham Citadel, UK, 1975) m 1976; Maj, IHQ (SALT Afr). b 17 Jun 44. MA. Served in UK.

ST-ONGE, Gilbert (Notre Dame, Montreal, QC, 1963); Lt-Col, Can. b 13 Nov 41, and **ST-ONGE, Marilynn J.** (née Hollingworth) (Barton Street, Hamilton, ON, 1963) m 1965; Lt-Col, Can. b 12 Sep 42.

STREET, Robert (Stotfold, UK, 1968); Comr, IS to CoS, IHQ. b 24 Feb 47, with **STREET, Janet** (née Adams) m 1967; Comr, WSWM, IHQ. b 19 Aug 45. Served in UK and Aus E (CS/ TSWM).

STRICKLAND, Ron (Santa Barbara, CA, 1978); Maj, USA W. b 7 Aug 45. BS (Bus Mgmt), and **STRICKLAND, Pamela** (née Fuss) (Minot, ND, 1969) m 1970; Maj, USA W. b 1 Dec 48.

STRISSEL, Dennis L. R. (St Louis Northside, MO, 1974); Maj, USA C. b 4 Mar 52, and **STRISSEL, Sharon** (née Olson) (Sioux City, IA, 1974) m 1975; Maj, USA C. b 7 Oct 51. Served in S Afr.

STRONG, Leslie J. (Kalbar, 1965); Comr, TC, Aus E. b 5 Apr 43. BAL, and **STRONG, Coral** (née Scholz) (Kalbar, 1966) m 1967; Comr, TPWM, Aus E. b 30 Mar 44. Served in Aus S (CS/TSWM).

SUNDIKA, Joel (Karambazungu, 1988); Maj, Zimb. b 1 Sep 56, with **SUNDIKA, Auxilia** (née Makanda) m 1985; Maj, Zimb. b 4 Apr 57.

SUSEELKUMAR, John (Pallickal, 1978); Maj, Ind SW. b 11 Oct 51, with **SUSEELKUMAR, Aleyamma** m 1976; Maj, Ind SW. b 15 Jun 52.

SUTHERLAND, Margaret (Sleaford, UK,

1968); Comr, Principal, ICO. b 22 Jul 43. MA, ARCO. Served in Zam, UK, Zimb (CS) and at IHQ (ISAfr).

SWAMIDHAS, Chelliah (Kannankulam, 1977); Maj, Ind SE. b 21 Apr 55, and **SWAMIDHAS Joice Bai** (Kaliancaud, 1973) m 1977; Maj, Ind SE. b 16 Feb 53.

SWANSON, Barry C. (Chicago Mt Greenwood, IL, USA C, 1978); Lt-Col, Nat CS, USA Nat. b 22 Apr 50. BS (Marketing), with **SWANSON, E. Sue** (née Miller) m 1975; Lt-Col, NSWM, USA Nat. b 13 Aug 50. BA (Soc Work). Served in USA C (CS/TSWM).

SWYERS, Philip W. (Dallas Temple, TX, USA S, 1968); Comr, TC, USA W. b 22 Apr 44. BBA, and **SWYERS, Patricia Lyvonne** (née Lowery) (Charlotte, NC, USA S, 1962) m 1968; Comr, TPWM, USA W. b 26 Aug 41. Served in USA C (CS/TSWM) and USA S (CS/TSWM)

T

TADI, Patrick (Bimbouloulou, 1984); Maj, Con (Braz). b 17 Apr 59, with **TADI, Clémentine** (née Bassinguinina) m 1982; Maj, Con (Braz). b 4 Apr 58.

TAMPAI, Yusak (Turen, 1993); Capt, Indon. b 25 Feb 66, and **TAMPAI, Widiawati** (Anca, 1995) m 1997; Capt, Indon. b 19 Apr 73.

TAN, Thean Seng (Penang, 1966); Lt-Col, Sing. b 24 Jul 45, and **LOO, Lay Saik** (Penang, 1966) m 1969; Lt-Col, Sing. b 12 Jul 47. Served at IHQ, in Sing (OC/CPWM) and HK (OC/CPWM).

TANAKA, Teiichi (Omori, 1983); Maj, Jpn. b 19 Feb 52, and **TANAKA, Chieko** (née Hirose) (Nishinari, 1977) m 1984; Maj, Jpn. b 22 Apr 48.

TARI, Samuel (Shantinagar, 1970); Maj, Pak. b 7 Sep 49, and **SAMUEL, Victoria** (née Khurshid) (Khanewal, 1971) m 1973; Maj, Pak. b 15 Oct 52.

TELFER, Ivor (Clydebank, 1982); Maj, UK. b 26 May 54. MSc (Strategic Management), with **TELFER, Carol** (née Anderson) m 1980; Maj, UK. b 26 Aug 59. Dip Post Traumatic Stress, Stress Consultant, CIPP.

THANHLIRA (Ratu, 1971); Maj, Ind E. b 15 Feb 49, and **THANTLUANGI** (Central, 1975) m 1975; Maj, Ind E. b 5 Jan 50.

THANRUMA, Jonathan (Saiha, 1981); Maj, Ind E. b 17 Aug 50, with

THANRUMA, Elizabeth (née Zoawii) m 1969; Maj, Ind E. b 5 Oct 56.

THEODORE, Sinous (Luly, 1981); Maj, Carib. b 20 Oct 52, and
  THEODORE, Marie Lourdes (née Doralus) (Port-au-Prince, 1981) m 1982; Maj, Carib. b 22 Sep 57.

THOMSON, Robert E. (Evansville Asplan Citadel, IN, 1971); Maj, USA C. b 20 Nov 50. BS (Soc Work), MSW, with
  THOMSON, Nancy (née Philpot) m 1972; Maj, USA C. b 4 May 50.

TILLSLEY, Mark W. (East Northport, NY, 1987); Maj, USA E. b 20 Nov 57. BA (Psychol/Sociol), MSW, with
  TILLSLEY, Sharon (née Lowman) m 1979; Maj, USA E. b 21 Jun 57. BS (Nursing).

TOLLERUD, Douglas (Santa Ana, CA, 1983); Maj, USA W. b 16 Mar 57, with
  TOLLERUD, Sheryl (née Smith) m 1978; Maj, USA W. b 12 Jan 59. BS (Organztnl Mngmnt).

TRAINOR, Iain (Orillia, Can, 1974); Maj, Aus S. b 18 Jan 45, with
  TRAINOR, Dawn (née McCormack) m 1965; Maj, Aus S. b 19 Jun 44. Served in Can.

TRIGG, Pamela S. (née Bowen) (Geelong West, 1971); Lt-Col, Aus S. b 17 Aug 43. Ww Capt Albert E., pG 1983. Served in HK.

TSANG, Alfred Hing-man (Kowloon Central, 1971); Lt-Col, OC, HK. b 12 Nov 41.

TSILULU, Dieudonné Nzuzi (Bandalungwa, 1997); Capt, Con (Kin). b 16 Dec 66, and
  TSILULU, Philippine Kiasala (née Ngudiankanga) (Kimbanseke 1, 1995) m 1998; Capt, Con (Kin). b 18 Nov 67.

TUCK, Trevor M. (Kensington Citadel, 1969); Comr, TC, S Afr. b 11 Sep 43, and
  TUCK, Memory (née Fortune) (Benoni, 1965) m 1968; Cmr, TPWM, S Afr. b 28 Apr 45. Served in S Afr (CS/TSWM) and PNG (TC/TPWM).

TURSI, Massimo (Naples, It, 1983); Maj, Ger. b 14 Nov 57, and
  TURSI, Anne-Florence (née Cachelin) (Bern 1, Switz, 1983) m 1983; Maj, Ger. b 25 Mar 59. Served in It and Switz.

TVEDT, Hannelise (née Nielsen) (Copenhagen Temple, 1976); Maj, Den. b 13 Dec 55. Served in Nor.

U

UDOH, Etim (Oboyo Ikot Ita, 1984); Maj, Nig. b 9 May 56, with
  UDOH, Ekerebong; Maj, Nig. b May 61.

UMOH, Smart (Ikot Akpan, 1974); Maj, Nig. b 18 Nov 50, with
  UMOH, Dorothy m 1971; Maj, Nig. b 12 Dec 56.

UNDERSRUD, Arne (Drammen, 1969); Maj, Nor. b 15 Mar 44, and
  UNDERSRUD, Anne Lise (née Bendiksen) (Finnsnes, 1969) m 1974; Maj, Nor. b 12 Feb 48. Served in UK.

UWAK, Udoh (Ikot Obio Inyang, 1992); Capt, Nig. b 2 Oct 66, with
  UWAK, Esther m 1990; Capt, Nig. b 12 Dec 73.

UZOHO, Stephen (Umuobom, 1974); Maj, Nig. b 22 Sep 49, with
  UZOHO, Edith; Maj, Nig. b 2 Jul 53.

V

VALE, John (Bairnsdale, 1981); Maj, Aus S. b 8 Jan 44, with
  VALE, Adele (née Brown) m 1965; Maj, Aus S. b 8 Dec 41.

VALLINSALO, Lasse (Pori, 1983); Maj, Fin. b 18 Jul 52, and
  VALLINSALO, Pirjo (née Kettula) (Pori, 1978) m 1983; Maj, Fin. b 1 Oct 54.

VAN BRUNT, T. Frederick (Arlington-Kearny, NJ, 1963); Lt-Col, USA E. b 22 Apr 41, and
  VAN BRUNT, Barbara (née Huntsman) (Niagara Falls, NY, 1964) m 1964; Lt-Col, USA E. b 27 Aug 43.

VAN DER HARST, Willem (Scheveningen, 1966); Comr, TC, Neth. b 13 Mar 44. Ww Capt Suzanne, pG 1985, and
  VAN DER HARST, Netty (née Kruisinga) (Amsterdam Congress Hall, 1984) m 1985; Comr, TPWM, Neth. b 15 Feb 58. Served in Cze R.

VAN HAL, Jeanne E. (Rotterdam Congress Hall, 1965); Maj, Neth. b 6 May 42. Served in UK and at IHQ.

VAN PELT, Hendrik (Rotterdam South, 1970); Maj, Neth. b 11 Mar 49, and
  VAN PELT, Wilhelmina (née Hoefnagel) (Rotterdam South, 1969) m 1972; Maj, Neth. b 4 May 47.

VAN VLIET, Johan C. J. (Baarn, 1975); Maj, Neth. b 17 Jul 52. D (Soc Serv Admin), with
  VAN VLIET, Maria E. (née de Ruiter) m 1971; Maj, Neth. b 9 May 51.

VANDER WEELE, Richard E. (Kalamazoo, MI, 1976); Maj, USA C. b 19 May 48. BS (Soc), MSW.

VANLALTHANGA (Ruallung, 1979); Maj,
Ind E. b 4 Jul 57, with
HMUNROPUII m 1977; Maj, Ind E.
b 25 Oct 59.

VARGHESE, Davidson (Trivandrum Central,
Ind SW, 1986); Maj, Zam. b 13 Dec 58. BA,
and
DAVIDSON, Mariamma (née Chacko)
(Adoor Central, Ind SW, 1985) m 1988;
Maj, Zam. b 1 May 65. Served in Ind SW.

VARUGHESE, Wilfred (Trivandrum Central,
Ind SW, 1985); Maj, Ind Nat. b 25 Mar 58.
BSc (Botany), and
VARUGHESE, Prema Wilfred (Anayara,
Ind SW, 1987) m 1987; Maj, Ind Nat.
b 25 May 60. BA, BD. Served in Ind SW.

VENTER, Alistair (Cape Town Citadel, 1981);
Maj, S Afr. b 19 Aug 58. ThA, BTh, and
VENTER, Marieke (née van Leeuwen)
(Benoni, 1988) m 1987; Maj, S Afr. b 31 Dec 62,
Assoc Theol, BCur.

VIJAYAKUMAR, Thumati (Denduluru, Ind C,
1970); Lt-Col, Ind Nat. b 10 Jun 49, and
VIJAYAKUMAR, Keraham Manikyam (née
Karuhu) (Denduluru, Ind C, 1970) m 1971;
Lt-Col, Ind Nat. b 17 Apr 53. Served in Ind C,
Ind SE and Ban (GS/CSWM).

VIRU, Zarena (Bhogiwal, 1973); Lt-Col, Pak.
b 1 Jan 52.

VOORHAM, Christina (The Hague South,
1970); Lt-Col, Neth. b 2 Sep 46.

VYLE, Bruce (Hamilton City, 1995); Capt, NZ.
b 5 Jun 46. MA, BA, DipT, with
VYLE, Elaine (née French) m 1968; Capt,
NZ. b 9 Jul 48.

W

WAFULA, John Wekesa (Lungai, 1977); Maj,
Ken. b 24 Apr 48, with
WAFULA, Hellen (née Olesia) m 1975;
Maj, Ken. b 25 Sep 52.

WAGHELA, Chimanbhai Somabhai
(Ratanpura, 1968); Comr, TC, Ind SW.
b 1 Jun 47, with
RAHELBAI, Chimanbhai Waghela, m 1972;
Comr, TPWM, Ind SW. b 1 May 52. Served in
Ind SE (CS/TSWO) and Ind E (CS/TSWO).

WAINWRIGHT, John (Reading Central,
1979); Maj, UK. b 13 Mar 51, with
WAINWRIGHT, Dorita (née Willetts)
m 1976; Maj, UK. b 19 Oct 51. Served in
E Afr and Zimb.

WALKER, Peter (Morley, 1982); Maj, Aus S.
b 2 Mar 54, with
WALKER, Jennifer (née Friend) m 1975;

Maj, Aus S. b 26 Feb 56. Served in Mlys.

WANJARE, Sanjay (Vithalwadi, 1994); Capt,
Ind W. b 10 Oct 67, with
WANJARE Sunita m 1992; Capt, Ind W.
b 1 Jun 70.

WARD, H. Alfred (Atlanta Temple, GA,
1971); Lt-Col, USA S. b 2 Aug 46. BA,
MBA, with
WARD, Mary M. (née Busby); Lt-Col,
USA S. b 13 Nov 47. BVA. Served in
Aus E.

WARD, Robert (Brock Avenue, Toronto, Can,
1970); Lt-Col, CS, Zimb. b 22 Apr 48.
MHSc (Health Mgmt), BA (Admin), and
WARD, Marguerite (née Simon) (Swift
Current, Can, 1970) m 1971; Lt-Col,
TSWM, Zimb. b 13 May 48. Served in Can,
Pak and S Afr.

WATT, Neil (Montreal Citadel, 1977); Maj,
Can. b 4 Nov 48, with
WATT, Lynda (née Westover) m 1968;
Maj, Can. Served in UK.

WHITE, Charles (Owensboro, KY, 1967);
Lt-Col, USA S. b 7 May 46, with
WHITE, Shirley (née Sanders) m 1962;
Lt-Col, USA S. b 24 Apr 43.

WHITE, Larry Wayne (Orlando, FL, 1972);
Maj, USA S. b 27 Aug 45, and
WHITE, Shirley Anne (née Knight) (Lake
Charles, LA, 1967) m 1969; Maj, USA S.
b 7 Mar 42.

WILLERMARK, Marie (Göteborg 1, Swdn,
1980); Maj, E Eur. b 18 Jun 54. Served in
Swdn and Den.

WILLIAM, Appavoo (N Karayankuzhy, 1969);
Lt-Col, Ind SE. b 2 Jun 48, and
DAVAMONY (Booth Tucker Hall, 1971)
m 1972; Lt-Col, Ind SE. b 18 Mar 47.

WILLIAMS, Michael (Bristol Easton Road,
UK, 1967); Lt-Col, IHQ. b 16 Dec 46. Served
in UK. m 1969; Lt-Col Ruth, ret 2004.

WOLTERINK, Theodoor (Hengelo, Neth,
1974); Maj, IHQ. b 16 Jun 47, with
WOLTERINK, Albertina (née Riezebos)
m 1970; Maj, IHQ. b 17 Feb 46. Served in
Neth.

WOODALL, Ann (Croydon Citadel, UK,
1969); Lt-Col, IHQ. b 3 Feb 50. MA, MSc,
FCCA, PhD. Served in Con, Zam, Zaï and
UK.

WOODWARD, Cecil (Coorparoo, 1969); Maj,
Aus E. b 3 Jun 46. MBA, and
WOODWARD, Catherine (née Lucas)
(Miranda, 1970) m 1970; Maj, Aus E.
b 20 Jan 48

Y

YAFELE, Jonathan (Chinyika, 1969); Maj, Zimb. b 6 Nov 46, and
YAFELE, Tandiwe (née Mhlanga) (Chinyika, 1985) m 1983; Maj, Zimb. b 13 Dec 49.

YAMANAKA, Masaru (Fukuoka, 1970); Maj, Jpn. b 10 Jul 44, and
YAMANAKA, Machiko (née Matsui) (Tenma, 1963) m 1973; Maj, Jpn. b 21 Jan 39.

YANDERAVE, Borley (Lembina, 1992); Capt, PNG. b 7 Jul 58, with
YANDERAVE, Iveme (née John) m 1984; Capt, PNG. b 25 Oct 66.

YANG, Tae-soo (Chun Yun, 1978); Maj, Kor. b 14 Feb 47, with
CHUN, Ok-kyung m 1968; Maj, Kor. b 14 Jul 47. Served in Sing.

YODER, Stephen (Dearborn Heights, MI, USA C, 1986); Maj, IHQ. b 4 Sep 64, and
YODER, Morag (Norridge, IL, USA C, 1989); m 1987; Maj, IHQ. b 15 Feb 59. Served in USA C.

YOHANNAN, C. S. (Kaithaparambu, 1975); Maj, Ind SW. b 8 Jan 54, and
YOHANNAN, L. Rachel (Pathanapuram, 1979) m 1978; Maj, Ind SW. b 31 Jul 55.

YOHANNAN, P. J. (Oollayam Kangazha, 1978); Maj, Ind SW. b 17 May 49, and

YOHANNAN, Annamma (Oollayam Kangazha, 1981) m 1981; Maj, Ind SW. b 31 Aug 55.

YOSHIDA, Makoto (Shibuya, 1969); Comr, TC, Jap. b 7 Dec 45. BS (Engin), and
YOSHIDA, Kaoru (née Imamura) (Omori, 1971) m 1974; Comr, TPWM, Jap. b 13 Jan 45. Served in Jpn (CS/TSWM) and at IHQ (IS/SWM, SPEA).

YOSHIDA, Tsukasa (Shibuya, 1982); Maj, Jpn. b 26 Nov 54, and
YOSHIDA, Kyoko (née Tsuchiya) (Kiyose, 1980) m 1982; Maj, Jpn. b 13 Oct 53.

Z

ZACHARIAH, Jupalli (Hutti, 1983); Maj, Ind C. b 6 May 54. BA, with
ZACHARIAH, Usha Rani (née Perumalla) m 1980; Maj, Ind C. b 15 Jun 65.

ZOLA, Ambroise (Kingudi, Con (Kin), 1979); Lt-Col, CS, Con (Braz). b 6 Sep 52, with
ZOLA, Alphonsine Kuzoma (née Nsiesi) m 1976; Lt-Col, TSWM, Con (Braz). b 2 Jan 57. Served in Con (Kin).

ZONDO, Bethuel Gubudu (Africa Central, 1965); Maj, S Afr. b 22 Feb 41, with
ZONDO, Thelma Thandiwe (née Mncube) m 1964. Maj, S Afr. b 10 Apr 43.

FROM India to Indonesia, from Ukraine to the USA, The Salvation Army is being used by God to change people's lives. For evidence and eye-witness reports pick up a copy of *All the World*, The Salvation Army's international magazine.

Published four times a year, *All the World* contains in-depth features on emergency relief, development and community work undertaken by Salvationists across the globe. Where there's a soup run, a house-building project, a rehabilitation scheme or a community programme *All the World* aims to be there, witnessing the often miraculous transformations brought about through the power of God and the dedication and sheer hard work of his people in The Salvation Army.

Copies can be purchased from any Salvation Army headquarters and subscriptions are available through Salvationist Publishing and Supplies, UK Territory. The online version of the magazine, including some down-loadable artwork, can be accessed at: www.salvationarmy.org/alltheworld

Retirements from Active Service

AUSTRALIA EASTERN

Maj Lynette Rushbrook (née Carter) from Upper Blue Mountains Corps on 1 Sep 2005

Majs Colin and Barbara Brownhill (née Phillips) from Greater West Division Chaplain to Refugees and Pastoral Care Officers, Auburn Corps, on 4 Jan,2006

Capt Steve Nelson from Wills and Bequest Office, Gold Coast, on 1 Feb 2006

Maj George Lingard from Commander, Recovery Services Command, on 1 Feb 2006

Majs Bill and Bev Mole (née Waterson) from Chaplain, Montrose Senior Citizens' Accommodation and Asst Officer, Child Sponsorship Programme, on 1 Apr 2006

Majs Bert and Jean George (neé Campbell) from Prison Chaplaincy, Canberra/Goulburn, and Chaplain, Mountain View and Burrangiri (Canberra), on 1 Jun 2006

Maj Joan Brown from Elizabeth Jenkins Place on 1 Jun 2006

AUSTRALIA SOUTHERN

Maj Beverley Watters from THQ on 1 Jul 2005

Lt-Cols Peter and Sandra Callander (née Paton) from THQ on 1 Aug 2005

Maj Paul Such from Victor Harbour Corps on 1 Aug 2005

Capt Carol Mechielsen (née Pollard) from Beechworth Corps on 1 Aug 2005

Majs Godefredus and Jean Janssen (née Farmer) from Family Stores and Glenelg Corps on 1 Sep 2005

Majs John and Diana Zilm (née Vaughan) from Hamilton Corps on 1 Oct 2005

Lt-Col Ian Smith from THQ on 1 Nov 2005

Majs Rodney and Irene Stevens (née Wheatley) from Melbourne Central Division on 1 Nov 2005

Maj Howard Davies from THQ on 1 Dec 2005

Majs Henry and Betty Greene (née Male) from THQ on 1 Feb 2006

Maj David Watson from Tanzania Command on 1 Feb 2006

Maj Bruce Foynes from Western Australia Division on 1 Feb 2006

Maj Ursula Jackson (née Geeves) from THQ on 1 Mar 2006

Capt Joan Buckle (née Brand) from Western Australia Division on 1 Mar 2006

Maj Alan Dale from Eastern Victoria Division on 1 Mar 2006

Majs Dennis and Olive Dell (née Turner) from Western Australia DHQ on 1 Mar 2006

Capt Judith Brown from South Australia DHQ on 1 Apr 2006

Maj Irene Dean (née Smithers) from South Australia DHQ on 1 May 2006

Maj Helen Newman from THQ on 1 May 2006

CANADA AND BERMUDA

Capt Myrna Tidd from THQ on 1 Sep 2005

Majs Weldon and Sally Carr (née McLean) from Toronto Hope Shelter on 1 Oct 2005

Majs Ronald and Joyce Stuckless (née Tilley) from Newfoundland and Labrador West DHQ on 1 Oct 2005

Majs Frank and Jean Johnson (née Hurley) from Pilley's Island Corps on 1 Feb 2005

Maj Barbara Bawks from THQ on 1 Jul 2006

Majs Eric and Wanda Brown (née Inder) from THQ on 1 Jul 2006

Majs Richard and Sandra Cooper (née Leach) from Bracebridge Community Church on 1 Jul 2006

Majs David and Donna Pitcher (née Howells) from THQ and Ontario Central DHQ on 1 Jul 2006

Majs Bernard and Ann Borden (née Bailey) from Newfoundland and Labrador West Division on 1 Jul 2006

Majs Samuel and Delores Fame (née Gass) from Vancouver Harbour Light on 1 Jul 2006

Majs Rolf and Joanne Guenther (née Church) from Oakville Community Church on 1 Jul 2006

Majs Robert and Joan Henderson (née Howard) from Stratford Community Church on 1 Jul 2006

Maj Grace Herber from The Honourable Ray and Helen Lawson Eventide Homen on 1 Jul 2006

Maj Margaret MacKenzie from The Honourable Ray and Helen Lawson Eventide Home on 1 Jul 2006

Majs Gary and Carolyn High (née Boorman) from Public Relations, Ontario North Division, on 1 Jul 2006

Maj Janice MacLean from THQ on 1 Jul 2006

Majs Edwin and Judy Mayo (née Brown) from the Newfoundland and Labrador East Division on 1 Jul 2006

Majs George and Margaret Perkin (née Allen) from Vancouver Belkin House on 1 Jul 2006

Maj Dianne Stevenson (née Knox) from THQ on 1 Jul 2006

Maj Roger Beaulac from Bathhust Community Church on 1 Aug 2006

Majs Max and Helen Bulmer (née Mills) from Public Relations and Development, Ontario East Division, on 1 Aug 2006

Maj Sandra Foster from Ontario Great Lakes DHQ on 1 Aug 2006

Majs Clyde and Helen Guy (née Tarrant) from Windsor Community and Rehabilitation Centre on 1 Aug 2006

Majs Raymond and Catherine Harris (née King) from College for Officer Training, St John's, Newfoundland, on 1 Aug 2006

Majs Malcolm and Barbara Robinson (née Tillsley) from Ontario Central DHQ on 1 Aug 2006

Majs Archibald and Marie Simmonds (née Drover) from Midland on 1 Aug 2006.

Maj Lillian West from Ontario East DHQ on 1 Aug 2006

Majs Larry and Eileen Williams (née Bowering) from Georgina Community Church on 1 Aug 2006

CARIBBEAN

Maj Eileen Colbourne from Regional Commander, Antigua, on 25 Jun 2006

CONGO (KINSHASA) & ANGOLA

Majs Gaston and Charlotte Lutumba on 31 Jul 2005

Maj Therese Dianzenza on 2 Jul 2006

DENMARK

Maj Edel Bjarkam from Frederikshavn on 22 Jun 2005

Maj Niels Andreassen from Århus on 30 Apr 2006

FINLAND AND ESTONIA

Maj Jaakko Rahkonen from Helsinki on 1 Oct 2005

Maj Tuula Halla-aho from Helsinki on 1 Feb 2006

Capt Mirja Nieminen from Kokkola on 1 Jun 2006

FRANCE

Maj Claude Etcheverry from Chaplain for Active Officers, THQ, on 1 Feb 2006

GERMANY AND LITHUANIA

Maj Willi Weiss from Essen Corps on 1 Jan 2006

Maj Ursula Bretzner (née Wiggert) from Kassel Corps on 30 Jun 2006

Majs Gerhard and Brigitte Rau (née Lämmel) from Frankfurt Corps on 30 Jun 2006

GHANA

Lt-Cols Paul and Doris Afful (née Oppongwaa) from THQ on 31 Aug 2006

Majs Emmanuel and Mary Duodu (née Otenewaah) from Central Division, on 26 Mar 2006

Maj Isaac Mensah Amofah from Nkawkaw Division on 30 Oct 2005

INDIA CENTRAL

Maj S. Suvarna Rao on 1 Jun 2005

Maj Prameela on 1 Jun 2005

Majs S. John Bhushanam and S. Penniamma on 1 Dec 2005

Lt-Cols S. Lukaiah and Saramma on 11 Dec 2005

INDIA EASTERN

Majs Lalchhuana and Lalngengi from Bethlehem Corps on 14 Apr 2006

INDIA NORTHERN

Majs Maharaj and Grace Masih from Gurdaspur on 31 Jan 2006

Majs Sulakhan and Santosh Masih from Batala on 31 Mar 2006

Majs Baboo and Shamwati Lal from Bareilly on 30 Apr 2006

Majs Safir and Margaret Masih from Gurdaspur on 30 Apr 2006

Majs Hamid and Rosie Masih from Moradabad on 31 Jul 2006

Majs Sadiq and Shanti Masih from Mukerian on 31 Jul 2006

INDIA SOUTH EASTERN

Lt-Cols Nallanayagam and Mabel Inbam from THQ on 15 May 2006

Majs V. Abraham and Esther from Chitharal on 15 May 2006

Majs G. Aruldhas and Florence Inbamony from Training College on 15 May 2006

Majs K. Mark and Santham from Kiliancode on 15 May 2006

Majs Perinbadhas and Chithravathy from Coimbatore DHQ on 15 May 2006

Majs Simon and Oithammal from Kolvai on 15 May 2006

Maj Nahomi from Girls' Hostel, Thuckalay, on 15 May 2006
Maj Christumoni from Kulasekharam DHQ on 18 May 2006

INDIA SOUTH WESTERN
Majs S. Raju and Chinnamma Raju from Kaduvapoke on 31 Jul 2005
Majs B. Joseph and Marykutty Joseph from Parabukonam on 31 Aug 2005
Majs T. M. Samuel and Rhankamma Samuel from Thuvayoor on 31 Aug 2005
Majs M. Joseph and R. Leela Joseph from Pethalakarikam on 30 Sep 2005
Maj Lillymary John from Kanikukulam on 31 Jan 2006
Majs C. M. George and Lillykutty George fromThuvayoor on 28 Feb 2006
Lt-Cols P. Johnson and Thankamma Johnson from Pallikal on 28 Feb 2006
Majs K. S. Das and Sosamma Das from Cheenthala on 31 Mar 2006
Majs Y. Noah and M. Gnanamma Noah from Kalayapuram on 31 Mar 2006
Maj Marykutty Moses from Narikal on 30 Apr 2006
Majs Mikhale and Omana Mickhayel from Kanniyakuxhy Old and New on 30 Apr 2006
Majs Y. James and Rajamma James from Pooyapally on 31 May 2006
Majs P. Mathew and Gracy Mathew from Elampally on 30 Jun 2006

INDIA WESTERN
Majs Shantilal and Sumitaben Jivabhai from Vatva Corps on 1 May 2006
Majs Arun and Chandrakala Waghmare from Training College on 1 May 2006
Capts Chhotalal Soma and Reginabai from Kunjarav Corps on 1 May 2006
Majs Premchand and Jayamala Borde from Shrirampur Division on 1 May 2006

INDONESIA
Majs Philimon and Dintjie Tohuro (née Jeman) from Poy Outpost on 1 Sep 2005
Maj Surniasih Salimin (née Kartosentono) from Lemah Bang Outpost on 27 Dec 2005
Majs Lesman and Nursiana Sinaga (née Siregar) from Mantikole 2 Corps on 1 Jan 2006
Majs Laurens and Paulona Lamanusu (née Bahasia) from Salua Corps on 2 Feb 2006
Maj Adriana Ngale from Manusi Clinic on 1 Jul 2006

Maj Bawaningdyahwijati Hohoy from Kupang Corps on 1 Jul 2006
Majs Aming and Miina Noerman (née Koesen) from Batujajar Corps on 1 Jul 2006

ITALY
Maj Giovanni Iannarone from Milan on 30 Jun 2006

JAPAN
Majs Yukio and Michiko Maruhata (née Yabuno) from Okayama on 30 Apr 2006
Comrs Nozomi and Kazuko Harita (née Hasegawa) from THQ (TC/TPWM) on 31 May 2006

KENYA
Majs Nelson and Judith Barasa (née Navalyo) from Ndakaru on 30 Sep 2005
Maj Ibramu Bitengo from Wabukhonyi on 1 Dec 2005
Majs Moses and Gladys Mumero (née Nanyama) from Endebes on 1 Dec 2005
Majs Lazarus and Christine Sirengo (née Nahimiyu) from Webuye on 1 Dec 2005
Majs Herman and Leonola Kabuty (née Wabule) from Madzuu on 13 Dec 2005
Majs Hezron and Janet Sande (née Keloya) from Kaptel on 13 Dec 2005
Majs Edward and Mary Ahujah (née Migide) from Chongoyi on 13 Dec 2005
Lt-Cols Daniel and Irene Musasia (née Mbango) from Kakamega Division on 1 Jan 2006
Lt-Cols Saul and Rose Cheroben (née Chemai) from Kenya THQ on 30 Apr 2006
Cols Bernard and Joyce Ndwiga (née Kagema) from sick leave and Kabete Children's Home on 30 Apr 2006
Majs Samson and Jerita Amalemba (née Ayieko) from Lurumbi on 31 Jul 2006
Majs Zakaria and Prisilla Imbali (née Khayasi) from Moi's Bridge on 31 Jul 2006

KOREA
Majs Shim, Sang-yong and Park, Hak-boon from Hong Sung Corps on 31 Dec 2005
Lt-Cols Han, Jong-suk and Kang, Tae-hyang from Choong Saw DHQ on 31 Jan 2006
Majs Park, Chong-kil and Ahn, Nam-soon from Syn Pyung Corps on 31 Jan 2006

MALAWI
Capts Eric and Elizabeth Mtengowalira from Zalewa Outreach Unit on 1 Dec 2005

THE NETHERLANDS AND CZECH REPUBLIC

Majs Bert and Gerda Kroon (neé de Bruijn) from Kampen on 1 Dec 2004

Lt-Col Hannie van Kesteren (neé Kramer) from Hilversum on 1 Jan 2005

Maj Henk Kooijman from La Salette on 1 Jun 2005

Maj Lo Spiering from Doesburg on 1 Aug 2005

Majs Feike and Gerrie Bergsma (née van der Klashorst) from Groningen on 1 Nov 2005

Maj Bauke Outhuijse from Enschede on 1 Dec 2005

Lt-Col Ben van Kesteren from THQ on 1 Dec 2005

Maj Niesje Schuppers (neé Wolfs) from THQ on 1 Jan 2006

Maj Hans Valster from Ede on 1 Feb 2006

Maj Hennie Spiering (née Hagedoorn) from Doesburg on 1 Mar 2006

Maj Herman Bolhoeve from Groot Batelaar on 1 Apr 2006

Majs Heinz and Anna Menge (née van der Zalm) from Nijverdal on 1 May 2006

Aux-Capt Coby Maasbommel from Ghana on 1 May 2006

Maj Coby Broekman from Lelystad on 1 May 2006

Maj Margriet Hogetoorn from Amersfoort on 1 Jul 2006

Majs Nico and Joke van der Made (née Schröer) from THQ on 1 Jul 2006

NEW ZEALAND, FIJI AND TONGA

Majs Neil and Merle Adams (née Stanton) from Midland DHQ on 12 Jan 2006

Majs David and Myrtle Clark (née Fitness) from Ashburton on 12 Jan 2006

Maj Lynne Thomson from Clifton on 12 Jan 2006

Cols Laurence and Margaret Hay (née Major) from IHQ on 28 Feb 2006

Lt-Col Lyn Buttar from THQ on 1 Mar 2006

NORWAY, ICELAND AND THE FÆROES

Maj Solveig Fosse from Grønland Corps on 31 Aug 2005

Maj Else Johnsen from THQ on 31 Dec 2005

Maj Irene Syversen from THQ on 31 Dec 2005

Maj Laila Waage from THQ on 28 Feb 2006

Maj Erna Djurhuus from Social Services on 31 Mar 2006

Maj Bjørg Davidsen from THQ on 31 Mar 2006

Maj Inger Nymoen from Mo i Rana Corps on 30 Apr 2006

Maj Kåre Georgsen from THQ on 30 Jun 2006

Maj Kai Clausen from THQ on 31 Aug 2006

PAKISTAN

Majs Ghulam and Joyce Jackson from THQ on 1 Feb 2006

Comrs Gulzar Patras and Sheila Gulzar from THQ (TC/TPWM) on 15 Sept 2006

PAPUA NEW GUINEA

Maj Win Ali (née Naime) from Training College on 4 Dec 2005

Majs Garo and Gora Rau (née Gudili) from Meirobu on 11 Dec 2005

SOUTHERN AFRICA

Majs Ogorogile and Keneilwe Nako from Ephraim Zulu Senior Citizens' Centre on 31 Dec 2005

Majs Aleck and Martha Ndlovu from Gauteng Corps on 31 Dec 2005

Majs Bethuel and Thelma Zondo from Eastern Kwa Zulu Natal DHQ on 28 Feb 2006

SRI LANKA

Majs G. A. and Manel Karunananda (née Perera) from Biyanwila on 14 May 2006

SWEDEN AND LATVIA

Maj Nanna-Greta Hjortfors from Dala-Järna on 1 Nov 2004

Maj Birgit Svensson from Göteborg on 31 Dec 2004

Maj Britt Boström from Luleå on 1 Mar 2005

Maj Gerd Boström from Gävle on 1 Mar 2005

Capt Lilian Dahnielsson from Tranås on 31 May 2005

Maj Birgit Eklund from Jönköping on 31 Jul 2005

Maj Ulla-Britt Johannesson from Umeå on 30 Apr 2005

Maj Allan Brodin from THQ on 30 Jun 2005

Capt Lilly Stefansson from Limhamn on 30 Jun 2005

Maj Lennart Johansson from Värnamo on 31 Jul 2005

Col Gunnar Nilsson from THQ on 31 Jul 2005

Comr Majvor Roos from THQ on 30 Sep 2005

Maj Ethel Forsell from THQ on 31 Dec 2005

Maj Yvonne Nilsson from Örnsköldsvik on 31 Dec 2005

Maj Ingrid Fröjd from Sala on 28 Feb 2006

Maj Barbro Wiberg from THQ on 31 May 2006

Maj Bernt Ahlström from Stockholm on
31 May 2006
Maj Charlotte Dahlström from THQ on
31 Aug 2006
Maj Dora Brodin from Umeå on 31 Aug 2006

SWITZERLAND, AUSTRIA AND HUNGARY

Maj Alice Landmesser from Beth Shalom,
Winterthur, on 1 Feb 2006
Maj Hanna Burch-Haller from Frutigen Corps
on 1 Mar 2006
Maj Ruth Frehner from Aarau Corps on
31 Jul 2006
Maj Roland Magnin from THQ on 31 Jul 2006

UNITED KINGDOM WITH THE REPUBLIC OF IRELAND

Lt-Col Gustave Allemand from IHQ on
1 Sep 2005
Majs Mervin and Margaret Baker (née Mallett)
from Northern DHQ on 1 Sep 2005
Lt-Cols Alan and Eveline Bateman (née Fenner)
from THQ on 1 Sep 2005
Majs Barry and Kathleen Elkin (née Moore)
from Ipswich Bramford Road on
1 Sep 2005
Capts Richard and Lynda Hutter (née Pearson)
from Wimborne on 1 Sep 2005
Maj Sheila McGill (née McNeill) from Royton
on 1 Sep 2005
Maj Valerie Smith (née Pockett) from William
Booth College on 1 Sep 2005
Maj Christine Cunningham (née Walton) from
Belfast Citadel on 1 Oct 2005
Maj Ruth Curtis from Mildred Duff Eventide
Home on 1 Oct 2005
Lt-Cols Alan and Valerie Hart (née Morgan)
from London North East DHQ and Bishop's
Stortford on 1 Oct 2005
Capts William and Diana Merritt (née
Stevens) from Herne Bay on 1 Oct 2005
Maj Alan Richards from THQ on 1 Oct 2005
Capt Sheila Harris (née Mugford) from Paignton
on 1 Nov 2005
Maj Gordon Dockerill from THQ on 1 Nov 2005
Maj Stephen Norman from West Midlands DHQ
on 1 Dec 2005
Majs Andrew and Shirley Halse (née Skinner)
from Torquay on 1 Dec 2005
Col Robert Cooper from IHQ on 1 Jan 2006
Maj Maureen Gill (née Calvert) from Sunderland
Millfield on 1 Jan 2006
Maj Marie Hickman (née Mason) from Millom
on 1 Jan 2006

Majs John and Maureen Luce (née McKinney)
from Blackpool South on 1 Jan 2006
Lt-Cols David and Kathleen Armistead (née
Miller) from Wm Booth College on 1 Feb
2006
Maj Brenda Austin (née Bury) from Bovington
Red Shield Club on 1 Feb 2006
Maj Joan Kirby from THQ on 1 Feb 2006
Maj Maurice Young from THQ on 1 Feb 2006
Capt Janet Penfold (née Ringer) from Ramsgate
on 1 Feb 2006
Maj Peter Exon from Chaplain, Bramwell House,
Blackburn, and HMP Manchester on
1 Apr 2006
Majs John and Lesley Jeeves (née Howie) from
Consett on 1 Apr 2006
Lt-Cols Colin and Barbara Tucker (née Mole)
from Clydebank on 1 Apr 2006
Maj Joan Bavis (née Miles) from Melton
Mowbray Red Shield Centre on 1 Jun 2006
Maj Jean Bradley from Mildred Duff Eventide
Home on 1 Jun 2006
Maj Wendy Burlinson from Shotton Colliery
on 1 Jun 2006
Maj Irene Houston (née Tominey) from
Chaplain, Davidson House Eventide Home
and The Pleasance, on 1 Jun 2006
Maj Jean Lacey from THQ on 1 Jun 2006
Maj Glenis Newton from THQ on 1 Jun 2006
Maj Maurice Porter from Chaplain, William
Booth Centre, Birmingham, and HMP Winson
Green, on 1 Jun 2006
Maj Wilma Sorley (née Robb) from Verwood
on 1 Jun 2006
Majs Leslie and Pauline Stanforth (née Peck)
from Maltby on 1 Jun 2006
Maj Sylvia Watchorn (née Moss) from
Shrewsbury on 1 Jul 2006
Majs Philip and May Wilbraham (née
Colquhoun) from Prison Chaplain, Yorkshire,
on 1 Jul 2006
Maj Margaret Anderson (née Perry) from
Sudbury on 1 Aug 2006
Maj Gillian Bruinewoud (née Walker) from
East Midlands DHQ on 1 Aug 2006
Maj Susan Cole from Brighouse on 1 Aug 2006
Maj Eileen Cook (née Moore) from Llanelli on
1 Aug 2006
Lt-Col Margaret Davis (née Conley) from East
Midlands DHQ on 1 Aug 2006
Comrs Paul and Margaret Du Plessis (née
Siebrits) from IHQ on 1 Aug 2006.
Majs Brian and Pamela Edwards (née Jones)
from Dereham Red Shield Centre on
1 Aug 2006

Maj Anne Finch from Walsall on 1 Aug 2006
Maj Margaret Goulding from Plympton on
1 Aug 2006
Lt-Cols John and Jane Hassard (née Robertson)
from Yorkshire DHQ on 1 Aug 2006
Majs Colin and Gillian Johnson (née Davidson)
from Nunhead on 1 Aug 2006
Lt-Col Valerie Jones (née Elvin) from Nelson
on 1 Aug 2006
Majs Peter and Carol Kendall (née Horncastle)
from Leeds West Hunslet on 1 Aug 2006
Maj Jean Leverett (née Milner) from Red
Shield, Marne Barracks on 1 Aug 2006
Majs Hugh and Margaret McCaig (née Martin)
from Stranraer on 1 Aug 2006
Maj Brian Miller from Gainsborough on
1 Aug 2006
Lt-Col Anwyn Mingay (née Dumbleton) from
Pokesdown on 1 Aug 2006
Maj David Scott from THQ on 1 Aug 2006
Lt-Cols Cedric and Barbara Sharp (née Hanson)
from Pakistan Territory (CS/TSWM) on
1 Aug 2006
Majs George and Jennifer Warren from
Harwich on 1 Aug 2006
Maj Margaret Watkins (née Lamb) from THQ
on 1 Aug 2006
Maj Pamela Wood from South Western DHQ
on 1 Aug 2006

USA CENTRAL

Maj Marilyn Riggs from Columbus, IN, on
30 Jun 2005
Maj Ruth Lohr from THQ on 31 Aug 2005
Majs Lloyd and Dorothea Hanton (née Saint)
from Kalamazoo, MI, on 31 Aug 2005
Majs David and Brenda Zahn (née Croghan)
from ARC Chicago, IL, on 31 Aug 2005
Majs David and Sandra Carr (née Wood) from
Heartland DHQ on 30 Sep 2005
Maj Cheryl Bailey (née Zeigler) from Wisconsin
and Upper Michigan DHQ on 31 Oct 2005
Maj Roy E. Rolling from Eastern Michigan DHQ
on 30 Nov 2005
Majs H. William and Donna Hurula (née
Larkins) from NHQ on 31 Jan 2006
Lt-Col Marlene Chase (née Cluff) from NHQ
on 28 Feb 2006
Majs David H. and Brenda Riches (née Watson)
from ARCC on 30 Jun 2006
Majs Allan and Caroline Irvine (née Cole) from
Midland DHQ on 30 Jun 2006
Capt Frederick and Maj Joyce Wakefield (née
Cooper) from Chillicothe, MO, on 30 Jun 2006
Majs Terrance and Sharon Nelson (née Wood)

from Western Michigan/Northern Indiana DHQ
on 30 Jun 2006

USA EASTERN

Majs James and Leann Klemowski (née Dell)
from New York, NY, ARC on 1 Sep 2005
Majs Ronald and Doris Dake (née Hill) from
Harrisburg, PA, on 1 Dec 2005
Majs Gary and Shirley Long (née Chiari) from
Rutland, VT, on 1 Dec 2005
Majs Harden and Marilyn White (née Hooper)
from NHQ on 1 Jan 2006
Lt-Cols Norman H. and Jeanne E. Voisey (née
Kittle) from Cleveland, OH, DHQ on
1 Feb 2006
Majs Glenn H. and Mary K. Avery (née
Fleming) from The Evangeline Residence,
New York, NY, on 1 Apr 2006
Majs James N. and Molly Shotzberger (née
Smith) from THQ on 1 Apr 2006
Comrs W. Todd and Carol Bassett (née
Easterday) from NHQ (Nat Comm/NPWM)
on 1 May 2006
Capt Paul and Maj Reta Hughes (née Remmers)
from Northwest Ohio Area Services, Toledo,
OH, on 1 May 2006
Lt-Col Sharon E. Berry from SFOT on
1 Jun 2006
Lt-Cols Norman E. and Louisa Wood (née
McIlwain) from Syracuse, NY, DHQ on
1 Jun 2006
Majs Richard and Dorothy Zander (née Foster)
from Indiana, PA, on 1 Jun 2006
Maj Jacquelin Triston from Framingham, MA
on 24 Jun 2006
Majs George and Linda Childs (née Abbott)
from Bronx, NY, ARC on 1 Jul 2006
Majs David and Jean Dlugose (née Farina)
from Greater New York, NY, DHQ, on
1 Jul 2006
Maj Faith Hasco from Pittsburgh (East Liberty),
PA, on 1 Jul 2006
Maj Josephine Howard from Pittsburgh (East
Liberty), PA, on 1 Jul 2006
Col Myrtle Ryder from NHQ on 1 Jul 2006

USA SOUTHERN

Lt-Cols Robert J. and Patsy Tritton (née
Allison) from Dallas, TX, DHQ on 1 Sep 2005
Majs Samuel and Linda Bivans (née Jordan)
from Charlotte, NC, DHQ on 1 Oct 2005
Maj Carol Sue Giffin from THQ on 1 Oct 2005
Lt-Col Evelyn Matthes from THQ on 1 Jan 2006
Lt-Cols Richard and Sharon Ulyat (née
Waiksnoris) from NHQ on 1 Feb 2006

Majs J. Ray and V. Carolyn Hudson (née Yaun) from Hot Springs, AR, on 1 Jul 2006
Comrs Philip D. and Keitha Needham (née Holz) from THQ (TC/TPWM) on 1 Jul 2006
Majs Thomas and Kareen Nicholls (née Boyer) from Atlanta, GA, ARC on 1 Jul 2006
Maj Catherine Hill from Tulsa, OK, on 1 June 2006

USA WESTERN
Maj Shirley Breukelman from Santa Cruz, CA, on 1 Sep 2005
Majs Arnold and Carol Hassler (née Wikle) from Oceanside, CA, on 1 Jan 2006
Maj Anna Wilson from Tucson (Amphi), AZ, on 1 May 2006
Majs Don and Rachele Bowman (née Holt)

from Billings, MT, on 1 Jul 2006
Majs William and Mary Dickinson (née Hester) from Auburn, CA, on 1 Jul 2006
Capts Christopher and Christine Giffey-Brohaugh (née Giffey) from Renton, WA, on 1 Jul 2006
Majrs Thomas and Sylvia Petersen (née Barry) from Reno, NV, on 1 Jul 2006
Majs Benton III and JoAnn Markham (née Tackett) from Spokane, WA, on 1 Aug 2006

ZIMBABWE
Majs Alfred Nubulu and Maria Moyo on 6 Feb 2006
Majs Godfrey and Stella Muringai on 15 Mar 2006
Majs Ngoni and Violet Sami on 30 Jul 2006

WORDS OF LIFE

THE Salvation Army's international Bible reading plan, *Words of Life* offers an invaluable aid to daily devotional study. The readings cover a wide selection of Scripture over a period of time and the comments offered give opportunity to build a lasting library for further study and reflection. Points for prayer and praise are a further enrichment to personal devotion. Retired General John Gowans begins a term as writer of *Words of Life* with the May-June 2007 edition.

WE BELIEVE IN SALVATION

'We are a salvation people. This is our speciality – getting saved and keeping saved, and then getting somebody else saved. . . . We believe in salvation! We believe in old-fashioned salvation. Ours is the same salvation taught in the Bible, proclaimed by prophets and apostles, preached by Luther, Wesley and Whitfield, sealed by the blood of the martyrs – the very same salvation which was purchased by the sufferings and agony and blood of the Son of God.' – *William Booth*

Retired Generals and Commissioners

The following list contains the names of retired Generals, commissioners and lieut-commissioners, and widows of lieut-commissioners and above, as at 31 August 2006

A

ADIWINOTO, Lilian E. (Malang, 1954); Comr. b 31 Jul 27. Served in UK, Indon (TC) and at IHQ.

ASANO, Hiroshi (Shizuoka, 1950); Comr. b 5 May 27. m Lt Tomoko Ohara (Kyoto, 1953) 1955. Served in Jpn (TC).

B

BASSETT, W. Todd (Syracuse Citadel, NY, USA E, 1965); Comr. b 25 Aug 39. BEd, with **BASSETT, Carol A.** (née Easterday) m 1960; Comr. BEd. b 10 Dec 40. Served in USA E, at IHQ (IS to CoS/ Mission Resources Sec) and at USA Nat (Nat Comm/NPWM).

BATH, Vida (née McNeill) (Moree, 1945); m 1951; Mrs Comr. Served in Sri Lan, Ind W, Ind NE, Ind SW, at IHQ and in Aus E. Ww Comr Robert, pG 2006.

BAXENDALE, David A. (Pittsburgh, PA, USA, 1954; Comr. b 23 Apr 30. MA (Col), BSc (Sprd), with Alice (née Chamberlain); BMus Ed (Syra). Served in USA E, USA W (CS), Carib (TC), S Am W (TC), ICO (Principla) and IHQ (IS Am and Carib).

BIMWALA, Zunga Mbanza Etienne (Central Hall, Kinshasa 1, 1959); Comr. b 29 Sep 32. Served in Zaï (TC/TPWO) and Switz. Ww Comr Alice, pG 2004.

BIRD, Patricia (Fulham, UK, 1958); Comr. b 7 Aug 35. Served in Nig, UK, Zam (TC) and at IHQ (IS Fin, IS Afr).

BOVEN van, Johannes (The Hague, 1955); Comr. b 9 Jan 35, and **BOVEN van, Klazina** (née Grauwmeijer) (Rotterdam, 1959) m 1960; Comr. b 22 Sep 35. Served in Neth (TC/TPWO).

BROWN, Jean (née Barclay) (Montreal Citadel, Can, 1938); Mrs General. Served at IHQ and in Can. Ww General Arnold Brown, pG 2002.

BUCKINGHAM, Hillmon (Waimate, NZ, 1960); Comr. b 20 Jan 36, with **BUCKINGHAM, Lorraine** (née Smith) m 1958; Comr. Served in Aus S, NZ (CS/TSWO) and Aus E (TC/TPWO).

B (continued, right column)

BURROWS, Eva Evelyn General (1986-93) (see page 25).

BUSBY, John A. (Atlanta Temple, GA, USA S, 1963); Comr. b 14 Oct 37. BA (Asbury), with **BUSBY, Elsie Louise** (née Henderson) m 1958; Comr. b 11 Jun 36. Served in Can (CS/TSWO), USA S (TC/TPWO) and USA Nat (NC/NPWM).

C

CACHELIN, Francy (Lausanne 1, Switz, 1944); Comr. b 4 Aug 23. Served in Switz, Belg, Frce (CS), Ger (TC), BT (Brit Comr) and at IHQ. Cross of the Order of Merit, Federal Republic of Germany (1985). m Lt Genevieve Booth, MA (Paris Central, Frce, 1947) 1951.

CAIRNS, Alistair Grant (West End, Aus E, 1942); Comr. b 12 Dec 16. AM, Order of Australia (1996). Served in Kor, Aus E (CS), at ITC and in S Afr (TC). Ww Mrs Comr Margery, pG 2006.

CAIRNS, William Ramsay (West End, Aus E, 1947); Comr. b 25 May 23. Served in Aus E (CS) and at IHQ (IS SPEA). AM, Order of Australia (1981). Ww Bernice, pG 1983. m Major Beulah Rae Ann Harris (Parramatta, NSW, Aus E, 1959) 1984.

CALVERT, Ruth (Port Hope, ON, 1955); Mrs Comr. b 8 Feb 35. Served in Aus E. Ww Comr Roy, pG 1994.

CAMPBELL, Donald (Highgate, WA, 1945); Comr. b 31 Oct 23. Served in NZ (TC) and Aus S (TC). m Capt Crystal Cross (Highgate, WA, 1944) 1947.

CHANG, Peter Hei-dong (Seoul Central, Kor, 1960); Comr. b 12 May 32. BD, STm (Union, NY), BTh MEd (Columbia, NY), and **CHANG, Grace Eun-Shik** (née Chung) (Seoul, Kor, 1963) m 1963; Comr. BA, BMus (Seoul Nat). Served in USA W (TC/TPWO), UK, Sing, HK, USA E, Kor (CS and TC/TPWO) and at IHQ.

CHEVALLY, Simone (née Gindraux) (Lausanne 1, 1947); Mrs Comr. Ww Comr Robert, pG 1989.

CHIANGHNUNA (Ngupa, 1951); Comr.
b 10 Jun 29. Served in Ind N (CS), E (CS)
and W (TC). m Maj Barbara Powell (Ware,
UK, 1948) 1968.

CLAUSEN, Siegfried (Catford, UK, 1958);
Comr. b 4 Mar 38, and
CLAUSEN, Inger-Lise (née Lydholm)
(Valby, 1958) m 1961; Comr. b 1 Oct 39.
Served in UK, S Am W, Sp (OC/CPWO),
L Am N (TC/TPWO), Ger (TC/TPWO) and
at IHQ (IS/SWM Am and Carib).

CLINCH, John H. (Fairfield, Vic, 1956); Comr.
b 30 Nov 30, with
CLINCH, Beth (née Barker); Comr. Served
in Aus S, Aus E (CS), at IHQ (IS SPEA) and
Aus S (TC/TPWO).

COLES, Alan C. (Harrow, UK, 1953); Comr.
b 2 Feb 25. ACIB. Ww Heather, pG 1978.
m Maj Brenda Deeming (Tipton, UK, 1959)
1980. Served in Zimb (TC) and at IHQ.

COLES, Dudley (North Toronto, ON, Can,
1954); Comr. b 22 Mar 26. m 2/Lt Evangeline
Oxbury (Powell River, BC, Can, 1954) 1956.
Served in Can, Ind Audit, Ind W, Sri Lan (TC)
and at IHQ (IS S Asia).

COOPER, Raymond A. (Washington
Georgetown, DC, 1956); Comr. b 24 May 37,
and
COOPER, Merlyn S. (née Wishon) (Winston
Salem Southside, NC, 1957) m 1959; Comr.
b 2 Sep 36. Served in USA C and USA S
(TC/TPWO).

COX, Hilda (née Chevalley) (Geneva, 1949);
Mrs Comr. Served in UK, Zam, Zimb, Frce,
Neth and at IHQ. Ww Comr Ron, pG 1995.

CUTMORE, Ian (Tamworth, Aus E, 1954);
Comr. b 27 Sep 33, and
CUTMORE, Nancy (née Richardson)
(Atherton, Aus E, 1957); Comr. Served in
Aus E, PNG, UK (CS), ICO (Prin) and NZ.

D

DAHLSTRØM, Haakon Adolf (Oslo 1, 1931);
Comr. b 7 Feb 07. Served in UK, Nor, Gha,
Nig (GS and TC), Fin (TC) and Nor (TC).
Knight, Order of St Olav (1975). m Capt Eili
Holme (Molde, 1937) 1946.

DALZIEL, Geoffrey Albert (Harrow, UK,
1934); Comr. b 10 Dec 12. Served in Aus S,
at ITC, in Aus E (CS), Can (CS), E Afr (TC)
and BT (Brit Comr). Ww Mrs Comr Ruth,
pG 1990.

DAVIS, Douglas E. (Moreland, 1960); Comr.
b 12 Feb 37, with
DAVIS, Beverley J. (née Roberts) m 1958;

Comr. b 23 Feb 38. Served in NZ, UK (CS/
TSWO) and Aus S (TC/TPWO).

DELCOURT, Raymond Andre (Montpellier,
1935); Comr. b 25 Oct 14. Served in BT and
Frce (TC). Croix de Guerre (1939-40),
Medaille Penitentiaire (1973), Medaille
d'Honneur de la Ville de Paris (1976),
Chevalier de la Legion d'Honneur (1978).
m Lt France Bardiaux (Lyon 1, 1943) 1943.

DEVAVARAM, Prathipati (New Colony, Ind C,
1964); Comr. b 15 Nov 46. MBBS, BSc, and
DEVAVARAM, P. Victoria (Bapatla Central,
Ind C, 1970) m 1974; Comr. b 25 Nov 49.
BSc, BEd, BLSc. Served in Ind C, at Ind Nat,
in Ind E and Ind SE (TC/TPWO).

DIAKANWA, Mbakanu (Poste Francais,
Kinshasa, 1949); Comr. b 1923. Officier de
l'Ordre du Leopard, 1981. Served in Zaï (TC).
Ww Mrs Comr Situwa, pG 1998.

DITMER, Anne (née Sharp) (Dayton Central,
OH, 1957) m 1992. Mrs Comr. Ww Comr
Stanley, pG 2003.

DU PLESSIS, Paul (Salt River, S Afr, 1968);
Comr. b 3 Jul 41. MB, ChB, MRCP, DTM&H,
with
DU PLESSIS, Margaret (née Siebrits);
Comr. b 17 Jul 42. BSoc Sc. Served in Zam,
Ind C (TC/TPWO), S Afr (TC/TPWO) and
at IHQ.

DURMAN, David C. (Bromley, UK, 1940);
Comr. b 21 Aug 20. Served in UK, Ind W (TC)
and at IHQ (Chancellor of the Exchequer and
IS S Asia). m Capt Vera Livick (South
Croydon, UK, 1942) 1949.

DWYER, June M. (Windsor, NS, Can, 1952);
Comr. b 28 Aug 32. Served in USA Nat, S Afr
(CS) and at IHQ (IS Admin).

E

EDWARDS, David (New Market Street,
Georgetown, Guyana, 1962); Comr.
b 15 May 41, and
EDWARDS, Doreen (née Bartlett)
(Wellington St, Barbados, 1957) m 1966.
b 4 Mar 35. Served in USA E, Carib
(TC/TPWO), at IHQ (IS/SWO Am and Carib)
and in USA W (TC/TPWO).

EGGER, Verena (née Halbenleib) (Solothurn,
1945); Mrs Comr. Served in Carib and C Am,
Zaï, Mex and C Am, S Am E and Switz.
Ww Comr Jacques E., pG 2001.

ELIASEN, Carl S. (Gartnergade, Den, 1951);
Comr. b 28 Mar 32. Served in Port (OC),
Brz (TC), S Am W (TC) and at IHQ
(IS Americas). Ww Comr Maria, pG 2003.

EVANS, Willard S. (Greenville, SC, 1949, w wife, née Marie Fitton); Comr. b 2 Sep 24. Served in USA S, USA E (CS) and USA W (TC). BA (Bob Jones Univ).

F

FEWSTER, Lilian (Lt Hunt, Hanwell, 1931); Mrs Comr. Served in UK, Can and Zimb. Ww Comr Ernest F., pG 1973.

FREI, Werner (Rorbas, Switz, 1965); Comr. b 6 Mar 40, and
FREI, Paula (née Berweger) (Heiden, Switz, 1965) m 1967; Comr. b 19 Mar 36. Served in Switz (CS/TSWO) and Ger (TC/TPWM).

FULLARTON, Frank (Bromley, UK, 1955); Comr. b 3 Mar 31. BSc, DipSoc, and
FULLARTON, Rosemarie (née Steck) (Croydon Citadel, UK, 1958) m 1959; Comr. BEd (Hons), MITD. Served at IHQ (CS to CoS and IS Eur), Soc S (GBI) (Leader) and in Switz (TC/TPWO).

G

GAUNTLETT, Caughey (Wood Green, UK, 1952, w wife, née Marjorie Markham); Comr. b 10 Aug 20. Served at ITC, in Zimb, Frce (CS), Ger (TC) and at IHQ (CoS).

GOODIER, William Robert Henry (Atlanta Temple, GA, 1941, w wife, née Renee L. Tilley); Comr. b 23 May 16. Served in USA S (CS), at USA Nat (CS), in Aus S (TC) and USA E (TC).

GOWANS, John General (1999-2002) (see page 26), and
GOWANS, Gisèle (née Bonhotal) (Paris Central, France, 1955) m 1957; Comr. Served in USA W, France (TPWO), Aus E (TPWO), UK (TPWO) and at IHQ (WPWM).

GRIFFIN, Joy (Maj Button, Tottenham Citadel, UK, 1957); Mrs Lt-Comr. Ww Lt-Comr Frederick, pG 1990.

GRINSTED, Dora (Lt Bottle, Sittingbourne, UK, 1950); Mrs Comr. Served in UK, Zam, Zimb, Jpn and at IHQ. Ww Comr David Ramsay, pG 1992.

H

HANNEVIK, Anna (Bergen 2, Nor, 1947); Comr. b 9 Aug 25. Served in Nor, UK, Swdn (TC) and at IHQ (IS Eur). Paul Harris Medal (1987), Commander of the Royal Order of the Northern Star (Sweden).

HANNEVIK, Edward (Oslo 3, Nor, 1954); Comr. b 6 Dec 32, and

HANNEVIK, Margaret (née Moody) (Newfield, UK, 1956) m 1958; Comr. Served in UK, Den (TC/TPWO), Nor (TC/TPWO) and at IHQ (IS/SWO Eur).

HARITA, Nozomi (Shibuya, Jap, 1966); Comr. b 10 May 39. BA (Mus), and
HARITA, Kazuko (née Hasegawa) (Shibuya, Jap, 1966) m 1969; Comr. b 19 Dec 37. BA (Ed). Served in Aus E and Jap (TC/TPWM).

HARRIS, Bramwell Wesley (Cardiff Stuart Hall, UK, 1948); Comr. b 25 Nov 28. m Capt Margaret Sansom (Barking, UK, 1949), 1955. Served in UK, Aus S (CS), at IHQ, in Scot (TC), NZ (TC) and Can (TC).

HAWKINS, Peter (Croydon Citadel, UK, 1948); Comr. b 16 Oct 29. FCIS, MBIM. m Lt Mary McElroy (Partick, UK, 1949) 1952. Served in UK and at IHQ (IS Finance).

HEDBERG, Lennart (Nykoping, Swdn, 1954); Comr. b 12 Oct 32, and
HEDBERG, Ingvor (née Fagerstedt) (Nykoping, 1955) m 1956; Comr. Served in Den, Swdn (TC/TPWO) and at IHQ (IS/SWO Eur).

HINSON, Harold D. (High Point, USA S, 1955); Comr. b 7 Sep 35, and
HINSON, Betty M. (née Morris) (New Orleans, LA, 1955); Comr. b 1 Jun 35. Served in USA C (TC/TPWO) and USA S (CS/THLS).

HODDER, Kenneth L. (San Francisco Citadel, CA, 1958); Comr. b 30 Oct 30. BA (Richmond), DSS (Hons) (Richmond) JD (California) and
HODDER, Marjorie J. (née Fitton) (San Francisco Citadel, CA, 1958). Served in USA W, USA C, Aus S (CS), USA S (TC/TPWO) and at USA Nat (NC).

HOLLAND, Louise (née Cruickshank) (Invercairn, UK, 1958); Mrs Comr. Served in UK, E Afr, Nig, Gha, Pak and at IHQ. Ww Comr Arthur, pG 1998.

HOOD, H. Kenneth (Denver Citadel, CO, 1954); Comr. b 27 Jan 33, and
HOOD, Barbara (née Johnson) (Pasadena, CA, 1952) m 1957; Comr. Served in USA W (CS), at USA Nat (CS/THLS) and in USA S (TC/TPWO).

HOWE, Norman (Dartford, UK, 1957); Comr. b 13 Aug 36, and
HOWE, Marian (née Butler) (Boscombe, UK, 1953) m 1959; Comr. b 9 Feb 30. Cert Ed. Served in UK, at ITC (Principal), in Aus S (TC/TPWO), Can (TC/TPWO) and at

IHQ (IS Prog Res/SWO Eur, General's Travelling Representative).

HUGUENIN, Willy (Le Locle, Switz, 1954); Comr. b 22 Sep 31, and
HUGUENIN, Miriam (née Luthi) (La Chaux-de-Fonds, 1953) m 1955. Served in Zaï (GS), Con (TC/TPWO), Switz (TC/TPWO) and at IHQ (IS/SWO Afr).

HUNTER, Denis (Poplar, UK, 1938); Comr. b 22 May 19. Served in Zimb (GS), NZ (CS), Scot (TC), at IHQ (IS S Pacific and Far East, IS Afr) and in BT (Brit Comr). MA (Cantab), O St J. Ww Mrs Comr Pauline, pG 2002.

I

IRWIN, Ronald G. (Philadelphia, PA, 1957); Comr. b 4 Aug 33. BS (Rutgers), MA (Columbia), and
IRWIN, Pauline (née Laipply) (Cincinnati, OH, 1953) m 1967; Comr. Served in USA W (CS/THLS) and USA E (TC/TPWO).

ISRAEL, Jillapegu (Peralipadu, 1957, w wife, Rachel née Amarthaluri); Comr. b 31 May 32. BA, BEd. Served in Ind M & A (CS/THLS), Ind N (TC/TPWO) and Ind SW (TC/TPWO).

K

KANG, Sung-hwan (Noh Mai Sil, Kyung Buk, Kor, 1973); Comr. b 15 Dec 39, with
LEE, Jung-ok m 1970; Comr. b 10 Nov 49. Served in Aus S and Kor (TC/TPWM).

KELLNER, Paul S. (Miami Citadel, FL, USA S, 1963); Comr. b 1 Sep 35. B Mus, with
KELLNER, Jajuan (née Pemberton); Comr. b 23 Feb 39. Served in USA S, Carib, Con (Braz) and Zimb (TC/TPWO).

KENDREW, K. Ross (Sydenham, NZ, 1962); Comr. b 7 Dec 38, and
KENDREW, Marion June (née Robb) (Wanganui, NZ, 1961) m 1964; Comr. b 8 Oct 39. Served in NZ (TC/TPWO) and Aus S (TC/TPWM).

KERR, Donald (Vancouver Temple, BC, Can, 1955); Comr. b 25 Oct 33, and
KERR, Joyce (née Knaap) (Mt Dennis, ON, 1955) m 1957; Comr. b 12 Jan 35. Served in UK (CS).

KIM, Suk-tai (Choon Chun, 1957); Comr. b 23 Jan 26. ThB, BA, MSoc. m Capt Lim, Jung-sun (Sudaemun, 1969) 1975. BMus. Served in Korea (TC).

KING, Margaret (Lt Coull, Fairview, 1936); Mrs Comr. Ww Comr Hesketh K., pG 1990.

L

LALTHANNGURA (Ratu, 1963); Comr. b 15 Sep 38. BA, with
KAPHLIRI; Comr. b 9 Sep 43. Served in Ind C (CS/THLS) and Ind E (TC/TPWM).

LANG, Ivan B. (Auburn, Aus S, 1967); Comr. b 18 Jul 40, with
LANG, Heather C. (née Luhrs) m 1961; Comr. b 8 Dec 42. Served in Sing (OC/CPWO), Aus E (CS/TSWO), at IHQ (IS/SWM SPEA) and in Aus S (TC/TPWM).

LARSSON, John General (2002-06) (see page 26), and
LARSSON, Freda (née Turner) (Kingston-upon-Thames, UK, 1964) m 1969; Comr. Served in S Am W (THLS), at ITC, in UK (TPWO), NZ (TPWO), Swdn (TPWO) and at IHQ (WSWM, WPWM).

LEE, Sung-duk (Cho Kang, 1963); Comr. b 10 Jun 35, with
CHO, In-sun (Taejon Central, 1963) m 1961; Comr. b 8 May 40. Served in Kor (TC/TPWO).

LIM, Ah Ang (Balestier Rd, Sing, 1954); Comr. b 30 May 32, and
LIM, Fong Pui Chan (Singapore Central, 1954) m 1958; Comr. Served in Sing, HK (OC/CPWO), Phil (TC/TPWO) and at IHQ (IS/SWO SPEA).

LINDBERG, Ingrid E. (Norrköping, Swdn, 1951); Comr. b 12 Dec 25. Served in Swdn, Zimb, Phil (OC), Den (TC) and Fin (TC).

LINNETT, Merle (Capt Clinch, Hindmarsh, 1947); Mrs Comr. Served in NZ, at IHQ, ITC, ICO and in Aus S. Ww Comr Arthur, pG 1986.

LOVATT, Olive (née Chapman) (Doncaster, UK, 1949); Mrs Comr. Served in UK, Aus S, Aus E & PNG and at IHQ. Ww Comr Roy, pG 2000.

LUTTRELL, Bill (Greeley, CO, USA W, 1958); Comr. b 4 Jul 38. BA Soc, and
LUTTRELL, Gwendolyn (née Shinn) (Long Beach, CA, USA W, 1961) m 1962; Comr. b 3 Sep 38. Served at IHQ (IS/SWO Am & Carib), in Can (TC/TPWM) and USA W (CS/TSWO and TC/TPWM).

LYSTER, Ingrid (Valerenga, Nor, 1947); Comr. b 7 Apr 22. Served in Nig, Zimb, Nor (CS) and at ICO (Principal). BA (S Afr).

M

MABENA, William (Bloemfontein, 1959); Comr, b 23 May 40, and
MABENA, Lydia (née Lebusho) (Bloemfontein, 1959) m 1960; Comr, b 25 Jun 39. Served in UK, S Afr (CS, TC/

THLS, TPWM), Gha (TC/TPWO) and at IHQ
(IS/SWO Afr).

MAILLER, Georges (Neuchatel, 1961); Comr.
b 9 Nov 36. BTh, with
MAILLER, Muriel (née Aeberli) m 1959;
Comr. b 15 Apr 35. Served at ESFOT
(Principal), in Frce and Switz (TC/TPWO).

MAKOUMBOU, Antoine (Bacongo, Con (Braz),
1968); Comr. b 2 Mar 40, with
MAKOUMBOU, Véronique (née Niangui) m
1967; Comr. b 30 Aug 46. Served in Con
(Braz) (TC/TPWM).

MANNAM, Samuel (Duggirala, 1946); Comr.
b 3 Jun 21. Served in Ind M & A (TC),
Ind W (TC), Ind SW (TC), Ind E (TC) and
Ind N (TC). Ww Mrs M., pG 1974.
m Maj Ruby Manuel (Leyton Citadel, UK,
1953) 1975.

MARSHALL, Marjorie (P/Lt Kimball) (New
York Temple, 1944); Mrs Comr. Served in
USA C, USA E, at USA Nat and at IHQ.
Ww Comr Norman S., pG 1995.

MARTI-JÖRGENSEN, Aase (née Jörgensen)
(Oslo, Nor, 1959); Comr. Served in Nor, Den,
Ger (TPWO) and Switz (TPWO). Ww Comr
Paul Marti, pG 1999.

MASIH, Mohan (Khundi, 1961); Comr.
b 29 Sep 39, with
MASIH, Swarni m 1958; Comr. b 14 Mar 42.
Served in Ind N (CS/THLS), Ind C (TC/
TPWO), Ind SW (TC/TPWO) and Ind W
(TC/TPWM).

MAXWELL, Earle Alexander (Orange, NSW,
Aus E, 1954); Comr. b 8 Jul 34. FCIS, ASA,
CPA, and
MAXWELL, Wilma (née Cugley)
(Camberwell, Vic, Aus S, 1956) m 1957;
Comr. Served in Sing (OC/CPWO), Aus E,
Phil (TC/TPWO), NZ (TC/TPWO) and at
IHQ (CoS/WSWO).

MILLER, Andrew S. (Newark, NJ, 1943);
Comr. b 14 Oct 23. Served in USA E, USA C
(CS), USA S (TC) and at USA Nat (NC).
BSc (Akron Univ, OH), Hon LLD (Asbury),
Hon LHD (Akron Univ, OH). m Lt Joan
Hackworth (Hamilton, OH, 1945) 1946.
Hon LHD (Wesley Biblical Seminary, MS).

MORGAN, K. Brian (Bairnsdale, Aus S, 1958);
Comr. b 5 Oct 37, and
MORGAN, Carolyn (née Bath) (Melville
Park, Aus S, 1958) m 1961; Comr. b 5 Mar 38.
Served in Rus/CIS (OC/CPWO), Aus S (CS/
TSWO) and Aus E (TC/TPWM).

MORRIS, Louise (née Holmes) (Charleston,
W VA, USA S, 1953) m 1957; Comr. Served

in USA S and Jpn (TPWO). Ww Comr Ted,
pG 2004.

MOYO, Gideon (Chikankata, 1963); Comr.
b 3 May 33. Served in Zam (GS) and Zimb
(TC). Ww Comr Lista, pG 2001.

MOYO, Selina (née Ndhlovu) (Bulayao Central,
1951); Mrs Comr. Served in Zimb (TPWO).
Ww Comr David, pG 2005.

N

NEEDHAM, Florence (née Jolly) (Baltimore 4,
MD, 1939); Mrs Comr. Served in USA S,
USA C, Carib and C Am, UK and at USA Nat.
Ww Comr John D., pG 1983.

NEEDHAM, Philip D. (Miami Citadel, USA S,
1969); Comr. b 5 Dec 40. BA (Rel), MDiv
ThM, DMin, with
NEEDHAM, Keitha (née Holz) m 1963;
Comr. b 9 Oct 41. BA (Ed). Served at ICO
(Principal), in USA W and USA S (TC/TPWM).

NELSON, John (Victoria Citadel, BC, Can,
1952); Comr. b 19 Aug 32, and
NELSON, Elizabeth (née McLean)
(Chatham, Ont, 1953) m 1956; Comr.
Served at IHQ (IS/SWO S Asia), in Can,
Carib and Pak (TC/TPWO).

NELTING, George L. (Brooklyn, Bushwick,
NY, 1942, w wife née Kathleen McKeag);
Comr. b 20 Jun 18. Served in USA E, at
USA Nat (CS), Neth (TC), at IHQ (IS Afr and
IS Far East) and in USA C (TC). Ww Mrs N.,
pG 1976. m Capt Juanita Prine (Cincinnati
Cent, OH, 1962) 1977.

NEWBERRY, Inez Margaret (Monroe, LA,
USA S, 1944); Comr. b 19 Mar 24. Served in
USA S, Sri Lan, Ind S, Ind NE, Ind M & A
(CS), Ind SE (TC) and Ind SW (TC).

NGUGI, Joshua (Nakuru, 1945); Comr.
b 29 Jan 16. Served in E Afr (TC). Ww Mrs
Comr Bathisheba, pG 2005.

NILSON, Birgitta K. (Boone, IA, USA C,
1964); Comr. b 2 Oct 37. AB (Chicago), MSW
(Loyola). Served in USA C, Swdn (TC) and at
IHQ (IS Eur).

NILSSON, Sven (Vansbro, 1940); Comr.
b 27 Jul 19. Served in Nor (CS), Den (TC)
and Swdn (TC). King's Medal (12th size),
Sweden (1983). m Capt Lisbeth Maria
Ohlqvist (Trelleborg, 1937) 1946.

NOLAND, Joseph J. (Santa Ana, CA, USA W,
1965); Comr. b 17 Jul 37. BA, MS, and
NOLAND, Doris (née Tobin) (Los Angeles
Congress Hall, CA, USA W, 1965) m 1966;
Comr. RN. Served in USA W, Aus E and USA
E (TC/TPWO).

NTUK, Joshua F. (Ibadan, 1969); Comr.
b 15 Jun 43, with
NTUK, Patience (née Ekpe); Comr. Served
in Nig (TC/TPWM).

NUESCH, Ruben D. (Rosario Cent, 1946);
Comr. b 28 Feb 21. Served in Brz (TC),
S Am W (TC) and S Am E (TC).
m 2/Lt Rosario Legarda (Bahia Blanca,
1946) 1948.

O

OLCKERS, Roy (Uitenhage, 1952); Comr.
b 16 Jul 29. Served in S Afr (TC). m Lt
Yvonne Holdstock (Fairview, 1952) 1955.

ORD, John (Easington Colliery, UK, 1948);
Comr. b 7 Sep 29. m Lt Lydie Deboeck
(Brussels, 1951) 1953. Served in Frce,
Belg (OC), at ITC, at ICO, in UK and
Nor (TC).

ORSBORN, Howard (Rutherglen, UK, 1940);
Comr. b 1 May 17. Served at ITC, in Can,
Aus S, NZ (CS), UK (CS), Swdn (TC) and
Aus E (TC). Ww Olive, pG 1967.
m Maj Amy Webb (Adelaide North, Aus S,
1951) 1968.

OSBORNE, James (Washington 3, DC, w wife
née Ruth Campbell, 1947); Comr. b 3 Jul 27.
Served in USA W (CS), USA S (TC) and at
USA Nat (NC).

ØSTERGAARD, Rigmor (née Hansen)
(Helsingør, 1944); m 1949; Mrs Comr. Served
in Fin, Den and at IHQ. Ww Comr Egon,
pG 2006.

P

PARKINS, May (Maj Epplett) (Seattle Citadel,
WA, 1951); Mrs Lt-Comr. Served in USA E,
USA S and USA W. Ww Lt-Comr William,
pG 1990.

PATTIPEILOHY, Blanche (née Sahanaja)
(Djakarta 1, 1955) m 1955; Mrs Comr. Served
in Indon. Ww Comr Herman G, pG 2000.

PATRAS, Gulzar (Punjgarian, Pak, 1973);
Comr. b 19 Aug 47, and
GULZAR, Sheila (née John) (Amritnagar, Pak,
1973) m 1973; Comr. b 22 Sep 46. Served in
Pak (TC/TPWM).

PENDER, Dinsdale L. (Bradford Temple, UK,
1953); Comr. b 22 Mar 32, and
PENDER, Winifred (née Dale)
(Godmanchester, UK, 1954) m 1955; Comr.
Served in NZ (CS/THLS), S Afr (CS/THLS
and TC/TPWO), Scot (TC/TPWO),
at IHQ, in Aus S (TC/TPWO) and UK
(TC/TPWO).

PINDRED, Gladys (Brig Dods, Kitsilano, BC,
1941); Mrs Comr. Served in Can and Carib.
Ww Comr Leslie, pG 1990.

PINTOS, Hugo D. (Patricios, S Am E, 1973);
Comr. b 15 Apr 53, and
PINTOS, Julia (née Duarte) (Del Puerto,
S Am E, 1972) m 1974; Comr. b 18 Dec 52.
Served in S Am E, L Am N (CS/TSWO) and
S Am W (TC/TPWM).

PITCHER, Arthur Ralph (St John's, NF,
1939); Comr. b 30 Oct 17. Served in S Afr
(CS), Carib (TC), USA S (TC) and Can (TC).
m Capt Elizabeth Evans (Bishop's Falls, NF,
1935) (b 1 Feb 14) 1942.

PRATT, William (Ilford, UK, 1947); Comr.
b 8 May 25. Served at IHQ, in BT (CS),
USA W (TC) and Can (TC). m Lt Kathleen
Lyons (Harlesden, UK, 1948) 1949.

R

RADER, Paul A. General (1994-1999) (see
page 25), with
RADER, Kay F. (née Fuller) m 1956; Comr.
BA (Asbury), Hon DD (Asbury Theol
Seminary), LHD (Hon) (Greenville) 1997,
Hon DD (Roberts Wesleyan) 1998. Served in
Kor (THLS), USA E (THLS), USA W (TPWO)
and at IHQ (WPWO).

RANGEL, Paulo (Rio Comprido, Brz, 1968);
Comr. b 19 Nov 41, Hon DD, and
RANGEL, Yoshiko (née Namba) (São Paulo,
Brz, 1967) m 1969; Comr. b 1 Sep 44. Served
in Brz (TC/TPWM).

READ, Harry (Edinburgh Gorgie, UK, 1948);
Comr. b 17 May 24. Served in UK, at IHQ,
ITC (Principal), Can (CS), Aus E (TC) and BT
(Brit Comr). m 2/Lt Winifred Humphries
(Mexborough, UK, 1948) 1950.

RIGHTMIRE, Robert S. (Cincinnati, USA E,
1946); Comr. b 23 Jun 24. Served in USA E,
S Afr (CS), Jpn (TC), Kor (TC) and USA C
(TC). m Capt Katherine Stillwell (Newark
Citadel, USA E, 1942) 1947.

RIVERS, William (Hadleigh Temple, UK,
1952); Comr. b 22 Dec 27. m 2/Lt Rose Ross
(Aberdeen Torry, UK, 1956) 1957. Served in
UK and at IHQ (IS Admin).

ROBERTS, William H. (Detroit Brightmoor,
MI, USA C, 1943); Comr. b 27 May 22.
Served in USA C, Aus S (CS) and at IHQ (IS
Americas and Carib and for Dev). BA (Wayne
State). m Lt Ivy Anderson (Marshalltown, IA,
USA C, 1943) 1945.

ROOS, Rolf (Uppsala, Swdn, 1962); Comr.
b 13 Nov 40, and

ROOS, Majvor (née Ljunggren) (Uppsala, Swdn, 1964) m 1965; Comr. b 15 Sep 38. Served in Fin (TC/TPWO) and Swdn (TC/TPWM).

RUTH, Fred L. (Shawnee, OK, 1955); Comr. b 21 Aug 35. BA (Georgia State), Dip Ed, MA (Counselling and Psychological Studies) (Trinity). Served in Kor, USA W, USA S , at USA Nat and IHQ (IS SPEA). Ww Sylvia (née Collins), pG 1990.

S

SAUNDERS, Robert F. (Philadelphia Pioneer, 1962); Comr. b 16 Jan 37. C Th (Fuller), and **SAUNDERS, Carol J.** (née Rudd) (Seattle Temple, 1966) m 1967. b 10 Sep 43. Served in Carib, USA E, USA W, Kor (CS/TSWO), Phil (TC/TPWO) and at IHQ (IS/SWO SPEA).

SCHURINK, Reinder J. (Zutphen, Neth, 1947); Comr. b 2 Dec 27. Officer Order of Orange Nassau (1987). m 2/Lt Henderika Hazeveld (Utrecht 1, 1950) 1951; pG 1961. Served in Ger (CS), Neth (TC) and Rus (Commander). Ww Mrs Comr Wietske, pG 1997. m Lt-Col Dora Verhagen, 1998.

SCOTT, Albert P. (Lawrence, MA, USA E, 1941); Comr. b 15 Oct 18. Served in USA E (CS) and at IHQ (IS Am and Carib, and IS Dev). Ww Mrs Dorothy, pG 1970. m Maj Frances O. Clark (Concord, NH, USA E, 1953) 1971.

SHIPE, Tadeous (Mukakatanwa, Zimb, 1969); Comr. b 13 Jul 43, and **SHIPE, Nikiwe** (née Jani) (Zimbara Zowa, Zimb, 1972) m 1972; Comr. b 24 Dec 49. Served in Zimb, Zam & Mal (TC/TPWM) and Zam (TC/TPWM).

SHOULTS, Harold (St Louis Tower Grove, MO, 1949); Comr. b 6 Mar 29. m Lt Pauline Cox (St Louis Tower Grove, MO, 1951) 1952. Served in USA E (CS), USA N (CS) and USA C (TC).

SKINNER, Verna E. (West End, Qld, Aus E, 1957); Comr. b 5 May 36. Served in Aus E, HK, Sri Lan (TC), Aus S (CS), at IHQ (IS Resources) and in E Afr (TC).

SMITH, Lawrence Robert (Portland Citadel, OR, 1936); Comr. b 28 May 15. Served in NZ (TC), at IHQ and in USA W (TC). m Lt Wilma Cherry (Portland Citadel, OR, 1937) 1939.

SOLHAUG, Karsten Anker (Sandvika, Nor, 1936); Comr. b 9 Nov 14. Kt, St Olav. Served in UK, Den (CS) and Nor (TC). Ww Else (née Brathen), pG 2006.

SUNDARAM, T. G. (Denduluru, 1963); Comr. b 1 Oct 35, with **SUNDARAM, Suseela** (née Thota) m 1955; Comr. b 16 Apr 36. Served in Ind C, Ind SE (TC/TPWO) and Ind W (TC/TPWO).

SWINFEN, John M. (Penge, UK, 1955); Comr. b 24 Jan 31. BA, Cert Ed, Chevalier de l'Ordre du Merite Exceptionnel (Congo), with **SWINFEN, Norma** (née Salmon); Comr. Served in Zimb, ITC, UK, E Afr (CS/THLS), Con (TC/TPWO) and at IHQ (IS/SWO Afr).

SWYERS, B. Gordon (Atlanta Temple, GA, 1959); Comr. b 25 Jul 36. BBA (Georgia State), and **SWYERS, Jacqueline** (née Alexander); Comr. b 25 Dec 29. Served in USA S and at IHQ (IS Admin/SWO SPEA).

T

TAYLOR, Margaret (née Overton) (Aylsham, UK, 1962); Comr. Served in UK, E Afr, Pak and at IHQ (IS Prog Res). Ww Comr Brian, pG 2004.

TAYLOR, Orval A. (Seattle Citadel, USA W, 1940); Comr. b 21 May 19. Served in USA W, USA S, USA N (CS), Carib (TC), at IHQ (IS Planning and Dev) and USA E (TC). m Capt Muriel Upton (Long Beach, USA W, 1937) 1943.

THOMPSON, Arthur T. (Croydon Citadel, UK, 1961); Comr. b 23 Dec 32. BSc, PhD, PGCE, Freeman of the City of London, and **THOMPSON, Karen** (née Westergaard) (Camberwell, 1961) m 1962; Comr. BA, PGCE. Served in Zimb, Zam, UK, NZ (CS/THLS) and at IHQ (IS Admin/IS Res, SWO Eur).

THOMSON, Robert E. (Racine, WI, w wife née Carol Nielsen, 1951); Comr. b 21 Feb 28. BM (St Olaf); Mrs T. BA (St Olaf). Served at USA Nat, in USA C (CS), at IHQ (IS Am and Carib) and in USA E (TC).

TILLSLEY, Bramwell Howard General (1993-94) (see page 25), with **TILLSLEY, Maud** (née Pitcher). Mrs General. Served in Can, at ITC, in USA S, Aus S (TPWO) and at IHQ (WSWO, WPWO).

TONDI, Roos (née Mundung) (Sonder, Indon, 1958) m 1967; Comr. Served in Aus S and Indon (TPWO). Ww Comr Victor, pG 2002.

V

VERWAAL, Sjoerdje (née Zoethout) (Zaandam, 1947); Mrs Comr. Ww Comr Cornelis, pG 2002.

W

WAHLSTROM, Astrid (Lt Gronlund, Helsinki, 1936); Mrs Comr. Served in UK, Fin, S Am E and at IHQ. Ww Comr Per-Erik, pG 1995.

WAHLSTRÖM, Maire (née Nyberg) (Helsinki 1, Fin, 1944); Mrs General. Served in Fin, Swe, Can and at IHQ. Ww General Jarl Wahlström, pG 1999.

WALTER, Alison (née Harewood) (Calgary Citadel, AB, 1955); Mrs Comr. Served in Zimb, E Afr, Can, S Afr and at IHQ. Ww Comr Stanley, pG 2004.

WATERS, Margaret (née Eastland) (Niagara Falls, 1953); Comr. b 1 Mar 34. Served in Can and at IHQ. Ww Comr Arthur W., pG 2002.

WATILETE, Johannes G. (Bandung 3, Indon, 1963); Comr. b 9 Sep 41. BA, MTh, DTh, DMin (HC) and

WATILETE, Augustina (née Sarman) (Bandung 3, Indon, 1962) m 1966; Comr. b 16 Aug 39. Served in Sing (GS/CHLS), Phil (CS/THLS and TC/TPWO) and Indon (TC/TPWM).

WATSON, Robert A. (Philadelphia Pioneer, PA, USA E, 1955); Comr. b 11 Aug 34, and

WATSON, Alice (née Irwin) (Philadelphia Pioneer, PA, USA E, 1956) m 1957; Comr. Served in USA E (CS/THLS) and at USA Nat (NC/NPWO).

WICKBERG, Eivor (Maj Lindberg, Norrköping 1, Swdn, 1946); Mrs General. Ww General Erik Wickberg, pG 1996.

WILLIAMS, Harry William George (Wood Green, UK, 1934); Comr. b 13 Jul 13. Served in Ind W, Ind NE, Ind S (TC), NZ (TC), Aus E (TC) and at IHQ (IS Am and Australasia, IS Planning and Dev). OBE (1970), FRCS (Edin), FICS. Ww Eileen M., pG 2002.

Y

YOHANNAN, Paulose (Kalayapuram, Ind SW, 1974); Comr, b 1 Dec 45. MA (Sociol), DD, PhD, with

YOHANNAN, Kunjamma (née Jesaiah) m 1966; Comr. b 15 Jun 47. Served in Ind SW, Ind E, Ind SE (TC/TPWM) and Ind N (TC/TPWM).

YOSHIDA, Ai (née Yamamoto) (Kyoto, Jap, 1934) m 1939; Mrs Comr. Ww Comr Shinichi, pG 2004.

The retirement thanksgiving service for General John Larsson and Commissioner Freda Larsson was held at International Headquarters in March 2006. During the informal gathering the Larssons' retirement certificates were presented by Retired General John Gowans (left), who paid warm tribute to his successor's multifarious gifts.

Promotions to Glory

AUSTRALIA EASTERN

Aux-Capt Olwyn Cantrill (née Packer) on
11 Aug 2005
Brig John Beasy on 18 Sept 2005
Mrs Lt-Col Kathleen Spillett (née Hill) on
25 Sep 2005
Mrs Brig Elsie McCabe (née Collins) on
25 Sep 2005
Maj Joyce Armstrong on 20 Oct 2005
Brig George Merton on 25 Oct 2005
Mrs Brig Ena Reeves (née Stace) on 25 Oct 2005
Maj Thomas Hubbard on 7 Nov 2005
Lt-Col Jean Todd (née Coleman) on
10 Nov 2005
Aux-Capt Pat Holley (née Pearson) on 24 Nov
2005
Mrs Major Miriam Pratt (née Cugley) on
1 Dec 2005
Mrs Brig Joyce Moore (née Collett) on
8 Jan 2006
Brig Marjorie Dinnes on 12 Jan 2006
Maj Edgar Smith on 20 Feb 2006
Mrs Lt-Col Lillian Whitehouse (née Miller) on
3 Mar 2006
Capt Abel Berry on 13 Mar 2006
Brig Fred Reeves on 22 Mar 2006
Comr Robert Bath on 7 Apr 2006
Mrs Brig Lorna Richards (née MacDonald) on
28 May 2006
Mrs Major Ruth Skinner (née Eldridge) on
3 Jul 2006
Mrs Brig May Prussing (née Shorney) on
5 Jul 2006
Mrs Lt-Col Lillian Schoupp (née Hemingway)
on 23 Jul 2006

AUSTRALIA SOUTHERN

Brig Roy Wright on 3 Aug 2005
Brig Jessie Barfoot on 5 Aug 2005
Maj Pearl Smith on 6 Aug 2005
Lt-Col Ruth Wilkins on 2 Sep 2005
Maj Aurial Austin on 9 Sep 2005
Maj Malcolm Messenger on 5 Oct 2005
Maj Kenneth Aumont on 31 Oct 2005
Lt-Col Peter Rigley on 3 Nov 2005
Brig Mavis Sapwell on 12 Nov 2005
Lt-Col Rowland Hill on 20 Jan 2006
Brig Winifred Sumsion on 28 Feb 2006
Maj Edna Exon on 13 Mar 2006
Col Eva Beasy on 15 Mar 2006
Brig Edgar Smith on 27 Apr 2006
Maj Douglas Christian on 25 May 2006
Maj Shirley Sampson on 26 May 2006

CANADA AND BERMUDA

Capt John Walter on 17 Sep 2005
Capt Darrell Newbury on 13 Oct 2005
Mrs Capt Elva MacKenzie on 11 Aug 2005
Brig Victor MacLean on 29 Sep 2005
Mrs Brig Effie Patey on 19 Oct 2005
Maj Albert Benjamin on 26 Oct 2005
Lt-Col James Sloan on 26 Oct 2005
Brig Ruth Naugler on 27 Oct 2005
Brig Alice Ebsary on 29 Oct 2005
Maj Bryn Jones on 14 Nov 2005
Maj Thomas Bell on 21 Nov 2005
Mrs Maj Dorothy Amos on 21 Nov 2005
Mrs Brig R. (Lorraine) White on 27 Nov 2005
Mrs Brig H. (Ruby) Corbett on 2 Dec 2005
Mrs Maj Ruth Gardner on 5 Dec 2005
Mrs Brig A. (Theresa) McInnes on
7 Dec 2005
Maj Lorne Jannison on 8 Dec 2005
Lt-Col John Smith on 6 Jan 2006
Maj Jose Garcia on 9 Feb 2006
Maj Phyllis Canavan on 18 Feb 2006
Mrs Brig P. (Sarah) Johnson on 8 Mar 2006
Mrs Aux-Capt W. (Norman) Young on
18 Mar 2006
Maj Keith Hall on 20 Mar 2006
Mrs Maj Clara Thompson on 24 Mar 2006
Maj Mrs Joyce Mitchell on 1 Apr 2006
Maj Evelyn Townsend on 1 Apr 2006
Mrs Maj Eva Brightwell on 7 Apr 2006
Brig Frances Hillier on 9 Apr 2006
Maj Allan Pittock on 9 May 2006
Lt-Col Melvin Hamilton on 15 May 2006
Maj Jean Cameron on 30 May 2006
Capt Victor Machado on 14 Jun 2006
Aux-Capt Gerald Hynes on 16 Jun 2006
Lt-Col J. Bramwell Meakings on 11 Jul 2006
Maj Connie van der Horden on 15 Jul 2006
Mrs Maj Isabella Peck on 24 Jul 2006
Aux-Capt Edwin Howell on 13 Aug 2006

CARIBBEAN

Maj Agatha Williams on 7 Jun 2005
Maj Mavis Tathum on 6 Mar 2006

CONGO BRAZZAVILLE

Maj Victor Sita on 9 Oct 2005
Maj Jean Taty on 11 Nov 2005

CONGO (KINSHASA) AND ANGOLA

Maj Madeleine Nsansi Kabeya on 9 Dec 2005
Maj Simon Lumanakio on 15 Feb 2006
Maj Henriette Masola on 21 Feb 2006

DENMARK
Brig Rosa Antvorskov on 2 Feb 2006
Comr Egon Østergaard on 26 Feb 2006

FINLAND AND ESTONIA
Maj Ritva Mäki on 25 Aug 2005
Maj Hjördis Backman on 13 Apr 2006

FRANCE
Lt-Col Mathilde Wälly on 23 Aug 2005
Commandant Henri Thöni on 19 Sep 2005
Maj Jean Kuhn on 16 Oct 2005
A/Capt Michel Chastagnier on 3 Dec 2005
Lt-Col Yvonne Escande on 23 Feb 2006
Maj Claude Kuhn on 21 Mar 2006

GERMANY AND LITHUANIA
Brig Ursula Büttner on 5 Apr 2006

GHANA
Maj Isaac Duku on 23 Mar 2006

INDIA CENTRAL
Lt-Col M.Rama Rao on 21 May 2005
Maj J. Premanandam on 26 Aug 2005
Maj T.Ahalyabai on 5 Oct 2005
Maj T.Devadas on 7 Mar 2006

INDIA EASTERN
Maj Thansanga on 19 Oct 2005
Maj Khumtea from Kolasib on 30 Nov 2005

INDIA NORTHERN
Mrs Brig Nannia Kundan Parshad on 28 Jul 2005
Maj Rahmat Masih on 19 Sep 2005
Maj Prakash Ghosh on 22 Oct 2005
Lt-Col Parveen Daniel on 12 Nov 2005
Lt-Col Rahmat Masih on 1 Feb 2006
Maj Inayat Masih on 19 Apr 2006
Maj Ajit Masih on 19 Apr 2006
Maj Santosh Sulakhan Masih on 11 Jun 2006

INDIA SOUTH EASTERN
Sen-Capt Chellammal on 9 Jun 2005
Maj Masilamony on 25 Jul 2005
Maj Dhayamony Arumanayagam on 19 Nov 2005
Maj Kamalam Swamidhas on 5 Dec 2005
Maj R Jacob (A) from Odupurai on 6 Feb 2006
Maj Nesabai Jacob on 26 Feb 2006
Maj Kamalam Gnanaseelan on 9 Apr 2006

INDIA SOUTH WESTERN
Lt-Col C. A. David on 2 Aug 2005
Maj Thankamma Joel on 3 Aug 2005

Brig Aley David on 1 Nov 2005
Maj M. D. Pathrose on 5 Nov 2005
Maj P. K. Devadasan on 20 Nov 2005
Maj P. M. Jose (A) from Mannamaruthy on 29 Dec 2005
Maj Rachel Mannuel on 29 Dec 2005
Maj Nesabai Francis on 18 Jan 2006
Maj M. D. Deveadas on 26 Feb 2006
Maj V. S. Samuel on 2 Mar 2006
Maj K. C. Peter (A) from Puthuchira on 12 Apr 2006

INDIA WESTERN
Mrs Brig Shantabai R. Kapadia on 9 Jan 2006
Maj Bhujang Salve on 6 Apr 2006
Mrs Maj Rangubai P. Ghadge on 14 Apr 2006
Mrs Maj Sumatibai D. Salve on 16 Apr 2006
Capt Michael Kadam on 19 Jun 2006
Maj Dashrath Gajbhiv on 23 Jun 2006

INDONESIA
Maj Mona Barani on 5 Jul 2005
Maj Matius Salimin (A) on 4 Sep 2005
Lt-Col Laura Tan Prasetyo on 20 Sep 2005
Sen-Captain Martina Agustina Leimena on 16 Oct 2005
Maj Martha Jatu on 28 Nov 2005
Lt-Col Estefanus Simatupang on 26 Mar 2006
Maj Saliy Higgi on 26 Apr 2006
Maj Peter Theosadrach on 16 Jun 2006

JAPAN
Brig Kazuo Nagura on 2 Sep 2005
Brig Kosaburo Soraoka on 4 Dec 2005
Brig Juzo Furukawa on 1 Jun 2006

KENYA
Maj Zakayo Kyengo on 16 Oct 2005
Mrs Comr Bathisheba Ngugi on 25 Nov 2005
Maj Elisheba Nyaga on 9 Jan 2006
Maj Naumi Kiduyu on 11 Jan 2006
Maj Joram Kapukha on 12 Mar 2006
Capt Wilson Ebiteru (A) on 25 Mar 2006
Maj Airen Mudanya (A) on 16 Apr 2006
Maj Francis Munyisia on 20 Apr 2006
Lt-Col Richard Simiyu on 2 Jun 2006
Maj Charles Aboka (A) on 8 Jun 2006

KOREA
Maj Kim, Ko-chul on 12 Jan 2006
Maj Oh, Taek-hwan on 16 Jan 2006

THE NETHERLANDS AND CZECH REPUBLIC
Lt-Col Jan Th. Ligtelijn on 27 Aug 2004
Brig Trijntje Stierman on 2 Sep 2004

Mrs Brig Maria C.E. van Erven (neé Bos) on
27 Nov 2004
Brig Johan A. Lodder on 4 Dec 2004
Maj Maria T. J. Bulterman on 13 Dec 2004
Mrs Brig Anje van Loon (neé Venema) on
7 Jan 2005
Maj Cornelis J. Spek on 1 Mar 2005
Brig Gerritje Visser on 6 May 2005
Maj Aaltje Nijhof on 13 Jun 2005
Maj Trijntje de Heus (née Visser) on 27 Jul 2005
Maj Jantje Veldman on 14 Dec 2005
Maj Dina C. J. Mekke on 26 Jan 2006
Maj Josephina Schram (née Copier) on
15 Mar 2006
Maj Fennechien Vos on 20 Mar 2006
Brig Johanna P. Akkerman on 21 Mar 2006
Brig Baukje Tjeertes on 2 Apr 2006
Maj Maria Liplijn on 7 Jun 2006
Maj Fokje Kuper (née Scholtens) on
19 Jun 2006

NEW ZEALAND, FIJI AND TONGA
Lt-Col E. Rodney Knight on 22 Aug 2005
Mrs Comr Lady Marjorie Goffin (née Barney)
on 19 Sep 2005
Brig A. Blanche Christopher on 27 Sep 2005
Brig Owen Ojala on 12 Oct 2005
Capt Janie Smith (A) (née Mettam) from
Christchurch on 12 Oct 2005
Aux-Capt Bruce White on 1 Nov 2005
Brig Nathaniel Jones on 13 Dec 2005
Brig Margaret Mounsey on 19 Jan 2006
Maj Edna Newton on 30 Jan 2006

NORWAY, ICELAND AND THE FÆROES
Maj Willy Olsen on 12 Aug 2005
Brig Jessie Adolfsen on 21 Oct 2005
Maj Anna Løwik on 17 Nov 2005
Maj Ågot Thalerød on 17 Dec 2005
Lt-Col Ole Andreas Evja on 21 Dec 2005
Brig Dagny Paulsen on 30 Dec 2005
Maj Fredrikke Nilsen on 24 Jan 2006
Maj Eva Olsen on 5 Feb 2006
Maj Jofrid Lavoll on 19 Feb 2006
Maj Gudny Rasmussen on 5 Mar 2006
Maj Ruth Wunderlich on 7 Mar 2006
Mrs Comr Else Solhaug on 8 May 2006
Mrs Brig Borgny Vinje on 7 Jun 2006
Maj Gudrun Bertheussen on 1 Jul 2006
Mrs Lt-Col Ruth Kvam on 11 Jul 2006

PAKISTAN
Capt Akeel Shakar (A) from Jhang on
17 Oct 2005
Maj Sana Ullah (A) from Lahore on 11 Nov 2005

Maj Ashiq Inayat (A) from Behar Colony on
6 Jun 2006

PAPUA NEW GUINEA
Maj Hane Ali on 21 Jan 2006

SOUTH AMERICA WEST
Lt-Col Jorge Nery, OF, on 15 Jul 2005
Maj Miguel Inostroza on 28 Apr 2006
Maj José Jacob on 2 May 2006

SOUTHERN AFRICA
Maj Andries Mlaba on 13 Jul 2005
Maj Dinah Mbhele in Aug 2005
Maj Annie Mngwenya on 11 Dec 2005
Maj Ernest Jones (A) from THQ on 1 Jan 2006
Maj Aaron Themba in Apr 2006
Maj Martha Masuku on 27 Apr 2006

SRI LANKA
Mrs Brig A. Devasagayam on 17 May 2006

SWEDEN AND LATVIA
Brig Eric Lindgren on 19 Oct 2004
Mrs Brig Astrid Kronberg (née Hedlund) on
5 Nov 2004
Mrs Brig Ingrid Åberg (née Olson) on
14 Nov 2004
Mrs Lt-Col Edith Lundell (née Lundberg) on
19 Nov 2004
Mrs Maj Elsa Arnefalk (née Österlund) on
2 Dec 2004
Mrs Brig Maria Karlsson (née Fjällström) on
3 Dec 2004
Lt-Col John Löfgren on 21 Dec 2004
Mrs Maj Karin Lyredahl (née Danielsson) on
30 Dec 2004
Mrs Maj Alice Ström (née Björk) on 8 Jan 2005
Maj Jan Holten on 23 Feb 2005
Brig Alfhild Andersson on 10 April 2005
Mrs Lt-Col Britta Lebenius on 14 Apr 2005
Brig Astrid Dalsgaard on 8 May 2005
Maj Maja Anderzon on 12 May 2005
Mrs Brig Runa Öberg (née Borg) on 6 Jun 2005
Brig Ingar Larsson on 21 Jul 2005
Sen-Capt Signe Sjöö on 16 Aug 2005
Mrs Brig Britta Janson (née Johansson) on
9 Sep 2005
Mrs Lt-Col Doris Nöjd (née Peterson) on
12 Sep 2005
Brig Margareta Bäckström on 26 Sep 2005
Mrs Brig Anna-Lisa Åkesson (née Karlsson) on
30 Oct 2005
Brig Mary Hagelin on 4 Dec 2005
Brig Elsie Andersson on 14 Dec 2005

Mrs Lt-Col **Eln Henriksson** (née Nilsson) on
  31 Jan 2006
Maj **Tora-Lisa Westman** (née Närlund) on
  1 Feb 2006
Mrs Brig **Stina Svensson** (née Lundbom) on
  8 Mar 2006
Brig **Stina Blomgren** on 12 Mar 2006
Maj **Ingrid Palmeroth** (née Westman) on
  13 Mar 2006
Maj **Elsie Pettersson** (née Ottoson) on
  19 Mar 2006
Maj **Margit Hjort** on 9 Apr 2006
Brig **Sonja Hofman** on 6 Jun 2006
Brig **Hilda Johansson** on 16 Jun 2006
Maj **Gunnel Elofsson** on 17 Jun 2006
Mrs Brig **Elisabet Ehnstedt** on 18 Jun 2006
Brig **Anna-Stina Högberg** on 18 Jun 2006
Lt-Col **Fred Byhlin** on 29 Jun 2006
Maj **Ulla Dahlberg** on 15 Jul 2006
Maj **Sture Öquist** on 9 Aug 2006

SWITZERLAND, AUSTRIA AND HUNGARY

Maj **Maria Hollenweger** on 5 May 2005
Maj **Elfriede Breiter-Ott** on 7 Jun 2005
Brig **Ruth Hanselmann-Vallotton** on 6 Sep 2005
Maj **Getrud Schütz** on 13 Oct 2005
Brig **Sophie Erzberger-Schulthess** on
  22 Oct 2005
Brig **Frieda Stalder-Schildknecht** on
  17 Nov 2005
Maj **Frieda Siegrist** on 15 Dec 2005
Maj **Katharina Jakob-Rupp (A)** from Thun on
  18 Jan 2006
Maj **Rosa Baumann** on 7 Mar 2006

UNITED KINGDOM WITH THE REPUBLIC OF IRELAND

Comr **Brian Taylor (A)**, IHQ, from Long Beach,
  California, USA, on 12 Oct 2004
Maj **Lynda Snaith (A)** from Coventry on
  18 Dec 2004
Maj **Patricia Hubbell (A)** from London on
  11 Mar 2005
Mrs Maj **Margaret Shaw** on 9 Sep 2005
Maj **Doris Turrell** on 17 Sep 2005
Mrs Brig **Miriam Turtle** on 17 Sep 2005
Col **Patricia Logan** on 19 Sep 2005
Mrs Maj **Eleanor Saltwell** on 23 Sep 2005
Mrs Lt-Col **Ethel Roberts** on 1 Oct 2005
Brig **Florence Morgan** on 7 Oct 2005
Mrs Brig **Brenda Ford** on 23 Oct 2005
Mrs Maj **Rose South** on 10 Nov 2005
Maj **Pearl Woodford** on 14 Nov 2005
Mrs Brig **Florence Spillett** on 18 Nov 2005

Brig **Charles Geleit** on 21 Nov 2005
Mrs Brig **Betty Wallace** on 4 Dec 2005
Maj **Reginald Watts** on 5 Dec 2005
Maj **H. Sydney Moore** on 7 Dec 2005
Maj **Stanley Wordley** on 10 Dec 2005
Maj **Lynda Snaith (A)** from Coventry on
  18 Dec 2004
Mrs Col **Muriel Holdstock** on 23 Dec 2005
Maj **Iris Port** on 27 Dec 2005
Brig **Kathleen Axon** on 4 Jan 2006
Brig **Alfred Chaloner** on 6 Jan 2006
Col **Colin Logan** on 8 Jan 2006
Lt-Col **William Boyes** on 9 Jan 2006
Mrs Brig **Mary Helm** on 12 Jan 2006
Mrs Brig **Jane Hollingworth** on 25 Jan 2006
Brig **Grace Raeside** on 25 Jan 2006
Brig **Joyce Jones** on 28 Jan 2006
Maj **Doris Slinn (A)** from Sutton on
  1 Feb 2006
Mrs Brig **Mildred Piper** on 3 Feb 2006
Mrs Maj **Elizabeth Murray** on 5 Feb 2006
Mrs Brig **Ruby Griffiths** on 6 Feb 2006
Mrs Brig **Gertrude (Ena) Parker** on 8 Feb 2006
Mrs Brig **Evelyn Johnson** on 18 Feb 2006
Mrs Maj **Ruth Saunders** on 21 Feb 2006
Brig **Gladys Old** on 27 Feb 2006
Mrs Maj **Kathleen Watts** on 4 Mar 2006
Maj **S. John Simons** on 6 Mar 2006
Maj **Raymond Harkcom** on 15 Mar 2006
Mrs Brig **Ellen Dunkley** on 20 Mar 2006
Col **Doris French** on 23 Mar 2006
Mrs Lt-Col **Mildred Long** on 30 Mar 2006
Maj **John Izzard** on 1 Apr 2006
Aux-Capt **Gordon Butcher** on 1 Apr 2006
Maj **Margaret Perryman** on 4 Apr 2006
Maj **Dianne Smith** on 5 Apr 2006
Maj **Leonard Cooper** on 8 Apr 2006
Maj **Kenneth Dixon** on 8 Apr 2006
Maj **William Eric Malpas** on 20 Apr 2006
Brig **Maud Flounders** on 28 Apr 2006
Maj **May Ramage** on 6 May 2006
Mrs Comr **Keren Ward** on 6 May 2006
Brig **Keith Anderson** on 13 May 2006
Mrs Brig **Elizabeth Bruce** on 24 May 2006
Lt-Col **Gordon Knapman** on 24 May 2006
Brig **Ena Catley** on 29 May 2006
Lt-Col **J. Alfred Holmes** on 30 May 2006
Maj **Albert Clifton** on 30 May 2006
Maj **Robert Huggins** on 11 Jun 2006
Mrs Brig **Edna Elliott** on 16 Jun 2006
Mrs Brig **Mary Mitchell** on 26 Jun 2006
Mrs Brig **Doris Snell** on 5 Jul 2006
Brig **Annie Duncan** on 19 Jul 2006
Col **Helen Kelman** on 20 Jul 2006
Mrs Brig **Helen Smith** on 28 Jul 2006

Maj Bramwell Bower on 13 Aug 2006
Maj Jess McAulay (A) from Stirling on
29 Aug 2006

USA CENTRAL
Mrs Maj Harold (Ida) Petrie on
25 May 2005
Maj John Anderson on 11 Jun 2005
Lt-Col Helen Waara on 23 Jun 2005
Mrs Brig Albert (Marjory) Koch on
26 Jun 2005
Brig Hubert Amick on 5 Jul 2005
Maj Mabel Frost on 8 Jul 2005
Maj Rothwell Stickley on 9 Jul 2005
Lt-Col Arthur E. Weir on 12 Jul 2005
Mrs Col John (Mildred) Paton on
31 Jul 2005
Maj Angel Rodriguez on 31 Jul 2005
Brig Dorothy Kemp on 16 Aug 2005
Maj Hallie Hickey on 29 Aug 2005
Maj Robert Greenleaf on 6 Sep 2005
Capt Sharon Young (A) from Scotts, MI, on
19 Sep 2005
Maj Pamela Phillips on 1 Oct 2005
Maj Roy Tompkins on 25 Sep 2005
Maj Mrs Louisa Merritt on 16 Nov 2005
Mrs Brig John (Maggie) Potter on
10 Dec 2005
Maj John G. Sullivan on 10 Dec 2005
Maj David Zahn on 10 Dec 2005
Mrs Sen-Maj Lawrence (Minnie) Hall on
18 Dec 2005
Lt-Col Merle L. Heatwole on 20 Dec 2005
Brig David M. Paton on 25 Dec 2005
Mrs Maj James (Nellie) Shiels on 1 Mar 2006
Mrs Maj W. Robert (Rosamond) Wilkins on
27 Mar 2006
Brig Albert E. Koch on 4 Apr 2006
Mrs Maj Arthur V. (Inger) Johnson on
7 Apr 2006
Maj Robert W. Stigleman on 8 Apr 2006
Lt-Col Pearl Norberg on 12 May 2006

USA EASTERN
Lt-Col Olof Lundgren on 17 Sep 2005
Mrs Brig Hannah M. Harvey on 20 Oct 2005
Mrs Brig Annie M. Van Gould on
20 Oct 2005
Maj Shirley H. Parkinson on 13 Nov 2005
Maj Mrs Dorothy Obitz on 24 Nov 2005
Maj Elizabeth A. Miles on 24 Dec 2005
Maj Edwin Beck on 29 Dec 2005
Maj Doris Davison on 4 Jan 2006
Mrs Brig Elzen Hawley on 24 Jan 2006
Mrs Brig Helen C. Eden on 21 Feb 2006

Brig Thelma L. Dundon on 18 Mar 2006
Mrs Maj Idabelle Crouch on 8 Apr 2006
Maj James R. Watson on 23 Apr 2006
Maj Barbara J. Wheeler on 26 Apr 2006
Mrs Brig Olive T. Hulihan on 22 May 2006
Brig Nathaniel F. Moody on 28 May 2006
Maj Gertrude A. Crawford on 13 Jul 2006
Mrs Brig Doris Hathorn on 27 Jul 2006
Maj Robert E. Waldron on 30 Jul 2006
Maj Kenneth C. Lance on 15 Aug 2006
Maj Mrs Helen Sinclair on 24 Aug 2006

USA SOUTHERN
Maj Mary Deveaux on 31 Aug 2005
Brig Janie Blanchard on 13 Sep 2005
Capt Devlin Thompson on 1 Oct 2005
Capt Matthew Mockabee (A) from Lufkin, TX,
on 1 Oct 2005
Mrs Maj Rachel Emily Hall on 6 Oct 2005
Brig Mary Eupha Gibson on 16 Oct 2005
Maj Otis Street on 28 Oct 2005
Mrs Brig Ruth Sheppard on 19 Dec 2005
Brig Elsie Shirley on 3 Jan 2006
Maj Olga Pinder on 26 Feb 2006
Maj Carlene Melton on 4 Mar 2006
Mrs Brig George (Mabel) Clendenan on
10 Mar 2006
Mrs Maj Helen Sigmon on 28 Mar 2006
Mrs Maj Arthur (Madeline) Kinlaw on
2 Apr 2006
Brig James H. Prout on 15 Jun 2006
Mrs Lt-Col Pauline Askey on 16 Jun 2006
Brig Dorothy Langston on 21 Jul 2006
Mrs Maj MaeBelle Tanner on 16 Jul 2006
Maj Earl Short on 13 Aug 2006
Mrs Maj Jeannette Frances Tritton on
27 Aug 2006
Mrs Maj Christine Wixon on 30 Aug 2006

USA WESTERN
Brig Joan Crombie on 18 Aug 2005
Maj Helen Nightingale on 25 Sep 2005
Lt-Col Muriel Collier on 8 Oct 2005
Brig James Watt on 28 Nov 2005
Brig Judy Watt on 24 Dec 2005
Mrs Capt Louise Helton on 2 Feb 2006
Aux-Capt Harlan Nelson on 8 Feb 2006
Capt Naomi Johnson on 14 Feb 2006
Mrs Brig Alta W. Kelso on 26 Feb 2006
Maj Herbert (Reg) Peacock on 2 Apr 2006
Mrs Comr Marion Westcott on 16 Apr 2006
Mrs Maj Grazia Graham on 12 May 2006
Maj Salvador Gomez on 2 Jun 2006
Lt-Col Charles M. McIntyre on 23 Jun 2006
Maj Larry Fankhauser on 18 Jul 2006

Maj Robert Pontsler on 28 Jul 2006
Brig Antonio Alquiza on 17 Aug 2006
Maj Dolores L. Bunch on 21 Aug 2006

ZAMBIA
Capt Henry Mapulanga on 24 Jul 2005

ZIMBABWE
Maj L. Seremwe (A) from Matabeleland
Division on 30 Jul 2005

Maj S. Tagwirei on 2 Aug 2005
Maj J. Chirebvu on 25 Sep 2005
Maj Kwaramba on 3 Oct 2005
Maj S.Nkomo (A) from Hurungwe Division on
14 Nov 2005
Envoy Kasaira (A) from Makonde Division
on 18 Nov 2005
Maj Tavarwisa on 23 Nov 2005
Maj N. Mavindidze on 30 Jan 2006
Capt N. Kandengwa in Jun 2006

PROMOTED TO GLORY

THERE are many descriptions to soften the harshness of the word 'death' but one of the most radical is the Army's descriptive phrase, 'promoted to Glory'. It sounds a triumphant, positive note in support of the Army's belief in eternal life, Heaven and an unending period in Glory with the Father. It declares incontrovertibly that death is not the end, but the beginning of a new and glorious experience for those redeemed by the blood of Jesus Christ.

The term was first used in *The War Cry* of 14 December 1882, at a time when so many other military phrases were being introduced following the advent of the name 'The Salvation Army' four years earlier. It seems to have found ready acceptance and soon entered common usage.

It was also consistent with the Founder's dislike of sombre black clothing as a sign of mourning. He believed that, while Christ sympathises with sorrow, he desires to make personal tragedy a stepping stone to greater faith by seeing death as a victory.

LEGACIES

THE Salvation Army is competent to receive bequests of money and property for its general purposes and for the benefit of any branch of its worldwide evangelical and social services. Further information about any aspect of Salvation Army work or advice regarding clauses providing bequests for specific objects will gladly be supplied on request to the Finance Secretary, The Salvation Army International Headquarters, 101 Queen Victoria Street, London EC4P 4EP, United Kingdom, or any territorial or command headquarters.

Abbreviations used in *The Year Book*

A

(A) (active officer pG); Acc (Accommodation); Afr (Africa); Am (America); AO (Area Officer); Apt (Apartment); Appt (Appointment); ARC (Adult Rehabilitation Centre); Asst (Assistant); Aus (Australia); A/Capt (Auxiliary-Captain).

B

b (born); Ban (Bangladesh); Belg (Belgium); B/M (Bandmaster); Braz (Brazzaville); Brig (Brigadier); Brz (Brazil); BT (British Territory).

C

Can (Canada and Bermuda); Capt (Captain); Carib (Caribbean); CIDA (Canadian International Development Agency); CO (Commanding Officer); Col (Colonel); Comr (Commissioner); Con (Congo); CoS (Chief of the Staff); CS (Chief Secretary); CWMO (Command Women's Ministries Officer); Cze R (Czech Republic).

D

DC (Divisional Commander); Den (Denmark); Dis O (District Officer); DO (Divisional Officer).

E

E Afr (East Africa); E Eur (Eastern Europe); ESFOT (European School for Officers' Training).

F

Fin (Finland and Estonia); Frce (France); FS (Field Secretary).

G

Ger (Germany and Lithuania); Gha (Ghana); GS (General Secretary).

H

HK (Hong Kong and Macau); HL (Home League); Hun (Hungary).

I

ICO (International College for Officers); IHQ (International Headquarters); Ind C, E, etc (India Central, Eastern, etc); Ind M & A (India Madras and Andhra); Indon (Indonesia); Internl (International); IS (International Secretary); It (Italy); ITC (International Training College).

J

JHLS (Junior Home League Secretary); Jpn (Japan).

K

Ken (Kenya); Kin (Kinshasa); Kor (Korea).

L

L Am N (Latin America North); Lat (Latvia); Lib (Liberia); Lt or Lieut (Lieutenant); Lt-Col or Lieut-Colonel (Lieutenant-Colonel); LOM (League of Mercy).

M

m (married); Maj (Major); Mal (Malawi); Mlys (Malaysia); Mol (Moldova); My (Myanmar).

N

Nat (National); Nat Comm (National Commander); Neth (The Netherlands and Czech Republic); NHQ (National Headquarters); Nor (Norway, Iceland and The Færoes); NZ (New Zealand, Fiji and Tonga).

O

OC (Officer Commanding); ODAS (Order of Distinguished Auxiliary Service); OF (Order of the Founder); O&R (Orders and Regulations).

P

Pak (Pakistan); pG (promoted to Glory); Phil (The Philippines); PINS (Persons in need of supervision); PNG (Papua New Guinea); Port (Portugal); PO (Provincial Officer); Pres (President); PRD (Public Relations Department); PS (Private Secretary).

R

RC (Regional Commander); ret (retired); RO (Regional Officer); Rus (Russia).

S

S/ (Senior); SAAS (Salvation Army Assurance Society); SABAC (Salvation Army Boys' Adventure Corps); S Afr (Southern Africa); SALT (Salvation Army Leadership Training); S Am E (South America East); SAMF (Salvation Army Medical Fellowship); S Am W (South America West); SAWSO (Salvation Army World Service Office); Scot (Scotland); SFOT (School for Officers' Training); Sgt (Sergeant); Sing (Singapore, Malaysia and

Myanmar); S/L (Songster Leader); Soc S (Social Services); Sp (Spain); SP&S (Salvationist Publishing and Supplies Ltd); Sri Lan (Sri Lanka); Supt (Superintendent); Swdn (Sweden and Latvia); Switz (Switzerland, Austria and Hungary).

T

Tai (Taiwan); Tanz (Tanzania); TC (Territorial Commander); tel (telephone); TCCMS (Territorial Community Care Ministries Secretary); THQ (Territorial Headquarters); TLWM (Territorial Leader of Women's Ministries); TPWM (Territorial President of Women's Ministries); TPWO (Territorial President of Women's Organisations); TSWM (Territorial Secretary for

Women's Ministries); TSWO (Territorial Secretary for Women's Organisations); TWMS (Territorial Women's Ministries Secretary).

U

Uga (Uganda); UK (United Kingdom); Uk (Ukraine); USA (United States of America); USA Nat, USA C, etc (USA National, Central, etc).

W

WI (West Indies); WSWM (World Secretary for Women's Ministries); Ww (Widow).

Z

Zai (Zaïre); Zam (Zambia); Zimb (Zimbabwe).

International Direct Dialling

Telephone country codes to territorial and command headquarters are listed below

In *The Year Book* the international prefix, which varies from country to country, is indicated by [square brackets]. Local codes are indicated by (round brackets)

Argentina	[54]	India	[91]	Portugal	[351]
Australia	[61]	Indonesia	[62]		
		Italy	[39]	Russia	[7]
Bangladesh	[880]			Rwanda	[250]
Belgium	[32]	Jamaica	[1876]	Singapore	[65]
Brazil	[55]	Japan	[81]	South Africa	[27]
				Spain	[34]
Canada	[1]	Kenya	[254]	Sri Lanka	[94]
Chile	[56]	Korea	[82]	Sweden	[46]
Congo (Democratic				Switzerland	[41]
Republic)	[243]	Liberia	[231]		
Congo (Republic)	[242]			Taiwan	[886]
Costa Rica	[506]	Mexico	[525]	Tanzania	[255]
		Malawi	[265]		
Denmark	[45]			United Kingdom	[44]
		Netherlands (The)	[31]	USA	[1]
Finland	[358]	New Zealand	[64]		
France	[33]	Nigeria	[234]	Zambia	[260]
		Norway	[47]	Zimbabwe	[263]
Germany	[49]				
Ghana	[233]	Pakistan	[92]		
		Papua New Guinea	[675]		
Hong Kong	[852]	Philippines (The)	[63]		

INDEX

A

Adler, Col Ines, 237
Advisory boards, 11, 14
Africa, 8, 39, 44, 47, 49, 93, 96, 116, 156, 168, 170, 188, 208, 223, 243, 245, 286, 289
Akpan, Comr Ime, 93, 94
Akpan, Comr Mfon Jaktor, 93
Alaska, 17, 277
Algeria, 3, 18
Alip, Maj Romeo, 168
All-Africa Congress, 20, 93, 208, 257, 287, 288, 289
All the World, 16, 18, 43, 320
Ambitan, Lt-Col Deetje, 148
Ambitan, Lt-Col Harold, 147
Americas and Caribbean, 44, 74, 78, 88, 163, 172, 214, 217, 255, 257, 263, 271, 277
Andaman Islands, 4, 134
Angola, 19, 27, 96, *see also* Congo (Kinshasa) and Angola 96-99
Antigua, 17, 27, *see also* Caribbean 88-92
Anzeze, Comr Hezekiel, 156
Argentina, 17, 27, 242, *see also* South America East 214-216
Asoegwu, Lt-Col Johnson, 188
Asoegwu, Lt-Col Veronica, 189
Australia, 3, 16, 17, 20, 23, 27, 41, 52, 141
    National Secretariat, 31, 52
    Eastern, 23, 24, 26, 31, 41, 48, 52, 53-59, 61, 198
    Southern, 23, 25, 31, 36, 41, 48, 52, 60-69, 77
Australian Agency for International Development (AusAID), 41, 52
Austria, 18, 27, 49, *see also* Switzerland, Austria and Hungary 237-240

B

BabySong, 102
Bahamas, 18, 27, *see also* Caribbean 88-92
Bailey, Maj Bradford, 227
Bailey, Maj Heidi, 227, 228
Baillie, Comr Joy, 257, 259
Baillie, Comr Kenneth, 257
Band of Love, 17
Bangladesh, 8, 9, 10, 19, 27, 48, 49, 70-71
Banks, Maj and Mrs Harvey, 5

Barbados, 17, 27, *see also* Caribbean 88-92
Bassett, Comr W. Todd, 21, 255
Belgium, 17, 27, 31, 48, 72-73
Belize, 18, 27, *see also* Caribbean 88-92
Bell, Lt-Col Debora, 279
Bell, Lt-Col Donald, 277
Berg, Lt-Col Grethe, 113, 114
Berg, Lt-Col Odd, 113
Bermuda, 17, 27, *see also* Caribbean 88-92
Bhutan, 4
Bolivia, 18, 21, 27, 39, *see also* South America West 217-222
Bond, Comr Linda, 43, 53, 218
Booth, Bramwell, 13, 16, 21, 36
    Catherine, 11, 13, 16, 34, 109
    Florence, 5, 6 (*see also* Florence Soper)
    Evangeline, 16, 18, 22, 23, 36
    William, 9, 11, 13, 16, 18, 22, 34, 36, 46, 109, 227, 247, 255, 327
Bosh, Col Gillian, 263, 265
Bosh, Col Larry, 263
Botswana, 20, 27, 289
Bramwell-Booth, Comr Catherine, 36
Braun, Comr Edouard, 237
Braun, Comr Françoise, 237, 238
Brazil, 18, 27, 31, 39, 48, 49, 74-77, 206
Bread for All (Switzerland), 41
Brekke, Col Birgitta, 195, 196
Brekke, Col Bo, 10, 195
Bringans, Col David, 210
Bringans, Col Grace, 210, 211
British Guiana, 17
British Honduras, 18
Brown, General Arnold, 19, 22, 24
Burkina Faso, 3
Burma, 18, 210, *see also* Myanmar
Burrows, Lt-Col David, 170, 287
Burrows, General Eva, 19, 22, 25
Burrows, Lt-Col Jean, 170, 171, 287
Burundi, 4
Bush, President George W., 21, 256, 258

C

Canada, 5, 16, 17, 20, 23, 24, 25, 27, 35, 41, 48, 138, 258
Canada and Bermuda, 24, 25, 31, 41, 78-87, 208, 257
Canary Islands, 227

Index

Caribbean, 31, 48, 49, 88-92
Carpenter, General George Lyndon, 18, 22, 23, 37
Carpenter, Mrs General Minnie, 35
Castillo, Lt-Col Aída, 215
Castillo, Lt-Col Luis, 214
Castor, Lt-Col Edmane, 97
Castor, Lt-Col Onal, 96
Celebes, 18
Cerezo, Maj Josué, 172
Cerezo, Maj Ruth, 173
Chandra Bai, Col T. Regina, 127, 128
Channel Islands, 16, see also United Kingdom, 247-254
Charan, Lt-Col Bimla, 141
Charan, Lt-Col Samuel, 140
Charlet, Col Helga, 113, 114
Charlet, Col Horst, 113
Chepkurui, Maj Grace, 243, 244
Chepkurui, Maj Stephen, 243
Chigariro, Comr Vinece, 286, 287
Chile, 18, 27, 39, 257, see also South America West 217-222
China, 3, 4, 18, 27, 52, 119, 120, 160 see also Hong Kong and Macau 119-124
Christian Mission, The, 5, 16, 42, 52, 247
Christian, Lt-Col Anandiben, 135
Christian, Lt-Col Paul Peter, 134
Christoffel Blindenmission (Germany), 41
Chronological Table, 16-20
Chun, Comr Kwang-Pyo, 159, 162
Clausen, Comrs Siegfried/Inger, 215
Clifton, Gen Shaw, 1, 2, 20, 21, 22, 26, 42, 44, 104, 226, 249
Clifton, Comr Helen, 1, 2, 7, 8, 44, 104
Cochrane, Lt-Col William, 45, 247
Colombia, 18, 19, 27, see also Latin America North 163-167
Community Care Ministries, 35
Community Development Projects, 40, 41, 44
Condon, Lt-Col James, 198
Condon, Lt-Col Jan, 199
Congo (Brazzaville), 18, 27, 31, 48, 49, 93-95, 96, 208
Congo (Kinshasa) and Angola, 18, 27, 31, 39, 48, 49, 96-99
Costa Rica, 18, 19, 27, see also Latin America North 163-167

Coutts, General Frederick, 19, 22, 24
Cox, Col André, 106
Cox, Col Silvia, 106, 107
Cuba, 18, 27, see also Latin America North 163-167
Curacao, 18, 176
Czech Republic (Czechoslovakia), 18, 19, 20, 27, 48, 49, see also Netherlands, The, and Czech Republic 176-180

D

Dali, Lt-Col Jessica, 117
Dali, Lt-Col Peter, 116
Dalziel, Geoffrey John, OF, 36, 61, 77
Dalziel, Lt-Col Peter, 176, 178
Dalziel, Lt-Col Sylvia, 178
Daniel, Lt-Col Edward, 229
Daniel, Lt-Col Lalitha, 230
Denmark, 17, 27, 31, 48, 100-102, 103
Devarapalli, Col Jayapaul, 131
Devarapalli, Col Yesudayamma, 131, 132
Devil's Island (French Guiana), 18
Dijkstra, Maj Pieter, 179, 180
Dispurse Foundation (Sweden), 41
Dixon, Maj Hester, 168, 169
Dixon, Maj Robert, 168, 169
Doctrines of The Salvation Army, 12, 16
Dominican Republic, 20, 27, 89, see also Latin America North 163-167
Downer, Lt-Col Gillian, 210
Duchêne, Col Alain, 109, 110
Dunster, Comr Robin, 2, 42, 45
Du Plessis, Comr Paul, 3, 4
Durston, Lt-Col Graham, 201
Durston, Lt-Col Rhondda, 203

E

East Africa, 20, 24, 48, 49, 243, 245
East Germany, 19, 49, 114
Eastern Europe, 3, 20, 31, 48, 49, 103-105
Ecuador, 19, 27, 83, 257, see also South America West 217-222
Egypt, 18
Eliasen, Lt-Col Deise, 75
Eliasen, Lt-Col Torben, 74
El Salvador, 19, 27, see also Latin America North 163-167
Emmanuel, Col Muthu Yesudhason, 127
England, 17, 19, 20, see also United

Index

Kingdom, 247-254
Ennis, Maj Wayne, 200, 298
Estonia, 18, 20, 21, 27, 49, *see also* Finland and Estonia 106-108
Europe, 44, 49, 72, 100, 103, 106, 109, 113, 151, 176, 191, 206, 227, 232, 237, 247
European School for Officer Training, 238
European Youth Congress, 20, 110, 151, 177, 191, 206, 238
Exbrayat, Maj Christian, 72
Exbrayat, Maj Joëlle, 72, 73

F

Fairbank, Lt-Col Jenty, 5, 6
Fair Trade, 9, 10
Færoes, The, 18, 27, *see also* Norway, Iceland and The Færoes 191-194
Feener, Comr Lenora, 271, 272
Feener, Comr Maxwell, 271
Fellowship of the Silver Star, 18, 35, 119
Ferreira, Col Adelina, 163, 164
Ferreira, Col Jorge, 163
Fiji, 19, 27, 49, *see also* New Zealand, Fiji and Tonga, 181-187
Finland, 17, 25, 27, 48, 102, 103, 106
Finland and Estonia, 21, 31, 33, 106-108
Flintoff, Lt-Col Ethne, 70, 71
Forster, Lt-Col Malcolm, 243
Forster, Lt-Col Valerie, 243, 244
Forsyth, Col Robin, 181
Forsyth, Col Shona, 183
Founders of The Salvation Army, 13
France, 16, 26, 27, 31, 48, 49, 109-112, 152
Francis, Comr Marilyn, 44
Francis, Comr William, 43, 44, 45, 89
Frans, Comr Arda, 44
Frans, Comr, Roy, 44, 45
Frei, Comrs Werner/Paula, 113
French Guiana, 18, 27, 88
Frisk, Lt-Col Kristina, 232

G

Gaither, Comr Eva D., 89, 96, 168, 243, 255, 256, 264
Gaither, Comr Israel L., 61, 89, 96, 168, 243, 255, 256 289
Gariepy, Col Henry, 32
General's Consultative Council, The, 42

Georgia, 27, *see also* Eastern Europe 103-105
Germany, 17, 24, 27, 41, 48
Germany and Lithuania, 31, 113-115
Ghana, 3, 18, 27, 31, 48, 49, 116-118
Gibraltar, 17
Global Exchange, 43
Gowans, General John, 20, 22, 26, 44, 335
Grenada, 17, 27, *see also* Caribbean 88-92
Guam, 200, 27, 255, 277
Guatemala, 19, 27, *see also* Latin America North 163-167
Guernsey, 27
Gulliksen, Comr Thorleif, 151
Guyana, 17, 27, *see also* Caribbean 88-92

H

Haiti, 28, *see also* Caribbean 88-92
Harding, Col Anne, 116, 117
Harding, Col Graeme, 116
Hawaiian Islands, 17
Herring, Lt-Col Alistair, 103
Herring, Lt-Col Astrid, 104
Herter, Dr Walter, 41
Higgins, Mrs Col Catherine, 5
Higgins, General Edward J., 18, 22, 23
High Council, 18, 19, 20, 21,22,23, 42, 249
Hills, Maj Cedric, 38, 44
Hiramoto, Lt-Col Naoshi, 153
Hiramoto, Lt-Col Seiko, 154
Hodder, Lt-Col Jolene, 157
Hodder, Lt-Col, Kenneth, 156
Hogan, Col Dianne, 172, 173
Hogan, Col Olin, 172
Holy Land, 17
Home League, 5, 6, 13, 17, 34, 97, 98, 117, 128, 164, 202, 243
Honduras, 20, 28, *see also* Latin America North 163-167
Hong Kong, 18, 20, 28, 48, 49, 119, 241
Hong Kong and Macau, 21, 31, 119-124, 160
Hope HIV, 40
Horwood, Capt Ted, 40, 44
Houghton, Comr Judith, 88, 89, 120
Houghton, Comr Raymond, 88
Howard, Comr Henry, 36, 46

Human trafficking, 7, 117, 189, 218, 248, 256

Hungary, 18, 19, 28, 49, *see also* Switzerland, Austria and Hungary 237-240

Hurricane Ivan, 89

Hurricane Katrina, 38, 155, 255, 263, 264, 271, 272, 276, 278, 285

Hurricane ita, 38, 278

I

Iceland, 17, 28, *see also* Norway, Iceland and The Faeroes, 191-194

In Darkest England and the Way Out, 13, 17

India, 8, 16, 17, 28, 38, 39, 40, 52

National Secretariat, 49, 125-126

Central, 31, 48, 49, 52, 127-130, 257

Eastern, 31, 33, 48, 49, 131-133

Northern, 28, 31, 48, 49, 126, 134-136

South Eastern, 31, 48, 49, 137-139

South Western, 31, 33, 48, 49, 126, 140-142

Western, 8, 31, 48, 49, 143-146

Indian Ocean tsunami, 4, 6, 20, 52, 126, 127, 137, 138, 140, 147, 150, 258

Indonesia, 17, 18, 28, 39, 48, 49, 147-150

Induruwage, Col Irene, 203

Induruwage, Col Malcolm, 201

International Centenary, 19

International College for Officers, 17, 19, 46, 50

International Commission on Officership, 20

International Conference of Leaders, 19, 20

International Congress, 16, 17, 18, 19, 20, 46

International Corps Cadet Congress, 19

International Headquarters, 2, 3, 10, 18, 19, 20, 23, 24, 26, 32, 33, 37, 38, 39, 40, 42-51, 247, 335

Administration Department, 43

Business Administration Department, 43

International Administrative Structure, 50-51

International Doctrine Council, 43

International Emergency Services, 38-39, 44, 157, 195, 202, 224, 229, 245

International Management Council, 42

International Personnel Department, 43

Programme Resources Department, 10, 43

International Projects and Development Services, 40, 44

Zonal Departments, 44

International Heritage Centre, 6, 250

International Literary and Publications Conference, 20

International Music and Other Creative Ministries Forum (MOSAIC), 20

International Poverty Summit, 20

International Sally Ann Council, 10

International Self-Denial Fund, 3, 48, 137

International Staff Band, 17, 249

International Staff Songsters, 19, 248, 249

International Statistics, 29-31

International Training College, 18, 24, 25, 26

International Youth Congress, 19

Iraq, 38, 39

Iraq Salvation Humanitarian Organisation, 39

Ireland, Republic of, 16, 23, 28, *see also* United Kingdom, 247-254

Isle of Man, 16, 27, 28, *see also* United Kingdom, 247-254

Italy, 17, 21, 28, 32, 48, 49, 151-152

J

Jamaica, 17, 28, *see also* Caribbean 88-92

James, Comr Susamma, 137, 138

James, Comr M. C., 137

Japan, 8, 17, 28, 32, 33, 48,153-155

Java, 17, 18, *see also* Indonesia 147-150

Jeffrey, Lt-Col Barbara, 272

Jeffrey, Lt-Col David, 271

Jeffrey, Lt-Col John, 60

Jeffrey, Lt-Col Judith, 62

Jersey, 27, 28

Jolliffe, Mrs Comr Fanny, 5

K

Kalai, Col Andrew, 198

Kalai, Col Julie, 198

Kartodarsono, Col Marie, 147, 148

Kartodarsono, Col Ribut, 147

Kashmir, 38, 126, 134

Kenya, 6, 9, 18, 20, 28, 32, 39, 48, 49, 52, 116, 156-158, 245

Index

Kerk in Actie (Netherlands), 41
Kim, Lt-Col Keum-nyeo, 160
Kindernothilfe (Germany), 41
Kitching, General Wilfred, 19, 22, 23
Kjellgren, Comr Christina, 44
Kjellgren, Comr Hasse, 44, 45
Knaggs, Comr Carolyn, 60, 62
Knaggs, Comr James, 60
Korea, 18, 25, 28, 32, 33, 48, 49, 104, 159-162
Korea, Democratic People's Republic of, 52, 159
Krommenhoek, Col Dick, 43
Krommenhoek, Col Vibeke, 21, 43
Krupa Das, Comr P. D., 125, 143
Kuwait, 4, 39

L

Lahase, Col Kashinath, 134
Lahase, Col Kusum, 134, 135
Lalhlimpuii, Comr, 44, 132
Lalkiamlova, Comr, 44, 45, 131, 132, 135
Lalkungi, Lt-Col, 132
Lalzamlova, Col, 229
Lang, Comrs Ivan/Heather, 230
Larsson, Comr Freda, 93, 106, 119, 153, 164, 177, 188, 271, 335
Larsson, General John, 20, 22, 26, 37, 93, 106, 119, 153, 164, 177, 188, 237, 271, 287, 289, 335
Latin America North, 19, 32, 48, 49, 163-167
Latvia, 18, 19, 28, 49, see also Sweden and Latvia 232-236
Laukkanen, Lt-Col Arja, 106
League of Mercy, 15, 17, 35, 78
Lecocq, Maj Noélie, 72, 73
Legacies, 344
Lesotho, 28, see also Southern Africa 223-226
Liberia, 19, 49, 116, 168-169
Ling, Maj Fona, 241, 242
Lithuania, 20, 28, 49, see also Germany and Lithuania 113-115
Ludiazo, Comr Jean B., 96
Ludiazo, Comr Véronique, 96, 97
Lukau, Lt-Col Angelique, 110
Lukau, Lt-Col Joseph, 109
Lydholm, Comr Carl, 191

Lydholm, Comr Gudrun, 191, 192

M

Mabena, Comrs William/Lydia, 224
Macau, 20, 28, see also Hong Kong and Macau 119-124
MacMillan, Comr M. Christine, 78, 80
McKenzie, Comr Garth, 181
McKenzie, Comr Merilyn, 181, 183
McMillan, Lt-Col Susan, 217
Maeland, Lt-Col Erling, 191
Maeland, Lt-Col Signe Helene, 192
Makina, Comr Amos, 44, 45, 245, 246, 287
Makina, Comr Rosemary, 44, 287
Malabi, Maj Florence, 208, 209
Malabi, Maj Joash, 208
Malawi, 5, 9, 28, 39, 47, 48, 49, 170-171, 257, 286, 287
Malaysia, 18, 28, see also Singapore, Malaysia and Myanmar 210-213
Mali, 3
Mallorca, 227
Malta, 17
Manam Islands, 6
Marshall Islands, 19, 28, 255, 277
Marvell, Col Ina, 100, 101
Marvell, Col Michael, 100
Masih, Lt-Col Bachini, 138
Masih, Lt-Col Bashir, 137
Masih, Maj Joginder, 70
Masih, Maj Shanti, 71
Mason, Lt-Col Raphael, 88
Mason, Lt-Col Winsome, 89
Matear, Comr Elizabeth, 89, 247, 249
Matear, Comr John, 89, 247
Mavundla, Lt-Col Mirriam, 224
Mavundla, Lt-Col Hezekiel, 223
Mexico, 18, 19, 28, 48, 49, 172-175
Micronesia, Federated States of, 20, 28, 277
Middles East, 4
Migration Department, 17
Miyoba, Lt-Col Grey, 286
Miyoba, Lt-Col Leniah, 287
Moldova, 28, see also Eastern Europe 103-105
Moretz, Comr Lawrence, 107, 173, 263
Moretz, Comr Nancy, 107, 173, 263, 265
Motor campaign, 17
Mozambique, 18, 28, 49, 116, see also

Index

Southern Africa 223-226
Mumford, Catherine, 13, 16
Mungate, Comr Hope, 188, 189
Mungate, Comr Stuart, 188
Mutewera, Comr Jannet, 289, 290
Mutewera, Comr Stanslous, 289
Myanmar, 18, 28, 48, 49, 52, *see also* Singapore, Malaysia and Myanmar 210-213

N

Namibia, 18
Nemkhanching, Col, 230, 231
Nepal, 4, 40
Nery, Col Jorge, OF, 21
Netherlands, The 17, 20, 28, 41, 48
Netherlands, The, and Czech Republic, 32, 41, 176-180
Newfoundland, 16, 25, *see also* Canada and Bermuda 78-87
New Zealand, 16, 17, 23, 27, 28, 48
New Zealand, Fiji and Tonga, 26, 32, 61, 181-187
Nicaragua, 3, 4
Nicobar Islands, 134
Nigeria, 18, 28, 32, 39, 48, 49, 116, 169, 188-190, 264
NORAD, 41
North Africa, 4
Norway, 9, 10, 17, 28, 35, 41, 48, 49, 138
Norway, Iceland and The Færoes, 32, 97, 103, 191-194
Nuesch, Col Nestor, 214
Nuesch, Col Rebecca, 214, 215

O

Ødegaard, Comr B. Donald, 43, 45
Ødegaard, Comr Berit, 9, 10, 43
Officer, The, 17, 43
Operation Desert Rose, 4
Operation One Day Work (Norway), 41
Order of Distinguished Auxiliary Service, 37
Order of the Founder, 16, 18, 36-37, 61, 77, 249
Order of the Silver Star, 18, *see also* Fellowship of the Silver Star
Orsborn, General Albert, 18, 22, 23
Overseas Service Funds, 48-49

Owen, Maj Graham, 100, 101
Owen, Maj Kirsten, 101
Oxfam, 41
Oxley, Brian, OBE, 21

P

Pakistan, 16, 26, 28, 32, 38, 48, 49, 195-197
Panama, 17, 28, *see also* Latin America North 163-167
Paone, Maj Jane, 151, 152
Paone, Maj Massimo, 151
Papua New Guinea, 6, 19, 28, 32, 48, 49, 61, 187, 198-200
Paraguay, 18, 28, 242, *see also* South America East 214-216
Pardo, Maj Magali, 164
Pardo, Maj Zoilo, 163
Park, Lt-Col Man-hee, 159
Parkhe, Lt-Col Nalini, 144
Parkhe, Lt-Col Sumant, 143
Paul, Lt-Col Emmanuel, 195
Paul, Lt-Col Gulzar Emmanuel, 196
Payne, Maj Diane, 245, 246
Payne, Maj Godfrey, 245
Pearce, Comr Lynette J., 43, 45
Peru, 9, 18, 28, 39, *see also* South America West 217-222
Philippines, The, 6, 8, 18, 28, 32, 39, 48, 49, 201-205, 257
Pobjie, Comr Barry, 103
Pobjie, Comr Raemor, 103, 104
Poke, Comr Roslyn, 232, 233
Poke, Comr Victor, 232
Poland, 3, 20, 21, 28
Portugal, 19, 28, 48, 49, 206-207
Portuguese East Africa, 18
Project Warsaw, 4, 20, 21, 43
Promoted to Glory, 15, 344
Puerto Rico, 19, 27, 28, 255, 263
Purdue, Brig Gertrude McClennan, OF, 36

R

Rader, General Paul A., 20, 22, 25
Radio Help (Sweden), 41
Rajakumari, Comr P. Mary, 143, 144
Rajan, Lt-Col Prema, 127, 128
Refstie, Comr Janet, 74, 75
Refstie, Comr Peder, 74

Regina, Col Chandra Bai, 127, 128
Reliance Bank Ltd, 17, 45
Roberts, Comr Nancy, 43
Roberts, Com William, 43, 45
Rohmingthanga, Lt-Col, 131
Romania, 20, 28, 39, *see also* Eastern
    Europe 103-105
Rowland, Lt-Col Elaine, 120
Rowland, Lt-Col Merv, 119
Royal Norwegian Ministry of Foreign
    Affairs, 41
Russia (Russian Federation), 18, 20, 28,
    see also Eastern Europe 103-105
Rwanda, 4, 20, 28, 39, 48, 49, 208-209

S

Sabah (East Malaysia), 20
St Helena, 116, 28, *see also* Southern
    Africa 223-226
St Kitts, 17, 28, *see also* Caribbean 88-92
St Lucia, 17, 28, *see also* Caribbean 88-92
St Maarten, 28, *see also* Caribbean 88-92
St Vincent, 17, 28, *see also* Caribbean
    88-92
Sally Ann, 9, 10
Sally Ann – Poverty to Hope, 10
Salvation Army
    Blue Shield Fellowship, 35
    Honours, 36-37
    International Trustee Company, 45
    Leaders Training College of Africa, 47,
        49, 171
    Medical Fellowship, 18, 35
    Scouts and Guides Jambouree, 20
    Students' Fellowship, 19, 35
Salvation Army Act 1980, 11, 19, 22
Salvation Army Australia Development
    Office (SAADO), 41, 148
Salvation Army World Service Office
    (SAWSO), 31, 48, 256
Salvation Story, 20
Scotland, 16, 23, 24, 26, 27, 192, *see also*
    United Kingdom, 247-254
Seiler, Lt-Col Carol, 259
Seiler, Lt-Col Paul, 257
Self-Denial Appeal, 15
    (*see also* International Self-Denial Fund)
Serém, Maj Alberto, 206
Serém, Maj Maria, 206, 207

Sex-trade trafficking, 7, 97, 144, 163, 256
Seymour, Lt-Col Geanette, 53
Shepherd, Col Eleanor, 80
Shepherd, Col Glen, 78
Sierra Leone, 3
Singapore, 18, 28
Singapore, Malaysia and Myanmar, 20, 32,
    48, 49, 143, 144, 210-213
Soldier's Covenant, 15
Solidarity Third World (Switzerland), 41
Solomon Islands, 3, 4
Soper, Capt Florence, 13
South Africa, 16, 17, 20, 28, 116, 289
    see also Southern Africa 223-226
South America East, 23, 32, 48, 49,
    214-216, 242
South America West, 21, 26, 32, 33, 48,
    49, 217-222, 257
South Asia, 44, 49, 70, 127, 131, 134, 137,
    140, 143, 195, 229
South Pacific and East Asia (SPEA), 44,
    49, 53, 60, 119, 147, 153, 159, 181, 198,
    201, 210, 241
Southern Africa, 20, 32, 33, 48, 49,
    223-226
SP&S Ltd, 10, 251
Spain, 19, 28, 48, 49, 152, 227-228
Sri Lanka, 8, 16, 25, 28, 32, 38, 48, 49,
    140, 229-231
Staite, Lt-Col John, 52
Stanley Thomas Johnson Foundation
    (Switzerland), 41
Steadman-Allen, Lt-Col Ray, OF, 248
Sterling, Maj David, 47
Street, Comr Janet, 44
Street, Comr Robert, 43, 45
Strong, Comr Coral, 53, 54
Strong, Comr Leslie, 53
Sub-Sahara Famine, 39, 157
Sudan, 3, 6
Sumatra, 18, 147
Sunbury Court, 19, 21, 251
Suriname, 18, 28, 176, *see also* Caribbean
    88-92
Sutherland, Comr Margaret, 46
Swanson, Col Barry, 255
Swanson, Col E. Sue, 256
Swaziland, 28, *see also* Southern Africa
    223-226

Index

Sweden, 9, 16, 17, 20, 23, 24, 25, 26, 28, 41, 48, 103, 104, 117
Sweden and Latvia, 32, 49, 232-236
Swedish Ecumenical Council for Women, 41
Swiss Government, 41
Swiss Solidarity, 41
Switzerland, 3, 16, 28, 41, 48, 52, 236
Switzerland, Austria and Hungary, 32, 52, 237-240
Swyers, Comr Patricia, 277, 279
Swyers, Comr Philip, 277

T

Taiwan, 19, 28, 32, 48, 49, 241-242
Tanzania, 9, 18, 28, 39, 48, 49, 208, 243-244
Tear Fund, 41
Tillsley, General Bramwell H., 19, 22, 25
Tobago, 28, *see also* Caribbean 88-92
Togo 116
Tonga, 19, 28, 40, 49, *see also* New Zealand, Fiji and Tonga 181-187
Trinidad, 17, 28, *see also* Caribbean 88-92
Tsang, Lt-Col Alfred, 119
Tsunami (*see* Indian Ocean)
Tuck, Comr Memory, 223, 224
Tuck, Comr Trevor, 223

U

Uganda, 6, 18, 20, 28, 39, 49, 208, 245-246
Ukraine, 28, 257, *see also* Eastern Europe 103-105
United Kingdom with the Republic of Ireland, 3, 8, 19, 21, 26, 28, 32, 33, 37, 38, 41, 48, 137, 247-254
United States of America, 8, 16, 17, 18, 19, 20, 21, 23, 27, 28, 35, 38, 41, 255-285
National, 19, 21, 32, 33, 255-256
Central, 5, 32, 48, 171, 257-262
Eastern, 25, 26, 32, 33, 48, 101, 152, 156, 168, 173, 215, 263-270
Southern, 25, 32, 36, 48, 49, 89, 104, 144,156, 271-276
Western, 21, 25, 26, 32, 33, 37, 48, 97, 104, 156, 241, 277-285
Uruguay, 17, 28, *see also* South

America East 214-216
USAID, 41

V

Van der Harst, Comr Netty, 113, 176, 177, 178
Van der Harst, Comr Willem, 113, 176, 177, 178
Venezuela, 28, *see also* Latin America North 163-167
Vietnam, 3
Virgin Islands, 18, 27, 28, 255, 263

W

Waghela, Comr Chimanbhai, 140
Waghela, Comr Rahelbai, 140, 141
Wahlström, General Jarl, 19, 22, 25
Wales, 16, 27, *see also* United Kingdom, 247-254
Ward, Lt-Col Marguerite, 290
Ward, Lt-Col Robert, 289
Wickberg, General Erik, 19, 22, 24
William Booth College, 18, 42, 151, 206, 250
Williams, Comr (Dr) Harry, OF, 37, 249
Wiseman, General Clarence, 19, 22, 24
Women's Corps Auxiliary, 5
Women's Ministries, 6, 8, 34, 44, 76, 132, 141, 189, 198, 200, 209, 287, 290
Women's Social Work, 13, 16
Words of Life, 44, 54, 327

Y

Year for Children and Youth (2005), 70, 78, 88, 93, 96, 114, 120, 124, 141, 143, 153, 159, 164, 181, 191, 198, 202, 216, 229, 243, 257, 258, 277, 289
Yoo, Comr Sung-Ja, 159, 160
Yoshida, Comr Kaoru, 153, 154, 199
Yoshida, Comr Makoto, 153, 199
Yugoslavia, 18

Z

Zambia, 18, 28, 47, 48, 49, 170, 286-288
Zimbabwe, 17, 20, 25, 26, 28, 32, 39, 47, 48, 49, 160, 170, 286, 289-291
Zola, Lt-Col Alphonsine, 94
Zola, Lt-Col Ambroise, 93
Zululand, 17, 223

TERRITORIES (T), COMMANDS (C) AND REGIONS (R) BY ZONES

AFRICA
Congo (Brazzaville) (T)
Congo (Kinshasa) and Angola (T)
Ghana (T)
Kenya (T)
Liberia (C)
Malawi (C)
Nigeria (T)
Rwanda (R)
Southern Africa (T)
Tanzania (C)
Uganda (C)
Zambia (T)
Zimbabwe (T)

AMERICAS AND CARIBBEAN
Brazil (T)
Canada and Bermuda (T)
Caribbean (T)
Latin America North (T)
Mexico (T)
South America East (T)
South America West (T)
USA Central (T)
USA Eastern (T)
USA Southern (T)
USA Western (T)

EUROPE
Belgium (C)
Denmark (T)
Eastern Europe (T)
Finland and Estonia (T)
France (T)
Germany and Lithuania (T)
Italy (C)
The Netherlands and Czech
    Republic (T)
Norway, Iceland and
    The Færoes (T)
Portugal (C)
Spain (C)
Sweden and Latvia (T)
Switzerland, Austria and
    Hungary (T)
United Kingdom with the
    Republic of Ireland (T)

SOUTH ASIA
Bangladesh (C)
India Central (T)
India Eastern (T)
India Northern (T)
India South Eastern (T)
India South Western (T)
India Western (T)
Pakistan (T)
Sri Lanka (T)

SOUTH PACIFIC AND EAST ASIA
Australia Eastern (T)
Australia Southern (T)
Hong Kong and Macau (C)
Indonesia (T)
Japan (T)
Korea (T)
New Zealand, Fiji and Tonga (T)
Papua New Guinea (T)
The Philippines (T)
Singapore, Malaysia and
    Myanmar (T)
Taiwan (R)